LAND AND POWER IN HAWAII
The Democratic Years

LAND AND POWER IN HAWAII

The Democratic Years

GEORGE COOPER   GAVAN DAWS

University of Hawaii Press
Honolulu

Paperback edition published by
University of Hawaii Press 1990

93 94 95   5 4 3

Originally published by Benchmark Books, Inc.

Library of Congress Catalog Card Number 85-72037
ISBN 0-8248-1303-0

CONTENTS

TABLES

AUTHORS' NOTE

THIS book is the first full-length study of land and politics in Hawaii in the Democratic years from the mid-1950s to the mid-1980s.

The book contains literally thousands of facts: the names of individuals and groups of people; how they might have been connected in politics and business; how those elected to office voted on land matters in the Legislature or in a Council meeting; the record of land rezonings and redistrictings by county planning commissions and the state's Land Use Commission; the amount of money for which a given parcel of land was bought before rezoning and the amount of money for which it was sold after rezoning; who the buyers and sellers were; who arranged the transaction; the timing of purchases and sales; who might have profited from the sale; and so on.

The research was done almost totally from the public record, meaning that the authors used government files accessible to the public, plus information publicly available in government and business publications, newspapers and periodicals.

In addition attempts were made, where necessary and possible, to check facts and clarify complicated situations by way of interviews.

It will immediately become clear to the reader that some ethnic groups figure in the book much more prominently than others. This is strikingly obvious—on virtually every page, in all the tables, and in the index. As anyone familiar with Hawaii over the last three decades will know, this is nothing more or less than a reflection of the facts of politics and land development in Hawaii in the Democratic years. If a book on land and power had been set in an earlier time, the ethnic distribution of names would have been different. By the same token, any book of this kind written, say, three decades into the future will almost certainly show a new and different ethnic distribution of land and power.

We have tried to present facts in sufficient quantity for readers to make up their minds concerning what these facts in the aggregate might mean about the land politics of the Democrats over the last thirty years. If a reader should want to check where the facts came from, there are notes at the end of the book.

We certainly hope that everything presented here as fact can be checked and substantiated by others. In the nature of a lengthy book constructed of so many interrelated details, it is possible that we have got some things wrong. We would hope such factual errors are few, and we would appreciate being informed of them so that they can be corrected in any future edition.

What we have tried to do is to describe the behavior of the Democrats in office in relation to land, and at least to some extent to explain this behavior. We have been sparing in offering opinions about the political, economic and social merits of this behavior, and even more sparing in making judgments. We hope readers will find our opinions to be based on adequate and clearly presented evidence. As for what this evidence might mean about the merits of the way the Democrats in power behaved concerning land, and, more generally, about the way Hawaii has been governed over the past three decades, our judgments are merely our own. It is inevitable that readers' judgments may differ from ours.

Inevitably, a percentage of those mentioned in this book are not public figures in the accepted sense. Because of the way real estate investments are made in Hawaii, there will often be found along with public figures other people who are more "private"—family members, friends, associates, perhaps a secretary or an aide. We have tried our best to be accurate and responsible in gathering information about these "private" people and sparing about setting it down in print; where possible, we have limited the use of their names in the book to occasions when they appeared in the public record, or when they were mentioned in relevant contexts by public figures whom we interviewed.

We believe the subject opened up in this book to be basic to the political and economic life of Hawaii in the last thirty years. We have tried to select topics for detailed discussion which throw a clear light on the overall general subject. At the same time we acknowledge that our treatment is not exhaustive. A single book, even as long as this one has turned out to be, cannot give encyclopedic treatment to three decades of political activity in relation to land. Thus, inevitably, we have been selective both in our choice and in our treatment of topics. In roughly the first half of the book, we discuss institutions that are significant in land and power statewide. Then we go on to discuss particular instances of the system in action, choosing cases which come from each of the counties of the state. On some subjects we write in relatively broad terms. In other instances, where in our opinion there is interest and significance in very detailed treatment, we go as deep as possible. Now, it may be that our particular approach, our particular angle of vision, has limited us so much that we have failed to see the overall subject whole and entire. Perhaps we are like the blind men trying to describe the elephant, touching different parts of the creature but never grasping the whole, offering descriptions that are accurate enough as far as they go but so partial and limited that they are misleading. We would like to think that this has not been so. Rather, we would like to think of the work that went into this book as being somewhat like the examination of an organism's cell structure, detailed work done at close range, which at the same time tells truths about the overall nature of the organism being examined, and the way its whole system operates.

The two authors between them have seen at least the public operation of the system with their own eyes over almost the entire period under study. Gavan Daws lived and worked in Hawaii 1958–1974, in other words from the early years of Democratic legislatures before statehood to the end of the third and final term of office of Gov. John A. Burns. Since then, Daws has on many occasions returned to Hawaii to do research for extended periods. George Cooper came to Hawaii in 1970, before Burns' final term began, and was still living and working here when this book was published in 1985—in other words from the time of George R. Ariyoshi as lieutenant governor to Ariyoshi's final term as governor. Cooper has firsthand knowledge of events discussed in several chapters of the book. He took part in obtaining and publishing the Leadership Homes memos discussed in the chapter on the ILWU. He was associated with two organizations mentioned in the chapter on Nukolii: the Committee to Save Nukolii, to which he was an advisor for a short time in 1977; and the Niumalu-Nawiliwili Tenants Association, to which he was an advisor almost from the start and for which he continues to do occasional work. Cooper also wrote from about 1973 to 1975 for the Kauai newspaper, *The Garden Island*, which is mentioned in the Nukolii chapter.

To check and calibrate our own perceptions, we have had the manuscript of the book read in part and in whole by people who could offer perspectives very different from our own. They include professional planners, community activists, attorneys for developers, public interest lawyers, economists and businessmen, union officials and rank-and-file members, journalists, public relations people for big firms, people in law enforcement, and people currently or formerly in politics and government at the state and county level. The institutions they are associated with range all the way from the Big Five to the Oahu Development Conference to Save Our Surf, from the Bishop Estate to Kokua Hawaii and the Save Nukolii Committee. Some did not wish to be acknowledged by name. This mention conveys our thanks to them.

The same range applies to interviewees. We tried to speak to people involved on all sides of major questions, and many times an initial interview demonstrated the need for more hours of conversation with them, or the need to make contact with yet other people. Most interviewing was done in Hawaii, though there were phone conversations with people as far away as Washington, DC; Texas; Florida; Oregon; Maryland; Idaho; Nevada; California; and Tokyo, Japan. Our thanks to them all. Some people chose to decline interviews on matters in which they played a substantive role; where this was the case it is noted in the text.

Overall, we have scores, even hundreds of people to thank for helping in all sorts of ways, large and small: sitting for interviews, answering detailed questions over the phone during and after working hours, arranging access to the public record, supplying documents for study, typing text and tables, reading early drafts of the manuscript, and seeing the book through the press. The staff of the Business Registration Division of the State Department of Commerce and Consumer Affairs was particularly helpful. A good deal of this book is based on files they maintain. There are few groups of people anywhere who were so consistently kind, whose information was so invariably accurate, and who were this way while under considerable work pressure. Our grateful thanks.

We wish to thank by name the following people: Mary Ann Akao, Herbert Arai, George R. Ariyoshi, Michael Belles, Dan Boylan, K. Napua Brown-Kamelamela, George Chaplin, Michaelyn P. Chou, Ph.D., Hugh Clark, Cornelius Downes, Charles Crumpton, David DeLeon, James B. Dooley, Kevin Doyle, Ramon Duran, Gay Eastman, Frances Fay Enos, Scott Ezer, Jim P. Ferry, Guy Fujimura, Mike Gillan, Julie Gordon, Karen Haines, Nelson Ho, John Hulten, Jean R. Imamoto, Edward A. Jaffe, Yasuto Kaihara, Joseph Kamelamela, Robert Kamins, Eric Kato, Bea Kaya, Noel Kent, Rene Kitagawa, David Kittelson, Hanako Kobayashi, Gary T. Kubota, Mark Kuklinsky, Rodney Lim, Laura Loftus, Lehua Lopez, Kem Lowry, Timothy Lui-Kwan, Robert McElrath, Dorothy McIntosh, Keith Nagaoka, Haruo "Dyna" Nakamoto, James Nishida, Joyce Oi, Maria R. Patton, Jeffrey Portnoy, David Rick, Carol Silva, Yoshito Takamine, Eddie Tangen, Edwin Tanji, Richard F. Thompson, Robert Wernet, Tamara Wong, Tom Yagi, Russel H. Yamashita. All these people between them helped greatly in getting the book started, keeping the research moving forward over a period of several years, bringing the work to a conclusion, and seeing the manuscript into print. The end product, of course, is solely our responsibility.

Finally, special thanks to our wives, Laureen K. K. Wong and Carolyn Kato Daws.

G. C. G. D.
Honolulu
May 1985

INTRODUCTION

THIS book asks a simple question:

What has been the connection between land and power in Hawaii in the Democratic years?

In 1954 Democrats won control of the Legislature for the first time in Hawaii's history. Except for a temporary loss of the Senate (1959–1962) they have controlled it ever since.

At the level of local government in this same period, most counties most of the time have had Democratic mayors, boards of supervisors and councils.

Until statehood in 1959 Hawaii was not entitled to elect congressional representatives or US senators. Instead the Islands, as a territory of the US, could elect one non-voting delegate to Congress. In 1956 a Democrat was elected delegate for the first time since World War II, and in 1958 he was re-elected. Ever since Hawaii's admission as a state in 1959 all but one of those sent to the House and the Senate from Hawaii have been Democrats.

Also before statehood Hawaii residents could not vote for governor; the governor was appointed by the president of the United States. In Hawaii's first gubernatorial election in 1959 the Democratic candidate was defeated. But he won in 1962, and again in 1966 and 1970. His last lieutenant governor succeeded him, winning election as governor in 1974, 1978, and 1982.

With statehood, Hawaii residents also for the first time could vote in American presidential elections. Hawaii has voted Republican only twice in the seven elections since, and both times it took national Republican landslides of historic proportions to defeat the Democratic candidate locally— Nixon over McGovern in 1972, Reagan over Mondale in 1984.

Thus, beginning in the mid-1950s, the Democrats took political power in what became an overwhelmingly Democratic state. They have held power for three decades.

The Democrats in power had to deal with other powerful groups who had strong vested interests in land in Hawaii: the Republican Party; the Islands' old landed estates and big businesses; a rising group of locally-born businessmen of Asian background; major US mainland and foreign businessmen looking to make money in Hawaii; labor unions, particularly the

International Longshoremen's and Warehousemen's Union (ILWU); and local organized crime.

These groups are discussed in this book, as are relatively powerless community and Hawaiian rights groups. There are books to be written about every one of them. But the focus here is strongly on Democratic politicians, Democratic governmental appointees, and their close associates.

So this book is centrally about a generation of politically successful Democrats and their involvement with land—and especially with land development.

* * *

In Hawaii, land has always been a political battleground and prize. Those who have held land have generally occupied the high ground in politics. If those out of political power have managed to come into power, they have usually set about using their new position to get hold of land.

This was true in traditional Hawaiian times, when one of the first acts of a Hawaiian chief victorious in battle was to seize land and redistribute it to his own advantage.

It was true in mid-nineteenth century when whites (*haoles*) became influential advisors to the Hawaiian monarchs. These *haoles* were leading members of a white community which, under the prevailing Hawaiian land system, chafed at not being able to buy and sell land and to obtain secure land tenure for businesses and homes. The advisors convinced a Hawaiian king to replace the traditional land system with a western one. By the end of the century through use of the new system *haoles* controlled, through ownership or lease, the bulk of the Islands' productive land and water rights.

It was true when *haole* revolutionaries overthrew the Hawaiian monarchy in 1893 and formed a government with the avowed intention of offering the Islands to the United States. By the act of taking over, the revolutionaries got control of Hawaii's government lands. They then confiscated the personal lands of the monarchs, called "crown lands," and added them to the government lands. Combined, these came to a total of about 43% of the surface area of the Islands.[1] Hawaii became a territory of the US in 1900. Although under the Organic Act establishing the new status the US government took title to those lands, the *haole* monied class that continued locally in control of government in Hawaii was able to make use of these lands largely to its own benefit.

* * *

The people who controlled land and politics in Hawaii at the turn of the century were *haole* Republicans, and Republicans remained in power in the Territory throughout the first half of the twentieth century.

The connection between land and political power in Hawaii in Republican times has been written about a great deal. It needs only the briefest of descriptions here, by way of background.

In the territorial Legislature from 1901 all the way up to World War II, Republicans outnumbered Democrats massively—almost five to one in the Senate, more than six to one in the House.[2] If there were times along the way when Democrats did better than usual at the polls, when the city of Honolulu had a Democratic mayor, or when a Democratic president in Washington appointed a Democrat to be governor of Hawaii, none of this altered the long-term, large-scale dominance of the Republicans in the Islands.

Republican politics in Hawaii was little else but the politics of business, big business. In fact it was true enough to say that government in Hawaii in the Republican years functioned avowedly as an arm of local big business, more particularly as an arm of the so-called "Big Five"—Castle & Cooke, Alexander & Baldwin, American Factors, Theo H. Davies, C. Brewer—plus a sixth, the Dillingham interests. (The Dillingham businesses were different from the others in that they revolved around construction and transportation, as distinct from the plantation agriculture that was the base of all the Big Five. But in terms of wealth and power, those who ran the Dillingham concerns stood on an equal footing with the heads of the Big Five.)

These long-established local companies, all dating from the nineteenth century, were heavily interlocked; that is, to a greater or lesser degree they shared officers and directors. As late as 1959, for example, Alexander & Baldwin had directors in common with American Factors and Castle & Cooke; American Factors, in turn, had a director in common with Brewer, and Castle & Cooke with Davies. The Dillinghams' Oahu Railway & Land Co. interlocked with all of the Big Five except Castle & Cooke. Matson Navigation Co. was Hawaii's economic lifeline, accounting in 1959 for more than 90% of all Hawaii-mainland public-carrier freight. Four of the Big Five owned 74% of Matson's stock and nine Big Five directors sat on Matson's board. Those nine, in turn, held a total of 105 directorships in 67 other Hawaii companies, for the most part the Islands' largest.[3] So throughout the first half of the twentieth century the Republicans were the party in power; they were the party of big business; and business and government were tightly controlled by a small elite.

In those decades, big business in Hawaii meant plantation agriculture—sugar and pineapple grown on land owned by the Big Five or leased either from government or from the great private estates.

Again, this situation has often been described. At the high point of the Republican era, before World War II, when Hawaii was not much more than a tightly-controlled plantation society that was very profitable to those on top, when the Big Five and Dillingham could go about their business effectively unchallenged, when the big companies and landed estates were more than content to maintain their enormous property holdings intact—at that stage in the history of Hawaii, almost half the total land area of the Islands was in the hands of fewer than 80 private owners. Government ownership accounted for most of the rest. As for productive agricultural land, most was in the hands of those same major private owners.[4]

This was an enormous concentration of wealth and power. Measure for measure there was nothing like it anywhere else in the United States. The consequence, in a place as small as Hawaii, was that once the big estates and corporations were accounted for, not much was left over for other people.

In Republican times, then, business power was one and the same as political power, and business power was land-based. A small minority, with *haoles* dominant, were rich and landed and powerful. The great majority were poor, without land, powerless. In Hawaiian politics money talked, the language it spoke was Republican, and the subject was land—land and the crops that were grown on it.

*   *   *

Right up through World War II and on into the early postwar period, there was no fundamental change in the situation of the large private landowners and no change in the land base of big business.

But in the late 1940s a great change was looming in the electoral politics of Hawaii, and there was nothing the Republican Party or the Big Five could do about it.

The sons and daughters of immigrant plantation laborers of Asian ancestry were coming to adulthood. Born in the Territory, these local-Asians were United States citizens by birth and had been taught democratic theories of government in Hawaii's public schools.

During the war they had seen military rule displace the Islands' old *haole* establishment, while many of Hawaii's young *nisei* (the first generation of Japanese ancestry born in the US, thus American citizens) fought with great distinction in Europe, simultaneously dispelling the myth of the *haoles'* local omnipotence and infusing the Islands' large Japanese community with tremendous pride and a determination to achieve a place in the political and economic sun.

Because of the war and the GI Bill of Rights that enabled veterans afterwards to pursue college degrees, many of the younger generation of local-Japanese traveled and lived in other parts of the nation and the world. They were exposed to different cultures and new ideas, and began to question social conditions in Hawaii.

Between 1944 and 1947 a militant labor union, the ILWU, organized the plantation industries and the waterfront for the first time. This was a shattering blow to Big Five economic dominance, one that reverberated at the polls as the union became active in electoral politics.

Also undermining the old ways was the urbanization of Hawaii's economy and the rise of a middle class—producing a bloc of people not directly beholden to the Big Five.

As the children of immigrants turned 21, they registered to vote. Most of their parents, previously barred from US citizenship by their East Asian birth, were now allowed to become naturalized citizens by virtue of the federal McCarran-Walter Act of 1952. A considerable percentage of them registered to vote. So did almost all ILWU members who were citizens.

There was no reason why plantation workers, East Asian immigrants and their children should vote for a party of plantation owners, and plenty of reasons why they would not. The new majority voted Democratic.

Whereas the Republican Party was dominated by *haoles* and supported by the ethnic Hawaiian vote, this new Democratic majority was made up of voters of many different ethnic backgrounds, with local-Asians predominant.

If there was one single decisive force in the new politics of Hawaii, it was the Japanese vote—perhaps 40% of the electorate in the early 1950s. The locally born Japanese of Hawaii were crucial to the so-called "Democratic revolution" of 1954, and to the generation of Democratic politics that followed.

* * *

The Democrats inherited a land system a century old, perfected over the years to protect and advance the interests of the large owners.

As the new party in power, the Democrats did not have to live with this system one hundred percent if they did not want to. If ever a group of politicians had a mandate for change, they did. The old "ins" were out—gone from the governor's mansion, from the leadership of both houses of the Legislature, from influential committee chairmanships, from the head offices of government departments. The new "ins" had a formidable base of popular support—all those multi-ethnic Democratic votes, virtually a guaranteed majority, good indefinitely. In other words, the Democrats of Hawaii had as much room for political maneuver as any party could hope for.

By national standards Hawaii's Democrats were very liberal, and they came into office promising broad reform. In all sorts of ways they intended to open up society to ordinary people and to promote civil liberties, and indeed there can be no question that they made Hawaii a vastly more open society than it had been under the Republicans. Public education, for example, got generous appropriations, and tuition levels in the territorial and later state university system were kept very low. In the labor area Hawaii developed a worker's compensation program (dealing with job-related disabilities) that has had among the highest payout rates of any state in the nation. Hawaii was the first state to adopt mandatory pre-paid health care for workers (1974). Only six states and Puerto Rico were ahead of Hawaii in abolishing the death penalty (1957). The Democrats made Hawaii the first state to legalize abortion (1970) and the first to ratify the proposed women's Equal Rights Amendment to the federal constitution (1972).

The Democrats came into office also promising land reform, meaning changes in the ownership, taxation, and use of land so as to benefit the ordinary person. And because there was no bigger item than land in Hawaii's politics, land reform was one of the biggest items on the Democratic agenda.

The record of the Democrats in power shows that they did make changes in land taxes and land use laws. During the 1950s and early 1960s they passed several important pieces of legislation in these areas. They raised taxes on the lands of the major landowners and in general made assessment practices more uniform for everyone. In 1957 they gave the outer island county governments the zoning powers that Oahu had had since 1939. And in 1961 House Democrats initiated a bill that gave Hawaii the first statewide land use law in the nation.

All these new laws cut away at the virtually unrestricted power of the old major landowners, but without addressing the fundamental issue of land ownership.

By Democratic lights Hawaii's massive concentration of land in the hands of a few score private owners was a huge social injustice. Land in large fee-simple parcels was virtually unavailable to anyone but a big estate or a Big Five company. And for a majority of Hawaii's families, even a modest house lot of their own was out of the question. This was not fair and it was not right, according to Democratic thinking.

If the Democrats in power wanted to fundamentally alter this situation, by one view they would have had to confront the radical issue of breaking up big land holdings, of forcing major owners to give up a good deal of their land.

There was no doubt that the Democrats had a popular mandate for a breakup. In 1958 the Republican Party commissioned a survey of voters on Oahu. The survey found that only 13% of those questioned opposed breaking up the major estates, as against 56% in favor, with local-Asians, the major segment of the Democrats' electoral base, most strongly in favor.[5]

This explosive issue was much discussed over the years of the Democrats' rise to power, and Democratic politicians kept talking about it after they took office.

But the large land holdings were never broken up. Nothing like that ever came close to happening.

Even if a majority of Democrats had seriously intended to break up big holdings without compensation and had passed laws to that effect, those laws would almost certainly have been struck down in the federal courts. The nation's powerful tradition of private property rights would never have tolerated such radical reform.

Just the same, the Democrats could probably have done far more than they did to shake up the big landowners, short of totally dispossessing them without payment:

For example, they could have tried out proposed laws that would have set a ceiling on the percentage of assets that various large landowning entities could hold in real property. The large trust estates, Bishop in particular, had almost 100% of their assets in real property. To stay within a ceiling requirement of, say, 30%–40% as proposed,[6] the estates would have been forced to sell large amounts of land, and this would have opened up the land market a great deal.

Or the Democrats could have forced the large owners to choose between either being assessed at market value for real property tax purposes, or having to sell to the government at below market value assessments. For years the large owners had obtained real property tax assessments that many Democrats believed were considerably lower than the open market value of the land. During the latter half of the 1950s and into the early 1960s Democrats introduced bills in the Legislature that would have required large owners to state annually to the Department of Taxation the value of their land. The government would then have had the right to condemn large tracts at or near those figures.[7] Inevitably there were constitutional questions raised about such bills; for whatever reasons one never passed until 1963. By this time assessments were much closer to open market value, and assessments were made merely a "rebuttable presumption" of value in a condemnation proceeding.[8]

Then too, the Democrats could have moved much earlier and more vigorously than they did to force landowners who were lessors of tracts of residential land to sell to their tenants in fee simple. So-called "Maryland bills" to force sales were regularly introduced in the Legislature from before the Democrats won control in 1954. It was not until the mid-1970s that a large number of legislatively induced sales actually began taking place.

In practical terms, then, some sorts of forced land reform were possible, even fairly far-reaching reform.

But though the Democrats in power did start out down the land-reform track in the general direction of social justice, it is a matter of public record that they did not proceed very far.

What happened was that a different and much more easygoing approach to land reform became dominant.

After only a few years in office most Democratic politicians pretty much abandoned forced land redistribution as a social goal, and, whether consciously and deliberately or not, opted instead for land development as an essential part of the way to broad social and economic reform.

The idea was that development would create new wealth for new groups of people in Hawaii. The living standards of middle and working-class people would rise. Thus rather than cut up the old pie of landed wealth in a different way, the idea was to make the pie grow rapidly and continually by developing land intensively, so that everyone could have more without anyone having to give up anything of significance.

Central to this equation was that major participants in the development process would be leading Democrats, plus their allies among the Islands' rising class of local-Asian businessmen.

Within as little as three years after winning control of the Legislature, major land deals were being struck between Democratic developers/ investors and Republican landowners. In other words, though the landed rich had been the avowed enemies of the Democrats for decades, now, almost overnight, Democrats became their partners in mutually profitable land deals.

Perhaps this sort of outcome was predictable. Certainly the odds against thoroughgoing land reform were long, in Hawaii as in the rest of the United States.

Aside from fundamental constitutional questions there were also matters of practical politics at work locally.

Like most political groups, the Hawaii Democrats were faction-ridden, and there was no way all factions could agree to implement every one of the policies that carried a Democratic label. Attempts at radical land reform would have generated tremendous resistance, in turn requiring a degree of party unity difficult to achieve.

Also, in the early Democratic years, by the natural operation of the existing American economic system of which Hawaii was a part, prosperity began to rise, especially after statehood in 1959. Overall, living conditions were steadily getting better for most people. This took away a lot of impetus from any drive for radical reform.

Then too, some of the party's more moderate land reforms were achieved. In part this occurred simply by Hawaii becoming a state and Democrats obtaining control of state government. When Hawaii became a territory all government lands were ceded to the US government. With statehood most were given back. Lands belonging to the new state of Hawaii made up about 39% of the Islands' surface area.[9] In office the Democrats set about rewriting policies on sale and lease of government lands, to make more acreage available for small farming and ranching and residential use.

The simple passage of time also took the edge off early Democratic appetites for radical reform. The Democrats, as noted, stayed in power after statehood and on through the 1960s and 1970s into the 1980s—a long, long time in politics. They came to office young, most of them, and they grew middle-aged and older in power. Youthful ideals waned, and near-term personal interests took precedence, things like getting re-elected, getting established financially, getting ahead.

In the medium to long term, the vast majority of Hawaii's elected Democrats turned out not to be revolutionaries, but just practical politicians with an eye to bringing some new social groups into positions of relative affluence and influence. As time went on it became clear that those favoring thoroughgoing land reform were in a minority—a minority which kept decreasing in size and was forced to the edges of the party.

The majority, the mainstream Democrats, clustered around the dominating figure of John A. Burns, a founder of the modern party and governor of Hawaii 1962–1974. Burns had been feared by Republicans as a potential radical before he took office. But in power he and his associates year by year found themselves more and more ready to do business with the old landowners and the Big Five, and with wealthy business newcomers to Hawaii. In time the Burns "consensus" government, as it was called, meaning a government that brought together in harmonious terms formerly disparate elements of the power structure, came to include practically everything but radicalism.

This is a familiar story in politics, and not just in Hawaii. It is also a very American story, and a very human story.

It is true that having power over land is not everything in life, nor even everything in political life. As noted, the Democrats in power did other things besides taking power over land. They set out to alter local society in many ways, and there are books to be written about what they accomplished along those lines. At the same time they were living their own individual lives, maturing and aging not just as politicians but as people with families and friends and neighbors in a changing community; and someday someone will write about this part of the life of the Democrats. But it is also true that these first-generation Democrats in power were practical professional politicians. To them power over land was crucial, and as individuals and as a group their drive to acquire real property was pronounced—as had been the case with every ruling group in Hawaii before them. There is no single subject more important in the last three decades of Hawaii's history, and that is what this book is about.

* * *

The fact that the Democratic political takeover occurred in the mid-1950s meant that, by lucky chance, the Democrats were firmly seated in power for the start of a long and spectacular economic boom that began about the time of statehood in 1959.

This was the biggest boom in Hawaii's history. It was partly a local boom, taking some of its impetus directly from the coming of statehood. But it was not only local. It was part of a nationwide boom which in turn was part of an international boom.

The opening years in Hawaii's economic takeoff were marked by two huge new forces bearing down on the Islands from outside:

The first was a mass tourist business, using the new commercial jet planes to fly in "visitors" by the hundreds of thousands each year, then by the millions.

The second was the result of the Cold War and then the involvement of the United States in a hot war in Southeast Asia—a buildup of the military establishment at Pearl Harbor and Schofield Barracks.

In the late 1950s military spending became the heaviest input into the economy of Hawaii, and in the 1960s tourism became number two, both far outstripping the old mainstays of sugar and pineapple. And the total economy grew by leaps and bounds.

The coming together of many things—strong prosperity generally in the developed world, statehood for Hawaii, and the big new inputs from mass tourism and the military buildup—produced local population and construction booms like nothing that had ever been seen in the Islands.

To put it impressionistically but accurately, the 1960s were the years when Hawaii, and especially Honolulu, went from rural to urban, from small-town to big-city, from low-rise to high-rise, from modest to gaudy, from slow-paced to hyperkinetic.

A few illustrations make the overall point. Between 1960 and 1970, the total population of Hawaii rose from 632,772 to 769,913, an increase of 22%, making Hawaii one of the fastest-growing states in the nation. Oahu, which held Honolulu, the capital and the only city in the Islands with a six-figure population, grew even faster than the state: up 26%. In 1965, when Honolulu was 54th in size among American cities, it ranked fifth in dollar value of building permits issued.[10]

For many of Hawaii's people, the combination of the economic boom and the far more open society of the Democratic years brought unprecedented opportunity and prosperity. There were new business ventures. In 1955, on the brink of the development boom, approximately 4,500 profit corporations and partnerships were registered in Hawaii; by 1965 there were about 10,300; by 1975 there were just under 25,000; and by mid-1983 there were just over 40,000. Personal after–tax income rose 125% in the 1960s. There were college educations and new professional careers. There were new homes. There were trips to Las Vegas, Disneyland, Japan. And on one of the most basic indexes of the American good life, Hawaii scored among the highest of the high. Between 1960 and 1970, the number of registered automobiles increased by 180%, from 199,829 to 358,255, so that in 1970 there was nearly one car in Hawaii for every two people—man, woman and child, serviceman and tourist.[11]

In short, in terms of disposable income and new ways to spend new money, life in Hawaii had never been so good.

In the process of this remarkable transformation, real estate values in the Islands shot up dramatically too: hundreds of percent on average, thousands of percent in specially favored places.

And all through these boom years the Democrats were in power.

In effect, they were right at the center of one of the most heated real estate markets in the world.

Of course they were not the only forces in the market. The land which was there to be bought was for the most part not the Democrats' to sell: it belonged to the big estates and corporations. And as for buyers, these were no longer just locals. Now they were appearing from the US mainland and from all over the world. Some of them were very big buyers indeed— industrialists and developers, insurance companies, oil companies, making even the Big Five look small.

Still, the Democrats were strategically placed—no one more so. They were the party in power. They made and administered land laws. In the strictly governmental sense it was for them to determine if, when, and how land in Hawaii might be developed.

In plain language, there were fortunes to be made in real estate in Hawaii, and anyone who wanted to do any sizable business in land had to deal with the Democrats.

* * *

And so we return to the basic question we ask in this book:

What has been the connection between land and power in Hawaii in the Democratic years?

In order to address this question, we set about getting down to cases by asking two other questions, very simple and obvious ones:

Who were the politically well-connected? And who were those who invested in real property and/or developed land?

We used a broad but practical definition for the politically well-connected: those elected to office, plus those appointed to government posts, plus their advisors and close associates, including family members.

These people were not hard to identify. Everybody in Hawaii knows who they are or can easily find out. The names of government appointees are a matter of public record: heads of departments and agencies, land use commissioners, judges, state and county attorneys, and so on. As for those who want to get elected to political office and stay there, they want everyone to know their names. Over the years they have paid out between them millions of dollars to make their names as widely known as possible. And the names of their close associates and advisors have become publicly known along the way.

Next, the investors and developers. To a large extent they too were easy enough to define and identify. For the most part their names are also on the public record.

In most cases when groups of investors in real estate in postwar Hawaii have publicly registered with the Territory or State, they have done so as a business *partnership*, as distinct from a *corporation*. This has mainly been because of certain tax advantages to the partnership arrangement when investing in real property.

In the local idiom of Hawaii such a partnership is often called a *hui*. This is a word that appears in the Hawaiian language and in major Chinese dialects. In both Hawaiian and Chinese it can mean a "group," which can be of many kinds. The meaning ordinarily understood in business dealings in Hawaii is something like "investment group," and this was probably taken from a South China dialect. As used in the Islands the word can also refer to small corporations. Whether the group registers with the territory or state has had no bearing on whether the word applies.

For this book the study of *huis* offered the most fruitful and comprehensive way of looking at connections between land and political power. All partnership annual statements, or reports, filed with the territorial and state governments were reviewed for the period mid-1954 to 1980. These totalled 57,636. Within these statements were to be found real estate *huis*, with the names of individual investors. This was our basic beginning source of information.

This list of names was supplemented with information selectively gathered about certain corporations, about individuals who have assisted with specific land investments and developments as attorneys and consultants, and about the ownership of particular areas of land, condominiums, etc.

So, with these two lists of names in hand—names of the politically well-connected and the investors/developers—we went back to the original question: What has been the connection between land and political power in the Democratic years?

When we put together the names of developers and the politically well-connected, the answer was immediately and strikingly obvious. In those real estate *huis*, among those real estate lawyers, among those groups of contractors, speculators, developers and landlords, are to be found the names of virtually the entire political power structure of Hawaii that evolved out of the "Democratic revolution."

The leaders of that "revolution," who by the early 1960s fully controlled the apparatus of government in the state, and who with their associates and successors maintained their control all the way into the 1970s and 1980s, have been, almost to a man, involved with real estate ownership and development.

By the 1970s, every major political and administrative institution was dominated by or contained many who had been involved in land deals, individually or as members of *huis*: the governor's office, the Legislature, the Land Use Commission, city and county councils, the mayors' offices, the Board of Regents of the University of Hawaii, the Board of Education, state and county administrative agencies, judges, police chiefs. Also included have been labor leaders and leaders of organized crime.

Many high-ranking government officials, and many at lower levels, set out to profit personally from the land boom, either by direct investment or by representing investors and developers as attorneys and in other ways.

And on the evidence of the public record the higher the rank in government, generally speaking, the more likely a politician or official is to have profited.

A further interesting truth emerges on closer inspection of the names in those land *huis*. After a while, adherence to stated political ideologies meant little. Not only is the full sweep of the post-World War II political leadership of Hawaii present, but there have been joint investments by political and business figures who on the face of things might have appeared antagonistic toward each other. All sorts of combinations appear. Democrats of feuding factions turn up as members of the same *hui*. Business interests cross party lines. Democratic politicians go into real estate deals with Republican politicians. Likewise Democratic politicians and Republican businessmen, Democratic businessmen and Republican politicians. Likewise labor and management have invested in the same *hui*. Likewise some who made their living out of administering justice in the courts of Hawaii and some who made their living out of organized crime.

In some of these cases the crossovers were apparently unknowing. A labor leader and a management official might invest in the same *hui* at the invitation of a third person, and each might not know that the other invested. The combination of the two is significant, nonetheless, for illustrating that people with such ostensibly antagonistic positions in life would have a trusted mutual acquaintance through whom each would invest in land. Most cases of crossovers between class and political affiliation in favor of real estate investment were knowing and conscious. Combinations of either kind, knowing or unknowing, make a sociological point: that after the early Democratic years a contemporary establishment emerged, constituted of elements new and old, but still heavily based on land.

To illustrate the kinds of combinations that occurred, here are a few examples from many that will be set down in the course of this book:

A land *hui* organized in the early 1960s included: the Democratic governor's chief aide on Maui; a gambler identified in court proceedings as being by 1970 the head of organized crime on Maui; a member of the old *haole* monied class. At some point a man joined who in the late 1960s went to work for Hawaii's largest government employees union and who also became a Democratic legislator.[12]

In 1966 a *hui* was formed in which the following people and groups invested: a large-scale financier who was close to the Democratic governor; two business executives who were part of the old Big Five establishment; an administrator at the East-West Center; a man who had been for 13 years the public relations director of a Big Five firm and who in the early 1960s became an aide to the Democratic governor; a Democratic politician who was at the time being appointed chief justice of the Hawaii Supreme Court; and a corporate investor, one of the Big Five in its own name.[13]

A *hui* was organized in 1973 which included: two children of the Democratic governor, one of whom later became a state judge; a former Republican Party official; several Democratic state and county officials on Maui; the Maui division director of the ILWU; a Big Five executive who helped negotiate the sale of land from his firm to the governor's chief aide on Maui who then organized the *hui* to own the land; and the director of the state department in charge of registering businesses.[14]

* * *

To say that there arose in the Democratic years a new establishment in relation to land is not to say that the various elements were always in accord.

For one thing, within the Democratic Party itself there were obvious factions. There were "mainstream" Democrats identified first with Gov. John Burns and later with his successor, Gov. George Ariyoshi. A liberal reform group of sorts was associated with Thomas P. Gill. And a dissident Democrat named Frank F. Fasi attracted a significant following. Both Gill and Fasi

at various times mounted serious but unsuccessful challenges to the Burns-
Ariyoshi dominance at the state level.

Then too, private enterprise segments of the new establishment by the
1970s believed government and unions (plus an environmental movement
that appeared in the early 1970s) to be extremely anti-business. A reporter
for the prestigious national business magazine, *Forbes*, wrote of Hawaii in
1983: "The 'paradise' state is a veritable purgatory for business, with a stag-
nant agricultural economy and a powerful political and labor union bu-
reaucracy that has smothered attempts at industrial development." He
quoted the regional director of the ILWU as saying: "We've got people on
the Land Use Commission, people all over, and the companies know if they
mess with us we can screw 'em. We've done it." *Forbes* also said that "Hawaii's
political leaders, led by Governor George Ariyoshi, could compete with the
Soviet Union's bureaucrats in their rigid regimentation of every facet of the
islands' economic life."[15]

To many all this sounded wildly overstated or inaccurate. The ILWU
director said he never made such statements to *Forbes*, though he did not
specifically deny holding the attitude that would underlie such statements.[16]
Others said they were misquoted. Most businessmen in Hawaii nevertheless
believed *Forbes* was right, although very few would say so publicly.

Perhaps paradoxically, this perceived anti-business environment made it
all the more necessary for businesses extensively regulated by
government—land developers, to pick a leading example—to make sure
that the politically well-connected and influential were included in a certain
number of deals, that legislators were put on the boards of directors of
banks, that attorneys with good ties to government were retained to deal
with agencies like the State Land Use Commission, and so on. And a fair
number of the politically influential, for their part, were quite willing to be
so included and retained.

                              *   *   *

It will become obvious in the course of this book that for the better part of
the last three decades in Hawaii, politically well-connected Democrats have
involved themselves, from start to finish, with the full range of buyers,
sellers, and developers of real estate.

In fact, in the Democratic years, overall public-private ties in land development have been so densely woven that rather than speaking of separate
entities which predominate in each sector, it is more accurate to speak of one
aggregate group involved in both government and land development.

What it comes down to is yet another repetition of that permanent truth
about politics in Hawaii. There never has been a ruling class or governing
group that has not drawn its strength and sought its continuing advantage
from land. In the Republican years land ownership meant political power.
The landowners controlled the government—they were the government.
In the Democratic years, political power gained at the polls meant a chance

to lay hold of a piece of that land power, reach out and manipulate land, buy title to large tracts, control the development rights to even larger acreage—and profit from it.

*   *   *

As an introduction to the nature and scope of the connections between political power and land development in the Democratic years, Table 1 below can be studied. It shows both Democratic and Republican officeholders, appointees, and other political figures and their associates, who appear on the public record as being associated with *huis* involved in real estate investment and development from the mid-1950s to the mid-1980s.

The table is not necessarily exhaustive—among other considerations, in Hawaii the public record does not tell the whole story about real estate dealings. But even with this qualification the table is long, and it tells its own story.

To repeat, that story is on the public record. What the reader sees in this table can be found by anyone who consults the public record, meaning government and business publications, newspapers and periodicals, and the documented information which is required by law, available in government files open to the public.

TABLE I

PUBLIC OFFICEHOLDERS AND POLITICAL FIGURES AS REAL ESTATE INVESTORS, DEVELOPERS, CONSULTANTS, ATTORNEYS, BROKERS AND SALESPERSONS

Note: The table is not exhaustive, merely representative. Names were chosen so as to include most top political leaders, a wide range of public offices, and an ethnic mix roughly the same as what existed in public officeholding in the years studied. Not every possible person is listed. Nor does the table show every office ever held by the people listed, just an indication of the range of their careers in public office. Nor is every single real estate investment they ever made or real estate activity they ever engaged in necessarily listed, just representative investments and activities. Participation in investments may be as a minor investor, a general partner, an officer in a corporation, and so on. In general the exact manner of participation is not indicated unless a large company is involved. Where an investment or activity is described as "in office," this can mean either that the person actually made the investment or engaged in the activity while in one of the offices listed, or that the investment or activity predated officeholding and continued while the person was in one or another office. Political party affiliation of elected officeholders is indicated by (D) for Democrat, (R) for Republican; this is shown for those elected to all offices except constitutional conventions and the Board of Education.

ABE, KAZUHISA (D). District Court Magistrate; Hawaii County Board of Supervisors; Senate including President; Hawaii Supreme Court. In office: helped organize 50th State Savings and Loan, which would specialize in home loans (denied federal insurance so never actually operated); Hilo Development Inc.; Robert T. Iseri and Assocs.; Kahi Inc. (general partner of Vacationland Assocs.); Kuwaye Bros. Inc. (general contractor); Kona Land Hui attorney before LUC 1963-64; attorney for LUC special-permit applicant 1965. After office: Taiyo Fudosan Kogyo Ltd. attorney before LUC 1976-77; Hitoshi Hoshi (Japanese businessman) attorney 1977 re purchase Diamond Head home for $1.4 million; Maui Bay View Estates attorney 1979; Kapalaoa Inc. attorney before LUC 1980-81; Yukio Hirai (Japanese country club owner) attorney before Honolulu Planning Commission 1981 re land client owned in Kahaluu, Oahu on which hotel was planned; attorney for Real Estate Finance Corp.

ACOBA, RAFAEL. Maui Police Pension Board; State Crime Commission. In office: SRG Hui; Ueoka Hui; Kihei Maui II Hui; Lower Main St. Hui.

ADUJA, PETER A. (R). District Court Magistrate; House; 1968 Constitutional Convention. In office: real estate broker; co-petitioner LUC application 1966-67. After office: Kawailani Hui.

AGSALUD, JOSHUA C. Director State Dept. of Labor and Industrial Relations. In office: wife held interest in Selected Investments.

AIONA, ABRAHAM (D). Maui Police Chief; Maui County Council. In office: real estate sales license; Tara Hui; Rick Medina Co.; Kahealani Ltd. Partnership.

AIU, JULIET K. Kauai Project Manager, State Dept. of Hawaiian Home Lands. In office: White Rock Ltd. Partnership.

AJIFU, RALPH K. (R). Board of Agriculture; State Land Use Commission including Chairman; House; 1968 Constitutional Convention; Senate. In office: Milolii Syndicate; ACF Hui; Wailea Ekahi II Apts. (a partnership); Tucker-Dale Building Investors; Kabbol Hui.

AKAHANE, GEORGE G. (D). Honolulu City Council including Chairman. Before office: Tampa Investments. In office: several investments and transactions with members and associates of Herbert K. Horita family; Royal Contracting Co. Ltd. employee.

AKI, RAYMOND X. (D). Kauai County Board of Supervisors including Chairman. In office: Kauai Resorts Development Inc. After office: Kailua Beach Venture.

ALAMEDA, FRANK A. Territorial Tax Assessor. In office: co-developer 26-acre residential subdivision Kaonoulu Beach, Maui.

ALCON, EMILIO S. (D). House. In office: real estate broker. After office: LR & I Development Two.

AMARAL, ALVIN T. (R). 1968 Constitutional Convention; House; Maui County Council. In office: Tara Hui; Amaral-Cole Land Co. Inc.; Wailea Ekahi II Apt. 23-D (a partnership); ACF Hui; manager Maui office Mike McCormack Realtors. After office: Kohala Makai I; Amaral-Cole Development Corp.

ANDERSON, DOMINIS G. "ANDY" (R). House; Senate; Honolulu City Managing Director. In office: Manaulu Assocs.; Anderson Enterprises (real estate partnership); invested in light industrial land Heeia, Oahu mid-1970s.

ANDREWS, LOIS M. Maui Police Pension Board; Maui Police Commission. In office: she or husband had shares Makena 700, ACF Hui.

ANSAI, TOSHIO (R). Maui County Board of Supervisors; Senate; Maui County Council. In office: Town Construction Co.; Tara Hui; Makena Beach Investors; Waikiki Grand Inc.; Kaanapali Landscapers Ltd.

ARIYOSHI, GEORGE R. (D). House; Senate; Lt. Governor; Governor. In office: George Ariyoshi and Assocs.; Hilolani Acres partner and attorney before State Board of Agriculture and Forestry 1960; member small hui that bought/sold 60 acres Kula, Maui; Milolii Syndicate attorney and partner; Royal Gardens attorney and partner; member four-man hui that 1964-66 acquired land, constructed and sold 18-unit apartment building near Queen's Hospital Honolulu; Terrace Apts. attorney before Honolulu City Council 1966; Mark Construction Inc. attorney in civil lawsuit 1966-67; C. Brewer attorney before Honolulu City Council on land use matter 1967; Coronet (a condominium) attorney before State Real Estate Commission 1968; Henry Haitsuka (general contractor) attorney before Honolulu City Council 1969; Reliance Industries Inc. shareholder; Real Estate Finance Corp. shareholder; investor miscellaneous houselots and condominium units Oahu and Big Island.

ARIYOSHI, JAMES M. Younger brother of George Ariyoshi. Career in banking, corporate finance, mortgage brokeraging, all generally with emphasis on development; also investor 1525 Partners; Kupono Assocs.; Union Title Insurance Agency.

ARIYOSHI, MITSUE. Mother of George and James Ariyoshi. Kawaihau Partners; Kupono Assocs.

ARRUDA, EARL A. Campaign manager Kauai mayoral candidate JoAnn A. Yukimura 1980, 1982. While holding that position: salesman Kauai Realty Inc.; Waipouli Ltd. Partnership.

ARZADON, JOHN J. Deputy Kauai County Engineer. In office: White Rock Ltd. Partnership.

BALDWIN, ASA F. Maui Board of Water Supply. In office: director Alexander & Baldwin; Pukalani Terrace Landco.

BAPTISTE, ANTHONY C. JR. (D). Kauai County Board of Supervisors; House; Kauai Planning Commission. After: office: RYM Venture 58.

BEPPU, HIROSHI. Maui Liquor Control Adjudication Board including Chairman. In office: Maui-Anchorage Hui; Resort 10; Romero Medical Building (a partnership); Wick Assocs.; Outrigger Maui (a partnership); Resort 5; Kamaole Hui; Kihei-Davis (a partnership); Kula 200; Murata Assocs.; Murata Hui. After office: Boulder-Maui Hui; Kamaole Two Hui; Kihei M Hui; Mid-Ten; Wells Four Hui.

BEPPU, TADAO (D). House; 1968 Constitutional Convention. In office: real estate salesman; International Development Co.; Heeia Development Co.

BICOY, BERNALDO D. (D). House. In office: Citrus Land Co.

BLAIR, RUSSELL (D). House. In office: attorney early 1980s for Kalua Koi Corp.

BRIANT, WALTER L. Chief Engineer Kauai County Water Dept. In office: Wailua Haven Inc. After office: Kilauea Gardens Ltd. Partnership; Wailua River Land Syndicate.

BROWN, GEORGE II. Board of Agriculture; Honolulu Zoning Board of Appeals. After office: Kawehi Place Hui; Honokawai Hui.

BROWN, KENNETH F. (D). Honolulu Redevelopment Agency; Gov. Burns' choice for lieutenant governor 1966; governor's aide; Senate; Hawaii Historic Places Review Board; Hawaii Community Development Authority (Kakaako redevelopment); East-West Center Board of Governors. In office: architect; Olohana Corp.; Kapiolani Park Land Co.; director Amfac; director Island Holidays Ltd.; developer Holiday Isle Hotel (Waikiki); Mauna Lani Resort Inc.; Ainamalu Corp. (co-developer high-rise office building downtown Honolulu at 1164 Bishop St.); landowner in own right, including in Pelekunu

Valley, Molokai, and near Diamond Head, where mid-1960s was officer Diamond Head Improvement Association, formed to promote high-rise development between Diamond Head and ocean.

BURNS, C.E.S. "FRANK" JR. Land Use Commission. In office: Amfac plantation manager and executive.

BURNS, JAMES S. Son of Gov. Burns; Circuit Court Judge; Intermediate Court of Appeals Judge including Chief Judge. Before office: appointed guardian for Campbell Estate minors 1968, Campbell Estate master 1976; law practice with miscellaneous land and development matters. In office: Rama and Assocs.; Nukolii hui.

BURNS, JOHN A. (D). Delegate to Congress; Governor. Before office: realtor. In office: Burns and Co., which owned small commercial building Kailua, Oahu.

CARRAS, JAMES R. Land Use Commission. In office: executive with Honolulu Iron Works Inc., which made building materials.

CASEY, BRIAN L. (D). Director Office of Information and Complaint City and County of Honolulu; Honolulu City Council; Deputy Director City Dept. of Auditoriums. In office: Mokuleia Investment; International Development Co.

CAYETANO, BENJAMIN J. (D). House; Senate. In office: attorney for Real Estate Finance Corp.

CHANG, ANTHONY K.U. (D). 1978 Constitutional Convention; hearings officer Dept. of Social Services and Housing; Senate. In office: CYC (a partnership).

CHANG, ROBERT W.B. (D). House; Circuit Court Judge. In office: Aupuni & Assocs.

CHIKASUYE, CLESSON Y. (D). Honolulu County Board of Supervisors and City Council. In office: Aina Assocs.; Hawaii Land Hui; Ala Ilima Apartments (a partnership); Pacific Real Estate Trust; wife was investor Pahoa Enterprise; law practice with miscellaneous land and development matters including, after office, serving as guardian for Campbell and Damon estates minors, and Bishop Estate master.

CHINEN, JON J. District Court Magistrate; US Bankruptcy Court Judge. In office: Pukoo J.V.; K&H Inc.; Crown Escrow Inc.

CHING, CLARENCE T.C. Chief campaign fundraiser for John Burns. While holding that position: general partner International Development Co.; real estate broker; Loyalty Enterprises; Loyalty Mortgage Co.; Loyalty Development Co.

CHING, DOROTHY K. Wife of Francis M.F. Ching (below), succeeded to certain of his interests after his death 1975. In her own right State Ethics Commission. In office: Kauai Ventures; Ocean View Ltd. Partnership; Kilauea Gardens Ltd. Partnership; Elysium Corp.

CHING, FRANCIS M.F. (R). Kauai County Board of Supervisors and Council; Senate; Kauai Mayor. In office: Ma-Ka-Poi Ventures; Kukuiolono Ventures. Between office: Kalaheo Assocs.

CHOI, WILBERT H.S. Land Use Commission including Chairman. In office: landscaper/nurseryman; Kaanapali Landscapers Ltd.; director Capital Investment Co.

CHOY, RICHARD B.F. Land Use Commission. In office: Waimanalo Acres; Hui Maluniu.

CHUCK, WALTER G. House, Senate Clerk; District Court Magistrate. In office: Waialae Nui Development Co. After office: Crown Land Corp.; Honolulu Trust Co. Ltd.; American Security Properties Inc.; Amity Waipahu Inc.; Kailua Towers (a partnership).

CHUN, DAI HO. East-West Center officer; University of Hawaii professor. In office: Pyramid Ranch Co.; Cal-Electric Investment Co.

CHUNG HARRY C.C. Honolulu Mayor Frank F. Fasi's chief fundraiser. While holding that position: Twentieth Century Furniture Inc.; Lakeview Gardens Assocs.

CHUNG, NORMAN K. Hawaii Employment Relations Board including Chairman; Honolulu Corporation Counsel. After office: Ben Tanabe & Assocs.; Kapiolani Development Co.; Moana Ebbtide Hotel Inc.; Kai Lani Manor Inc.; law practice involving miscellaneous land and development matters, such as in 1962 testifying before legislative committee on behalf Kaiser Hawaii Kai Development Co., Trousdale Construction Co., and Oceanic Properties (Castle & Cooke subsidiary).

CHUNG, WILLIAM C.H. Brother of Harry C.C. Chung; Honolulu Police Commission. In office: Lakeview Gardens Assocs.; Kona Highlands Development Co.

CLARK, CHARLES G. Honolulu Managing Director; State Superintendent of Schools; Director State Dept. of Health. In office: Hui Kala.

COBB, CHRISTOPHER. Chairman Board of Land and Natural Resources. Before office: attorney for miscellaneous land and development matters, including for Kalua Koi Corp., Boise Cascade, Signal Properties Inc., Oceanic Properties Inc. In office: Smith & Cobb (a land investment partnership); Ahualoa Land Co.

CORREA, MAXINE J. (D). Kauai Planning Commission and County Council. In office (she and/or husband): JP Enterprises; White Rock Ltd. Partnership; Hiku Assocs.; Nonou Mountain Estates Inc.; Nonou Mountain Estates (a partnership).

CRAVALHO, ELMER F. (D). House including Speaker; Mayor of Maui. In office: officer, shareholder MDG Supply Inc., which had building materials department and which invested in resort land in Kihei and Makena, Maui; in own right invested in several small lots Maui.

CUSKADEN, EVERETT L. Land Use Commission. In office: attorney, one of whose firm's specialties was real estate and condominium law, including as clients, for example, Association of Apartment Owners of Yacht Harbor Towers Condominium.

DAHLBERG, JAMES L.K. (R). Hawaii County Council. In office: realtor; Lalamilo Assocs.; Kohala Makai I.

DE LA PENA, RAMON. Director Kauai Office of Economic Development. In office: Carpp Enterprises.

DE LUZ, FRANK III (D). Hawaii County Council. In office: Kailua-Kona Land Assocs.; Gold Coast Investments; NSBL Partnership.

DEVENS, PAUL. Honolulu Managing Director, Corporation Counsel. After office: Whiteacre Investments; law practice with miscellaneous land and development matters, including representing Oceanside Properties Inc. before Honolulu city government.

DEVEREUX, DOROTHY L. (R). House; 1968 Constitutional Convention. In office: Pau Hana Hui.

DOI, HERBERT T. Kauai Director Dept. of Personnel Services. In office: Kauai Ventures; White Rock Ltd. Partnership.

DOI, NELSON K. (D). Hawaii County Attorney; 1950 and 1968 Constitutional Conventions; Senate including President; Circuit Court Judge; Lt. Governor. In office: M&D Investors; Nusite Developers; Keolu Partners; Komohana Investors.

DOI, REGINALD Y. Kauai Planning Commission. In Office: Kundo Assocs.; Thomas Baker Assocs.; Hanapepe 7.

DURAN, RAMON A. Director Advanced Planning Division Honolulu Planning Dept.; State Land Use Commission executive officer; Honolulu Dept. of General Planning deputy planning officer; Director Honolulu Dept. of Parks and Recreation. In office: Simon & Seafort Venture; Kaneohe Woods Ltd. Partnership.

ESPOSITO, O. VINCENT (D). House including Speaker; Senate. In office: Hilton-Burns Hotels Co. Inc.; Hawaiian Village Inc.; attorney handling miscellaneous land and development matters, including 1960 Honolulu City Council rezoning of land for Kahala Hilton Hotel. After office: KBH Co.

FASI, FRANK F. (D). Senate; Honolulu City Council; 1968 Constitutional Convention; Mayor of Honolulu. In office: Frank F. Fasi Supply Co. (buy/sell new/used buildings and construction materials); Fasi family 1954 purchased 4.5 acres near Oahu Prison for Fasi Supply Co., later leased for miscellaneous light industrial/commercial operations.

FELIX, JOHN H. Administrative Assistant to Gov. William F. Quinn; Honolulu Civil Service Commission; Honolulu Redevelopment Agency including Chairman; Honolulu Board of Water Supply including Chairman; Honolulu Planning Commission including Chairman; Honolulu Police Commission; Honolulu Board of Parks and Recreation including Chairman. In office: Park Surf (a partnership); Monte Vista Development Co.; Windward Partners.

FERNANDES, JOHN B. SR. (D). Kauai County Board of Supervisors; House; Senate. In office: F&M Bros. After office: JB Assocs.

FERNANDES, WILLIAM E. (D). House; Senate; Deputy Director State Dept. Agriculture; Kauai County Council. In office: F&M Bros.; Toshiharu Yama Assocs.; JB Assocs.

FERRY, JAMES P. Chairman Board of Land and Natural Resources. Before office: real estate broker; tract manager Joe Pao Realty; Ferry and Assocs.; Jim P. Ferry & Richard A. Botelho Realty Co. After office: planning consultant, including on Joe Pao LUC application regarding Mount Olomana, Oahu 1969-70; Manaulu Assocs.; JB Properties; director Kanoa Estate Inc.

FONG, HIRAM L. JR. (R). House; Honolulu City Council. In office: part of father's businesses, outlined below.

FONG, HIRAM L. SR. (R). House; 1950 Constitutional Convention; US Senate. In office: principal of a constellation of development, finance and law firms that over time led to Fong becoming one of wealthiest men in Hawaii. Development projects included creation of residential community on Campbell Estate land at Makakilo, and two speculative subdivisions on Hawaii: Fern Forest Vacation Estates and Royal Hawaiian Estates.

FREITAS, ANDREW S. Maui Deputy Police Chief. In office: co-developer 26-acre residential subdivision Kaonoulu Beach, Maui.

FUJITA, ARTHUR S. 1973-74 Kauai Charter Review Commission; Kauai Planning Commission. In office: Kauai-Kamuela Assocs.; Kilauea Gardens Ltd. Partnership; Lucky Twenty-Five.

FUJIUCHI, GUY Y. Dean of Student Services Kauai Community College. While holding that position: Kaumualii Investment Co.; White Rock Ltd. Partnership.

FUJIYAMA, WALLACE S. University of Hawaii Board of Regents; Aloha Stadium Authority. In office: Apartment Partners 71; Kailua Towers (a partnership); Kapalama Investment Co.; V&F Investments; Punchbowl Properties Investors; as attorney handled miscellaneous land and development matters, including for Seibu Group Enterprise's Prince Hotels of Hawaii Inc. before Maui Planning Commission 1979, Hasegawa Komuten (USA) Inc. beginning 1982 regarding its Nukolii, Kauai resort, Grove Farm Co. before Kauai Planning Commission 1983, and Real Estate Finance Corp.

FUKUNAGA, CAROL (D). 1978 Constitutional Convention; House; aide to Lt. Gov. John D. Waihee III. In office: Intent Hawaii.

FUKUOKA, S. GEORGE (D). District Court Magistrate; Maui County Board of Supervisors and Council; Senate; Circuit Court Judge. In office: Heeia Development Co.; B&F Enterprises; Maui-Anchorage Hui; Upten; Waipao Joint Venture; Kam 5; Mid Ten; Puuone Seaview Partnership; Maui Beach Hotel Inc.; Valley Isle Realty Inc.; Shirley Yokouchi Hui; Maui Development Co. Ltd.; investor various parcels Kihei, Maui.

FUNAKI, JAMES T. House Majority Chief Attorney. In office: O&T Investors; as attorney had extensive practice before LUC, including on behalf of Oceanic Properties Inc., Kalua Koi Corp., and Kamehameha Development Corp. (wholly-owned subsidiary Bishop Estate).

GAGE, REGINALD P. Real Property Assessor State Dept. of Taxation, then Kauai Finance Dept. While holding that position: White Rock Ltd. Partnership.

GARCIA, RICHARD (D). House. In office: real estate salesman's license; industrial relations Alexander & Baldwin; as of 1978 owned 5 pieces property Oahu collectively valued at $940,000.

GILL, THOMAS P. (D). House; US House of Representatives; Lt. Governor. In office: Thomas P. Gill Trust half owner 27,000 square-foot lot Waikiki on which Seaside Towers leasehold condominium built; as attorney occasionally handled land matters, such as in early 1960s application to rezone 26,000 square feet Kaneohe to hotel-apartment.

HAAKE, RICHARD H. Maui Police Captain. While holding that position: Haake First Hui; Ueoka Hui.

HAGINO, GERALD T. (D). 1978 Constitutional Convention; House; Senate. In office: Intent Hawaii.

HALE, HELENE H. (D). Hawaii County Board of Supervisors including Chairman; County Council. In office: Hawaii Isle Realty Ltd.

HAMASU, EDGAR A. Hawaii County Planning Director; staff of State Dept. of Education; Deputy to Chairman Board of Land and Natural Resources. In office: H&H Partners; Apartment Partners 71.

HANAPI, EMPEROR A. Honolulu City Clerk. After office: Prime Garden Venture; Aloha Foster Venture.

HARA, STANLEY I. (D). House; Senate. In office: Robert T. Iseri & Assocs.; Vacationland Assocs.; Hilo Hawaiian Investors; Kona Hawaiian Resorts Investors; Sea-Pac Properties; Komohana Estates Development; Akahi Investors; Kona Palisades Assocs.

HARDING, KENNETH R. Kauai County Public Information Officer; Director Kauai Office of Economic Development. Before office: Kalani Runne Assocs. In office: Olohena Ridge Assocs.

HARE, C. MICHAEL. Lawyer representing Waiahole-Waikane Community Association. While representing WWCA: CS VIII.

HARUKI, BARBARA T. Circuit Court assistant clerk. While holding that position: Kauai Land Holding Co.

HASEGAWA, EDITH M. Secretary to Councilman Matsuo Takabuki. While holding that position: bought two apartment-zoned lots Salt Lake; later resold.

HASHIMOTO, HENRY H. Principal Kauai High and Intermediate School. In office: White Rock Ltd. Partnership.

HATA, FRANK J. Leading fundraiser Gov. Ariyoshi. While holding that position: University Village Apartments (a partnership).

HATAISHI, VALENTINE K. Executive Secretary Kauai Liquor Control Commission. In office: Lawai Ventures; Kauai Ventures.

HAWKINS, ALLEN R. District Court Magistrate; Honolulu Prosecutor; Circuit Court Judge. After office: Windward Partners; Enchanted Lake Partners.

HEEN, ERNEST N. JR. (D). House. In office: Project coordinator for principal developer Kaneohe Ranch Co. land; real estate salesman's license.

HEEN, ERNEST N. SR. (D). Honolulu City Clerk; Senate; Director Territorial Dept. Public Welfare; Honolulu Board of Supervisors and Council. In office: real estate broker's license.

HEEN, WALTER M. (D). House; Senate; Honolulu City Council; District Court Judge; Circuit Court Judge; US Attorney; US District Court Judge; Hawaii Intermediate Court of Appeals Judge. In office: WSL Assocs.; Delpy Developers Assocs.; as attorney handled miscellaneous land and development matters.

HEEN, WILLIAM H. (D). Circuit Court Judge; Honolulu City Attorney; Senate including President; 1950 Constitutional Convention. In office: Moses Akiona Ltd.; Market Place Ltd.; law firm had extensive land and development practice, including on behalf of Capital Investment Co., Waianae Development Co., Trade Wind Development Co., Hawaiian Trust Co.

HEFTEL, CECIL (D). US House of Representatives. In office: Heftel (12.5%), Heftel Broadcasting Corp. (84.3%), plus one other individual (3.1%) 1977-78 bought/sold 154-acre parcel Kamaole Homesteads, Maui.

HENDERSON, RICHARD (R). Senate. In office: The Realty Investment Co. Ltd.; Riverside Assocs.; Leilani Investors; Realty Finance Inc.; Leilani Estates Inc.; Kapoho Land and Development Co.

HEW, JEROME Y.K. (D). Kauai County Council and Clerk. In office: White Rock Ltd. Partnership; miscellaneous small investments.

HIGA, KASE. Maui County Attorney; District Court Judge; Circuit Court Judge. In office: Nukolii hui; Kula Venture; Shirley Yokouchi Hui.

HILL, WILLIAM H. (R). Senate including President. In office: The Realty Investment Co.; director C. Brewer.

HIMENO, STANLEY T. Honolulu Planning Commission. After office: STH Land Assocs.; Kawela Development Co.; Kuhio East Joint Venture; Rainbow Developers; bought/sold several apartment-zoned lots Salt Lake.

HIRAI, SEICHI "SHADOW." Senate Clerk. In office: Heeia Development Co.; Ethereal Inc.; Leilani Estates Joint Venture; Luke Yasaka et al Partnership; as attorney represented miscellaneous land and development matters, such as LUC application for Damon Estate 1966.

HIRAMOTO, MILDRED K. Circuit Court administrative assistant. While holding that position: Waipouli Ltd. Partnership.

HIYANE, GEORGE. 1973-74 Kauai Charter Review Commission. In office: White Rock Ltd. Partnership.

HONDA, EDWIN H. Board of Education; Director Dept. of Regulatory Agencies; District Court Judge; Circuit Court Judge. In office: Nukolii hui; David Kong Hui.

HONG, HERBERT. Honolulu Finance Dept. While holding his position: Milolii Syndicate.

HONG, TANY S. Director Dept. of Regulatory Agencies; Attorney General; District Court Judge. Before office: N&H Co. In office: VCCK Hui.

HOUGHTAILING, GEORGE K. Honolulu Planning Director. After office: frequent appearances before government land use agencies on developing land; Partners of Hawaii XVI; Partners of Hawaii XVII.

HULTEN, JOHN J. SR. Senate including President. In office: real estate sales license; real estate appraiser; Hawaiian Escrows Ltd.

IHA, PETER S. (D). House. After office: Jack H. Ujimori Development.

IIDA, RONALD B. Kauai Board of Water Supply. In office: Waipouli Ltd. Partnership; White Rock Ltd. Partnership; Poipu Sands Ltd. Partnership.

INABA, GORO. Land Use Commission. In office: manager small hotel Kona; brothers very active in land investing and developing Big Island, brother Norman especially.

ING, ANDREW T.F. Director Dept. of Budget and Finance. Before office: Loyalty Enterprises; Loyalty Mortgage Co. In office: bought apartment-zoned lot Salt Lake, sold after left office. After office: Garden Investors; director Maui Land and Pineapple Co.; Kulana-Nani.

ING, LAWRENCE N.C. Hawaii Housing Authority; Assistant US Magistrate. Before office: Waipuilani Hui Assocs. In office: Ueoka Hui; Kawehi Place Hui; Ala Kai Assocs.; HIIMMS Hui; LVGV Hui; PCC Apt. No. 1404 Hui; 2133 Wells St. Investors; plus extensive other real estate investments and, as attorney, handling of land and development matters.

ISHIMOTO, ARTHUR U. State Adjutant General. In office: Royal Gardens.

IZUMI, FRANCIS M. Deputy State Attorney General assigned to the Board of Land and Natural Resources. In office: Aloha Maui Co. Inc. After office: extensive law practice in area of land and development, representing number of clients before government agencies, including Amfac before the LUC.

IZUMI, JAMES M. Assistant House Clerk; Maui Personnel Director. In office: Waipao Joint Venture; Valley Isle Realty Inc.; Hui Akamai; Miyaki Hui.

JITCHAKU, RICHARD M. (D). Hawaii County Board of Supervisors; aide to Sen. John Ushijima. In office: Kona Highlands Development Co.; GHR Investment Co. After office: extensive developer Hawaii Housing Authority projects on Hawaii.

KAGAWA, CLAY A. 1973-74 Kauai Charter Review Commission; Kauai Deputy County Engineer. In office: Kundo Assocs.; White Rock Ltd. Partnership.

KAGE, KAZUO. Maui Planning Commission. In office: The Puuhala Assocs.; Waipao Joint Venture; Shirley Yokouchi Hui.

KAITO, BEN F. (D). Honolulu City Council; Honolulu Charter Review Commission early 1970s; per diem District Court Judge; hearing officer State Dept. of Health. In office: Moki & Assocs.; Punchbowl Plaza (a partnership); BL Assocs.

KAITO, FRANK M. Honolulu Chief Treasurer. In office: Milolii Syndicate.

KAMAKA, HIRAM K. (D). House; 1968 Constitutional Convention; Director State Dept. of Finance; Honolulu Chief Budget Officer. In office: Kaena Management Co. Inc.; attorney for miscellaneous small developments, generally in windward Oahu. Between office: attorney for Real Estate Finance Corp.

KAMALII, KINAU BOYD (R). House; Senate; Hawaiian Claims Study Commission. In office: ACF Hui.

KAMO, JAMES H. Senate Clerk. After office: Hirano Bros. Ltd. & Assocs.

KANAZAWA, KINJI. Honolulu Planning Commission. In office: Elko Terrace Development Co. of Hawaii; Nuuanu Ventures; HSM Ventures; Manoa Ventures; realtor. After office: SGP Ventures; Venture Six; HKH Ventures; Oceanview Ventures; 835 Kapaakea Apartments (a partnership); Palmer Joint Venture; Pearl III Venture; JCY & Assocs.

KANEMOTO, SHIGETO. House Assistant Clerk, Clerk. In office: Alani Development Co.

KATO, HIROSHI (D). House; 1968 Constitutional Convention; Circuit Court Judge. In office: Heeia Development Co.; Lakeview Manor; K&M Assocs.; Kalihi-Ashford Assocs.

KAUAHI, CHRISTOPHER O.H. Captain, Criminal Investigation Division, Kauai Police Dept. In office: White Rock Ltd. Partnership.

KAUHANE, CHARLES E. (D). House including Speaker; 1950 and 1968 Constitutional Conventions. After office: Akamai Development Inc.

KAWAHARA, WILLIAM S. (D). Hawaii County Council. In office: realtor.

KAWAKAMI, NORITO (R). District Court Magistrate; House; Circuit Court Judge. In office: Kahili Development Co. Inc.; wife invested in Kauai Ventures, Momoyo Kuboyama Assocs.

KAWAKAMI, RICHARD A. (D). Kauai Charter Commission; 1968 Constitutional Convention; House. In office: Lihue Industrial Development Co.; Kauai Ventures; Kahili Development Co.

KAWASAKI, DUKE T. (D). In office: realtor; developer; Wiliwili Nui Ridge Subdivision (a partnership); HIG Enterprise.

KEALA, FRANCIS A. Honolulu Police Chief. Before office: Kipsy Assocs.

KEALOHA, JOSEPH G. JR. Office of Hawaiian Affairs. Before office: Waipuilani Hui Assocs.; Puuone Development (a partnership). In office: Kilolani Hui; Ponahawai Ltd. Partnership; Ueoka Hui.

KENNEDY, EUGENE F. (R). Honolulu Police Captain; Honolulu Board of Supervisors and Council. In office: developer; real estate broker; Robert T. Iseri & Assocs.; Eugene F. Kennedy Co.; Eugene F. Kennedy & Assocs. et al Hilo Venture.

KIDO, MITSUYUKI (D). House; Honolulu Board of Supervisors; Senate. In office: realtor; developer; Moiliili Developers; Century Investments; International Development Co.; Loyalty Investments; Cal-Electric Investment Co.; Waialae-Kahala Medical Building (a partnership); Eastern Building Co.; Heeia Development Co.; Hung Wo Ching Realty Co.; Waical Development Co.; Contractor's Building Supplies; Hale Hui Ltd.; Hawaii Engineering Supplies; Rural Investments Inc.; Leeward Development Corp. After office: director Hawaiian Pacific Industries Inc.; L&K Assocs.; Hui o Kauai I; M&H Assocs.; Al Watanabe and Assocs.; Monte Vista Development Co.; Wailua Rise (a partnership); Windward Partners; Enchanted Lake Partners; Heeia Assocs.; MSW Ltd.

KIDO, SUNAO. Brother of Mitsuyuki. Assistant House Clerk; Deputy to Chairman and then Chairman Board of Land and Natural Resources; Public Utilities Commission. In office: real estate salesman's license; Heeia Development Co.; Rural Investments Inc.

KIM, KE NAM. Head Dept. of Accounting and General Services; Deputy Director Honolulu Dept. of Transportation Services. In office: Waikele Estates; Hale Makahuena Investors.

KIM, WALLACE S.W. Honolulu Deputy Planning Director; planner with Board of Land and Natural Resources. In office: bought apartment-zoned lot Salt Lake, later resold.

KING, SAMUEL P. District Court Magistrate; Circuit Court Judge; US District Court Judge. In office: MKG Corp; Marine Surf Waikiki Hotel (a partnership).

KIYABU, KEN S. (D). House. In office: realtor.

KOBAYASHI, ANN H. (R). Honolulu Police Commission; Senate. In office: Pensacola Assocs.

KOGA, GEORGE M. (D). House; Honolulu City Council. In office: Alani Development Co.; investor apartment-zoned lots Salt Lake.

KOMO, RICHARD R. District Court Magistrate and Judge; Circuit Court Judge. In office: Hawaiian Island Pacific Properties Investments Enterprises; Maui Palms Hotel; wife invested in Ueoka Hui.

KONDO, RALPH W. Director Dept. of Taxation. In office: KIC, A Partnership.

KONDO, RONALD Y. (D). House; Maui County Council; Gov. Ariyoshi's representative on Maui. In office: 934 Ventures; real estate broker's license; Maui Realty Co. Inc.; Laulima Inc.

KOSHIBA, JAMES E.T. Judicial Selection Commission including Chairman. Before office: Waipuilani Hui Assocs.

KUBOTA, ERNEST H. District Court Magistrate and Judge; Circuit Court Judge. In office: Waiehu Heights Assocs.; Lee Construction Inc.

KUNIMURA, TONY T. (D). Kauai County Board of Supervisors; House; Mayor of Kauai. In office: real estate salesman's license.

KUTAKA, MASAO. Kauai County Engineer; Kauai Charter Commission; Kauai Board of Ethics. In office: consulting engineer; Wailua Haven Inc.

LEE, ANDREW S.O. Deputy State Attorney General, often working on major land and water cases. In office: Thurston-Lees Co.

LEE, HERBERT K.H. (D). House; Senate including President. In office: co-developer Professional Center; subleased lot Waikiki, on which built Hawaiian King Hotel during last year in Legislature. After office: Herbert K.H. Lee and Assocs.; Kaimoku Partners; business associate Henry J. Kaiser in developing Hawaii Kai.

LEE, SAMUEL S. Dept. of Land and Natural Resources, Land Agent on Kauai. While holding that position: Kauai Ventures.

LEWIS, ALFRED JR. Kauai Planning Commission. After office: Kauai Land Holding Co.

LOO, FRANK W.C. (D). House; Honolulu City Council. In office: Eugene F. Kennedy Co.; Robert T. Iseri & Assocs.; Aloha Loans and Mortgage Co.; miscellaneous small investments.

LOUIS, LEIGHTON S.C. Honolulu Planning Commission and Director. After office: LL & Assocs.; Makiki Realty Inc.; real estate consultant.

LUM, HERMAN T.F. House Clerk; US Attorney; Circuit Court Judge; Hawaii Supreme Court including Chief Justice. In office: Lumleong Enterprises; Waialae-Kahala Medical Building (a partnership); leasing one acre Bishop Estate commercial property Kakaako, subleased to miscellaneous tenants.

LUNA, B. MARTIN. Hawaii Housing Authority; Democratic Party Chairman Maui. In office: Ueoka Hui; Ulupalakua Hui; SNTLU Assocs.; Lower Main St. Hui; D&L Venture; SNL Assocs.; 2133 Wells St. Investors; LST Partners; Hoyer Hawaii Corp.; Kahili Ltd. Partnership; law practice extensively involved with representing land and development interests before government agencies.

MARK, SHELLEY M. Director Dept. of Planning and Economic Development. In office: Magnolia Shopping Center Inc.

MARUMOTO, MASAJI. Supreme Court. In office: Cal-Electric Investment Co. After office: attorney handling miscellaneous land and development matters, such as for Amfac mid-1970s in effort to erect hotel at Poipu, Kauai that would exceed county building height limit.

MASUNAGA, DR. NOBUICHI. Board of Land and Natural Resources and its territorial predecessor. In office: International Development Co.; Hirotoshi Yamamoto and Assocs.; Waianae Assocs. After office: Leeward Venture; Bayview Venture; Kauai Ventures.

MASUOKA, GEORGE M. Hawaii Public Broadcasting Authority Board; per diem District Court Judge. In office: Kumukahi Assocs.; Banyan Tree Hui.

MATAYOSHI, HERBERT T. (D). Hawaii County Board of Supervisors and Council; Mayor. In office: Kaohu St. Building Co.

MATSUI, YOSHIKAZU "ZUKE." Maui Planning Commission including Chairman; Deputy Planning Director. In office: Valley Isle Realty Inc.; Nukolii hui; Waipao Joint Venture; YM Venture; Hui Akamai; Miyaki Hui.

MATSUKAGE, DANIEL R. Honolulu Planning Commission. Before office: Alani Development Co.; member four-man hui that included George Ariyoshi that built/sold 18 unit apartment building near Queen's Hospital Honolulu. In office: Real Estate Finance Corp. After office: Makawao Inc.

MATSUNAGA, SPARK M. (D). House; US House of Repesentatives; US Senate. In office: Poki Apartments (a partnership); attorney handling miscellaneous land and development matters, such as representing Ruddy Tongg and others before Honolulu city government 1957 on rezoning for medium-rise buildings near Diamond Head.

MAU, CHUCK (D). Honolulu Board of Supervisors; Tax Appeal Court Judge; 1950 Constitutional Convention; First Circuit Court Judge. After office: Territorial Investors; International Development Co.; Monte Vista Development Co.; Wadco Inc.; Loyalty Enterprises; Town Investment; Union Title Insurance Agency; Kawela Development Co.; co-buyer/seller four apartment-zoned lots Salt Lake; as attorney handled miscellaneous land and development matters.

McCLUNG, DAVID C. (D). House; Senate including President; State Chairman Democratic Party. In office: Wiliwili Nui Ridge Subdivision (a partnership); interest in land under pineapple cannery in Lahaina; wife had interest Fong Assocs.; as attorney handled miscellaneous land and development matters, such as for Signal Properties Inc. After office: Leialoha Assocs.; Maui Waiohuli Partners.

MEDEIROS, JOHN J. (R). House. In office: Manaulu Assocs.; realtor.

MEDINA, RICARDO (D). Maui County Council. In office: Tara Hui; Rick Medina Co.

MINK, PATSY T. (D). House; Senate; US House of Representatives; Honolulu City Council including Chair. Between offices: early 1960s attorney Yoshikawa Development Co. Ltd.

MIURA, TAD T. SR. Administrative Assistant to Mayor of Kauai; County Clerk. In office; KY II Enterprises. After office: salesman Kauai Realty Inc.

MIYAHIRA, ETHEL M. Circuit Court administrative assistant. While holding that position: M. Seki Hui.

MIYAHIRA, WINSTON S. Director Maui Dept. of Liquor Control. In office: RMB Hui; Waipao Joint Venture; Shirley Yokouchi Hui; Yokouchi Hui.

MIZUGUCHI, HARRIET K. University of Hawaii Board of Regents. In office: Hui NKM.

MIZUGUCHI, NORMAN K. (D). House; Senate. In office: Nukolii hui.

MIZUHA, JACK H. (R). Kauai County Board of Supervisors; District Court Magistrate; University of Hawaii Board of Regents; Circuit Court Judge; Attorney General; Supreme Court. In office: Oroville Investment Co.; wife in Royal Gardens. After office: director Kyo-ya Co. Ltd. (vehicle by which wealthy Japanese businessman Kenji Osano owned several hotels Waikiki).

MOLINA, MANUEL S. (D). Maui County Council; Maui Office of Council Services. In office: F&D Hui; Tara Hui; Rick Medina Co.

MORIOKA, THEODORE T. (D). House; 1968 Constitutional Convention. In office: real estate sales license; All Hawaii Investment Corp.; Waikiki Land Development Co.

MORISAKI, LANNY H. (D). Maui County Board of Supervisors and Council including Council Chairman. In office: Valley Isle Realty Inc.; Nukolii hui; Miyaki Hui; Maui Development Co. Ltd.

NAGATA, BARTON H. Kauai District School Superintendent. After office: salesman Kauai Realty Inc.; Ocean View Ltd. Partnership.

NAGATA, RUSSEL S. Various top posts Dept. Regulatory Agencies/Dept. Commerce and Consumer Affairs. In office: Liko's Hui.

NAKAMOTO, ROY K. District Court Magistrate. In office: Waipio Properties; Kona Highlands Development Co.; Yasuo Kuwaye and Assocs.

NAKAMURA, EDWARD H. University of Hawaii Board of Regents; Supreme Court. In office: Nukolii hui.

NAKAMURA, GEORGE T. District Court Magistrate and Judge. In office: Surf and Sand Apartments (a partnership); Century Development Inc.; Ujimori Development Ltd.; Beretania Plaza (a partnership); Kohou Assocs.

NAKAMURA, HOWARD K. Maui Planning Director; Maui Managing Director. In office: ACF Hui; INT Investment Co.; SNL Assocs.

NAKAMURA, MILDRED M. Secretary to Honolulu Councilman Clesson Chikasuye. While holding that position: bought/sold two apartment-zoned lots Salt Lake as head of hui.

NAKASHIMA, SUMIO (D). District Court Magistrate; House. After office: Kona Palisades Assocs.; Hawaiian Island Pacific Properties Investment; Kona Tradewinds; Royal Gardens; 2 K's; Kona Hawaiian Resorts Investors; Highland Terrace Unit #1; Kona Heavens; Alaska-Hawaii Venture.

NAKASONE, ROBERT H. Maui County Council including Chairman. In office: paint business; bought/sold two farm lots totalling 4.4 acres; wife had share Kula-Lahaina Partners.

NAKEA, CLIFFORD L. Kauai District Court Judge. In office: Kauai-Kamuela Assocs.

NAPIER, ALEXANDER J. JR. Land Use Commission. In office: officer Kahua Ranch Ltd. which planned resort on portion of its land.

NIITANI, GEORGE T. Dept. of Land and Natural Resources Parks Superintendent on Kauai. In office: Kundo Assocs.

NISHIMURA, SHIRO "SALLY." Land Use Commission. In office: Kukuiolono Assocs.; Opaikaa Assocs.; Hui o Kauai I. After office: Lawai Development Co.; Konohiki Estates.

NORWOOD, WILLIAM R. Honolulu Planning Commission; Labor and Industrial Relations Appeals Board; administrative assistant to Gov. Burns; High Commissioner Trust Territories of the Pacific. In office: Pyramid Ranch Co. After office: Black Construction Corp.

NUROCK, DR. ARNOLD B. Kauai Director State Sea Grant Program. While holding that position: Kilauea Gardens Ltd. Partnership.

O'CONNOR, DENNIS E.W. (D). 1968 Constitutional Convention; House; Senate. In office: Waialae Enterprises; Kai Iki Corp.; one of principal attorneys for residential lessees seeking to convert possession of their lots to fee simple.

OGATA, THOMAS S. (D). Senate; Circuit Court Judge; Supreme Court. In office: Pukalani Terrace Landco.

OHATA, ROBERT O. Maui Planning Director. After office: 2133 Wells St. Investors.

OKAMURA, THOMAS (D). Aide to Honolulu Councilman George Akahane; 1978 Constitutional Convention; Board of Education; House. In office: Intent Hawaii.

OMORI, MORIO. Administrative assistant US Sen. Daniel K. Inouye. In office: Francis I. Tsuzuki & Assocs.; King Kalani Apartment Hotel (a partnership); Colorado Land Investors; Broomfield 103 Acres; Constructors Hawaii Inc.; law practice extensively involved with land and development, including on behalf of Chinn Ho concerns, and Bishop and Austin estates before the LUC in late 1960s.

OSHIRO, ROBERT C. (D). House; Democratic Party Chairman; key campaign strategist in gubernatorial campaigns John Burns 1970 and George Ariyoshi in 1974, 1978 and 1982; East-West Center Board of Governors. In office: as attorney represented several major businesses, including Castle & Cooke's Lanai Co. before the LUC in 1974, and Amfac in its efforts in the late 1970s-early 1980s to obtain government approval for a garbage-to-energy plant in Waipahu.

OSORIO, ELROY T.L. SR. (R). Hawaii County Board of Supervisors. In office: General Realty Corp.

OTA, CHARLES S. (D). Land Use Commission; University of Hawaii Board of Regents; Maui Planning Commission; Maui County Council. In office: Waipao Joint Venture; Nukolii hui; Valley Isle Realty Inc.; real estate broker's license; Kamuela Assocs.; Hui 3YO; Shirley Yokouchi Hui; Yokouchi Hui; Hale Kaanapali (a partnership); Pukalani Terrace Landco.

OURA, MITSUO. Land Use Commission. In office: business agent Carpenters Union Local 745.

PACARRO, RUDOLPH (D). House; Honolulu City Council including Chairman. In office: realtor; Manoa Realty; Real Estate Hale Inc.; miscellaneous transactions with Hirotoshi Yamamoto or with Yamamoto's "Manoa" companies, for example Yamamoto 1966 sold Pacarro and two others a 21-acre parcel in Kalihi Valley, which they resold 1971.

PARK, ARTHUR Y. Administrative assistant Lt. Gov. Thomas Gill. After office: Kaimalu Partners.

PASCUA, GEORGE R. Land Use Commission. In office: employee Amfac Distribution Co., a building materials supplier.

PENCE, MARTIN. Hawaii County Attorney; Circuit Court Judge; US District Court Judge. In office: Waimanalo Acres; Melmo Partners.

PETERS, HENRY H. (D). House including Speaker. In office: Dura Constructors Inc.; Panin North America Inc.; Bishop Estate trustee.

PORTUGAL, CESAR C. 1973-74 Kauai Charter Review Commission; Kauai Liquor Control Commission. In office: consulting engineer and surveyor; Nonou Mountain Estates; White Rock Ltd. Partnership; Hiku Assocs.

QUINN, WILLIAM F. Governor. After office: director Oceanic Properties Inc.; director Bishop Investment Corp.

RICHARDSON, WILLIAM S. (D). Senate Clerk; Lt. Governor; Chief Justice Supreme Court. In office: Pyramid Ranch Co. After office: Bishop Estate trustee.

ROEHRIG, STANLEY H. (R). House. In office: Partners Investment Co.

ROHLFING, FREDERICK W. (R). House; Senate. In office: Manaulu Assocs.; Fiji Pacific Partners; Squaw Ranch Partners.

RUTLEDGE, ARTHUR A. Honolulu Planning Commission. After office: Windward Partners.

SAKAHASHI, STANLEY K. Land Use Commission. In office: miscellaneous small investments Oahu. After office: Kauai-Kamuela Assocs.

SAKAI, HIROSHI. Counsel/Chief Clerk House and Senate Judiciary, Finance, and Ways and Means committees. In office: Milolii Syndicate. After office: Woodlawn Ventures; JYI Co.; KKK Ventures; King Kalani Apartment Hotel (a partnership); Hirano Bros. Ltd. and Assocs.; attorney for intended developer of Ota Camp area in Waipahu, Oahu early 1970s.

SAKIMA, AKIRA (D). House. In office: Lawai Development Co.

SAMESHIMA, MUNEO (D). Hawaii County Council. In office: real estate broker.

SAN DIEGO, JOHN S. SR. Maui Police Chief. Before office: Kipsy Assocs. In office: Kalihi-Uka Hui #1; Kona Kai Hui.

SEGAWA, HERBERT A. (D). House. In office: Ka Ulupala.

SERIZAWA, TOSHIO (D). Kauai County Board of Supervisors; 1950 Constitutional Convention; House. In office: Nusite Developers.

SETO, MASAO (R). Kauai County Board of Supervisors and Council; Kauai Finance Director and Public Information Officer; Kauai Liquor Control Commission. In office: Kukuiolono Ventures; RYM Venture 58; Kauai Ventures; Kukuiolono Assocs.

SHIBANO, TOM T. University of Hawaii Board of Regents including Chairman. In office: STC Land Assocs.; S-T-C Venture; The Puuhala Assocs.; Pauwela Heights Association; Pearson Hui; Waipao Joint Venture; Yokouchi Hui.

SHIMODA, WALTER T. District Court Magistrate. After office: Kelawea Hui; trustee for Nukolii hui; William Okamoto et al; as attorney handled miscellaneous land and development matters, for example for Valley Isle Realty Inc., and for developers of the Makena Surf condominium before the Maui Planning Commission.

SHIRAISHI, CLINTON I. (R). District Court Magistrate; Territorial Board of Public Lands; House; Senate; Kauai County Board of Supervisors; 1973-74 Kauai Charter Review Commission. In office: Milolii Syndicate; Wailua River Land Syndicate; White Rock Ltd. Partnership; Twelve Investors Hui; Waimea Valley Land Syndicate; Ocean View Ltd. Partnership; Valley of Two Falls Ltd. Partnership; Nonou Mountain Estates; Kamuela Assocs.; Kilauea Gardens Ltd. Partnership; Kauai Realty Inc.; A.C. Nominee Inc.; Kanzaki Realty Inc.; JO Developers Inc.; The First Kauai Development Corp.; Kauai Investment Assocs. Inc.; Kauai Land Co. Inc.; M.S. and Joy Properties Inc.; Wailua Haven Inc.; Western Shore Apartments Inc. After office: Poipu Sands Ltd. Partnership; Kauai Land Holding Co.; Twenty-Five Investors Hui; Waipouli Ltd. Partnership; KCMTS Venture; The Ouli Investment Ltd. Partnership; Kauai-Kamuela Assocs.; Elysium Corp.; Kaumualii Investment Co.

STATTS, MARY BETH. Daughter of Gov. John Burns. Nukolii hui; her and husband 1965-66 bought/sold two apartment-zoned lots Salt Lake.

SUWA, JACK K. (D). House; Deputy Director and then Director Dept. of Agriculture. In office: Vacationland Assocs.; Kalapana Corp.; investor in houselots Puna, Hawaii; community relations Amfac.

TAJIRI, HARVEY S. (D). Hawaii County Council. In office: Komohana Hui; Kahalani III Hui; Kawailani Assocs.

TAKABUKI, MATSUO (D). Honolulu Board of Supervisors and City Council; one of Gov. Burns' closest advisors. In office: 1961 filed this disclosure of interest: "I have investments in corporations, partnerships and joint ventures in Waialua, Waianae, Waipahu, Kaneohe, Heeia, Makaha, Niu Valley, Moanalua, Waikiki, Airport area in Damon Tract, and Liliha, and I have clients who have interests in land and business in all parts of the City and County of Honolulu." Also in office: Heeia Development Co.; Tropicana Village-Waipahu (a partnership); West Coast Realty Inc.; Tropicana Investments Inc.; attorney for various Chinn Ho interests such as Makaha Valley Inc., Capital Investment Co. and the Ilikai Hotel. After office: Bishop Estate trustee.

TAKAHASHI, SAKAE (D). Honolulu Board of Supervisors; Territorial Treasurer; 1968 Constitutional Convention; Senate. In office: Moiliili Developers; Hirotoshi Yamamoto & Assocs.; Waianae Assocs.; Yorktown Ventures; Honolulu Merchandise Mart (a partnership); Wulff & Takahashi; Al Watanabe & Assocs.

TAKEYAMA, ROY Y. Deputy State Attorney General assigned to Land Use Commission; special assistant to President University of Hawaii; UH Board of Regents Secretary. In office: Ahualoa Land Co.; Kalaheo Ltd. Partnership; Ranch View Partners; Fiji Marina Partners; Kamuela Assocs.; Airport Inn Partners; Kilauea Gardens Ltd. Partnership; KCMTS Venture; The Ouli Investment Ltd. Partnership. After resigned from Attorney General's office had extensive law practice regarding land and development matters, including representing Herbert Horita before the LUC.

TAKUSHI, MORRIS T. State Elections Administrator. In office: K&H Land Co. II; Takushi & Takushi; Ward Development Co.; D&M Enterprise.

TAM, EDWARD F. (D). Maui Board of Supervisors including Chairman. In office: Kihei Land Co.; real estate sales license.

TANAKA, WARREN I. Assistant to Mayor of Kauai. In office: Kauai Land Co. Inc.

TANGEN, EDWARD M. Land Use Commission including Chairman. After office: worked as development consultant for Environmental Land Concerns Inc.; 10% share in hui that owned 20 acres Kilauea, Kauai.

TASAKA, YURIKO N. Chairperson Citizens Advisory Committee for Kauai General Plan Update. In office: saleswoman Kauai Realty Inc.

THOMPSON, DONNIS H. State Superintendent of Schools. In office: The Triangular D.

THOMPSON, MYRON B. Land Use Commission; aide to Gov. Burns; Director State Dept. Social Services and Housing. In office: executive director Liliuokalani Trust, which owned about 10,000 acres; real estate salesman's license. After office: Bishop Estate trustee.

TOKITA, TURK. Chief campaign organizer on Kauai for John Burns 1954-70 and George Ariyoshi 1974-82; aide to Kauai County Board of Supervisors and Council. In office: MSW Ltd.

TOYOFUKU, GEORGE H. (D). Kauai County Board of Supervisors; House; Senate. In office: Ma-Ka-Poi Ventures.

TSUKIYAMA, TED T. Chairman Hawaii Employment Relations Board; Labor and Industrial Relations Appeal Board. In office: Pono Assocs.; Pyramid Ranch Co.

UEOKA, MEYER M. (D). District Court Magistrate; 1968 Constitutional Convention; Board of Education; House. In office: Ma-Ka-Poi Ventures; UKOWU; Maui Shores Syndicate; Pukalani Terrace Landco; Ueoka Hui; Mana Kai-Maui Hotel Association; F&D Hui; D&L Venture; Five Man Hui; The Ouli Investment Ltd. Partnership; Nine Man Hui; Ueoka Two Man Hui; Kihei Properties Inc.; Akina II; Akina III; Paniolo Venture; Kahana Land Hui; Hawaii Omori Corp.; bought/sold miscellaneous condominium units Maui; law practice extensively involved with land and development and representing developers before government agencies.

USHIJIMA, CHARLES T. (D). House. In office: Kiyoshi Kinjo & Assocs.; Kalihi-Uka Hui No. 5.

USHIJIMA, JOHN T. (D). Senate including President; 1968 Constitutional Convention. In office: Kona Highlands Development Co.; MUK Co.; Safeguard Enterprises Inc.; Kona Estates Inc.; Valley of the Gardens Inc.; as attorney handled miscellaneous land and development matters, including before the LUC for Boise Cascade and Mauna Kea Sugar Co.

UWAINE, CLIFFORD T. (D). Senate. In office: Hawaiian Land Investment Partners.

WAIHEE, JOHN D. III (D). 1978 Constitutional Convention; House; Lt. Governor. In office: Intent Hawaii.

WAKATSUKI, JAMES H. (D). House including Speaker; Circuit Court Judge; Supreme Court. In office: Ventura Co.; interest in project in Delta City, Arizona; Aloha Surf Hotel Inc.; as attorney represented Herbert Horita family, Star Markets Ltd. and Amfac Financial Corp. on land use matters before Honolulu City Council.

WILSON, JOHN H. (D). Mayor of Honolulu. In office: Wilsonite Brick Co. Ltd.

WONG, DICK YIN. State Tax Appeal Court Judge; Circuit Court Judge; US District Court Judge. In office: Cal-Electric Investment Co.; Kawela Development Co.; Mahukona Properties; Park Terrace Condominium Inc.

WONG, FRANCIS A. (D). House; Senate. In office: real estate broker; Mainline Harbor Properties; Queen St. Building Assocs.; Graham & Wong Queen; Queen's Barristers; Waimaha Pacific Partnership I; Waimaha Pacific Partnership II; Maquoia Assocs.; The Mahana Model Hui; Graham Wong Hastings Co.; Kauai Beach Partners; KBP Ltd. Partnership; Waikiki Beach Partners.

WONG, GORDON Y.H. Director State Dept. of Taxation. Before office: Waipuilani Hui Assocs.

WONG, RICHARD S.H. (D). House; Senate including President. In office: real estate sales license; Manoa Estates Ltd.; RSHW Corp.; VP Syncap Inc.; WRBS Sandpiper Inc.; WUC Inc.; KKK Investments.

WUNG, LESLIE E.L. Land Use Commission. In office: real estate salesman's license.

YADAO, JOSEPHINE R. (D). Hawaii County Council. In office: Manaulu Assocs.

YAGI, THOMAS S. Maui Board of Adjustment and Appeals; Board of Land and Natural Resources. In office: Nukolii hui.

YAMADA, DENNIS R. (R then D). House. In office: Ocean View Ltd. Partnership; Twenty-Five Investors Hui; member of law firm with extensive land and development practice, whose clients included Amfac Inc. or Amfac subsidiaries, Grove Farm Co., and Leadership Homes of Hawaii.

YAMADA, ROBERT M. (D). Hawaii County Planning and Traffic Commission, Board of Supervisors and County Council. In office: YS Rock; active in land investment, for example 1958 sold tract in Puna to developers who created Hawaii's first large scale speculative subdivision, called Hawaiian Acres; later developed own such subdivisions or built roads for them, such as in Eden Roc and project called Hawaiian Parks, Beaches and Shores.

YAMAMOTO, EUGENE H. Assistant Superintendent State Dept. of Education. In office: Ocean View Ltd. Partnership.

YAMAMURA, TANJI. Land Use Commission. In office: Waikiki Bali Hai Assocs.; Makena 700. After office: Mueller Capitol Plaza-Sacramento (a partnership).

YAMASAKI, MAMORU (D). House; Senate. In office: Hui o Nakane; Heeia Development Co.; The Group.

YANAGI, SANFORD Y. Hawaii County District Tax Administrator. In office: Kona Highlands Development Co.

YANAGI, WALLACE T. Assistant Administrator then Administrator Maui Memorial Hospital. In office: Nukolii hui; Waipao Joint Venture; Kauai Ventures; Hui Akamai; Kuliouou Valley Assocs. Ltd. Partnership; Pearson Hui; Valley Marketplace Partners.

YANAI, EDWARD K. Land Use Commission. In office: Hui 86.

YANO, VINCENT H. (D). Senate; running mate Thomas Gill 1970 gubernatorial race. In office: developer; member small hui that included George Ariyoshi that bought/sold 60 acres Kula, Maui.

YEE, WADSWORTH Y.H. (R). House; Senate. In office: Haleiwa Surf Assocs.; M-Y Properties; Finance Factors Building Ltd.; developer Kawela Plantation subdivision Molokai.

YOKOUCHI, MASARU "PUNDY." Gov. Burns' Maui representative; Chairman State Foundation on Culture and Arts. In office: realtor; developer; active land investor; Heeia Development Co.; Hale Kaanapali Assocs.; Pukalani Terrace Landco; Nukolii hui; Kamuela Assocs.; Seaside Developers; Valley Marketplace Partners; Kauai Ventures; West Maui Partners; Crown Corp.; Waipao Joint Venture; Valley Isle Realty Inc.; Kula Venture.

YOSHINAGA, NADAO (D). House; Senate. In office: real estate broker; Valley Isle Realty Inc.; M. Yokouchi/W. Yanagi; immediate family had several shares Nukolii hui; he or immediate family in Mondrian Inc., Rousseau Inc., Ethereal Inc.

YUASA, ERNEST T. Director Honolulu Building Dept. In office: Westgate Enterprise.

YUDA, GEORGE S. Hawaii First Assistant Corporation Counsel. In office: Yasuo Kuwaye and Assocs.; Kona Highlands Development Co.

YUEN, WILLIAM W.L. Land Use Commission including Chairman. In office: Mountain View Investments; attorney whose firm represented several landowners/developers, including Alexander & Baldwin, Grove Farm Co., Waitec Development Inc.

ZALOPANY, LEONARD H. SR. Kauai Planning Commission. In office: Poipu Shores Hotel Apartment (a partnership).

Sources: Gwenfread E. Allen, ed., *Men and Women of Hawaii: A Biographical Directory of Noteworthy Men and Women of Hawaii* (Honolulu, 1966); Betty F. Buker, ed., *Men and Women of Hawaii 1972: A Biographical Directory of Noteworthy Men and Women of Hawaii* (Honolulu, 1972); Department of Commerce and Consumer Affairs, Business Registration Division; State of Hawaii, Legislative Reference Bureau, *Directory of State, County and Federal Officials: Supplement to Guide to Government in Hawaii* (published occasionally, most recently annually); Chamber of Commerce of Hawaii, *Who's Who in Government State of Hawaii* (various years); miscellaneous state and county public officials' personal financial disclosure statements, on file with State Ethics Commission and offices of county clerks; State of Hawaii, Land Use Commission, miscellaneous files; Hawaii State Archives; files of county planning departments; miscellaneous references in newspapers and periodicals.

1

LAND REFORM

In the 1950s when the Democrats went looking for places to launch their attack on the old land system, one of the obvious starting points was Hawaii's property taxes.

Hawaii's wealthy were landed. Everyone in the Islands could see that, just by looking around. The United States Internal Revenue Service demonstrated it with figures. In a study based on 1962 data the IRS found that, nationwide, deceased persons with estates valued at $60,000 or more had 25% of their estates in real property (land and buildings). In Hawaii the figure was 42%.[1]

But when it came to collecting taxes, the figures were turned around. As of about 1956, mainland states on the average got 37% of their tax revenues from real property. Hawaii got only 17%.[2]

The Hawaii Republicans had arranged territorial and county taxes to keep their landed wealth intact, at the same time keeping society the way they liked it.

To begin with, the Republicans had put a ceiling on the amount of revenue the counties were allowed to collect through real property taxes. So even after World War II, when real property values began to rise markedly, taxes did not go up correspondingly for lands whose use was not intensified, such as plantation land. Indeed, quite often they went down. For example, between 1948 and 1956 the value of Ewa Plantation Co.'s land doubled, but its annual tax bill dropped, from $79,000 to $52,000.[3]

This tax revenue ceiling was a great built-in protection for major landowners and lessors in Hawaii. And when they came to have their lands assessed for tax purposes, they were equally well protected. Amazing as it may seem looking back from the present day, major agricultural interests were able to suggest to government what their own real property assessments should be. The government usually accepted the figures, and taxes paid were simply a multiple of assessments. In effect then, the government did not tell these landed businesses how much real property tax they should pay—they told the government. A government consultant, Public Administration Service, wrote in 1958: "The assessor thus finds himself in the unen-

viable position of having delegated such an essential part of his responsibility that he does not have control of the situation."[4] Small property holders,
though, were not in such a happy situation. A husband and wife who both
had to work to make mortgage payments were not permitted to suggest to
the government how much tax they should pay on their house and lot—the
government told them what they must pay.

Property tax assessments appeared to routinely favor big landowners
over small. In the last days of these old arrangements, the mid-1950s, the
Republican mayor of Honolulu hired a land economist to survey tax assessments on Oahu. The economist, John J. Hulten Sr., who happened to be a
Democrat, reported that, based on a survey of vacant land sales in 1956,
small parcels on Oahu (less than an acre) were being assessed on the average
58% more severely than large parcels (10 acres or more).[5]

When the government wanted to condemn private land, big landowners
got favorable consideration. Both landowner and government knew that
the value put on land for tax assessment purposes was artificially low, often
ridiculously so. If the government paid only that price when it condemned
land, it would be getting the property dirt cheap. So in a condemnation
proceeding the large landowner was allowed to argue that his land was really worth much more than the tax assessment value, and he got a much
higher figure when his land was condemned than when it was assessed. All
this without being assessed for back taxes.

The same disparity existed in private sales by the big owners. As Hulten
pointed out, 1,074 acres of Damon Estate land assessed in 1957 at $184 an
acre were sold that year for about $9,650 an acre.[6]

Finally, if a big landowner wanted to, he could remove land from taxabil-
ity altogether. He could put appropriate land into "forest reserve," on which
no property tax at all was levied. He did not have to leave the land there for
any set length of time, and he could take it out again and put it to profitable
use whenever he wanted, without penalty of any sort. A *Honolulu Star-
Bulletin* reporter wrote in 1957 that "persons close to the situation will admit privately that certain estates put some of their land into forest reserve
purely and simply to keep it tax-free for the time being." For whatever reasons the arrangement was extensively used: as of 1956 65% of the 122,000
acres in forest reserve belonged to large private owners like the Bishop and
Campbell estates and Castle & Cooke.[7]

These arrangements suited the big landowners very well socially as well
as financially. Owners of sugar and pineapple plantations made good
profits, even during the Depression, and they were very well pleased with
life at the top of a plantation society. The trustees of the big private estates
were making very respectable money for themselves and their beneficiaries,
who also lived at the top of society. None of these well-to-do people had any
particular reason to want change.

The Democrats, of course, saw in this tax system inequity amounting to
drastic abuse. As long as big landowners got off so easily at tax time, small

landowners—and those who owned no land at all, meaning most people—had to pick up an unfair share of the total tax burden.

Beyond this, as the Democrats saw things, there was a broader social dimension to tax policy. As long as Republicans in power kept real property tax rates low for the perpetual benefit of an already wealthy landed minority, Hawaii would never have the public money to fund large-scale social programs for the benefit of the great un-landed, un-wealthy majority.

Education was a case in point. The children of the big landowners went to richly endowed private schools, paid for out of the profits of sugar and pineapple. But Hawaii's public schools, where ordinary children went, were poorly funded—partly because the rich were paying such low taxes on their land. The US Bureau of Education, for example, in 1920 did a national survey of public schools. It found that Honolulu, while much above the average in taxable wealth among the cities studied, ranked "considerably below the average city in point of tax rate and far below the average in the amount expended for school purposes."[8] This was still so after World War II. Obviously, as long as the Republicans stayed in power, tax policy would not change, and neither would social policy.

In the year of the Democrats' great electoral victory, 1954, their party platform pledged to "revise thoroughly Hawaii's antique tax laws by: (1) shifting the tax burden from those least able to pay to those who are most able to pay, (2) eliminating the inequitable ceiling on real property tax and levying that tax in accordance with true market value, (3) plugging the loopholes which have favored certain special interests."[9]

There were tax targets other than real property. For example, Hawaii had a flat 2% personal income tax which weighed more heavily on the poor than on the rich. In 1957 the Democrats succeeded in instituting a progressive personal income tax.

As far as real property tax laws and practices were concerned, in the late 1950s and early 1960s there were parallel reforms. The ceiling on real property tax revenues was abolished. Major agricultural interests were no longer allowed to help set tax assessments on their own land. The old "forest reserve" arrangement was abolished. Real estate was no longer assessed merely at its existing use or even less, but at its "highest and best" possible use—meaning that condemnation and private sale prices were brought more nearly in line with open market value.

When John Burns took office in 1962 as Hawaii's first Democratic governor, the "highest and best use" approach was intensified. Also, in the Legislature of 1963 a new land tax law was passed, intended to stimulate construction. This was the so-called "Pittsburgh Law," modeled on an assessment approach used in Pittsburgh, Pennsylvania. Under this plan, buildings were assessed at lower rates than land. This was meant to create an incentive to build. The Pittsburgh Law, as well as "highest and best use," were at the same time deliberate strategies to persuade the big landowners to develop their land—or sell to someone who would.

One result of tax reform was that in 1960 the assessed value of cane lands jumped 20% statewide. Where cane and other large tracts of land had high potential for urbanization the jump was even higher. For example, some Bishop Estate land in Aiea went from $402 an acre in assessment to $7,000; some Kaneohe Ranch Co. land went from about $1,000 an acre to $7,500.[10]

*   *   *

It is clear that all of these Democratic tax measures meant change for the benefit of the ordinary person. And it is just as clear that on the whole the changes were rather modest.

The Democrats made much of the sales tax, which was the greatest single source of tax revenue, since it fell hardest on working people. But the Democrats made only a short-term moderate reform here, one that was later abandoned. In 1952 sales taxes accounted for 39.5% of total county and territorial tax revenues. By the late 1960s the percentage was down somewhat, to 35%. But thereafter the figure started to rise, and in 1982 it exceeded the 1952 figure, reaching over 42%.[11]

On the other hand, in the area of personal income taxes inroads were made in the old, regressive tax structure. From 1952 to 1982 the percentage of Hawaii's total territorial, state and county tax revenues accounted for by personal income taxes went from 13.6% to 20.7%, with a far more progressive rate system imposed.[12]

At the same time, though, corporate income taxes as a percentage of overall receipts actually declined, from 5.6% in 1952 to 2.9% in 1982.[13]

As for land-related taxes, although the large owners or their lessees had to start paying more, in the long run nothing fundamental changed with respect to the place of real property taxation in Hawaii's overall taxing scheme. In 1952 real property tax receipts made up 14% of total territorial and county tax revenues. During the 1960s and 1970s the figure fluctuated around 16%-17%. In 1982 it was 18.6%.[14]

There had been some theorizing about raising assessments to force development, which in turn was to make the large owners sell off lands they could not develop themselves. This hardly occurred, however, and apparently was never a real threat anyway. In an interview for this book, a senior staff member for one of the large estates said that much of the major owners' land was leased out to others, and it was the lessees, not the owners, who had to pay the property taxes. His point is substantiated by a report published in 1957 by the Legislative Reference Bureau. The LRB wrote that as of 1955, some 66% of the lands of six selected major owners were leased out to others, such as sugar plantations.[15] Three of these six owned much of the land that was in the natural path of Honolulu's expansion and therefore stood to be reassessed upwards—and indeed eventually it was. But since the lessees paid the property tax, a number of the major owners were insulated from "highest and best use" and Pittsburgh assessment approaches.

*   *   *

A similar picture emerges in examining the Democrats' record on laws proposing alterations in patterns of land ownership in Hawaii—a retreat from early ideals.

A good many Democrats in the early years talked about breaking up the big landholdings. For example, bills were introduced that would give residential lessees the right to purchase the fee interest in their house lots; that would establish a Hawaii Land Development Authority (HLDA) to condemn large tracts for housing, commercial and agricultural development; that would set a limit on the percentage of assets that the great landed estates and corporations could hold in real property, with the large owners having to sell off the balance. There were also bills that would have allowed the territorial and state governments and even private developers to condemn land from the large owners at or near the extremely low tax assessment rates that they had been able to obtain during the Republican era, and that would break up the extensive interlocking of directorates of Hawaii firms that were direct competitors, and even non-competitors, in land-related and other businesses.[16]

The overall track record on these measures indicates a retreat from the extreme land reform liberalism or even radicalism of the Democrats' early years.

It took the Democrats two decades in office to pass a residential lease-to-fee conversion bill and necessary follow-up legislation. The first Democratic governor, John Burns, opposed such laws and refused to process conversions. His successor, George Ariyoshi, as a state senator in 1963 cast the tie-breaking vote against a conversion bill. Eventually, in 1975, under mounting pressure, legislation was passed that prodded all but one of the old residential lessors to start selling off most of their house lots to their tenants.

Land development opportunities for members of the new local-Asian middle class were opened up slightly and indirectly by the passage of a state anti-trust law in 1961. That, plus the first interest in anti-trust issues in Hawaii ever shown by the US Department of Justice, soon ended extensive interlocks among major old-line businesses that had been direct competitors in real estate financing, among other things. As a result the Hawaii economy of the mid-1980s had, by comparison with the Republican era, relatively few interlocks between competitors. The 1961 law was one of many signals to the old companies that they had better cut others in on business opportunities. Together with other measures and trends, this ended the propensity of old-money *haoles* to deal almost totally among themselves in major business ventures.

On the other hand, not passed in 1961 was the far more stringent House Bill 906 that would have ended many interlocks between medium and large corporations whether they were in competition with each other or not. This bill was signed for introduction by nearly every Democratic state representative. It would have allowed the state to take 50% of a corporation's annual income above $200,000 whenever it had a common director with two other corporations, provided the annual gross of each was at least $200,000. This was irrespective of whether any of the three were in the same lines of business—so great did some Democrats feel was the evil of separate businesses having common directors.

Such a measure as HB 906 had no chance of becoming law in 1961, with Republicans in control of the Senate and with a Republican governor. But even in later sessions when Democrats controlled both houses and the governor's office as well, the bill was either never introduced, or if introduced then never passed.

Also, in 1962 the state attorney general's office, during a Republican state administration, proposed a rule that would have required corporations with assets of at least $50,000 and with directors who sat on two or more boards to disclose the interlocks, as an aid in policing the interlocking of competitors.[17] Following a great deal of criticism by businessmen the proposal was rejected and no later Democratic state administration ever imposed it either. Furthermore, the state agency charged with registering businesses—then the Department of Treasury and Regulation, as of 1985 the Department of Commerce and Consumer Affairs—never indexed businesses by the names of people involved, or even by companies in the same lines of enterprise. The net effect of all this is that there has never been a systematic and direct way of knowing what interlocks might exist between companies, whether competitors or non-competitors, short of reviewing a literal mountain of corporate and partnership annual reports filed with the state.

After several years of trying, a bill tying land tax assessment value to condemnation price did finally pass in 1963. By then, however, due mainly to agitation by Democrats, assessments much more nearly reflected actual market value; so its impact was minimized. Also, the bill as finally adopted merely made tax assessments a "rebuttable presumption" of market value, rather than automatically the price or near the price at which the government could purchase if it so chose.

A Hawaii Land Development Authority bill also passed, in 1959. Its sponsors had drafted in a mechanism for private builders to initiate condemnation proceedings for lands that they thought had development potential but which the large owners refused to develop. Initially there was also a provision allowing the price paid by either the government or private developers to be tied to tax assessment figures. The bill that finally passed contained neither provision. Also cut were sections allowing lands to be condemned for commercial and agricultural purposes. In the end the watered-down bill applied only to residential development by the government and only on Oahu.

Of all the land legislation of those years, this omnibus land condemnation/development bill would probably have gone the furthest to implement the Democrats' land reform program. But heavy amendment led one of the bill's authors to call what passed "nothing but a ghost." Another said that "the great elephant for lo these many months did labor and give birth to a mouse."[18] Furthermore, after passage no administration, whether Republican or Democratic, ever used the law in the sweeping manner that its proponents had envisioned.

No bill ever passed that would have fixed the upper limit of the assets that a trust or corporation could hold in land. In some respects bills of this sort would have been the most radical in terms of forcing the large owners to divest themselves of much of their holdings. Most of the great charitable and private trust estates had little but real estate in their portfolios, and some of these bills would have held to levels like 30% and 40% the amount of assets that could be held in real property.

* * *

On balance it was the bills most feared and opposed by the major owners, those that would have entailed large-scale condemnation or divestiture of land, that either never passed or were never used.

What started out as an extremely liberal or even radical land reform program became, in the end, quite moderate.

2

LAND AND THE NEW POLITICAL ESTABLISHMENT

HAWAII's post-World War II political transformation had some of its origins in a socio-economic development that went back well before the war:

In the long twentieth-century shift from the plantations into urban and suburban society, many locally born Asians moved into middle-class jobs. Especially after the war they moved in great numbers into the teaching profession and the civil service. They were also moving into the more prestigious professions of medicine and dentistry, architecture and engineering.

After World War II they also went heavily into the legal profession. Many who made this move were members of the famous Japanese-American US Army units, the 100th Battalion and the 442nd Regimental Combat Team, which fought with such distinction in Europe. As veterans, they used the GI Bill to put themselves through law school.

For a sizable number, a law degree was a step along the road to a career in politics. And for the great majority of these, the Democratic Party was the inevitable and natural choice.

Among Democratic legislators, especially in the late 1950s and throughout the 1960s, there were heavy concentrations of lawyers. In 1955, in the first Democratic legislature, nearly half of all Democrats were attorneys. In 1960, the first full session following statehood, the figure was nearly two-thirds. (Thereafter the number trended down. In 1970 it was 40%. In 1980 it was 18%.)[1]

Just as attorneys stood out professionally among Democratic legislators, Japanese stood out ethnically. From 1960 to 1980, Japanese averaged 50% of the total membership of both houses. From 1955 to 1980, the percentage of Japanese Democrats in the Legislature was twice the percentage of Japanese in Hawaii's population. In 1960, when Japanese were 32% of population, they were 67% of Democratic legislators in both houses. In 1970, with 28% of population, they were 58% of Democratic legislators. In 1980, with 25% of population, they were 60% of Democratic legislators.[2]

Locally-born Chinese too were strongly represented on the Democratic side of the Legislature. In 1940, Chinese were 7% of population, 20% of Democratic legislators. In the 1950s and 1960s, they were less strongly present as legislators—the same percentage as in the population. But in the

1970s they were again more strongly present; and in 1980, when they were 5% of population, they were 10% of Democratic legislators.[3]

Just as Japanese and Chinese were "over-represented" as Democratic legislators, so *haoles* and Hawaiians and part-Hawaiians were "under-represented." In 1960, when *haoles* were about one-third of population, they were only 10% of Democratic legislators. As late as 1980 there were still, percentage-wise, twice as many *haoles* in the population as among Democratic legislators. As for Hawaiians and part-Hawaiians, in 1960 they were 16% of population but only 4% of Democratic legislators. By 1980 these numbers were even more extreme, 18% versus 3%. (A reversal of this trend set in in the early 1980s, however.)[4]

Hawaii's other large ethnic group, Filipinos, was severely under-represented among Democratic legislators until the 1980s. Not until 1984 did the percentage of Filipino Democrats in both houses match Filipinos in the population.[5]

Japanese strength among the ruling Democrats in the Legislature tended to mean that Japanese rose to leadership positions in great numbers: senate president, house speaker, chairman of a finance, judiciary, or ways and means committee. Between 1955 and 1984 42 men and one woman held these positions. Of the 43, 55% were Japanese—about double the average percentage of Japanese in the population over that period.[6]

Of those Japanese leaders, some 63% were attorneys. Also just about 63% were born on the outer islands. Of the Japanese leaders 1955–1975, 39% were veterans of the 442nd or 100th. (By 1975, most though not all of these veterans had left the Legislature.)[7]

So a picture emerges of the typical successful legislator of the post-World War II period: a Burns Democrat; of Japanese background; *nisei*; likely to have been born on an outer island, meaning essentially in a plantation community; an attorney; often with war service.

Among well-known names fitting this pattern are Spark M. Matsunaga, John T. Ushijima, and Nadao Yoshinaga. Matsunaga became a congressman and US senator, Ushijima president of the state Senate, Yoshinaga one of the leading legislators of the entire post-World War II era. Among other well-known names, Matsuo Takabuki fits in every way except that the plantation community where he was born was in rural Oahu rather than on an outer island. Takabuki for years was one of John Burns' closest political advisors, a leading member of the Honolulu Board of Supervisors and later City Council, and then a Bishop Estate trustee. US Sen. Daniel K. Inouye fits in every way except that he was born not in a plantation community but in a working-class district of Honolulu. Sakae Takahashi, also a major figure in the Legislature for many years, fits in every way except that he parted company with the Burns majority about 1970 in favor of the Gill faction. Tadao Beppu, a House speaker, fits in every way except that he was not an attorney.

These men and dozens of others like them were the politicians who took over from the Republicans in the 1950s and led Hawaii into the boom years of statehood and beyond. They were the ones who set out to take apart the old land system, examine its workings, and put it together again so that it worked as rewardingly for Democrats and their supporters as it had for Republicans.

* * *

In the eyes of Democratic politicians and their associates Hawaii's big landowners were yesterday's men. In their view the officers and directors of the big corporations and the trustees of the great estates were tied to the past, oblivious of the great changes that were looming in the 1950s: the growth starting to occur in tourism and military spending, the big increase in population waiting just around the corner. These things were going to work radical changes in the size and shape of Hawaii's economy, and the big landowners could not see it, in the opinion of the Democrats.

Without question the big landowners were chronically reluctant to let go of land, or even to use land for anything other than the traditional sugar, pineapple, and ranching.

In a few instances prior to the mid-1950s, if land was not profitable for planting and ranching, it might just possibly be available for sale. That was how, for example, the local-Chinese businessman Chinn Ho got hold of a big parcel of land at Makaha, along Oahu's Waianae coast. In 1946 the Big Five firm of American Factors sold to an investment group organized by Ho a 9,150-acre sugar plantation and ranch that had become unprofitable.[8] Likewise in the early 1950s along the ocean in Maalaea, Maui, Alexander & Baldwin sold off small parcels of what was considered wasteland.[9]

But for the most part, outright sale was uncommon, and even the possibility of developing land while still holding on to the title seemed slow to make an impression on the major landowners. In 1959, O. Vincent Esposito, a liberal Democratic political leader and attorney, was appointed by a circuit court judge to review the 1958 annual accounting of the trustees of Campbell Estate. In his report Esposito wrote that up to 1952 the trustees' handling of their lands "left much to be desired. The lands were put to little use and there was very little imaginative long-range comprehensive planning. The income was low. The prospects were low."[10]

But if the change to a development orientation on the part of the big landowners came late, it came quickly.

It had to come. The combined outside pressures of tourism and military spending were simply undeniable, with the Korean War and Cold War military buildup in Hawaii beginning in the early 1950s, followed by statehood in 1959, and then the US military escalation in Vietnam in the 1960s.

Esposito pinpointed 1958 as the year the Campbell trustees began to move from the "old coupon-clipping philosophy" to a "progressive and relatively modern move to get the estate assets nearer to a goal of highest and best use."[11]

The same thing was happening with the other major owners. In 1959.

the year of statehood, Richard J. Lyman Jr., a Republican senator who himself was a relatively large landowner and who was about to become a Bishop Estate trustee, acknowledged the dawning of the day of development. Speaking of the large owners in general, he said: "We've been stupid. We've held down the value of our lands to avoid taxes, and crippled our ability to develop. We have to realize that land value is collateral for loans."[12]

* * *

By the late 1950s, then, the big landowners were getting ready, like it or not, for a new era, one of land development. Local-Asians were looking toward development too, with appetite. In fact their political and business leaders were already forcing the pace.

As the development boom began and gathered momentum, Democratic politicians and their associates were on the alert for ways to take part. The most forward-looking and aggressive saw great opportunities in real estate development: homes, hotels, office buildings, shopping centers, industrial baseyards.

For local-Asians who did not themselves own land in quantity, the way into large-scale land development had to be by association with the big landowners.

A main road to that destination went through politics.

Thus when the Campbell Estate in 1957 entered into a residential development agreement covering 118 acres in Ewa, Democratic Sen. Mitsuyuki Kido was a corporate treasurer and director of the company that signed the agreement, Leeward Development Corporation. Another company officer was Taro Suyenaga, at that time a law partner of Democratic Sen. Sakae Takahashi and Democratic Chief Clerk of the House Herman T. F. Lum. (Lum much later rose to the position of chief justice of the Hawaii Supreme Court.)

Also in 1957 the Damon Estate sold 1,074 acres in Salt Lake and Moanalua to a consortium, one of whose heads was Clarence T.C. Ching, and which included as investors Mitsuyuki Kido and Chuck Mau. Both Kido and Mau had been in the five-man founding core of the modern Democratic Party organized just after the close of World War II. Ching later served as John Burns' finance chairman for his first two successful gubernatorial campaigns.[13]

Bishop Estate in 1959 entered into a development agreement with mainland industrialist Henry J. Kaiser covering 6,000 acres in east Oahu. Several months later, Democratic Senate President Herbert K. H. Lee announced his retirement from politics and went to work for Kaiser.[14] (Lee made a brief political re-entry in 1962, first announcing for the governor's office and then instead running unsuccessfully for Congress.)

The Kaneohe Ranch Co. in those years owned about 10,000 acres in windward Oahu, and much of the area's residential development occurred on its lands. The company that contracted to do the ranch's principal development work hired Ernest N. Heen Jr. about 1960. In 1963 Heen was made projects coordinator and continued in that capacity until 1968. As of 1960

Heen's father was a member of the Honolulu Board of Supervisors (predecessor to the Honolulu City Council), and had been a prominent Democrat for several decades. His uncle, William H. Heen Sr., had been one of the leading figures in the Democratic Party throughout the first half of the twentieth century, and senate president in 1955 and 1957. Ernest Jr.'s brother as of 1960 was a state representative. He himself in 1962 was elected to the House, where he remained until 1970.[15]

These and other well-connected Democrats were becoming involved with development for several reasons:

One was that from early on a number of Democrats had been aligned in business and politics with certain non-*haole* developers and financiers like Clarence Ching, K. J. Luke, Hung Wo Ching, Chinn Ho and Joseph R. Pao: men who represented a new entrepreneurial force in Hawaii, with the drive and willingness to take risks in large-scale land development before it was clearly profitable to do so. As these new businessmen moved into and then up in the development business, so also did certain of their political associates who invested in their companies or did legal or consulting work on their projects.

Another reason was that the Democrats in power had their hands on the levers of control by which government approved or disapproved much that had to do with development. If the old landowners and non-Democrat-affiliated developers tried to keep things exclusively in their own hands, their proposals could be—would be—delayed, obstructed, and perhaps disapproved. Once the large owners became committed to construction, they or their developers often felt a need to link up with men who had Democratic ties.

All this was obvious, a fact of political life. Most of the big landowners did not have to be told about it, at least not more than once.

* * *

So, by the end of the 1950s, while the Democrats' land reform package was still making its way through the Legislature, leading Democrats as individuals and in groups were beginning to take part in land development on a significant scale.

As mentioned, a natural consequence was that they acquired ties to the big landowners.

Thus among the Democrats were men who were debating land reform bills on the floor of the Legislature and at the same time, in their private capacities as businessmen or attorneys, were setting out to make money directly from development in association with the big landowners.

In time this played a role in deflating the Democrats' enthusiasm for land reform.

* * *

This pattern may be studied by looking at possible connections between the development of lands at Heeia, on the windward side of Oahu, and a move in the legislature to raise the annual fees paid to trustees of charitable trusts:

In 1959, in the last territorial legislative session before statehood, Republicans in both the Senate and House proposed amending the law that set fees paid to trustees of charitable trusts, including the Bishop Estate, the biggest single private landowner in Hawaii.

In 1959 Democrats were solidly in control of the Legislature and no Republican-sponsored bill could pass without their support.

In the previous session, that of 1957, a number of Republican bills passed, according to William F. Quinn, Republican governor of Hawaii 1957–1962, who was interviewed for this book. In 1959, though, according to Quinn, rather few Republican measures passed. He thought this may have been because statehood was imminent, with elections immediately following. Quinn thought the Democrats might have put the brakes on Republican bills in 1959 in order to downplay the effectiveness of Republicans in office, as a bit of election propaganda.

In the 1959 session a total of 3,212 bills were introduced in both houses. Of these, about 400 were Republican. Of the 3,212 introduced, 279 passed and became laws. Of those that became law exactly 12, or 4%, were Republican measures—that is, bills introduced solely by Republicans. Looking at Republican bills offered as compared with those passed, Republicans enjoyed a success rate of 2.4%.[16]

The Republican success rate was meager not only as judged by the numbers but also by substance. In the order in which they became laws this is what ten of their bills pertained to: free funerals for indigent veterans; procedural changes in what to do with unclaimed shareholder funds after a corporate dissolution; how to apportion expenditures for an alcoholism clinic; changing the wage and hour law so as to make clear that what was meant in one section where the word "persons" appeared was "employees;" deleting the requirement that the governor personally approve the merger or consolidation of non-profit corporations; amending a law to make clear that when a partnership applied for a liquor license, those who made up the partnership were to be called "partners" rather than "members;" slightly amending a law on qualifications for embalmers; allowing territorial-chartered banks to buy stock in the federal national mortgage association; amending a law to increase the amount of sick leave that government employees could accrue; making relatively minor changes in procedures to be followed by the Public Utilities Commission.

An eleventh Republican bill that became law was of some substance: it raised the pay for supreme court justices and circuit court judges.

The twelfth that became law was the estate trustees' fees bill.[17]

On the face of things, this particular bill did not seem to have much of a chance, since any Republican bill in the 1959 session was going to have only a 2.4% chance of success.

Beyond that, why should Democrats vote to increase the pay of people like Bishop Estate trustees, who embodied the old Republican land system the Democrats had come into office to dismantle?

Yet two of the 1959 session's most powerful Democratic senators, one of them Mitsuyuki Kido, quietly lobbied for the increase, according to two other legislators whose support for the bill was crucial and who were interviewed for this book.

It should be noted that all four—the two who were lobbying and the two who were lobbied—were of the Burns faction. In other words the comments of the two interviewed were apparently not cases of political enemies telling stories about each other. Moreover, both who were interviewed noted that in 1959 they thought it odd that Democrats like Kido would argue for passage of such a bill.

Kido had been in the five-man group, including John Burns, that just after World War II laid the foundation for Hawaii's contemporary Democratic Party. Initially a schoolteacher by profession, Kido by the later 1950s was a developer. From 1953 to 1957 he had been a member of the Honolulu Board of Supervisors, predecessor to the City Council. In the 1959 Legislature he was a member of the Senate Judiciary Committee, one of two committees which would handle the bill on trustees' commissions. He was also chairman of the Oahu Select Committee, which reviewed and made recommendations on all state monies to be appropriated by the Legislature for capital improvement projects on Oahu—highways, parks, etc. (Several months after the close of the regular 1959 legislative session Kido became Burns' unofficial running mate in Hawaii's first gubernatorial election.)

Those who supported the bill argued that the pay of Bishop trustees— about $13,000 per trustee in fiscal 1959—was not commensurate with their responsibilities. It was pointed out, for example, that in 1957 the trustees of Campbell Estate, a private non-charitable trust, were paid nearly three times as much as Bishop trustees, yet Campbell trustees handled only one-third the volume of income. With this underpayment of Bishop trustees, it was argued, why would competent men be willing to serve?

Supporters also pointed out that the then-current fee schedule had been set as far back as 1943, when several part-Hawaiian Democratic senators, upset with the operation of the Bishop Estate, attempted to slash fees drastically, and did succeed in reducing them somewhat.

In 1943 Sen. William H. Heen had been chairman of the Judiciary Committee, which that year was the main body probing the matter of fees paid trustees of charitable trusts. Heen and Sen. David K. Trask Sr., both part-Hawaiians, were among the committee's most active members on this issue.

A Judiciary Committee report said that it was necessary to amend the law on trustees' commissions because of "the method of administration of the Bernice P. Bishop Estate."[18]

The beneficiaries of the estate were two schools operated primarily for Hawaiian children, the Kamehameha Schools.

The report compared Kamehameha with Punahou, the *haole* elite school, in terms of income, expenditures, and numbers of students educated. The committee wrote that Punahou 1936–1941 had an income of $2 million, of which $1.7 million, or 85%, was spent on education, and that 5,730 students were taught. Kamehameha, on the other hand, through the Bishop Estate took in $4.3 million, of which $1.5 million, or only 35%, was spent on education, and educated only 3,719 students. Although Kamehameha outspent Punahou on a per-student basis (about $400 to $300), still the drafters of the committee report seemed appalled at how little Bishop Estate/Kamehameha was spending in comparison with what could be spent.

Part of the differential was attributed to what the committee saw as inordinately high administrative costs incurred by Bishop—25% of Bishop's income over the previous decade. No figure was provided for Punahou, but presumably it was far lower, since during the previous five years 85% of income had gone to educational expenses.

The committee concluded "that the exorbitant cost of administering the Bishop Estate, the limited benefits received by the beneficiaries for whom Bernice P. Bishop created the trust, have rendered long overdue this amendment to the statute awarding commissions to the trustees of charitable trusts."

Bishop trustees in fiscal 1942 were earning at a rate of about $10,250 a year. Heen and Trask had set out to limit the total that could possibly be paid a trustee to about $2,000 per year. A compromise was achieved in the 1943 session that altered the formula for determining fees, cutting them roughly in half. By the late 1950s, due to an increase in Bishop Estate income, the fees went back up to and then exceeded what they had been before the 1943 amendment, though in the meantime there had been some inflation.[19]

For Sen. Kido and others the 1959 fee bill was, in part, undoing a past wrong. Kido said that the 1943 Legislature "had slashed the commission rates for the Bishop Estate trustees, and they were getting really a very nominal amount for the tremendous responsibility they had."[20]

In 1943 the Legislature provided that trustees would be paid 10% of the first $1,000 earned by the trust, 7% of the next $4,000, 5% of the next $100,000, 3% of the next $100,000 after that, 2% on the next $300,000, and 1% on anything else. As things went through the late 1950s the last step was of no account. Most or all trustees' fees came from the first five steps.[21]

The 1959 act got rid of the last two steps. In their place it provided for payment of 2% on everything over $205,000.

While these percentages might seem insignificant, they brought tangible rewards when applied to the income that Bishop Estate was starting to make in the land boom that had just gotten underway. In essence the 1959 bill would cause the fees paid to Bishop trustees to double.

Because of the new schedule and the development boom, each Bishop trustee got about $35,000 in 1960; in 1962 about $44,000; and by the early

1980s the five Bishop trustees between them were getting more than $1 million a year.[22]

These new pay levels were roughly equal with those obtained by trustees of major private estates. For example, a Bishop trustee who was in office for the full fiscal-year 1983, which comprised the latter half of 1982 and the first half of 1983, was paid $238,000. He was also entitled to an additional $41,000 but all Bishop trustees chose to waive this extra money. In 1982 trustees of the Campbell Estate were each paid $298,000. Trustees of the smaller Damon Estate received $175,000 each.[23]

To return to the specifics of the 1959 session: was there a connection between land development and the passing of the 1959 law to increase payments to the trustees of charitable trusts?

The two legislators interviewed for this book who reported being lobbied by several fellow Democrats said that sometime after the 1959 session they wondered if there was a link.

One of the two said he was lobbied by Kido. He wondered whether the lobbying had anything to do with a Bishop Estate development agreement awarded to Kido. The second of the two wondered about the fact that the fellow legislator who lobbied him turned up in a *hui* organized by Kido to develop part of the Bishop land. And both who had been lobbied wondered about the fact that a large number of prominent Burns Democrats also invested in Kido's *hui*.

The timing of events concerning Kido's obtaining the agreement and the passage of the trustees' fees bill lent some credence to the questions raised by these men.

The first public announcement that Bishop and Kido had been negotiating and reached agreement came in a press statement in February 1960. The signing of a formal agreement came in July. It covered 520 acres of *mauka* lands (toward the mountains) in Heeia, in windward Oahu. At the same time Bishop signed a companion agreement with another developer, Thomas F. McCormack (father of latter-day realtor/developer Michael T. McCormack) covering the rest of Bishop's lands in Heeia, those *makai* or toward the sea.

In an interview for this book Kido said that actually his agreement had been fully wrapped up no later than 1958.

In fact Kido's statement was inaccurate. Nor would the public announcement in 1960 help in understanding when the critical events occurred.

Heeia in those years was still largely undeveloped, about 71% of it being in agricultural use in 1959, according to a City Planning Department study.[24]

But the land boom was beginning to get under way. In 1957 Bishop Estate had commissioned a study of the district's development potential, believing that it was only a matter of time before Heeia, along with much of the windward coast, became urbanized as commuter suburbs for Honolulu.[25]

In the interview Kido also said that Bishop first approached a business partner of his, Joe Pao, about developing part of the Heeia lands, but that

Pao was too tied up with a project in Kailua, and so recommended Kido. Kido said then "one of the trustees called me." Kido indicated to the trustee an interest in negotiating. What resulted was that Kido was to provide a personal financial statement. This was done by Central Pacific Bank, of which Kido was then a vice-president.

Kido said that after the financial statement was submitted, the trustees asked him to submit a proposed development agreement, which he did, together with a business partner.

The trustees' fees bill was introduced in the Legislature in mid-March 1959.

Kido's letter to Bishop containing his proposal was dated April 14.

Final legislative approval of the bill came on May 2.

On May 5 the Bishop trustees agreed in principle to award an agreement to Kido (and to the *makai* developer, McCormack).

The governor signed the bill into law May 27.

*   *   *

Was there any connection between the development agreement and the legislative act?

Kido said absolutely not.

He also said that the two were entirely separate timewise. In fact, though, they were not.

In addition, although negotiating with Bishop while supporting the fees bill, Kido did not publicly disclose the fact of the negotiations. Nor did the 1959 Senate Journal indicate that he publicly attempted to abstain from voting.

Bishop Estate's side of the story on any possible connection between the fees bill and the development agreement could not be made available for this book. At the time research on Heeia was done, all but one of the men who had been Bishop trustees in early 1959 were dead. The one still living was extremely old. A request to interview him was not granted.

As with so many stories of this kind a final resolution is elusive. Who knows what really happened?

Conceivably, as Kido asserted, the Heeia negotiations and the fees bill were just two ships passing in the daylight.

And if the two events interacted, it is just as conceivable that this was not deliberate, that it was a case of interests naturally flowing together, of events placing people in situations where they wanted to help each other out and could, without calculated forethought.

And then there is this question: if indeed Sen. Kido felt in some way impelled to reciprocate for the opportunity that Bishop was offering him, what impact would his support for the fees bill have had?

Obviously it would have made some difference. Kido had great stature in the Democratic Party faction then in control of both houses. He sat on the committee that considered the bill in the Senate, and he chaired the committee that made recommendations on the apportionment of state capital improvement projects money—a fact of some consequence to fellow legislators from Oahu interested in obtaining monies for their districts.

Moreover, in those days the Legislature met for only three months every two years. During session there were virtual floods of bills to consider. The fees bill was only one of 3,212 in 1959. Visible support by someone like Kido would have lifted the fees bill out of the pack. Once it was known that Kido supported it, the merits might have been more readily accepted by Democrats, or at least there may have been less Democratic opposition.

One clear consequence of Sen. Kido obtaining the agreement with Bishop was that it played a role in his voting "no" in 1963 on a Democratic Party lease-to-fee conversion bill. The bill was to allow homeowners whose houses stood on lease land to compel their landlords to sell them the fee interest in the land. Kido attempted to abstain from voting, based on the fact of his agreement with Bishop, which called for the creation of a large number of residential leasehold lots. But the senate president ruled that Kido had to vote and he voted "no." The bill was defeated in the Senate by one vote.[26]

The story of Heeia development and Bishop Estate trustees' fees also stands for the fact that as early as 1960 the business and governmental activities of prominent Democrats and the large landowners were becoming intertwined in mutually-profitable relationships based on land.

Underscoring this point is that in the months following his obtaining an agreement with Bishop, Kido organized a large *hui*, Heeia Development Co. (HDCo.), to capitalize the residential portion of the project. In that *hui* at various times were some of the top and mid-level leadership of the Burns faction of the Democratic Party, which at the time was steadily moving into greater control of the entire apparatus of government in Hawaii. Furthermore, many of the known investors in HDCo. were born on Maui, where Kido came from, which underlines another point: that many who made Hawaii's "Democratic revolution" came from plantation communities, especially on the outer islands.

Hui members included Matsuo Takabuki, then a leading member of the Honolulu Board of Supervisors and one of Gov. Burns' closest advisors. (Just prior to the 1959 legislative session Takabuki had led the Burns faction in a successful fight over the House speakership.) Three investors who were from Maui were 1959 Senate Ways and Means Committee Chairman S. George Fukuoka and two of his committee clerks, Mamoru Yamasaki, who later that year was elected to the House from Maui, and Yoshikazu "Zuke" Matsui, who later served for many years on the Maui Planning Commission and was then appointed its deputy director. Also investing was Masaru "Pundy" Yokouchi, one of the leaders of the Democratic Party on Maui who in 1962 started heading up Burns' campaigns there. Also joining the *hui* was James M. Izumi, who had managed Burns' congressional delegate campaign in 1956 on Maui and was now the county's deputy civil service director.

Former assistant senate clerk Seichi "Shadow" Hirai was another Maui-born man who put in money. He worked in Burns' Washington office 1956-1958. In 1963 he became Senate Clerk and held that position till his death in 1982. Another investor was K. K. Lee, whose brother, Herbert, was senate president in 1959. The 1959 House Judiciary Committee chairman Hiroshi Kato also joined, as did Maui-born Rep. Tadao Beppu, chairman of the House Statehood Committee.[27]

*   *   *

In other places besides Heeia, leading Democrats were acquiring business ties with the large landowners.

They earned fees for doing legal work for estate developments, and fees for acting as court-appointed attorneys reviewing the affairs of the great estates. They made straight-out investments and became partners with other politically well-connected Democrats—judges, senior civil servants, and so on—in development plans based on estate land.

Several Democratic politicians and businessmen closely associated with the Democrats, in fact, became estate trustees and Big Five directors. Local-Chinese businessman Chinn Ho, close to the Democratic leadership, was made managing trustee of the Mark A. Robinson Trust in 1954. In 1961 he was elected to the board of Theo. H. Davies. Also in 1961 Honolulu City Council leader Herman G. P. Lemke was named a Robinson trustee. In 1962 Hung Wo Ching, a Chinese businessman closely associated with the Democratic Party, was elected to the board of Alexander & Baldwin. In 1968 Ching was appointed a Bishop Estate trustee, as was Matsuo Takabuki in 1971. In later years, part-Hawaiian William S. Richardson, a Democratic Party leader, and Myron B. "Pinky" Thompson, also part-Hawaiian and a former aide to Gov. Burns, were appointed Bishop trustees.

The following table (Table 2) shows how common it had become by 1970 for members of the Democratic Legislature, the Democratic administration, and their close associates to benefit in these ways.

——————————————————— **TABLE 2** ———————————————————

BURNS AND OTHER MAINSTREAM DEMOCRATS AND DEMOCRATIC
APPOINTEES WHO BY 1970 HAD TIES TO MAJOR LANDOWNERS

Note: The year 1970 was chosen as representing a time by which such arrangements were well in place. This table lists Burns Democrat politicians, appointed government officials and one family member, plus other mainstream Democratic politicians and officials, who by 1970 had: obtained development agreements from Hawaii's major landowners; purchased large tracts from them or represented the purchasers; invested in huis that had the agreements or had made the acquisitions; leased commercial property from major lessors; represented big landowners before government agencies and in labor/community matters; obtained court appointments to review the financial affairs of the great estates (year indicated is year of appointment); become estate trustees. Government/political position listed in this table is as of 1970.

ARIYOSHI, GEORGE R. Lieutenant Governor. Attorney C. Brewer 1967 before Honolulu City Council on land use matter.

BURNS, JAMES S. Governor's son. Campbell Estate minors guardian 1967.

BEPPU, TADAO. House Speaker. Investor Heeia Dev. Co. which had development agreement with Bishop Estate on 520 acres windward Oahu.

CHING, CLARENCE T.C. Gov. Burns' chief fundraiser 1962 and 1966 campaigns. One of principals International Dev. Co. in 1957 purchase of 1,074 acres in Salt Lake and Moanalua, Oahu, from Damon Estate through Territorial Investors.

FONG, ARTHUR S.K. Former Assistant State Attorney general. Campbell Estate master 1969.

FUKUOKA, S. GEORGE. State Circuit Court Judge. Investor Heeia Dev. Co.

HEEN, WALTER M. Honolulu City Council Chairman. Campbell Estate minors guardian 1966.

HIRAI, SEICHI "SHADOW." Senate Clerk. Officer and director Ethereal Inc., which had agreement 1965-67 with Amfac to buy fee interest 102 lease lots Waipahu, Oahu and resell to tenants; attorney for Damon Estate before Land Use Commission 1966.

IZUMI, JAMES M. Maui County Personnel Director. Investor Heeia Dev. Co.

KAMAKA, HIRAM K. State Finance Director. Campbell Estate minors guardian 1965.

KATO, HIROSHI. House Judiciary Chairman. Investor Heeia Dev. Co.

KAWASAKI, DUKE T. State Senator. Investor Wiliwili Nui Ridge Subdivision (a partnership), which had development agreement with Bishop Estate.

KIDO, MITSUYUKI. Former State Senator and Honolulu Supervisor; along with John Burns one of founders of contemporary Democratic Party. Former officer and director Leeward Dev. Corp. which developed Leeward Estates, a Campbell Estate leasehold subdivision. General partner Heeia Dev. Co. Head of sub-hui within International Dev. Co.

KIDO, SUNAO. Chairman State Board of Land and Natural Resources. Brother of Mitsuyuki. Investor Heeia Dev. Co.

LEMKE, HERMAN G.P. Former Honolulu City Council Chairman. Trustee Mark A. Robinson Trust.

LUM, HERMAN T.F. State Circuit Court Judge. Since 1963 held Bishop Estate lease to half-acre office-building site Kahala Shopping Center. Since 1969 held Bishop Estate lease to 1 acre Kakaako, site of three office buildings.

MATSUI, YOSHIKAZU. Chairman Maui County Planning Commission. Investor Heeia Development Co.

MAU, CHUCK. Former Honolulu Supervisor and Circuit Court Judge; along with John Burns one of founders of contemporary Democratic Party. Limited partner International Dev. Co.; attorney for buyers of Damon Tract from Damon Estate 1956.

McCLUNG, DAVID C. Senate President. Investor Wiliwili Nui Ridge Subdivision.

OMORI, MORIO. Aide to US Sen. Daniel K. Inouye. Attorney for Bishop and Austin estates before Land Use Commission 1967-69 on major residential developments leeward Oahu.

OSHIRO, ROBERT C. State Representative; chief campaign strategist Gov. Burns' re-election 1970. Campbell Estate master 1963.

TAKABUKI, MATSUO. Leading advisor to Gov. Burns; former Honolulu City Councilman. Leased Robinson trusts lands Waipahu 1965, subleased to various commercial ventures. Investor Heeia Dev. Co. Campbell Estate minors guardian 1962, master 1964.

TOKUNAGA, MICHAEL N. Deputy Director Department of Accounting and General Services. Investor International Dev. Co. sub-hui.

USHIJIMA, JOHN T. Senate Judiciary Chairman. Officer and director Ethereal Inc.

YAMASAKI, MAMORU. State Senator. Investor Heeia Dev. Co.

YOKOUCHI, MASARU "PUNDY." Gov. Burns' chief campaign organizer and chief representative Maui. Chairman State Foundation on Culture and the Arts. Unpaid consultant to Amfac approximately 1967 in settling labor and community problems Lahaina area, Maui, which to extent resulted in subsequent land sales to Yokouchi by Amfac. President Ethereal Inc.

YOSHINAGA, NADAO. State Senator. Officer and director Ethereal Inc. Campbell Estate master 1965.

Sources: Gwenfread E. Allen, ed., *Men and Women of Hawaii: A Biographical Directory of Noteworthy Men and Women of Hawaii* (Honolulu, 1966); Betty F. Buker, ed., *Men and Women of Hawaii 1972: A Biographical Directory of Noteworthy Men and Women of Hawaii* (Honolulu, 1972); Department of Commerce and Consumer Affairs, Business Registration Division; State of Hawaii, Legislative Reference Bureau, *Directory of State, County and Federal Officials: Supplement to Guide to Government in Hawaii* (published occasionally, most recently annually); Chamber of Commerce of Hawaii, *Who's Who in Government State of Hawaii* (various years); miscellaneous state and county public officials' personal financial disclosure statements, on file with State Ethics Commission and offices of county clerks; State of Hawaii, First Circuit Court, equity files on court-supervised affairs of Campbell, Damon and Bishop estates; State of Hawaii, Land Use Commission, miscellaneous files; Hawaii State Archives; files of county councils and planning departments; miscellaneous references in newspapers and periodicals.

The next table (Table 3) shows legislative leaders as the term has been previously defined—Senate president, House speaker, chairman of finance, judiciary, or ways and means committees, 1955-1984—and their involvement in land development.

Leaders of all major Democratic factions in those years were privately involved with land and development. Three leading members of the liberal Gill faction, O. Vincent Esposito, Vincent H. Yano, and Sakae Takahashi, all had extensive involvement, though Esposito's involvement was apparently greater in the years after he left leadership. Nadao Yoshinaga, Nelson K. Doi, and Kazuhisa Abe were three who contended with each other for leadership at various times; each was involved with real estate, particularly Yoshinaga and Abe.

The number of Republicans who were legislative leaders was very small—three out of 43. Two of the three, William H. Hill and Yasutaka Fukushima, were extensively involved with land and development.

Of the 43, only seven apparently had no simultaneous involvement with
real estate or the development business. Two who served in the 1970s and
early 1980s, Benjamin J. Cayetano and Kathleen Stanley, showed no interests in real estate in their financial disclosure statements (though Cayetano
at some point was an attorney for Real Estate Finance Corp.). Three—
Toshio Serizawa, Charles E. Kauhane, and Noburo Miyake—held their
leadership positions early in or prior to the land boom. Once the boom got
under way, two of these three took part in at least small ways. Serizawa, who
held a leadership position in 1955, in 1960 became a partner in Nusite Developers. Kauhane, after ceasing to be a legislative leader, became in 1971
president of Akamai Development Inc. Kenneth S. Kiyabu, who served in
1983–1984, had been a realtor immediately prior to entering leadership.
Anthony K.U. Chang, who served in 1984, had been a partner in CYC.

———————————————— TABLE 3 ————————————————

LEGISLATIVE LEADERS 1955–1984 REAL PROPERTY INVESTMENT AND
DEVELOPMENT ACTIVITY, AFFILIATIONS WITH MAJOR LANDOWNERS
AND DEVELOPERS

Note: All business activities cited below overlap in time with the leadership positions
held.

ABE, KAZUHISA. Senate President 1965–66, Senate Judiciary Chairman
1959 regular session, Senate Ways and Means Chairman 1955–57. President,
director, shareholder Hilo Development Inc. (developer Orchid Land Estates in
Puna, Hawaii). Secretary, director, shareholder Kuwaye Brothers Inc. (general
contractor). Limited partner Robert T. Iseri & Associates (developer Kaumana
Terrace, Hilo). Secretary, director, shareholder Kahi Inc. (general partner Vacationland Associates, which developed Vacationland subdivision, Puna, Hawaii).

ARIYOSHI, GEORGE R. Senate Ways and Means Chairman 1963–64. Attorney and limited partner Royal Gardens (developer Royal Gardens subdivision,
Puna, Hawaii). Attorney and limited partner Milolii Syndicate (developer Milolii Beach Lots Subdivision, Hawaii). Member small hui owning 60 acres, Kula,
Maui. Member 4-man hui that constructed and later sold 18-unit apartment
building near Queen's Hospital, Honolulu. Invested in several house lots
Moanalua, Oahu and Puna, Hawaii.

BEPPU, TADAO. House Speaker 1968–74. Held real estate license. Member
sub-hui International Dev. Co. (developer Salt Lake and Moanalua, Oahu).
Member sub-hui Heeia Dev. Co. (developer residential portion of 520 acres Heeia, Oahu).

CARPENTER, DANTE K. Senate Judiciary Chairman 1981–84. Public affairs
director C. Brewer & Co. Ltd. (Brewer was one of largest landowners and a
developer on Carpenter's home island of Hawaii.)

CAYETANO, BENJAMIN J. Senate Ways and Means Chairman 1979–80. No
known involvement while in leadership position.

CHANG, ANTHONY K. U. Senate Judiciary Chairman 1984. No known involvement while in leadership position.

CHANG, ROBERT W. B. House Judiciary Chairman 1959 regular session—
1964. His law firm represented Pacific Electrical Contractors Association;
Plumbing and Mechanical Contractors Association; State Tile Ltd.

CRAVALHO, ELMER F. House Speaker 1959–67, House Finance Chairman 1956. Officer, director, shareholder MDG Supply Inc. (MDG had building materials department.) Investor several small agricultural lots.

DOI, NELSON K. Senate President 1963–64, Senate Judiciary Chairman 1957. Limited partner Nusite Developers. President, director, shareholder M&D Investors Inc.

ESPOSITO, O. VINCENT. House Speaker 1957, House Judiciary Chairman 1955. Law firm handled several minor development matters, e.g. before Honolulu Board of Supervisors 1955 on construction of small office building.

FUKUOKA, S. GEORGE. Senate Ways and Means Chairman 1959 regular session, Senate Judiciary Chairman 1963–64. Partner B & F Enterprises. Partner 3-man hui 1959–64 owning 6 acres, Kihei, Maui. One of 3 partners 1959–1968 owning 3.5 acres Kihei, now under Menehune Shores condominium. One of 2 partners 1960–68 owning 12 acres Kihei, now under Kihei Kai Nani and Kihei Akahi condominiums. One of 2 partners 1960–65 owning 13.3 acres Kihei, now under Keawakapu condominium. Member subhui Heeia Dev. Co. Shareholder Valley Isle Realty Inc. Director, shareholder Maui Enterprises Ltd. (development finance). As attorney, involved in miscellaneous land and development matters.

FUKUSHIMA, YASUTAKA. Senate Judiciary Chairman 1959–62. As attorney had extensive development practice, including appearances before Honolulu City Council on behalf of clients.

GARCIA, RICHARD. House Judiciary Chairman 1977–78. Held real estate license, at Graham Realty Inc. Owned 5 pieces real property Oahu. Industrial relations for Alexander & Baldwin.

HARA, STANLEY I. House Finance Chairman 1959–64. Limited partner Robert T. Iseri & Associates (developer Kaumana Terrace, Hilo). Treasurer, director, shareholder Kahi Inc. (general partner, Vacationland Associates which developed Vacationland, Puna, Hawaii). President, director Hilo Factors Inc. (company business included real estate). Secretary, treasurer, director, shareholder Akahi Painting Corp. Director Hilo Dev. Inc. (developer Orchid Land Estates, large subdivision Puna, Hawaii).

HEEN, WILLIAM H. Senate President 1955–57. Assistant secretary, director Moses Akiona Ltd. (general contractor). Shareholder Capital Investment Co. Ltd. (major Oahu landowner and developer). President, director, shareholder Market Place Ltd. Law firm had extensive development practice. Clients included Capital Investment Co. and Waianae Dev. Co. in developing Waianae; Trade Wind Dev. Co. in building hotel in Waikiki; Halemaumau Land Co. and Kanau Dev. Co. re subdivision Niu Valley, Oahu; C. S. Wo & Sons on road matter with Honolulu city government; Hawaiian Trust Co. re eminent domain matter with Honolulu city government; Kalama Land Co. Ltd.

HILL, WILLIAM H. Senate President 1959 special session—1962. Major shareholder Realty Investment Co. Director C. Brewer & Co. Ltd. (major landowner on Hill's home island, Hawaii).

HULTEN, JOHN J. SR. Senate President 1967–68, Senate Ways and Means Chairman 1969–70. Held real estate license at Joe Pao Realty. Real estate appraiser and economic development consultant. Treasurer, director Hawaiian Escrows Ltd.

KAMAKA, HIRAM K. House Appropriations Chairman 1965–68. President, director, shareholder, attorney Kaena Management Co. Inc. Attorney for small developments, generally in windward Oahu.

KATO, HIROSHI. House Judiciary Chairman 1959 regular session, also 1967–70. Member sub-hui Heeia Dev. Co. Limited partner Kalihi-Ashford Assocs. Attorney for occasional development matters, e.g. Heeia Dev. Co. before Honolulu City Council 1969 rezoning.

KAUHANE, CHARLES E. House Speaker 1955. No known involvement while in leadership position.

KIYABU, KENNETH S. House Finance Chairman 1983–84. No known involvement while in leadership position.

KUNIMURA, TONY T. House Finance Chairman 1981–82. Held real estate broker license at Yoneji Realty Inc.

LEE, HERBERT K. H. Senate President 1959 regular session, Senate Judiciary Chairman 1955. Subleased lot Waikiki 1957; he in turn sub-subleased 1958; Hawaiian Prince Apts. built on lot. Built Hawaiian King Hotel, Waikiki, 1959 on land subleased 1958, in all of which he assigned his interest 1963. As attorney handled miscellaneous development matters, e.g. represented "wealthy Honolulu business interests" 1959 re option on 90 acres near San Francisco, according to Honolulu Star-Bulletin.

MATSUNAGA, SPARK M. House Judiciary Chairman 1957. Partner Poki Apts. approx 1957–59. Law firm handled miscellaneous development matters, including major Diamond Head rezoning 1957 for Ruddy F. Tongg and others.

McCLUNG, DAVID C. Senate President 1969–74. Partner Wiliwili Nui Ridge Subdivision. Second V-P, director Fong Construction Co. Ltd. Interest in land under pineapple cannery Lahaina, Maui. Attorney Signal Oil & Gas Co. re major resort on Big Island.

MIYAKE, NOBURO. Senate Ways and Means Chairman 1959 special session—1962. No known involvement while in leadership position.

MORIOKA, THEODORE T. House Finance Chairman 1980. Held real estate sales license. Treasurer, director All Hawaii Investment Corp.

NAKAMURA, YOSHIRO. House Judiciary Chairman 1981–82. Investor small number residential properties Wahiawa, Oahu and Lawai, Kauai. As attorney handled minor development matters.

NISHIMURA, DONALD S. Senate Judiciary Chairman 1975–78. Small real property holdings.

O'CONNOR, DENNIS E. W. Senate Judiciary Chairman 1979–80. One of principal attorneys for residential lessees seeking to convert their lots to fee simple.

PETERS, HENRY H. House Speaker 1981–84. Director industrial relations Dura Constructors Inc. Director Panin North America Inc. (Hong Kong-owned company formed to do real property business in Hawaii). Bishop Estate trustee.

ROEHRIG, STANLEY H. House Judiciary Chairman 1975–76. Member of Partners Investment Co. Miscellaneous land holdings on Hawaii.

SERIZAWA, TOSHIO. House Finance Chairman 1955. No known involvement while in leadership position.

STANLEY, KATHLEEN. House Judiciary Chairman 1983–84. No known involvement while in leadership position.

SUWA, JACK K. House Finance Chairman 1971–79. Director community relations Amfac (major landowner on Suwa's home island of Hawaii and throughout state). Limited partner Vacationland Assocs. (Puna developers). As of 1979 owned 6 lots Kurtistown, Hawaii.

TAKAHASHI, SAKAE. House Judiciary Chairman 1965–66. Partner Yorktown Ventures. Partner Hirotoshi Yamamoto & Assocs. Partner Waianae Assocs. Partner Honolulu Merchandise Mart. Director, secretary Makaha Reef Inc. Partner Moiliili Developers. Partner Wulff and Takahashi. Director Nuuanu Memorial Park Ltd. Miscellaneous other holdings.

USHIJIMA, JOHN T. Senate President 1975–78, Senate Judiciary Chairman 1967–74. V-P, director, shareholder, attorney Ethereal Inc. Limited partner Kona Highlands Dev. Co. (developer 250-lot subdivision Kona, Hawaii). V-P, director Safeguard Enterprises Inc. (Kona Highlands general partner). Partner, attorney MUK Co. Secretary, director Kona Estates Inc. Had miscellaneous small real property holdings Hawaii, Maui, Kauai. Attorney for major developer Boise Cascade Home & Land Corp., also for smaller companies and projects such as Kona Dolphin condominium, and Allied Aggregates Corp. (rock quarrying and crushing).

WAKATSUKI, JAMES H. House Speaker 1975–80, House Finance Chairman 1969–70, House Judiciary Chairman 1974. Partner Ventura Co. Shareholder Capital Investment Co. (developer resort Makaha, Oahu). Interest in Delta City, Arizona project as of 1974. Attorney before Honolulu City Council on land use matters for Amfac Financial Corp, also for Star Markets Ltd.

WONG, RICHARD S. H. Senate President 1979–84, Senate Ways and Means Chairman 1975–78. Held real estate license. Partner Manoa Estates Partners Ltd. President, director, shareholder RSHW Corp. (real estate agency). V-P Syncap Inc. (property management). V-P, treasurer, director, shareholder WRBS Sandpiper Inc. President, secretary, treasurer WUC Inc. Partner KKK investments. Consultant 1976 to Warren Corp. (sand mining, quarrying, trucking).

YAMADA, DENNIS R. House Judiciary Chairman 1979–80. Partner Ocean View Ltd. Partnership. Partner Twenty-Five Investors Hui. Law firm represented two of his home island of Kauai's largest landowners on development matters: Amfac and Grove Farm. Law firm had extensive practice many aspects of land and development.

YAMASAKI, MAMORU. Senate Ways and Means Chairman 1981–84. Member Hui o Nakane.

YANO, VINCENT H. Senate Ways and Means Chairman 1967–68. Developer. Partner Kapiolani Center. Member small hui owning 60 acres Kula, Maui.

YOSHINAGA, NADAO. Senate Ways and Means Chairman 1965–66, 1971–74. Held real estate broker's license. Partner M. Yokouchi/W. Yanagi. Various immediate family members had interests in Yanagi Nukolii Hui. V-P, director, shareholder Ethereal Inc. V-P, director, shareholder, broker Valley Isle Realty Inc. Part-owner 25 acres Kalihi Valley, Oahu. Wife was partner Gordon Miyaki Hui. Wife plus 2 others 1959–69 owned 24 acres Kihei, Maui. Wife president, shareholder, director Aloha Maui Co. Wife sole owner Rousseau Inc. Wife sole owner Mondrian Inc.

Sources: Gwenfread E. Allen, ed., *Men and Women of Hawaii: A Biographical Directory of Noteworthy Men and Women of Hawaii* (Honolulu, 1966); Betty F. Buker, ed., *Men and Women of Hawaii 1972: A Biographical Directory of Noteworthy Men and Women of Hawaii* (Honolulu, 1972); Department of Commerce and Consumer Affairs, Business Registration Division; State of Hawaii, Legislative Reference Bureau, *Directory of State, County and Federal Officials: Supplement to Guide to Government in Hawaii* (published occasionally, most recently annually); Chamber of Commerce of Hawaii, *Who's Who in Government State of Hawaii* (various years); miscellaneous state and county public officials' personal financial disclosure statements, on file with State Ethics Commission and offices of county clerks; State of Hawaii, Land Use Commission, miscellaneous files; Hawaii State Archives; files of county planning departments; miscellaneous references in newspapers and periodicals.

Not only did legislative leaders get extensively involved in development, but in their land business and their other enterprises they crossed lines of political party, political faction, and social class.

The 15 men listed in Table 4 below were all Democratic legislative leaders. The business associations listed occurred while they were legislators, and most occurred while they were legislative leaders. Most though not all associations involved land.

──────────────── TABLE 4 ────────────────

DEMOCRATIC LEGISLATIVE LEADERS IN BUSINESS ARRANGEMENTS
WITH REPUBLICANS, MEMBERS OF THE OLD ESTABLISHMENT, AND
MEMBERS OF RIVAL DEMOCRATIC FACTIONS

Note: In most cases the business activity cited overlaps in time with the holding of the leadership position. In all cases there is overlap between the business activity and holding legislative office.

ABE, KAZUHISA. Law firm of Republican Rep. Yasutaka Fukushima 1958 incorporated Hilo Dev. Inc., of which Abe was president. Abe 1963 helped organize 50th State Savings and Loan Assoc., of which he was president, Pepeekoo Sugar Co. manager Herbert M. Gomez V-P. Abe 1965 was elected director Hilo Electric Co.; president was Republican Sen. William H. Hill; officers and directors included members of old Shipman and Lyman families.

ARIYOSHI, GEORGE R. Invested 1960-67 in small hui with Vincent H. Yano, against whom in 1970 he ran for lieutenant governor. Ariyoshi 1963 was elected director First National Bank of Hawaii; most of bank board was establishment haole; was elected by nomination of Damon Estate trustees who were members of board. Elected director 1965 Honolulu Gas Co. Ltd; most other board members were from old haole firms. Elected director 1966 Hawaiian Insurance & Guaranty Co. Ltd., wholly-owned subsidiary of C. Brewer. As attorney represented Brewer 1967 before Honolulu City Council re improvement district matter involving Brewer downtown Honolulu property.

CARPENTER, DANTE K. For years employee C. Brewer subsidiary; in 1981 became C. Brewer director of public affairs.

FUKUOKA, S. GEORGE. Director Maui Enterprise Ltd.; other directors included William H. Balthis, Bank of Hawaii V-P for Maui, and Raymond R. Lyons, Maui Electric executive V-P and general manager, who also served on boards of several Baldwin family companies.

GARCIA, RICHARD. Industrial relations assistant Alexander & Baldwin.

HARA, STANLEY I. Assistant treasurer 50th State Savings & Loan; V-P was Pepeekoo Sugar Co. manager Herbert M. Gomez.

HEEN, WILLIAM H. Law firm represented Hawaiian Trust Co. before Honolulu Board of Supervisors 1957.

KAMAKA, HIRAM K. Associate mid-1960s law firm Chuck & Fujiyama. Walter G. Chuck was Republican-appointed Clerk of House of Representatives

1951-54, Clerk of Senate 1959-61. Chuck previously was member law firm Republican politician Hiram L. Fong. Wallace S. Fujiyama active Republican 1950s-early 1960s, including chairman Oahu County Young Republicans mid-1950s.

LEE, HERBERT K.H. V-P, director, shareholder Hawaiian Memorial Park Ltd. Other officers, directors, shareholders included members and business associates of Castle family, Kaneohe Ranch Co., Hawaiian Trust Co.: James C. Castle, Virginia Castle Baldwin, Horace W.B. White, Marshall M. Goodsill. Lee also subleased 2 apartment lots from Waikiki Dev. Co., a company composed of some of same people as Hawaiian Memorial Park.

MATSUNAGA, SPARK M. Shared law offices 1955 with Republican Masaji Marumoto, who was appointed 1956 to Territorial Supreme Court by Republican administration.

SUWA, JACK K. For many years employee of Amfac sugar company subsidiary. Became Amfac director of industrial relations 1973, rising to assistant V-P 1979.

USHIJIMA, JOHN T. Attorney 1966 for Mauna Kea Sugar Co. before Land Use Commission. Director American Security Bank 1975 when he became Senate President. Republican counterpart in Senate, Minority Leader Wadsworth Y.H. Yee, was also American Security director.

WAKATSUKI, JAMES H. Attorney for Amfac Financial Corp. 1972 before Honolulu City Council.

YAMADA, DENNIS R. Was Republican but switched to Democrat mid-1970s. Law partner Clinton I. Shiraishi was former Republican officeholder, leading Republican figure on Yamada's and Shiraishi's home island of Kauai. Law firm represented Amfac and Grove Farm on development matters.

YANO, VINCENT H. Organized small hui 1960 including George R. Ariyoshi, against whom Yano ran for lieutenant governor 1970.

Sources: Gwenfread E. Allen, ed., *Men and Women of Hawaii: A Biographical Directory of Noteworthy Men and Women of Hawaii* (Honolulu, 1966); Betty F. Buker, ed., *Men and Women of Hawaii 1972: A Biographical Directory of Noteworthy Men and Women of Hawaii* (Honolulu, 1972); Department of Commerce and Consumer Affairs, Business Registration Division; State of Hawaii, Legislative Reference Bureau, *Directory of State, County and Federal Officials: Supplement to Guide to Government in Hawaii* (published occasionally, most recently annually); Chamber of Commerce of Hawaii, *Who's Who in Government State of Hawaii* (various years); miscellaneous state and county officials' personal financial disclosure statements, on file with the State Ethics Commission and offices of county clerks; State of Hawaii, Land Use Comission, miscellaneous files; Hawaii State Archives; files of county planning departments; miscellaneous references in newspapers and periodicals.

It was, of course, not only legislative leaders who crossed political and social class lines in private business. The following are other examples:

Democratic Gov. John Burns chose former Republican Kenneth F. Brown as his lieutenant-gubernatorial running mate in 1966. Brown was a member of an old landed family and a director of Amfac.

A small tour company, Maui Island Tours Ltd., was incorporated in 1954. Deputy Maui County Attorney Thomas S. Ogata, a Democrat, was its vice-president. Shareholders included Republican Sen. Benjamin F. Dillingham II and C. Brewer director and former president Philip E. Spalding. Ogata was elected to the state Senate in 1959, appointed an Oahu circuit court judge in 1965, and an associate justice of the Hawaii Supreme Court in 1977.

Ogata in the early 1960s also became an investor in and attorney for Pukalani Terrace Landco, a *hui* organized to do a big residential subdivision in Pukalani, Maui. Landco was a large *hui* with a number of unregistered sub-*huis*. Frequently members were unaware of who else had invested. In any case, besides Ogata, included were members of the old Maui Baldwin family; Masaru "Pundy" Yokouchi, who 1962–1973 was Gov. John Burns' chief campaign organizer and representative on Maui; Takeo Yamauchi, a gambler who for many years was reputed by law enforcement authorities to run illegal gambling and organized crime on Maui; and at some point Gerald K. Machida, who from the late 1960s worked for HGEA, a white-collar government employees union, and who became a legislator in the 1970s.

Entrepreneur Hung Wo Ching in 1957 organized a company to build a shopping center on the US mainland, Magnolia Shopping Center Inc. A vice-president, director and shareholder was Sakae Takahashi, a prominent Democratic politician then in the Senate and aligned with the Burns Democrats. Takahashi in the mid-1960s began to break with the party majority, and in 1970 actively supported liberal Democrat Thomas P. Gill in an unsuccessful attempt to unseat Burns, the incumbent governor. At the time Takahashi began breaking away, other shareholders in Magnolia included Burns' brother, Edward, whom Burns had appointed director of the State Department of Taxation 1962–1969; William S. Richardson, who had been Burns' lieutenant governor 1962–1966, when Burns appointed him chief justice of the Hawaii Supreme Court; Mitsuyuki Kido; Shelley M. Mark, whom Burns appointed director of the State Department of Planning & Economic Development 1962–1974; and Matsuo Takabuki.

Hawaii National Bank was organized in 1959. Former Democratic politician Chuck Mau, one of the founders of the modern Democratic Party, was the secretary and a director. Clarence T. C. Ching, one of the bank's organizers, was a vice-president and director. Ching in 1962 and 1966 was John Burns' chief campaign fundraiser. Another vice-president and director was J. Garner Anthony, an attorney for the Bishop Estate. Campbell Estate trustee George M. Collins was a director. John H. Felix, a former aide to Republican Gov. William F. Quinn, joined the board several years later.

*   *   *

The following table (Table 5) is of lawyers who, beginning in 1963, were appointed by judges and state attorneys general to review the internal business affairs of three of the largest trust estates: Bishop, Campbell, and Damon. (The year 1963 was chosen because that was the first in which the governor, who selected the attorneys general and judges involved, was a Democrat.)

Of the 90 appointments, 90% could be identified as having gone to government or political figures, mostly Democrats and usually of some note, or to men who represented the ILWU, which throughout this period was a central part of the political power structure.

The basis for the appointments was highly discretionary. A judge or attorney general could choose from a large field of attorneys in private practice. But as the table shows, the appointing authorities handed out what were small but moderately desirable plums almost exclusively to members of the Democratic establishment. This example of the system at work shows the Democrats doing what the Republicans had done before them—fashioning a relatively tight-knit political elite and sharing the spoils of office.

The founders of the Bishop, Campbell, and Damon estates owned great amounts of land. The founders' wills ordered their lands held in trust for their beneficiaries. Estate management on such a scale was complex. In order to protect the interests of the beneficiaries as much as possible and to ensure proper guidance of the trustees, the founders also ordered that courts oversee the trusts. Basically, circuit court judges appointed special masters to review annual accounts, and guardians to represent interests of minors. Masters and guardians reported to the appointing judge. In addition, the state attorney general was required to help oversee Bishop Estate, with the authority to hire outside counsel to assist.

Bishop, Campbell, and Damon estates were selected for study because they were three of the four largest land-based trusts in Hawaii in the Democratic years, and they involved ongoing court supervision. (The fourth, actually a group of trusts, arose out of the will of Harold K. L. Castle, who died in 1967. In his will Castle set up a charitable foundation and two private trusts. None of these involved ongoing court review, however.)

Bishop is a perpetual charitable trust with a school for Hawaiian children as its beneficiary. The Campbell Estate is a private trust set up to last until 20 years after the death of the last of the four daughters of the estate's founder, James Campbell. He died in 1900. As of the early 1980s there was one surviving daughter in her late eighties. The Damon Estate is also a private trust, to last until the death of the last of the grandchildren of the estate's founder, Samuel M. Damon. He died in 1924. In the early 1980s there were four surviving grandchildren, aged between 60 and 70.

For an attorney, the job of reviewing an estate was a plum—only small to medium-size, but prestigious in its way, without being particularly stressful, since the estate staffs were knowledgeable, some of the spadework was done by accountants, and, with certain notable exceptions, the results of the attorneys' review were not the subject of controversy.

The fees overall were not particularly large because the work did not usually take long, but such time as was spent was generally billed at or near the attorneys' regular rates. Furthermore, unlike most private law work billed by the hour, with attorneys accounting to their clients in detail for how time is spent, here the lawyers normally did not even indicate to the judge the gross number of hours spent. Instead the appointees simply, when the work was done, told the court that they ought to be paid such and such an amount. Supervising judges routinely ordered the estates to pay whatever was indicated. Also, the estates paid their bills, and did so promptly, a fact of no small importance to private attorneys, particularly those who practiced alone or in small firms as did many of those men appointed. All this made the work relatively rewarding for the time required.

Besides, the chance to get a look at the internal workings of a big estate and to meet the trustees was normally valuable to an attorney with a personal and professional interest in real property investment and development—which many appointees had.

It should be noted that not all "political" appointees were Democrats. Former Republican Gov. William F. Quinn, for example, was appointed a Damon guardian in 1963.

There are two main reasons why some Republicans show up. One is that it took several years of Democrats in office before the terms of Republican-era judges expired or they retired, to be replaced mostly by Democrats. The other is that one circuit court appointee in the Democratic years who was a Republican, Yasutaka Fukushima, for a period of time was probate judge and thus responsible for appointing masters and guardians. He appointed a number of Republicans.

In the main, though, the names below are of Democrats.

──────────────── **TABLE 5** ────────────────

PRIVATE ATTORNEYS
APPOINTED BY COURT AND ATTORNEY GENERAL
TO REVIEW BISHOP, CAMPBELL AND DAMON ESTATES
1963-1984

Note: Government or political position is as of year of appointment to review estate. Each separate account or annual report or other matter that was to be analyzed is counted as one "appointment."

AYABE, SIDNEY K. Former deputy attorney general. Campbell master 1975.

BURNS, JAMES S. Governor's son. Campbell guardian 1968. Campbell master 1976.

CHIKASUYE, CLESSON Y. Former Honolulu councilman. Campbell guardian 1977, 1982. Damon guardian 1978 (3 accounts). Bishop master 1979.

DAMON, C.F. JR. Former director State Dept. of Labor and Industrial Relations, former assistant to Republican US Sen. Hiram L. Fong. Campbell guardian 1968 and 1974.

DODGE, ROBERT G. Former Senate attorney, former vice-chairman Honolulu Charter Commission, former Democratic Party official. Bishop special deputy attorney general 1965.

DOI, MASATO. Former circuit court judge, former Honolulu councilman. Campbell guardian 1980.

DYER, JOHN F. Former circuit court judge. Bishop special deputy attorney general 1966.

FONG, ARTHUR S.K. Former assistant attorney general. Campbell master 1970.

FUKUDA, ROBERT K. Former State representative. Campbell guardian 1964.

GELBER, DONALD J. Campbell guardian 1972 (2 appointments).

HARE, C. MICHAEL. Formerly active Young Democrats. Bishop special deputy attorney general 1975 (5 reports to review).

HEEN, WALTER M. Honolulu Council legislative lobbyist, former State representative. Campbell guardian 1967.

HUSTACE, FRANK W. Former Territorial public land commissioner. Bishop master 1971.

KAITO, BEN F. Former Honolulu councilman. Damon guardian 1975 (3 accounts). Campbell master and guardian 1977-78 (4 appointments).

KAMAKA, HIRAM K. State representative. Campbell guardian 1966.

KATO, HIROSHI. Former circuit court judge, former State representative. Bishop master 1983.

KIMURA, GEORGE Y. Campbell guardian 1969.

KING, JAMES A. ILWU attorney. Bishop master 1970.

KING, SAMUEL P. Former circuit court judge. Campbell guardian 1970.

LEBB, EDWARD R. Campbell guardian 1973.

LIM, KWAN HI. Formerly law partner of or shared offices with Democrats such as Bert T. Kobayashi Sr., Russell K. Kono, Edwin H. Honda, Roy Y. Takeyama, Donald S. Nishimura. Bishop master 1982 (2 appointments). Bishop master 1983 (2 appointments).

LUM, LESLIE W.S. Former Democratic Party officer. Campbell master 1967.

LUM, RICHARD M.C. Per diem district court judge. Bishop master 1977.

LYONS, SAMUEL A.B. Campbell guardian 1973.

MARUMOTO, MASAJI. Former Hawaii Supreme Court justice. Campbell guardian 1965.

MARUMOTO, WENDELL H. Son of Supreme Court justice. Bishop master 1971.

MIHO, JON T. Former assistant to Republican US Sen. Hiram L. Fong. Law firm had a number of members, including Fong, who achieved high elected and appointed governmental positions. Campbell guardian 1975.

MINAMI, WAYNE K. Former attorney general, former director State Dept. of Regulatory Agencies. Campbell guardian 1981.

MIZUHA, JACK H. Former Supreme Court justice, former attorney general. Campbell master 1968. Campbell guardian 1969. Bishop master 1970.

NAITO, YUKIO. Former legislative attorney. Bishop master 1976.

NAKAMURA, HIDEKI. ILWU attorney. Campbell master 1973.

QUINN, WILLIAM F. Former governor. Damon guardian 1963.

REINWALD, ARTHUR B. Campbell guardian 1972.

ROHLFING, FREDERICK W. Republican State representative. Campbell guardian 1963. Republican State senator. Campbell guardian 1971.

RUBIN, BARRY J. Former assistant Senate clerk. Law partners include State representative and governor's son. Campbell guardian 1965.

SAKAI, HIROSHI. Former clerk for key legislative committees. Campbell guardian 1971.

SASAKI, RICHARD S. Former executive director Public Utilities Commission. Bishop special deputy attorney general 1967.

SCHULZE, RICHARD P. District court magistrate. Bishop master 1970.

SHIM, ALVIN T. Both he and wife very active in Democratic Party. Formerly in law firm with prominent Democrats Thomas P. Gill and David C. McClung. Damon guardian 1971.

SHINN, MELVIN Y. Former aide Republican US Sen. Hiram L. Fong, served in various capacities Honolulu Redevelopment Agency, former chief clerk Senate Judiciary Committee. Campbell guardian 1976.

SPITZER, ARTHUR H. Former tax court Judge. Campbell master 1963.

STEINER, KEITH J. Former district court magistrate, delegate 1968 constitutional convention. Campbell guardian 1976.

SUYENAGA, TARO. Former law partner Sen. Sakae Takahashi and US Attorney Herman T.F. Lum, former business associate Sen. Mitsuyuki Kido. Campbell guardian 1966.

TAKABUKI, MATSUO. Honolulu Councilman. Campbell master 1965.

TAKAHASHI, SAKAE. State senator. Campbell master 1971.

TAKAYESU, BEN G. Former district court magistrate. Bishop special deputy attorney general 1964.

TANIGUCHI, BRIAN T. State representative. Damon guardian 1981 (3 accounts).

TAYLOR, CARROL S. Campbell guardian 1979.

TITCOMB, FREDERICK J. Campbell master 1974.

TSUKIYAMA, TED T. Chairman Hawaii Employment Relations Board. Damon guardian 1967. Damon guardian 1969. Campbell guardian 1970.

UEHARA, JOHN J. Former Territorial Loyalty Board member. Campbell master 1969.

VENTURA, JAMES F. Campbell guardian 1975.

WIIG, JON. Former federal judge. Damon guardian 1963.

WOLFE, STUART E. Son-in-law chief justice Hawaii Supreme Court. Bishop master 1975 (4 reports to review).

WONG, DICK YIN. State tax appeal court judge. Bishop special deputy attorney general 1963.

WONG, GORDON Y.H. Former director State Dept. of Taxation. Campbell guardian 1983. Bishop master 1984.

YAMANE, ERNEST Y. Former Republican Party official. Campbell guardian 1965.

YOSHINAGA, NADAO. State senator. Campbell master 1966.

Sources: State of Hawaii, First Circuit Court, equity files for court-supervised matters regarding Bishop, Campbell and Damon estates; Gwenfread E. Allen, ed., *Men and Women of Hawaii: A Biographical Directory of Noteworthy Men and Women of Hawaii* (Honolulu, 1966); Betty F. Buker, ed., *Men and Women of Hawaii 1972: A Biographical Directory of Noteworthy Men and Women of Hawaii* (Honolulu, 1972); State of Hawaii, Legislative Reference Bureau, *Directory of State, County and Federal Officials: Supplement to Guide to Government in Hawaii* (published occasionally, most recently annually); Chamber of Commerce of Hawaii, *Who's Who in Government State of Hawaii* (various years); miscellaneous reference in newspapers and periodicals.

Another example of the kind of pattern seen in the above table was provided when Gov. George Ariyoshi in 1982 nominated Circuit Court Judge Arthur S.K. Fong to the state appeals court.

During several recent years Fong had been the so-called "motions" judge on Oahu—a kind of "traffic cop" position for circuit court civil cases. In that capacity Fong disposed of preliminary matters, and could summarily decide cases if there were no factual matters in dispute but only conflicting views on the applicable law.

Frequently foreclosure cases involving real property were capable of summary disposition. In such cases Fong then appointed someone to take charge of the property involved, sell it, and repay the party bringing the foreclosure action as well as others who may have been owed money.

The work paid well and was not considered particularly difficult; generally it was desirable to be appointed a commissioner.

The Senate Judiciary Committee held a hearing on Fong's nomination. During the hearing several private attorneys criticized Fong's record as a circuit court judge. Most criticism focused either on allegations that Fong had been reversed on appeal an abnormally large number of times, or that in various ways he had displayed favoritism.

One private attorney charged that Fong had displayed favoritism in selecting foreclosure commissioners. Following the charge the committee asked for a list of people Fong had appointed. A judiciary system administrator prepared a list of all of Fong's appointees from January 1977 through May 1980. There were approximately 140 names on the list.[28]

Fong told the committee that "the list . . . reflects a cross section of the real estate, business and the law profession." He also said that "all were selected on the basis of merit alone," and that many had been suggested by the parties involved in particular foreclosure cases.[29]

Under questioning by senators Fong also "acknowledged that most of the people on the list were personal friends," according to a newspaper story.[30]

Honolulu Advertiser reporter James Dooley studied the list and found that "many of the names . . . were politicians or men with strong political connections to the state and city." Dooley also determined that three of Fong's nephews were on the list. In addition Dooley found a former supreme court justice, Jack H. Mizuha, with whom Fong had shared law offices 1970–1974, and

Honolulu Police Commission Chairman William C. H. Chung, who had been Fong's client when Fong was in private practice.[31]

Although several judges and prominent political figures publicly endorsed Fong's nomination, the publicity, especially concerning the list of commissioners, was so adverse that the committee decided to recommend that the full Senate deny Fong's appointment. Before that could occur, Gov. Ariyoshi withdrew the nomination. Fong then continued to serve as a circuit court judge until 1984, when he retired from the bench.

*　*　*

It is useful to compare in terms of politics the types of appointments listed in the above table of estate masters and guardians, plus those of Fong's foreclosure cases, with run-of-the-mill guardian and criminal case appointments.

Large estate work and foreclosure cases ordinarily paid attorneys at or near their regular hourly rates. Kwan Hi Lim, a Bishop Estate master in the early 1980s, said that he put in 273 hours for which he billed and was paid $25,000, a rate of about $92 an hour. Lim indicated $92 was somewhat on the low side for him, since at the time his usual hourly rate was between $100 and $125 per hour. (It should be noted that Lim's assignment was unusually large—reviewing four Bishop accountings simultaneously—and this was in part responsible for what was also an unusually large bill. By way of contrast, former circuit court judge Hiroshi Kato in 1983 was appointed master for one Bishop accounting, for which he was paid $9,000.)[32]

Ordinary court-appointed guardianship work as of early 1984 paid $30 an hour out of court; $40 in court. There was a $1,000 ceiling, though judges had the authority to raise it in special circumstances. Court-appointed criminal defense work paid $30 an hour out of court and $40 in court. For class A felonies there was a $2,000 ceiling. For classes B and C it was $1,500. As with guardianship work judges could raise the criminal fee ceiling.[33]

Most experienced lawyers considered such levels of pay as somewhere between low and abysmally low. For some perspective: a court-appointed murder defense could pay up to $2,000. For the same work an experienced defense lawyer, privately retained, might have demanded a flat fee of $25,000 or more.

Ordinary court-appointed guardianships and criminal defense work generally went to lawyers who asked for it. Appointing judges maintained lists which attorneys asked to be put on. Those who sought, or at least accepted, this work were generally young attorneys who needed the money, however small, and the experience.

In this group it was very unusual to find names of the kind that appeared in the table of estate masters and guardians or on Judge Fong's list of foreclosure commissioners.

*　*　*

The subject of land and Hawaii's new establishment had other dimensions as well. One had to do with efforts by major US mainland and foreign business interests to break into the development business in Hawaii.

In the 1960s, after statehood, development money started flowing into Hawaii from outside in unprecedented quantities, first from the US mainland and somewhat later from the rest of the world, Japan especially, starting in the early 1970s.

Among the outside developers were some very big names indeed. Hilton Hotels International about 1959 began planning for the Kahala Hilton in Honolulu, which became a place where United States presidents and movie stars stayed. The industrialist Henry J. Kaiser in 1959 entered into an agreement with Bishop Estate to develop 6,000 acres in east Oahu—the start of Hawaii Kai. Weyerhauser, a big American wood products firm, helped finance Chinn Ho's resort at Makaha Valley, Oahu. Laurance S. Rockefeller developed the Mauna Kea Beach Hotel at Kawaiahae on Hawaii in the mid-1960s. Boise Cascade Home and Land Corporation, self-described as the United States' largest homebuilder and third largest land developer, took an option in 1967 on 31,000 acres along the Big Island's South Kohala coast. Leadership Housing Systems Inc., a subsidiary of the multinational mining firm Cerro Corporation, and describing itself as "among the nation's top fifteen residential real estate and land developers," attempted several projects around the state in the early 1970s, the largest being a proposed 1,185-acre resort at Poipu, Kauai.

Three mainland firms entering development in Hawaii were in the oil and gas business: Signal Oil & Gas Co., which in 1967–1968 through its Signal Properties bought and leased 54,000 acres near Boise's land on Hawaii; Consolidated Oil & Gas, which in 1968 bought most of the 11,000-acre Princeville Ranch at Hanalei, Kauai, from a subsidiary of Amfac; and Louisiana Land & Exploration Co., which in 1969 went into joint venture with Molokai Ranch Co. to build a big resort on the west end of Molokai.

Two Japanese conglomerates, Mitsubishi and Tokyu, jointly developed the Mauna Lani Resort at South Kohala on the Big Island. Daichi Kanko in 1973 bought much of the developed property of Chinn Ho's Makaha Valley resort. Seibu Group Enterprises in 1973 bought 1,000 acres at Makena, Maui, for a resort. Hasegawa Komuten went into a number of resort projects, the most visible being a highly controversial development at Nukolii, Kauai. Japanese multimillionaire Kenji Osano became by 1974 the largest single hotel owner in Waikiki, having acquired one-fourth of all rooms.

These and other outside developers were playing for big stakes in Hawaii by previous local standards, scores of millions of dollars, hundreds of millions.

Sensibly enough, from the beginning they took to hiring politically well-placed Island residents to help their projects through the maze of Hawaii government regulations.

The following table (Table 6) shows politically well-connected Hawaii residents and their associations with large outside developers. As usual, Burns Democrats predominate, but Democrats from other factions also appear, as do Republicans.

―――――――――――――――――― TABLE 6 ――――――――――――――――――

MAJOR OUTSIDE DEVELOPERS AND THEIR LOCAL REPRESENTATIVES

Note: The name of the local resident appears first, then his position in politics or government prior to or while working for the developer, then the name of the outside developer or financier, then the action taken by the local for the outsider. Where an individual local resident represented more than one outside developer, the information is repeated in the same order.

ABE, KAZUHISA. Former Senate president and Supreme Court associate justice. Taiyo Fudosan Kogyo Ltd.; successfully resisted downzoning by Land Use Commission 1974, 280 acres Kahului-Puapuaa, Hawaii. Pacific Basin Resorts Inc. and Taiyo Fudosan Kogyo Ltd.; obtained from Land Use Commission 1976 urban districting 145 acres Kona, Hawaii, for residential project.

BLAIR, RUSSELL. State Representative, 1975 chaired House committee reviewing shoreline protection bill that, when passed, established special management area (SMA) permit system. Louisiana Land & Exploration Co.; as attorney helped obtain SMA permit 1982 from Maui Planning Commission for Louisiana Land subsidiary for access road to condominium project at Kawakiu, Molokai.

BROWN, KENNETH F. Gov. Burns' running mate 1966, governor's aide 1966-68, State Senator 1968-74, Chairman Hawaii Community Development Authority beginning 1977. Laurance S. Rockefeller;Brown 1964 became V-P, director Rockefeller development firm in Hawaii, Olohana Corp., developer of land Kawaiahae, Hawaii, containing Mauna Kea Beach Hotel. Mitsubishi Corp.-Tokyu Tochikaihatsu Co. joint venture; Brown 1974 became director, later president of the joint-venture company, eventually named Mauna Lani Resort Inc., building Mauna Lani Resort in South Kohala, Hawaii.

ESPOSITO, O. VINCENT. State Senator, former House speaker. Hilton Hotels Corp.; attorney before Honolulu Council 1960 on behalf of local developer joint-venturing with Hilton to build Kahala Hilton Hotel. In 1961 became assistant secretary of two Hilton-related corporations, Hilton-Burns Hotels Inc., and Hawaiian Village Inc.

FUJIYAMA, WALLACE S. University Board of Regents 1974-1982, close associate of Gov. George Ariyoshi. Seibu Group Enterprises; attorney 1979 before Maui Planning Commission for hotel at Makena. Hasegawa Komuten (USA) Inc.; attorney starting 1982 regarding resort at Nukolii, Kauai.

HONG, WALTON D.Y. Former deputy state attorney general assigned to Land Use Commission. Consolidated Oil & Gas Co. Inc.; as attorney before Land Use Commission 1974 unsuccessfully sought urban districting for 877 acres Hanalei, Kauai, for Princeville resort undertaken by Consolidated's Hawaii subsidiary. Moana Corporation; as attorney before Land Use Commission and Kauai County agencies late 1970s obtained approvals for 457-acre resort Poipu, Kauai. Pacific Standard Life Insurance Co. and Hasegawa Komuten (USA) Inc.; Pacific Standard 1974 bought 60-acre resort site Nukolii, Kauai and proceeded with a partner to develop 25 acres; Hasegawa 1980 bought out the 25 acres. Since 1977 Hong represented project before State and Kauai County agencies.

LEE, HERBERT K.H. Former Senate president. Henry J. Kaiser; several days after announcing retirement as Senate President 1959, Lee joined Kaiser's firm in developing Hawaii Kai, east Oahu.

LEE, KENNETH K.L. Former State Representative. Panin Development (Hong Kong) Ltd.; Panin was Hong Kong conglomerate, some of whose principals bought stock mid-1970s in American Security Bank (later renamed First Interstate Bank), and asked Lee to sit on board of directors as one of 2 Hawaii representatives. Panin North America Inc. established 1982 as Hawaii corporation to find real estate investments, with Lee president.

McCLUNG, DAVID C. Senate President. Signal Oil & Gas Co.; as attorney lobbied Hawaii County agencies 1968 for Signal Properties, which 1967-68 acquired 54,000 acres in fee and lease South Kohala, Hawaii, for major resort.

MIRIKITANI, PERCY K. State Senator. Hawaii Daichi Kanko Inc.; attorney for the company's 1973 purchase Makaha Inn and 2 golf courses Makaha, Oahu, from Capital Investment Co. of Hawaii Inc.

MIZUHA, JACK H. Former territorial Attorney General and former associate justice State Supreme Court, close advisor to Honolulu Mayor Frank F. Fasi. Kenji Osano; Mizuha director Osano's Hawaii company, Kyo-ya Co. Ltd., which by 1974 owned 1/4 all hotel rooms Waikiki.

MURAI, DR. ERNEST I. Among early founders modern Democratic Party. Kenji Osano; director Osano's Kyo-ya Co. Ltd.

OMORI, MORIO. Aide to US Congressman and then US Sen. Daniel K. Inouye 1959-78, shared law offices 1958-65 with Honolulu City Councilman Matsuo Takabuki. Weyerhauser Co.; attorney before Honolulu Council 1960s for resort Makaha, Oahu, of which Weyerhauser was major investor. Attorney before state agency, Kauai Task Force, 1974 for group of primarily mainland investors who owned bulk of lands of old Kilauea Sugar Co.

PETERS, HENRY H. House Speaker. Panin Development (Hong Kong) Ltd.; Hong Kong conglomerate some of whose principals bought stock in American Security Bank (later renamed First Interstate Bank). Panin asked Peters to sit on bank board, beginning 1982. Peters 1983 became director Panin North America Inc., Hawaii corporation locating real property investments for Panin.

SHIGEMURA, JAMES Y. State Representative, Chairman House Tourism Committee. Signal Oil & Gas Co.; co-counsel with Senate President David C. McClung for Signal Properties, which 1967-68 acquired 54,000 acres fee and lease South Kohala, Hawaii, for major resort.

SHIRAISHI, CLINTON I. Chairman Kauai County Charter Review Commission, also former State Senator, Kauai county supervisor, Representative, district court magistrate. Leadership Housing Systems Inc.; attorney 1974 before various state and county agencies in unsuccessful attempt to begin major resort Poipu, Kauai.

UEOKA, MEYER M. State Representative, member State Board of Education at various times, former Maui district court magistrate. Masao Omori; director Hawaii Omori Corp. which late 1970s-early 1980s built West Maui Center, Kaanapali Alii condominium, Wili Ko Professional Building, all in west Maui.

USHIJIMA, CHARLES T. State Representative. Asahi Development Hawaii Corp.; V-P, director Asahi, which built Royal Kuhio Condominium, Waikiki, and The Rose Condominium near Punchbowl, Oahu.

USHIJIMA, JOHN T. State Senator, Chairman Senate Judiciary Committee. Boise Cascade Home & Land Corp.; attorney before Land Use Commission 1968. Boise 1967 had obtained option 31,000 acres South Kohala Hawaii, for major resort.

YOKOUCHI, MASARU "PUNDY." Gov. Burns' representative on Maui. Seibu Group Enterprises; assisted 1974 getting urban districting for 500 of 1,000 acres bought 1973 Makena, Maui, for major resort.

Sources: Gwenfread E. Allen, ed., *Men and Women of Hawaii: A Biographical Directory of Noteworthy Men and Women of Hawaii* (Honolulu, 1966); Betty F. Buker, ed., *Men and Women of Hawaii 1972: A Biographical Directory of Noteworthy Men and Women of Hawaii* (Honolulu, 1972); Department of Commerce and Consumer Affairs, Business Registration Division; State of Hawaii, Legislative Reference Bureau, *Directory of State, County and Federal Officials: Supplement to Guide to Government in Hawaii* (published occasionally, most recently annually); miscellaneous state and county public officials' personal financial disclosure statements, on file with State Ethics Commissions and offices of county clerks; State of Hawaii, Land Use Commission, miscellaneous files; Hawaii State Archives; files of county planning departments; miscellaneous references in newspapers and periodicals.

Overall, these local representatives were skilled in their professions. To that extent they would have been useful to outside investors and developers irrespective of background in government or politics. But the fact is they did have inside knowledge of local government, and generally had an ability to deal effectively with the many politicians, bureaucrats, commission members and so on involved in the multitude of development approvals. In short, they had contacts and connections.

In some instances the connections gave the appearance of being very close indeed:

When Democratic Sen. O. Vincent Esposito represented Hilton Hotels and local developer Charles J. Pietsch Jr. before the Honolulu City Council in 1960 on the matter of the Kahala Hilton, he was sharing law offices with Councilman Clesson Y. Chikasuye. On all three Council readings of the hotel rezoning bill, Chikasuye not only voted in favor but also seconded the motion to approve.[34]

When the Japanese hotel owner Kenji Osano put former Hawaii Supreme Court Justice Jack H. Mizuha on the board of Osano's Hawaii corporation, Kyo-ya Co., Mizuha was one of the closest advisors to the then-mayor of Honolulu, Frank F. Fasi. Osano's local holdings were in Waikiki which, in terms of land use controls, was primarily under the jurisdiction of the Honolulu city government which Fasi led. At the same time Osano gave a board seat to Dr. Ernest I. Murai, one of the founders of the modern Democratic Party which controlled state government. Finally, the law firm that Osano used, Kashiwa & Kashiwa, included Shiro Kashiwa, the first attorney general of the state of Hawaii, 1959–1962, who thus had served a Republican administration. Whether by design or coincidence Osano was hedging his bets extremely well.[35]

Rep. Russell Blair in 1982 represented a local subsidiary of Louisiana Land in obtaining a shoreline management area permit. Blair had entered politics in the early 1970s with an interest in environmental issues. In 1975 he chaired the House Environmental Protection Committee, which worked on the legislation that gave rise to such permits.[36]

When Seibu retained Masaru Yokouchi as a consultant, he was Gov. Burns' chief unofficial representative on Maui, whose powers included providing the governor with names of Maui people suitable for appointment to state boards and commissions, including the Land Use Commission, the first major hurdle Seibu had to clear. When Seibu applied to the LUC in 1974, Yokouchi arranged private meetings between Seibu representatives and several commissioners, including the Maui commissioner, who had been appointed in 1969 on Yokouchi's recommendation.[37]

When Kenneth Brown in 1974 joined the board of the joint venture of Mitsubishi and Tokyu, he was a state senator. Brown was also a director of Amfac, a major hotel owner along the same coast of the Big Island where the two Japanese companies were planning their Mauna Lani Resort. He had previously been an officer and director of the Laurance Rockefeller company that in the mid-1960s built the Mauna Kea Beach Hotel just to the north of Mauna Lani.

Former Sen. Clinton Shiraishi represented Leadership Housing before the Land Use Commission in 1974. The Leadership executive who retained him believed Shiraishi was simultaneously handling five other petitions before the LUC that concerned projects in which sitting LUC members were secretly involved financially. (Shiraishi later denied this, and no evidence ever came to light substantiating the executive's belief.)[38]

One thing distinguishing Shiraishi from most of the rest was that he was a Republican. This, however, did not rule out his having good Democratic Party ties. Beginning in the early 1960s Shiraishi became perhaps the most active and successful local developer on his island of Kauai. In *huis* he organized were an extraordinarily large number of Democratic officeholders and jobholders in Democratic administrations.[39] Also, the man who in 1969 became his law associate and later partner, Dennis R. Yamada, in 1970 became a Republican state representative. In 1974 Yamada ran for and won a House seat as a Democrat, and as such continued to hold a seat through 1982, chairing the powerful House Judiciary Committee 1979–1980, and rising to the post of House majority leader 1981–1982 before retiring from the House in 1982.

As noted previously, two others on the list, Percy Mirikitani and Jack Mizuha, were also Republicans. Mizuha was close to dissident Democrat Frank Fasi, mayor of Honolulu 1968–1980. And Mirikitani, like Shiraishi, was a veteran of the 442nd Regiment.

Large outsider companies apparently did not always retain or bring onto their boards Hawaii residents with solid ties to government. When, for example, Consolidated Oil & Gas first approached the Land Use Commission in 1969 and obtained urban districting for 995 acres at Princeville, the company apparently had no one on its payroll with local political ties or experience in government. (Thereafter this changed, though.)

This also appeared to have been the case with Laurance Rockefeller, who only by accident obtained a politically well-connected corporate officer and director in Kenneth Brown:

Rockefeller was one of the first major outside businessmen to size up Hawaii resort potential, and his capital and know-how were welcomed by all kinds of political, labor and community leaders. The Mauna Kea Beach Hotel he built in Kawaihae was cited for years afterward as one of Hawaii's best luxury hotels, with consistently high occupancy rates. To achieve this Rockefeller apparently did not need special influence, beyond that of his own name.

Brown was an independently wealthy member of an old Hawaii family. In 1964 he was a Republican, but not active in politics. Although over rounds of golf he was then developing a close friendship with Democratic Gov. Burns, still Kenneth Brown in 1964 was not a politically influential person.

When Rockefeller in 1964 registered his Olohana Corporation to build a resort at Kawaihae on the Big Island, he named Brown a vice-president and director. In an interview for this book Brown said that Rockefeller did so partly in exchange for development rights to some land held by Brown and several others. Then in 1966 Gov. Burns chose Kenneth Brown as his running mate, and from then on Brown was politically influential.

At times the pairing of political insiders with big-money outsiders came about because the outsiders were in joint ventures of some sort with local businessmen who used politically well-connected attorneys. This was the case with Weyerhauser, also with Hilton in building its Kahala hotel.

As another variation, there were off-the-record arrangements, meaning it is not possible to know the full extent to which outsider developers obtained help from political insiders. For example:

Louisiana Land, from the inception of its development work on Molokai, saw the supply of potable water as one of its most critical needs. The State Board of Land and Natural Resources (BLNR) had jurisdiction over a water plan put forward by Louisiana Land and Molokai Ranch in the early 1970s. An ILWU officer was a BLNR member, and the union had substantial influence with the governor, who appointed all BLNR members. According to current and former ILWU officers interviewed for this book, Louisiana Land and the ILWU struck a private agreement whereby the union would use its influence to help obtain BLNR approval for the water plan, and then, as the resort became operational, the company would agree to the ILWU representing its workers.[40]

But if there were variations on the pattern, still the pattern was pronounced: in most cases the large outsiders hired politically well-connected Hawaii residents.

Underscoring what an outside developer wanted from an insider in the way of contacts and connections is the fact that in several known cases the outsiders used not one but two sets of attorneys—a "non-political" law firm to handle routine legal work, and a "political" lawyer for highly discretionary dealings with government.

Charles J. Pietsch Jr., joint developer of the Kahala Hilton, had two attorneys for a long time. One was William B. Stephenson of Stephenson & Ashford, an outsider to the Democratic establishment. The other was Democratic Sen. O. Vincent Esposito. In an interview for this book a Pietsch associate said that Stephenson was used "for thinking," Esposito "for talking."

Leadership Housing retained Ashford & Wriston, the successor firm to Stephenson & Ashford, to do day-to-day work and routine litigation. To represent Leadership before the Land Use Commission, Clinton Shiraishi was hired. Other attorneys known to have been considered by Leadership for LUC representation were: former Honolulu councilman Ben F. Kaito; Francis M. Izumi, in the 1960s a deputy state attorney general assigned to the State Land Board; US Sen. Daniel K. Inouye's aide, Morio Omori; and Kenneth R. Saruwatari, a per diem state district court judge and longtime state and Honolulu city attorney who 1965-1967 held the number two post in the state attorney general's office.[41]

Boise Cascade retained Jenks Kidwell Goodsill & Anderson, a prominent *haole* firm whose practice included a good deal of work for old-line local businesses. Also on Boise's payroll for a time was Sen. John T. Ushijima. Boise vice-president Ronald K. Duplanty told *Honolulu Star-Bulletin* reporter Tom Coffman that "Ushijima was hired to assist us at the state level. He spoke for us several times. He gave us an education as to the ins and outs of government, whom to see for what."[42]

The work done for pay by political insiders on behalf of outside developers inevitably raised questions of possible conflict of interest.

This became a public issue in 1969. Two cases were looked at closely: John Ushijima working for Boise Cascade; and Senate President David McClung and Rep. James Shigemura working for Signal Oil, all as private attorneys.

Both senators were highly placed—Ushijima through holding two influential committee chairmanships, McClung as Senate president and chairman of the State Democratic Party. Shigemura was chairman of the House Tourism Committee.

Ushijima represented Boise before both state and Hawaii County agencies. McClung represented Signal before Hawaii County agencies. He also appears to have assisted Ushijima on behalf of Boise. In exactly what capacity Shigemura represented Signal was never made clear.[43]

Under a 1967 ethics law, legislators and other state officials had to submit information about their private law practices and business dealings to the recently created State Ethics Commission. First submissions were made in 1968.

The Commission was looking for cases of conflict of interest. Were any public officials conducting private business in conflict with their public responsibility and trust?

McClung said, when the fact of his work for Signal became public and a conflict-of-interest question was raised, that he "would be disappointed" to think that his position as Senate president gave him any special entree when he appeared on Signal's behalf before the Hawaii County Council and the Hawaii Planning Commission.

The *Honolulu Star-Bulletin*, in an editorial, remarked that "if McClung is not influencing anyone, it would appear that Signal Properties is wasting the money that McClung will be paid."

The editorial went on to observe that county officials had "a tremendous vested interest in the attitudes of the State Legislature." For example, the Legislature appropriated state grants-in-aid that went to counties, and these monies were "crucial to the county governments' operating effectiveness." Also, the paper pointed out that the Legislature effectively controlled the financial base of the counties by passing the laws under which real property tax rates were set. The counties received most of their income from real property taxes. Also, more or less simultaneous with McClung's lobbying for Signal, the Legislature considered and then approved funding for a pay increase for county employees and council members. Finally, only months before McClung lobbied in Hawaii County for Signal, he had, as State Democratic Party chairman, coordinated the Democrats' statewide election effort, under which the Big Island's mayor and all Democratic county council members (six of the Council's nine) were elected.[44]

In other words, McClung had more than a little to say about the Hawaii County Democrats' capacity to deliver on promises to their voters; about the chances of county Democrats getting elected; and about how much money county politicians and workers were paid.

Ushijima's client, Boise Cascade, was a paper products outfit. Boise's ownership or cutting rights to large numbers of trees led it into home construction and the land business on the mainland about a year before Boise established itself on the Big Island.

A number of Boise's mainland projects were already-developed second home, recreational and retirement communities, acquired by Boise by way of acquiring the companies that built them. In addition Boise did some of its own developments of this kind.

In an effort to see what Boise's Big Island project might eventually look like, *Honolulu Star-Bulletin* reporter Tom Coffman in 1970 visited several Boise developments in California. What in general he found were big rural subdivisions, remote from population centers, with house lots generally lacking normal residential subdivision amenities like sewers, water lines, public roads, electricity, and phone lines. The lots were purchased mostly by small buyers, apparently for speculation. After several years few buyers had actually built homes. This low build-out rate was in line with an article Coffman saw in a Boise publication, which said that in the company's "recreational communities" the annual homebuilding rate was about 1% per year. Of Boise's Rancho Calaveras Coffman wrote that "after three years it remains almost a ghost town: miles of prairie cut by miles of roads."[45]

If indeed these were remote subdivisions that would remain mostly empty, they could pose severe financial hazards to local governments. The problem was that usually at least a handful of people would move in and build, and they would want the usual government services: schools and school buses, police protection, hospitals and ambulances, and so on. Because these new residents would be few in number and far from existing towns, the unit cost of providing services would be prohibitively high.

When Boise went into the land business on the Big Island in 1967, Hawaii County had already been through a rush of speculative subdividing of this sort beginning in 1958, and had just gotten around to tightening its subdivision standards—precisely to guard against the creation of any more of this kind of project.[46]

Boise had the strong appearance of intending to do on the Big Island what Coffman believed he saw on the mainland. Not long after obtaining its option on 31,000 acres on the South Kohala coast, Boise privately presented Hawaii County's planners with a proposal showing relatively small-lot subdivision of the entire tract.[47] On an island with 75,000 already-existing vacant home lots, prospects for immediate settlement of such a large new subdivision were minimal, to put it mildly.

By the time Boise made its plans public, the number of lots had been scaled down considerably. But it was still a very big project.

It came in two related parts, a resort on Anaehoomalu Bay and a housing subdivision about 1.5 miles inland.

Did Boise really mean to build the resort, or was this just a come-on to attract house lot buyers to the subdivision? And what was the real purpose of attracting buyers to the subdivision? Was Boise really going to do a community development project? Or was it just going to run a land sales scheme?

The company's first major hurdle in obtaining development approvals was at the state level: the Land Use Commission.

Boise's LUC presentation was a story all by itself:

In the first place Boise only held an option on the land, and did not exercise the residential portion of it until favorable LUC action was obtained.[48]

In addition, the Boise development subsidiary that was to undertake the Big Island project did not register to do business in Hawaii until after LUC redistricting.

The company's attorney at the LUC hearing was John Ushijima. At that time Ushijima chaired one of the Senate's most powerful committees, Judiciary, to which bills of great interest to Boise were referred in 1968 and 1969. He also chaired the Senate Hawaii Select Committee, which made recommendations on the apportionment of state capital improvement project (CIP) money on the Big Island. The sum of the authority vested in Ushijima by these two chairmanships gave him unusual entree with top-level state administration officials. Thus in his LUC testimony Ushijima could report that "in a conversation with Dr. Matsuda [director of the State Department of Transportation], it was learned that every effort will be made to expedite the construction of the highway all the way into Kawaihae from Kailua, Kona." When built this highway linked Boise's property with the state airport in Kona.

Also at the hearing, in support of the view that the South Kohala-North Kona so-called "Gold Coast" was appropriate for major resort development, Ushijima cited "the considerable sums of money already expended by legislative action for the area."[49]

This statement caused the Star-Bulletin's Tom Coffman to write two years later: "Ushijima qualifies as an expert witness on such state spending. As chairman of the Big Island's Senate Select Committee he reviews and makes recommendations on all State projects on the Big Island."[50]

Boise's written materials were given commissioners in leather-bound volumes—a touch nearly unheard of in the history of the LUC. Commissioners were shown a 15-minute color film on the company, narrated by NBC-TV news anchorman Chet Huntley.[51]

To counter critical views of Boise held by the executive director of the LUC, the company hired Robert I. Bush. Bush was a planner who as a consultant had worked for Hawaii County in preparing a general plan for the region that contained the land now at issue.[52]

In many other ways Boise apparently attempted to influence groups and institutions whose activities had some bearing on the success of its Big Island project. The Honolulu Advertiser's Big Island correspondent since 1963, Walt Southward, retired from the paper in 1970, at which time he was hired by Boise to do media relations. Around this time Ed Sheehan was doing television commercials for Boise in Hawaii. Sheehan had been on radio and TV in Hawaii for the past dozen years. Since 1965 he had written a column for the Honolulu Advertiser, and he was a co-author of the coffee table book The Hawaiians.[53]

At some point Boise also hired former land use commissioner Robert G. Wenkam to handle community relations. Wenkam was a strong conservationist. In 1970 after he had quit working for Boise and become an arch-critic of Ushijima's efforts on behalf of the company, Wenkam said he believed that he had been hired to neutralize conservation groups in Hawaii that might oppose Boise.[54]

When Tom Coffman investigated Boise on the mainland he came away thinking such hiring practices typical of the company. Coffman cited the fact that a senior partner in the law firm handling Boise's Lake Tahoe, Nevada project was US Sen. Allan Bible (D-Nev), and that media relations there were handled by a man who at the time was also the local correspondent for two Reno, Nevada newspapers, as well as for the San Francisco Examiner and United Press International.[55]

However it happened, Boise acquired ties to Hawaii's power structure that were manifold, extending as well to local big business. In 1968 Boise acquired a 14.65% interest in one of the Big Five, Theo. H. Davies, reportedly to help rescue Davies from an unfriendly takeover attempt. From 1967 to 1969 Boise's parent company president held a seat on the board of another Big Five corporation, Castle & Cooke. Both of these Big Five firms had a major presence on the Big Island where between them they owned four sugar plantations and one ranch, encompassing many thousands of acres of land.[56]

Boise also attempted to influence people favorably at the community level. In 1970 upon completion of an access road to the site of the residential subdivision, Boise gave a party. Some 1,000 people attended. Boise served them free steak and beer and provided free entertainment.[57]

It seems fair to say that in Boise's early years in Hawaii there were few other major development proposals with so much form and so little apparent substance.

The Land Use Commission staff and the LUC's private planning consultant looked at Boise's record on the mainland, the number of vacant houselots already on the Big Island, and the amount of land on Boise's side of the island already districted urban but still lying vacant and undeveloped. The staff wrote: "These vacant lots and the vacant Urban lands indicate that the Commission has more than satisfied the urban growth needs in this location based on a 10-year projection." The consultant concluded that "the proposed Recreation Village Sector [the subdivision] is a land sales scheme rather than a community development scheme."[58]

In any case, the LUC redistricted 2,550 acres to urban for Boise.

* * *

Beyond this favorable result, if Boise's plans were to succeed, the company needed the state to spend considerable money in the vicinity of Boise's Big Island land to make the resort and the subdivision accessible and attractive.

Boise's project would benefit greatly by a small boat harbor at Honokohau and a new airport at Keahole. And a new state highway from Kailua to Kawaiahae was actually indispensable, because otherwise the only access to Boise's land (and Signal's too, for good measure) was by jeep.

In 1967 the Legislature appropriated $434,000 for the highway and $1.4 million for the harbor. In 1968, $4.7 million was appropriated for the airport, $200,000 for the harbor, and $41,000 for the highway. In 1969, appropriations included $14.3 million for the airport, $250,000 for the harbor, and $855,000 for the highway.

* * *

Boise now had LUC approval to develop 2,550 acres, and the Legislature was putting sizable money into the area.

But in another respect, the timing of events may have been against Boise.

The Big Island's recently-tightened county subdivision standards meant that Boise would have to put in normal residential amenities, of the sort demanded in places·where people were actually going to move in and live.

This meant that if Boise was in fact planning to mass-market inexpensively-developed rural house lots to middle-class speculators, it would have to lay out more money up front than it may have planned on, to cover the cost of the standard amenities that Hawaii County was now demanding.

The alternative for Boise would be to try to move the cost of improvements elsewhere.

Boise's opening strategy was to attempt to offload this expense onto its lot buyers.

The path to this goal ran through the Legislature.

In early 1968 Senate Bill 439 was introduced which would give large developers like Boise powers previously unknown in Hawaii—to tax land and sell quasi-government bonds to develop roads, water lines, and other infrastructure.

The bill was introduced by John Ushijima.

Since mid-1967 Ushijima had handled various legal matters for Boise from time to time, and he continued to do so through at least the end of 1968.[59]

Unknown to many in the Legislature, the bill that Ushijima introduced was not drafted in his office or anywhere else in the Legislature, but was actually written by Boise's attorneys in California. In 1969 a *Honolulu Star-Bulletin* reporter interviewed a Boise executive who "said Boise Cascade did introduce a bill through Ushijima, which was drawn up by the California law firm of O'Melveney and Myers."[60]

In other words, the bill was tailored directly to Boise's interests, and Ushijima, who in and around that time was being paid as a private attorney ·by Boise, was acting on the floor of the Senate directly in Boise's interests.

For his part Ushijima said publicly that his efforts on behalf of the bill and another quite like it in 1969 were strictly in the public interest. Ushijima also said that "any kind of suggestion that I got paid to do this is nothing but baloney."[61]

The bill would have allowed developers of Boise's size to create something called a "special public facilities construction and taxation district." The directors of such districts would be elected from among landowners in the development, and voting would be on the basis of one vote per one dollar's worth of land—meaning that at the beginning of development, the developer would control the majority of votes. The directors would be able to sell tax-free bonds to finance improvements in the development, and lot buyers would be taxed to repay the bonds. Collateral would be land in the subdivision rather than any other assets the developer might have.

In brief, the argument in favor of the bill was as follows. Very large developers were coming to the state of Hawaii. For the outer islands, their projects required infrastructure outlays on an unprecedented scale. County government could not meet the total cost of the amenities normally provided by county governments, like local roads and water lines. The Boise-Ushijima bill was designed to allow developers to borrow infrastructure money, using their projects' land as collateral—thus making very large developments possible.

This approach pushed by Boise was distinct from that taken by virtually all other large Hawaii resort developers in those years, who themselves covered all infrastructure costs that government could not or would not pay for.

The Boise-Ushijima bill came before the Senate in 1968 and again in 1969, the second time with some added provisions in favor of the developer. The 1969 version, Senate Bill 259, would have forbidden a county council to refuse to allow the establishment of a district as long as those wanting it complied with the technical provisions of the bill. And a district could dissolve itself whether a county government liked it or not—after which all public facilities would be turned over to the county to maintain.

In other words a large developer like Boise could act in its own best financial interests concerning improvements, for just as long as it wanted, then drop the responsibility, leaving the county to pick up the cost and maintain the infrastructure of the development at public expense, out of taxes.

When Tom Coffman went to California in 1970 and looked at several Boise subdivisions there, he also talked with California government officials about the kind of projects he believed he saw Boise doing. A California deputy state attorney general specializing in investment fraud told him: "We have had considerable bad experience with these developer-controlled districts." Among other things, some developers had defaulted on their bonds, and this had "adversely affected the sales of municipal bonds in this state."[62]

In both 1968 and 1969 the Boise bill introduced by Ushijima was referred for study to the Judiciary Committee, which he chaired.

Ushijima in 1968 reported the bill favorably out of Judiciary and managed it all the way to passage through the full Senate. The bill then failed to pass the House.

In 1969 the bill was also referred to the outer island Senate select committees, presumably for recommendations on the impact of the bill on the use of state construction money. Ushijima was chairman of the Hawaii Select Committee. The select committees issued a joint report authored by Ushijima, recommending passage. The bill then went to Ushijima's Judiciary Committee, and for whatever reason it never left. The 1969 bill thus never went to the full Senate for a vote, nor into the House for consideration.

The upshot was that Boise was not going to be able to raise infrastructure money through the Legislature.

(A postscript: In 1970 Sen. George Ariyoshi introduced "by request" two bills that would allow Boise to establish the Waikoloa Sanitary Sewage Co. and the Waikoloa Water Co. Neither bill, however, provided the sweeping powers that the two Ushijima bills had. Neither passed.)[63]

* * *

Boise, still faced with the prospect of having to make considerable cash outlays to start up its subdivision according to the Big Island's new and stricter standards, next tried to have those standards lowered.

The mayor of the Big Island, Shunichi Kimura, was disinclined to waive requirements for things like curbs, gutters and sidewalks, but about 1969 Boise prevailed on the County Council to go along over the mayor's veto.

In 1976 Boise tried again to lessen its financial load, asking the county to create what would have been the largest public improvement district in the Big Island's history, selling county bonds to pay for the resort portion of the infrastructure. The bonds would be repaid by projects within the resort.[64]

The improvement district idea was eventually dropped. Published reports held that the cause was county officials being leery of Boise not wanting to collateralize the bonds with any of the company's assets except its Big Island land. A former Boise official in an interview for this book said, rather, that Boise itself grew cool to the idea. He said Boise did so when told the company could not itself maintain the roads, but would have to let the County do it. Boise disliked this idea, he said, because roads within a resort had to be kept immaculate, and Boise was afraid the County might not do a good enough job.

Boise in the end did put in subdivision amenities such as curbs and gutters. As with the dropping of the improvement district idea, there were different versions of why this happened. In an interview for this book a former Big Island planning official said the curbs and gutters went in following an unusually heavy rain that clearly demonstrated the need. The man who became the Boise Big Island project director in 1970, Willis H. Sanburn, said in an interview for this book that upon taking over he voluntarily offered to put them in to make peace with the Big Island mayor.

In the end the residential subdivision, Waikoloa Village, developed essentially as promised. By mid-1984 about one-third of its 968 houselots had homes, residences that in most cases were substantial.

Boise also in the early and mid-1970s made efforts to get the resort portion of its project off the ground—the resort which some had said was only a come-on for a speculative subdivision. But the company was hampered by a legal challenge over title to the oceanfront land at Anaehoomalu; and by the time that was cleared up, the money market had tightened. On the mainland Boise about 1972 had decided to get completely out of the land and development business, and began to sell off its real estate holdings. In 1979 it sold its Big Island property—at a reported loss: Boise's figures were that the company invested about $42 million and would get back only about $15 million from land sales.

Interviews for this book with several current and former Boise officials, and with persons formerly in news media and currently and formerly in the Big Island county government, indicated that Boise had a two-phased existence in Hawaii, with respect to whether its development was primarily for speculation or for actual use. This may have been the case with Boise nationally as well.

When Boise first came to the Big Island its behavior was to a great extent that of a company out to do a huge cut-and-run subdivision, and on top of that to spend much less up front than most major Hawaii developers.

The appointment of Willis Sanburn in 1970 appeared to signal a new phase. In an interview for this book Sanburn said that he voluntarily gave up the curbs variance to heal a rift between Boise and the Hawaii County administration. In his view the problem had originated in an insensitive approach to local government on the part of his predecessor, as well as attempted power plays and grandiose, unrealistic representations. In 1971 Sanburn told a reporter: "You can't just walk into a state and tell people you're going to run it. We got burned for this and we deserved it."[65]

About this time at the national level the magazine *Business Week* reported on a Boise management shakeup that had to do with the image or the reality that Boise had been in the land business developing speculative projects, and now was going to change. A Boise executive was quoted as saying: "We decided . . . that we were not in the business for speculation. We were going to sell a product for use."[66]

Furthermore, however it happened, the empty Boise subdivisions Tom Coffman saw on the mainland in 1970 were by early 1985 building out at about the same rate as Waikoloa on the Big Island, and had most or all of the standard amenities. Indeed Boise public relations official Samuel Donaldson said in an interview for this book that Coffman's *Star-Bulletin* articles were one of the major reasons for a change in Boise's orientation nationally.

* * *

A question remains concerning Sen. Ushijima's relations with Boise in the late 1960s:

The Ethics Commission opinion on Ushijima (and on Sen. David McClung and Rep. James Shigemura with their paid work for Signal Oil) noted that Ushijima and McClung were powerful members of the Senate, and that Shigemura, by being co-counsel with McClung, was by extension also powerful.

The Commission's opinion said that "any action these legislators should take . . . on bills of importance to their clients, such as voting or processing . . . within committees, may constitute a use of position in violation of Section 7."[67]

Ushijima, as chairman of the Senate Judiciary Committee and chairman of the Hawaii County Select Committee, had been doing just that.

* * *

Ushijima's actions in the Senate on ethics bills themselves are worth noting:

When the 1967 Legislature took up the matter of an ethics law, it was the House that first passed a bill. This bill, among other things, would have forbidden a state employee who was also an attorney in private practice to process matters that came to his state department from his private law firm. (For example, the head of the Business Registration Division of the Depart-

ment of Regulatory Agencies would not have been allowed to process articles of business incorporation filed by his law firm for a client.) But the
House bill of 1967 would have allowed the law partner of an elected legislator to lobby the Legislature on behalf of a client. In other words, the House
was prepared to be more lenient about the private interests of legislators
than about the private interests of state employees.

The House bill came over to the Senate and was referred to the Judiciary
Committee. Under Ushijima the committee left in place this lenient treatment of legislators and their law partners.

Ushijima's committee also altered a provision in the House bill that would
have forbidden both state employees and legislators to represent clients as
private attorneys before state and county agencies on a contingency fee basis. (A "contingency fee" meant that the attorney got paid only for a win,
with the fee a percentage of the winnings.) Ushijima's committee changed
this so that the restriction on contingency fee work applied only to state
employees, leaving legislators free to work that way in their capacity as private attorneys. In other words, Ushijima's committee was again making it
possible for legislators to treat themselves more leniently in ethical terms
than state employees were allowed to do. In this form the ethics bill passed
the Senate and was signed into law by Gov. Burns.

In the following session, 1968, three bills were introduced that would
have prohibited contingency fee work by legislators. All three bills died in
Ushijima's Senate Judiciary Committee. In 1969 a contingency fee bill was
introduced and was referred to Ushijima's Hawaii Select Committee—
which was odd, in that select committees usually dealt not with ethical matters but with state construction spending. In any case, the bill never left this
other Ushijima committee either.

Not till 1972 did the Legislature finally extend the contingency fee prohibition to legislators, and also bar legislators from representing private interests before the Legislature in which they sat.[68]

At the same time as the Hawaii Legislature was setting out to frame an
ethics law, and going easy on attorneys who were also legislators, the American Bar Association was revising its code of ethics for lawyers.

This set of ethical standards was adopted by the Hawaii Supreme Court
as applicable to Hawaii attorneys starting in 1968.

A Bar Association committee opinion issued on the mainland took the
view that "a law firm could not accept employment to appear before a legislative committee while a member of the firm is serving in the Legislature. A
full disclosure before the committee would not alter this ruling, nor would it
be changed by the fact that the member of the Legislature would not share
in the fee received thereby."[69]

In sum, in the matter of ethics, the Hawaii Legislature, with its numerous
attorney members, was seemingly prepared to be more lenient with itself
than the American Bar Association and the Hawaii Supreme Court indicated should be the case.

* * *

There are significant postscripts to the Ushijima/Boise Cascade/Ethics Commission episode:

Whatever embarrassment Ushijima may have suffered, it apparently caused no major damage to his political standing, either with his colleagues in the Legislature or with the voting public. Each time he came up for re-election he was returned to office. In the eyes of a *Honolulu Star-Bulletin* writer who covered the Legislature in 1973, Ushijima in the early 1970s distinguished himself as "one of the upper body's most liberal forces." This assessment was echoed the next year by a liberal news magazine, the *Hawaii Observer,* which picked Ushijima as one of that year's best legislators: "Ushijima is not an exceptional orator, but he runs his committee with efficiency and dispatch. As a member of the inner clique of the Senate, he sometimes sacrifices democratic procedure for efficiency, and in the past has engaged in some questionable lobbying practices. However, on balance, especially during the last two sessions, he demonstrated a desire to work for the overall welfare."[70]

Ushijima continued to chair the powerful Senate Judiciary Committee through 1974, and in 1975 rose to the Senate presidency, a post he held until 1978. He retired from the Senate in 1982.

3

THE LAND USE COMMISSION

FROM the standpoints of land, development and the power structure of Hawaii in the Democratic years, few pieces of legislation were as central as the State Land Use Law (LUL) of 1961.

The LUL, based on laws adopted in England to regulate reconstruction after World War II, had the distinction of being the first statewide zoning measure in the United States.

If it was innovative nationally, it was in many ways a logical planning step for Hawaii to take. "State control," as University of Hawaii planning professor G. Kem Lowry Jr. wrote in 1980, was "viewed as a response to conditions unique to the fiftieth state: a relatively small land mass, concentrated ownership of land, and a history of centralized government."[1]

In the minds of the law's advocates, prime among them liberal Democratic Rep. Thomas P. Gill, the need for statewide regulation was clear.

Gill and others saw excesses in the early years of Hawaii's land boom that were beyond the powers of the counties' small and not well-organized planning bodies to control.

Foremost among these excesses was the scattering of urban subdivisions in prime agricultural lands, not only undercutting Hawaii's farming potential but also leading to inefficiencies in providing government services to new communities that were spread all over the place.

On the Big Island a speculative subdividing boom was creating tens of thousands of house lots on remote lava fields, often in volcanic hazard zones, with practically no improvements, without basic amenities such as county-standard roads and utilities. These lots were being bought, usually sight unseen, mostly by amateur speculators from Oahu and the US mainland who had no intention of ever living there. From the standpoint of conventional planning principles these subdivisions were bizarre, to say the least; but the Big Island county government was showing no signs of calling a halt.

At that time, Oahu was the only other island where a great deal of development was taking place. This activity, unlike the Big Island's, was mostly genuine, a response to rapid population growth. But some of it struck a discordant note of another kind. Oahu was only 10% of the state's total land area, yet it held some 54% of all prime agricultural land, most of it in central

Oahu,[2] a natural westward growth area for the city of Honolulu. Urban population was beginning to move in that direction. If the trend persisted, much prime agricultural land would be buried forever under subdivisions, roads, shopping centers and parking lots.

Bearing in mind this situation, the LUL was written with two principles uppermost: make urbanization efficient in the use of all types of resources; and preserve agricultural and conservation lands as much as possible. These twin principles gave the LUL in its early years the name "greenbelt law," since it intended urbanization to be compact rather than scattered, with belts of green agricultural and conservation land all around.

The law called for the creation of a Land Use Commission (LUC), to be appointed by the governor with Senate approval. The Commission was authorized to district and redistrict every bit of land in the Islands—in essence a statewide zoning board.

The LUC had nine members. From 1961 through 1975 two of the nine were the heads of the state departments dealing with, respectively, state lands and planning. One commissioner was appointed from the general public in each of the six state senatorial districts; the ninth was appointed at large. In 1975 the Legislature changed this to one commissioner from each of the four counties, the other five from the public at large.

In a place and time where urban development was so central to the economic well-being of the population and to economic and political power, the influence of the LUC was very great indeed.

*   *   *

In the overall theory and practice of land use control by government in Hawaii in the Democratic years, the LUC became the top layer, the one that initially placed all land in broad classifications.

At first there were three categories: urban, agricultural and conservation. In 1963 the Legislature added a fourth, rural, a low-density residential classification allowing half-acre lots. In 1964 when the LUC adopted the first permanent districts, 52% of the Islands' area was districted agricultural, 45% conservation. A little less than 3% went into the urban district, less than 1% into rural.[3]

Two decades later these figures had not changed appreciably. As of January 1983 the agricultural and conservation districts each held about 48%, the urban district 4%, and the rural district less than 1%.[4]

Once land was districted by the LUC, other land use agencies became involved as well. Conservation land came under the jurisdiction of the State Board of Land and Natural Resources. The subdivision of agricultural lands was regulated by city and county governments, usually at the levels of planning departments and planning commissions. The LUC also had certain jurisdiction over development within the agricultural district, through the issuance of special permits. The counties and the LUC had similar dual authority over rural lands. Development within urban districts was con-

trolled by city or county governments, with generally the greatest reposi-
tory of power at that level in the hands of the councils.

* * *

The political behavior that brought about passage of the Land Use Law
in 1961 and then produced repeated attempts throughout most of the
1960s to repeal it or cut back on its reach, is a story all by itself.

Essentially a combination of House Democrats and Senate
Republicans—the two opposite ends of the political spectrum in those
years—brought about passage of the law.

The bill that became law was a Democratic Party bill originating in the
House. It passed there 27–22 with two excused. All but one of the 27 were
Democrats. Every Republican in the House but one voted "no."

Some senators wanted to make changes. A conference committee of representatives and senators was appointed to propose a draft acceptable to
both houses. That draft then passed the Senate 18–6 with one excused.
Roughly half of the Senate's Democrats voted against. Of the 18 in favor 12
were Republicans. Only one Republican voted "no." The House then voted
on this final draft. It passed nearly unanimously.

Apparently accounting for these twists were four quite disparate factors:
liberal political ideology applied to land use; some ignorance of the law's
probable impact on the Islands' then-freewheeling development practices;
Democratic Party discipline; and a tax break for owners and lessors of large
tracts of agricultural and conservation land.

The bill was fundamentally the work of Tom Gill, one of the most liberal
politicians of stature during the Democratic years. It was in the classic mold
of twentieth-century liberal thought, in extending government authority
broadly throughout the economy to minimize what were perceived to be
excesses of the marketplace, and to rationalize market activity in the public
interest.

The majority House Democrats at that time were still by and large committed in principle to a party program that was progressive and widely supported
by Hawaii's have-nots. To a great extent they were elected by grass-roots efforts
organized by their party, not beholden to large campaign contributors. The
House Speaker, Elmer F. Cravalho, was strong on party discipline. All this made
for cohesion on bills proposed by Democratic leaders.

Gill, looking back on the passage of the Land Use Law, said in an interview for this book that party discipline in those years meant that at times
Democrats were willing to vote somewhat blindly. According to him, many
who voted for the bill did not understand it fully, not realizing the extent to
which it would impede some of the development practices then standard.
Gill also said he deliberately did not explain this at the time, believing that if
he had, the law might never have passed.

Some who, in any case, may have been paying attention were Senate
Republicans—more than any other legislators the representatives of the old
landed class. Of the 12 Senate Republicans who voted in favor, seven worked

for the old companies and estates, most of them in middle and upper-level positions: an Alexander & Baldwin department manager; a Bishop Estate trustee; a Damon Estate trustee; a C. Brewer director; a Parker Ranch "recreational advisor;" a First National Bank of Hawaii (later First Hawaiian Bank) assistant cashier; and an executive assistant to the president of Hawaiian Telephone Co.[5]

These men supported the law partly because it could provide a tax break for owners and lessors of agricultural and conservation land—in other words, mainly the big landowners.

The thrust of Democratic tax policy regarding large tracts of privately-owned non-urban land had been to force assessments upwards. This was partly to make the large owners pay more tax, also to try to force development of lands that were idle or that the Democrats considered under-utilized. To cite a prime example: plantation lands that adjoined heavily developed lands and were in the natural path of urban expansion tended to be considered "under-utilized."

The principal way assessments were raised was to calculate a property's highest potential monetary return irrespective of existing use. This approach was called "highest and best use."

Once the land boom was well under way there was considerably less need to pressure owners to develop. Indeed with the possibility of losing large amounts of valuable agricultural land to urban use, inducements seemed warranted to some to keep land in agriculture.

In any case, the Land Use Law allowed owners and long-term lessors of lands districted agricultural or conservation to dedicate these lands for 10 years to uses normal in such districts. Once dedicated, the land was assessed and taxed according to its actual use, rather than at its highest and best use.

Whatever the planning or economic wisdom of this tax law change, without it, in political terms, the Land Use Law might not have passed.

* * *

The Senate Democrats who voted "no" in 1961 were all from the outer islands. This was a harbinger of things to come throughout the 1960s in the Legislature with respect to the Land Use Law.

Part of the Democrats' land reform program of the 1950s was to give outer island counties the same zoning authority as Oahu had had since 1939. In 1957, over Republican objections, Democratic legislators extended zoning powers to the outer islands.

Now the Land Use Law modified that situation by superimposing a layer of state-level land use control.

This second level had a disproportionately great impact on the outer islands. With the LUL in place, it was a foregone conclusion that the lands in and immediately around the city of Honolulu would be made urban. Beyond that, in the years ahead, major Land Use Commission decisions would be concerned with which other lands would be moved out of the agricultural, and to some extent conservation, districts into the urban district.

Thus it was the undeveloped parts of the state—in other words, the outer islands especially—where LUC control would have the most impact.

What made this particularly hard for outer-island Democrats to take was that they were looking heavily toward urbanization to improve not only their islands' then-flat economies but also, in the case of many, their own personal incomes as well. These men opposed what they saw as outside interference in this process.

So opposed were the outer-island Democrats that after the Land Use Law was passed in 1961, they introduced bills in 1963, 1964, 1965 and 1967 to repeal the law or cut back on its powers.

They came closest to succeeding in 1967 when a bill was introduced in the House to abolish the Land Use Commission altogether, leaving the counties in charge of the districting process.

A number of Oahu Democrats were by 1967 also dissatisfied with the law. A leading Democratic legislator of that period said in an interview for this book that many Democrats considered that even though all commissioners were by then Burns appointees, nevertheless the large landowners had a disproportionately great amount of influence over the whole process. This feeling, paired with the outer-island Democrats' continued disaffection with a state agency having so much to say about the location and pace of development on their islands, nearly brought about passage.

The bill passed the House 27–23 with one excused. All 27 were Democrats, and among them were 13 of the 14 from the outer islands. Among those voting "no" were 11 of the House's 12 Republicans.

The bill died in the Senate. In the end all efforts during the 1960s at repeal or major modification failed. Not until 1975, following heavy criticism of the LUC by liberals, radicals, community activists and environmentalists, and public disruption of LUC proceedings, was the law overhauled.

*   *   *

Among the early warnings of the avalanche of criticism that was to come in the mid-1970s were conflicts that began occurring in the late 1960s between the politically appointed commissioners and their professional planning staff.

The 1960s were a time of rapid and exuberant economic growth in Hawaii. Gov. John Burns rather uncritically welcomed the material results of growth, and most of his appointments to the LUC reflected his views.

At the same time an undercurrent of opposition to growth was beginning to gather strength. The Commission staff—professional planners who tended to be younger than the appointed commissioners and not necessarily part of the Democratic establishment—started to reflect this countervailing trend.

A group of three redistricting applications filed in mid-1967 covering 2,330 acres of sugar cane land in central Oahu highlighted the conflict.[6]

As mentioned, Oahu's central plain held about half of the state's prime agricultural lands. This fact was an essential element in the conflict.

The LUC initially denied the redistricting of all but four acres. Then, about a year later, all three applications were refiled. This time the applicants succeeded. Most of the lands that were actually developable, based on such things as terrain, were made urban—1,228 acres, about half the total.

The LUC staff strongly—even bitterly—opposed all three applications both times around, and no one more than the staff director, Ramon A. Duran.

When the applications were first filed the State was revising its general plan. Based on data from the revision, the LUC staff said that population growth projections for the part of Oahu in which the applications fell indicated a need through 1985 of an additional 1,397 urban acres. But the general plan research indicated there were already 3,152 vacant urban acres available. "Thus," the staff report summed up, "it would seem that even though the Urban District boundaries [as first established in 1964] were predicated upon the inclusion of sufficient reserve areas to accommodate a 10 year growth period, the State General Plan revision study indicates that there is ample land to accommodate a 20 year growth period."[7]

To Duran the fact that the LUC would nevertheless redistrict more prime agricultural land to urban in such quantity was outrageous. He became an outspoken critic of the Commission. For example, on the occasion of one of the revotes he read an acidic staff report which among other things said: "The vast plain of prime agricultural land in Central Oahu will be sacrificed to urban use as fast as leases expire, withdrawal clauses are exercised, development contracts are signed and bulldozers can move." Several months later, when the LUC redistricted yet more central Oahu agricultural land, Duran attacked the Commission itself for allegedly going along with everything of consequence that was being proposed: "The last time the Land Use Commission denied an urban zoning request on Oahu . . . was two and a half years ago," and that, he said, concerned only a minor application.[8]

The three Central Oahu applications demonstrated a basic fact of LUC life in the late 1960s—how deeply the political establishment, and members of the LUC themselves, were tied up in the development business:

The lands in question were owned by several trusts and leased to Oahu Sugar Co. One of the landowners was a combination of several Robinson trusts. One Robinson trustee was Honolulu Council Chairman Herman G. P. Lemke. Another was financier-developer Chinn Ho, who was closely aligned with the Burns Democrats, and whose son, Stuart, was then sharing law offices with another Council leader, Matsuo Takabuki, who was one of Gov. Burns' closest advisors. The lawyer representing the Robinson trusts and its developer before the LUC, Kinji Kanazawa, was a former Honolulu planning commissioner who used to share offices with Takabuki. Another landowner involved was Bishop Estate, whose developer initially was to be a joint venture of Amfac and Joe Pao, later Amfac alone. Pao, like Ho, had close ties to the political establishment. Pao's first cousin and former employee, James P. Ferry, was now head of the State Board of Land and Natural Resources and, as such, also on the LUC. The attorney for the third landowner, the Austin Estate, was the principal aide in Hawaii to US Sen. Daniel K. Inouye and a brother-in-law to Land Use Commissioner Keigo Murakami from Maui. This was Morio Omori, who also used to share offices with Takabuki.[9]

Oahu Sugar Co. leased all the land involved, and in general was legally committed to release it for urbanization and even to cooperate in urbanization. The company, for example, in 1967 wrote to the Robinson trusts saying: "Oahu Sugar Co. further acknowledges that the Robinson Trusts' lands mauka of Parcel 2 . . . will be progressively urbanized in an orderly manner and will therefore cooperate with and assist in any such future urbanization should the Robinson Trusts or their developers apply for the reclassification or rezoning for urban use." Oahu Sugar was an Amfac plantation, and Amfac also was to be a developer of the Bishop Estate land involved. An Amfac executive, C. E. S. Burns Jr. (no relation to Gov. Burns), was a land use commissioner.[10]

Finally, as of the second go-round on the three applications, the ILWU had an agreement with the developer of the Robinson land that the union would reverse its previous opposition to redistricting, in exchange for a housing program for ILWU members in the Waipahu area. As of the second LUC vote on the Robinson application, ILWU officer Edward Tangen was a commissioner who voted in favor.[11]

* * *

The occasion for the attacks on the LUC in 1974 was the second of what were called "five-year boundary reviews."

The Land Use Law called for the Commission, every five years after initial establishment of permanent district boundaries, to review all those boundaries at one time—essentially a statewide review of land use.

The LUC first established permanent districts in 1964, so the first five-year review came in 1969.

The 1969 review was relatively uneventful in terms of public participation. There was still strong pro-growth sentiment throughout the state; proposed redistrictings to urban did not seem dramatic and were not viewed negatively; and trends leading to a strong anti-eviction and environmental movement were still about a year from coalescing.

The 1974 review, in its turn, came at the height of the environmental and anti-eviction movement. Additionally, during this review landowners and developers were apparently proposing more urban redistricting than in 1969 (though it is impossible to be certain of this since no accurate totals exist for 1969).

At the suggestion of LUC chairman Eddie Tangen, all major landowners were contacted at the start of the 1974 review and asked to write letters of intent stating their development plans—a "wish list." The idea was for the Commission to have before it all conceivable development plans so as to be in a position to plan as comprehensively as possible.

This approach yielded 167 separate proposals. As the *Honolulu Advertiser* observed while letters were still coming in, those proposals that would convert land to urban represented the "equivalent of most of urban Honolulu between Pearl City and Hawaii Kai."[12] Included were plans that could lead to mass evictions in Waiahole and Waikane valleys in windward Oahu, and in Niumalu on Kauai.

Also up for consideration were proposals for major resorts along then undeveloped or hardly developed coastlines which were favorites among local residents for fishing, swimming, and camping: Makena on Maui, Kilauea on Kauai's north shore and Mahaulepu on the south, and in the Ewa area of Oahu.

A fair amount of good agricultural land was proposed for urban districting as well.

All this, coming as it did in the midst of a land and environmental movement that was strongly anti-establishment, made for some real commotion at LUC public hearings—hearings that also were far longer and much more tedious than anything the LUC had ever experienced.

The upshot in terms of LUC decisions was that most redistrictings that were heatedly protested were denied. Based on the numbers, the Commission's decision record was moderate. Of the total acreage proposed to go from agricultural and conservation to urban, 5,436 acres, or 39%, were approved. Moreover, there had been downzonings proposed, a good number of them by the LUC itself. (Over and above the 167 redistrictings proposed by landowners and developers the LUC itself proposed 61, many of which were downzonings.) Those downzonings that passed put 4,056 previously urban acres into agricultural and conservation—making for a net urban increase of only 1,380 acres.[13]

The controversy had been heavy. Perhaps inevitably, it spilled over into the Legislature.

Two lines of thinking emerged to deal with what were seen as a host of problems surrounding the LUC.

The first appeared to go along with criticisms by liberals and community activists who had come to believe the Commission could not be trusted to be apolitical and impartial, that it was over-ready to redistrict land to urban. These critics objected to what were believed to be inordinately large profits that some developers were making from the beauty of Hawaii. A bill emerged that would remove redistricting power from the LUC and give all its major decision-making authority to the Legislature. The Commission would continue to exist merely to advise the Legislature. The proponents of this bill also suggested that all profits from upzoning be made the property of the State.[14]

The second line was aimed more at the disruptions that some members of the public had caused during the 1974 review public hearings, also at the fact that much public testimony was repetitious. Following this line of thought, a bill emerged to make Commission proceedings "quasi-judicial," meaning that hearings would be conducted like civil court trials. This bill also mandated the Commission to follow somewhat more explicit planning guidelines on what should and should not be redistricted. Commission Chairman Eddie Tangen later explained that such changes would help "to avoid such disruptive demonstrations in Land Use Commission hearings as occurred last year."[15]

This approach appeared to mean that there would be far less direct public input at LUC hearings. The Commission would have to certify in advance whether each speaker had a sufficient interest in the matter to have the right to testify, and then whether the speaker's testimony was relevant, non-duplicative, and so on. It might even be, as Kauai Planning Department staff planner Gregory Kamm later observed, that those wanting to speak would need attorneys. The "small man" would be "precluded from effective participation."[16]

Largely because of a recent Hawaii Supreme Court decision, the Legislature was forced to consider the quasi-judicial approach. In *Town v. Land Use Commission* the court held that the LUC was a type of government agency whose proceedings had to be quasi-judicial. What was unclear, though, was whether the LUC could, on a particular proposed redistricting, conduct both a quasi-judicial hearing and a hearing of the more informal sort that it had previously held. *Town* had been decided early in the 1974 review and this was the approach taken as a result. Furthermore this was the approach that the State Public Utilities Commission had used for years.[17]

Then, to some, there was the possibility of amending the laws on which the Supreme Court had based its decision so as to exempt the LUC from quasi-judicial requirements.

In the end the bill that would have put the Legislature in charge of land use districting died. The bill that turned the Land Use Commission into a sort of civil court passed.

By and large it had been *de facto* coalitions of liberal Democrats, often from Oahu, and Republicans that had made possible the passage of the Land Use Law in 1961 and protected it from repeal or major weakening by outer-island Democrats through 1967. Now, by some accounts, it was outer-island Democrats, generally aligned with the ILWU, plus Republicans, who killed the bill that would have put the Legislature in charge of the LUC. By most accounts virtually all legislators, except for a few liberal independents like Rep. Neil Abercrombie and Sens. Richard S. H. Wong and Jean S. King, supported the quasi-judicial bill.

An early public indication of how forces may have been grouping themselves over LUL legislation in 1975 came when reports surfaced that the bill that would put the Legislature in charge of the LUC was bogged down in a House Democratic caucus.

The *Honolulu Advertiser* reported that a scheduled House vote was being deferred. "The deferral came in the face of growing opposition from labor-aligned legislators and the House's 16 Republicans." The *Advertiser* explained that several participants in the caucus said opposition came from legislators aligned with the ILWU. The paper said that this was because "the union has considerable clout on the commission, as Commission Chairman Eddie Tangen is the ILWU's international representative," the implication being that the union had more control over land use decisions if made by the LUC than by the Legislature. The paper said Republicans "are against the measure because they say it violates the concept of separation of powers."[18]

By 1975 it was impractical to talk seriously of killing the LUL, even if anyone still wanted to do it. Environmental consciousness was at high tide, with its emphasis on increasing, not decreasing, regulation of business as it affected the natural environment. The question for most legislators, then, in reacting to the mass of criticism and turmoil that had come to surround the LUC, was how to make the Land Use Law more effective.

A threshold question was: more effective at what?

To liberals it was a matter of being more responsive to the popular will. One bill introduced in 1975 along these lines would have required all proposed redistrictings of conservation land to be voted on by the general public. Other bills would have given the Legislature final say over most or all proposed boundary amendments. The theory was that the Legislature, being a popularly elected body, was more accountable to the public than an appointed body like the LUC.

To those who opposed the public or the Legislature having final say, it was partly a matter of efficiency. Having the Legislature decide, meeting as it did only once a year for three months, and already having to handle literally thousands of bills, would have been unwieldy, not to mention extremely political.

To those who favored the quasi-judicial approach the question was partly one of law and order. The preamble to their bill read in part: "Under existing procedures the land use commission has been unable to reconcile in an orderly and rational manner the increasingly hostile and conflicting points of view which surround land use decisions."[19]

Democratic legislators in 1975 between them represented a wide variety of special and public interests: developers, environmental activists, unions, and so on. For each the question was how best to achieve their objectives through the land use districting process.

But if the Democratic spectrum was wide, the Democratic center now rested on development and the local-Asian business establishment. This fact perhaps more than any other shaped the character of amendments to the Land Use Law in 1975.

A representative socio-economic profile of mainstream Democrats as of 1975 could be seen in the two who chaired the House and Senate committees that processed the LUL bills that session.

Rep. Richard A. Kawakami of Kauai chaired the House Committee on Water, Land Use Development & Hawaiian Homes. His father, H. S. Kawakami, founded what by 1975 was the largest retailing group on Kauai, owning about 20 stores, selling food, furniture, and general merchandise. Richard participated in running these operations. In terms of real estate, Richard as of 1975 was a partner in the Lihue Industrial Development Co. and a director of the Kahili Development Co. Inc.[20]

Sen. Francis A. Wong of leeward Oahu chaired the Senate Economic Development Committee. His father, Francis Y. Wong, was a realtor and developer who for a period of time in the 1940s was secretary-treasurer of Chinn Ho's Capital Investment Co. Francis Jr. was a realtor/lawyer/developer. He had been a real estate broker since 1962, and was now principal broker for Francis A. Wong and Associates. As of 1975 or just previously he held interests in: Mainline Harbor Properties, Queen Street Building Associates, Graham & Wong Queen, Queen's Barristers, Waimaha Pacific Partnership I and II, Maquoia Associates, The Mahana Model Hui, Heritage Development, Heritage Homes, Ala Wai Plaza Associates, Nanakai Development Co., and Mid-Pacific Homes Ltd. In addition some of Wong's legal work was development-related.[21]

Putting the Legislature in charge of districting land would have made what was already a slow process a really cumbersome one, one which for many Democrats would have directly affected their own incomes as well as those of many people with whom they associated in business or were allied in politics.

The ILWU, for its part, through the existing LUC, had a voice in districting far out of proportion to the size of ILWU membership within Hawaii's overall population. This was because the appointing authorities—first Gov. Burns and then Gov. Ariyoshi—depended heavily in their election campaigns on the outer island vote, which was anchored by the ILWU. No other organization of any kind over the entire life of the Commission obtained as many appointments as the ILWU's four. Since 1969 the LUC had had at least one ILWU man as a member. Between 1977 and 1981 two members were ILWU men. The LUC chairman 1973–1977 was ILWU officer Eddie Tangen, a particularly intelligent and able person whose weight on the Commission as a result was usually considerably greater than that of merely one vote.

Furthermore, the popular power bases of both the ILWU and mainstream Democrats were now visibly in decline. As so often happens in democracies when popular bases erode, leaders who came to power on those bases were now increasingly relying on their accumulated influence over administrative and judicial agencies—those, in other words, somewhat removed from immediate popular accountability.

As to the Republicans at this juncture, their position was one of both ideology and self-interest—ideology in that Republicans generally opposed the extension of government regulation into the economy, and self-interest because Republicans were part of the business establishment and as such objected to laws that impinged on their ability to make money.

What it all meant by 1975, as could be seen across the political board in Hawaii, was that a new establishment based on land had formed, and mainstream Democrats were right in the middle of it.

* * *

If, as time went by, the interests and political positions of Republicans and various Democrats concerning the Land Use Commission underwent some changes, one constant was how each group behaved when they were in charge.

Compare the first set of commissioners and their adoption in 1962 of temporary district boundaries, with those commissioners of 1974 and their handling of the redistricting items that generated all the protest that year.

At the time the law passed in 1961 the governor was a Republican, William F. Quinn. The law allowed him to nominate seven of the nine commissioners from the general public, the other two being the heads of the state departments dealing with state lands and planning. The Senate was to confirm his nominations, and the Senate was then controlled by Republicans.

Governor Quinn's 1961 LUC nominees showed as plainly as could be the extent to which the Republican Party in those years was the party of business, big business especially.

Of the seven nominated from the general public in 1961, a majority (four) were in executive positions with large landowners: the Parker Ranch land manager; the Dole Corporation land manager; the manager of an Amfac sugar plantation on Kauai; and the president of Dillingham Investment Co. Another was a past president of the Chinese Chamber of Commerce. Another was president of several medium-sized businesses.[22]

On the day in 1962 when these men were to adopt temporary district boundaries, they first met for lunch at the Pacific Club, an enclave of old *haole* money and the Republican Party.

During lunch, so the *Honolulu Star-Bulletin* reported, "various subdividers went to the club to present their views before the Commission was scheduled to meet."

After lunch the LUC went to a state office building to gather in formal session.

But first they huddled in small groups outside the meeting room. This went on for about two hours. They then met in closed session. At this point Democratic Rep. David C. McClung, Chairman of the House Lands Committee, attempted to break into the meeting with two members of the news media. LUC chairman Ralph K. Ajifu either attempted to or did kick them out, saying: "We're not in session, this is a caucus." Eventually the commissioners came out, met for about five minutes, and without explanation as to how they had made their decisions, adopted temporary district boundaries for the entire state.[23]

After John Burns was elected Hawaii's first Democratic governor in 1962 he was able to appoint commissioners. As of 1974 those men appointed by him (and by George Ariyoshi, who took over as acting governor in late 1973 when Burns fell terminally ill), consisted of the following: an ILWU officer; an owner of a small general merchandise store on Kauai who was a loyal Burns Democrat and a small real estate investor; a sales manager in Hawaii for Japan Airlines (in about 1974 Japanese companies were making their first appearances in quantity before the LUC); a business agent for the Carpenters Union; an independent pineapple grower on Maui who was also an occasional land investor; an executive with Honolulu Iron Works, which was a supplier of building materials; and an executive with a Big Island ranch.[24]

This, in snapshot form, was what the "consensus" government of the Burns and Ariyoshi administrations looked like. Compared with the LUC of 1962, it was a far broader across-the-board grouping. But if more diverse socio-economically, the Democratic LUC was as pro-development as the Republican one had been. There was little room on the LUC for conservationists. One, Robert G. Wenkam, was appointed by Burns in 1963. Burns renominated him in 1967. At that point Senator Nadao Yoshinaga, a Burns Democrat who was also a real estate broker, blocked Wenkam's reappointment by not allowing it out of a committee he chaired. Of this the *Honolulu Star-Bulletin* wrote that "Yoshinaga said he feels that Wenkam's statewide activities and speeches in behalf of conservation were not compatible with his position as a member of the Land Use Commission."[25]

In the area of off-the-record discussions, whether with proponents or opponents of development, the LUC of 1974 bore similarity to that of 1962. For example, following the 1974 proceedings an environmental activist group, Life of the Land, sued to overturn all decisions. In a pre-trial deposition one commissioner discussed the fact he had met privately on a redistricting matter with Robert C. Oshiro, attorney for Lanai Co., a subsidiary of Castle & Cooke. The *Honolulu Advertiser* wrote that the commissioner also "admitted that such meetings with petitioners outside of Land Use Commission proceedings happened about fifty per cent of the time."[26]

* * *

Robert Oshiro was not just any lawyer. He was at that time one of the most politically influential people in Hawaii outside of government. A former state representative, he had been the key strategist in John Burns' successful election campaign in 1970. He was just as important in 1974 to George Ariyoshi, then making his first successful run for governor—at the very time Oshiro was representing Lanai Co. before the LUC.[27]

The fact that people like Oshiro were involved in applications was a reason why the LUC was now tolerable to Burns-Ariyoshi Democrats.

Throughout the life of the LUC there was a heavy involvement of politically well-connected people like Oshiro, mostly mainstream Democrats, as investors, developers and developers' paid representatives.

For this book there were examined all petitions ever filed for redistricting aimed at profit-making, involving at least about five acres, proposed to go into urban or rural, and decided upon by mid-October 1984. (Petitions by government agencies and non-profit organizations such as the ILWU were not included in this study. Also excluded were redistricting items considered during the two statewide LUC reviews of all districts, in 1969 and 1974. The files generated in those reviews are incomplete and somewhat disorganized, especially those of 1969. Also not included were special permit applications. These tended to be special case matters—for example, a quarry operation in an agricultural district—and generally did not involve large tracts of land.) The proposed major additions to the urban district involved by far the most land. They were of greatest concern to the Commission, and are thus most pertinent to the main subject of this book.

A total of 264 petitions met these criteria. Of them 70% had current or past government officials and employees involved as investors, corporate officers, partners, attorneys, and consultants, or had land use commissioners with some kind of interest in or tie to the applicant. (See Tables 7 and 8.) The overwhelming majority of these officials were Democrats, or men who worked for Democratic state and county administrations.

Petitions involving the politically well-connected were approved at a higher rate than those without: 82% as against 63%.

One sub-category did better still. If a current or former state attorney or former top county attorney was involved in the petition, the success rate was 91%, against about 73% for all other petitions studied.

A number of the attorneys concerned were former deputy attorneys general who, while working for the state, had been assigned to the Land Use Commission: Roy Y. Takeyama, Walton D. Y. Hong, Michael R. Marsh, and Harry S. Y. Kim.

Also in the group of current and former government attorneys appearing before the LUC were former State Land Board lawyer Francis M. Izumi and longtime House Majority Chief Attorney James T. Funaki.

Two of this group—Takeyama and Hong—had a 100% record of full or partial approval of redistricting petitions they represented as private attorneys before the LUC.

TABLE 7

GOVERNMENT OFFICIALS AND POLITICAL FIGURES INVOLVED IN
PRIVATE CAPACITIES WITH LAND USE COMMISSION APPLICATIONS
1962-84

Note: Material is arranged by county. Only applications listed below are those meeting specifications indicated in the text and involving then-current or former officials. The year the application was filed is given first, with the application number. Next comes the name of the person with the governmental or political position; the position is as of when the application was processed. Next is the nature of the person's involvement with application, then land use districts concerned (AG = Agricultural, C = Conservation, R = Rural, U = Urban), then acreage, and finally result (A = Approved, PA = partially approved, D = Denied).

HONOLULU

1962/3. TAKAHASHI, SAKAE. Senator. Member of partnership which is applicant. AG to U. 168 acres. PA.

1962/4. HOUGHTAILING, GEORGE K. Former Honolulu planning director. Consultant. AG to U. 398 acres. PA.

1962/5. KIDO, MITSUYUKI. Senator. Member of partnership which is applicant. HOUGHTAILING, GEORGE K. Former Honolulu planning director. Consultant. AG to U. 215 acres. PA.

1962/24. CHUCK, WALTER G. District court magistrate; former clerk Senate, House. Chuck's law associate, Henry H. Shigekane, was attorney. AG to U. 2,300 acres. PA.

1963/38. CHUNG, NORMAN K. Former Honolulu Corporation Counsel. Attorney. HOUGHTAILING, GEORGE K. Former Honolulu planning director. Consultant. AG to U. 2,000 acres. PA.

1963/58. HONDA, EDWIN H. State Board of Education. Attorney. C to U. 106 acres. PA.

1963/60. OMORI, MORIO. Aide US Sen. Daniel K. Inouye. Attorney. AG + C to U. 575 acres. PA.

1964/71. FERRY, JAMES P. Land use commissioner. Applicant's former employee. BURNS, CALEB E. S. JR. Executive with company which is co-applicant. C to U. 16.5 acres. PA.

1965/84. CASTRO, ALEXANDER H. Former chairman territorial Public Welfare Board; delegate 1950 Constitutional Convention. Trustee of estate which is applicant. AG to U. 65 acres. A.

1965/99. TSUKIYAMA, TED T. Chairman Hawaii Employment Relations Board. Attorney. AG to U. 25 acres. A.

1965/100. TAKABUKI, MATSUO. Honolulu councilman. Attorney. AG to U. 1,400 acres. PA.

1965/101. YANO, VINCENT H. Senator. Attorney. AG to U. 30 acres. A.

1965/102. KASHIWA, SHIRO. Former attorney general. Attorney. C to U. 5 acres. A.

1966/119. HOUGHTAILING, GEORGE K. Former Honolulu planning director. Consultant. AG to U. 35 acres. PA.

1966/123. SUNN, FRANKLIN Y. K. Former land use commissioner. President of engineering firm which is consultant. U to AG 48 acres, AG to U 48 acres. A.

1966/140. McCLUNG, DAVID C. Senator. Member of partnership which is applicant. KAWASAKI, DUKE T. Senator. Member of partnership which is applicant. ESPOSITO, O. VINCENT. Former senator. Attorney. C to U. 10 acres. A.

1966/145. FUNAKI, JAMES T. Chief Majority Attorney House of Representatives. Attorney. BURNS, CALEB E. S. JR. Land use commissioner. Executive with company whose affiliate is lessee. AG to U. 56.5 acres. A.

1967/158; 1968/197 (same application filed twice). LEMKE, HERMAN G. P. Chairman Honolulu City Council. Trustee of landowner. KANAZAWA, KINJI. Former Honolulu Planning Commissioner. Attorney. AG to U. 352 acres. PA.

1967/160. FUNAKI, JAMES T. Chief Majority Attorney House of Representatives. Attorney. C to U. 5 acres. A.

1967/161; 1968/201 (same application filed twice). HOUGHTAILING, GEORGE K. Former Honolulu planning director. Consultant. OMORI, MORIO. Aide US Sen. Daniel Inouye. AG to U. 702 acres. PA.

1967/162; 1968/202 (same application filed twice). OMORI, MORIO. His brother-in-law Keigo Murakami is land use commissioner; Omori is also aide US Sen. Daniel Inouye. HOUGHTAILING, GEORGE K. Former Honolulu planning director. Consultant. AG to U. 1,276 acres. PA.

1967/163. CASTRO, ALEXANDER H. Former Chairman Territorial Public Welfare Board; Delegate 1950 Constitutional Convention. President company representing applicant. AG to U. 7 acres. A.

1967/165. LOUIS, LEIGHTON S. C. Former Honolulu planning director. Attorney. AG to U. 10 acres. A.

1968/182. HASHIMOTO, SIDNEY I. Former director Dept. Regulatory Agencies. Attorney. SUNN, FRANKLIN Y. K. Former land use commissioner. President of engineering firm which is consultant. AG to U. 26 acres. A.

1968/205. TAKEYAMA, ROY Y. Secretary University of Hawaii Board of Regents; former deputy attorney general assigned LUC. AG to U. 18 acres. A.

1969/210. HOUGHTAILING, GEORGE K. Former Honolulu planning director. Consultant. AG to U. 16 acres. A.

1971/273. TAKEYAMA, ROY Y. Secretary University of Hawaii Board of Regents; former deputy attorney general assigned LUC. Attorney. AG to U. 9 acres. A.

1971/275. TAKEYAMA, ROY Y. Secretary University of Hawaii Board of Regents; former deputy attorney general assigned LUC. Attorney. AG to U. 228 acres. PA.

1971/281. MYATT, JOHN C. Former director Highways Division State Dept. of Transportation. Officer/director of company that is engineering consultant. AG to U. 7 acres. A.

1971/283. IZUMI, FRANCIS M. Former deputy attorney general assigned Dept. of Land and Natural Resources. Attorney. HOUGHTAILING, GEORGE K. Former Honolulu planning director. Consultant. AG to U. 620 acres. D.

1971/311. AKI, RAYMOND X. Former Kauai supervisor. General manager of company which is applicant. C + AG to U. 35 acres. PA.

1972/330. LEE, FREDERICK K. F. Former Honolulu planning director. Consultant. MAU, CHUCK. Former circuit court judge; former Honolulu supervisor. Member of partnership which is applicant. KIDO, MITSUYUKI. Former senator; former Honolulu supervisor; brother is land use commissioner. Member of partnership which is applicant. IWAI, DONALD K. Former Honolulu deputy corporation counsel. Attorney. C to U. 30 acres. D.

1972/342. NAPIER, ALEXANDER J. JR. Land use commissioner. Declared conflict of interest. AG to U. 324 acres. A.

1972/344. ARIYOSHI, JAMES M. Brother of lieutenant governor. Officer of company which is applicant. AG to U. 229 acres. A.

1975/403. HOUGHTAILING, GEORGE K. Former Honolulu planning director. Consultant. AG to U. 25 acres. A.

1976/414. FUNAKI, JAMES T. Chief Majority Attorney House of Representatives. Attorney. AG to U. 48 acres. A.

1976/421. KIM, HARRY S. Y. Former deputy attorney general assigned LUC. Attorney. HOUGHTAILING, GEORGE K. Former Honolulu planning director. Consultant. AG to U. 830 acres. PA.

1976/423. KIDO, MITSUYUKI. Former senator; former Honolulu supervisor. Member of partnership which is applicant. HAWKINS, ALLEN R. Former circuit court judge. Member of partnership which is applicant. Attorney. AG to U. 429 acres. D.

1976/424. OMORI, MORIO. Aide US Sen. Danial Inouye. Attorney. HOUGHTAILING, GEORGE K. Former Honolulu planning director. AG to U. 7 acres. D.

1976/427. FUNAKI, JAMES T. Chief Majority Attorney House of Representatives. Attorney. AG to U. 590 acres. A.

1978/444. IZUMI, FRANCIS M. Former deputy attorney general assigned Dept. Land and Natural Resources. Attorney. C to U. 8 acres. A.

1978/445. FUNAKI, JAMES T. Chief Majority Attorney House of Representatives. Attorney. AG to U. 227 acres. D.

1979/469. KIM, HARRY S. Y. Former deputy attorney general assigned LUC. Attorney. AG to U. 181 acres. A.

1980/485. FONG, HIRAM L. SR. Former US senator. Chairman of board of company which is applicant. AG to U 113 acres, U to AG 124 acres. PA.

1980/487. ISHIDA, LINCOLN J. Former Honolulu deputy corporation counsel. Attorney. TUCK AU, HENRY. Former Honolulu chief traffic engineer. Consultant. C to U. 72 acres. PA.

1983/551. FUNAKI, JAMES T. Chief Majority Attorney House of Representatives. Attorney. AG to U. 256 acres. A.

1983/558. KIM, HARRY S.Y. Former deputy attorney general assigned LUC. Attorney. AG to U. 181 acres. A.

1983/560. FUNAKI, JAMES T. Chief Majority Attorney House of Representatives. Attorney. C to U. 6 acres. A.

MAUI

1962/10. CHING, CLARENCE T. C. Chief fundraiser John Burns 1962 gubernatorial campaign. Officer of company which is applicant. HOUGHTAILING, GEORGE K. Former Honolulu planning director. Consultant. AG to U. 830 acres. A.

1962/11. OGATA, THOMAS S. Senator. Attorney. AG to U. 24 acres. A.

1962/25. JENNINGS, WILLIS C. Former land use commissioner. Officer of company which is applicant. AG to U. 10 acres. A.

1963/31. UEOKA, MEYER M. Member State Board of Education. Attorney. AG to R. 42 acres. D.

1963/42. OGATA, THOMAS S. Senator. Attorney; his law firm owned part of company which is applicant. MUNOZ, FRANK. Former member Maui County Board of Water Supply. Member of partnership which is applicant. UEOKA, MEYER M. Member State Board of Education. His law firm represented applicant, owned part of company which is applicant. AG to R. 460 acres. A.

1965/91. KIDO, MITSUYUKI. Senator. Member of partnership which is applicant. AG to R. 401 acres. A.

1965/98. UEOKA, MEYER M. Member State Board of Education. Attorney. R to U. 32 acres. D.

1966/112. SODETANI, DOUGLAS R. Chairman Maui Charter Commission; former member Maui Planning and Traffic Commission; former member State Civil Service Commission. Agent. AG to R. 7 acres. D.

1966/120; 1967/164 (same application filed twice). IGE, EDWIN T. Member Maui County Police Commission. Applicant. AG to R. 58 acres. A.

1966/134. BURNS, CALEB E. S. JR. Land use commissioner. Executive with company whose affiliate is bonding applicant. AG to U. 49 acres. A.

1966/135. UEOKA, MEYER M. Member State Board of Education. Attorney. AG to R. 5 acres. A.

1966/143. SODETANI, DOUGLAS R. Chairman Maui Charter Commission; former member Maui Planning and Traffic Commission; former member State Civil Service Commission. Agent. AG to R. 7 acres. A.

1967/148. QUINN, WILLIAM F. Former governor. Director of company which is applicant. AG to U 20 acres, U to AG 6 acres. A.

1968/173. PRYOR, TAYLOR A. Former senator. Officer of company which is applicant. AG to U. 20 acres. A.

1968/176. SHIMODA, WALTER T. District court magistrate. Attorney. AG to U. 14 acres. A.

1968/189. BURNS, CALEB E. S. JR. Land use commissioner. Executive with company which is applicant. AG to U. 26 acres. A.

1968/190. BURNS, CALEB E. S. JR. Land use commissioner. Executive with company which is applicant. AG to U. 48 acres. A.

1969/215. MUNOZ, FRANK. Former member Maui County Board of Water Supply. Member of partnership which is applicant.

1969/216. IZUMI, FRANCIS M. Former deputy attorney general assigned Dept. of Land and Natural Resources. Attorney. AG to U 764 acres, C to U 36 acres. PA.

1969/218. UEOKA, MEYER M. District court magistrate. Attorney. AG to U. 50 acres. PA.

1969/222. OHATA, ROBERT O. Former Maui county planning director. Consultant. AG to U. 450 acres. PA.

1969/242. IZUMI, FRANCIS M. Former deputy attorney general assigned Dept. of Land and Natural Resources. Attorney. R + C to U. 39 acres. A.

1971/293. PRYOR, TAYLOR A. Former senator. Officer with company which is applicant. AG to U 20 acres, U to AG 20 acres. A.

1971/294. KONDO, RONALD Y. State representative. Officer of company holding land under sale agreement. AG to R. 15 acres. A.

1972/352. FERRY, JAMES P. Former land use commissioner. Consultant. AG to R. 8 acres. A.

1975/386; 1975/401 (same application filed twice). IZUMI, FRANCIS M. Former deputy attorney general assigned Dept. of Land and Natural Resources. Attorney. AG to U. 65 acres. A..

1975/399. SODETANI, DOUGLAS R. Former Chairman Maui Charter Commission; former member Maui Planning and Traffic Commission; former member State Civil Service Commission. Officer of company which is agent. TOKUNAGA, DONALD H. Former member Hawaii Housing Authority. Officer of company which is agent. AG to U. 28 acres. D.

1975/401. IZUMI, FRANCIS M. Former deputy attorney general assigned Dept. of Land and Natural Resources. Attorney. AG to U. 65 acres. A.

1975/405. UNEMORI, WARREN S. Former engineer with State Dept. of Transportation, also with Maui County Dept. of Public Works. Consultant. CROCKETT, WILLIAM F. Former member Maui County Charter commissions. Attorney. AG to R. 27 acres. A.

1976/416. KAMAKA, HIRAM K. Former director State Dept. of Budget and Finance; former state representative. Attorney. C + R to U. 85 acres. D.

1977-429. ABE, KAZUHISA. Former justice Hawaii Supreme Court; former senator. Law firm represented applicant. AG to R. 242 acres. A.

1978/437. TAKEYAMA, ROY Y. Former deputy attorney general assigned Land Use Commission; former secretary University of Hawaii Board of Regents. AG to U 5.5 acres, R to U 15 acres. A.

1978/442. UEOKA, MEYER M. State representative. Attorney. AG to R. 6 acres. A.

1978/443. UEOKA, MEYER M. State representative. Attorney. AG to U. 30 acres. A.

1979/451. SODETANI, DOUGLAS R. Former member Maui County Charter Commission; former member Maui Planning and Traffic Commission; former member State Civil Service Commission. Agent. AG to U. 27 acres. A.

1980/480. UNEMORI, WARREN S. Former engineer State Dept. of Transportation, also with Maui County Dept. of Public Works. Consultant. AG to U. 99 acres. PA.

1980/483. YUEN, WILLIAM W. L. Land use commissioner. Declared conflict of interest. AG to U. 625 acres. D.

1981/511. CROCKETT, WILLIAM F. Former member Maui County Charter commissions. Attorney. ING, ANDREW T. F. Former state budget director, lieutenant governor. Director of company which is applicant. AG to U. 8.5 acres. A.

1981/514. LUNA, B. MARTIN. Chairman Democratic Party on Maui; former member Hawaii Housing Authority. Attorney. AG to U. 29 acres. A.

1981/517. HEFTEL, CECIL. US Congressman. Heftel Broadcasting Corp. was 84.3% owner of land, Heftel himself was 12.5% owner, under agreement of sale to the applicant. AG to U + R. 148 acres. D.

1981/520. MANCINI, PAUL R. Former Maui corporation counsel. Attorney. AG to U. 91 acres. PA.

1982/528. MANCINI, PAUL R. Former Maui corporation counsel. Attorney. AG to U. 29 acres. A.

1982/532. IZUMI, FRANCIS M. Former deputy attorney general assigned Dept. Land and Natural Resources. Attorney. AG to U. 50 acres. A.

1982/535. MANCINI, PAUL R. Former Maui corporation counsel. Attorney. AG to U. 680 acres. A.

1982/536. MANCINI, PAUL R. Former Maui corporation counsel. Attorney. AG to U. 190 acres. A.

1982/542. FUNAKI, JAMES T. Chief Majority Attorney House of Representatives. Attorney. U + AG to R, AG to U. 1,015 acres. PA.

1982/543. MANCINI, PAUL R. Former Maui corporation counsel. Attorney. AG to U. 9 acres. A.

KAUAI

1964/76. SHIRAISHI, CLINTON I. Senator; former district court magistrate; former territorial representative. Attorney. AG to U. 37 acres. A.

1964/79. BURNS, CALEB E. S. JR. Land use commissioner. Manager of company whose parent substantially or entirely owned applicant. AG to U 17 acres, U to AG 11 acres. PA.

1965/85. KAWAKAMI, NORITO. District court magistrate; former territorial representative. His law firm represented applicant. AG to R. 6 acres. A.

1965/86. KAWAKAMI, NORITO. District court magistrate, former territorial representative. His law firm represented applicant. AG to R. 13 acres. A.

1965/93. BURNS, CALEB E. S. JR. Land use commissioner. Manager of company whose parent owned block of applicant's stock. AG to U 44 acres, U to AG 50 acres. A.

1965/94. BURNS, CALEB E. S. JR. Land use commissioner. Manager of company whose parent owned block of applicant's stock. AG to U 8.5 acres, U to AG 5.5 acres. A.

1966/114. MEDEIROS, EDWARD. State tax assessor and collector for Kauai; former Kauai county planning commissioner; former member Kauai County Charter Commission. Spokesman for applicant. AG to R. 18 acres. A.

1966/121. FERNANDES, WILLIAM E. Senator. Applicant. AG to R 55 acres, U to R 5 acres. PA.

1968/203. SHINSATO, MORRIS S. District court magistrate; Chairman Kauai County Charter Commission; former member University of Hawaii Board of Regents. Attorney. AG to U. 32 acres. PA.

1968/206. SHINSATO, MORRIS S. District court magistrate; Chairman Kauai County Charter Commission; former member University of Hawaii Board of Regents. Attorney. AG to U. 12 acres. PA.

1969/213. SHINSATO, MORRIS S. District court magistrate; former Chairman Kauai Charter Commission; former member University of Hawaii Board of Regents. Attorney. AG to R. 16 acres. D.

1969/217. TAKEYAMA, ROY Y. Secretary to University of Hawaii Board of Regents; former deputy attorney general assigned LUC. Attorney. AG to U. 53 acres. PA.

1969/233. TEXEIRA, JOHN D. Former district court magistrate. Consultant. AG to U. 29 acres. D.

1969/235. SHINSATO, MORRIS S. District court magistrate; former Chairman Kauai County Charter Commission; former member University of Hawaii Board of Regents. Attorney. AG to R. 23 acres. D.

1969/238. KAWAKAMI, TORU. Former member Kauai County Charter Commission. Applicant. AG to U. 22 acres. A.

1970/246. KUTAKA, MASAO. Former Kauai county engineer; former member Hawaii Housing Authority. His engineering firm was consultant. SAKAI,

HIROSHI. Former chief clerk/chief counsel key legislative committees. Attorney. AG to U. 37 acres. D.

1975/397. TAKEYAMA, ROY Y. Secretary to University of Hawaii Board of Regents; former deputy attorney general assigned LUC. Attorney. IZUMI, FRANCIS M. Former deputy attorney general assigned Dept. of Land and Natural Resources. Attorney. AG to U. 30 acres. A.

1975/402. IZUMI, FRANCIS M. Former deputy attorney general assigned Dept. of Land and Natural Resources. Attorney. AG to U. 34 acres. A.

1975/410. HONG, WALTON D. Y. Former deputy attorney general assigned LUC. Attorney. R to U. 6.5 acres. A.

1976/411. IZUMI, FRANCIS M. Former deputy attorney general assigned Dept. of Land and Natural Resources. Attorney. AG to U. 103 acres. A.

1976/417. HONG, WALTON D. Y. Former deputy attorney general assigned LUC. Attorney. AG to U. 11 acres. A.

1976/418. HONG, WALTON D. Y. Former deputy attorney general assigned LUC. Attorney. AG to U. 457 acres. A.

1976/422. TAKEYAMA, ROY Y. Secretary to University of Hawaii Board of Regents; former deputy attorney general assigned LUC. Attorney. SHIRAISHI, CLINTON I. Former senator; former district court magistrate; former county supervisor; former territorial representative. Applicant. AG to R. 62 acres. A.

1976/425. HONG, WALTON D. Y. Former deputy attorney general assigned LUC. Attorney. AG to U. 36 acres. A.

1977/431. NAKEA, CLIFFORD L. Former Kauai deputy county prosecutor. Attorney. AG to R. 34 acres. A.

1978/436. SHIRAISHI, CLINTON I. Former senator; former district court magistrate; former county supervisor; former representative. Attorney. AG to U. 7 acres. A.

1978/438. SHIRAISHI, CLINTON I. Former senator; former district court magistrate; former county supervisor; former territorial representative. Attorney. AG to U. 61 acres. A.

1979/456. SHIRAISHI, CLINTON I. Former senator; former district court magistrate; former county supervisor; former territorial representative. Attorney. AG to U. 14 acres. A.

1979/466. HONG, WALTON D. Y. Former deputy attorney general assigned LUC. Attorney. AG to U. 6 acres. A.

1979/467. TSUCHIYA, BURT K. Kauai county councilman. Spokesman. SHIRAISHI, CLINTON I. Former senator; former district court magistrate; former county cupervisor; former territorial representative. Attorney. AG to U. 86 acres. A.

1981/513. TAKEYAMA, ROY Y. Former secretary to University of Hawaii Board of Regents; former deputy attorney general assigned LUC. Attorney. AG to U. 5 acres. A.

1981/516. SALLING, MICHAEL R. Wife and law partner is senator. AG to U. 5 acres. D.

1981/519. WONG, DONALD K. O. Former deputy attorney general. Attorney. AG to U. 52.5 acres. A.

1982/530. SHIRAISHI, CLINTON I. Former senator; former district court magistrate; former county supervisor; former territorial representative. Attorney. AG to U. 78 acres. PA.

HAWAII

1962/6. NAKASHIMA, SUMIO. Former representative, former district court magistrate. Attorney. AG to U. 9 acres. A.

1962/8. NAKASHIMA, SUMIO. Former territorial representative; former district court magistrate. Attorney. AG to U. 45 acres. A.

1963/47. KIMURA, SHUNICHI. Former Honolulu deputy corporation counsel; one law partner is senate president. Attorney. AG to U. 99 acres. PA.

1963/50. ABE, KAZUHISA. Senator. Attorney. AG to U. 29 acres. D.

1964/68. OSORIO, ELROY T. L. SR. Hawaii County supervisor. Agent. AG to U. 352 acres. D.

1964/69. NEVELS, LUMAN N. JR. Senior Judge Wake Island Court; former circuit court judge. Attorney. AG to U. 7 acres. A.

1964/75. NEVELS, LUMAN N. SR. Senior Judge Wake Island Court; former circuit court judge. Attorney. AG to U. 18 acres. A.

1965/82. HILL, WILLIAM H. Senator. Director of company which owns applicant. AG to U. 11 acres. D.

1965/105. KAI, ERNEST K. Former territorial attorney general. Attorney. AG to U. 262 acres. A.

1966/109. USHIJIMA, JOHN T. Senator. Attorney. AG to U. 43 acres. PA.

1966/122. THOMPSON, MYRON B. Land use commissioner. Executive director of trust which is applicant. AG to U 14.5 acres, U to AG 1.5 acres. A.

1966/126. NEVELS, LUMAN N. JR. Senior Judge Wake Island Court; former circuit court judge. Attorney. AG to U. 112 acres. PA.

1966/141. KAI, ERNEST K. Former territorial attorney general. Attorney. AG to U. 41 acres. A.

1966/146. ADUJA, PETER A. State representative; former district court magistrate. Co-applicant. AG to U. 20 acres. A.

1967/153. KUWAYE, YASUO. Former Hawaii county planning commissioner. Co-applicant. USHIJIMA, JOHN T. Senator. Law firm represented applicant. AG to U. 33 acres. A.

1967/154. USHIJIMA, JOHN T. Senator. Law firm represented applicant. AG to U. 21.5 acres. A.

1967/170. GREENWELL, SHERWOOD R. H. Hawaii County supervisor. Officer of company which is applicant. AG to U. 300 acres. PA.

1967/172. USHIJIMA, JOHN T. Senator. Attorney. AG to U. 24 acres. D.

1968/175. KAI, ERNEST K. Former territorial attorney general. Attorney. C to U. 165 acres. A.

1968/188. HENDERSON, RICHARD. Former member Board of Agriculture; political protege of Sen. William H. Hill. Agent. AG to U. 32.5 acres. PA.

1968/194. USHIJIMA, JOHN T. Senator. Attorney. AG + C to U. 5,850 acres. PA.

1968/208. NAKAMOTO, ROY K. District court magistrate; law partner is senator. Attorney. INABA, GORO. Land use commissioner. Brother was surveyor for applicant. AG to U. 143 acres. PA.

1969/220. NAKASHIMA, SUMIO. Former territorial representative; former district court magistrate. Agent. AG to R. 11 acres. D.

1969/224. HILL, WILLIAM H. Senator. Director of company which is applicant. AG + C to R + U. 5,400 acres. PA.

1969/228. TAJIMA, PAUL. Former planner Dept. of Land and Natural Resources. Consultant. AG + C to U + C. 428 acres. D.

1969/231. GREENWELL, SHERWOOD R. H. Hawaii County councilman. Officer of company which is applicant. AG to U. 12.5 acres. D.

1969/234. INABA, GORO. Land use commissioner. Declared conflict of interest. AG to U. 5 acres. A.

1969/236. KUSHI, MASANORI. District court magistrate. Attorney. AG to U. 41 acres. D.

1970/252. KANEMITSU, CYRIL. Former Hawaii County deputy corporation counsel. Attorney. AG to U. 9 acres. D.

1970/255. NAKAMOTO, ROY K. District court magistrate. Attorney. INABA, GORO. Land use commissioner. Declared conflict of interest. AG to U. 8 acres. PA.

1970/257. YAMADA, ROBERT M. Hawaii County councilman. Applicant. AG to U. 24 acres. D.

1970/263. INABA, GORO. Land use commissioner. Brother was surveyor for applicant. AG to U. 6 acres. A.

1971/292. MENOR, BARNEY B. Former state representative. Applicant. INABA, GORO. Land use commissioner. Brother was surveyor for applicant. AG to R. 18 acres. A.

1971/319. FERRY, JAMES P. Former land use commissioner. Consultant. AG to U. 14 acres. D.

1972/325. TAJIMA, PAUL. Former planner Dept. of Land and Natural Resources. Consultant. IZUMI, FRANCIS M. Former deputy attorney general assigned Dept. of Land and Natural Resources. Attorney. AG to U. 290 acres. PA.

1972/327. ARINAGA, CLIFFORD I. Former deputy attorney general. Officer of company intending to develop. AG to U. 100 acres. PA.

1972/343. NAPIER, ALEXANDER J. Land use commissioner. Filed conflict of interest. AG to U. 15 acres. D.

1973/365. KENNEDY, EUGENE F. Former Honolulu councilman. Officer of company which is applicant. AG to U. 13 acres. A.

1973/373. NAKAMOTO, ROY K. Former district court magistrate. Attorney. YUDA, GEORGE S. Deputy Hawaii county corporation counsel. Member of partnership which is applicant. AG to U. 40 acres. A.

1975/406. YAMADA, ROBERT M. Hawaii County councilman. Member of partnership which is applicant. AG to U. 5 acres. A.

1976/412. ABE, KAZUHISA. Former supreme court justice; former senator. Law firm represented applicant. AG to U. 145.5 acres. A.

1978/440. NAKASHIMA, SUMIO. Former territorial representative; former district court magistrate. Consultant. C to U. 90 acres. D.

1979/461. FUNAKI, JAMES T. Chief Majority Attorney House of Representatives. Attorney. AG to U. 880 acres. PA.

1979/462. DOI, NELSON K. Former lieutenant governor; former circuit court judge; former senator. Law firm represented applicant. AG to U. 212 acres. A.

1979/463. KEALOHA, JOSEPH G. JR. Trustee Office of Hawaiian Affairs. Applicant and intended developer. YANAI, EDWARD K. Land use commissioner. Declared conflict of interest. AG to U. 10 acres. PA.

1979/468. MIHO, JON T. Former aide US Sen. Hiram L. Fong; belonged to law firm that contained large number current and former Republican officeholders, including Hiram Fong Sr. and Jr. Attorney. AG to U. 156 acres. A.

1979/470. KAWAKAMI, NORITO. Former circuit court judge. Attorney. MARSH, MICHAEL R. Former deputy attorney general assigned LUC. AG to U. 175 acres. PA.

1979/471. FUNAKI, JAMES T. Chief Majority Attorney House of Representatives. Attorney. AG to U. 26 acres. A.

1980/482. FUNAKI, JAMES T. Chief Majority Attorney House of Representatives. Attorney. C to U. 240.5 acres. PA.

1980/494. ABE, KAZUHISA. Former supreme court justice; former senator. Law firm represented applicant. AG to U. 131 acres. D.

1980/498. FUNAKI, JAMES T. Chief Majority Attorney House of Representatives. Attorney. AG to U. 166 acres. D.

1980/500. ABE, KAZUHISA. Former supreme court justice; former senator. Law firm represented applicant. C to U. 16 acres. D.

1981/505. TAKEYAMA, ROY Y. Former deputy attorney general assigned LUC. Attorney. AG to U. 40 acres. A.

1981/524. TAKEYAMA, ROY Y. Former deputy attorney general assigned LUC. Attorney. C to U 65 acres, U to C 65 acres. A.

1981/525. LUM, CLIFFORD H. F. Former Hawaii county corporation counsel. Attorney. AG to U. 411 acres. PA.

1983/556. HIGASHI, ROLAND H. Member Board of Land and Natural Resources. President of corporation which is general partner of applicant. AG + C to U. 9 acres. A.

Sources: Gwenfread E. Allen, ed., *Men and Women of Hawaii: A Biographical Directory of Noteworthy Men and Women of Hawaii* (Honolulu, 1966); Betty F. Buker, ed., *Men and Women of Hawaii 1972: A Biographical Directory of Noteworthy Men and Women of Hawaii* (Honolulu, 1972); Department of Commerce and Consumer Affairs, Business Registration Division; State of Hawaii, Legislative Reference Bureau, *Directory of State, County and Federal Officials: Supplement to Guide to Government in Hawaii* (published occasionally, most recently annually); Chamber of Commerce of Hawaii, *Who's Who in Government State of Hawaii* (various years); miscellaneous state and county public officials' personal financial disclosure statements, on file with State Ethics Commissions and offices of county clerks; State of Hawaii, Land Use Commission, miscellaneous files; Hawaii State Archives; miscellaneous references in newspapers and periodicals.

--------------------------------- TABLE 8 ---------------------------------

LAND USE COMMISSION DISTRICT BOUNDARY AMENDMENTS 1962-1984
SHOWING INVOLVEMENT OF CURRENT AND FORMER PUBLIC
OFFICIALS

	OAHU	HAWAII	KAUAI	MAUI	STATE
total applications	61	97	41	65	264
total approved partially or completely	52	64	33	53	202
% approved partially or completely	85%	66%	80.5%	81.5%	77%
total denied	9	33	8	12	62
% denied	15%	34%	19.5%	18.5%	23%
total applications with officials	48	56	34	47	185
% with officials	79%	58%	83%	72%	70%
total without officials	13	41	7	18	79
% without officials	21%	42%	17%	28%	30%
total approved with officials	43	40	29	40	152
approval rate with officials	90%	71%	85%	85%	82%
total approved without officials	9	24	4	13	50
approval rate without officials	69%	58.5%	57%	72%	63%
total with state and top county attorneys	17	12	14	11	54
total approved	14	11	13	11	49
approval rate	82%	92%	93%	100%	91%

Sources: State of Hawaii, Land Use Commission, miscellaneous files; Gwenfread E. Allen, ed., *Men and Women of Hawaii: A Biographical Directory of Noteworthy Men and Women of Hawaii* (Honolulu, 1966); Betty F. Buker, ed., *Men and Women of Hawaii 1972: A Biographical Directory of Noteworthy Men and Women of Hawaii* (Honolulu, 1972); Department of Commerce and Consumer Affairs, Business Registration Division; State of Hawaii, Legislative Reference Bureau, *Directory of State, County and Federal Officials: Supplement to Guide to Government in Hawaii* (published occasionally, most recently annually); miscellaneous state and county public officials' personal financial disclosure statements, on file with State Ethics Commission and offices of county clerks; Hawaii State Archives; files of county planning departments; miscellaneous references in newspapers and periodicals.

There were many threads linking applicants and their representatives to government and to the LUC itself. Ties ran the other way as well, linking commissioners with development.

From 1963 to 1984, 34 commissioners were appointed. (There were two sets of commissioners appointed previously, in 1961 and 1962, but their tenure was brief and their work not of great importance.) Among the 34 were a handful of non-establishment individuals: for example, a conservationist, a liberal woman, proponents of Hawaiian rights issues. But overall, the ties of commissioners ran to virtually every major segment of the development business: landowners, airlines, investors, building material suppliers, realtors, unions with special interests in development, attorneys whose firms did development-related work, a major landscaper, and a supplier of food to hotels. Further, of the nine commissioners appointed in 1963, four had a realtor's license when appointed or obtained one before their term expired. (See Table 9.)

─────────────── **TABLE 9** ───────────────

LAND USE COMMISSIONERS 1963-1984 OCCUPATION AT TIME OF APPOINTMENT, AFFILIATIONS WITH DEVELOPMENT

Note: Names are listed in order of appointment. Where several were appointed in the same year, names are listed alphabetically.

BURNS, C. E. S. JR. (1963–1969). Manager Oahu Sugar Co., an Amfac Inc. plantation; Amfac was a major landowner and developer.

FERRY, JAMES P. (1963–1968). Chairman State Board of Land and Natural Resources, therefore by law at the time a member of LUC; 1957–1959 tract manager for Joe Pao Realty, an affiliate of one of then-largest residential developers in Hawaii; obtained real estate broker's license 1958, still held 1984; 1959–1963 affiliated with real estate firm of Jim P. Ferry and Richard A. Botelho Realty Co.

INABA, GORO. (1963–1973). Manager small hotel in Kona; brothers were very active in investing in and developing land, Norman especially, in these years one of Big Island's most active developers of residential tracts; Goro himself invested at least once.

MARK, SHELLEY M. (1963-1974). Director State Department of Planning and Economic Development, therefore by law at that time a member of the LUC; at least once made small investment, in Magnolia Shopping Center Inc., which was to build shopping center on US mainland.

NISHIMURA, SHIRO "SALLY." (1963–1969). Kauai chicken farmer who became one of island's more active land investors, including, during LUC tenure, in Kukuiolono Associates, Opaikaa Associates, Hui o Kauai I.

OTA, CHARLES S. (1963–1965). Real estate broker and insurance salesman; 1961 became president of Valley Isle Realty Inc., whose officers-directors-shareholders were mostly high-ranking Maui Democrats of the Burns faction; obtained real estate broker's license 1964.

THOMPSON, MYRON B. (1963–1967). Executive director Queen Liliuokalani Trust, a charitable trust for Hawaiian children owning about 10,000 acres of land held for lease and development; obtained real estate salesman's license 1956.

WENKAM, ROBERT G. (1963– 1967). Photographer and conservation activist.

WUNG, LESLIE E. L. (1963– 1973). Big Island rancher; obtained real estate salesman's license 1971.

MURAKAMI, KEIGO. (1967– 1969). Employee Maui Publishing Co.

CHOI, WILBERT H. S. (1967– 1970). Nurseryman-landscaper; landscaped major developments such as Ala Moana Center, Mauna Kea Beach Hotel, Fort St. Mall; shareholder Capital Investment Co., became a director 1969; Capital Investment was one of Hawaii's larger developers in 1960s, built resort Makaha, Oahu, in which Choi was to be co-creator of international botanical garden; Choi died before garden project could get under way.

NAPIER, ALEXANDER J. JR. (1968– 1975). Officer Kahua Ranch Ltd., which was on Hawaii; during LUC tenure Kahua sought to have resort built on portion of its lands; ranch president, J. Atherton Richards, was Bishop Estate trustee.

KIDO, SUNAO. (1968– 1974). Chairman State Board of Land and Natural Resources, therefore by law at that time also member LUC; obtained real estate salesman's license 1960; also 1960 joined two land development businesses: Heeia Development Co., which was to develop the residential portion of a 520-acre project on Bishop Estate land in windward Oahu; and Rural Investments Inc., to undertake development of industrial land; brother Mitsuyuki was prominent Democratic politician and one of most active land developers of his time.

TANGEN, EDDIE. (1969– 1977). ILWU.

YAMAMURA, TANJI. (1969– 1976). Maui pineapple farmer, land investor; during LUC tenure held investments Makena 700, which bought-sold 700 acres in Makena, Maui, also Waikiki Bali Hai Associates, which apparently invested in a Waikiki condominium.

SAKAHASHI, STANLEY K. (1970– 1978). Owner small general merchandise store Kauai; held small real estate investments on Oahu.

CARRAS, JAMES R. (1973– 1979). Executive Honolulu Iron Works Inc., which made building materials.

OURA, MITSUO. (1973– 1981). Business agent Carpenters Union Local 745.

YANAI, EDWARD K. (1974– 1982). Hawaii sales manager Japan Air Lines; investor Hui 86; 1980 bought part-interest unit Maui Vista condominium Kihei, Maui.

DUKE, CHARLES W. (1975– 1981). Food broker-distributor, including hotel accounts.

MACHADO, COLETTE Y. (1975– 1979). Honolulu Community College outreach counselor; Hawaiian rights activist.

WHITESELL, CAROL B. (1975– 1982). Officer League of Women Voters.

MIYASATO, SHINSEI. (1976– 1984). ILWU.

NAKAGAWA, SHINICHI. (1977– 1981). ILWU.

PASCUA, GEORGE R. (1978– 1981). Employee Amfac Distribution Co. Ltd., building materials supplier.

YUEN, WILLIAM W. L. (1979–). Attorney Case Kay & Lynch, whose clients during his LUC tenure included landowners-developers such as Alexander & Baldwin, Molokai Ranch Co., Grove Farm Co., Waitec Development Inc.

CHOY, RICHARD B. F. (1980–). President Paradise Optical Inc.; also investor in Waimanalo Acres and Hui Maluniu.

CUSKADEN, EVERETT L. (1981–). Attorney Oliver Cuskaden & Lee, one of whose specialties was real estate and condominium law; one client as of 1983 was Association of Apartment Owners of Yacht Harbor Towers Condominium.

TAMAYE, ROBERT S. (1981–). Truck farmer.

TACBIAN, TEOFILO. (1981–). Account executive First Insurance Co. of Hawaii Ltd.

CHUN, LAWRENCE F. (1982–). Hawaii public relations director United Airlines.

WHITTEMORE, FREDERICK P. (1982–). Retired officer First Hawaiian Bank.

RUBIN, WINONA E. (1982–). Executive director Alu Like Inc., Hawaiian rights organization.

SUZUKI, TORO. (1984–). ILWU.

Sources: Gwenfread E. Allen, ed., *Men and Women of Hawaii: A Biographical Directory of Noteworthy Men and Women of Hawaii* (Honolulu, 1966); Betty F. Buker, ed., *Men and Women of Hawaii 1972: A Biographical Directory of Noteworthy Men and Women of Hawaii* (Honolulu, 1972); Department of Commerce and Consumer Affairs, Business Registration Division; State of Hawaii, Legislative Reference Bureau, *Directory of State, County and Federal Officials: Supplement to Guide to Government in Hawaii* (published occasionally, most recently annually); miscellaneous state and county public officials' personal financial disclosure statements, on file with State Ethics Commissions and offices of county clerks; State of Hawaii, Land Use Commission, miscellaneous files; Hawaii State Archives; miscellaneous references in newspapers and periodicals.

Perhaps inevitably, these overlapping public sector-private sector ties led to potential or actual conflicts of interest when commissioners voted on particular redistricting petitions.

In 1970 the state attorney general cited three current and former commissioners for alleged conflict-of-interest voting.[28]

Of the three the most publicized case was that of Kauai chicken farmer Shiro "Sally" Nishimura.

Nishimura was a 10% owner and general partner of Hui o Kauai I, which in March 1969 bought for $325,000 137 acres of old pineapple plantation land in Kalaheo, Kauai, from Alexander & Baldwin.

The purchase took place near the start of the LUC's 1969 five-year district boundary review. Some 45 of the 137 acres were in the urban district, the balance of 92 in the agricultural district. As part of the review the 92 agricultural acres were proposed for urban redistricting.

The LUC's consultants supported the proposal. Their written explanation was that the general region "possesses great potential for future residential development based on the proximity to the Koloa-Poipu resort area;

the physical characteristics of the area, such as climate, topography and orientation; and the availability of land in fee simple ownership."

The Kauai Planning Director and the Planning and Traffic Commission, while they might have endorsed the general regional analysis, were opposed to redistricting Hui o Kauai I's land, saying its "terrain is too rugged and access to properties seems difficult."[29]

Unlike the 1974 review, landowners in 1969 could not formally request to have their lands considered for redistricting. Only commissioners could do that.[30]

Apparently it was Nishimura himself who initiated consideration of the 92 acres for redistricting and was the primary reason that the LUC consultants supported the change. Consultant Howard B. Altman told a reporter in 1970 that "he recalls Nishimura suggesting urban zoning of Kalaheo lands [both the *hui*'s as well as others]."[31] In an interview for this book a man who in 1969 was on the LUC staff said that there "is no question [but] that Nishimura initiated" the proposed redistricting. The former staff member explained that it was normal practice during the 1969 review for each island's commissioner to initiate all proposals for his island.

The local commissioners reportedly played similar roles when it came to the consultants' recommendations on each proposal. LUC staff director Ramon Duran told a reporter in 1970 that the "consultants relied heavily on local commissioners in making their island-by-island recommendations."[32]

In July Nishimura took part in a unanimous decision to redistrict the land to urban. Having paid $325,000 in March 1969, now in March 1970 his *hui* resold all 137 acres, without having made any physical changes to it, for $900,000. The apparent gross profit to Nishimura alone was $57,500.[33] According to newspaper reports and the court records of a State Ethics Commission case involving Nishimura, just about the time that his *hui* bought the property the Ethics Commission began investigating him, and may have filed some kind of preliminary conflict-of-interest charge. Exactly what the Commission was focusing on at the time is impossible to say, since the Commission's file on a matter of this kind is not a public record. Nor do the court records explain. In any case, over a year later, Gov. Burns said that in early or mid-1969 he ordered his attorney general to investigate Nishimura. Burns said the inquiry had nothing to do with Kalaheo. Rather, he said he wanted to have reports looked into that Nishimura had been bragging about "fixing things" or "getting things done" on Kauai as a land use commissioner.[34]

About two months after the redistricting in 1969 Nishimura resigned from the LUC, saying he had had a slight heart attack. The date of his resignation nearly coincided with the completion of an investigation of Nishimura by the attorney general's office.[35] Whatever caused the resignation, in about July or August 1970 a *Honolulu Star-Bulletin* reporter was given a tip about the transaction and vote. He wrote a story. This led to stories by the *Star-Bulletin* and the *Honolulu Advertiser* about two other commissioners having engaged in alleged conflict-of-interest voting, all at about the time of yet another investigation by the attorney general's office. This investigation resulted in an opinion citing for conflicts of interest two of the three who had been subjects of newspaper stories, plus a fourth who had not. The attorney general wrote specifically of Nishimura that he violated the state ethics code by his "active participation" in the Kalaheo redistricting.[36]

If this all sounds scandalous in retrospect it did not seem so to many people at the time.

Nishimura in an interview for this book said that he had not done anything wrong. He pointed out that the LUC vote which redistricted Hui o Kauai I's land was simultaneously on all proposed redistrictings for Kauai at the close of the five-year review, and not just on the *hui* property. He indicated that had the vote been item-by-item, he would not have taken part: "I knew better than not to vote on your own land."

Also, Nishimura's behavior in buying and selling the land was not necessarily that of a person who was being devious. For example, although he did not disclose his investment in connection with his vote, neither did he make any attempt to keep the fact of his interest off the public record. The *hui* was registered with the state, and the registration papers, listing Nishimura as an investor, were available for public inspection. Nishimura was one of the general partners. As such his name appeared on maps concerning the property prepared and made available to the public by the State Department of Taxation. Also, conveyance documents pertaining to both purchase of the property by Nishimura's *hui* and resale were publicly recorded.

Indeed it was apparently all this public recording that led someone who knew of Nishimura's being on the LUC to also learn of his financial interest.

The general reaction by the state government and leading Burns Democrats was that the Nishimura episode was not a big issue. For example, the redistricting was not canceled, despite Kauai planners having opposed it. Also, just a few months after issuance of the attorney general's opinion, Nishimura helped organize a small land *hui*, MSW Ltd. Two of its other three members were leading Burns Democrats: former Sen. Mitsuyuki Kido and Burns' chief campaign organizer on Kauai, Turk Tokita.

Burns himself went no further than saying Nishimura committed "an indiscretion." And although Nishimura was the apparent initiator both of LUC consideration and the consultants' favorable recommendation on his own land, Burns refused to concede that the profit Nishimura made was anything but fortuitous: "Nishimura did not make any money out of his position on the commission," Burns told reporters. "He just took a chance" on an investment that happened to go well.[37] A majority on the Hawaii Supreme Court in 1972 went even further in Nishimura's favor. They suggested that a State Ethics Commission proceeding against Nishimura, apparently based in part on the Kalaheo matter, might have been politically motivated. This was a charge that Burns Democrats also hurled at the media that had given the issue such attention.

The ethics case had been underway since early 1969, according to court records. The *Star-Bulletin* disclosure in August 1970 apparently gave the case impetus and a further basis for proceeding. But late in 1970 Nishimura, who was now off the LUC, went to state circuit court on Oahu to attempt to halt the ethics case. He took the position that the Ethics Commission lost jurisdiction over state employees when they left state government. A circuit court judge agreed and ordered the case stopped. The Ethics Commission appealed. The Supreme Court upheld the circuit court.

The Supreme Court majority opinion said that Nishimura's "fear that the commission's action in this case may have been politically motivated may not have been entirely frivolous." As evidence the justices cited Nishimura's lawyer saying that while an initial Ethics Commission charge had been filed in March 1969, it was amended in September 1970 during a gubernatorial election campaign in which one candidate was making much of the Nishimura episode. The justices quoted Nishimura's lawyer: "Was such amended charge based on political or publicity reasons?"[38]

(Although it is impossible to be sure since none of the ethics files in question are public records, it would seem that if the amended charge had to do with the Kalaheo land, and if the Ethics Commission first learned of the Kalaheo matter in the newspaper, then the reason Nishimura was not charged on this point until September 14 1970 was that the newspaper report had come on August 14 1970.)

Nishimura's legal representation is a small study in itself. At the circuit court level, where the judge was Republican Yasutaka Fukushima, Nishimura was represented by a prominent Republican who was a former Supreme Court justice, Jack H. Mizuha. On appeal before an all-Democrat group of justices Nishimura was represented by Mizuha and Arthur S. K. Fong, with whom Mizuha shared law offices. Fong had just recently resigned as the number two man in Burns' state attorney general's office, and was soon to be appointed a state circuit court judge.

Actually, the whole thing did not seem to mean a lot to most people. The newspaper revelations came late in a primary election campaign in which liberal Democrat Lt. Gov. Tom Gill was challenging John Burns for the governorship. Gill was making much of land use issues and integrity in government. He hit the Nishimura case hard. Gill, for example, talked of Nishimura and others in possible conflict-of-interest situations as having "a sleazy sense of ethics." Of Nishimura specifically Gill said that he "unfortunately is another of the Governor's most alarming friends. His self-serving action on the commission—and the Governor's apparent acceptance of it— underscores the need for a new look at ethics in government."[39]

Many in the electorate were apparently not paying much attention to Gill or the media, however. Nor, if they were, did they blame Burns for anything that might be wrong. Tom Coffman in his book about the 1970 gubernatorial election, *Catch A Wave*, wrote that a Burns poll found less than half of all voters statewide were even aware of the Nishimura incident, despite massive media exposure. Also, of those surveyed who had heard of the case, an insignificant 7% blamed Burns.[40]

Indeed some felt that Gill's attacks on Burns were backfiring politically. Coffman wrote that the Burns campaign surveyed voters on the question: "Do you feel that Lt. Gov. Tom Gill is justified in his accusations against Gov. Burns?" The result was that 72% said "no." Furthermore, of Japanese voters only 4.5% saw Gill as justified. Japanese, although only 28% of Hawaii's population, were to account for 46% of Democratic voters in the 1970 primary.[41]

*   *   *

Other commissioners cited in the media or by the attorney general in 1970 for alleged conflict-of-interest voting were Amfac executive C. E. S. Burns Jr., Kahua Ranch Ltd. executive Alexander J. Napier Jr., and nurseryman/landscaper Wilbert H. S. Choi.

Regarding Burns, the attorney general wrote that while he abstained from voting in two cases involving Amfac in 1968, nevertheless he voted six times 1964–1965 on applications filed by Amfac subsidiaries or by an independent corporation of which Amfac owned 18%, Grove Farm Co. In two of the six the application would not have passed without Burns' vote. The attorney general said that Burns' voting in the six cases "clearly indicates a conflict of interest." At the same time the attorney general suggested that the problem might have been one of confusion over whether it was permissible to vote in cases involving subsidiaries or affiliated companies.[42]

Napier was cited not for voting—he abstained—but for lobbying. Just prior to or during the 1969 boundary review Kahua Ranch sold 4,150 acres of its *mauka* (inland) lands and 132 acres *makai* (toward the sea) to a developer from Pennsylvania. In the sale agreement the price of the *makai* property was made contingent upon LUC action—with urban districting the price would double. Prior to the vote Napier publicly disclosed his affiliation with the application and declined to vote on it. But, according to an interview he gave the attorney general's office, "Napier did admit that informally in conversations outside of hearings he did venture opinions [to other commissioners] on the soundness of the proposal."[43]

*   *   *

Choi's case was in some respects the most complicated. Although the facts are not altogether clear, this is what appears to have happened:

Choi was a nurseryman and landscaper by profession. For several decades he owned and operated the Makiki Nursery in the very back of the residential portion of Makiki Valley on Oahu.

In 1946 Choi obtained a 20-year lease from the territorial government on about 5.5 acres in the area. He already owned an adjacent 18,000 square-foot lot. At the same time Choi obtained a variance from the Honolulu city government, covering both the lease and fee land. The variance included a landscape design office and the display and sale of plants in a residential zone. The variance was to last as long as the lease.[44]

When the Land Use Commission in 1964 established Hawaii's first permanent district boundaries, the 18,000 square-foot lot was made urban. The land just beyond, in the direction of the mountains, was districted conservation.

In 1966 Choi obtained a variance from the city to build two houses on his urban lot. They went up about 1968–1969.[45]

Also in 1966 the 20-year lease expired. Choi continued to hold the five acres on a revocable permit basis—a short-term arrangement, in other words.

In early 1969 the LUC five-year review was underway. In May the Commission held a hearing on Oahu. At the hearing the LUC displayed a map showing proposed redistrictings for Oahu. The map indicated the 18,000 square-foot lot was to remain in urban.

In June, because the City was considering acquiring the lot plus the lease land, a city inspector took a look at the property. The inspector reported a violation of a city code, apparently the zoning code. Choi's 1946 variance was to have lasted as long as the lease, but since the lease ran out in 1966, the inspector believed the variance was no longer any good. The nursery operation, in a residential zone, would therefore be illegal.[46]

Choi disputed this interpretation, saying he still had an agreement with the state—his revocable permit. Apparently Choi's view prevailed. The city file that describes the violation reads "case closed," as of June 23, 1969.[47] At some point between that May LUC hearing and another LUC meeting in August, the Oahu map was changed to show Choi's lot as proposed to go from urban to conservation. Exactly who did this, when and why were never established.

Choi, for his part, later said he opposed the proposal, but agreed to it at the insistence of other commissioners who thought it was logical to designate plant nursery land on the edge of existing conservation district lands as conservation.[48]

Whether or not Choi opposed the proposal, about two weeks before the LUC's August meeting he sent a letter to the LUC regarding the 18,000 square-foot lot. He wrote: "I request property dedication to Conservation for a period of ten (10) years."[49] He did not explain why he wanted such a designation, nor did he apparently understand that such a step was not possible—the LUC did not reclassify temporarily.

Perhaps what he thought he was doing was attempting to obtain reduced real property taxes. State law then allowed a plant nursery in an urban district to dedicate the land to that use for 10 years. Such dedicated land was assessed for real property tax purposes according to the land's actual use as a nursery, rather than at its "highest and best use." Normally an actual use assessment was lower, even much lower, than "highest and best use."

There was a problem with the letter, though, if Choi's aim was to make use of this law. The LUC had no authority to dedicate his land. It was the province of the director of the State Department of Taxation.

In any event, two weeks after writing his letter Choi voted along with all other commissioners present to adopt in one motion all proposed redistrictings for Oahu. Included was reclassification of the 18,000-square foot lot from urban to conservation.

At about this time the two houses for which Choi obtained a variance in 1966 were being completed. Apparently a neighbor or passerby noted this, and noted as well that they were in an area which had the physical attributes of a conservation district, and inquired or complained to the City. However it happened, in early 1970 mayoral aide Mason Altiery, a former TV newsman, made a written request to the City Building Department to investigate whether the two houses were legal.[50]

The city building inspector who had checked the homes upon their recent completion and given them full approval, Hiromi Horimoto, went back out to Choi's property. Horimoto now believed he found a violation of the zoning code. He found that Choi was using part of one house as an office when the approved plans had shown its purpose as strictly residential. Horimoto wrote that "field investigation shows an office use for the building instead of a rumpus room as shown on approved plans."[51] Since the possible violation had to do with the zoning code, which was overseen by the City Planning Department, Horimoto recommended that the matter should be referred there.

But then someone discovered or realized the land was now in the state conservation district. Thus the State Department of Land and Natural Resources (DLNR), which ordinarily governed use of conservation district land, might have been the appropriate agency to follow up. City Building Superintendent Edward Y. Hirata in the fall of 1970 wrote Land Board Chairman Sunao Kido, apprising him of the possible violation.[52] Kido wrote back that any violation would have predated conservation districting, and was "therefore subject to laws and regulations which then applied to this parcel." It was the City's jurisdiction, in other words.[53] Hirata replied no, it was the State's. Since the land was now conservation, "the City is in no position to take any action on the use of the Makiki Nursery property."[54]

Whoever had the jurisdiction and whether there was a zoning code violation or not, no citation was ever issued, according to state and city files, and according to DLNR and City Building Department employees interviewed for this book.

It was in August 1970, just after the *Honolulu Star-Bulletin* ran its Nishimura story, that the *Honolulu Advertiser*'s Harold P. Hostetler wrote a story about Choi voting in 1969 to redistrict his lot.

Hostetler near the beginning of the story wrote that "it is unclear just what was gained by the rezoning."[55]

But he also wrote about both zoning code violation matters in such a way as to not make clear, if indeed he realized, that at the time of Choi's letter requesting conservation districting and at the time of Choi's vote, there were no code violation cases outstanding. This apparent misunderstanding became widespread. It was reflected in a summarization of the Choi episode by then-*Star-Bulletin* reporter Tom Coffman, who wrote two years later in

Catch A Wave: "Choi . . . had, like Nishimura, voted to rezone his own land. But in this instance, the land had been downzoned to conservation use from urban zoning. However, there was a hooker on which the *Advertiser* pegged its story: Choi's land was used for a nursery in open space, and he had a building on the land which violated the city government's zoning code. By transferring the land to a conservation zone, the land reverted to state zoning control, thereby solving Choi's violation of the city zoning ordinance."[56] But the documentary evidence is that at the time of Choi's letter and vote he had no zoning code problem. The file on the first possible violation reads "case closed" as of June 1969. Choi wrote his letter in July and the vote came in August. The second code problem did not arise till early 1970. Also, Building Inspector Horimoto, who indicated in an interview for this book that he would have been one of the first to know of the second potential violation, said he was not aware of that problem until he was ordered to take a look in 1970.

Thus, although it is impossible to be sure, the evidence suggests that, whatever it was that made Choi request conservation reclassification, it may not have been to eradicate city zoning code problems, as the *Advertiser* and other media made it appear.

On the other hand, there is a chance that although Choi did not write his letter till after the first code case was resolved, nevertheless it might have been he who initiated the proposed LUC map change, and he might have done it before the first case was closed. Moreover, regardless of who initiated the change and when, Choi, having just had one brush with the City on a zoning code matter, might have wanted to remove the property from the City's jurisdiction to prevent a recurrence of the problem. Choi might also have seen the reclassification as moving the property out of "enemy territory" and into friendly hands. The head of the state department with primary jurisdiction over conservation land was Sunao Kido, a fellow land use commissioner and reportedly Choi's friend. Honolulu's mayor at the time was Frank Fasi, an arch-enemy of the state government of which Choi was a part.

And irrespective of whether Choi was concerned with what government agencies had jurisdiction over land use matters concerning his lot, there is the appearance that he attempted to get the Land Use Commission, of which he was a member, to lower his property taxes.

Given the fact that Choi as a land use commissioner had voted on his own property, given that Hostetler's story followed the one on Nishimura, and given the volatile political atmosphere at the time of the 1970 gubernatorial primary election, Choi was viewed by many, especially in the Gill camp, as another of Gov. Burns' "alarming friends."

Choi, who previously had at least one heart attack, now, several weeks after the Hostetler article, had another, which was fatal. Whether fairly or unfairly, Burns attributed Choi's death in part to the media. At Choi's funeral Burns said: "In his actions as a commissioner, Mr. Choi even voted to downzone his own property into the conservation class . . . While this resulted in a loss to him personally, it led to a misinformed news article which caused him strain."[57]

* * *

An item of interest in the Nishimura case apparently not discovered by the media or the attorney general was that another commissioner had a connection to that application. Commissioner Sunao Kido's brother, Mitsuyuki, was sole owner of S&M Investments Inc., which had a $5,000 share in Nishimura's *hui*. Sunao voted to approve.[58]

On two other occasions in 1969 Sunao apparently voted on matters involving his brother. In the first, Mitsuyuki was a director of Joe Pao's Hawaiian Pacific Industries Inc. (HPI), which made the request. In the second, Mitsuyuki was a director of Pao's Island Construction Co. Inc., which was in joint venture with another company. In the first, HPI obtained urban districting for 181 acres in windward Oahu near Mt. Olomana. The second involved making urban six acres of Bishop Estate land near Leeward Community College.[59] The first involved Sunao voting on the HPI matter as part of voting simultaneously on all proposed redistrictings for Oahu at the end of the five-year review. The second involved a vote on a single application standing alone.

In an interview for this book, Sunao Kido said that he never discussed his official duties with his brother insofar as they affected his brother's private business affairs. Mitsuyuki in 1970, discussing the Mt. Olomana application, told a reporter the same thing.[60]

Whether Sunao was aware of Mitsuyuki's involvements with the Nishimura, HPI, and Island Construction redistrictings is unclear. Although interviewed once for this book about having taken official action on matters affecting his brother, Sunao declined a second interview in which he was going to be asked about these three redistrictings. (He declined before it was possible to tell him what the specific subject of the interview was to be.)

In any event, in at least one case Sunao voted against an applicant, International Development Co. in 1973, in which Mitsuyuki was an investor.[61]

Research for this book indicates there were other cases of commissioners voting on matters that involved relatives. Commissioner James Ferry in 1965 voted on an HPI application to redistrict 5.4 acres in Niu Valley on Oahu from conservation to urban. Pao was his first cousin and former employer.[62] Keigo Murakami in 1968 voted "yes" on an unsuccessful application concerning 1,276 acres of Austin Trust land in Waimalu. His brother-in-law, Morio Omori, was the trust attorney.[63] Goro Inaba once in 1969 and twice in 1971 voted on Big Island applications with which his brother, Yoshio, was involved as a surveyor or engineer.[64]

It should be noted that research done for this book indicates that, in general, voting that directly affected relatives other than a spouse or dependent child did not violate existing state ethics rules.

* * *

What then did all of these overlaps and ties mean?

One easy answer was obvious: as in most other land-related matters in the Democratic years, interconnections were so extensive that such distinctions as "public sector" and "private sector" had no important meaning.

The more difficult issue, though, had to do with how all of this affected LUC decision-making.

Several researchers have taken stabs at objective appraisals of LUC performance.

Kem Lowry studied, among other things, all petitions filed 1964–1975 for redistricting to urban.[65] He first consulted the LUC rules that set standards by which commissioners were to judge applications—economic feasibility of the proposal, whether prime agricultural land was involved, etc. He turned the standards into a checklist. He then looked at LUC staff analyses of each petition to determine the petitions' characteristics—did the staff think that the proposal was economically feasible, etc? The idea was to see how standards and characteristics matched up.

Lowry listed the results as approved, partially approved, or denied. Thus he knew, for example, that in some particular number of cases in which petitions were approved, the characteristic of, say, economic feasibility, was present. This allowed him to weight each of the individual standards by the extent to which they appeared to have actually guided decisions.

Looking at the results, Lowry wrote that "the most striking characteristic (of most of the petitions) is that in spite of the express goal of the law to protect agricultural land, agricultural suitability does not appear to have been a major factor in Commission decision-making."[66]

This finding would seem to be supported by the 1980 legislative testimony of John Farias Jr., Chairman of the State Board of Agriculture. Farias said, as paraphrased by a reporter: "The State Agriculture Department has come out the loser nearly every time it has gone before the Land Use Commission to oppose redistricting of agricultural land for urban use."[67]

But in other respects, Lowry went on, decision-making with regard to the majority of applications was "generally consistent with the intent of the law. Several measures of the location of the proposed additions to the urban district—proximity to employment, consistency with the county general plan, and the avoidance of scattered urban development—emerged as crucial variables . . . "[68] In Lowry's findings there was thus something of a tilt in the direction of one of the original Land Use Law's two most fundamental principles as against the other—efficient urbanization over preservation of farm lands.

Would the presence in applications of so many with political ties have anything to do with this?

The fact that so many people in politics and government, mostly Democrats, were involved with LUC petitions was at least in part a reflection of how extensively Democrats were privately involved in economic development in post-World War II Hawaii, and how central the urbanization of land was to this process.

Whether the great extent of this involvement led to distortions in LUC decision-making is impossible to know in any empirical way.

If Lowry's findings and the views of liberal and radical critics of the LUC were to the effect that the Commission was over-ready to redistrict land to urban, there was another side to the story.

From where many businesses sat, the LUC was obstructionist: it inhibited economic development and/or made it more expensive. For example, at the suggestion of the state's Hawaii Housing Authority, it became standard practice beginning in the late 1970s for the Commission in approving major residential projects to require that 10% of the project's units, or some equivalent value, be set aside for low and moderate income housing. In the case of major resort developments a requirement was generally imposed that 10% of the project's value be set aside for employee housing.

A 1983 *Forbes* magazine article that called Hawaii "a veritable purgatory for business" indicated that to a great extent this was because land use boards like the LUC were overly protective of agricultural lands to the detriment of economic growth. Many businessmen from at least the early 1970s expressed the opinion that, as American states went, Hawaii was an extremely difficult place in which to do business.[69] Restrictions and added costs imposed on land development such as those required by the LUC were repeatedly cited as evidence.

On balance the LUC came off looking like what it was: an enormously powerful government agency, though one whose discretionary leeway was trimmed somewhat by the 1975 amendments to the Land Use Law; sitting in a position between the imperative of economic growth and the conflicting need for some sort of preservation; with a tilt in the direction of growth, but not enough to satisfy business; and with many of those who got their projects approved having ties to the same political establishment through which commissioners were appointed.

4

THE HONOLULU CITY COUNCIL

NEXT to the Land Use Commission no government agency was so central to the practical real-world workings of land development in the Democratic years as the Honolulu City Council, the local legislative body for the City and County of Honolulu, which included the whole island of Oahu.

Oahu in 1940 had 60% of Hawaii's population of 422,301. In 1960 it had 80% of the Islands' expanded population of 630,401—and nearly every bit of the new military money of Pearl Harbor and Schofield Barracks, as well as almost all of the new mass tourist money of Waikiki.[1]

Oahu was therefore where the great bulk of new development and construction was taking place, and it remained so even when development spread to the outer islands in the 1960s.

So tightly controlled was the development process that virtually everything that was built on Oahu had at some stage to pass through the Honolulu City Council. This was especially so by the 1970s as layers of Council land use controls proliferated—special design districts, interim control ordinances, shoreline management area permits, development plan amendments, and so on.

Moreover, from the start of the boom and continuing through the 1980s, no power the Council had was more important than its land use authority. A Council member of the 1970s and 1980s once said: "We're not energy, we're not education, auto parts or anything else . . . We're land use."[2]

The Democrats took over the Council as part of their general takeover of government in Hawaii.

As tourism and military spending mounted, the Democrats used the Council to forward development, and to try to ensure that the benefits went heavily to local-Asian developers, lawyers, contractors, architects, and, to a lesser extent, homebuyers.

At the same time most councilmen—and Council leaders especially— were personally involved with land and development.

Many councilmen of the 1960s and 1970s invested in real estate directly. Several were developers. Some had relatives who were investors in land. One had a realtor husband, another an architect brother. One of the most powerful councilmen of the 1970s had extensive property dealings with one of Oahu's major developers. Another, who was a leader for a part of that decade, was started in politics and the real estate and finance businesses by a prominent developer/financier. One council leader of the 1960s was an accountant whose firm handled the books of one of Oahu's biggest developers. Many councilmen and most council leaders of the 1960s were attorneys. Often they shared law offices with other attorneys who handled rezoning applications before the Council. And over this entire period a great deal of the money spent in the increasingly expensive Council election campaigns was contributed by contractors, architects, engineers, realtors, real estate attorneys, large landowners, developers, and financial institutions, plus current or prospective city employees. Most successful candidates simply could not have been elected without development money, particularly after the mid-1960s when campaign costs took off.

In brief, with the Honolulu City Council in the Democratic years, the connection between politics and land development was powerful.

* * *

The origin of the Council's power over land use on Oahu was the 1959 Honolulu City Charter, which shifted effective control over development from the city's Planning Commission to the Council.

The Planning Commission was set up in 1915. It was purely advisory until 1939, when it acquired most of the important land use authority on Oahu. In the period 1939–1959 it took five of the seven members of the Council's predecessor, the Board of Supervisors, to override a Commission decision.[3] The way things went, the Commission, appointed by the mayor and in turn appointing the city planning director, controlled land use.

The Democrats, after they started winning seats on the Board of Supervisors, began to agitate for more power over land use. Throughout the 1950s there were jurisdictional disputes, which the Commission usually won. Then in 1956, as consideration was being given to a new city charter, three leading Democratic supervisors pushed to have the Board of Supervisors' land use decisions hold sway over those of the Commission. They reportedly had some support from the mayor, who under the proposed new charter would appoint the planning director. They all got their wish. The Planning Commission in the 1959 charter was made a mostly advisory body (as is the case in most American cities). A planning director was appointed by the mayor. And a new nine-member City Council made the primary land use decisions.[4]

The adoption of the new charter in 1959 thus gave the Council control of Oahu's development approval process right at the beginning of Hawaii's biggest boom ever, putting the Council in a box seat to be involved in development on a massive scale.

* * *

An overview of the personal, business and professional links with land development held by most of the 29 people elected to the Council from the first post-statehood races in 1960 up to but not including the 1982 elections shows the density of connections between the Council and land development during this period.

The case of Matsuo Takabuki, an attorney who was on the Board of Supervisors and Council 1953–1968, was notable in this respect. In 1961 Takabuki filed with the City Clerk a disclosure of interest statement which read: "I have investments in corporations, partnerships and joint ventures who have interests in real property in Waialua, Waianae, Waipahu, Kaneohe, Heeia, Makaha, Niu Valley, Moanalua, Waikiki, Airport area in Damon Tract, and Liliha, and I have clients who have interests in land and businesses in all parts of the City & County of Honolulu."[5]

During Takabuki's 16 years on the Council, probably his most important client was Chinn Ho, one of Oahu's largest and most active land developers. Takabuki represented Ho's principal business entity, Capital Investment Co., as well as his major development ventures in Makaha Valley on the west coast of Oahu, and the Ilikai Hotel in Waikiki. Ho was one of Takabuki's major campaign contributors. Takabuki's law office was for many years in Ho's Capital Investment Building on Merchant St. in downtown Honolulu. During Takabuki's last few years on the Council, he took in Ho's oldest son, Stuart T. K., as a law associate. In 1966 the Council hired Stuart to lobby on its behalf in the State Legislature that session. After Takabuki was defeated in the elections of 1968, Ho made him a vice-president of Capital Investment and a director of Ilikai Inc.[6]

Takabuki was at the center of Democratic politics not only at the city level but at the state level as well. The *Honolulu Star-Bulletin* in 1960 called him "the strong man of the City Council." He was also widely considered to be John Burns' closest advisor during the 1950s and 1960s. In 1959, Takabuki reportedly led the Burns forces in a fight over the position of speaker in the Territorial House of Representatives—and Takabuki was not even in the House. In 1962, when Burns won the governorship for the first time, the *Honolulu Advertiser* considered Takabuki to be "not only the Number 2 man in the City government—he's the Number 2 man in the State government, now that John Burns is elected." A year later the *Star-Bulletin* estimated that Takabuki, a regular at the governor's private working breakfasts, had "more influence on the Governor in the matter of appointments than any other person in the state."[7]

When Takabuki lost his Council seat in 1968, Burns invited him to become state attorney general. Takabuki declined. Then in 1971 Takabuki was appointed a trustee of Bishop Estate. A seat on the Bishop board was one of the true pinnacles of power in Hawaii. Trustees were appointed by the Hawaii Supreme Court, and the Hawaii Supreme Court was appointed by the governor. At the time of Takabuki's appointment all five Supreme Court justices were Burns appointees. In this sense Burns appointed Takabuki.

* * *

When Takabuki was a supervisor and councilman he also had a law practice that was in itself a small study in the new power structure of Hawaii.

Takabuki at one time or another was in partnership or shared office space with: Daniel K. Inouye, Morio Omori, Stuart T. K. Ho, Gov. Burns' son James, Kinji Kanazawa, Ben G. Takayesu, Richard S. Sasaki, Donald K. Iwai, and Shiro Kashiwa.[8]

All of these men either at the time of their association with Takabuki or afterward obtained public office, in most cases high office. Inouye was a territorial legislator who became a US congressman and senator. Omori became Sen. Inouye's aide. Ho became a state representative; Burns a state judge; Kanazawa was a Honolulu planning commissioner; Takayesu became a district court magistrate; Sasaki became executive director of the Public Utilities Commission; Iwai a deputy city attorney; and Kashiwa the first state attorney general.

During Takabuki's years on the Board and Council, most of these men as private attorneys, either during or after their law associations with Takabuki, made Board and Council appearances, generally regarding development matters for their clients. Most of their requests were granted.[9] Whether this had anything to do with a relationship with Takabuki is impossible to say. It appears that a majority of requests filed by all persons in those years was approved. On the other hand most people petitioning for such major items as zoning and general plan changes, and even for many lesser matters, were represented by lawyers who, like Takabuki's then-current and former law associates, were politically well-connected.

Takabuki's law partner for much of the 1950s, Ben Takayesu, made occasional Council appearances on land use matters.[10]

The Kashiwa brothers made many appearances. Takabuki went to Waialua High School for two years with Genro, and during World War II they served in the same company of the 442d Regiment. After Takabuki graduated from law school he worked for a short time for Shiro.[11]

At times Takabuki and his attorney associates made land investments together, as in 1962, when Takabuki and Morio Omori invested, along with several other people, in West Coast Realty Inc., which was set up for development in California.

Omori was perhaps the most active of this group of attorneys in representing development interests before the Council. On occasion, since Takabuki as a sitting councilman could not make on-the-record appearances for Chinn Ho, Omori would appear. Omori represented Ho in 1961 in the matter of the city adopting a general plan for Waianae, where Ho had extensive holdings. Omori also represented a large number of small property holders in their various requests to the Council.[12]

Takabuki, Omori and Inouye shared office space 1958–1965. During the last two years of this association, attorney Richard Sasaki and realtor-attorney Kinji Kanazawa joined them.

Kanazawa was active in seeking rezonings for clients throughout the

1960s. His applications included one in 1962 for apartment zoning on Metcalf St. near the university, and another in the same year for apartment zoning on Sea View Avenue, also near the university.[13]

Kanazawa was appointed to the City Planning Commission in 1963 (the year before he joined Takabuki, Omori and Inouye) and served until 1966. He made no Council appearances on private land use matters while on the Commission, but, following his resignation in 1966, he began again, seeking industrial zoning for a client in Kalihi in 1967, and apartment zoning the same year on Lusitana St. for another client.[14]

In the 1970s Kanazawa advised Council leader George G. Akahane on some of Akahane's property investments with the Horita family, major Oahu developers. Kanazawa also joined Horita land *huis*, serving, for example, as a general partner in Oceanview Ventures, formed to build Newtown Estates in Waimalu.[15]

Another attorney with whom Takabuki shared office space was Donald Iwai. This association was in the mid-1950s, just after Iwai graduated from law school. Iwai became a deputy city attorney in the early 1960s. He went on to become a partner in the law firm of Hong & Iwai. Iwai represented a prominent and politically well-connected developer, Hirotoshi Yamamoto, in matters concerning Yamamoto's Manoa Investment Co. during Council consideration of a proposed Comprehensive Zoning Code in 1968. Iwai also represented other major concerns, such as Pearl Harbor Heights Developers in 1963, plus miscellaneous smaller clients seeking land use changes in the 1960s.[16] Iwai's firm represented developer Clarence T. C. Ching's large-scale rezoning in 1965 of the Salt Lake area for apartments. In addition, in 1966 Iwai represented Loyalty Enterprises before the Council on a Salt Lake-Moanalua land use matter.[17]

*   *   *

Just what Takabuki's professional relationship might have been with those he shared office space with was open to interpretation. For example, Takabuki referred to Omori on occasion as "my associate." The 1960 Hawaii Bar directory listed Takabuki, Omori, and Inouye as "associates." And, as already noted, Omori represented Chinn Ho's interests on the floor of the Council when Takabuki could not. On the other hand, Takabuki once wrote that "each of us [Takabuki, Omori, Inouye, Kanazawa] is independent of the others on all matters and share only the expenses incurred for office rental and janitorial service."[18] Whatever the degree of closeness, the picture was that of a number of Takabuki's current and former law associates frequently representing development applications before a Council which Takabuki dominated.

What were the ethical considerations in all this?

The city attorney in the early 1960s offered an opinion that an office-sharing arrangement was too insubstantial a relationship for a conflict-of-interest situation to arise.[19]

At the same time, though, the American Bar Association in those years appeared to look with disfavor on the Takabuki-Omori type of relationship. An ABA committee on the mainland decided the propriety of a particular office-sharing case. Its decision was included, by way of elucidating a general ethical rule, in the ABA ethics code, by which in those years Hawaii attorneys were bound. The committee took the view that office-sharers, even though not in partnership, might cause the public, "knowing of their intimate relation as office associates, [to] infer that there is some influence operating in their establishment." This was where one was a government official and the other either represented clients before him or obtained clients because of his official actions.[20] The issue in Hawaii came to a head in 1965, during a sharp fight Takabuki had with then-Councilman Frank F. Fasi over the propriety of Takabuki's arrangements with his associates. Takabuki disclaimed the existence of any relationship except the physical sharing of office space. Fasi complained to the Hawaii Bar Association about Takabuki, and about other attorney-councilmen with similar arrangements. A Hawaii ABA committee ruled that such arrangements should cease, saying they tended "to create a general impression in the public mind that any one of the lawyers in such office arrangement would be more influential or more effective in representing a client before a public body or commission of which another attorney in the same office is a member."[21]

The ruling led to the break-up of the following: Takabuki/Omori/ Inouye/Sasaki/Kanazawa; Councilman Clesson Y. Chikasuye/Sen. O. Vincent Esposito; Councilman George M. Koga/Judge Dick Yin Wong/Richard C. Lo/Wilfred H. C. Youth; and Councilman Ben F. Kaito/Rep. James H. Wakatsuki.[22]

Takabuki and the others had never felt a need to hide or apologize for their private-public professional relationships. All of these locally born Asian, Democrat-connected attorneys, politicians, and developers, whether in politics or private business or both at the same time, saw themselves joined together in a fight to break the old *haole* Republican elite's stranglehold on business and government. To non-*haole* Democrats, it made the best sense in the world to get into power positions wherever they could, and then to coordinate their activities. That was how business and political opportunity could be maximized. If it followed that certain Japanese and Chinese attorneys and their business colleagues seemed to be getting preferential treatment, so be it. Non-*haoles* had a lot of catching up to do in Hawaii. If the Democrats ran the Council, they could help persuade Hawaii landowners of the old elite to let locals have the development rights to their land. Local architects, builders, electricians, attorneys, plumbers, contractors of all kinds would get work and get ahead.

* * *

Just how common was it in the boom years for politically well-connected attorneys to represent development-related matters before the Council?

To take a sample, a study was made for this book of all lawyers practicing before the Council 1968–1969 on private land use matters. (See Table 10.)

Altogether in that period, as indicated by the Council's subject indices, which logged on an annual basis all business the Council handled, 27 attorneys appeared on 32 separate items.[23]

Of the 27, 33% were state legislators, either at the time or previously, mostly in leadership positions. As usual, Burns Democrats predominated, but other Democratic factions were represented, as were Republicans. Twenty-two percent were former law partners or associates of councilmen before whom they were appearing. And of those handling major matters of zoning and general plan amendments (as compared with minor matters such as getting permission for a pedestrian gate in a building) 100% had clear governmental or political affiliations.

The group picture that emerges is yet another snapshot of a part of the new power structure, indicating new origins, new achievements, new connections—though old forms. For example, of the 27, some 50% appeared in either the 1966 or 1972 editions of *Men and Women of Hawaii*, a kind of Who's Who for the Islands published since early in the Republican era. Thirty-seven percent attended the national elite law schools of Harvard, Yale or Stanford. And one of the 27, Asa M. Akinaka, was chosen in 1968 as one of the first two local-Asians ever admitted to membership in the Pacific Club, an old-money establishment which had had a long-standing policy against admitting Asians.[24]

───────────────── **TABLE 10** ─────────────────

ATTORNEYS APPEARING BEFORE THE HONOLULU CITY COUNCIL ON PRIVATE LAND USE MATTERS 1968–1969

Note: Government or political position listed is as of 1968–1969.

AKINAKA, ASA M. Former aide US Sen. Oren E. Long. Representing Electric Sales & Service Ltd. for sign variance Nimitz Highway.

ARIYOSHI, GEORGE R. Senate Majority Leader. Representing building contractor supporting another company's rezoning in Heeia.

BURGESS, H. WILLIAM. Representing trustees York International Building Inc. on installation of pedestrian gate to building.

CHUCK, WALTER G. Former clerk of House, then of Senate; former Honolulu district court magistrate. Representing Reed & Martin Investment Corp. re planned development housing Kapiolani Blvd.

CHUN, EDWARD Y. C. Associate Fong, Miho, Choy & Robinson. US Sen. Hiram L. Fong was former partner, now "of counsel;" partner Katsuro Miho former Honolulu planning commissioner; partner Katsugo Miho State representative; partner Herbert Y. C. Choy former Territorial attorney general; partner Clarence W. H. Fong former Territorial representative; associate Barry J. C. Chung soon to be Honolulu city prosecutor. Representing Wigwam Co. Inc. on improvement district Kapalama; representing Foodland owner on amending improvement district ordinance.

CHUNG, BARRY J. C. Associate Fong, Miho, Choy & Robinson, then appointed Honolulu City Prosecutor. Representing individual on electrical hookup in Toomey & Wright Subdivision prior to dedication of roads to City.

ESPOSITO, O. VINCENT. Legislator 1951–66, former House speaker, formerly shared law offices with Councilman Clesson Y. Chikasuye. Representing Rose H. Smith Estate on proposed extension city road in Kalihi.

HASHIMOTO, SIDNEY I. Director State Dept. of Regulatory Agencies 1963–66, former Territorial representative, formerly associated in law practice with Council Chairman Walter M. Heen. Representing Imperial Hotel on zoning code amendment re amount floor area that could be devoted to accessory uses.

IWAI, DONALD K. Former deputy city corporation counsel, formerly shared law offices with Councilman Matsuo Takabuki. Representing Kaiser Hawaii Kai Development Co. and Manoa Investment Co. in commenting on City's proposed Comprehensive Zoning Code; representing Kaiser Hawaii Kai Dev. Co. on land exchange with City; representing Kaiser Hawaii Kai Dev. Co. re right of entry to City land for developing Lunalilo Agricultural Subdivision.

KAMAKA, HIRAM K. State Representative, Chairman House Appropriations Committee. Representing client to clarify drainage matter re client's Hauula rezoning.

KAMO, JAMES H. Former Senate clerk. Representing Lemon Tree nightclub, Kalakaua Ave., re enclosing a lanai.

KANAZAWA, KINJI. Former Honolulu planning commissioner; formerly shared offices with Councilman Matsuo Takabuki, US Sen. Daniel K. Inouye. Representing individual asking review of proposed City plan re road near client's property.

KATO, HIROSHI. State Representative, Chairman House Judiciary Committee. Representing Heeia Dev. Co. re rezoning to light industrial Heeia.

MARUMOTO, WENDELL H. Son of associate justice Hawaii Supreme Court. Representing Thomas F. McCormack re rezoning to commercial Heeia.

OMORI, MORIO. Executive assistant to US Sen. Daniel K. Inouye. Representing Honolulu Sash and Door re improvement district Sheridan Tract.

PLEWS, JOHN H. R. Representing self and family members. Commenting on City's proposed Comprehensive Zoning Code affecting family property.

PYUN, MATTHEW S. K. JR. Deputy City Corporation Counsel 1965–66. Representing medical doctor re minor rezoning to allow commercial use of building.

ROBINSON, EARL S. Partner Fong, Miho, Choy & Robinson. Representing Choy Subdivision Kalihi Valley re easement and roadway.

ROSEHILL, AMBROSE J. Chairman Honolulu City Liquor Commission, former State representative, deputy city prosecutor, deputy city attorney. Representing Motor Supply Ltd. re street alignment in improvement district.

SHIGEKANE, HENRY H. Former Honolulu district court magistrate, former deputy city corporation counsel. Representing Honolulu Scenic Tours Ltd. re redesignating a parking area.

SHIGEMURA, JAMES Y. State Representative. Representing Manoa Finance Co. Inc. and Makaha Surfside Development Co. in general plan amendment for resort use Waianae.

TAKAYESU, BEN G. Former district court magistrate, Honolulu deputy corporation counsel, deputy state attorney general. Representing individual re rezoning land to resort Waianae; representing individual re obtaining easement for sewer line.

TASHIMA, VERNON T. Deputy Honolulu Corporation Counsel 1951–59. Representing Greenhaven Memorial Park, Kaneohe, re City purchasing land for road or issuing building permit.

TSUKIYAMA, TED T. Chairman Hawaii Employment Relations Board, former deputy city attorney, former Honolulu Redevelopment Agency attorney. Representing individual in realigning easement.

WAKATSUKI, JAMES H. State Representative, formerly shared law offices with Councilman Ben F. Kaito. Representing Herbert K. Horita re rezoning for apartments Kalihi; representing Star Markets Ltd. re building permit for new store Kaneohe.

WICHMAN, CHARLES R. Representing several upper-class haole landowners re improvement district Sheridan Tract.

YANO, VINCENT H. State Senator, Chairman Ways and Means Committee, formerly associated in law practice Councilman George M. Koga. Apparently representing self in rezoning to hotel-apartment.

Sources: Gwenfread E. Allen, ed., *Men and Women of Hawaii: A Biographical Directory of Noteworthy Men and Women of Hawaii* (Honolulu, 1966); Betty F. Buker, ed., *Men and Women of Hawaii 1972: A Biographical Directory of Noteworthy Men and Women of Hawaii* (Honolulu, 1972); Department of Commerce and Consumer Affairs, Business Registration Division; State of Hawaii, Legislative Reference Bureau, *Directory of State, County and Federal Officials: Supplement to Guide to Government in Hawaii* (published occasionally, most recently annually); Hawaii State Archives; Honolulu City Council subject indices (1968, 1969); Oahu telephone books yellow pages section on attorneys (various years); miscellaneous references in newspapers and periodicals.

It was normal for major developers in the Democratic 1950s and 1960s to have some connection with one or more councilmen. It was normal for councilmen to have some private involvement with development. And usually, the higher up a councilman was in the Council's power structure, the more likely he was to be investing in land or working privately for development interests.

Matsuo Takabuki was perhaps the most notable example, but there were others:

Herman G. P. Lemke (on the Board of Supervisors/Council 1955–1968) was an accountant. One of his early clients was John Burns, before Burns won public office (he was running a small liquor store). In 1954 Burns encouraged Lemke to run for supervisor and Lemke, to his amazement, won in that Democratic landslide year.[25]

Lemke became, along with Takabuki, one of the leaders on the Council, and during his last term, 1965–1968, served as Council chairman.

Lemke's clients included Joe Pao & Associates, and Pao's Island Construction Co. and Hawaiian Pacific Industries Inc. Pao was one of Oahu's principal land developers from the beginning of the building boom to his death in 1977. Lemke also did work for Kamaaina Realty Inc.; Island Lumber Co.; realtor Marion Blair; paint store owner James K. Woolsey; the Albert Lovett Co., a developer; Konini Corporation, a developer; Fearon-Cross Inc., a real-estate brokerage and management firm; Sans Souci Inc., which managed a Diamond Head cooperative apartment building; and two construction workers unions, PECA-IBEW (electrical workers) and PAMCAH-UA (plumbers and pipe fitters). In addition Lemke was a trustee, along with Chinn Ho, of the Mark A. Robinson Trust Estate, a medium-sized landowner.[26]

Councilman Clesson Y. Chikasuye (1957–1974), was Finance Committee Chairman 1965–1968, and Council vice-chairman 1971–1974. As an attorney, Chikasuye represented at various times First Financial Savings & Loan Association and Allied Masons Inc. He was a shareholder in Midtown Development Corporation and a director of Aloha Airlines, along with developers Sheridan C. F. Ing, Hung Wo Ching, Clarence T. C. Ching, and K. J. Luke. Aloha Airlines depended heavily on the tourist industry, a key element in development.[27]

Chikasuye at one stage shared office space with Democratic politician O. Vincent Esposito, who in 1960 successfully represented developer Charles J. Pietsch Jr. in his application to have land in Waialae-Kahala rezoned to build the Kahala Hilton Hotel. Chikasuye voted to approve the application, which passed unanimously.[28] Chikasuye was one of only two Council incumbents beaten in elections in the 1970s, losing to Marilyn Bornhorst in 1974. His loss may have been based in part on publicity surrounding a City Ethics Commission ruling that he acted unethically by receiving a fee from a developer in 1973 and then, without disclosing this, voting to approve the developer's project, the Makana Kai Marina. The fee was only $245, and Chikasuye was not representing the developer but a small property owner who had a dispute with the developer. The developer agreed to pay Chikasuye's fee, however. Then Chikasuye reportedly denied receiving it. In the public eye the denial was perhaps the worst part.[29]

Ben F. Kaito (1961–1970) was a leading member of the Takabuki-Lemke group that controlled the Council during the 1950s and 1960s. Immediately after Kaito was elected to the Council, he became vice-chairman of the pivotal Public Works Committee, which processed rezonings and capital improvement expenditures. In 1964 he became chairman of this committee, and he held the chair until retiring from the Council in 1970.

Kaito was elected to the Council from leeward and central Oahu. An attorney, he shared offices 1962–1965 with leeward legislator James H. Wakatsuki. Wakatsuki, elected to the House in 1959, rose in the mid-1970s to be speaker.

In the Kaito years, Wakatsuki first petitioned the Council on a land matter in 1962. The city planning director had denied industrial zoning for an individual on Kamaile St. near McKinley High School in Honolulu, and Wakatsuki successfully urged reversal of the denial.[30]

Wakatsuki's clients included the Horitas, a leeward-based family which by the late 1960s had become one of Oahu's largest developers, especially of leeward land. According to the Council's subject indices, Wakatsuki first appeared before the Council on behalf of the Horitas in 1964. In 1967 he obtained residential rezoning for them on Kaneohe Bay Drive over the strong objections of many area residents. In 1968, on Wakatsuki's application for the Horitas, the Council rezoned some Kalihi land for apartments. Wakatsuki also made an appearance in 1969 for Star Markets Ltd., of which he was then secretary.[31]

From 1970 onwards, Kaito was in partnership with former city deputy corporation counsel Lincoln J. Ishida. During Kaito's last year as a councilman, and just after Ishida resigned his city job, Ishida represented Heeia Development Co. before the Council. Heeia Development had as one general partner Mitsuyuki Kido, himself a former city supervisor and state legislator.[32]

Upon Kaito's retirement from the Council in 1970, he was tapped to work for the State a number of times: as a Health Department hearing officer, a special deputy state attorney general, a labor arbitrator, and a *per diem* district court judge.[33] He also served on a city charter review commission.

George M. Koga, vice-chairman of the Council 1969–1971, chairman 1971–1975, and vice-chairman again 1975–1978, was a moderately active property investor. Koga told a reporter that in 1968 he obtained from Salt Lake developer Clarence Ching an option on six adjacent parcels. In 1971 Koga exercised the option. Koga also bought and sold individual condominium units in buildings such as the Chateau Waikiki, the Sakura in Nuuanu, the Waikiki Keoni Ana Apartments, and the Marco Polo. His wife was half-owner of Ritz Stores, and also owned several apparently small properties around Oahu.[34]

Koga, an attorney, at various times in the 1960s was associated in the practice of law with prominent Democratic politician Vincent H. Yano, and with Dick Yin Wong, then a part-time state judge. In 1968 after they were no longer associated, Yano came before the Council, successfully seeking hotel zoning, and in 1970 seeking a permit for a labor union building in Kalihi. (Yano himself had extensive personal interests in development, serving, for example, as a director of Camacho Realty Ltd. in the early 1960s.) The firm of Wong, Lo & Koga in 1965 represented a property owner seeking commercial zoning in Manoa. The successor firm of Lo, Youth & Ikazaki in the early 1970s represented Headrick Development Co. in rezoning Melemanu Woodlands.[35]

George Akahane was generally regarded as the single most powerful councilman in the 1970s. First elected in 1970, he held the Planning & Zoning Committee chairmanship during most of his tenure, and was Council chairman 1975–1976. His private investments on the public record were small, though all within the Horita family orbit. *Honolulu Star-Bulletin* writer Stirling Morita gave details in 1978: "A longtime Horita friend, Akahane bought his old Waipahu home from a Horita *hui* [HSM Ventures in 1968]. He sold it back to another Horita *hui* [Oceanview Ventures in 1975]. He bought his [current] Newtown Estates home from Oceanview Ventures, had a three-year investment until 1971 in a Horita general partnership [Tampa Investments], and bought a Nuuanu condominium through a Horita associate [Kenneth Nakamura, in 1973]." In 1976 Akahane, stating that he was acting as a nominee, or front, for someone else, sold a unit in the Marco Polo condominium to the Horitas.[36]

Akahane at times used the legal services of the former law associate of Matsuo Takabuki, Kinji Kanazawa, who was a general partner in the Horitas' Oceanview Ventures.[37]

Akahane worked for some years in the late 1970s for State Savings & Loan Association, which lent extensively to land investors and developers as well as to individual home buyers. Its customers included builder Jack H. Ujimori; Sunny Investments Inc.; Hanson Development Co. Ltd.; Central Pacific Development Corporation; Ahuimanu Joint Venture; Pearlridge Square Development Ltd.; and Real Estate Finance Corporation. For a time in the early 1980s Akahane worked for Royal Contracting Co. Ltd.[38]

What the Horitas were to George Akahane, Hirotoshi Yamamoto was to Councilman Rudy Pacarro. Pacarro was within the Council's ruling group for most of the 1970s. He was floor leader 1972–1975, chairman of the Planning & Zoning Committee 1975–1977, and Council chairman 1979–1982. Yamamoto, an active investor and developer, was head of a group of "Manoa" companies: Manoa Finance Co. Inc.; Manoa Investment Co. Inc.; and Manoa Realty Inc. Pacarro has said that Yamamoto got him started in politics, encouraging his successful run for the state House in 1962. Pacarro worked for Manoa Realty, and Pacarro has said that Yamamoto helped him establish his own firms in real estate and finance: Real Estate Hale Inc. and First Filipino Finance Corporation.[39]

Most of Pacarro's known property dealings were with Yamamoto. For example, Yamamoto in 1966 sold Pacarro, State Sen. Nadao Yoshinaga, and another individual a 21-acre parcel of land in the back of Kalihi Valley, which the three resold in 1971 to Shigeru Horita and a business associate.[40]

Over the years, Pacarro borrowed money from Yamamoto. Manoa Investment helped Pacarro start a laundromat in Waianae in 1975. In 1977 Pacarro sold his penthouse condominium at Salt Lake to Manoa Investment.[41]

Pacarro in 1975, along with Hawaii Midas Muffler franchise holder Edward K. Kageyama, leased commercial space in Kukui Plaza. This city redevelopment project soon came under withering criticism for such activities as circumventing agreements to sell a certain number of its residential units to moderate income buyers, instead selling to people connected with the city administration. There was no evidence of Pacarro receiving preferential treatment, however.[42]

Toraki Matsumoto, first elected to the Council in 1968, was in leadership during most of his tenure, chairing finance-type committees most of the time. His brother, Takeo, was an architect retained by such companies as Makaha Reef Inc., Makiki Venture Project, and the company that owned the Pacific Hotel. Their father occasionally invested in real estate or development-related ventures, such as Land Research & Investment Co.[43]

Daniel G. Clement Jr., first elected as a Republican and later a Democrat, was an estate planner with Bishop Trust Co., of which he was a vice-president throughout his years on the Council (1972–1982). Bishop Trust was a major manager of real estate in Hawaii. During his last term Clement chaired the Finance Committee and for a time was Council vice-chairman.[44]

Andrew K. Poepoe, who served 1979–1982, worked in management with Dole Co. Dole's parent company, Castle & Cooke, had another subsidiary that since the 1960s had been developing its extensive land holdings in central Oahu. Although a Republican, Poepoe was for a time chairman of the Zoning Committee.[45]

Hiram L. Fong Jr., Republican, who served during the same period as Poepoe, had probably the most pervasive ties with development of all Council members of his time. Through stock ownership, directorships, and as an attorney, Fong was closely tied with the financial and real estate empire of his father, former US Sen. Hiram L. Fong Sr. Prior to his election Hiram Jr. appeared before the Council as an attorney in an effort to preserve a building permit for the Hobron, a Waikiki highrise. Fong's law firm represented clients such as Finance Realty, Highway Construction Co., the engineering firm of Alfred Yee & Associates, the Ala Moana Hotel, Finance Factors, and Royal Development Co. Fong sat on the boards of companies such as American Security Bank, which lent extensively in the development field. Although a Republican, Fong appeared to work moderately well with the majority Democrats.[46]

Councilmen who did not hold top leadership positions tended to be less active and less well-connected in development than were Council leaders. There was also some tendency of this sort regarding councilmen altogether outside the governing blocs, though in this latter, wider group it was not always the case that not being in a governing group correlated with not being involved in some way with real estate.

For example, Yoshiro Nakamura (1961–1968), never greatly influential on the Council, was an officer, director, and attorney for Crown Waipahu Inc., which built apartments.[47]

Also, James Y. Shigemura (1971–1974), an attorney, represented Makaha Surfside Development Co. while in the Legislature but before becoming a councilman. In those years he was also co-counsel with Senate President David C. McClung on behalf of Signal Oil & Gas Co. in its proposal to build a large resort at South Kohala on the Big Island. Shigemura was solidly a part of the Democratic establishment; while a councilman in 1974 he was appointed a state district court judge. But during his Council tenure Shigemura never held an important committee chair, an apparent indication of his not having been in top leadership on the Council.[48]

Other council members not in top leadership but who had some involvement with real estate included Eugene F. Kennedy (1957–1958, 1965–1968), a Republican who was himself a realtor and small developer; Republican Mary George (1969–1974), later a state senator, whose husband was a real estate broker; Brian L. Casey (1969–1970), who was a limited partner in Clarence Ching's International Development Co., which was then developing Salt Lake. Frank W. C. Loo (1971–1982) had a small mortgage company, and made real estate investments, as in the Holiday Gardens Apartments, Kaumualii Park Apartments, and beachfront property at Mokuleia. In the late 1960s while a deputy city clerk, Wilbert S. "Sandy" Holck (1975–1978) invested in apartment-zoned land at Salt Lake.[49]

Council members without obvious involvement in real estate were also those who most seldom held leadership posts or posts of real substance; for example Kekoa D. Kaapu (1965–1968, 1975–1978), Herman J. Wedemeyer (1969–1970), and Charles M. Campbell (1969–1970). Marilyn Bornhorst, first elected in 1974, was a dissident member who ultimately became Council chairman, though in her case the chair was stripped of most of its usual prerogatives of power.[50] On the evidence, then, there was a correlation, if not a perfect one, between power on the Council, stature within the wider political establishment, and a propensity to be involved with real estate and development.

*   *   *

One of the most remarkable cases of intertwining business, family and political relationships involving the Board of Supervisors and Council in the Democratic years was that of the Chinese-Hawaiian Heen family.

As a family the Heens were virtually everywhere in government and all over the Democratic political map.

There were two Heens on the Board of Supervisors or Council at different times, Ernest N. Sr. (1949-1950, 1959-1964), and his son, Walter M. (1969-1972).

Ernest Sr. was a leader of the Democratic Party before the Burns era. By 1950 he was a "right wing Democrat," according to the *Honolulu Star-Bulletin*, opposing the Burns and ILWU people who were becoming strong in the party. He was Honolulu City Clerk 1933-1944, and served in the Senate 1945-1948. For a few years in the early 1950s he was director of the territory's Department of Public Welfare. He died in 1965.[51]

Walter was Council chairman for two years. He was later appointed, in this sequence: a state district court judge, state circuit court judge, United States attorney, temporary federal district court judge, and Hawaii Intermediate Court of Appeals judge. Prior to being a councilman Walter had been in the House and Senate for a total of 10 years. In 1962 he was named Outstanding Young Man of the Year by the Junior Chamber of Commerce. That year he was also Oahu County Chairman of the Democratic Party.[52]

If Ernest Sr. was on the right wing of the Democratic Party by the 1950s, Walter was to the left. During the House speakership fight in 1959 Walter was part of the liberal Gill-Esposito group, like his father standing opposed to the Burns-ILWU faction, though from a different orientation. In the 1960s Walter at times took extremely liberal positions, supporting, for example, the presidential candidacy of Vietnam dove Eugene McCarthy in 1968, a most unusual thing for a successful Hawaii politician to do at that time. In the late 1960s Walter's name was mentioned as a possible running mate for Tom Gill in Gill's 1970 attempt to unseat Gov. Burns. But Walter did not burn bridges to the Burns side of the party. In an interview for this book Walter said that by the time he was on the Council (1969), he and Burns were "quite close." This helped account for Walter's string of Democratic political appointments to state judgeships and high federal positions beginning in 1972.[53]

Another of Ernest Sr.'s sons, Ernest Jr., was a state representative from 1963 to 1970, and for a time afterwards worked on contract for the State Department of Land and Natural Resources in developing a park in Kahana Valley in windward Oahu.

One of Ernest Sr.'s two daughters, Marion H., was active in the Gill wing of the Democratic Party, in 1962 coordinating Gill's successful congressional campaign. Marion's husband, attorney Alvin T. Shim, was for a time Gill's law partner, and was also politically active. For many years Shim's law firm represented the large white-collar government workers union, the Hawaii Government Employees Association (HGEA). Marion herself held various government jobs.[54]

The achievements of Ernest Sr.'s family were diverse: his other daughter, Claire, in 1951 was Miss Hawaii.[55]

Ernest Sr. had an older brother, William H. Sr., who was in the Senate 1926-1957, serving as Senate president his last two sessions. He had previously been a circuit court judge and Honolulu city attorney. William Sr. for many years prior to and at the start of the "Democratic revolution" was a major power within Hawaii's Democratic Party. Like his brother Ernest Sr., he was toward the end of his career part of the Democratic old guard. He died in 1973.

One of William Sr.'s law partners, Robert G. Dodge, served as vicechairman and often chief spokesman for the Honolulu Charter Commission, which drafted the charter that shifted effective land use power in city government to the Council. Two of William Sr.'s sons had state jobs. In the early 1960s, for example, William Jr. was a fiscal officer for the Department of Social Services, and Curtis N. was an analyst for the Department of Budget and Review.[56]

The Heen family was also involved with land and development. Ernest Sr. was a licensed real estate broker from 1947 until his death in 1965. He also advised and represented development interests, as when the Yoshikawa Development Co. in 1958 offered to sell the city for playground use a parcel within the company's Waipio subdivision.[57] Ernest Jr. held a real estate salesman's license from 1956. From about 1960 to 1968 he worked for Centex-Trousdale Co., mainland developers operating in Hawaii, serving as project coordinator much of that time. The company was one of Oahu's major homebuilders in those years, as principal developer of Harold K.L. Castle's extensive holdings in windward Oahu. After leaving Centex-Trousdale, Ernest Jr. was a consultant to a number of other windward developers.[58] Walter's law practice included handling miscellaneous development matters. He also represented development-related unions of electrical workers and plumbers. In 1969 he filed statements with the City Clerk indicating he represented the "PECA-IBEW (electricians) Administrative Office in collection cases against contractors," and the trustees of the PAMCAH (plumbers) Trust Funds in similar matters. Walter also had *hui* investments. When running for Congress in 1964 he disclosed that in 1960 he had invested $10,000 in WSL Associates, and in 1961 $1,500 in Delpy Developers Associates.[59]

William Sr., during the years his brother and nephew were councilmen, was senior partner in a law firm that had an extraordinary range of clients and connections, concentrating somewhat in the Chinese community. In particular the firm represented Chinn Ho's various companies. William in addition sat on various Ho boards, such as Capital Investment Co., which was the Waianae coast's major developer in the 1960s and 1970s, and which participated in building the Ilikai Hotel in Waikiki. Also as a Ho associate William Sr. in the early 1960s became an officer and director of a company that owned the *Honolulu Star-Bulletin*, plus a television and radio station. This law firm also occasionally represented such old-line concerns and people as the Hawaiian Trust Co., and in 1962 then-Republican businessman Kenneth F. Brown's Pacific Network Inc. The firm also represented miscellaneous developers, such as Trade Wind Development Co. in building a hotel in Waikiki, and Halemaumau Land Co. and Kanau Development Co. regarding a subdivision in Niu Valley on Oahu.[60]

The Heens' private-sector activity lapped over extensively into the Council, including while two family members were councilmen:

As mentioned, Ernest Sr. in 1958, just before taking a seat on the Board of Supervisors, as a real estate broker represented Yoshikawa Development Co. with the city government. Subsequently as a councilman in 1961 he voted to approve a mayor's recommendation that Yoshikawa be reimbursed by the city for one-third of the cost of installing street lights within a subdivision.[61] (Coincidentally, the lawyer who represented Yoshikawa before the City from about 1959 to 1963 was future Council chairperson Patsy T. Mink. Mink was elected to Congress in 1964 and served through 1976. In 1982 she won a Council seat.[62])

Ernest Sr.'s most politically prominent sons, Ernest Jr. and Walter, each represented development interests before the Council during their father's Council tenure, as did Ernest Sr.'s brother's law firm. Ernest Sr. in general participated in all of these Council matters involving his family.

Ernest Jr. in those years appeared many times as spokesman for Centex-Trousdale. On one occasion in 1963 the question arose as to whether it was proper for the father to vote, given the son's interest. The *Honolulu Advertiser* reported that "Councilman Heen has previously stated that he saw no conflict of interest in the situation. He [also] said he didn't think any father should stand in the way of his son's career."[63]

The occasion was that of a possible City condemnation of Kawainui Marsh in Windward Oahu, where Centex-Trousdale planned a 4,000-lot subdivision. A number of conservation groups strongly supported government purchase in order to preserve the area as a habitat for wetland wildlife, also for open space and flood control.

Initially Ernest Sr. openly opposed condemnation. In 1962 he voted against a resolution directing the mayor to apply for federal funds to help the city with the purchase, though the resolution passed 5-4. In 1963, with the rest of the Council split 4-4 on a bill to authorize condemnation, and with the spotlight on Ernest Sr., he successfully moved for deferral. A small storm ensued, with focus on the father-son relationship. For whatever reason, Ernest Sr. subsequently voted for condemnation. (In 1964 the city bought 750 acres at Kawainui, and later bought more.)[64]

If Ernest Sr. routinely voted on matters involving his sons without declaring a conflict of interest, for some reason he did declare a conflict on one occasion when his brother, William Sr., had an interest. The matter concerned a height variance in 1960 for the Ilikai Hotel. William Sr. was a director of and shareholder in Capital Investment Co., the hotel builder. Council rules permitted a councilman who declared a conflict to then vote anyway, which Ernest Sr. did. The variance was approved unanimously by those voting. (Councilman Matsuo Takabuki also declared a conflict. He was the Ilikai's attorney, and he said he also had an involvement with a corporation which might later take part in the project. Takabuki did not vote.)[65]

Ernest Sr. also voted on other matters in which family members had interests, as follows:

The Council in 1961 concluded work on a general plan for the Waianae coast. Ernest's son Walter, then a state representative, and Walter's law associate, Sidney I. Hashimoto, a former representative who two years later was appointed Gov. Burns' first Department of Regulatory Agencies director, between them had half a dozen clients owning 12 parcels within the affected area. Walter and Hashimoto asked the Council to designate all 12 commercial. In general all were in areas that made commercial use logical. Ten of the 12 were so classified, with Councilman Heen voting in favor of the general plan that contained these classifications.[66]

Also included in the plan as adopted were miscellaneous urban zonings for Chinn Ho's large holdings in Makaha. Councilman Heen's brother William Sr. was involved as a director of Ho's Capital Investment Co., the entity that oversaw Ho's Waianae Coast concerns. William Sr. was also president of Ho's Waianae Development Co., a water utility outfit set up to facilitate overall development. In addition William Sr.'s law firm at times represented Ho's businesses, though the on-the-record appearances for Ho before the Council in 1961 on the Waianae general plan were by Morio Omori, who was sharing law offices with Councilman Takabuki.[67]

Other instances of overlapping family/Council activities during Ernest Sr.'s tenure were Walter in 1961 representing Shada Pflueger Bryan in an apparently unsuccessful attempt to rezone for apartments an acre on the ocean in Wailupe; Walter in 1962 successfully petitioning the Council to ask the city administration to issue a building permit to an individual; William Sr.'s law firm in 1962 representing Kenneth F. Brown's Pacific Network Inc. in a dispute with a Henry J. Kaiser company over coaxial cable TV lines being installed in parts of east Oahu; the firm in 1962 representing general contractor Moses Akiona Ltd. in an apparently unsuccessful attempt to rezone a half acre in Kalihi; and the firm in 1963 representing Akiona with regard to several city construction contracts in Palolo Valley.[68]

When Walter served on the Council (1969-1972) there were similar overlaps. In 1970 he voted "yes" on a zoning code amendment for the Imperial Hotel in Waikiki, whose attorney was Sidney Hashimoto, Walter's former law associate from about 1959 to 1965. In 1972 Walter voted for apartment zoning on Dole St. near the university. Here the lawyer was another former associate, Ronald Y.C. Lee. Walter's uncle's law firm in 1970 represented an individual in selling an oceanfront lot at Diamond Head to the city for a park; Walter voted in favor of the appropriation.[69]

In an interview for this book Walter Heen said he saw nothing ethically improper about participating in these matters. It should be noted, furthermore, that most Council matters involving the Heens which were researched for this book did not succeed or fail on just one vote, a Heen vote—most were unanimous or decided by wide margins.

What these numerous ties indicated was that the Hawaii power structure as modified by the Democrats was still small and close-knit, peopled by those who worked for and with each other in a variety of ways over the years. In the process many interconnections developed.

In such a situation it followed that hiring or putting on a board of directors a councilman's son/brother/uncle/law associate would tend to facilitate getting things done. Such a person was *ipso facto* an insider, often a decision-maker who could get the ear of at least one of the other decision-makers involved with the matter at hand. As Walter Heen put it, when interviewed for this book, he and his former law associates "remained personal friends" even after they went their separate ways in law. When his former associates later came before him as a councilman, "I would have to say their statements would be accepted at face value [by me]." At times such acceptance could make a difference in the outcome of a question, particularly given, in turn, interconnections among the councilmen themselves. Walter Heen, for example, in the mid-1950s had been a roommate at Georgetown University Law Center with fellow-councilman George Koga, and had been friends since childhood with fellow-councilman Ben Kaito. In, say, 1969, Heen chaired the Council, Koga was vice-chairman and floor leader, and Kaito chaired the Public Works Committee, which handled land use, among other things. In such a situation, if someone had a development project needing Council approval, retaining a former law associate of Heen's could be a definite advantage.[70] This would be the case whether or not the client knew in advance and in detail of the personal-professional interconnections between Council members and the attorneys in private practice who appeared before the Council on real estate matters.

*   *   *

Possibly the most significant case of intertwining family connections involving the two senior Heen brothers, Ernest and William, came during an early skirmish in what became Hawaii's biggest battle over development in the 1960s: whether to build a high-rise resort complex between Diamond Head and the ocean.

Unlike the Ilikai situation the Heen private interest here was apparently never publicly declared or known.

In June 1961 the City Council and the City Planning Commission were simultaneously considering different measures bearing on development near Diamond Head.

The Council was working on a bill concerning building densities in hotel-apartment zones Oahu-wide. The Commission was processing a proposed resolution to expand the hotel-apartment zone near Diamond Head from the existing 11 acres to 17.

During Council deliberations the Diamond Head area came up. Ought there to be more hotel-apartment zoning there? Since the Planning Commission was then reviewing that very question, Councilman Heen took the occasion to send a signal to the Commission. He moved that the Council state a general position on the area's hotel-apartment zoning, namely to "look with favor" on expanding it from 11 to 40 acres, in an area he verbally outlined. This was 23 acres more than the Commission was considering. The motion carried. It did not have the effect of actual rezoning, but it did suggest what the Council might do when the matter would later come before it.[71] Loud protests erupted from conservationists, and from some well-to-do *haole* residents for whom parts of the extremely lovely area between Diamond Head and the ocean were a kind of privileged residential preserve.

In the hubbub it was pointed out that Councilman Heen's own home was within the 23 additional acres. In other words, if the Council actually did change the zoning to hotel-apartment as Heen suggested, he stood to increase the value of his own real estate substantially.

The house was on an 8,000-square-foot lot at the foot of Makalei Heights. Elizabeth L. Heen had bought the property in 1943. Following her death in 1946 Ernest Sr. had received a one-seventh interest from her estate. Over the ensuing years he bought up other fractional interests, including four 1955-1959. As of 1961 he had a roughly one-half interest.[72]

Although there was some grumbling among development opponents about Heen's possible conflict of interest, nevertheless there was nothing hidden about his potential financial benefit.

On the other hand there was a potential benefit to his brother that was not generally known.

Just five months before Ernest Sr.'s Council motion, William Sr. obtained an interest in an oceanfront parcel a block away from Ernest Sr.'s house, also in the 23 additional acres.

Back in January 1961 a company called Market Place Ltd. traded property outside the Diamond Head area to Texaco Inc., taking in exchange a 55,894-square-foot lot just below the seaward face of Diamond Head crater. William Sr. was a vice-president of Market Place, an owner of 9% of the stock and a co-trustee of another 84%. The Diamond Head lot was already among the choicest real estate anywhere in Hawaii; if it got hotel-apartment zoning it would be hundreds of percent more valuable.[73]

There was no public disclosure of this trade in connection with Councilman Heen's motion, though it is conceivable he never knew about it. Nor apparently was it ever picked up by the media or by opponents of development around Diamond Head. At most there was a mention in the *Honolulu Star-Bulletin* several months after the Council action, that William was affiliated with a family called Otani in a business that was unrelated to Diamond Head, and that the Otanis owned land in the 23-acre area.[74] Market Place Ltd. was an Otani company, though Market Place was not mentioned in the *Star-Bulletin* story.

As it turned out the area that included the Heen home and the Market Place land did not ultimately get the zoning.

But Councilman Heen's motion that the Council "look with favor" on the construction of apartments on the seaward face of Diamond Head turned out to be an early event in the biggest fight over development in Hawaii in the 1960s.

* * *

Immediately at stake in the Diamond Head fight was the southern face of an extinct volcanic tuff cone, one that looked to Hawaiians like the head of an *ahi* (tuna), hence *Lae-ahi* in Hawaiian, later spelled Leahi. It acquired its *haole* name early in the period of western contact when British sailors found calcite crystals there which they mistook for diamonds.[75]

Behind the controversy stirred up by the prospect of development was the overall economic and social history of Diamond Head and Waikiki.

Anchoring Waikiki's eastern extremity, Diamond Head overlooked a sunny but not-too-hot area of white sand beaches and gentle surf, favored for rest and recreation since the days when Hawaiians alone inhabited the Islands.

Waikiki began to develop as a western-style resort toward the end of the nineteenth century, and became twentieth-century Hawaii's tourism center, holding as of the mid-1980s about half of all the Islands' hotel rooms.[76]

As Hawaii became integrated into world travel networks, Diamond Head became its best-known sight, a famous landmark, virtually the symbol of the Islands.

At about the same time that Waikiki was getting started as a resort, Kapiolani Park was developed at its east end, in the morning shadow of Diamond Head.[77]

The location of the park meant that future resort facilities were to be located in the central and western sectors of Waikiki, except for a small strip of hotels and apartments near Diamond Head, between the eastern end of the park and the ocean.

The furor over Diamond Head that reached a peak in the 1960s focused on whether this strip should extend east along the coast to the narrowest point between Diamond Head and the sea, and slightly up the crater's southwest slope.

Altogether about 40 acres were at issue, including by the 1960s existing as well as proposed new hotel-apartment areas.

In or near the disputed 40 acres were some of Hawaii's most expensive homes, including the residence of Walter F. and Louise G. Dillingham, for many years Hawaii's social "first family." The lavish Dillingham estate was called "La Pietra" after an Italian villa in which the couple was married in 1910. (After the Dillinghams died, La Pietra was given in 1964 to the elite private school, Punahou, and in turn in 1968 to Hawaii School for Girls.)[78]

At its nearest point toward Waikiki the contested 40 acres started on the ocean, just east of the Waikiki Aquarium and the World War I War Memorial Park with its now-decrepit Natatorium, a salt-water swimming pool surrounded by a seawall and concrete bleachers.

Immediately to the east of these facilities was a popular local beach, between one and two acres in size, called Sans Souci, after a hotel by that name first opened nearby in 1893.[79]

From there the area ran eastward about a mile along the ocean toward a Coast Guard lighthouse on the Kuilei Cliffs, which was due south of Diamond Head and at its nearest point to the sea.

About halfway between Sans Souci Beach and the cliffs, just to the east of Kapiolani Park, the 40 acres bulged inland several hundred yards, running slightly up the slopes of Diamond Head, taking in two subdivisions from the 1920s. Diamond Head Terrace, with about 100 lots, had been created in

1924 by the Henry Waterhouse Trust Co. In 1927 Bishop Trust Co. created Makalei Tract, also known as Makalei Heights, with about 20 lots.[80]

Diamond Head Terrace was a subdivision of relatively small lots, generally with no views to speak of, except for the lots on the ocean and the inlandmost lots on the lower slopes of Diamond Head. Except for the people on the choice real estate of the slopes, Terrace residents in the main were middle class. After some ambivalence in the late 1950s, Terrace home owners in the 1960s came to constitute a nearly solid pro-development bloc.

An exception here were Terrace residents living higher up the slopes, and the Dillinghams who lived nearby. Most or all of these people had wonderful views of the ocean, the city of Honolulu, and west Oahu. In general this group opposed high-rise development.

Makalei Heights was also higher up the slopes than most of Diamond Head Terrace. Lots were larger and views generally excellent. Residents were fewer and considerably wealthier than most in Diamond Head Terrace. For home owners in Makalei Heights, as for people like the Dillinghams, there was little incentive to favor hotel-apartment zoning anywhere in the vicinity. As far as their own financial interests were concerned, most in Makalei Heights were already well-off. Why should they push for rezoning so they could sell their lot at a profit to some developer? Even if there were big profits to be made, they would lose their home, meaning they would have to move out and live somewhere else. But where in Hawaii—indeed where in the world—could they find a place nicer to live than Diamond Head? And if they looked beyond their own lot boundary, high-rise construction on the oceanfront would ruin their view. Not surprisingly, residents of the heights generally lined up against high-rise development anywhere in the area.

                              *   *   *

The first hotel-apartment zoning anywhere in the 40 acres came in 1940 when the Honolulu Planning Commission approved a 6.7-acre piece between Sans Souci and the Elks Club, about a hundred yards from the western boundary of Diamond Head Terrace. In 1942 the Commission added 1.7 acres right at the boundary, leaving unzoned 1.8 acres between the 1.7 and the 6.7 acres. Then in 1946 the Commission backfilled, zoning this third piece for hotel-apartment use also.[81]

By 1946, then, the entire strip from Sans Souci Beach to the border of Diamond Head Terrace was zoned hotel-apartment.

Diamond Head Terrace itself was the next place in the firing line for development.

From 1947 through 1957 a half-dozen or so rezoning applications were filed for hotels and apartments in Diamond Head Terrace on or near the ocean.

The Planning Commission denied them all. Reasons usually cited by the Commission were that this was a residential area and should be left as such, and that roads in the area were too narrow to support more intensive development. Some residents who protested development also said the beauty of

Diamond Head would be desecrated by any more medium and high-rise buildings nearby.[82]

In 1957 the owners of most of the three acres constituting the Diamond Head Terrace oceanfront lots applied as a group to the Commission for hotel-apartment classification.

This was the first highly controversial application. It more or less split the wider Diamond Head Terrace community. It also generated petitions and letters to the Commission in numbers that foretold tumult in the coming decade.

The Commission turned down the group application. But at the same time the Commission indicated it thought the area proper for hotel-apartment use, and invited individual landowners to re-apply if and when they had definite plans.[83]

Immediately Ruddy F. Tongg, an owner who had been a spokesman for the Diamond Head Terrace oceanfront group, made an application, and in late 1957 he was given approval for what became the Kainalu cooperative apartment building, at the extreme eastern end of the Diamond Head Terrace oceanfront lots.[84]

This approval caused the hotel-apartment zone that in 1940 had begun at Sans Souci Beach to leapfrog from the extreme west end of Diamond Head Terrace to the extreme east.

People who in those years opposed hotels and apartments in this general area had been especially against the Kainalu for the foot-in-the-door effect it might have. Their worry turned out to be well founded.

Thereafter, in 1959, the Commission allowed four more projects in Diamond Head Terrace. Early in 1961, by which time zoning authority had shifted to the City Council, a fifth was allowed. (This one, as things eventually turned out after all the coming battles, was the last ever allowed, and the only one not on the ocean.)[85]

Diamond Head Terrace's oceanfront land was now zoned and used about half for single family homes, half hotel-apartment.

* * *

If the Diamond Head Terrace community was split in 1957, thereafter it never really was. A realtor about 1959 proposed that the lot owners band together and jointly offer a long-term lease to a developer. As of mid-1960 the owners of about 82% of the lots had agreed. In the controversies of the 1960s most Diamond Head Terrace residents favored rezoning their property and selling out.[86]

On the other hand the minority of wealthy, old-*haole* Diamond Head residents such as the Dillinghams, generally living up on the slopes, saw wisdom in preservation. Thereafter they formed the most consistent anti-development bloc among the residents.

A third group remained split throughout. They owned the oceanfront property on Diamond Head Road just below the crater's nearest point to the sea, *the* choicest land from a development standpoint. In this group *haoles* from Hawaii's old elite tended to oppose development, local-Asians and Portuguese favored it.

Adding it all up, among Diamond Head residents the most consistent factors in sorting out opponents of development from proponents were ethnicity and social class. Put simply if crudely: old-money *haoles* were most likely to be against development. Anybody else was likely to be for it.

Pro-development people argued that old families like the Walter Dillinghams were being dogs in the manger. They had it made already, and of course they wanted to stay put.

Anti-development residents, on the other hand, took the view that if their neighbors were prepared to sell out for profit and allow multi-story buildings so close to Hawaii's most famous landmark, well, then, they were grasping and entirely without a sense of history or esthetics.

The fact that families like the Walter Dillinghams constituted a major opposition group did present certain ironies. For example, in 1960, Walter's brother, Harold, sold a large Diamond Head oceanfront property, which had been his home, to Jiroichi Otani. Otani took up residence there and became active among the non-*haoles* seeking rezoning.[87]

Another active opponent of high-rises was Muriel Damon. Her husband's nephew, Samuel R. Damon, in 1957 as a trustee of the Damon Estate, had participated in selling 1,074 acres in Moanalua, containing a salt lake unique in Hawaii, to a local non-*haole* development group. Muriel and her husband, Cyril, had no part of the Damon Estate. But just the same this Damon family sale set the wheels in motion for Hawaii's other enormous development controversy of the 1960s—whether to land-fill most of the lake for a golf course which was to become a centerpiece for a very large complex of high-rise apartments. (The lake was eventually 86% filled, the golf course was constructed, and the apartments were built.)[88]

Then there was Walter Dillingham himself. Probably no other individual had done more to set the stage for the intensive development of Waikiki. In the 1920s he obtained a major contract from the territorial government to dredge and fill the wetlands of Waikiki, thus making possible the heavy urbanization of the post-World War II era. Dillingham had been able to look down on all this taking place from the wealthy seclusion of his home at La Pietra. Now intensive development was threatening to lap into his front yard.[89]

* * *

In 1961 the Planning Commission recommended, and in 1962 the Council approved, a general plan classification of hotel-apartment for the entire seven acres making up the portion of Diamond Head Terrace on the ocean side of Diamond Head Rd. This brought the total number of hotel-apartment acres to about 14.[90]

The day of the Council vote a suit was filed by three extremely wealthy *haole* women who were Diamond Head residents and property owners, together with a middle-class woman who lived in the Kainalu, all later to be joined by the Walter Dillinghams. They were represented by J. Russell

Cades, a partner in one of Hawaii's most prestigious law firms, whose clients included the Islands' largest businesses. They asked the court for an order prohibiting zoning that would implement the new Diamond Head Terrace general plan classification until the City adopted a general plan for the entire island of Oahu. The 1959 charter required that zoning be carried out only after a comprehensive general plan was prepared. No such plan existed, yet individual rezonings were occurring.

Cades put on evidence to the effect that the City frequently and at times somewhat arbitrarily rezoned land, without reference to an overall general community development plan.

Circuit Court Judge Ronald B. Jamieson found in favor of Cades' clients. In the existing ad-hoc approach to zoning Jamieson saw potential for bad planning and corruption. He wrote that if "zoning changes must conform to and implement a general plan . . . such changes will be less likely to be contrary to good planning and less likely to result from favoritism, personal interest, corruption or bribery."[91]

The then-Honolulu planning director, Frederick K.F. Lee, in an interview for this book indicated that one reason why there had been as yet no general plan was that councilmen were resisting the adoption of one. Lee believed they feared it would cut into their then-great leeway to rezone land. Councilmen, as did "all politicians, depended on contributions and votes," he said, and "if there was no plan," then in rezoning to please political supporters and contributors, "it would be happy days, here we go."[92]

Judge Jamieson in his order went beyond the seven acres at Diamond Head, and said that there would be no rezoning anywhere on Oahu until the City adopted a comprehensive general plan.

This was Hawaii's first major judicial decision on land use. It was also a remarkable and rather brave step for a judge to take at a time when most of the community at large, and certainly the political and business establishment, were strongly and uncritically pro-development.

The Hawaii Supreme Court in 1964 reversed Jamieson, saying he had gone too far when he included the entire island.[93]

By then, though, the City had adopted Oahu's first overall general plan.

In preparing the plan, the Planning Commission recommended that the seven acres on the ocean at Diamond Head, whose reclassification to hotel-apartment in 1962 had precipitated the suit, be made single-family residential.

The Council, however, by a 5-3 vote again made them high-density.

Again there were many who protested.

About this time a mayor's citizens advisory committee was appointed to study the entire Waikiki area. Development around Diamond Head was held in abeyance while the committee worked. The committee's report, completed in 1966, set the stage for the grand finale of the Diamond Head controversy.

The committee proposed that the western half of a strip of land just seaward of Diamond Head crater—bounded by Diamond Head Terrace on the west, Diamond Head Road on the north, the Coast Guard lighthouse on the east, and the ocean on the south—be designated for medium-density apartments. The committee proposed that the other half be left in residential use and ultimately acquired for a park. The entire Diamond Head Terrace subdivision was proposed for apartments.[94]

As this plan came to the Planning Commission and Council, several owners within the strip proposed that a 2,000-unit high-rise resort complex be built using the entire strip.

In their active lobbying for rezoning, these owners formed themselves into a non-profit corporation called the Diamond Head Improvement Association (DHIA).

The DHIA proposal had considerable appeal from the standpoint of economic development. It also had a good deal of political weight behind it.

But public opinion was strenuously against it. At the height of the controversy, for example, Councilmen Takabuki, Lemke, and Kaapu between them reported receiving 370 letters in the space of only a few days, most or all favoring preservation of Diamond Head.[95]

When the Council held a hearing on Diamond Head in 1967, some 500 people literally packed the Council chambers. Fifty-four spoke, most against development. On a land use issue Hawaii had never seen anything like it.

Moreover virtually every group imaginable opposed development; the opposition was one of the most diverse aggregations ever to agree on an environmental issue in Hawaii. Included were some of the wealthiest women of Hawaii and the US mainland; the ILWU, which only a few years before had been Marxist and revolutionary; a number of other labor organizations including the Honolulu Building and Construction Trades Council; conservation and beautification groups like the Conservation Council and the Garden Club; a community association from the sugar plantation town of Waipahu in Central Oahu; professional associations of planners, engineers and architects; and all kinds of chambers of commerce, including Japanese and Chinese.[96]

It was all so large and heated that the issue got into the national press. *Time* and *Newsweek* ran stories. The *New York Times* weighed in with an editorial favoring preservation.[97]

It had taken a massive threat to the unique landmark of Diamond Head to generate this degree of opposition to development. Perhaps no other site in Hawaii could have focused the issue so sharply.

The Council was virtually forced to pay attention. It did, and as a result, for the first time in the boom period, anti-development sentiment prevailed on a major issue.

The Council declined to adopt *any* further land use map at that time for Diamond Head, and made moves to start buying oceanfront land for park use.

In 1968 Gov. Burns was persuaded to nominate Diamond Head to the US Department of Interior as a National Natural Landmark, and it became so designated. This gave part of the long-disputed area a certain protected status. The practical result was that no more development would be permitted on the exterior of the crater or on a publicly owned strip of land extending to the sea.

Thereafter, until 1981, there was left intact the 1964 general plan classification of apartments for the seven acres of Diamond Head Terrace on the seaward side of Diamond Head Road. But the outcry against high-density construction had been so loud that apparently no landowner or developer ever made a serious attempt to implement that classification. Then in 1981 the City adopted a development plan covering Diamond Head that officially froze all apartment zoning at where it had been in 1961. This in essence permitted apartments only on those lots that already had them. A follow-up zoning map adopted in 1982 was identical in this respect to the 1981 development plan.[98]

In the mid-1980s, of the 40 acres that had been in dispute, the strip of land that was the western half, running from Sans Souci Beach to the eastern end of Diamond Head Terrace, held about 19 medium and high-rise structures. Zoning for these had all been approved 1940-1961. They were mostly cooperative apartments, though there were some condominium and hotel units too. Anchoring the end of the strip nearest Waikiki was the Colony Surf Hotel, which was a combination cooperative, condominium and hotel, with Michel's French restaurant on its ground floor overlooking the ocean. Next door on the Waikiki side were the Sans Souci cooperative and the New Otani Kaimana Beach Hotel. Next door on the other side were the Elks and Outrigger Canoe clubs. Holding down the extreme east end of the strip was the Kainalu cooperative. Near it on the ocean, sandwiched between buildings called 3019 Kalakaua Ave. and the Seabreeze Apartments, were still a number of single-family homes built a half century earlier.

*　*　*

Because development in Hawaii in the Democratic years was political in the fullest sense of the term, because development was so bound up with the socio-economic advancement that much of the "Democratic revolution" was about, thus did construction around Diamond Head involve the politically well-connected.

Two of those most interested in developing Diamond Head were part of the "revolution" on the business side of things—Chinn Ho and Ruddy Tongg.

Chinn Ho made history when in 1946 he organized an investment group to buy the 9,150-acre Waianae sugar plantation from the old Big Five firm of American Factors. This was the first time ever that a large piece of land had been sold by the old elite to a local-Asian. Ho's intent in part was to subdivide some of the land for sale to non-*haoles*.[99]

In the mid-1960s Ho, a Diamond Head property owner, became president of the organized pressure group, the Diamond Head Improvement Association, that urged high-rise development in the area.

Ruddy Tongg was another local Chinese businessman who made history just after World War II. In 1946 he organized a group of local-Asian businessmen to found an inter-island airline—the predecessor to Aloha Airlines. This was a progressive step in several respects. It challenged the monopoly on inter-island air travel then held by Hawaiian Airlines, which was owned by an old-money company. It was also anti-racist. Until 1946 Hawaiian had employed no local-Asians as pilots, stewardesses or at ticket counters. Tongg's venture helped put an end to such practices.[100]

In 1957 Tongg sought apartment zoning for several oceanfront parcels at the extreme east end of Diamond Head Terrace. This was part of a group application that covered all oceanfront lots within Diamond Head Terrace. The application had been preceded by a decade of solid denials for apartments in that area. Tongg himself had been turned down twice, in 1947 and 1954.

Attorneys representing Tongg in 1957 before city agencies were, first, Daniel K. Inouye, and later, Spark M. Matsunaga. Inouye had served in the 442d Regiment during World War II, Matsunaga in the 100th Battalion. By 1957 the two were territorial representatives and leaders of the Democratic Party. Inouye was House majority floor leader. Matsunaga chaired the powerful Judiciary Committee. (In 1959 Inouye was elected to Congress, and in 1962 to the US Senate, where he was still serving in 1985. Matsunaga was elected to Congress in 1962 and to the Senate in 1976. He too was still serving in 1985.)[101]

What difference the involvement of Inouye and Matsunaga made in this pivotal rezoning is impossible to know. At the same time it is improbable that it made no difference.

Tongg succeeded in getting approval for what became the Kainalu. As mentioned, this decision was highly precedential in terms of opening up the question of high-density development deep into areas around Diamond Head that had previously been off-limits.

Also involved with the Kainalu was David A. Benz, who in the late 1940s and early 1950s was part of the core group of the Democratic Party faction led by John Burns.[102]

Benz in the 1960s also handled much of the contact with city agencies for Kalakaua Land Development Inc. regarding various projects in the Diamond Head area.[103]

A Kalakaua Land Development lawyer was Matsuo Takabuki, who in 1961 did a merger for the company. As a councilman in 1962 Takabuki voted to approve the seven-acre general plan amendment covering the Diamond Head Terrace land on the ocean side of Diamond Head Road. Kala-kaua Land owned three of these lots and leased two others. The company planned to erect a twin-tower apartment building. Takabuki apparently made no disclosure of interest in connection with his vote.[104]

At the same time in 1957 that the city was deliberating on Ruddy Tongg's Kainalu, Manuel Gomes was also getting approval, and also taking some flak from nearby residents, for an eight-acre low-rise apartment project on the western slope of Diamond Head, in and around Pualei Circle. His realtor was George F. Centeio, then on the Planning Commission. Also involved as attorney and economic consultant, respectively, were Vincent H. Yano and John J. Hulten Sr., neither of whom were yet in politics but both of whom were elected to the Senate in 1962. US Sen. Hiram L. Fong's Finance Investment Co. actually did much of this development.[105]

Former territorial attorney general Ernest K. Kai from 1959 through about 1962 represented several projects in the Diamond Head area. His law partner was William H. Heen Sr., brother of Ernest Sr., on the Council 1959-1964, who in general voted on these matters concerning Kai. In 1970 Ernest's son Walter was on the Council and voted to appropriate money to buy for park use a Diamond Head oceanfront lot whose owner Kai was representing in dealing with the city.[106]

One item involving Kai was a bill in 1962 to keep alive a variance for a high-rise which, if built, would tower over the Sans Souci from behind, blocking its view of the mountains. Not extending the life of the variance would mean that anything built on the property would have to be much smaller. The Sans Souci manager protested the extension. At the time the Sans Souci accountant was Councilman Herman Lemke, who on the bill's first two readings was the only one to vote "no." The bill was later defeated unanimously.[107]

Attorney Genro Kashiwa in 1962 represented the Kaimana Hotel in successfully requesting the Council allow building permit applications filed by a certain date to avoid the requirements of a new ordinance on building heights and densities that was about to take effect. Councilman Takabuki and Kashiwa, as mentioned, were high school classmates, and served together in the 442nd Regiment. Takabuki had worked for a short time as a lawyer for Genro's brother Shiro, who was now State Attorney General.[108]

The most publicized case of a governmental-business overlap regarding Diamond Head was that of structural engineer Alfred A. Yee in 1965.

Yee was on the Planning Commission. He voted to recommend that the Council approve a cluster of 16-story apartment buildings planned by Oceanside Properties Inc. on an acre of land near the Kainalu.

Prior to the vote Yee disclosed that about two and a half years earlier he had worked on the project. The Commission chairman ruled that Yee could nevertheless vote now, which he did.

When making his disclosure Yee did not mention that at the time of the vote his firm had ongoing involvement with two other Oceanside projects. A reporter later discovered this, and Yee received heavy criticism for this non-disclosure from opponents of development and from newspaper editorial writers.[109]

On the Council, however, no mainstream Democrat took Yee to task. His only vocal critic there was the dissident Democrat Frank F. Fasi.

(Later, in the early 1970s while Fasi was mayor, Oceanside Properties, with the same president, Hal J. Hansen Jr., undertook a major city urban renewal project, Kukui Plaza. In 1977 in connection with this project Fasi was indicted for bribery. The indictment was obtained largely on the grand jury testimony of Hansen. Subsequently Hansen refused to testify at trial, causing the charge to be dismissed.)[110]

The Diamond Head Improvement Association (DHIA) had Kenneth F. Brown as vice-president and Chinn Ho as president.

Brown, a wealthy part-Hawaiian from an old landed family, had changed his party affiliation from Republican to Democrat and run for lieutenant governor with John Burns in 1966. Several key Democratic councilmen campaigned for him. Brown lost in the primary to Tom Gill, but went on in the next election to win a State Senate seat. During the height of the Diamond Head controversy in 1967, Brown was an aide to Gov. Burns.

An extremely successful businessman, Chinn Ho over the years had attracted a wide variety of people, particularly from the new local-Asian middle class, to buy stock in his companies. By the early 1960s investors in two, Capital Investment Co. and Latipac International Inc., included Big Island Councilman Herbert T. Matayoshi, who later became Hawaii County mayor; Rep. James H. Wakatsuki, later House speaker; Amy C. Richardson, whose husband, William S. Richardson, was in sequence lieutenant governor, chief justice of the Hawaii Supreme Court, and a Bishop Estate trustee; Federal District Court Judge C. Nils Tavares and former federal judge Delbert Metzger, who was also a longtime Democratic politician; *Honolulu Advertiser* editor George Chaplin; banker Kan Jung Luke; Wilbert H.S. Choi, who in 1967 became a member of the Land Use Commission and in 1969 a director of Capital Investment; and Matsuo Takabuki.

As mentioned above, for years Takabuki had been Ho's attorney, and as of 1967 was also a director of Ho's Ilikai Inc. Stuart, Ho's oldest son, who at times spoke for DHIA, since 1965 had been sharing law offices with Takabuki. The Council, of which Takabuki was a leading member, in 1966 hired Stuart as one of its two lobbyists for that legislative session. Later in the year Stuart himself won a House seat.

DHIA's planning consultant was former City planning director George K. Houghtailing. He had just finished serving as chairman of the mayor's citizens advisory committee which drew up the Waikiki-Diamond Head plan that in 1966-1968 was before the Planning Commission and Council. A Ho corporate officer, Alta Mae Goffin, had been an advisory committee member.[111]

DHIA's lawyer was former Clerk of the Senate James H. Kamo. His law partner, Hiroshi Sakai, represented Oceanside Properties, a developer in the Diamond Head area. Like Kamo, Sakai had worked in the Legislature. From 1957 through 1964 he had held a series of clerkships for key committees, including House Finance and Senate Ways and Means.

Also speaking in favor of hotels and apartments in 1967 as a property owner in the affected area was Ernest Heen Jr., now a state representative.

*   *   *

The Diamond Head development controversies of the late 1950s and throughout the 1960s were classics, given what was at stake and who took part. As much as any case study one could choose, they illustrate how thoroughly the new political establishment and the development business were interconnected.

They also signaled changes that were underway in the politics of Hawaii.

The Diamond Head battles pitted many business and political leaders of the "Democratic revolution" against members of Hawaii's old monied class—but not only the old monied class, because now, for perhaps the first time, a reasonably broad spectrum of the public emerged as being against development. In this instance the opposition was only to developing Diamond Head. But anti-development sentiment grew over the next several years, place by place, incident by incident, episode by episode, until by the 1970s there was something sizable enough to be called an anti-development or even an environmentalist movement. It was heterogeneous and not well organized overall, but it existed and it made its presence felt. Diamond Head was an early sign that something of the sort might be in the making. Certainly it signaled that a gap was beginning to open up between mainstream Democrats—popular insurgents of the early post-World War II era—and part of their base. In the usual way of the world what had happened was that formerly low-income, progressive, grassroots leaders of an earlier day had become moderately affluent. They were now taking an increasingly great interest in their own incomes and the material desires of their families. Formerly powerless and without organization, they had created and wrapped themselves inside a new power structure, one that linked government and business. They remained committed to policies—intensive urbanization, in this case—that had earlier been seen as benefiting everyone, including themselves. Now, when certain groups in the community began to say that they could not see benefits in a particular application of this policy, as at Diamond Head, the Democrats in power pushed on anyway—in this instance to collision and unprecedented defeat.

In early 1968, a few weeks after the City Council's climactic 1967 hearing on Diamond Head, Matsuo Takabuki sat for a wide-ranging interview on the evolution of politics in Hawaii. He said that "basically, it's the same kind of problem for the Democrats now that the Republicans had in 1954." Back then "we were aggressive and maybe even a little irresponsible." But now "the same people have been the leaders for the past 13 to 15 years . . . We're not old chronologically but we have been in this game for a long time." Partly as a result "there isn't the sense of urgency and zeal for change that we had. This may be a part of the affluence existing now. Some of us have grown, economically as well as in other ways. You might call us more conservative." There was also now "a more evolutionary change being favored by the Democrats," and "the difference between the two parties grows less and less."[112]

In that year's elections Takabuki was voted out of office. It was his first defeat since entering politics as a candidate in 1952. His loss was widely attributed to voter dissatisfaction with the Burns-Democratic establishment.

Diamond Head in the early 1960s provided an example of the difference between Republicans and Burns Democrats growing "less and less." Differences between leaders of both sides now seemed less significant than an emerging gap between leaders in general on the one hand and a growing segment of the public on the other.

Take the case of J. Russell Cades, the lawyer who represented that small group of mostly wealthy women in overturning the Diamond Head Terrace zoning in the early 1960s:

Back in 1957, several who were to be his clients signed a petition opposing high rises on all Diamond Head Terrace oceanfront lots. One, Martha A. Gerbode, wrote the Planning Commission saying "the erection of tall apartment houses and hotels at the foot of Diamond Head would be unsightly."[113]

In 1962, while Cades was representing these people, he became a minor shareholder in Kapiolani Park Land Co., which about 1960 had built a high-rise project on the first oceanfront lot inside of Diamond Head Terrace going toward Diamond Head. Another investor was Kenneth Brown, who several years later was named vice-president of the Diamond Head Improvement Association. Also several years later Brown switched party affiliation and became Gov. Burns' 1966 running mate. Also in the early 1960s Cades was trustee for three of Chinn Ho's children in the matter of some stock ownership in Ho's Capital Investment Co. Ho became the DHIA president.[114]

All this was not to say there were no antagonisms between various sectors of Hawaii's new establishment. For example, old money could still find new politicians crude and insufferable. In 1960 one of Cades' future Diamond Head clients, Mrs. Walter Dillingham, a leading figure in Honolulu's *haole* social circles, opposed deep Council participation in running a city-owned auditorium that was Hawaii's center for the performing arts. "What can the councilmen know," she said, "about symphony orchestras and culture?"[115]

But while there were certain differences between the old and the new in the power elite that now governed Hawaii, there was agreement on fundamental questions, like the general importance of intensive urbanization and of protecting property rights.

There would never be such affinities in the major land use fights of the

1970s, where activists battling mass evictions and development were often Marxist-oriented, and where opponents of eviction and development often saw themselves as standing radically against the entire establishment.

*   *   *

Diamond Head was a spectacular case. What happened in other less widely publicized instances of opposition to development?

On the evidence, over the years, down to the 1982 elections, when a development was contested before the Council, development interests generally prevailed. The following newspaper accounts from the 1960s and 1970s give some of the flavor:

1960: "Over strong Army objections, the City Council yesterday unanimously agreed to rezone for industrial use a portion of land adjacent to Fort Shafter at Moanalua."[116]

1961: "About 100 angry Manoa Valley residents stormed city hall yesterday protesting what they called an unjust burden on them for [a] controversial street improvement." The Council subsequently approved it anyway, though later reversed itself, after a developer who stood most to benefit said he no longer desired the improvement.[117]

1965: "The Planning Commission action [recommending rezoning near Diamond Head] brought an avalanche of protests from residents and civic organizations, but most councilmen seemed unmoved."[118]

1968: "The City Council has approved an apartment-park complex in Ewa Beach, despite the protests of community leaders."[119]

1971: For a portion of Sand Island the Council approved industrial zoning and a sewage treatment plant, "which had been bitterly opposed by community groups" because of park plans for the whole island.[120]

1976: "Despite opposition from residents, the City Council gave final approval yesterday" to a high-density residential project in Hawaii Kai.[121]

1979: "The Council allowed the 184-lot Bethany Gardens subdivision to go ahead despite opposition from city agencies, the city Planning Commission and a host of community groups."[122]

To a great extent the more highly visible land use conflicts of the early 1960s involving the Council had to do with opening up areas that had been the preserves of moderately prosperous or wealthy *haoles*. The Council was setting out to force open such places to create business and home-buying opportunities for the new, local-Asian segment of Hawaii's middle class; to stimulate Hawaii's economy in general; also, at times, to simply provide public access. Lines of ethnicity, party affiliation and social class were fairly clear in these controversies. The Democratic Council stood with working and middle-class local-Asians against middle and upper-class Republican *haoles*. Also, so small and tight was the leadership of the pro-development Democratic side in these fights, and so similar the ideologies of both public officials and business interests on this side, that it was normal for the developer, if there was one in the picture, to have a direct business tie to at least one councilman.

An early example of this pattern was an application in 1960 to rezone Waialae-Kahala land for the Kahala Hilton Hotel. Nearby residents included many well-to-do *haoles*. Among them were a large number who opposed the hotel. A petition in opposition generated some 3,000 signatures. The Planning Commission, appointed by a Republican mayor, by a vote of 5-1 recommended denial. But the Council voted unanimously for approval, and then overrode a mayoral veto.[123] The applicant had an important connection to the Council. Councilman Clesson Chikasuye, who on all three readings of the rezoning bill seconded the motion to approve, as a private attorney was sharing office space with attorney/Democratic politician O. Vincent Esposito, who represented the applicant before the Council.

At about the time of the Kahala Hilton approval, the Council began an ambitious program of acquiring beach rights-of-way around Oahu. A great deal of development was starting to take place on the shoreline. During discussion of the proposed Kahala Hilton, Lemke had said concerning Oahu: "It is predicted that ultimately all beach frontage will have to be zoned for hotel-apartments."[125] The acquisition of beach rights-of-way was thus seen as important to preserve access for ordinary working or middle-class people who could not afford oceanfront property, and who without public rights-of-way were going to have an increasingly hard time getting to the beach.

Opposition to acquisition came primarily from well-to-do *haoles* who owned beachfront homes. The most highly publicized instance involved Lanikai, in windward Oahu. The president of the Lanikai Community Association explained his position: "It's a private community, and there is absolutely no reason for the public to be in Lanikai." The association retained as its attorney to oppose City acquisition the same J. Russell Cades who was soon to represent several old-money *haoles* with homes and property at Diamond Head in opposing further high-rise development there.

Another such conflict was over a proposed street widening in Manoa Valley 1960-1961. The Council, by establishing an improvement district, proposed to widen Manoa Road from the very back of the valley, near where Paradise Park was later to go, to just above the Waioli Tea Room. In some places the widening would be to four lanes, in others six. Development in the back of the valley would mean a great increase in the number of cars passing through the lovely, sedate, tree-lined, *haole* center of the valley. The homes that were ultimately built in the back were populated largely by local-Asians.

One of the developers who stood most to profit was Joe Pao. In addition to planning to build in the back of the valley, Pao had a half-million dollar contract with the City to do the street widening.

Councilman Lemke's accounting firm at the time was doing accounting work for several of Pao's companies, a fact which Lemke duly disclosed.

About 1,800 Manoa residents signed a petition against the street widening. This represented a very large percentage of affected residents, a substantial number of them *haole*. The Council in the first couple of ballots nevertheless voted in favor of the widening. Then Pao himself announced he would be satisfied with less widening. A ballot in the Council then went 5-4 against the original large-scale widening, on the changed vote of Clesson Chikasuye. He explained that there was no point persisting on the larger scale if Pao was satisfied with less, since "the developer stood most to benefit."[126] (The portion of Manoa Road in question ultimately became no wider than a spacious two-lane street.)

Another Manoa development matter somewhat in this pattern came in late 1964, and caused loud protest from the community in the lower valley. This involved an application for apartment zoning in a quiet, single-family residential neighborhood on Sea View Avenue near the university.

Unlike the Manoa Road widening issue, the community here was predominantly local-Asian.

A *Honolulu Star-Bulletin* reporter wrote that this was "a neighborhood where sewers, streets and other public utilities were already overloaded." For these reasons, and also to preserve the existing character of the community, nearby residents were strenuously opposed to the apartments. Joining them were the Manoa Valley Community Association and the Oahu Development Conference. (The ODC was composed principally of executives of large *haole* businesses and estates.)[127]

A week after that fall's general election the Council approved the rezoning 5-4. Three of the majority votes came from lame-duck councilmen, two of them just beaten for re-election and serving out their terms, the third voluntarily retiring. One of the three, Richard M. Kageyama, said the owner of the land in question had been active in his campaign.[128]

Mayor Neal S. Blaisdell vetoed the rezoning, however, and the Council could not summon the necessary six votes to override.

So it often went through the early 1960s in cases where there was opposition, though as the 1960s wore on it was, as indicated, not only *haoles* in affected communities who might protest. In 1965 the Council rezoned six acres in Aikahi for a shopping center, with Morio Omori and Ernest Heen Jr. representing developer Centex-Trousdale. Heen was a state representative. Omori shared law offices with Councilman Takabuki. The *Star-Bulletin* wrote that this "has been a long-fought battle in the Kailua and Windward communities," with a number of community associations opposing the project. In 1966 46 acres near Kailua High School were rezoned for 12 high-rise apartment buildings. Joe Pao was to be one of the developers. Pao was at the time or had been a major client of Councilman Lemke's accounting firm. (This project was scaled down considerably in the wake of the 1969 *Dalton* decision by the Hawaii Supreme Court.) The former law firm of Circuit Court Judge Masato Doi, council chairman 1961-1964, was able in 1966 to obtain apartment zoning for about four acres in Foster Village, though as the *Star-Bulletin* wrote, "most residents of Foster Village have supported a year-long campaign to have the land zoned for park use." Councilman Kaito shared law offices 1962–1965 with state Rep. James H. Wakatsuki. As a private attorney representing the Horita family, Wakatsuki in 1967 obtained increased density on 18 acres of residentially zoned land along Kaneohe Bay Drive. The *Star-Bulletin* reported that the rezoning came "over protests from the community groups in the area and the City Planning Commission."[129]

*   *   *

By the end of the 1960s, the heyday of obvious connections and close cooperation between Burns Democrat councilmen and developers, leading to easy Council approvals, was coming to an end.

In the 1970s, business connections and political power were less intensely concentrated, and rezoning applications were less certain to pass.

Now a good deal of the much-enlarged community opposition to development started to come from non-*haoles*. This trend came into focus in 1971, with the arrest of about 30 members of Kokua Hawaii, a radical Hawaiian-led organization. The 30 had staged a civil disobedience sitdown protesting the eviction of locally born working people from Kalama Valley in east Oahu, where the landowner, Bishop Estate, and its developer planned a middle and upper-middle-class residential development.

Beginning especially in the early 1970s developers wanting Council approval were put under pressure to do things like concede park land or scale down planned buildings.

Democratic dissident Frank F. Fasi, elected mayor in 1968, played a substantial part in this trend, giving vocal expression to growing undercurrents of opposition to the Burns Democrats. Fasi drew several key Democratic Council leaders of the 1970s away from a close affiliation with the Burns organization, and he vetoed rezonings if he was not satisfied with what a developer was offering the City in such things as parks and highway improvements.

Two land use decisions in 1971 foreshadowed these changes of direction. Both involved a good deal of environmental criticism coming mainly from non-*haole* working and middle-class people, as a result of which there were public-interest concessions. Yet both harked back to the 1960s. Although suffering initial setbacks, both developers ultimately prevailed, and both had a connection to one or more councilmen.

The most hotly contested involved an application by Makaha Surfside Development Co. for zoning of 5.5 acres of oceanfront land in Waianae for a resort condominium. The property had city general plan and detailed land use map (DLUM) designations that allowed such a project, but not the appropriate zoning.

Investors in Makaha Surfside, which was buying the land by agreement of sale, included a large number of locally born middle-class Japanese and Chinese. Until just some months before Council consideration of the project, Councilman Rudy Pacarro had been an employee of Manoa Realty, an affiliate of Manoa Finance Co., the company that was selling the land. Councilman James Shigemura had represented Makaha Surfside prior to his election to the Council half a year earlier. Before becoming a councilman he was a state representative and chairman of the House Tourism Committee. Now the developer's attorney was Hiroshi Sakai, who had been a deputy city attorney in the 1950s, had once been a Democratic Party officer, and had held high appointive positions with the state Legislature.[130]

As against all this, a city agency poll showed that 90% of the community in the Waianae area opposed any more development seaward of Waianae's coastal highway, including the Manoa Finance/Makaha Surfside land.[131]

The Council at first denied the rezoning, and went on, in a reversal of attitude which would have been unthinkable in the 1960s, to consider the downzoning of all resort-zoned land in Waianae seaward of the coast road.

The Council did not think it could deny the Makaha Surfside rezoning, however, without buying the land for a park. This was despite the fact that when the developer bought the property, there was no legal guarantee of rezoning, even though the land had apartment classifications in the general plan and on the area's DLUM. Indeed, after the Council denied the rezoning, the developer went to court in an effort to have the City ordered to zone the land in conformance with the general plan and DLUM. State Circuit Court Judge Yasutaka Fukushima declined to do so.[132]

Mayor Fasi refused money for park purchase. He agreed, however, to the developer giving the city 2.8 acres for a park that would go right beside the development. On this basis Makaha Surfside went ahead. The other downzonings talked about by the Council were forgotten, though not by people in the Waianae community, who were furious.

The second fight was over a request to downzone 2.25 acres of resort-zoned land at Haleiwa. Two of the would-be developers were Kenneth F. C. Char and Sheridan C. F. Ing. Both were officers or directors of Aloha Airlines, as was Councilman Clesson Chikasuye. Republican Sen. Wadsworth Y. H. Yee was also part of the development group.[133]

The downzoning request came from the Waialua Community Association and was put to the Council by Councilman Toraki Matsumoto. At the height of the fight, with the developers intensively wooing the community association, the association was still 126–48 against. The Council eventually killed the downzoning, though some concessions were extracted, such as lowering the planned buildings from four stories to three, and getting a promise from the developer to preserve most of the property's large trees. The 51-unit Haleiwa Surf was subsequently built on the site.[134]

*   *   *

Another way in which the 1970s differed from the 1960s was that connections between individual councilmen and individual projects occurred less frequently, or at least less visibly.

This was partly because there were now far more people involved with development, many of them new, mainland *haoles*. Given the greater numbers the statistical probability of an individual developer-councilman link was declining.

Partly the decreasing frequency or growing obscurity of these links was due as well to a rising volume of public criticism of such relationships.

Still, the actual record of approvals in the 1970s, and beyond into the early 1980s, was not much different from earlier years.

And even when the Council was giving the appearance of restraint, this was not necessarily the case. For example, in early 1976, following several years of environmentalist and community agitation over development standards, the Council adopted the Waikiki Special Design District. There were then in Waikiki 22,500 hotel rooms, and under existing standards a further 68,000 could have been built. The Special Design District cut the number of allowable new rooms from 68,000 to 26,000, and reduced hotel building densities—units per acre—by 30%.[135] This might have seemed like a dramatic downzoning. But there were no real objections from Waikiki's large landowners and builders, because even with the reductions they could still double the number of rooms, meaning they still had as much expansion capability as they could possibly use for the foreseeable future—and this in an area which most independent commentators said was already overdeveloped.

In 1981, while passing the Oahu Development Plans, the Council attached about 70 last-minute changes, most or all favoring development interests.[136]

This provoked a backlash in certain communities and in the media. The *Honolulu Star-Bulletin* took the opportunity to review Council activities over the past three years. The paper's finding was that out of 16 major land use decisions, only one had gone against the developer. A *Star-Bulletin* reporter wrote: "At the heart of the current controversy, and always a part of past uproars [involving the current Council], has been the Council's apparent willingness to go along with changes sought by development interests."[137]

* * *

Overall no Council from statehood until the 1982 elections could be described, on balance, as anything but "pro-development."

The Councils of the 1960s had behind them a broad community consensus in support of rapid development. This was the heyday of exuberant economic growth. By about 1970 this consensus had become less solid. By the mid-1970s a noticeable segment of public opinion had shifted against development of the 1960s kind.

This change was perhaps indirectly reflected in opinion polls that tested general community approval/non-approval of councils over the years. In the initial Democratic surge of the 1950s, members of the Board of Supervisors, like members of the early Democratic legislatures, were regarded by large segments of the voting public as something like folk heroes. In 1969, though, a poll taken on Oahu showed that only 32% of those sampled approved of the job the Council was doing, and 37% disapproved. In 1980 only 31% approved and 50% disapproved.[138]

In other words, a large bloc of the Council's constituents had gone from enthusiastic support to ambivalence and discontent. And since to a great extent what the Council did concerned land use, this change probably had something to do with community perceptions of development.

But over those same years, the tie between councilmen and developers remained constant, even grew tighter in some ways.

One area in which this could be seen was the financing of Council election campaigns, or at least the campaigns of successful candidates:

In Hawaii, as in other places in the United States, money buys votes. And in Council campaigns, the winners are usually financed by development interests: architects, contractors, attorneys, realtors, engineers, landowners, bankers, investors. To read through the list of major contributors to winning candidates is like reading a "Who's Who" of Oahu land development. So great and consistent has been the interlock that Rudy Pacarro said in 1977 that if he had to declare a conflict of interest every time a land use matter came before the Council that involved a contributor of his, then he would be making declarations "all the time."[139] He did not, of course, make declarations all the time. Neither did other councilmen.

The political and financial equation was a simple and well-understood one, as true for Hawaii as for any other place in the United States:

Former councilman Yoshiro Nakamura said in an interview for this book that "in the palms of the City Council is a tremendous power—the power to create wealth overnight by rezoning land."[140] For this reason developers contributed to Council candidates in the hope of obtaining a measure of influence on the Council.

And the Council's general response was relatively straightforward, at least according to former Council chairman Herman Lemke, who said for publication in 1966: "The person who gives you a good $100 check has more influence on you than someone who might be your constituent."[141]

A good $100 check might have been something, but a good four-figure check was just that much better, because over the years it came to cost a great deal to get elected to the Council. In Hawaii, as everywhere in the United States, political campaigning was becoming a matter of such things as computerized research, demographically-sorted mass mailouts, and heavy advertising, none of which came cheap.

At the same time pressures on potential contributors were growing. By the mid-1960s the Big Five, previously passive in land development, were much more active, and mainland developers were appearing in force. So from then on there was a larger crowd of developers, meaning more competition for limited land, perhaps smaller profit margins, and a general need to speed up the rate at which an investment paid off, in a generally speeded-up society.

Then, by the early 1970s, with something like a new environmental consciousness being partially translated into regulations, the hurdles a developer had to jump were proliferating: shoreline management area permits, certificates of appropriateness, conditional use permits, etc.

Then again, as the 1970s wore on, development, which had been virtually a sure thing in the good days of the 1960s, got more risky in pure economic terms. As American world economic supremacy was threatened by other nations, and the US economy began to falter under the impact of inflation caused first by the Vietnam war and then by oil price increases, the Hawaii tourist business began to wobble, and with it the whole development business in Hawaii.

Added to this was the fact that the Councils of the 1970s were not as cohesive as those of the 1960s.

In the 1960s the great majority of councilmen were straight-ahead mainstream Burns Democrats. When John Burns was making his first successful run for the governorship in 1962, eight out of nine councilmen went on television as a group to urge his election. (The ninth was out of town.) Following the elections of 1960 and 1964, the Council organized itself, sorting out power positions and committee assignments, with initial organization lasting as long as the Councils' terms of office. When powerful men left the Council they could go on to high appointive positions either in or connected with state government. Former Council chairman Masato Doi became a circuit court judge. Matsuo Takabuki was offered the post of state attorney general but turned it down. Subsequently he was appointed a Bishop Estate trustee. Ben Kaito, Public Works Committee chairman through most of the 1960s, received a variety of state appointments.[142]

This consistency and solidity departed with the 1968 elections, which caused a changing of the political guard at city hall. Takabuki was defeated. Mayor Neal S. Blaisdell retired. A Republican, Blaisdell had nevertheless got along well with Burns Democrats. Two Burns councilmen, Chairman Herman Lemke and Kekoa D. Kaapu, ran for mayor but lost to Councilman Frank Fasi, a Democrat but an arch-foe of Burns people. As mayor, Fasi fought constantly with the Council. Incumbent Democratic Councilman Yoshiro Nakamura was defeated. Six of the nine elected in 1968 were new to the Council. Where there had been but a single Republican on the previous council, now there were two. There was also a black man and the first woman ever to be elected. The new chairman was Walter Heen, a Democrat, but not just then a one hundred percent Burns man. Heen was to be mentioned as a possible running mate for liberal Democrat Tom Gill in Gill's attempt in 1970 to unseat Gov. Burns. One of the six new councilmen, Brian L. Casey, became something of an ally of Fasi's. After Casey's Council term expired, Fasi appointed him deputy director of the City Department of Auditoriums.

Thus the Council was unsettled and remained so throughout the 1970s. Before the end of 1969 there was already an attempt to unseat Chairman Heen. The council that took office in 1971 saw several attempted insurgencies, with George Akahane attempting to oust Chairman George Koga. Akahane finally succeeded in 1975, but was unseated a year later. Council isolate Marilyn Bornhorst was then installed as chairman because no single faction had enough votes to put its leader in the chair; but Bornhorst was stripped of many of the prerogatives of real power and had to reign without ruling. In 1979 Rudy Pacarro became chairman. He in turn had to face several insurgencies, including one that prompted a major reorganization of committee chairmanships and assignments.[143] All this factionalism made things more difficult for developers. They could no longer simply talk to a single powerful figure such as Matsuo Takabuki. They had to talk to many Council members. Perhaps as a consequence they had to distribute money in more directions, and more money overall.

Finally, there was the fact of the rising antipathy of at least part of the public to development, and declining Council popularity.

For a variety of reasons, then, from the late 1950s on, there was ever more incentive on the part of development interests to pay, and ever more need for candidates to spend, if they really wanted to win.

In 1960 most candidates, winners and losers alike, spent on average $6,400. (This and all the following figures on Council campaign expenditures are in 1978 dollars.) In 1964 the figure stood at about $10,000, again for both winners and losers.[144]

But in the late 1960s there was a sharp rise in costs and a divergence in amounts being spent by winners as compared with losers. In 1968 winners' expenses averaged $21,200 and losers $18,800. In 1978 winners spent almost $36,000. Losers that year averaged only $9,500.[145]

Now also fewer candidates were running for the Council. In the four elections 1960–1970 there was an average of 39 candidates per campaign (primary and general combined). In the elections of 1974 and 1978 there was an average of 24.[146] This partially had to do with money again. If a candidate could not win without money, it did no good to run without it.

A parallel trend was that increasingly the same people were being returned to office. They served for longer periods, or else served in some other public office before turning to the Council. Incoming Council members of the 1960s had, prior to being sworn in, served an average of 4.6 years on the Council/Board of Supervisors or in another elective office. For the 1970s the figure rose to eight years.[147]

At the same time the average ages of incoming Councils was rising. The average for the 1960s was 42 years old; for the 1970s it was 47.[148]

Going along with all this was an apparent decline in the rate at which the public voted in Council elections. Research was done for this book to estimate, of those Oahu residents legally entitled to register and vote in Hawaii elections, what percentage actually did register and vote in contested Council races during general elections. "Contested" meant there were at least two candidates to choose from. Research indicated that in such races in 1960, about 57% of people who could register did so and voted. From there the figure trended upwards to 67% in 1964 and slightly down in 1968 to 64%. Thereafter, through the 1978 election the figure trended steadily down— 61% in 1970, 53% in 1974, and 48% in 1978.[149]

The 1982 Council elections were widely seen as a test of voter satisfaction/dissatisfaction with the land use policies of the incumbents, particularly the handling of the Oahu development plans in late 1981.

The election results appeared to indicate a degree of dissatisfaction. They may also have signaled a change in the evolutionary direction of the Council, though if so, only a partial change.

Some of the fundamental characteristics of the Council elected in 1982 were quite in line with its recent predecessors. The average age of the 1982 Council was 47—the same as the overall average for the 1970s although down a year from the council elected in 1978. The average time spent by the 1982 Council in elected office, nine years, was also down from 1978, which was 10.4 years, but higher than anything at least as far back as 1960. Likewise campaign spending in 1982 was similar to that of 1978. Indeed winners' average expenditures in 1982 were almost exactly those of 1978— about $36,000. Losers in 1982, however, spent about $14,000, as compared with some $9,500 in 1978. And the participation rate of potential voters continued to decline. In 1978 it had been 48%. In 1982 it was 35%.[150]

(Nor, apparently, would the voter participation rate numbers have been higher if research for this book included contested primaries as well as generals. Two very hard-fought 1982 primary races saw Democratic challenger Welcome S. Fawcett beat incumbent Daniel G. Clement Jr., and go on to win easily in the general; and Democratic challenger Leigh-Wai Doo beat incumbent Thomas T. Nekota, and likewise win an easy general victory. In the Fawcett/Clement primary a total of 22,116 votes were cast. In the general Fawcett and her opponent received a total of 31,052 ballots. In the Doo case the primary and general numbers were, respectively, 21,357 and 28,732.[151])

Nevertheless the 1982 Council race and the nine members elected were in some respects dramatic departures. To an extent there was the appearance of greater vitality and independence.

For one thing there were a total of 31 candidates. This was a number that harked back somewhat to 1970 and earlier. For another, during the entire period studied, there had never been so many incumbents beaten by non-incumbents—three—as in 1982. In 1974 and 1978 there had been one each. There were no incumbents beaten in 1970, though there were two each in 1968 and 1964.

What perhaps most set the 1982 Council apart from all others studied for this book was its relative lack of affiliations with development interests, particularly concerning investments and paying work outside the Council. This, in all probability, reflected a degree of popular disenchantment with the virtually solid development ethic of the Democratic establishment.

* * *

Taking the long view of the Honolulu City Council over the Democratic years, what it all suggests is that following the "Democratic revolution" of the early 1950s a new power structure began to form. In time it became resistant to change. It started recycling old members rather than continually pulling new participants up from the grassroots from which the founders emerged. Its elected leaders more and more relied on the money of the "haves." In time they themselves became "haves."

5

LAND AND LABOR: THE ILWU

FROM the beginnings of large-scale plantation agriculture in Hawaii in the late nineteenth century, all the way up to World War II, the Big Five essentially controlled the land on which sugar and pineapple were grown.

They also controlled the flow of immigration which brought laborers to Hawaii, and the conditions under which these laborers worked the land.

Then, basically between 1944 and 1947, the International Longshoremen's and Warehousemen's Union (ILWU) successfully organized the Hawaii sugar and pineapple plantations industry-wide, as well as the waterfront.

The result was momentous. From then on, big business in the Islands had big labor to contend with, in the form of an organization that was Hawaii's first multi-racial union, Marxist-oriented, tightly organized, led by men who were highly motivated, capable and militant, with a membership that grew to a peak of 37,000.[1]

The very existence of the union, and the principled and uncompromising way it operated from the beginning, changed many things in Hawaii irreversibly, including the question of who ultimately had effective control of the use of agricultural land, both in the short term and in the long term.

For more than a decade, through 1958, the ILWU went head to head against the Big Five. Battles between labor and management in Hawaii's basic industries were fought out on plantation land and on the waterfront.

The union had powerful weapons, which struck at the old economic establishment in the most fundamental ways. The ILWU was able and willing to bring its tens of thousands of members out on strike, over the right to exist as a union, over pay, over work conditions, over the prosecution of its top Hawaii leader for allegedly belonging to the American Communist Party. And if a major strike went on long enough, an entire sugar or pineapple crop could be threatened. Or the union could close down the waterfront, meaning that sugar and pineapple could not be shipped out and turned into cash.

The Big Five might still have fee simple title or long-term leases on great stretches of agricultural land. But with the ILWU as an adversary they no longer had sole undisputed control over the way the land was worked, how and when crops were harvested, and how and when they were shipped out.

The ILWU could tie up plantation agriculture altogether if it wanted to, and if it could do that, it could tie up the economy. In other words, the union was now right at the heart of land and power in Hawaii.

*   *   *

The union also made a major entry into politics, and made a fundamental impact there as well.

In the late 1930s the man who several years later came to lead the ILWU as Hawaii regional director, Jack W. Hall, began taking an interest in electoral politics—not as a candidate but as a power broker. In 1944, when ILWU membership began to take off, the union threw itself directly into territorial elections and claimed credit for the success of several candidates. In the early postwar years, when the ILWU came to the height of its numerical strength, it became extremely active inside the Democratic Party. Indeed in these years the union accounted for many of the party's organizers and a significant part of its electoral base.

This program of working inside the party ended in 1949 when Jack Hall and other ILWU leaders resigned their party posts. Thereafter the union kept away from any formal affiliation with the Democrats. "It is much more advantageous for us," Hall said, "to be on the outside and influence elections . . . To commit ourselves entirely to the Democratic Party is wrong."[2]

The ILWU nevertheless remained very close to the Democratic Party, and it continued to be the case that most election candidates who got the support of the union were Democrats. This was because ILWU leaders and most of the new wave of Democratic politicians were of the same generation, came out of similar socio-economic backgrounds, and had similar world views. But when it suited the union, the ILWU made deals and endorsed others, including on occasion conservative Republicans.

From the start John Burns and the ILWU were close. This was a function of shared visions and practical politics. Of all factions in the majority party, the Burns Democrats were closest to the union in angrily rejecting the Republican-Big Five past. And at the same time they were the most willing to make political deals and keep promises.

Aside from the Democratic old guard in those years, there was one other main Democratic Party faction, led by O. Vincent Esposito and Thomas P. Gill. This amounted to the liberal wing of the party. They might have been further left in some respects than the Burns Democrats—for example they usually favored a greater forced redistribution of wealth than did the Burns group—but this did not necessarily bring them closer to the union. Partly this was due to the personal style of Gill, an intelligent man with a sharp tongue that alienated many people throughout his political career. Also this group, if basically sympathetic to the aims of organized labor, was against what it considered ILWU attempts to dictate to politicians who had union endorsement.

Burns first stood for an elected post in 1948, running for the office of Hawaii's delegate to Congress. Although Burns was close to the ILWU, the union endorsed his Republican opponent, Joseph R. Farrington. Farrington was a well-known incumbent with a pro-statehood stand that the ILWU liked. The union believed Farrington was going to win easily anyway, so it made additional sense to support him in order to be on the winning side. Burns, an unknown at the time, was swamped.

Burns ran again for delegate in 1954, this time against Farrington's widow. Now Burns got an ILWU endorsement, and he lost by less than 1,000 in an election in which 140,000 cast votes. Although the ILWU endorsed Burns, still some of his closest supporters blamed the loss on the union, saying it did not do enough for Burns.

In the 1956 delegate race the ILWU again endorsed Burns and, by all accounts, worked hard for his election. Burns won. Again in the 1958 delegate race, and ever afterwards in his gubernatorial campaigns, the ILWU was a staunch and key supporter, as it was in the campaigns of Burns' chosen successor, George Ariyoshi.

Even at its height in terms of membership, the ILWU controlled nothing like a majority of Hawaii's work force. And as late as 1958 over one-third of the union's 23,500 members were aliens, according to a newspaper report.[3] Translated into political numbers this meant that, even as the percentage of aliens later declined, the union could never command anything like a majority at the polls. In the first election in which Burns won the governor's seat, for example, 1962, ILWU members accounted for only about 9-10% of the electorate.

But the union had a tight organization that was an invaluable political weapon. ILWU members were highly disciplined, probably more so than any other group of voters in Hawaii. This was because plantation communities were small, isolated, and socially stable—thus, as neighborhoods and communities went in the Islands, those of the plantations were particularly suited to efficient political organization. Also, workers on the plantations and the waterfront learned quite early to trust the union, because it had given them a previously unknown sense of dignity, and was delivering higher pay and better working conditions. In return the ILWU leadership could and did "deliver" the ILWU vote.

In many cases, a political candidate's endorsement by the ILWU was crucial to victory, particularly on the outer islands where most of the plantations were located. Most "ILWU Democrats" thus were elected from the outer islands.

In the early Democratic years the ILWU's outer-island political base was an especially great advantage, because the outer islands were over-represented in the territorial and then the state Legislature. Though population was shifting at a quite rapid rate away from the outer islands and rural Oahu into Honolulu, the House, and even more so the Senate, were not being automatically reapportioned to reflect this trend. Thus, as late as 1966, out of 25 state senators, 15 were from the outer islands. With only about 20% of Hawaii's civilian population in 1966, the outer islands thus had 60% of the state's senators. The 51-member House was not so extreme; in 1966 15 members—29%—represented the outer islands.

In 1967 as a result of reapportionment the number of outer-island senators dropped from 15 to 6. The number of outer-island representatives stayed at 15.

In elections for governor the margin for victory was often the outer island vote, meaning to a great extent the plantation vote, meaning the ILWU vote. This was true for John Burns himself and later for George Ariyoshi.

Taking the two men together as the Democratic gubernatorial candidates 1959-1982, they ran a total of seven times. There was a defeat in 1959 but then six wins in a row. In three of the six—1966, 1974, 1978—the critical race, which was sometimes the primary, sometimes the general, was lost on Oahu but then won on the outer islands by a big enough margin to bring overall victory.

In the one gubernatorial election Burns lost, 1959, he carried the outer islands, but by the smallest margin ever for either him or Ariyoshi. If Burns in 1959 had won there in numbers anything like he and Ariyoshi did in virtually every other election, he might well have won the governorship that year.

In 1970, in a critical primary race against Tom Gill, Burns carried Oahu only by 2,879 votes—as against his margin of more than 10,000 on the outer islands.

In the other two elections of the seven, the 1962 and 1982 generals, the outer islands were not crucial to victory. In 1962 Burns carried Oahu by the greatest margin by which either he or Ariyoshi ever would in a sharply-contested gubernatorial race, until 1982. In 1982 there was a three-way contest in which those voting for Ariyoshi's opponents rather evenly divided themselves.

Even if not critical in 1962 and 1982, the outer island vote was there to be counted on, a fact that in 1982 might have made the kind of difference it had in other races, if one of Ariyoshi's two opponents had dropped out in favor of the other, as one publicly suggested.

The plantations, with their ILWU constituency, anchored the outer-island vote for Burns and Ariyoshi. This could be seen by looking at two districts on the Big Island, one of them a classic sugar plantation area, the other not:

The Hamakua Coast for a long time had been almost exclusively a sugar-growing area. So strongly ILWU was its population that its territorial and state representative 1959-1984 was an ILWU officer, Yoshito Takamine. His son Dwight became a labor lawyer, and when Yoshito retired from the House in 1984, Dwight won his seat.

Kona had relatively few ILWU members in its population. For many years it was a remote area of coffee farmers. By the 1980s its economy depended on tourism and marijuana growing.

In the three races which Burns or Ariyoshi won based on the outer-island vote, these two districts voted for them as follows: 1966—Hamakua 65%, Kona 53%; 1974—Hamakua 54%, Kona 46%; 1978—Hamakua 60%, Kona 49%.[4]

In capsule form, those figures exemplify the political debt which the Burns Democrats and later the Ariyoshi Democrats incurred to the ILWU. This debt was paid off on a continuing basis throughout the Democratic years.

* * *

The ILWU established itself as a new and formidable force in the economy and politics of Hawaii, one with a staying power that even the employers came in a grudging way to accept. This led finally to a cooling off in the labor wars that had begun back in 1946 with Hawaii's first industry-wide strike.

A sugar strike in 1958 was the watershed event in this new era of labor-management relations.

The strike lasted four months and cost the industry fully half its crop from 1958 through 1960. Henry A. Walker Jr., who had been with Amfac since the 1940s and rose to be president in 1967, recalled in 1983: "Both sides of the table were shocked by the enormity of the '58 strike and I think both were resolved never to let such a thing happen again." He said that thereafter "negotiations with the union assumed a greater atmosphere of professionalism. The old on-the-record negotiating sessions [meaning the media was given details of talks following each session], which served simply as occasions for both sides to make speeches, which nobody believed, were slowly abandoned. Negotiations were always finally concluded by off-the-record sessions anyway, and therefore, why not start out that way in the beginning?"[5]

Two other moderating influences on the ILWU were the land boom and the fact that their closest political allies, the Burns Democrats, were rapidly making an accommodation with development and other business interests.

With the boom there was suddenly enough money around for business to make good profits. Union members could be better paid without gigantic and exhausting struggles and strikes of the old kind. Liberal Democratic government programs could be financed. Members of the new Democratic power structure could get ahead financially on their own account.

This all came under the heading of the "consensus" politics of the Burns administration, which brought together in a more or less cooperative spirit the old business establishment, the Burns Democrats, and the ILWU.

* * *

The ILWU from the very earliest days set itself to exercise influence across the widest possible range of politics, government, business and labor matters.

The union, for example, throughout the Democratic era was instrumental in the passage of territorial and state labor laws, among the most progressive in the United States.

Aside from basic matters such as wages and labor legislation, the ILWU took a broad view of its members' needs and of its role in society. Thus as the ILWU began to arrive at a position of political power and demanded in return representation on government boards, it sought appointments to bodies as diverse as police commissions and the school board. This was in part to be involved in all sectors of society, in part to look out for specific interests of the union. With police commissions the specific interest was that in the past, police had been used by employers against unions—to break up strikes, to beat up organizers, etc. The ILWU now wanted representation in an effort to make the police act more neutrally. In the case of the school board the union wanted to ensure that rural schools, where most children of ILWU workers got their education, were treated as well as urban schools.[6]

Going beyond such things, the union was also willing to take strong positions, on principle, on social and economic questions that did not directly affect its members. For example, the ILWU was always a strong supporter of minimum wage legislation, even though its own members' pay was set by contract. Again, according to a former ILWU officer interviewed for this book, the union about 1973 helped secure land for a group of Kauai farmers who wanted to raise papaya, even though there were no ILWU workers involved. Besides the union helping obtain land for what became the Moloaa Farmers Cooperative, ILWU officer Edward M. Tangen in the mid-1970s, as chairman of the state-financed Kauai Task Force, organized to promote economic development in the wake of actual and potential plantation closings on Kauai in the early 1970s, supported and voted for the awarding of low-interest state loans to the papaya farmers. The ILWU believed it good social and economic policy to promote diversified agriculture in Hawaii, provided sugar and pineapple lands were not involved.[7]

With this sort of wide-ranging approach, it was inevitable that the ILWU would demand a voice in high-level decisions about land. Land was of vital concern, both to the union and to society in general.

In 1965, with exhausting organizational battles and massive strikes a thing of the past, and with the standard of living of union members considerably improved, the ILWU announced that it was turning some of its energies to quality-of-life matters, involving itself in the broadest of statewide land-related issues. Eddie Tangen said that "planning is the most serious problem facing us today." At an ILWU convention in 1965 he decried the "architectural junkyard of Waikiki." Also that year the union wrote the State Department of Land and Natural Resources asking for a halt to a plan to fill a reef area off Waikiki because it would endanger surfing sites. In 1966 the ILWU announced opposition to a plan to fill Oahu's Salt Lake for a golf course, and called as well for height limits on buildings around Honolulu's Punchbowl Crater, which contained the National Memorial Cemetery of the Pacific. In 1967 an ILWU spokesman told the Honolulu City Council that the union opposed a plan to build high-rises along the seaward face of Diamond Head.[8]

Beginning in the early 1970s, the union became an advocate of somewhat slower growth for Hawaii than it had supported in the 1960s. From the start of Gov. Ariyoshi's efforts to master-plan the operation of the whole state, the ILWU supported this idea.

All this makes the ILWU sound like an organization of great stature that acted on the scale almost of a second government. And indeed this was near enough to being the case.

A study of leadership on Oahu completed in 1967 indicated that Jack Hall of the ILWU was perceived by other community leaders as the second most influential man on the island, meaning for all intents and purposes in the state at large—behind one particular corporate president but ahead of Gov. Burns.[9] And this on an island where the ILWU had comparatively few members.

When it came time to choose a running mate for Burns in the 1970 elections, with more than a possibility that this person could become Burns' successor, apparently several of the men in the political inner circle who eventually chose George Ariyoshi were ILWU leaders, including ILWU lobbyist Eddie De Mello.[10]

Through the 1970s the ILWU continued to have great influence. For example, when the union in about 1972 mounted an organizing drive at the Kuilima resort on Oahu, sitting legislators sometimes accompanied the organizers as they went about contacting workers. (The drive turned out to be unsuccessful. The tactic had previously been used about 1966 when the ILWU successfully organized employees at the Mauna Kea Beach Hotel on the Big Island.)[11]

On into the 1980s the ILWU continued to have deep and wide representation in government appointments. In 1983 25 ILWU officers or members sat on state boards and commissions. This included one ILWU man on the powerful Land Use Commission. From the appointment in 1963 of the first set of land use commissioners to serve out full terms, down to early 1985, there were four ILWU men chosen. No other institution or organization saw more of its members appointed to the LUC.

In 1983-1984 *Hawaii Business* researched the question of who were the most influential people in each of Hawaii's three outer-island counties. The magazine concluded that each county's ILWU division director ranked high. Maui's Thomas S. Yagi, who was also a member of the State Land Board, ranked in the top five; Kauai's Alfred Castillo ranked number four behind the mayor, the editor of Kauai's main newspaper, and developer-attorney Clinton I. Shiraishi; and the Big Island's Yoshito Takamine, who was also a member of the House of Representatives, where he chaired labor committees 1961-1980, ranked number one.[12]

* * *

At the same time as the union was taking the high ground in statewide land and planning matters, it took the closest possible interest in specific land development projects that might affect ILWU members.

Thus, for all sorts of reasons, the ILWU wanted union members on county planning commissions and on the state-level Land Use Commission and Board of Land and Natural Resources.

One of the most visible and important ILWU appointments was that of International Representative Eddie Tangen to the Land Use Commission 1969-1977. Tangen rapidly became the LUC's most influential member. The *Honolulu Advertiser* wrote in 1971 that he was "already considered the most powerful member of the Land Use Commission and normally acts as its spokesman and principal negotiator and principal interrogator during regular meetings."[13] Obtaining Tangen's support for a development project was normally good for securing one and sometimes two of the other six LUC votes needed for amending a district boundary, that is, for upzoning. In 1973 Tangen was elected chairman, and he held the post until he left the Commission in 1977. During these years Tangen worked almost full-time as a commissioner, the only LUC member who had the time to do so.

ILWU membership on land-related commissions and boards meant that in practical terms, beginning in the early 1960s, companies planning a major development that needed governmental approvals, particularly approvals by the state government and outer-island counties, had to contemplate the prospect of negotiating with the union for its support.

In general the ILWU's role in supporting or opposing a particular land development project could be characterized as reactive and pragmatic. Government agencies generated such things as general plans. Developers played the key role in initiating particular projects. Then, as plans and projects were proposed and processed, the union looked at them in terms of what concretely could result for its members.

One of the union's perennial concerns was good housing for its members. The union at times was prepared to offer its support for a particular development in return for the promise of low-cost housing—with good results. In fact, through shrewd use of its political and economic muscle, and through plain hard work by its staff, the ILWU created perhaps the single most effective housing program for working-class people in the history of Hawaii, better in its own terms than anything private enterprise or government was able to manage.

When the union organized the sugar and pineapple industries, workers were living in camps, in units rented from the plantation owners. As time went by several forces began to operate to end the camp era.

In the old days, to have workers in housing that the plantation owned was a great instrument of control. Those days were gone. Once the ILWU organized the workers such control became effectively impossible. As well, plantation camps everywhere in Hawaii were by, say, the 1960s, getting old and expensive to maintain. Whatever income tax depreciation value they once had was used up. The ILWU, for its part, bargained hard to keep camp housing rents low, and succeeded. From 1946 on there was only one increase, which did not come till the 1980s; and then it was only $5 a month. Also by the 1960s and 1970s, several camps had turned into health hazards and were cited by the state's Health Department. So overall the camps had become an unprofitable nuisance to the owners.[14]

In a number of cases the ILWU used its governmental position to help make new, fee simple housing possible for its members and retirees at relatively low cost:

For example, in 1967-1969 some Robinson trusts land near Waipahu in central Oahu was before the Land Use Commission for redistricting. The developer, a Herbert K. Horita company, initially asked that 352 acres be redistricted urban. Much of the land was in sugar and considered agriculturally prime. The ILWU opposed development. The head of the Waipahu Community Association at the time was an old ILWU organizer, Hideo "Major" Okada, who on behalf of the association asked that the project be delayed two years. The LUC staff was against the development altogether. The staff said that a state general plan revision study then underway found that population projections indicated 1,397 acres were needed for new development in the Waipahu area through 1985, yet there were already 3,152 acres zoned, vacant and available. The Land Use Commission voted 6-2 against, though it did allow four acres to become urban.[15]

A little over a year later the developer refiled his petition, this time for 316 acres. The LUC staff continued to be opposed. But at some point, according to a former ILWU officer interviewed for this book, Horita and the ILWU made an agreement that housing for ILWU members would be provided if the union endorsed the project and it was approved. For the ILWU in this instance obtaining union housing outweighed protecting cane land.

Just a month before the second vote, ILWU officer Eddie Tangen was appointed to the Land Use Commission. According to a *Honolulu Star-Bulletin* paraphrase of his remarks, Tangen explained that "the ILWU had changed its position in opposing the land use change . . . because there is a desperate need for housing for plantation workers in the Waipahu area."[16]

The LUC vote now went 7-0 for approval with Tangen one of the seven.

In interviews for this book two former ILWU officers said that Horita subsequently delivered on his promise of housing for the union. One also said that the union played no part in other commissioners changing their votes. An attempt was made to interview Horita for this book but he declined.

On Maui there were several instances of ILWU support for resort development in return for an agreement by the developer to build housing for ILWU members:

One case had to do with Amfac's Kaanapali resort. About 1967 the Maui County Planning Department was revising its general plan of the Lahaina-Kaanapali area. Amfac as well prepared a revised master plan of its own lands in the region. The ILWU initially opposed Amfac expanding further at Kaanapali, based on chronically bad labor relations at Amfac's adjacent Pioneer Mill plantation. The union subsequently reversed itself, however, primarily in exchange for an employee housing program, according to three men interviewed for this book: a former Amfac executive involved with Kaanapali at the time; a man who was the governor's chief representative on Maui then and who was involved with Amfac-ILWU negotiations over Kaanapali; and a former ILWU officer.

Several years later Maui Land & Pineapple Co., a longtime subsidiary of the Big Five firm of Alexander & Baldwin which in 1969 became an independent company, was planning through one of its own subsidiaries to develop a major resort to the north of Kaanapali, to be called Kapalua. The old Honolua plantation camp was in the middle of the proposed development. Obviously ML&P wanted the camp to go. The State Health Department also wanted the camp closed because its raw sewage was flowing into Oneloa Bay. According to several former ILWU officers the union agreed to support ML&P's resort for several reasons, including low-cost housing on ML&P land for the workers who would have to move out of the camp. Maui Mayor Elmer F. Cravalho was also insistent that ML&P participate in providing new housing for the camp residents. In 1974 the new Napilihau housing project opened and ML&P workers began moving there.[17]

Maui provided another example of the ILWU's bargaining strength on housing, plus its moral authority in the community. In the mid-1970s C. Brewer's subsidiary Wailuku Sugar Co. sold to an ILWU-organized partnership some land in or near Wailuku for what a former union leader said was about half price. The partnership later turned the land over to the County, which developed the 65-house-and-lot Ho'ohui Ana subdivision. A former ILWU officer has said that the union was able to induce several of Maui's top professionals in planning, engineering, and real estate to help out, without charge or at cut rates, as a kind of public-interest donation of their time and skills. Most or all who bought the relatively inexpensive homes that resulted from all this were ILWU members.

*   *   *

ILWU bargaining for housing in return for helping developers obtain government approvals continued right through the Democratic years into the 1980s.

A complicated case, one that also had to do with keeping alive a marginal sugar plantation, involved Alexander & Baldwin's Maui Lani, a very large proposed residential development in the Kahului-Wailuku area of Maui.

In the early post-World War II years, Hawaiian Commercial & Sugar Co.

(HC&S) was a 30,000-acre A&B plantation that dominated the central Maui plain. According to an A&B publication, the management of HC&S in 1947 began planning a fee simple residential subdivision at the extreme north end of the plain, to be called Dream City. HC&S workers were then living in company camps spread all over central Maui, but with the recent onset of unionization A&B was looking to get out of the housing-rental business. The first new houses were occupied in 1950. According to A&B, "most of [these] new homeowners were HC&S employees, and they were given special discounts."[18]

This was the start of the town of Kahului, which by 1970 held 21% of Maui's people, most of them living in fee simple single-family housing on former HC&S land. As of about the end of 1983, A&B wrote that "of 3,159 homesites [that A&B ever] developed in Kahului, more than 2,000 were sold to employees and pensioners of HC&S and other A&B organizations."[19] In general, sales to A&B workers and retirees were on better-than-open-market terms.

In the early 1970s, with Maui's population starting to increase rapidly due to the then-booming growth of the tourist industry on the island, A&B began to consider where the next increment of Kahului might go. The company finally decided on an approximately 1,000-acre arc of land abutting Kahului on the south, and filling in the space between Kahului and Wailuku. The project was eventually called Maui Lani. It was to contain about as many lots as A&B had developed in all its previous increments at Kahului put together.

Unlike most or all previous increments, A&B said this time "the primary goal was to provide housing for the general public. There would be no discounts for A&B employees."[20]

According to A&B, from the early 1970s all the way to the early 1980s, the project was stalled by land use laws and government planning programs. The County had to process its Wailuku-Kahului General Plan; then A&B sought to amend the plan since, as adopted, it provided for little or no residential use in the proposed Maui Lani area; then, due to a new state law, A&B had to prepare an environmental impact statement; next, because of the State General Plan Act, the County had to prepare a new general plan; finally, because most of the land was in the state agricultural district, A&B had to seek urban districting from the Land Use Commission.[21]

About 1978, while the County was preparing its second general plan, a complex group of negotiations took place that affected Maui Lani, involving Mayor Elmer F. Cravalho, the ILWU, A&B, Maui Land & Pineapple Co. (ML&P), and Amfac.

There are several versions of what was discussed and agreed to by participants. What all said, though, was that an understanding was reached regarding plantation lands owned by some of the companies and leased in a chain to others. A&B was leasing to ML&P, and ML&P to Amfac for its Pioneer Mill.

Pioneer was a marginal plantation, with relatively little cultivable acreage. The loss of its ML&P lease land might be a fatal blow. An objective of the understanding was to prevent this from happening.

The linchpin was A&B. If A&B withdrew lands from ML&P, ML&P in turn would feel compelled to compensate by withdrawing from Pioneer Mill. In 1978, at the conclusion of the negotiations, A&B President Gilbert E. Cox wrote Mayor Cravalho a letter saying A&B would not withdraw lands from ML&P, "unless there is a major change in circumstances affecting the parties."[22]

The letter made no mention of any other agreements—housing for A&B employees, or County administration support for resort or residential developments, for example. Nor apparently did any other letter or document, except perhaps documents internal to the organizations involved.

But Cravalho, in an interview for this book, said there were several connected understandings involving the County, A&B, the ILWU, and Amfac. He said they included County and ILWU support for Maui Lani; A&B committing 32 acres within the project to ILWU housing; the County supporting the construction of a Hyatt hotel at Amfac's Kaanapali; and Amfac building or helping to build subsidized employee housing in west Maui. Cravalho said "A&B would get Maui Lani, and within Maui Lani was the concept of" ILWU housing. He also said Amfac gave assurances that Pioneer Mill would remain in business. "On this basis we approved the Hyatt" within Amfac's adjacent Kaanapali resort, and "we also put in the package" that Amfac would participate in building employee housing in west Maui, near Kaanapali and Pioneer Mill.

Such a large and complex deal, if indeed it was made, involving multiple public and private sector benefits, would have been very much in the Cravalho mold. Of all mayors in the history of contemporary Hawaii, Cravalho was among the most insistent on large landowners and developers providing substantial community benefits as a price of getting county support for their projects. His years running Maui County, 1967-1979, saw repeated instances of this sort of arrangement, though seldom if ever on the scale of the reported agreement linking the 1000-acre Maui Lani, a Hyatt hotel, two employee housing projects, and several thousand acres of plantation land.

Likewise it would have been very much like the ILWU to demand housing for union members as part of any large agreement that would provide new profits for employers due to various land activities. In any case, a former high-ranking ILWU officer on Maui interviewed for this book said, as did Cravalho, that there was a collateral agreement with A&B concerning 32 acres within Maui Lani for ILWU members' housing.

Others remember things differently. Two men who were A&B executives in the late 1970s, who were involved either with the five-party talks or with Maui Lani, and who were interviewed for this book, said that as far as they knew there was no such 32-acre agreement. They said there was no commitment, period, on housing for the ILWU. These two were Hannibal Tavares, who was involved with the negotiations at least insofar as they concerned plantation leases, and Robert K. Sasaki, in charge of property development for A&B. Sasaki said the ILWU had asked for union housing, but that, to his knowledge, A&B had never agreed.[23]

*   *   *

From the standpoint of obtaining major land use approvals from government for Maui Lani, A&B's strategy had been to get the required county general plan designation first, then, in effect, with county endorsement, to go to the State Land Use Commission. But in 1980, A&B, saying it was tired of waiting for Maui County to finish its new general plan, applied to the State Land Use Commission for urban districting for 620 of Maui Lani's planned 1,000 acres.[24] (The other 380 or so acres were already in the urban district.)

Also at about this time, A&B's HC&S was experiencing better than expected results with drip irrigation, then still in its first decade of use in the sugar industry in Hawaii. As a result the plantation was now looking for additional lands to plant—drip, being so efficient, meant that with the same amount of water HC&S could make use of more land.

In December 1980, according to A&B's lease agreement with ML&P, A&B had the right to withdraw 1,000 acres in north central Maui at Haiku-Haliimaile that ML&P had in pineapple, and convert it to cane. A&B had promised Cravalho in 1978 not to withdraw this land "unless there is a major change in circumstances." To A&B its success with drip irrigation constituted "a major change." Also, Amfac was developing or attempting to develop some of the plantation land that it owned in fee simple. Hannibal Tavares in 1981 asked "was it fair to expect A&B to subsidize Pioneer Mill when Amfac was developing caneland?" Thus, sometime in 1980 apparently, A&B notified ML&P that the lands would be retaken. ML&P in turn gave notice to Pioneer Mill.[25]

Pioneer Mill in the late 1970s was classified a "distressed plantation" by sugar industry analysts.[26] Eddie Tangen in testimony to the Land Use Commission in 1980 said that in recent sugar negotiations, "the workers at Pioneer Mill went along with the pleas of the industry and recognized the fragility of the plantation and agreed to take a less favorable wage settlement than some other plantations and even gave up the right to strike in the following year."[27]

If Pioneer was one of the state's poorer sugar plantations, HC&S was the richest or one of the richest; in any case, as measured by production, HC&S was the largest. In 1980 Pioneer produced about 50,000 short tons of sugar; HC&S produced 188,000. HC&S's output that year accounted for 18.4% of the total for the entire industry. HC&S operating profits for 1980 accounted for about 45% of A&B's profits.

As of 1980 Pioneer had about 8,600 acres in cultivation. If A&B withdrew from ML&P, then ML&P would compensate by withdrawing from Pioneer, leading to a net reduction of 750 acres available to Pioneer. Pioneer manager Robert T. Vorfeld in an interview for this book said that the ILWU in 1980 asked him how many cultivable acres Pioneer needed to remain viable. He said that he told the union a minimum of 8,200. The 750 acres Pioneer stood to lose to ML&P included some non-cultivable lands. Most were usable, though, and in Vorfeld's judgment at the time, the loss would have put Pioneer in a precarious position. He told the Land Use Commission in 1980 that "there is the danger that Pioneer Mill will no longer be viable."[28]

In these years Pioneer's chances of survival, however, depended not only on the amount of cultivable acreage available, but also, and perhaps mostly, on the profitability of Amfac's adjacent Kaanapali resort, and on Amfac's willingness to use Kaanapali profits to underwrite sugar losses.

For example, at about the time the Maui Lani application was filed with the LUC, Hawaiian Airlines filed an LUC special permit application to build a small inter-island airport. The application covered 124 acres near Lahaina belonging to Pioneer Mill, some 90 of which were in cane. (In 1981 the LUC approved the permit, but it was later cancelled or withdrawn as a result of litigation.)[29]

Whether A&B, the County and the ILWU made a 32-acre housing agreement remains in dispute. In any case, there certainly was an understanding regarding leases of plantation land.

Given that, as of 1980 when Maui Lani was being reviewed by the LUC, the ILWU considered A&B to have reneged both on housing and on plantation land lease agreements, the ILWU decided to oppose Maui Lani before the LUC, according to two men interviewed for this book who were ILWU officers at the time.

Here the ILWU faced several apparent dilemmas relating to the union leadership's practice of not telling the general public about ILWU bargaining for union housing or other benefits in return for supporting major developments.

Thus when ILWU officer Eddie Tangen went before the LUC to testify against Maui Lani, he did not say anything about ILWU housing (though he indicated in several interviews for this book that this was at least in part because his main concern was with the issue of the plantation leases). Also, Tangen apparently did not believe he could publicly argue that the LUC should hold Maui Lani hostage in order to force A&B to not withdraw lands from ML&P. Such an argument would probably have been seen as off to one side of the matter directly at hand. So instead Tangen testified that urbanization of the Maui Lani lands would be the sole and direct cause of the A&B withdrawal from ML&P. He told the Commission: "We have information that leads us to believe that A&B intends to withdraw substantial acreage, they own, presently under lease to Maui Land & Pine to replace acreage involved in the subject petition."[30]

But this was unlikely. According to several LUC witnesses, as of 1980 the Maui Lani area held only a 65-acre seed cane operation and five acres in passionfruit, both of which would be relocated elsewhere should Maui Lani be built. Otherwise the area was nothing but scrub trees and bushes, and had apparently never been used for much of anything, except perhaps as a low-grade pasture. The State Department of Agriculture wrote that the Maui Lani soil's "agricultural productivity is low." The US Soil Conservation Service wrote that most of the area consisted of "excessively drained sandy soil." Besides being sandy, meaning water quickly ran away and nutrients leached out rapidly, the Maui Lani area was windy.[31]

An A&B witness told the LUC that there had never been "the slightest possibility that any part of that Waialae pasture land which is [to be used] for Maui Lani, could be used for cane production for HC&S." In an interview, Pioneer Mill manager Robert Vorfeld also said that as far as he could see, the fact that Pioneer was about to lose cane land due to the three-way lease arrangement had "no relation to Maui Lani" not being available for possible agricultural use.

Shinsei Miyasato, an ILWU member who worked at HC&S and who was on the Land Use Commission at the time, was asked for this book if he thought the Maui Lani land had important potential for raising sugar, and, if so, whether this was why Tangen spoke against urban districting. Miyasato said Tangen's statement was "only an excuse," that Tangen's words to the LUC were "phony statements."

On the agricultural potential of the Maui Lani area, Tangen counterargued before the LUC that the ILWU was "far from satisfied that if it were necessary, that this land could not be put into productive caneland." In rebuttal, A&B's vice-president for agriculture, Kobe Shoji, said that in the early 1970s, when drip irrigation was new to the Hawaii sugar industry and plantations were eager to test its useful limits, Wailuku Sugar Co. leased from A&B some land in or immediately adjacent to the Maui Lani area. In an interview for this book, another A&B man, Richard H. Cox, said Wailuku Sugar also had the right to lease additional Maui Lani land. But both Shoji and Cox said that after several years and using drip, Wailuku Sugar gave up efforts to grow cane in this area as uneconomic.

For passage, land use district boundary amendments required six of the LUC's nine members to vote yes. The chairman of the LUC, William W.L. Yuen, was a lawyer whose firm was on retainer to A&B. He abstained. Among the other eight, on a motion to approve, the vote went 5-3. A&B lost.

To what extent the defeat was brought about by the ILWU is unclear. ILWU leaders lobbied several commissioners, and Miyasato said that "Eddie Tangen really put the pressure on" four commissioners.

Of the three who voted "no," one was an ILWU member from Oahu, Shinichi Nakagawa. He declined to be interviewed for this book.

Another who voted against was Edward K. Yanai. In an interview he said that no one from the ILWU talked to him, and that, regarding Tangen's testimony: "I did not take that into consideration." Yanai said he voted "no" because "I just felt that the project did not really contribute to that extent to the low-income housing for the people of Maui." Yanai cited the fact that a golf course was then to go in the center of Maui Lani, and that, in his view, residential developments around golf courses were normally for relatively high-income people. Yanai also indicated the union may have thought it unnecessary to attempt to talk him into voting "no," since "I think I gave out some signals that I wasn't that completely happy with the application."

The third commissioner who voted "no," George R. Pascua, said in an interview that he was lobbied by Eddie Tangen, and that although his vote had nothing to do with ILWU influence, nevertheless "I think the union had a little to do with" how the LUC voted.

Pascua was probably right.

ILWU man Miyasato voted "yes." This fact was pointed to by many who wondered whether indeed the ILWU opposed Maui Lani; or, if so, whether there was a split in the union over this project; or whether the fact of the union's opposition meant all that much in the outcome of the vote.

For his part, Miyasato said he did not know that the ILWU back about 1978 may have extracted a promise from A&B for housing within Maui Lani. In an interview he said all he knew was that as of about 1978, ILWU leaders "Tom Yagi and Eddie Tangen said they were for" Maui Lani. Miyasato said that as of 1980 he was too: "I think it was a very good plan for the low-income people." Miyasato reportedly also said that, prior to the vote, he had committed himself to voting "yes," that when he did so he knew nothing about any deal for ILWU housing, and that he was going to keep his word and vote for the project as proposed, without attempting to pressure A&B into committing land, or additional land, for ILWU housing.

Miyasato and a former A&B executive attributed ILWU opposition mainly to sour grapes on the part of Tangen and Yagi. In an interview for this book, the former A&B man said that Tangen, just prior to the LUC vote in February 1981, asked that A&B hire him as a consultant who would work to break the ILWU-A&B impasse. In May Tangen was to retire from the union, after which he was going to work as a private planning consultant. The former A&B executive said A&B rejected Tangen's offer. The A&B man said this upset Tangen, and was the reason that Tangen then worked to defeat Maui Lani before the LUC. In an interview Miyasato said "I'm pretty sure what the [A&B man] told you . . . that's the fact."

With Yagi, the A&B man said the problem was this: the ILWU endorsed Tavares in 1979. Still, Tavares was a Republican with an electoral base that did not rest so heavily on ILWU membership as had that of his predecessor, Elmer Cravalho. Tavares did not allow Yagi the access to county admininstration decision-makers that Yagi used to have in the Cravalho days, according to the A&B man, also to a Maui Planning Department official interviewed for this book. The planner and the former A&B executive said this annoyed Yagi, and played a role in Yagi's opposing Maui Lani.

Tangen and Yagi in interviews for this book both strongly denied these charges. Tangen also pointed to the fact that at the time he was said to have approached A&B on the consultancy, it was still several months before he was due to resign from the union. Thus even if he wanted to be retained he was not available.

* * *

The LUC's turndown of Maui Lani in 1981 caused something of an uproar. The project had a fair degree of public support. It was generally perceived to be a development for middle and working-class people—in other words local Maui people, for the most part. It of course would generate jobs. The Maui Lani soil was quite sandy and so the land appeared to have little or no other viable economic use. The fact that it would fill in an area between two urban regions, Wailuku and Kahului, was another point that made it a logical choice for urban districting. Redistricting was supported by both the Maui Planning Department and the State Department of Planning and Economic Development's Land Use Division.

The ILWU either did not make public its claim that it had opposed redistricting because A&B had reneged on a housing agreement, or reporters did not pick up on this fact. The union's position that it acted to protect Pioneer Mill was duly noted, but apparently did not carry much weight in public opinion. In the public eye the ILWU looked fairly obstructive.

A year after denial A&B refiled its petition. This time the company asked for urban districting for 680 acres.

The ILWU gave the second petition qualified, grudging support. An ILWU business agent on Maui read a statement to the LUC, saying "at this time we are not opposing" the project.[32]

Referring to the possible demise of Pioneer Mill due to lease withdrawals, he said that "is no longer a threat." By this time, according to a former ILWU officer interviewed for this book, the union had obtained assurances that lease withdrawals would not be the reason that Pioneer might close. This was despite the fact that withdrawals in the amount contemplated around the time of the first LUC hearing indeed were going to or did take place.

On the question of a dispute over housing for the ILWU, the business agent suggested that A&B to an extent might have won out. Regarding what the ILWU indicated to be only a vague commitment of housing for the union, his statement said that "this commitment does not assure us affordable housing . . . We [thus] wish to propose a stronger commitment on the part of A&B Properties, Inc. to provide affordable housing for its employees."[33]

The farthest A&B was willing to go at this time, according to an A&B publication, was to modify "the [Maui Lani] sales program by setting priorities for [A&B] employees, giving them opportunity to purchase homesites before the general public." [34]

The LUC approved the application 8-0. What possibly made the difference from the first time was that, besides lack of ILWU opposition now, the three commissioners who voted "no" in 1981 were no longer on the Commission. The project also continued to be endorsed by the Maui Planning Department and the state Land Use Division, and it still enjoyed a fair amount of community support.

According to a former ILWU officer in an interview, at some point, apparently after the hearing at which the ILWU business agent testified, A&B finally agreed to provide approximately the 32 acres that he said had been promised originally. Elmer Cravalho, now a private citizen, agreed. In an interview Cravalho said "I think they [the ILWU] got a deal." In part Cravalho thought this might have been accomplished by eliminating the proposed golf course and substituting a park that would use a smaller area, thus freeing up more land for urban uses.

An A&B executive, Robert Sasaki, said however that there was still no such deal. He did point out, though, that the LUC, as a condition of approval, had required A&B to commit 10% of the units within Maui Lani, or some equivalent, to low and moderate cost housing for the general public, and that conceivably some who would ultimately benefit from this would be ILWU members.

Whatever the truth of the matter, the story concluded happily for Pioneer Mill, though it was a qualified happy ending.

At the time of the first LUC hearing on Maui Lani in 1980, Pioneer had some 8,600 acres in cultivation. Given the existing financial and technological picture, the plantation manager, Robert Vorfeld, believed he needed at least 8,200 acres to remain viable—to break even or make a small profit. But in an interview for this book he said that Pioneer's use of new cane varieties and drip irrigation in the early and mid-1980s helped the plantation's production and income situation more than anticipated. Due mainly or entirely to the return of land to ML&P, Pioneer was down to about 8,000 acres by the end of 1984. But Vorfeld said that Pioneer led the Hawaii sugar industry in yield per acre 1983-1984; and in income Pioneer had broken even or made a small profit.

Also as mentioned, during the early 1980s Amfac top management was reportedly willing to run Pioneer Mill at a loss, if necessary, subsidized by the Kaanapali resort. But Vorfeld said that by the mid-1980s the company was no longer willing to underwrite sugar losses if it ever appeared that losses would be perpetual. The continued existence of Pioneer Mill was no longer guaranteed.

*   *   *

Sorting out the contradictory statements made over the course of the Maui Lani episode and deciding what it all meant is not easy. Yet at least this much seems so:

A shift in the base of the political establishment on Maui had been underway for some time, with plantation employment shrinking, and large numbers of people moving to Maui from the US mainland. Key establishment organizations like the ILWU and the Democratic Party were losing cohesion and vigor. In large part this was simply because they were aging; the Maui ILWU division director as of the early 1980s was the same man who had held the job since 1952.

Re-elected in 1978, Mayor Cravalho, a key leader of the "Democratic revolution" throughout Hawaii, in 1979 abruptly resigned from office. A&B executive Hannibal Tavares, a Republican, then won a special mayoral election.

Tavares' win meant that for the first time on Maui since the start of the Democratic years, a man closely affiliated with the Big Five was running the County administration. Tavares won again in 1982.

The man he beat epitomized what mainstream Democratic leaders on Maui had been for three decades now. He was Robert H. Nakasone—Maui-born, Japanese, Democratic chairman of the County Council, a small businessman who also made small real estate investments with people who were politically well-connected, and who was strongly backed by the old Democratic forces, including the ILWU.

The ILWU had endorsed Tavares in 1979, but he did not need their support, or at least the support of ILWU leaders, the way his predecessor did. Tavares' electoral base included the new *haole* element in west Maui and along the Kihei coast—an element that, ironically, the ILWU's fairly consistent support for development had done so much to create.

Tavares as mayor worked hard for approval of Maui Lani. He publicly fought with the ILWU leadership on this issue, and he strenuously opposed much or any ILWU housing within the project, though he strongly supported a good deal of low and moderate income housing in general within the development. Tavares also endorsed A&B's desire to retake lands from ML&P.

This all meant that Maui now had a mayor who, together with A&B, was willing to defy the ILWU on major land issues in ways that, for three decades on Maui, would have been unthinkable.

* * *

The base on which ILWU strength was built was plantation agriculture. But in the long term, meaning the whole Democratic period, that base was being eroded.

Starting before World War II mechanization had been shrinking the plantation workforce. Then, from 1939 to 1949 alone, sugar employment dropped 46%, due mainly to mechanization.

Mechanization continued to lessen both the sugar and pineapple workforces into the 1960s and 1970s, when other factors began to affect Hawaii plantations as well.

For one thing, the Islands' plantations were becoming steadily less competitive with plantations in the Third World, where labor was far cheaper.

An extensive use of artificial sweeteners also eroded sugar jobs. So did the appearance of "sugar-free" products and the belief that it was unhealthy to eat processed sugar. Congress in 1974 allowed the Sugar Act to lapse, and thereafter gave the US domestic sugar industry far less help than it had during the 37-year life of the act. In seeking continued federal protection the Hawaii industry now had to contend with a large artificial-sweetener lobby, plus senators and members of Congress with urban and suburban constituencies that wanted cheap sugar. These problems in Washington tended to undermine the willingness of Hawaii sugar plantation owners to stay in business or to expand.[35]

As a result of all this, by the mid-1980s sugar workers under ILWU contract were down from about 25,000 just after World War II to about 7,000, and pineapple workers under contract were down from 7,200 to about 3,600.[36]

These trends and events were occurring in the years when Hawaii's population boom was creating ever-increasing pressure to move land out of plantation crops and put it into housing, and when the rapidly growing tourist business was making heavy demands on land for resort development.

Though the ILWU might oppose some developments that would withdraw land from plantation agriculture, more and more the union was coming to the position that development had to be accommodated, even if at times sugar and pineapple lands were lost. Development was a fact of life. It was not going to go away. In fact there was going to be more and more of it.

From the beginning the union attitude was that development in itself was not a bad thing, even intensive development. In rural areas the big resorts were seen as a means for wives to have jobs as well as their husbands who worked for the plantations; as replacement employment when plantations reduced their workforces or went altogether out of business; and as a way for the children of local working people to rise in the world. For every so many base-level jobs there would in turn be so many mid-level managers, accountants, doctors, attorneys, county engineers.[37] (This was conspicuously not a radical view of what might constitute a good society. On this subject the ILWU by now was sounding like another version of the Burns Democrats.)

Also, when faced with the reality of rapidly growing development in years of steadily declining agriculture, the union supported certain developments on the promise that some of the profits would go to offset sugar's losses. This was so at Ninini Point on Kauai; and it was true on Maui, where Amfac's Pioneer Mill, at times running at a loss, as mentioned above, was kept in existence alongside Amfac's very successful resort at Kaanapali.

Another way the union used its bargaining powers was in trying to ensure that the new jobs created by development went to some extent to ILWU members or their families.

For example, a former ILWU officer said in an interview for this book that in the mid-1970s the union agreed to support developer Herbert

Horita in his plans for a major resort at West Beach in Ewa. He said this was in exchange for Horita's promise that when Horita hired workers to build and operate the resort, he would give priority to people living in parts of Ewa that the ILWU designated. Included would be former ILWU members, their families, and other working-class people in the area who, if they could find work in Ewa, would thus be spared the long drive into Honolulu.

*   *   *

At times the ILWU lost major land use decisions outright:

C. Brewer in the early 1970s closed the Kilauea Sugar Co. on the north shore of Kauai, throwing ILWU members out of work.

Shortly thereafter Brewer and a joint venturer sought county approval for a mass subdivision proposal that ostensibly would have created many small farms, but which the County rejected as a land speculation scheme. Brewer and its partner then sold the land in large, unsubdivided parcels, mostly to US mainland investors.

Through 1974 little use was made of the old plantation lands and no resolution of their long-term use was decided. There continued to be some unemployment in Kilauea.

At that point the ILWU endorsed a plan under which lands of marginal or no farm value could be developed for resort or expensive residential use, in exchange for landowners dedicating the good agricultural land to farming for a defined period of time. A large California agribusiness was waiting in the wings if long-term leases were obtainable, which they would be if the plan was approved. The California firm would provide permanent jobs for some former ILWU plantation workers who either were unemployed or were having to drive far to new jobs. The union considered having one large outfit operating on the basis of a long-term arrangement much preferable to small farming on short-term leases, which was the only use the lands were being put to in the meantime.

A number of Kilauea's small independent farmers opposed the plan, however. To them the areas that would be subdivided were big; urban land would be in amongst farm land and the contrasting land uses might clash; and urban use would inevitably expand and drive out agricultural use, as it seemed to be doing all over Hawaii.

As for others interested and involved, some community activists did not want to see an essentially rural community invaded by resort and expensive residential development. Their position to some extent spilled over into, and to an extent reflected, the feelings of former workers at Kilauea plantation, who were divided. Kauai in general was then at a high tide of anti-development feeling, making it a hard time for anyone to propose a big urbanizing project.

The ILWU leadership generally, and especially Eddie Tangen, then-chairman of the Land Use Commission, made concerted efforts in 1974 to get LUC approval, but failed. Then Gov. Ariyoshi, elected in 1974 with ILWU support, turned against the partial urbanization plan. The ILWU went to great lengths to change his mind, but failed again.[38]

* * *

Although the ILWU at times made clear, straight deals with large land-owners and developers over particular projects, it was not always a case of *quid pro quo*, of an explicit something for something, particularly between the ILWU and the large old Hawaii companies and estates. At times the ILWU simply assumed that its help on a project would later be taken into account.

For example, Amfac attempted 1975–1978 to get approval from the Kauai Planning Commission for an extremely controversial hotel at Poipu, one that would exceed the county's building height limit of four stories. When the first vote was taken in 1975 over an eight-story hotel, the ILWU had two members on the seven-person Commission. Amfac apparently made no approach to them. The Commission turned Amfac down, 4–2, with the two ILWU members voting against Amfac. In 1977 Amfac came back with a six-story proposal. The same two ILWU members were on the Commission. This time Amfac got approval 6-1, with the two ILWU members voting yes. There was evidence that this time Amfac would not have needed the ILWU votes anyway, a majority for approval having been found without them. Just the same, according to a former ILWU officer interviewed for this book, one ILWU Commission member suggested to Amfac after the vote that the union should be remembered for its support.[39]

(The six-story hotel was never built. A citizens' group sued to overturn the Planning Commission decision, and a related group made the first-ever use of Kauai's initiative law to attempt to strip the Commission of its authority to allow buildings of more than four stories. In June 1978, with the lawsuit and the initiative pending, Amfac withdrew its six-story plan and substituted one of four stories, and on that basis the luxurious 434-unit Waiohai Hotel was later built. In the 1978 general election the initiative was on the ballot; with 13,326 votes cast it lost by 38.)[40]

Likewise if one of the old companies agreed to an ILWU request, that might be remembered later on. Amfac about 1973 agreed to lease land at Moloaa, Kauai, for a papaya cooperative, partly at the request of the ILWU. The ILWU officer who dealt with Amfac on this said in an interview for this book that it was understood that down the line the union would remember Amfac's cooperation in getting the papaya project off the ground.

* * *

Another example of ILWU leverage in land matters could be found in the way the union dealt with large mainland firms which were in the process of establishing themselves in Hawaii.

In 1974 Leadership Homes of Hawaii Inc., a subsidiary of Leadership

Housing Systems Inc., one of the largest homebuilders in the United States at the time, asked LUC approval for a 1,185-acre resort near Poipu on Kauai. In exchange for support, the ILWU got Leadership to agree to relatively inexpensive worker housing. A Leadership in-house memo stated that the proposed redistricting would "carry the support of the ILWU."[41] Apparently connected to this promise was discussion of worker housing. A subsequent memo said that a Leadership executive "committed to Eddie Tangen . . . The inclusion of between 30 and 60 residential sites within our Poipu parcel for 'worker housing' subsidized by us . . ."[42]

The LUC turned Leadership down, however, due to substantial community opposition on Kauai. The opposition was led primarily by David C. H. Chang and the Wong sisters, Napua, Tamara and Paula, all lifelong residents of nearby Koloa. At the time they defeated one of the nation's largest homebuilders they were aged respectively 24, 23, 19, and 17.

*   *   *

The youth of the opposition to Leadership at Poipu raised a point about the aging of the ILWU as an institution in Hawaii.

When in the 1950s and early 1960s the ILWU was becoming part of the power structure in Hawaii, there was growing up behind the union a cohort of young people who by around 1970 came to be vocal critics of the ILWU's place in the new establishment, and of its role in the development of the Islands.

Ironically it was in large part because of the high material standard of living achieved by American industry and labor, and the broad democratic rights secured in part by the labor movement, that there could afford to appear in the 1960s a youth culture that stood opposed to mainstream adult values and institutions.

Another irony concerning the ILWU in particular was that of all organizations and institutions that made up Hawaii's new power structure, the ILWU was by far the most like the anti-establishment people among the young in terms of egalitarianism, positions on world politics, and attitudes toward government and big business.

In 1960, before there was anything called a New Left, ILWU officer Newton K. Miyagi visited Fidel Castro's Cuba and returned home publicly praising Cuban socialism. The ILWU came out against the Vietnam War long before this was fashionable. When in 1968 there was turmoil at the University of Hawaii over anti-war activism, the ILWU's executive board supported an anti-war sit-in, against general opinion in the community. An ILWU statement read in part: "We are not going to knock the students for using dramatic tactics. We used a few ourselves when we were first establishing our union and fighting for changes which brought more freedom and democracy to Hawaii. A lot of people called us trouble-makers then, but most agree Hawaii is a better place today because of the 'trouble' we made 25 years ago."[43] Union officers in 1974 joined a demonstration organized by young community and labor activists against a Chilean ship, the *Esmeralda*, in protest against the military overthrow of the elected president of Chile, the socialist Salvador Allende. Throughout its history in Hawaii, the ILWU consistently opposed nuclear weapons.[44]

For all this, on the local scene, problems arose over attitudes toward development between the ILWU on the one hand and New Left and community activists on the other.

Related in part to simply having been born at different times, union leaders and youthful opponents of development approached the question of urbanization differently. Union leaders and older union members had known scarcity. They had worked hard for what they got. Typically they had come to look on proposed developments in terms of potential new jobs, or a chance to get a break on badly-needed new housing.

Most of the young of the 1960s and 1970s, on the other hand, had known only relative affluence and economic security. They did not have the experience of the Great Depression or of World War II. Their emphasis was rather on preserving Hawaii's natural beauty and easy-going lifestyle, keeping the beaches as uncrowded as possible, protecting surfing sites; also on preventing the eviction of locally born working and middle-class people to make way for more intensive development.

Thus for various reasons the politically left among the young, a number of whom harked back to the same Marxist ideas that had driven the ILWU leaders when they themselves were young, were almost always anti-development. The ILWU was often on the other side.

A factor that aggravated the situation at times was that, among adults, some of the anti-development youths' most vocal allies were mainland *haoles* who wanted the beauty that brought them to Hawaii preserved—who thought, now that they had arrived, that growth controls were a good idea. This group tended to be middle or upper-middle class, and not particularly sympathetic to unions.

On the other hand there were also among adults opposed to development Hawaii-born non-*haoles* who were threatened with loss of their rented homes and/or farms to make way for development. This last group produced some of the most tenacious opposition to development in Hawaii, particularly the Waiahole-Waikane Community Association on Oahu in the mid-to-late 1970s, and the Niumalu-Nawiliwili Tenants Association on Kauai in the early-to-mid 1970s. And at times these and at least one other association clashed sharply with the ILWU leadership over development. The disagreements were usually over how much urbanization to concede to the landlords involved, in return for a halt to evictions. The ILWU tended to take a more pragmatic approach to these problems, which would lead to allowing more development than the community associations wanted, which led to the clashes.[45]

In terms of alienating the young in particular, there was also the willingness of the ILWU leadership by the mid-1960s to work closely with business and political leaders. In 1965, local newspapers ran a photo of three Hawaii labor leaders, including Jack Hall of the ILWU, smiling broadly during a five-way handshake that included Gov. John Burns and businessman Lowell S. Dillingham, president of Dillingham Corporation, one of Hawaii's largest companies. The occasion was a benign one: the kick-off of the year's Aloha United Fund drive.[46] Still, to young left-wing activists, such a grouping could confirm suspicions that the ILWU had sold out.

Then there was the matter of the ILWU tying some of its positions on controversial developments to secret agreements. For various reasons, the union did not favor explaining itself publicly. Even the union rank and file was not always told about specific arrangements made with politicians and developers, though members were generally provided general reasons for such things as campaign endorsements by the ILWU's Political Action Committee, and ILWU support for major developments.[47]

Among opponents of development there was a consistent demand for openness in government decision-making. There were deep-running suspicions—sufficiently well founded, as it turned out—that some large projects and even some relatively small ones got government approval based in part on secret deals or implicit understandings among influential people. The ILWU had come to be perceived as part of that deal-making world. The fact that more often than not the union was bargaining for affordable housing for working people, or bargaining to save jobs or create new employment, did not matter much to critics. It was the secrecy that was seen as important—and seen as obnoxious.

The case of Leadership Homes on Kauai was an example of this. There, as it appeared in in-house corporate memos obtained by opponents of development and turned over to the media,[48] Eddie Tangen of the ILWU was secretly bargaining his Land Use Commission vote and his general support in return for worker housing.

There was never any evidence that anything more was involved on Tangen's part—bribery, for instance; and a State Ethics Commission proceeding involving Tangen and Leadership found no ethics violation.

But publication of the memos caused an uproar. The picture that emerged was of Tangen, with other high government officials and several attorneys, secretly attempting to orchestrate approval of a major resort that was highly unpopular with many in the most affected community, Koloa.

Tangen was depicted as suggesting which attorneys Leadership should hire to handle representation before the Land Use Commission; providing Leadership with strategic information such as where opposition to the project might surface; and making suggestions as to the content of Leadership's proposal.

The Leadership executive on Kauai, John Slayter, reported that in a series of meetings with the mayor and other Kauai County administration officials he was assured of not only their support but also the mayor's willingness to orchestrate county and state approvals from behind the scenes.

Thus, since "the approval of the [county] General Plan amendment has already been virtually assured by Kauai County officials," Slayter wrote, "our strategy becomes one of providing to the public the rationale for the Planning Commission's favorable action."[49]

Part of what the memos pictured as behind-the-scenes work involved Leadership's attorney on Kauai, Clinton I. Shiraishi. Slayter wrote of Shiraishi that "his technique of operating is to do extensive groundwork prior to actual hearings to the extent he and the Commission know exactly what is going to take place at the hearing. Consequently . . . he has never represented a client where it was not known considerably before the public hearing exactly what the outcome would be."[50] (It should be noted that this was solely Slayter's assertion.) In a later memo Slayter said he was "extremely pleased with Shiraishi's performance and ability to work totally behind the scenes."[51]

Leadership also arranged or attempted to arrange legal representation before the LUC in Honolulu. At one point the Honolulu attorney was to have been a former Honolulu city official.

Slayter wrote that Eddie Tangen and Kauai Mayor Francis M. F. Ching approved of this man being retained. Several weeks later Slayter wrote that "our Kauai attorney, Clinton Shiraishi, informed me that the recommended Honolulu attorney . . . would require a fee of approximately $500,000." For comparable or more work Shiraishi was to get $60,000, with a $30,000 bonus if the LUC approved the application.[52]

Slayter wrote that he then asked James A. Wriston Jr., another Honolulu attorney retained by Leadership, what he thought of the proposed half million dollar fee. Slayter wrote that Wriston replied that "a fee of the size quoted . . . obviously provided for participation with others unknown whereas Shiraishi's fee was obviously net to him alone." Wriston was also reported as saying that "the payment of any fee as high [as $500,000] . . . could serve as the basis for charges of unethical practice by Leadership should it ever become known."[53] The lawyer who was the former City official was apparently not retained.

Slayter wrote further that Shiraishi, who was to represent Leadership before the LUC on Kauai, was at the same time representing eight other applicants before the LUC. Slayter wrote that "I discovered that five of the eight . . . were on behalf of State Land Commission members themselves."[54] If this was so it was news to the public, because no LUC members at that time were on record as declaring conflicts of interest.

Slayter, Tangen, Shiraishi and Ching later denied or qualified most of the assertions made in the leaked memos. Tangen also said that he knew nothing about information contained in the memos that did not pertain to him.[55] The lawyer who was the former City official who reportedly asked for the half million dollar fee was asked to comment for this book on his role. He declined to do so.

The Slayter memos, leaked to the media, were the sole original source for this tangled story. The truth of what actually transpired was never really established. Nonetheless, in the eyes of many on Kauai, and for that matter statewide, wherever people read newspapers and listened to radio news and watched TV, the damage to the credibility of these men was great.

Furthermore the memos were deliberately released in the middle of an election campaign in which development was a major issue.[56] The intent in large part was to defeat Mayor Ching, who was considered extremely pro-development by those who opposed Leadership, who also did not like a great many other developments then planned for Kauai. Ching did lose, by 208 votes to Councilman Eduardo E. Malapit, apparently to an extent due to the Leadership episode. Slayter much earlier had written "that the politics of the County of Kauai will hinge this year on our Poipu project."[57] Ironically it was not only the Leadership project but also his memos that played a part.

Tangen's participation, as seen through the memos, was to bargain his LUC vote and influence to Leadership in return for housing for ILWU workers. As innocuous or even laudable as that might be, it was lost on many people.

Later, the State Ethics Commission investigated Tangen's part in the affair and found no ethics violation. But under state law such decisions could not be made public. Also, this all occurred during a period of rising public distrust of leaders in general—the Leadership memos excerpts were published about two months after Richard M. Nixon resigned as president as a result of the Watergate scandal. Tangen overall ended up looking poorly in the public eye.

*　*　*

What further complicated the secrecy question regarding ILWU leaders in general was that people were coming to wonder if perhaps some union leaders were using their position and influence for personal enrichment.

A case in point concerned some land at Nukolii on Kauai:

There Tom Yagi, the Maui ILWU division director, owned a share in a large unregistered *hui* that included several people in or close to the top leadership of the state government.[58]

A close friend of Yagi in 1973 signed an agreement to buy from Amfac 60 acres of raw oceanfront land at Nukolii for $1.2 million. The friend organized a *hui* to take over purchasing the property, and Yagi was invited to join. About two-thirds of a year later, without any intervening rezoning or construction, the *hui* resold to a Hawaii subsidary of a mainland American insurance company for $5.25 million—a 400% profit.[59]

Neither the sale nor resale agreements were publicly registered until about four years later, and then the sale document that was publicly filed did not indicate who the actual buyer had been.

Despite widespread protest beginning in 1977 against building on the land, most government officials called upon to rule on development there approved it.

The *Honolulu Advertiser* in 1980 made public the *hui*'s existence, also that several of its members were in government or were politically well-connected.[60] In view of the mainland insurance company having paid such a markup and then having succeeded so well with local government in the face of great community opposition, it appeared to many that, as part of the resale agreement, political insiders sold their influence with government to the insurance company. This seemed all the more likely since the *hui* had apparently tried to hide its presence.

In applying this theory of insider influence to Yagi, there was the fact that a fellow-ILWU officer and a personal friend, Eddie Tangen, was then LUC chairman. Tangen voted in favor of redistricting.

There were plausible points made by a *hui* spokesman in defense of what happened.[61] For one thing, it really was not clear whether the *hui* had been under legal obligation to register. For another, although most approvals would have to come and did come at the county level, there were no Kauai County officials known to be involved as investors. If the intent in lining up investors was to wire in the development, surely some Kauai officials would have been included, so the argument went. Yagi, for his part, denied having approached Tangen. Tangen confirmed this, and also said he had not even been aware of Yagi's investment.

As with the Tangen-Leadership case, the public in the end was left hanging. What exactly happened with Nukolii was never fully established. Did the insurance company believe that its purchase included political help? Were any LUC members lobbied by any politically influential *hui* members?

Given the apparent secrecy elements of it all, suspicions lingered in the minds of many that the answer to questions like these was "yes."

And again, an ILWU official came away looking poorly.

Aside from secrecy considerations there was also the fact that Yagi, by investing in Nukolii, wound up putting himself, and thus in a sense the ILWU, in a directly adversarial position against a grassroots community group that vehemently opposed development there. Yagi though, did not know this would happen at the time of his investment, since at that point there was no public knowledge that Nukolii was being contemplated for development, hence there could be no opposition to development.

In 1975 leaders of two other unions made investments that put them at considerable odds with another grassroots organization. Arthur A. Rutledge of the Hawaii Teamsters and Harold Lewis of the Operating Engineers Union bought shares in a partnership to develop the windward Oahu valleys of Waiahole and Waikane. The development was strenuously opposed by almost all residents of the valleys, most of whom were working-class. Unlike Nukolii, in this case, according to publicly filed business records, investments came after community opposition surfaced.[62]

Given the radical political origins of most of the union officials involved, such investments were a sign of how far they and their generation—and Hawaii—had traveled since the start of the Democratic years.

* * *

However the tangled story of Nukolii was viewed, the fact of Yagi's investment and its lucrative return illustrated a trend in the later history of the ILWU in Hawaii: a number of union officials were becoming investors in land and development.

They generally invested with friends who were businessmen and politicians, usually of local-Asian extraction.

Nukolii was not Yagi's only real estate investment. Over the years he occasionally invested small amounts of money in other projects with some of the same people who organized the Nukolii *hui*. Another ILWU official from Maui, Mamoru Yamasaki, who was also a member of the state Legislature, made several investments, in Hui o Nakane, The Group, and Heeia Development Co., this last a large *hui* with a membership including many leading Maui Democrats. Goro Hokama, an ILWU steward who beginning in 1959 represented his home island of Lanai on the Maui County Board of Supervisors and later the County Council, had a small investment in the Pearson Hui, which, like Heeia Development, contained a number of government officials. In 1982 Eddie Tangen, after he retired from the union, and ILWU Secretary-Treasurer Newton K. Miyagi each bought a two-acre lot in Republican Sen. Wadsworth Y. H. Yee's Kawela Plantation agricultural subdivision on Molokai. Tax records indicated that each paid $91,400 for his lot. Also after retiring Tangen bought a 10% interest in a *hui* that purchased a 20-acre parcel in Kilauea, Kauai.

(In an interview for this book, Tangen said that he never invested in real estate until after he resigned from the ILWU in 1981, although he said he had offers to do so.)

In Danny P. S. Fong *et al*, an eight-member partnership organized in 1975, there were listed the names of the wife of the ILWU's then-education director, who herself had once been in the labor movement in Hawaii, also two longtime ILWU insurance consultants, one of whom was once in the labor movement on the mainland, and the head of the Pacific Maritime Association (PMA), Edward J. Flynn. The PMA was a West Coast and Hawaii shipping employers' association with which the ILWU negotiated longshore contracts. Flynn told a reporter that he was unaware of the investment by the wife of the ILWU officer.[63] Whether the ILWU man likewise was unaware of Flynn's involvement was unclear.

Danny P. S. Fong *et al* was a sub-*hui* within Kauai Ventures, organized by Masaru Yokouchi, who organized the Nukolii *hui*. As with Nukolii, the land was purchased from Amfac; the *hui* was not publicly registered until after the *Honolulu Advertiser*'s James Dooley in 1980 did stories about unregistered *huis*; and the *hui*'s agreement of sale with Amfac was initially unrecorded.[64]

The ILWU education director whose wife bought a share in Danny P. S. Fong *et al* was David E. Thompson. He and his wife, Mitsue, in the same year also invested in Alawaena Road Hui, which bought a 49-acre parcel in South Hilo. Another investor in Alawaena was the wife of Big Island ILWU Division Director and state legislator Yoshito Takamine. Takamine also later invested in a *hui* that bought a 25-acre parcel in the Kalopa Homesteads area of the Big Island. Two of the three original general partners in Alawaena, meaning those who ran the venture, were Big Island ILWU business agents Akira Omonaka and Francisco Latorre. Others in Alawaena as limited partners were a public school teacher, a county parks employee, and small businessmen.

Of course ILWU officials were not the only labor leaders investing in land and development. Anthony Rutledge of the Hawaii Teamsters and Harold Lewis, financial secretary of the Operating Engineers Local 3, each had shares in Enchanted Lake Partners, organized in 1976. As mentioned above, Lewis and Anthony's father, Arthur A. Rutledge, for years the head of both the Teamsters Union in Hawaii and the Hotel, Restaurant Employees and Bartenders Union, Local 5, in 1975 invested in Windward Partners, which intended to develop the windward Oahu valleys of Waiahole and Waikane. State Sen. Clifford T. Uwaine, who was also an aide to the state director of the United Public Workers, had a share in Hawaiian Land Investment Partners, which invested in 1979 and 1980 in one condominium unit in The Chandelier in Salt Lake and one in the Makiki Plaza in Makiki, both on Oahu.

The Maui head of the Hawaii Government Employees Association, Gerald K. Machida, had as of 1980 investments in real estate in Kihei and Pukalani, both on Maui. Machida also invested in Pukalani Terrace Landco, a *hui* whose membership was a cross-section of Hawaii's contemporary power structure.

* * *

The ILWU was once *the* union in Hawaii. In the middle of the 1940s the ILWU represented nearly everyone who belonged to a union. But by the time of statehood in 1959 the ILWU's membership accounted for only about one-third of organized labor. By 1980, the ILWU's share was one-fifth, and ILWU members accounted for only 5% of the total work force, down from about 19% in the late 1940s.[65]

These trends had political ramifications. When John Burns first won the governorship in 1962, ILWU members accounted for 9–10% of the electorate. In the governor's race of 1982, this figure was down to about 5%. And the accelerated decline of plantation agriculture in Hawaii since about 1970 threatened not only to make the 5% figure smaller still, but to remove altogether the most reliable element of the ILWU political base—plantation workers.

The ILWU was not only declining in relative size, so was organized labor in general, both in Hawaii and nationwide. Unions in Hawaii hit their peak about 1976 in terms of percentage of the work force they represented—some 40%. As of 1980 this was down to 28%. Nationally in 1980 unions represented about 25% of all workers, down from about 30% a decade earlier.[66]

Several factors accounted for the decline in organized labor:

Due to such things as continuing technological innovations and the export of capital abroad, the United States' domestic economy for a long time had been shifting from basic industries, like steel in Pittsburgh and sugar in Lahaina, to high technology and service industries, like microcomputers in Sunnyvale and tourism at Kaanapali. White-collar and service workers were much less interested in union representation than their parents had been in the 1930s and 1940s. Unions by the 1980s tended to be viewed by prospective members in a non-ideological way, as one more professional service to be bought and paid for; and for various reasons many workers had come to think unions were not worth it.

Other factors operating specifically in Hawaii were that a large proportion of the organized work force was in government, and government employment in the difficult economic times since the mid-1970s was leveling off rather than expanding. Further, construction in Hawaii, so buoyant in the boom days of the 1960s, was especially hard hit by the on-and-off economic recessions of the 1970s and 1980s. Many union construction workers lost jobs, and non-union workers were leery of putting their jobs at risk by voting to bring in unions, which might impose extra costs on their employers.

Employers in Hawaii, for their part, had become more sophisticated than the plantation managers and *lunas* (foremen) whose harshness helped drive so many workers into the ILWU 30 and 40 years before. In Amfac hotels, for example, non-union workers were offered wage rates similar to those in union shops.[67]

Then there was the fact of generally uniform safety requirements prevailing in non-union and union shops because of federal legislation.

But when push came to shove, as it did in bad economic times after the collapse of the Hawaii boom, employers were still hard-nosed. Many resisted union organizing bids. Some apparently went to considerable lengths to get rid of existing unions. For example, there were "alter ego" cases where a company shut down, laid off all employees, changed as much of its appearance as possible—company name, officers, directors—then reopened as an ostensibly new outfit and with no union.

Over the same years, Hawaii unions were conducting a declining number of organizing drives. Elections were down from 184 in 1975 to 53 in 1982 and 31 in 1983—and of those 53 in 1982, fully 20 were either petitions to get rid of existing unions, or were "raids," in which one union was trying to take members from another union.[68]

Indeed, in the competition for union membership, there were times when nobody won, at least as far as organized labor was concerned. In an organizing fight in the early 1980s between the ILWU and the Hotel Workers Local 5 over the Sheraton Coconut Beach on Kauai, there were two elections. In the first, Local 5 got 57 votes, the ILWU 27, and 56 voted for no union. That is, a majority of workers voted in favor of some union representation, but neither union got an absolute majority. So there had to be a run-off with only the winner of the first vote, Local 5, on the ballot. This time a majority voted for no union at all.[69]

There were some organizing successes in these years. For example, in 1980 the ILWU won a representation election at the large Hyatt Regency Maui, which brought in a unit that later rose to about 1,000 union members.[70]

But there were a good many other cases where, in trying to get new members, the unions, among them the ILWU, lost out altogether. Of the 21 petitions filed by all unions in 1982 to organize workers—not raids or efforts to get rid of existing unions, in other words—12 were defeated on the votes of workers, and the remaining nine successful petitions yielded only slim pickings—a total of 143 new members for organized labor in Hawaii.[71]

* * *

Part and parcel of these years, and an indication of a decline in the moral authority of unions in Hawaii, was a succession of criminal convictions of labor leaders in the late 1970s through the mid-1980s, and the revelation of links between certain union leaders and organized crime.

It is worth noting that with one small exception these involved unions other than the ILWU. By and large the ILWU was a clean union, both in Hawaii and on the US west coast. As such it stood in contrast to the International Longshoreman's Association, which represented dock workers on the east coast and the Gulf of Mexico. The ILA had been mob-ridden since nearly its inception prior to World War II, having been associated with such notorious *Cosa Nostra* figures as Albert Anastasia, the leader of Murder Inc. from the 1930s through the mid-1950s.

But although clean, without doubt the ILWU suffered in public perception—a kind of unfair guilt by association.

The foremost name in the Hawaii labor-organized crime scene was that of Henry W. Huihui, former official of the International Brotherhood of Electrical Workers (IBEW), Local 1186, and former secretary-treasurer of the Honolulu Building and Construction Trades Council. In 1984 Huihui pleaded guilty to a series of syndicate-related crimes, including extorting building contractors and in 1977 soliciting the murder of Josiah Lii, then head of the Inland Boatmen's Union in Hawaii.[72]

Also under indictment in 1984 in connection with Huihui's allegedly criminal activities was Gordon Yabui, longtime president of the IBEW in Hawaii.[73]

Yabui was also an officer of six companies set up in 1977, most of whose members were relatives and associates of Huihui's. Another member of several of these companies was Shinichi Yoshikawa, at the time a Carpenters Union business agent, and several of the corporations listed their address as that of the Carpenters Union. The companies were described by the *Honolulu Star-Bulletin* and by Carpenters Union leader Walter Kupau as dummy corporations, established by Huihui to launder illegal money.[74]

Kupau himself was convicted of perjury in 1984, for having lied in an affidavit he filed with the National Labor Relations Board. Several lesser Carpenters officials were convicted earlier of perjury in connection with the same events. These perjury convictions grew out of a Carpenters organizing drive, the target being a small contractor on Maui, who said that he came to believe that his life was in danger for working with law enforcement authorities in prosecuting Kupau and the others. As a result the contractor felt forced to go into hiding under federal protection, a move that entailed a good deal of publicity, some of it at the national level.[75]

The president of the Hawaii Meat Cutters Union, Local 594, Ivanhoe K. Naiwi, pleaded guilty in 1984 to embezzling from the union, and to not reporting for federal tax purposes some income he received as union president. Meat Cutters business agent Koho Uyehara also was charged with embezzlement but acquitted by a jury.[76]

In 1983–1984 Democratic State Sen. Clifford Uwaine was prosecuted for allegedly conspiring to register voters illegally for a political protege of his, Ross Segawa, who was a House candidate in the 1982 elections. Uwaine, as well as being a politician, was aide to the state director of the United Public Workers Union. Uwaine's trial ended in a hung jury. In the 1984 elections, he lost his Senate seat. As of early 1985 he had not been retried.[77]

Segawa, after stories broke about possible illegal voter registration, obtained jobs first with the Carpenters Union and then the Building and Construction Trades Council. And even after a plea of no contest in his own prosecution Segawa continued to hold a job with the Carpenters. He was subsequently sentenced to a year in jail.[78]

The one case involving the ILWU was that of long-time sugar business agent Benito Apostadiro. For years Apostadiro was reputedly involved with running chickenfights and other illegal gambling operations in leeward Oahu and along the Waianae coast. He was arrested in 1971 in connection with charges that he owned a gambling arena in Maili. He was jailed for 30 days in 1975 for evading federal taxes on income he received from allegedly running cockfights in Waianae in 1970. In 1976 Apostadiro was arrested in Ewa on gambling charges. In 1981 he and several others were sued in civil court by the Honolulu prosecutor's office to close and demolish a cockfight arena which they were allegedly running at the Korean Camp plantation village in Ewa. A co-defendant was Penrod "Tommy" Fanene, a nephew of former Oahu syndicate leader Alema Leota and a former member of the Earl K. H. Kim gang. Eventually the arena was bulldozed with the agreement of the owner and the lessor of the land, Campbell Estate and Oahu Sugar Co.[79]

On the occasion of the prosecutor's suit, a *Honolulu Advertiser* reporter wrote in reference to Apostadiro working for the ILWU: "Sources said Oahu Sugar has been reluctant to try to stop the cockfights because it didn't want to run afoul of its own employees, or of the ILWU, which represents many of its employees."[80]

In an interview for this book Apostadiro said that his involvement with chickenfighting was always "a personal thing and had nothing to do with the ILWU." He said that "I never relied on the ILWU supporting me on that point."

Apostadiro also said that he "had nothing to do with racketeering," that he was in cockfighting just because he enjoyed it.

Apostadiro was asked for this book whether the chickenfights and other gambling operations he had taken part in running over the years nevertheless paid off to and in other ways cooperated with organized crime. In reply he equivocated. At various times he said "no," "maybe," "yeah I guess so," and "maybe you are right" that they paid off.

Chickenfights in Hawaii were to an extent a cultural thing; they were popular in the Philippines and Apostadiro was Filipino. But his involvement gave the ILWU a black eye because chickenfights and other organized gambling events on Oahu for most of the years Apostadiro was known to have been involved had in fact been paying off to, and to an extent were run by, organized crime. The cockfights thus supported men who in the ordinary course of business committed murder.

* * *

The changing situation of the ILWU in terms of land and power in contemporary Hawaii was brought into sharp focus by a change in the employment base of the island of Molokai in the 1970s.

In this instance the ILWU was willing and able to use its political influence for union objectives that were also seen as having public interest benefits. And a major mainland developer involved had to come to terms, at least to some extent, with the local power structure, which on Molokai included the ILWU.

This particular Molokai development came along at a time when plantation agriculture on the island was failing—a matter of tremendous concern to the ILWU statewide, causing the union to make strenuous efforts to find replacement employment. And the ILWU found itself in sharp competition with another union to represent workers at the new development.

Molokai through most of the twentieth century was half pineapple plantation on the west end of the island, Hawaiian homesteading in the center, and some subsistence living on the east end.

The pineapple workers since the end of World War II were predominantly Filipino. The homesteaders and many of those living at subsistence level were Hawaiian. There were smaller groups of Japanese and *haoles*, usually in middle-class managerial and professional jobs. In 1970 the population of the island broke down as 36% Hawaiian, 32% Filipino, 15% *haole*, 14% Japanese.

From the mid-1940s the pineapple workers had been represented by the ILWU.

Since at least the early 1960s pineapple in Hawaii had been in long-term decline, particularly canned pineapple, underpriced by cheaper labor in tropical parts of the Third World. For example, in 1973 with labor costs accounting for about half of the costs of production, a Hawaii worker got $2.79 an hour for harvesting pineapple; in Taiwan the same work was being done for 17 cents. Against this background, Hawaii's share of world pineapple production 1950–1973 dropped from 72% to 33%.[81]

By the late 1960s Libby, McNeil & Libby's operation on Molokai was faltering. In 1969–1970 Castle & Cooke's Dole Co. took it over. Then in 1972 and early 1973 both Dole and the other pineapple company operating on Molokai, Del Monte Corporation, announced that they would shut down by 1975.[82]

This was nothing short of devastating. On an island with a total population in 1970 of 5,261, the pineapple companies provided 520 full-time year-round jobs and 1,200 seasonal jobs.[83] In addition the pineapple companies leased land from Hawaiian homesteaders—another part of the population dependent on pineapple. Other than pineapple there was no industry of any size on Molokai. And even before the announcement of the closings, unemployment was a problem—16% in 1972 as against a state average of 7.5%.[84]

Dole closed in 1975 as planned. Del Monte lingered on for several years. In 1982 the company announced it would be finally closing on Molokai at the same time as it would be shutting down its cannery on Oahu. Then in December 1983 Del Monte announced it would keep about half its Molokai acreage in production for the fresh fruit market, employing about 85 workers.[85]

What could replace pineapple as a generator of employment on Molokai? To many people, in government, in business, and in the labor force, the only effective alternative seemed to be tourism—resort development.

Actually, as long ago as about 1960, tourism was being contemplated by the Molokai Ranch Co., which was owned primarily by the old *haole* Cooke family.

The ranch's holdings were in the western part of Molokai, pineapple country, and amounted to 46% of the total land area of the island.

Tourist resorts in Hawaii were typically on southerly and westerly coasts of the islands, sunnier and drier than windward coasts to the north and east, hence much favored by tourists. The south and west sides also tended to have more of the white sand beaches that tourists liked. The basis of white sand was coral, and coral grew best in shallow seas not subject to heavy fresh-water runoff from rain as were the windward sides of most Hawaiian islands. Molokai's west end was in this pattern, sunny, dry, with fine beaches; so the west end had some of the basic components of successful resort development.

Molokai Ranch commissioned a planning study, and a plan was publicly announced in 1967 looking forward to a 20,000-acre resort community, with 4,000 hotel rooms and 30,000 residents.[86]

In 1969 a joint venture was formed between Molokai Ranch and Louisiana Land & Exploration Co. to carry out the development, under the name of Kalua Koi Corporation (in 1983 renamed Kaluakoi Corporation). Louisiana Land's principal lines of business were oil and gas exploration, land reclamation and heavy industrial development. In the Molokai endeavor Louisiana Land was to supply the money and skills, the ranch was to provide the land.

The insistence of tourists on dry sunny weather gave resort developers everywhere in Hawaii a perennial problem: where to get fresh water. Molokai was no exception. The west end was dry. Thus in 1967 when the west Molokai development was announced, a spokesman said that success depended in part on the State helping to supply water.[87]

In the early 1970s, this need of the resort for water ran head-on into fears by some Hawaiian residents of Molokai that the island was not big enough for both the local community and such a large tourist community. The figures seemed on the face of things to be cause for concern: just over 5,000 local residents as against a planned 30,000 newcomers.

Where would the water come from for these 30,000 prosperous people with their many bathrooms and showers and dish washers and lawn sprinkler systems and golf courses?

In the early 1960s the State had begun building a major agricultural water system on Molokai, funded by state and federal money, the cost of which was to be repaid by users. By the late 1960s the system was in operation.[88]

Under state law, the Hawaiian homesteaders of central Molokai were to be given preference for use of up to two-thirds of the system's capacity.

Kalua Koi wanted to be able to make use of this state system along with the Hawaiian homesteaders. Kalua Koi could raise water from wells in central Molokai. What the company needed was a way to get that water to its resort on the west end. The state system included a pipeline that ran much of the distance, with unused capacity sufficient for the resort's foreseeable needs. So it made economic sense to Kalua Koi to rent the unused space in the state's pipeline rather than go to the expense of building a line of its own.

Now, the water from Kalua Koi's wells in central Molokai was too salty for drinking. US Public Health Service standards allowed a maximum of 250 parts per million of salt content, and Kalua Koi well water measured 446. Kalua Koi had two options: build a desalinization plant; or mix its salty water with that of the State and the homesteaders, which had but 12 parts per million, making the Kalua Koi water drinkable.

It was overwhelmingly in Kalua Koi's interest to be able to tap into the existing water system and transmission line, thus avoiding having to build a desalinization plant and separate system and line. Kalua Koi proposed to the State to be allowed to tap in.[89]

But was this mixed use of the transmission line in the interest of the home-steaders? Not necessarily. Several Hawaiians opposed Kalua Koi's proposi-tion. There was fear of what the increased salinity might do to agriculture, even though the mix would be within Health Service maximums for safe farming and drinking. Other and perhaps greater fears loomed. Home-steader James Zablan, who was then also a member of the Hawaiian Homes Commission, was worried because "being farmers, we figure that if the time comes when water becomes tight and there are people [meaning thousands of tourists] down there on the west end, they're going to get priority."[90]

* * *

The State Land Board was the agency that would rule on the Kalua Koi water plan. The company believed it could benefit from political influence in dealing with the Board, and the ILWU believed it could benefit from providing influence. Thus, according to ILWU sources, Kalua Koi and the union struck a deal.

The ILWU strongly supported the creation of the resort anyway, to re-place pineapple jobs that were being lost. So the union offered to quietly intercede on Kalua Koi's behalf with the Board.

In exchange, according to several former ILWU officers interviewed for this book, when it came time to organize the resort workers, the ILWU wanted no resistance from Kalua Koi.

Specifically, according to the ILWU, Kalua Koi agreed to recognize the ILWU as their workers' collective bargaining agent via a "cross-check" or "card-check" recognition procedure. This meant that when the ILWU be-gan organizing, and reached a point where more than 50% of the employ-ees had signed cards calling for a federally-supervised representation elec-tion, then, after a neutral third party determined that indeed more than 50% had signed, Kalua Koi would simply agree to ILWU representation.

(For this book an attempt was made to locate and interview the Kalua Koi project manager or general manager with whom two ILWU officers said the union reached the water/cross-check agreement. According to a Kalua Koi executive interviewed for this book, the man had apparently left Hawaii sometime in the mid-1970s and his whereabouts were unknown.)

Subsequently Maui ILWU Division Director Tom Yagi spoke personally with Gov. Burns in favor of Kalua Koi. Yagi would probably have gotten a cordial hearing in any case, because the Burns administration also sup-ported the resort development and believed the water plan was necessary for the project's viability.

The Land Board in due course voted to approve. According to the min-utes of the action meeting, the ILWU member of the board, Newton Miyagi, did not arrive until after the Kalua Koi vote. Opponents of the plan spoke against it following the vote; but the Board, now with Miyagi present, de-clined to reconsider its vote.[91]

So Kalua Koi had permission to use the state water line.

Legal challenges followed, from a Hawaiian group on Molokai and an Oahu-based environmental organization, Life of the Land. These held up matters for several years, but the plan was eventually implemented, and ground was broken by Kalua Koi in 1975 for a 298-room Sheraton hotel.[92]

By that time, in a move to ward off local opposition, Kalua Koi had acquired from Del Monte a well in central Molokai with relatively low salt content—70 parts per million. This was the water Kalua Koi ultimately put through the state line. It raised the overall salt content of the mixed water in the line from 12 to only 16 parts, pure enough for drinking as well as for agriculture.[93]

So, despite early misgivings by some Hawaiians, use of the mixed water by homesteaders wound up causing no known problems and led to no formal complaints—though concern persisted about over-development on the west end, and about the preemption of prime Hawaiian shoreline by tourism.

In 1976, when the golf course at Kalua Koi was opening and had hired 36 employees, the ILWU began organizing. The union got signed cards from more than 50% of the workers. Kalua Koi then agreed to recognize the ILWU as collective bargaining agent through the cross-check procedure.[94]

The ILWU at this point was entitled to believe that its support for Kalua Koi's water supply and the resort in general had paid off in the form of easily obtaining representation of Kalua Koi's workers.

In fact it may not have been a case of a *quid pro quo* at work. The Kalua Koi vice-president who agreed to uncontested ILWU representation said in an interview for this book that he had arrived on the scene only in 1976, and was unaware of a possible earlier water deal. He said he agreed to ILWU representation for several reasons. He pointed out that the ILWU had supported the entire resort proposal, not just the water line, actively organizing for it and speaking at public hearings. Many of the resort's workers had been ILWU members on the pineapple plantations and would probably vote to have the ILWU represent them at the resort anyway, he believed. And in the short time he had been in Hawaii he said he had come to respect the ILWU overall.

In any case, several months later, with the hotel getting ready to open and hotel workers being hired, difficulties arose for the ILWU. Now the ILWU was not dealing with a well-disposed Kalua Koi vice-president. The employer here was not Kalua Koi the developer but Sheraton the hotel operator; and Sheraton, by a cross-check, recognized and signed a collective bargaining agreement not with the ILWU, but with a rival union.[95] The ILWU was furious.

The other union was Local 5 of the Hotel, Restaurant Employees and Bartenders Union, AFL-CIO, then led by the ILWU's old enemy in Hawaii, Art Rutledge. Local 5 at that time represented employees of all unionized Sheraton hotels in Hawaii. For this and other reasons the ILWU took the view that Sheraton and Local 5 had developed a sweetheart relationship and had conspired to bring Local 5 into the Sheraton Molokai.

There was evidence to support the ILWU view:

In an interview for this book, a man who was a Local 5 business agent involved with organizing the Sheraton Molokai said "I think we had an edge [over the ILWU]." This was because he thought Sheraton believed that one union or another was going to obtain representation, and that Sheraton preferred Local 5 since it was already having to deal with Local 5 elsewhere in Hawaii. The business agent indicated that Sheraton helped out Local 5 in the Molokai case by hiring certain off-island personnel favorable to his union. He said that "some of the people who went into training [at the Sheraton Molokai] were friends [of Local 5]." As circumstantial evidence of there having been a sweetheart relationship, the business agent said that in general "you cannot get a card check without the cooperation of the employer."

This all fitted with the ILWU view of things. The ILWU newspaper charged that "Sheraton apparently connived with Local 5 to grant recognition and to make it look legitimate by conducting a cross-check of membership cards before the ILWU had a chance to petition for an election. The action was timed for a weekend when the NLRB [National Labor Relations Board] office was closed."[96]

For this book an attempt was made to interview the man who had been Sheraton's vice-president for industrial relations in 1977, Richard Hashimoto. He declined.

The NLRB's version of things was that the Local 5-Sheraton collective bargaining agreement was signed the very same day that the ILWU submitted an election petition to the NLRB, and that at the time Sheraton signed the agreement it did not know the ILWU petition had been filed. Thus the NLRB later ruled that the agreement was valid.

The ILWU did not take this sitting down, but set about collecting signed workers' cards of its own. In three weeks it said it had 73% of the hotel workers signed up, which meant that a good many must have switched from Local 5. But the NLRB subsequently ruled that this was all too late, and Local 5 was recognized.[97]

The ILWU leaders believed they had been deceived. Certainly they were outmaneuvered.

It was a far cry from the great organizing drives of the 1940s and the huge strikes of the 1940s and 1950s.

*   *   *

In making a deal with Kalua Koi in the early 1970s, the ILWU was using political influence built up in earlier times but now eroding.

In fact, looked at objectively and with the benefit of hindsight, the ILWU probably peaked in the 1960s and began declining in its power base.

As early as the 1950s, reapportionment of the Hawaii House of Representatives, reflecting population shifts away from the outer islands to Oahu, began to chip away at the number of representatives from the rural strongholds of the ILWU. Then in 1967, the very year in which Jack Hall was judged to be the second most influential man on Oahu, meaning essentially statewide, reapportionment caused the number of outer-island senators to go from 15 to 6 in the 25-member Senate.

Over this same period, sugar and pineapple were going into decline, and this hit hard in the 1970s, when a number of plantations, mills and canneries began to close. Public announcements of closures came one after the other: Kilauea Sugar Co. on Kauai in 1970; Kohala Sugar Co. on the Big Island and Kahuku Plantation Co. on Oahu in 1971; Hawaiian Fruit Packers on Kauai and Dole Co. on Molokai in 1972, with Dole announcing at the same time that its Oahu pineapple acreage would be cut 50% over the next three years; and Del Monte Corporation on Molokai in 1973. (Del Monte, as mentioned above, delayed closing, then announced in 1983 it would go on with about half its Molokai acreage—but at the same time announced it was closing its Oahu cannery.)[98]

Causing further instability was Congress's 1974 decision to allow the Sugar Act to lapse, reducing Hawaii sugar's ability to compete with Third World sugar, produced with cheap labor and allowed onto the American market at low prices for foreign policy reasons, alongside heavily subsidized sugar from European Economic Community countries. Then there were the artificial sweeteners. US per capita consumption of sugar 1972–1982 dropped 25%, and leaders of the Hawaii sugar industry blamed this largely on the sweeteners.

In part due to these trends and events yet another sugar plantation, the Big Island's Puna Sugar Co., began closing in 1982, and was shut down for good in the fall of 1984.[99]

Another major trend putting the ILWU more and more at the mercy of forces it could not control was that the bulk of Big Five ownership and operations were no longer confined to Hawaii. Worldwide business expansion and diversification meant among other things that the areas of operation of Hawaii's plantation owners were now vastly wider than the ILWU's. Thus the fact that the ILWU could strike Hawaii's sugar industry or mount an effective lobbying effort in the Hawaii Legislature meant much less to, say, the Amfac of the early 1980s, with some 80% of its revenues coming from non-Hawaii operations, than it did to that company in the early 1960s, when all or almost all of its revenues came from Hawaii.

Many people believed this trend was also bringing about a tougher bottom-line attitude on the part of sugar industry executives, and a greater willingness to consider getting out of sugar altogether. Thus Amfac Board Chairman Henry A. Walker Jr. told an ILWU convention in 1983 that "as ownership and management authority gradually move away from the Hawaiian center of gravity the notion of a permanent sugar industry becomes harder to perpetuate."[100]

Also changing was the social composition of the ILWU membership, somewhat undermining the union's position in the power structure of Hawaii.

When the union first started in Hawaii, most of its members were plantation workers. Although since the late 1950s the ILWU had held steady at around 22,000 members in full-time jobs, by the 1980s only about half were in sugar or pine. The next largest group was in tourism, and after that came workers in all manner of enterprises—everything from hospitals to newspapers and car dealerships.[101]

The non-plantation members did not live in close-knit communities like the plantation workers of an earlier era, and they tended to not stay with one employer as long as plantation workers—who often stayed a lifetime. The younger workers grew up after the ILWU and other unions had been organized, and so did not know what it was like to live without the basic securities the unions provided. Those who were teenagers in the 1960s grew up in an atmosphere that was rather hostile to authority figures of all types. At the same time, over the long haul, the ILWU leadership was becoming somewhat bureaucratized, middle-class, and less vigorous. All this led to the evolution of a membership somewhat less responsive to leadership. Among other things this meant a declining willingness for members to vote as the ILWU Political Action Committee suggested, in turn undermining the ability of ILWU leadership to bargain effectively with politicians.

Also somewhat undercutting the old unity of the ILWU's early years were some of the union's own greatest successes. As mentioned the ILWU created probably the single most effective housing program for working-class people in Hawaii. The ILWU also made Hawaii's plantation workers among the highest paid agricultural workers in the world. All this was not to say that the average Lihue Plantation Co. employee living in his own home in Hanamaulu, Kauai was on a financial par with the average resident of Menlo Park, California or Fairfax, Virginia. But that person in Hanamaulu for several decades now had been doing well enough that he felt less constrained to be a down-the-line union man when voting in local and national elections.

And then, as mentioned, ILWU members were a declining percentage of the electorate, down from 9–10% in 1962 to 5% in 1982.[102]

All of which, to get back to the subject of labor as a significant element in land and power in Hawaii, was undermining the position of the ILWU, creating a somewhat more fragmented and decentralized political scene, at a time when Hawaii itself was coming more and more under the sway of remote and impersonal forces of the world economy.

6

LAND AND BIG BUSINESS: THE EXAMPLE OF AMFAC

THERE is a story told about the Big Five firm American Factors in the late 1950s on the eve of the land boom. One of the company's directors, Howard Butcher III, a mainlander, a Philadelphia banker, was urging the sale of some land to help finance the development of a resort. Another director with strong Hawaii ties rebuffed him in words that became celebrated: "But, Mr. Butcher, we in the Islands don't sell land."[1]

This had been essentially true for American Factors and others of the Big Five for many decades. Having acquired land, they held it. They did not like to sell.

But what worked satisfactorily in the second half of the nineteenth century and the first half of the twentieth was not necessarily good business in the changing times that came upon Hawaii with such things as the land boom, statehood, and the era of conglomerates and multinational corporations. Whether American Factors and the rest of the Big Five initially wanted to or not, they found that they had to get involved in land sales, and land development, on a large scale. The times demanded it.

* * *

In this chapter, the example of American Factors (renamed Amfac in 1966) will be used as a way to look at the workings of big business of local origin in terms of land and power in Hawaii in the Democratic years. Others of the Big Five will be referred to for general context.

The business that became Amfac started out in 1849 as H. Hackfeld & Co., a German-owned firm with a small general store on the Honolulu waterfront.[2]

As the sugar industry became established in Hawaii, Hackfeld began servicing the sugar plantations: obtaining capital, labor and supplies for them; selling their sugar; representing them with the government. Hackfeld's first such arrangement dated from 1853, with Koloa Plantation on Kauai (Hawaii's first sugar plantation, begun in 1835).

Hackfeld and other leading Honolulu merchants were considered better qualified for these jobs, and certainly they were much better located to handle them than, say, the men running Koloa on the remote south coast of Kauai.

Toward the end of the nineteenth century, sugar middlemen like Hackfeld, known as "factors" or "agents," were beginning to take over the plantations they were servicing.

Essentially this was because the factors had larger and more regular supplies of money. The industry needed capital for expansion, especially after 1876, when a reciprocity treaty between Hawaii and the United States came into effect. The treaty allowed Hawaii sugar into the United States duty-free. This set off rapid growth in the Islands' sugar industry. In 1875, the last year before the treaty took effect, Hawaii exported about 25 million pounds of sugar; ten years later, some 171 million pounds were exported. The Honolulu factors were in a position to provide or obtain the capital the planters needed, by making direct investments in plantation companies, by lending from their own funds, by allowing lines of credit on supplies, and by negotiating financing from banks.

In between boom periods there were depressions, problems with drought, changes in US laws on sugar imports, and so on. Planters who found themselves in hard times, even facing bankruptcy, often turned over to their factors quantities of stock in their plantation companies, rather than go out of business altogether.

In 1948 a Harvard economist summed up this process: "The vital lack of capital, and the superior access which the commercial houses [factors] had to capital, gave them a strategic advantage in their dealings with the plantations . . . A near crisis from acute stringency [shortage] of capital during the vast expansion following 1876, and several later depressions in which plantations were faced either with bankruptcy or the necessity of turning over stock to their factors, have led to the complete domination of the sugar industry by the largest factors."[3]

In time the largest factors came to be called "the Big Five." Besides Hackfeld there were Alexander & Baldwin (A&B), Castle & Cooke, C. Brewer, and Theo. H. Davies.

The Big Five's domination of the plantations, if initially a result of uncontrollable things like the weather and business cycles, may later have taken on a more consciously exploitative character. A federal labor investigator wrote in 1906: "These companies [the factors] take a profit on nearly all the freight that passes the plantation boundaries in either direction. Their commissions, which are very liberal, are collected in bad as well as good years. Moreover, they are the plantations' bankers, and have the pickings of their financial transactions. In addition to the plantation agencies, there are transportation companies, both land and marine, and irrigation companies, all living off the plantations and taking their profits in lean years as well as fat ones. The stock of all these companies is owned by the men who are the most heavily interested in plantation stocks. These inside investors are therefore often making a comfortable income out of the sugar industry in years when the outside investor is receiving no return on his capital."[4]

*   *   *

At the beginning of the twentieth century a pineapple industry was also established in Hawaii. In time the Big Five achieved a major position in this business as well, in part through starting their own pineapple operations, in part through taking over others. The Big Five, though, never attained the utter control of the pineapple industry that characterized sugar. In pineapple from early on large US mainland companies took part: Libby, McNeill & Libby; California Packing Corporation (in 1967 renamed Del Monte Corporation); and later Stokely-Van Camp Inc. There were small independent growers as well.

If pineapple's story in Hawaii differed from sugar's with respect to the extent of Big Five control, still there were similarities when it came to Big Five behavior. In this regard there is a famous story of a Big Five company taking over a large independent grower:[5]

James D. Dole was a Boston-born distant relative of the missionary Doles whose son, Sanford, became president of the government established in the wake of the overthrow of the Hawaiian monarchy in 1893, and later the Territory of Hawaii's first governor.

James Dole arrived in Hawaii in 1899. In 1901 he incorporated the Islands' first successful pineapple business, to produce canned pineapple.

Dole's Hawaiian Pineapple Co. Ltd. became over the next quarter century the largest or one of the largest pineapple packers in the world, and pineapple became established as Hawaii's second biggest industry.

In 1931 Hawaiian Pineapple accounted for about 38% of the Islands' production, as measured by cases of canned pineapple produced.

Through 1931, Matson Navigation Co. had been the sole shipper of all Hawaii pineapple. That year a Matson rival offered to ship Dole's pineapple for less than what Matson was charging. Dole welcomed and accepted the offer because the Great Depression was on and his firm was reportedly facing bankruptcy; among other things Hawaiian Pineapple had loans outstanding that the company was having difficulty repaying.

Two of Dole's board members at the time were top officers of Castle and Cooke. According to historian Lawrence H. Fuchs, they may have conveyed the fact of the rival's offer to Matson since Castle & Cooke was an "agent and substantial owner" of Matson. However it happened, talks subsequently took place involving officers of Matson and Castle & Cooke, the upshot being, according to Fuchs, that "Dole soon found that banks in San Francisco as well those in Honolulu were unable to renew his loans. [Then] in October 1932, Hawaiian Pineapple was reorganized to avoid catastrophe, and Dole was replaced as general manager by Atherton Richards, a former treasurer of Castle & Cooke . . ."[6]

By around the end of World War II Castle & Cooke owned 18% of Hawaiian Pineapple. By the late 1950s the Castle & Cooke interest was 52%. In 1972 the business that James Dole founded 71 years earlier became part of the food division of Castle & Cooke.[7]

There is a postscript to this story: because during the first half of the twentieth century the name of the company's founder had become synonymous with pineapple products in the United States, in 1960 Hawaiian Pineapple Co. was renamed Dole Corporation; in 1964 the name became Dole Co.

*   *   *

H. Hackfeld & Co. also underwent a change of ownership and a change of name, though for different reasons. As a result of World War I, German-owned businesses in the US had their assets seized by the federal government. Hackfeld was sold to a group of prominent Hawaii businessmen of non-German extraction, and the firm took on the patriotic name of American Factors. (The company's clothing store, B.F. Ehlers, became Liberty House.) The businessmen taking over were affiliated with others of the Big Five; and until after World War II when some of these affiliations ended, American Factors was something of a stepchild to the rest.

On down through World War II and into the postwar years the Big Five continued to increase their ownership interests in their sugar and pineapple plantations, as had Castle & Cooke in Hawaiian Pineapple Co., to achieve greater control, also for reasons such as better centralization of operations and increased borrowing capacity.

Then the land boom hit Hawaii in the later 1950s.

By having either founded or taken over most of Hawaii's plantations over the course of the last 100 years, hence having acquired vast tracts of sugar and pineapple land, the Big Five were positioned to take part in the boom.

Some Big Five companies were more fortunate in this respect than others.

Due to a set of coincidences of economic history, the plantation lands of Amfac (as the firm will be referred to for the rest of this chapter) were situated so as to have some of the best urbanizing potential of any Big Five land in the Islands.

Foremost among the Amfac plantations in this respect were Lihue Plantation Co., Oahu Sugar Co., and Pioneer Mill Co. Lihue Plantation owned most of the land in and around the Kauai county seat of Lihue, stretching north along the coast to well above the relatively large town of Kapaa—a natural urban-growth corridor that included some beautiful oceanfront land. Lihue Plantation also owned the 11,000-acre Princeville Ranch in lush Hanalei on Kauai's north shore; most of the ranch was sold in 1968 to a buyer who in the 1970s started a major resort there. Oahu Sugar owned lands around the town of Waipahu in leeward Oahu, in the natural path of westward urban expansion from Honolulu. Pioneer Mill owned immensely important lands in west Maui, in and around Lahaina, on which Amfac later built the Islands' first and most successful destination resort, Kaanapali. Amfac also owned a plantation and ranch in Waianae on Oahu which, however, it sold in 1946. These lands included Makaha Valley, later the site of a resort, and some beachfront land developed for condominiums.[8]

A&B and Castle & Cooke also had plantation lands with good development potential. A&B's were primarily on Maui. They included much of central Maui, hence a great deal of what became the fairly large town of Kahului. The property on which A&B's Wailea resort was built was not plantation land; it was originally owned by Ulupalakua Ranch, sold in the late 1950s to Matson Navigation Co., then obtained by A&B when A&B acquired a controlling interest in Matson as a result of settling a federal antitrust case in 1964. A&B built Wailea in joint venture with Northwestern Mutual Life Insurance Co.

A&B for a time also controlled the pineapple plantation land at the north end of west Maui which became the Kapalua resort in the 1970s. These lands were purchased mainly for ranching by one of the founders of A&B in the late nineteenth century. In time he incorporated as Baldwin Packers and planted pineapple. He died in 1911, and over the next several decades his heirs sold off about 25% of the company stock to A&B. Meanwhile, by the 1940s and 1950s Baldwin Packers was becoming uneconomical as a pineapple business. As a result, in 1962 it was merged into Maui Pineapple Co., of which A&B owned a majority interest. A&B now also owned a majority of the surviving company, thus had a controlling say in the use of the approximately 23,000 acres in west Maui that Baldwin Packers owned and brought into the company. In 1969, however, Maui Land & Pineapple Co. (ML&P) was carved out of A&B when the Cameron branch of the Baldwin family successfully moved to exchange their stock in A&B for certain A&B assets, which they put into ML&P. Among these were the Kapalua lands. The resort at Kapalua thus was a creation of the Cameron family through a subsidiary of ML&P.[9]

The Castle & Cooke plantation lands of greatest urbanizing potential were pineapple lands in central Oahu. Beginning in the 1960s a Castle & Cooke development subsidiary built Mililani Town there. Most or all of the lands used were obtained by Hawaiian Pineapple Co. in 1948 when it bought the 10,000-acre *ahupua'a* of Waipio from the John Papa Ii Estate.[10]

Brewer and Davies were not so fortunate as the other three of the Big Five. Brewer's lands were remote from population centers. An attempt in the 1970s at a resort near Ninole on the Big Island, Seamountain, was largely a failure. Davies had little property with development potential; for the most part the company was limited to relatively small commercial and light industrial holdings near the Hilo waterfront.[11]

*   *   *

For most of the Big Five, the era of intensive land development in Hawaii was also a time for diversification and expansion outside of Hawaii.

Amfac under a new president in 1967, Henry A. Walker Jr., Hawaii-born but willing to look beyond the Islands in business terms, began a major program of this sort. Over the ensuing years the company came to hold interests as diverse as a flower business in South Carolina, mushrooms in California, potatoes in Oregon, a mail-order business in South Dakota, pharmaceuticals in Alabama, a hotel in the Grand Canyon, and so on.

Amfac eventually was doing business in a majority of the 50 states, and joined the ranks of the *Fortune* 500—the country's 500 largest companies.[12]

By about 1970 more than half Amfac's annual revenues were coming from mainland operations. In 1983, by which time a very high percentage of annual revenues was being earned on the mainland, and only about 18% of stock was held by persons and institutions residing or based in Hawaii, the company moved the office of its president/chief executive officer and its administrative headquarters to San Francisco. (See Table 11.)

────────────────── TABLE 11 ──────────────────

DISPERSAL OF AMFAC OWNERSHIP, MANAGEMENT AND OPERATIONS
TO US MAINLAND, 1955—1983

1955. Mainland investor Harry Weinberg begins buying Amfac stock;   by 1966 owns 4% and gains seat on board of directors for one year.

1957. Philadelphia investment banker Howard Butcher III obtains enough stock to gain seat on board of directors, which he retains until antitrust charge forces resignation 1962.

1962. Approximately the first year in which more than half the company's stock is owned by mainland and foreign investors.

1965–67. Chase Manhattan Bank owns 8% of shares; mainland lumber company, Georgia-Pacific, considers acquiring Chase shares in possible takeover bid; Los Angeles insurance executive H. Leslie Hoffman 1966 buys the 8%, gains seat on board of directors.

1967. Amfac listed on New York and Pacific Coast stock exchanges as part of program to rapidly diversify and acquire mainland companies.

1970. Approximately the first year in which more than half the employees reside on mainland, more than half revenues come from mainland operations.

1973. Gulf & Western Industries Inc. surfaces as major shareholder with 7% of stock; as of 1983 owns 24.5%; as of 1983 Bass family of Fort Worth, Texas owns 11%.

1973. 71% of revenues come from operations outside Hawaii.

1974. Amfac president tells reporter he fears unfriendly takeover by company based in Persian Gulf.

1978. Board of directors vice-chairman, who is also chief financial and administrative officer, moves office to San Francisco.

1978. 80% of revenues come from operations outside Hawaii.

1980. First time annual shareholders meeting held outside Hawaii; held in San Francisco.

1981. Listed on London Stock Exchange.

1982. Hawaii shareholders control only about 18% of Amfac stock.

1983. Company president/chief executive officer relocates office to San Francisco.

Sources: Amfac Inc. annual reports to shareholders (various years); Frederick Simpich Jr., *Dynasty in the Pacific* (New York, 1974); miscellaneous references in newspapers and periodicals.

Among others of the Big Five, and the Big Sixth, Dillingham, there were
both similarities and variations on the path followed by Amfac:

As with Amfac, Castle & Cooke and Dillingham eventually set up administrative headquarters in San Francisco.

In 1982 only 9% of Castle & Cooke's stock was owned by Hawaii residents.
In 1983 Dillingham stockholders approved the sale of the company to a
private group of investors, most or all of whom were mainland-based.[13]

Two others of the Big Five came to be 100% owned outside Hawaii. Da-
vies was taken over in 1973 by Jardine, Matheson, a British firm based in
Hong Kong; and Brewer in 1978 became a subsidiary of Philadelphia-based
IU International Corp.[14]

Only Alexander & Baldwin stayed very much at home in Hawaii. As late
as 1982, 95% of A&B's revenues came from Hawaii operations (though the
company was reportedly looking to increase its mainland holdings); and
about half A&B's shares were still in the hands of Hawaii-based individuals
and institutions, with some 20% of the company still family-owned.[15]

All of the Big Five remained among Hawaii's largest businesses during
the Democratic years. Amfac, though, distinguished itself in this regard,
eventually outdistancing the rest of the Big Five, and everyone else for that
matter, in amount of gross annual revenue. Using this measure, by the early
1970s Amfac became Hawaii's largest locally based company, and remained
so until it ceased to be local with the move to San Francisco in 1983. Amfac
in 1974 became the first Hawaii corporation to earn $1 billion in a year, and
in 1981 became the first to earn $2 billion. A document Amfac filed with the
federal Securities and Exchange Commission in 1984 showed Amfac Sugar
Company as the largest Hawaii producer of raw sugar, accounting in 1983
for 31% of the industry total. Amfac was the only company with plantations
on all four major islands through 1984, when it closed its sole plantation on
the Big Island. In 1983 Amfac also said it was "the third largest operator of
resort hotels in Hawaii managing eight hotels and resorts with almost 3,150
rooms on the four major islands." And in terms of Hawaii land holdings,
Amfac reported that it owned about 60,000 acres and leased another
92,000 acres.[16]

* * *

The expansion that Amfac underwent starting in 1967 generally occurred through buyouts of existing companies that sold their businesses to
Amfac in exchange for Amfac stock.

There was a Hawaii land tie-in to how and why this occurred:

For most buyers of stock in the US the key indicator of value was earnings
per share. Thus for Amfac to be able to make attractive buyout offers it was
important to keep earnings up.

Achieving steady and high earnings was a function of such things as continually applying new technological innovations, operating efficiently, and
diversifying in order to be as broadly based as possible to better withstand
the vagaries of business cycles.

Selling real property was another way for Amfac to generate earnings, and a relatively easy one.

Amfac, like other Big Five companies, was "land-heavy." Furthermore it had acquired much of its land at least a half-century earlier, and since then land values in Hawaii had risen astronomically, so that when sales were made in, say, the 1960s and 1970s, very large profits were realized.

Another dimension to land-heaviness was that, by one view, it tended to invite unfriendly takeover attempts:

Like others of the Big Five, Amfac generally carried its lands on the company books at values set by prices originally paid for the property. A 1973 Amfac report explained: "Over a period of more than 100 years, Amfac has accumulated real estate assets whose total value at any point in time is not possible to determine . . . At the end of 1973, the book value of the approximately 65,500 owned acres in Hawaii was $10,793,000."[17]

$10.8 million for that much land, which included tracts in such urbanizing areas as Lihue on Kauai, Kaanapali and Lahaina on Maui, and Waipahu on Oahu, was a low figure indeed for 1973.

By one theory, an extremely low book value for an asset like land, if undeveloped and owned in great quantity by a corporation whose stock is publicly traded, tends to invite takeover. Although a corporation may have a lot of valuable land, still, as mentioned, the price of the company's shares usually depends on corporate earnings. If for some reason earnings are low, this tends to deflate stock prices. If the stock price is low in relation to what a prospective raider believes to be significant unrealized value in assets such as tracts of raw or agricultural land, then the raider may be willing in a takeover bid to pay higher than listed market price for the stock.

Amfac reportedly experienced two potential takeover scares in the mid-1960s and one in the mid-1970s. Amfac President Walker in 1974 discussed one with a *Honolulu Star-Bulletin* reporter, who wrote: "Like some other asset-heavy companies whose assets, particularly land, are carried on their books at their original purchase cost and not their true value, Amfac is a 'sitting duck' for a raid, Walker said." Walker also told the reporter that he was "scared stiff" of a takeover attempt by a company which he would not name, though he indicated it might be based in a Persian Gulf country. Walker said that he feared a takeover might be followed by dismemberment of Amfac, with the buyer selling off assets for cash.[18]

So Amfac, from the start of the land boom, and especially following the ascent of Walker to the presidency in 1967, sold land. The first large sale in the Walker era came in 1968, with the sale to an oil company of all but about 50 acres of the 11,000-acre Princeville Ranch.

The sales helped boost earnings. To an extent this helped keep up stock prices and ward off unfriendly takeovers. At the same time healthy earnings, which had a variety of causes, made it possible for Amfac to be the one doing the buying out, though apparently always on a non-hostile basis. Sales of land also at times meant higher dividends for stockholders. In addition

land sales provided expansion capital: to the extent that proceeds were reinvested, real property which had been appreciating in value but not earning
money was converted into income-producing assets.

During these years Amfac also developed land, most notably at Kaanapali. Land development in Hawaii had become a profitable business, and
one that moved non-income producing properties into the cash-generating
category.

Thus the lands that Hackfeld & Co. had obtained by taking over plantations to a great extent became the basis for a major and successful entry by
Amfac into the fast-paced and highly diversified business world that Hawaii
entered in the Democratic years.

                                *   *   *

When Hawaii's big landowners took the leap into selling land or developing land for new purposes, they were entering a business the likes of which
they had never known.

With the Democrats in power a new political day dawned in Hawaii,
bringing into government people whom the old companies did not automatically control. This political shift was especially felt in the land business,
since beginning in the 1960s there were new governmental land use regulations, and state and local governments were given a lot of say over development. By the 1970s these new rules were proliferating rapidly, creating a
time-consuming and expensive obstacle course for developers.

Organized labor, particularly the ILWU, also constituted a formidable
new presence. Later another important new element appeared: grassroots
community opposition to business activities, directed mostly against land
developments.

Also, in the early 1960s a major antitrust attack was mounted on the old
ways of doing business in Hawaii, one which also affected the land business.
The Islands' old *haole* elite had always been a tight group. Since the middle
of the nineteenth century their businesses, which is to say most business in
Hawaii, had been extensively interlocked by the sharing of officers and directors. This had been a key device for coordinating major business decisions and keeping not only business power but all power in Hawaii closely
held among a few wealthy men, often enabling the Big Five to act as the Big
One. Now, using antitrust laws, the state and federal governments attempted the dis-interlocking of most or all large businesses in Hawaii that
were direct competitors.[19]

Also in these years, in part due to antitrust efforts, there came to be a
more open business climate in Hawaii. Businesses from the US mainland
and other countries—including especially Japan from the early 1970s—
could now more readily enter the Hawaii scene and compete. Some of these
new entrants were very big players indeed.

The response of the big Hawaii corporations to these new realities was
pragmatic and businesslike. When objecting or resisting might make a difference they did so, but overall they adjusted.

On the largest scale, as mentioned, they began to expand and diversify.

The reasons for this were predominantly other than local-political. For purely business reasons it came to be thought preferable to be more broadly based geographically. But as well, executives of the large old firms began to feel that Hawaii had become a difficult place in which to do business.

In the antitrust area the Big Five yielded to much of the agitation and ended the interlocking of competitors, though years later some of this crept back.

At the same time the Big Five started to spread local business opportunities among men other than members of the old elite. Under steady pressure from the ILWU the Big Five also shared the wealth a bit more with their employees. Along the way the old companies acknowledged the power and the apparent permanence of the union in a wide variety of political and community matters.

The Big Five forced themselves to live with the new era of land regulation. Though they often complained, as did almost everyone in the development business, they ultimately resigned themselves to preparing the seemingly endless development applications and documentation required by government: environmental impact statements, district boundary amendment applications, county general plan amendment petitions, and so on.

The Big Five also came to terms with the apparently permanent Democratic political regime. They made the required donations to the election campaign war chests of Democratic politicians as well as to their old Republican allies, now the minority. They hired local-Asians and put them on their boards of directors to give their companies a less *haole* look, though most top slots and nearly all the power remained in *haole* hands. They developed more of a benign and responsible public face in local communities where they did business, especially where they had land development plans. They began to spend time doing community organizing and public relations work for their projects. Land was donated for public facilities like schools, parks and low-cost housing, to an extent as bargaining chips for the rezoning they needed as the Big Five went into land development.[20]

And, as important as anything else in their tactics and strategy, the Big Five hired or entered into development agreements with politically well-connected local businessmen and professionals who could give them back the immediate access to government that they had lost when the Democrats came into power.

*   *   *

This point about new connections is illustrated by Amfac's dealings with Joseph R. Pao:

Born on Kauai of Portuguese descent and born poor, Pao rose from literally nothing to become one of the largest homebuilders in post-World War II Hawaii.

After some years in the development business Pao and Amfac became joint venturers. One of their early projects came in 1959, when they teamed up to do a 100-acre residential development in Manoa Valley on Oahu. The next year they announced one of the most ambitious housing projects ever contemplated in Hawaii: a 25,000-home development on 13,500 acres of Bishop Estate and Bishop Museum land near Pearl Harbor, in and around Halawa, Waiawa and Waiau. Amfac was to provide building supplies and some of the financing. Pao's Lakeside Development Corp. was to build the houses. Another Pao outfit was to sell them.[21]

Included in Pao's duties was dealing with government. This was something he was well equipped to do. Pao was among that group of locally born, non-*haole* businessmen in favor with the new political establishment, one of "the former have-nots who were to be given every consideration," as he was described by Kekoa D. Kaapu in an interview for this book. Kaapu from the early 1960s through the mid-1970s was an aide to Gov. Burns, then a Honolulu city councilman, then Honolulu's urban renewal coordinator, and again a councilman. He said that when someone like Pao petitioned the government, it was understood that he should be accommodated. And "normally something like that wouldn't even have to be spoken. The idea is just he's one of our guys kind-of-thing, our friends."

Pao had ready enough access to Gov. Burns. He was also a close personal friend of Honolulu Mayor Neal S. Blaisdell. For example, Blaisdell and Pao and their wives, plus one of Blaisdell's political advisors and his wife, took a trip together to Las Vegas in 1960.[22]

Blaisdell was a politician not unwilling to favor his friends. One of Blaisdell's planning directors, Frederick K. F. Lee, said in an interview for this book that Blaisdell once told him that in reviewing a proposed development, if the situation was black and white, Lee was to go by the book. But, said Blaisdell, "if there's a grey area and you can lean toward my friends, OK, do it."

Beyond Pao's useful entree to the governor's office and the mayor's chambers, he had business ties across the political board, with Democrats and Republicans, liberals and conservatives, *haoles* and Japanese and Portuguese, as indicated by the following table (Table 12). The usefulness to Amfac of such a well-connected man is obvious.

─────────────── TABLE 12 ───────────────

JOSEPH R. PAO BUSINESS AND PERSONAL TIES WITH POLITICS AND GOVERNMENT

Note: All companies listed were organized and/or owned by Pao. The table's time focus is late 1950s through 1960s, thus some persons' later governmental positions are not indicated.

BLAISDELL, NEAL S. Honolulu mayor 1955–68. Personal friend; took Las Vegas trip together 1960; Pao 1960 sold Blaisdell house in Enchanted Lake for Blaisdell's daughter and son-in-law.

CLARK, CHARLES G. Honolulu city managing director till 1962. After he left city government 1962 Pao turned over 106-lot area for him to sell.

FERRY, JAMES P. Chairman State Board of Land and Natural Resources 1963–68. Pao's first cousin; tract manager Joe Pao Realty 1957–59; Pao planning consultant several projects after 1968.

HOUGHTAILING, GEORGE K. Honolulu city planning director 1942–57. Pao's planning consultant after leaving city government.

HULTEN, JOHN J. SR. Land and tax consultant to Democratic legislators and to city; Senate 1963–78 including senate president 1967–68. Kailua Heights investor approximately 1956; real estate salesman's license at Joe Pao realty 1964–69; son was Pao attorney/officer.

KIDO, MITSUYUKI. Territorial Senate 1957–59; candidate for lieutenant governor 1959; State Senate 1963–66. Kailua Heights investor approximately 1956; Enchanted Lake investor 1958; Queen Emma Associates 1960; Windward Partners 1975–83.

LEE, KAM TAI. Territorial treasurer 1950s; former legislator. Queen Emma Associates investor 1960.

LEMKE, HERMAN G.P. Honolulu supervisor and councilman 1955–68; council chairman 1965–68. Lemke's accounting firm became Pao's accountant beginning 1961.

MARUMOTO, MASAJI. Associate justice Supreme Court 1956–60, 1967–73. Director Hawaiian Pacific Industries Inc. early 1960s; Pao attorney in state antitrust case 1962.

STEADMAN, ALVA E. Judge First Circuit Court and Land Court 1927–32; former chairman territorial Board of Labor and Industrial Relations. Chairman Hawaiian Pacific Industries Inc. starting 1960.

Sources: Gwenfread E. Allen, ed., *Men and Women of Hawaii: A Biographical Directory of Noteworthy Men and Women of Hawaii* (Honolulu, 1966); Betty F. Buker, ed., *Men and Women of Hawaii 1972: A Biographical Directory of Noteworthy Men and Women of Hawaii* (Honolulu, 1972); Department of Commerce and Consumer Affairs, Business Registration Division; State of Hawaii, Legislative Reference Bureau, *Directory of State, County and Federal Officials: Supplement to Guide to Government in Hawaii* (published occasionally, most recently annually); Chamber of Commerce of Hawaii, *Who's Who in Government State of Hawaii* (various years); Hawaii State Archives; miscellaneous references in newspapers and periodicals.

The emergence of people like Joe Pao also illustrated the changing sociology of Hawaii business and political leadership in the late 1950s and 1960s. In, say, 1965, while implementing his big joint venture agreement with Amfac near Pearl Harbor, Pao might want to see Gov. Burns about state capital improvement plans; Mayor Blaisdell about plans for extending city services into the new urban area; City Council Chairman Herman Lemke and possibly other councilmen about zoning; or Bishop Estate trustee Herbert J. Keppeler about lease policies. Keppeler, Burns, Blaisdell, Lemke plus two other councilmen that year, Pao's consultant and former Honolulu planning director George Houghtailing, and Pao himself, had all gone to a largely working-class Catholic high school, St. Louis in Kaimuki. No longer were the graduates of the old *haole*-dominated elite Punahou School the only people in a position to make big decisions about land in Hawaii.

* * *

Another case of Amfac making new connections in the Democratic years had to do with Masaru "Pundy" Yokouchi and Amfac's major development at Kaanapali in west Maui:

Kaanapali until the early 1960s was several hundred acres of dry, sunny cane and pasture land belonging to Amfac's Pioneer Mill Co. Amfac in 1957 announced its intention to build there Hawaii's first master-planned resort. Amfac itself was to develop the land and, generally, sell or lease the building sites to others.

The relationship between Amfac's tourism development at Kaanapali and its sugar operation at Pioneer Mill said a lot about changing balances in the economy and politics of Hawaii, all the way from the 1950s to the 1980s. Over that period, resort development at Kaanapali became profitable and sugar at Pioneer Mill unprofitable. In 1981 Pioneer had even higher costs per pound of sugar produced than did Amfac's plantation at Puna on the Big Island, which was about to be phased out as uneconomic. For the Hawaii sugar industry in general in 1981 there were 8.5 employees per ton of sugar produced. For Puna the figure was 9.1, for Pioneer 11.64. Yet Pioneer continued in production.[23]

In part this was in deference to state and county government and the ILWU, all of which wanted the plantation kept in business because of the jobs it provided. Amfac needed the good will of all three entities: the union because workers at all other Amfac plantations were union members, and because ILWU men sat on various state and county boards with which Amfac had to deal; and government because Amfac had a great deal of developable land and development in Hawaii was intensively regulated by state and local authorities.

Besides, if anyone wanted to look at it that way, and Amfac had to, Pioneer Mill provided a picturesque visual backdrop to the big resort at Kaanapali. Amfac Board Chairman Henry Walker in late 1982 or early 1983 told a reporter that Pioneer's "sugar has value as ground cover if nothing else."[24]

By the mid-1980s the situation at Pioneer Mill was symptomatic of yet something else. Even with the plantation using new technologies which brought it back to the break-even point or slightly into profit, top management at Amfac was no longer committed to keeping Pioneer open indefinitely, should the plantation again start to lose money and have no apparent prospect of remaining profitable in the long term. By 1985 the possibility of a total phaseout of the Hawaii sugar industry was not a new thought, and with policy decisions like this at Amfac it was one that seemed to be steadily gaining ground.

* * *

The first hotel at Kaanapali opened in 1961. Development continued through the mid-1960s. Then, about 1967, Maui County began revising its general plan for Kaanapali and nearby Lahaina. Amfac revised its own master plan as well.[25]

Amfac at that point ran into trouble from various directions: from the ILWU unit at Pioneer Mill; from Maui-born small businessmen who were property owners in Lahaina; and from politicians who reflected the views of these two groups.

The Pioneer Mill management and the ILWU, according to both Amfac and ILWU men, had a long history of bad relations. Now the union, in retaliation for problems on the plantation, was trying to block Amfac's expansion at Kaanapali.

The Lahaina small businessmen were upset because Amfac was proposing the town be designated for historic preservation—meaning, preserve old Lahaina as a draw for tourists staying at the Amfac resort at Kaanapali. That might have made sense from an overall tourist-oriented Kaanapali-Lahaina view; and of course Amfac, which itself owned property in and around Lahaina town, could afford not to develop every square foot to the fullest. But for small businessmen historic preservation meant, among other things, severely limiting building heights; and that was no good for people other than Amfac who might want to go in for intensive development on their own account.

All this represented something of an impasse, and Amfac needed the impasse broken.

That a Big Five firm could not automatically and effortlessly get what it wanted in a matter of land use—that it had to go looking for help—was in itself an indication of how much times had changed.

And the person Amfac approached, Masaru Yokouchi, embodied those changes:

Yokouchi was Gov. Burns' campaign manager and unofficial representative on Maui. He was widely respected. He was well-connected with both county and state governments. He was a good friend of the head of the ILWU on Maui. And, like most of the union leaders and the Lahaina small businessmen, he was Japanese. Part of Amfac's problem was that their executives were *haole*. They communicated poorly with locals, and indeed were viewed with deep suspicion at Pioneer Mill and in Lahaina.

A former Amfac official involved with Kaanapali in the late 1960s pointed out in an interview for this book that Amfac was a political outcast on Maui at the time, so that Yokouchi's apparent influence in government was crucial to the company approaching him. The former official said he believed that Yokouchi "had the Council very well wired," and he "had the ILWU" as well. Thus, "as far as I was concerned, there wasn't any other way to go" but to try to hire Yokouchi.

Measuring a person's political influence is an imprecise business. An indicator, though, of the extent to which Yokouchi was closely connected with people in politics and government was the makeup of a realty company he headed as of 1967, about the time Amfac came to see him regarding Kaanapali. The following table (Table 13) shows all Valley Isle Realty Inc. officers, directors and shareholders in that year. Of a total of ten, nine at the time held some sort of government position; the tenth had previously been a state employee. Besides Yokouchi himself, who was close to the governor, the nine included two state senators, a member of the Maui County Board of Supervisors, a county planning commissioner, and a county department head.

TABLE 13

VALLEY ISLE REALTY 1967 SHOWING CONNECTIONS WITH POLITICS AND GOVERNMENT

YOKOUCHI, MASARU. President, director, shareholder. Governor's representative on Maui.

OTA, CHARLES S. V-P, director, shareholder. Maui member of University of Hawaii Board of Regents.

IZUMI, JAMES M. Secretary, director, shareholder. Director County Dept. of Personnel Services.

YANAGI, WALLACE T. Treasurer, director, shareholder. Assistant administrator Maui Memorial Hospital.

YOSHINAGA, NADAO. Director, shareholder. State senator.

MORISAKI, LANNY H. Director, shareholder. County supervisor.

CHING, ELMER J. Director, shareholder. District overseer County Dept. of Public Works.

MATSUI, YOSHIKAZU. Director, shareholder. County planning commissioner.

FUKUOKA, S. GEORGE. Director, shareholder. State senator.

WATANABE, WINSTON T. Director, shareholder. No current government position; formerly area sanitarian, State Health Dept.

Sources: Gwenfread E. Allen, ed., *Men and Women of Hawaii: A Biographical Directory of Noteworthy Men and Women of Hawaii* (Honolulu, 1966); Betty F. Buker, ed., *Men and Women of Hawaii 1972: A Biographical Directory of Noteworthy Men and Women of Hawaii* (Honolulu, 1972); Department of Commerce and Consumer Affairs, Business Registration Division; State of Hawaii, Legislative Reference Bureau, *Directory of State, County and Federal Officials: Supplement to Guide to Government in Hawaii* (published occasionally, most recently annually); Chamber of Commerce of Hawaii, *Who's Who in Government State of Hawaii* (various years); Hawaii State Archives; miscellaneous references in newspapers and periodicals.

With the personal approval of Gov. Burns, Yokouchi became Amfac's representative in working on the Kaanapali-Lahaina problem.

For the benefit of the ILWU, Yokouchi helped persuade Amfac to initiate a worker housing program and other community programs. This won ILWU support for Amfac at Kaanapali. Having testified against Kaanapali expanding at an early county hearing, at a later hearing the ILWU came out in support of Amfac.[26]

Yokouchi was able at the same time to convince the small businessmen of Lahaina that making the town a historic district would not harm them, but rather would be in their interest. According to Yokouchi in several inter-views for this book, he asked them if they were businessmen first or devel-opers. If businessmen, then the building height limitation that was their sharpest concern was really no worry. He said preserving the physical charm of old Lahaina would guarantee that tourists would come there from Kaanapali, and the shops they would frequent would be at street level, where customers could easily walk in. The small businessmen eventually came around. Partly in consequence, the town was designated a historic preservation district.[27]

Apparently all concerned benefited. Lahaina filled up with tourist-oriented shops in buildings old and new, all low-rise, mostly reflecting building designs that harked back to the nineteenth century. And virtually all the local Japanese property owners whom Yokouchi talked to later be-came absentee landlords, collecting high rents from tenants who were mostly mainland *haole* small businesspeople.

Simply as property owners the local Lahaina people generally did well. The Taketaro T. Takeuchi family, for example, in 1961 bought for $21,000 an old fishmarket on a 6,418-square-foot parcel near the waterfront. For the next 20 or so years the family ran a small tourist-oriented retail outlet there. In 1983 the Takeuchis sold the property to ABC Discount Stores for $995,000.[28]

The historic district designation was not without its critics, among them the Takeuchis. Taketaro's son George, who came to run the family opera-tions, told this story:

In 1962 his father leased an old plantation store near the fishmarket. At some point afterwards his father had his old friend Tadashi Sato make mu-rals or wall panels on its front, using coral, stones, shells and white cement. Sato was perhaps contemporary Hawaii's most celebrated painter, who oc-casionally worked in other media. In 1969 the Takeuchis obtained the fee interest in this property, and in the mid-1970s they undertook major reno-vations. At that time a County Planning Department staff member told their architect that the Sato panels would have to be removed before the town's historic commission would approve the renovation. The problem was that Sato's materials were not current during the period of Lahaina's his-tory that the town's buildings had to reflect. According to the Takeuchis, to remove Sato's work intact they would have had to cut out entire sections of walls, something they considered prohibitively expensive. So the panels were jackhammered off the walls, and in the process they disintegrated. George Takeuchi found it ironic that, in the name of historic preservation, work by one of modern Hawaii's most famous locally born artists was de-stroyed.

* * *

Kaanapali became Maui's—and all of Hawaii's—first, largest, and peren-nially most successful destination resort, a standard against which to mea-sure others that followed. It played a major part in sparking the extensive development of Maui beginning in the late 1960s. Kaanapali was a turning point in Maui's modern economic history, and in the history of tourism in all of Hawaii for that matter.

The Amfac executive in charge of Kaanapali in the late 1960s said in an interview for this book that Masaru Yokouchi "was instrumental in a lot of our success in the Lahaina community" at that time, hence, to an extent, in the longterm success of Kaanapali.

Yokouchi's association with Amfac was something of a turning point for him as well. In part as a result of this relationship, within a decade he became one of Maui's financially more successful men. Up through the mid-1970s, for example, the Yokouchis lived in a pleasant but modest house in a suburb of Wailuku. But then in 1976 they moved to a large Tudor-style home on a 16-acre estate in Kula on the slopes of Haleakala, the total market value of which Yokouchi in the mid-1980s placed at about $1 million.

By his own account, Yokouchi was not particularly sophisticated when he started out in the land business. He never went to college. For 17 years of his adult life he worked in the family bakery in Wailuku, spending a lot of his free time coaching sports.

To some extent Yokouchi's later financial success came from a natural skill in investing. He also had the good fortune to move into investment in the place where he had lived all his life, and at a time when property values were appreciating rapidly.

Another part of Yokouchi's success may have come from the fact that he was generally considered a particularly unselfish person, someone who shared business opportunities with many friends. His personal manner was kind and fairly direct. Because of all this Yokouchi tended to be trusted, thus accommodated when he needed a favor.

In part, too, Yokouchi's longterm success came from his connections with Amfac. And his connections with Amfac came to him in the first instance because of his close connections with the Burns Democrats.

In several interviews for this book, Yokouchi outlined his career in real estate development from the time Amfac approached him. He said that when he agreed to represent Amfac at Lahaina the company offered him a fee. He declined. As it was, being no more than an unpaid spokesman for Amfac around Lahaina, he did not think he would be well received by local non-*haoles*. In fact an ILWU man called him "another *haole*" for working with Amfac. Actually being in Amfac's pay, Yokouchi believed, would have diminished his credibility to the point of ineffectiveness.

Yokouchi did tell an Amfac executive, though, as well as others who asked him why he was representing Amfac, that in return he hoped Amfac would later be willing "to do business with him." By his own account, often during his career in land investment and development he was asked to give advice or render a service such as he did for Amfac. Normally he did not ask for or accept a fee for this kind of thing. Rather, as with Amfac, he either suggested or simply hoped to himself that his help would be remembered later, that the person or company he helped would throw some business his way.

In the case of Amfac, Yokouchi hoped the company would sell him land.

Yokouchi from the late 1950s had been investing in land, usually through *huis* that he organized. Since 1960 he had had a real estate business, Valley Isle. But he had never bought Amfac land. And he had never built on land he owned.

Amfac on six occasions from 1970 to 1978 sold Yokouchi land with development potential, totalling approximately 105 acres, as Table 14 indicates. By 1973–1974 Yokouchi and his *hui* partners in transactions with Amfac were dealing in land values in the millions of dollars.

TABLE 14

AMFAC LAND SALES TO MASARU YOKOUCHI

1970. 3 acres Lahaina town on which Yokouchi built shopping center early 1970s. $492,664.

1971. Two half-acre parcels in light industrial section Lahaina town. $88,600. Resold raw 1973 for $160,000.

1973-74. Two abutting parcels totaling 60 acres oceanfront land at Nukolii, $1.2 million. Yokouchi bought and then organized a hui that became the owner; resold raw two-thirds of a year later for $5.25 million.

1975. 17 acres raw, residential-zoned land Lihue, Kauai. $1.5 million. Yokouchi bought and then had a hui organized that became the owner; resold raw 1978 for $2.1 million. Payments to hui were temporarily interrupted by bankruptcy of buyer in 1980; eventual payout to hui members represented poor return on investment.

1978. 8-acre building site within Kaanapali resort. $9 million. Yokouchi negotiated purchase mainly on behalf of Japanese businessman Masao Omori. Yokouchi also had small interest. Kaanapali Alii condominium subsequently built.

1978. Two adjacent parcels totaling 16.2 acres, surrounded by golf course, in Kaanapali resort, $2.5 million. Amfac later became interested in developing historic theme park on site. Negotiations in progress with Yokouchi mid-1980s.

Sources: City and County of Honolulu, Department of Finance, Real Property Assessment Division; State of Hawaii, Bureau of Conveyances; interviews with Masaru Yokouchi.

In each case Amfac of course was selling land because it was in the interest of the company to sell. Yokouchi noticed, for example, that at times the sales came at the end of a financial year when, he believed, Amfac had a use for cash before closing its books.

With each purchase, Yokouchi said, he paid what any other buyer would have had to pay. For example, he agreed to buy Nukolii in 1973 for $1.2 million. That was the price recommended a half year earlier by an independent appraiser, according to a document given to the authors of this book by a former Amfac executive, C. Earl Stoner.

With several of the Amfac properties that Yokouchi purchased, he said that they had first been offered to and turned down by someone else before he entered the picture. Yokouchi also said that as far as he knew, the prices that Amfac quoted to him were the same as those quoted to the prospective buyers who were in the picture before him.

In the case of one of the six purchases, the two half-acre parcels in Lahaina bought in 1971, Yokouchi said he purchased these at a public sale.

In three cases, Yokouchi alone was the buyer. In two others, after negotiating purchase, he organized *huis* that became the owner. In the sixth case he was basically representing Japanese businessman Masao Omori, though Yokouchi also took a small ownership interest.

All the acreage Amfac sold to Yokouchi was raw—that is, without buildings. In three instances Yokouchi resold the land raw, usually realizing good profits, though in one case he and a *hui* of his either lost money or only broke even. In two other cases development took place. In the sixth case, negotiations for development were under way in the mid-1980s.

*   *   *

All this began with Yokouchi's help to Amfac at Lahaina in 1967–1968. Clearly Amfac was grateful for that help, and saw Yokouchi as someone of stature and influence with whom an ongoing relationship would be useful. Indeed in subsequent years Yokouchi was willing and able to help Amfac in its dealings with government statewide, according to a former Amfac officer interviewed for this book, because Yokouchi "had a good deal of influence throughout the state." Therefore, the former officer said, Yokouchi's "importance [to Amfac] went far beyond" the Lahaina matter of the late 1960s.

As a result, Yokouchi entered a kind of Amfac inner circle of people to whom the company would readily sell land, a circle based on such things as previous business and political associations—and of course on ability to pay.

Within this group there were far bigger players than Yokouchi. For example, Harry Weinberg, who developed a sizable interest in Alexander & Baldwin, became as well one of Amfac's most regular land customers, and the value of his purchases greatly exceeded Yokouchi's.

At the same time, according to Yokouchi, his helping Amfac and the land sales that later occurred were not strictly speaking a straight *quid pro quo* situation. For example, he said that if Amfac really wanted to "take care of him," the company should have offered to sell him land immediately after he rendered the service in 1967–1968. Also, Amfac should have offered to sell him property with clear and certain income-producing potential—for example, an already developed shopping area—rather than raw land.

Yokouchi also said that his relationship with Amfac was a "two-way street," citing the following case. In the late 1970s Amfac sold Yokouchi an option on a 40-acre residentially zoned parcel near Kaanapali. Prior to exercising the option, Amfac asked him to relinquish it and instead buy a 16-acre area inside Kaanapali, which Yokouchi did. Then Amfac decided it might like to construct an historic theme park on the 16 acres. So, as a courtesy to Amfac, Yokouchi for several years held his own plans for the site in abeyance while Amfac decided what to do.

Amfac's willingness to sell land to Yokouchi and Yokouchi's ability to pay were sometimes two different things. For example, although Amfac provided him several million dollars interim construction financing for his 3-acre Lahaina shopping center, Yokouchi had to find long-term financing elsewhere to make the project go. Yokouchi's account of how he found the money is as follows:

He was negotiating with a California lender, Gibraltar Savings & Loan Association. Because at the time Yokouchi did not look to be a substantial developer, Gibraltar was driving a hard bargain. In the middle of negotiations Yokouchi went to the mainland for a golf tournament, and by coincidence he and the president of Gibraltar were in the same foursome. When the Gibraltar man found out who Yokouchi was, he said he would see that the loan went through without Yokouchi having to make any more concessions. This chance meeting on a golf course had nothing to do with Yokouchi's access to Amfac; yet without the Gibraltar loan Yokouchi would not have been able to build his shopping center.

On the other hand there was the Nukolii sale, where many believed that the price Yokouchi paid Amfac was rigged low by a secret side deal with an Amfac officer, Earl Stoner.

Stoner and Yokouchi had first worked together in settling Amfac's community problems in the Lahaina area in the late 1960s. It was Stoner who handled initial negotiations for the Nukolii sale on Amfac's behalf. Yokouchi paid Amfac $1.2 million for raw land whose zoning allowed essentially no development. He then organized a *hui* that became the owner, with himself as manager. Two-thirds of a year later, with the land still raw and unrezoned, the *hui* resold for $5.25 million.

A *Honolulu Advertiser* reporter in 1980 discovered and then wrote that Stoner at some point joined the Nukolii *hui*.[29] (Stoner told the reporter that he joined after he left Amfac, which was in 1975. In interviews for this book, however, both Stoner and Yokouchi admitted that Stoner had actually been invited to join and did join before leaving Amfac.)

Many who read the newspaper account believed Stoner deliberately obtained far too little from Yokouchi on Amfac's behalf, doing so because he was going to be allowed to invest in Yokouchi's *hui*.

After the *Advertiser* story, Amfac conducted an internal study of the transactions. The company said the study showed Stoner had obtained a fair price from Yokouchi.[30] Also, as mentioned, Stoner gave the authors of this book a copy of an appraisal of Nukolii done for Amfac in late 1972 that suggested as a price exactly what Yokouchi was charged in mid-1973. Furthermore, Stoner and Yokouchi pointed out in interviews for this book that other Amfac officials senior to Stoner had to approve the sale, indicating it would have been difficult or impossible for Stoner and Yokouchi on their own to connive on the sale terms.

* * *

Like all other major landowners and developers in the Democratic years, Amfac had to go before government agencies to get permission to urbanize lands.

And like most others, Amfac used politically well-connected people to represent the company in these matters.

This was especially so where government decision-making was highly discretionary—in other words, where members of agencies and commissions operated under laws that gave them a good deal of leeway about how to decide.

The State Land Use Commission, in ruling on land use district boundaries, was a body engaged in highly discretionary decision-making that was often crucial to Amfac's development plans. Being a Big Five company, therefore owning a great deal of plantation land, Amfac had most of its lands districted agricultural or conservation. Before attempting to develop such land, Amfac normally had to go to the LUC for urban districting.

To observe the extent to which Amfac used politically well-connected people before the LUC, and to calculate the company's success rate with the LUC, there were studied for this book all Land Use Commission district boundary amendment applications filed by Amfac, either solely or in joint venture, and decided upon up to September 1984. These totaled 17. (See Table 15.)

In such matters as parcel size and intended land use, the 17 applications divided themselves reasonably neatly into two groups:

The first group, with eight applications, included four for worker housing, one downzoning from urban to agricultural, and three concerning areas from 4.5 to 11 acres, apparently intended for single-family residential housing to be sold on the open market. Applications in this category, in other words, were either of the public interest variety or involved rather small projects. Little or no great potential profit was involved, and relatively easy LUC passage could be expected.

The second group, with nine applications, included parcels larger than 11 acres, ranging up to hundreds of acres, usually intended for major residential development, or commercial, resort, or industrial use. Large-scale applications of this sort often drew the close attention of government, the ILWU and community activists. Normally this sort of application encountered harder going, no matter who the applicant was.

Looking at the two groups of applications in terms of the involvement of politically well-connected people, the following could readily be observed:

Of the group of eight minor applications, 37% involved people with ties to government—for example, an Amfac executive sitting on the LUC at the time, or a former state attorney representing Amfac.

In the second group, involving larger acreages, high development costs, and projected returns ranging up into the millions, with possibly more difficulty in getting approval, Amfac had politically well-connected people representing them in 100% of cases.

All of the first group were approved fully or in part. So also, eventually, were all but one of the second group.

Amfac's overall approval rate was therefore 94%—as against an overall approval rate for all redistricting requests by all LUC applicants through September 1984, of about 77%.

In other words, Amfac did markedly better than average before the LUC, even in cases where "political" difficulty might have been expected. And this overall very high success rate in "political" cases was associated 100% with the presence of politically well-connected people.

These Amfac associates with political/governmental ties included men like developer Joe Pao, who joint-ventured with Amfac; Amfac plantation manager and then executive Caleb E.S. Burns Jr., an LUC commissioner in the 1960s; Amfac Distribution Co. employee George R. Pascua, an LUC commissioner in the 1970s; and Amfac planning consultant George K. Houghtailing, previously Honolulu city planning director for many years.

Amfac also retained politically well-connected attorneys such as Clinton I. Shiraishi and Francis M. Izumi:

Izumi, while attending law school at George Washington University in Washington, D.C. in the late 1950s, worked nights for then-Hawaii Congressional Delegate John Burns. Maui-born, Izumi came home in 1959 to work as a deputy Maui county attorney. In 1962 he was the Democratic Party's election campaign manager for Maui. From 1963 to 1968 Izumi was a deputy state attorney general assigned to the State Land Board. Throughout these years he was also a member of land *huis* that included politically well-connected people such as Masaru Yokouchi and State Sen. Nadao Yoshinaga. For example, Izumi, Yokouchi, and Yoshinaga were all officers and/or directors of a development company called Aloha Maui Co. Izumi's brother James started working in 1956 in the Maui County Department of Personnel Services. He rose to the directorship in 1962 and held the post into the 1980s. James was also active in land *huis* with Maui political figures, and served as an officer in Yokouchi's Valley Isle Realty, as did Yoshinaga and others in politics and government on Maui.

Shiraishi, also born on Maui, was in himself a study in power and influence in Hawaii in the Democratic years. A member of the 442nd Regiment, Shiraishi was decorated with four battle stars and a Purple Heart. After the war he went to college and then law school. Upon coming back to Hawaii, Shiraishi moved to Kauai and made it his home.

About that time or possibly earlier, Shiraishi did something unusual for his generation of Hawaii-born Japanese—he joined the Republican Party.

In 1954, the year of the great Democratic sweep of the Legislature, Shiraishi, the same day that he was sworn in to practice law in Hawaii, was appointed a district court magistrate for the town of Koloa. For a number of years down through 1962 he was a magistrate. In the later years his jurisdiction extended to Lihue as well.

In 1958 Gov. Quinn appointed Shiraishi to the territorial Board of Public Lands. Later that year he was elected to the territorial House of Representatives. In 1962 he won a seat in the state Senate. In 1966 he won election to the Kauai Board of Supervisors. In 1973-1974 Shiraishi served as chairman of the county's Charter Review Commission.

Shiraishi rose over the years to be one of Kauai's most influential people. In 1984 *Hawaii Business* magazine, in a study of Kauai's 15 most influential people, rated Shiraishi number three, behind the mayor and the editor of Kauai's principal newspaper.

In part this prominence was owing to Shiraishi's success in land matters.

As did so many of his fellow 442d and 100th Battalion veterans who became lawyers and then politicians, Shiraishi became an active real estate investor and developer when the land boom hit Hawaii. As most of the Big Five were well positioned to benefit from the boom because of their land, so too were men like Shiraishi, because they knew their way around government and they had stature in the non-*haole* community. Moreover, the same drive that brought these men through the war in Europe, that gave them the stamina to work for political change at home, gave them the appetite to take opportunities to get ahead personally through the land boom.

Beginning in about the early 1960s, Shiraishi became an active organizer of land *huis* on Kauai. He also started a real estate sales firm. As an attorney he did work in land and development. Overall from the early 1960s through the mid-1980s there was probably no individual on Kauai more active in land than Shiraishi.

In examining the makeup of his *huis*, in looking at the people who worked for his real estate business, and who were his law partners and associates and clients, it can be seen how thoroughly well connected Shiraishi was to the political establishment on Kauai, which in general was a Democratic Party establishment. Beyond that it can be seen how well connected he was all across the power spectrum on the island.

Simply with respect to people who were public officials or employees with duties affecting development, and who simultaneously had interests in *huis* he organized, Shiraishi's ties were manifold. Councilman Jerome Y.K. Hew owned a share in White Rock Ltd. Partnership ("*shiraishi*" in English means "white rock"); Planning Commissioner Maxine J. Correa and/or her husband were in White Rock, also in Nonou Mountain Estates (Correa later was elected to the Council); Planning Commissioner Arthur S. Fujita in Kilauea Gardens Limited Partnership, Lucky Twenty-Five, and Kauai-Kamuela Associates; Deputy County Engineer Clay A. Kagawa in White Rock; Board of

Water Supply member Ronald B. Iida in White Rock, also Waipouli Ltd. Partnership; state and then county real property appraiser Reginald P. Gage in White Rock; County Water Department Chief Engineer Walter L. Briant in Wailua Haven Inc.; Deputy County Engineer John J. Arzadon in White Rock; Chairman of the Board of Supervisors Raymond X. Aki in Kauai Resorts Development Inc.; State Transportation Commissioner Mark K. Tanaka in Waipouli Ltd. Partnership; Kauai Project Manager for the State Department of Hawaiian Home Lands Juliet K. Aiu in White Rock; and Kauai director of the state's Sea Grant Program Dr. Arnold B. Nurock in Kilauea Gardens Ltd. Partnership.

Among those selling real estate at Shiraishi's Kauai Realty Inc. over the years were April F. Shigemoto, whose husband was county deputy planning director; the woman who chaired the Citizens Advisory Committee for the Kauai General Plan Update, Yuriko N. Tasaka; Earl A. Arruda, who in 1980 and 1982 was campaign manager for mayoral candidate JoAnn A. Yukimura; former County Clerk Tad T. Miura, who was also a former mayoral aide; former state superintendent of schools on Kauai, Barton H. Nagata; and Mark Tanaka, serving on the State Transportation Commission.[31]

A similar picture emerges in looking at Shiraishi's law practice. The man who was his associate beginning in 1968 and later his partner, Dennis R. Yamada, served in the Hawaii House of Representatives 1971–1982. Elected initially as a Republican, he later became a Democrat, thereafter rising in the House hierarchy to chair the Judiciary Committee in 1979–1980, and to serve as Majority Leader in 1981–1982. An associate member of Shiraishi & Yamada who at times handled criminal cases for the firm, Calvin K. Murashige, was a former deputy county prosecutor. Kauai District Judge Clifford L. Nakea invested in Shiraishi's Kauai-Kamuela Associates. Shiraishi and others in the firm made frequent appearances in Nakea's court. Two of several on the staff in circuit court on Kauai invested in Shiraishi *huis*: Barbara T. Haruki in Kauai Land Holding Co., and Mildred K. Hiramoto in Waipouli Ltd. Partnership.

The range of Shiraishi's clients was wide, including Floro V. Villabrille, who for most of the 1960s and 1970s ran Kauai's largest chickenfight near his home in Keapana. Shiraishi represented the Villabrille family on private business matters.[32]

When the mainland builder Leadership Homes came to Kauai about 1974 to attempt a major resort development near Poipu, the Leadership executive in charge on Kauai wrote that, upon asking the mayor to recommend an attorney to represent the company on the island, the mayor recommended Shiraishi.[33]

Another of Shiraishi's many clients on development matters was Amfac, whom he represented in the late 1970s and early 1980s before the Land Use Commission in cases of the kind described above as highly discretionary, involving substantial acreage and possible profits in the millions.

—————————————— **TABLE 15** ——————————————

AMFAC LAND USE COMMISSION APPLICATIONS 1964-1984

Note: LUC district boundary amendment application number is shown first, then the island, then acreage and intended use, then governmental/political ties/background of various individuals involved, then LUC action. AG=Agricultural. C=Conservation. R=Rural. U=Urban. A=Approved. PA=Partially approved. D=Denied. "Intended use" is indicated either by actual, physical type of land use—residential, for example—or by state land use district.

1964/71. Oahu. 16 acres. Residential. Commissioner James P. Ferry was first cousin and former employee of Amfac joint venturer's chief executive Joseph R. Pao. John J. Hulten Jr., attorney for joint venturer, was son of state senator. PA.

1964/79. Kauai. Switching 17 acres to U, 11 acres to AG. Applicant was Amfac subsidiary. Amfac executive Caleb E.S. Burns Jr. was commissioner who voted to approve. State attorney general wrote 1970: "this clearly indicates a conflict of interest." PA—AG to U portion only.

1965/92. Hawaii. 1 acre. Employee housing. Amfac executive Burns was commissioner who voted to approve, and was subsequently found by attorney general in conflict of interest for having done so. A.

1966/124. Kauai. 4.5 acres. Residential. Applicant was Amfac subsidiary. Amfac executive Burns was commissioner who voted to approve, and was subsequently found by attorney general in conflict of interest for having done so. A.

1967/161, 1968/201 (2 successive applications for approx. same area). Oahu. 702 acres and 615 acres respectively. Residential. Amfac was joint venturer. Bishop Estate was owner. Former Honolulu planning director George K. Houghtailing was joint venture consultant. US Sen. Daniel K. Inouye's aide Morio Omori was attorney for Bishop on second attempt. PA on second attempt.

1968/189. Maui. 25.7 acres. Employee housing. A.

1968/190. Maui. 11 acres. Residential. A.

1969/210. Oahu. 16.2 acres. Residential. Amfac was joint venturer. Former Honolulu planning director Houghtailing was joint venture consultant. A.

1971/283. Oahu. 620 acres. Residential. Amfac was joint venturer. Former State Land Board attorney Francis M. Izumi was joint venture attorney. Former Honolulu planning director Houghtailing was joint venture consultant. D.

1971/296. Maui. 4.6 acres. Employee housing. A.

1972/335. Kauai. 26.4 acres. U to AG. A.

1975/397. Kauai. 30 acres. Commercial and multi-family. Amfac subsidiary was landowner, in process of selling to HRT Ltd. Former State Land Board attorney Izumi was Amfac attorney. Former LUC attorney Roy Y. Takeyama was HRT attorney; also secretary to University of Hawaii Board of Regents. A.

1975/401. Maui. 65.4 acres. Residential. Amfac was developer. Former State Land Board attorney Izumi was Amfac attorney. A.

1978/444. Oahu. 8.4 acres. C to U. Amfac was joint venturer. Former State Land Board attorney Izumi was joint venture attorney. A.

1979/454. Maui. 8 acres. Employee housing. A.

1979/456. Kauai. 13.7 acres. Residential. Amfac subsidiary was owner. Subsidiary to sell land if application approved. Former elected and appointed government official Clinton Shiraishi was attorney and head of hui planning to buy. Amfac Distribution Co. Ltd. employee George R. Pascua was member of LUC. LUC chairman ruled Pascua could vote; he voted to approve. A.

1982/530. Kauai. 78 acres. Resort and industrial. Amfac was landowner, developer. Former elected and appointed government official Clinton Shiraishi was attorney. PA.

Sources: State of Hawaii, Land Use Commission, miscellaneous files; Gwenfread E. Allen, ed., *Men and Women of Hawaii: A Biographical Directory of Noteworthy Men and Women of Hawaii* (Honolulu, 1966); Betty F. Buker, ed., *Men and Women of Hawaii 1972: A Biographical Directory of Noteworthy Men and Women of Hawaii* (Honolulu, 1972); Department of Commerce and Consumer Affairs, Business Registration Division; State of Hawaii, Legislative Reference Bureau, *Directory of State, County and Federal Officials: Supplement to Guide to Government in Hawaii* (published occasionally, most recently annually); Hawaii State Archives; miscellaneous references in newspapers and periodicals.

It was not just in dealing with the LUC that Amfac retained politically well-connected attorneys and consultants. In the mid-1970s, in attempting to get Kauai Planning Commission approval for a hotel in Poipu that would exceed the county's building height limitation, Amfac hired Clinton Shiraishi, plus former Hawaii supreme court justice Masaji Marumoto. Former Republican Party official John E.S. Kim, a business associate of well-connected Democrats such as Gov. Burns' chief fundraiser of the 1960s, Clarence T.C. Ching, worked from the late 1960s through the early 1970s for the board chairman of Amfac in dealing with government agencies on Oahu. Former Honolulu city corporation counsel Paul Devens in 1978 represented Amfac before the City on a proposed ordinance regulating building densities on Oahu. In 1975 Albert C. Zane, former Honolulu chief city engineer and former chief of the Highways Division of the State Department of Transportation, was spokesman for a study done for Amfac, Hawaiian Electric Co., and the City on the feasibility of converting garbage to electricity. Government, especially at the city level, was central to whether the project could proceed. In order to further sell the idea to government authorities and the public, Amfac about 1979 hired attorney Robert C. Oshiro, a former state legislator who was a chief architect of Gov. Burns' successful campaign in 1970 and of Gov. George Ariyoshi's three successful campaigns 1974– 1982.

The retaining of well-connected attorneys and consultants was not something Amfac invented. All through the Democratic years it was a routine part of doing business in Hawaii. And for all Amfac's apparently high success rate with government agencies, even the hiring of well-connected help was no ironclad guarantee of success. Amfac failed to prevail on its eight-story hotel application at Poipu despite the involvement of Clinton Shiraishi and Masaji Marumoto, retreating to six stories, and ultimately settling for four, the legal height limit. The company was initially rebuffed on the garbage-to-electricity project despite the involvement of Robert Oshiro. And Amfac lost a major decision before the LUC in 1973 when, despite the representation by Francis Izumi and George Houghtailing, a proposed 620-acre residential development in leeward Oahu was denied.[34]

Where Amfac succeeded, there were multiple causes in addition to the political character of its legal and planning representation. Amfac's attorneys and consultants were usually very competent professionals in their own right. The firm had the money and depth of experience to be thorough in its presentations, and the enlightened self-interest to make public-interest concessions as they appeared necessary. Besides, Amfac was locally based, with land in all parts of the state. To an extent it could choose its moment, acting when it considered it had the best chance of success.

How much difference was made by the hiring of a Clinton Shiraishi or a Francis Izumi, as opposed to an equally competent attorney with little or no influence in government, cannot be precisely known—although the striking success rate of projects in which the politically well-connected were involved would suggest that it was prudent to keep on hiring them.

At the same time it must be pointed out that most large firms such as Amfac believed they were mistreated by government in Hawaii, that far from having things greased, they were obstructed to extremes by the Democratic government, as well as by organized labor and some sectors of the community at large. If Amfac's apparent success rate was high in the projects the company proposed, it came at great expense of time and money. Furthermore, Amfac's outward success rate with the LUC did not reflect the fact that some projects, which might have appeared economically feasible to Amfac executives, may simply never have been proposed for fear that someone might object strenuously enough to make the effort to develop not worth the trouble.

What in any case was clear on balance was that the practice of hiring men such as Shiraishi or Izumi gave back to Amfac links to government that the firm lost at the time of the Democratic takeover in the 1950s.

* * *

Locally based big business in the Democratic years had to adjust to great changes on the economic scene—local, national and global. In the course of this adjustment big business underwent great changes in its relationship to land and power in Hawaii.

The power of the Big Five locally was clearly curbed and relatively diminished. In 1967 a University of Hawaii political science student setting out to study Oahu's power structure began with the hypothesis that the Big Five still "made every major decision in all areas." Her research technique was essentially to poll mid-level and then top-level leaders as to who were

Honolulu's most powerful people. Of the 12 men her research indicated to be the power structure's inner circle, only one was a Big Five chief executive. Among 31 secondary leaders there were only two Big Five presidents. To her these findings suggested "the passing of the Big Five's domination of political processes in Honolulu."[35]

What also happened, as early as the mid-1960s, was that the Big Five became enmeshed in a set of connections amounting to a land-based reuniting of elements of the power structure that the initial Democratic takeover temporarily broke up. There coalesced a new power structure, with new relativities of power and wealth.

On the national and global scene, Hawaii's old companies were experiencing not only the opportunity but the necessity to diversify and expand. Once the biggest of fish in a tiny isolated pond, they were now small to medium-sized fish in an ocean that was as big as the world and contained sharks that could swallow them whole. Two were swallowed in the mid-1970s (Brewer and Davies); and as of early 1985 a third, Castle & Cooke, was in financial extremities, possibly faced with having to go through a merger in which its shareholders might not come out well.

In this new period of diversification and outside ownership it was a distinct possibility that in Hawaii land matters the Big Five would make decisions for reasons that had little or nothing to do with local considerations.

Still, it continued to be true that if Amfac and the other big firms were far less concentrated in Hawaii than they used to be, their economic presence in the Islands remained great. The magazine *Hawaii Business* in 1984 ranked by 1983 gross earnings most businesses that originated in or were based in Hawaii. Amfac was number one, Castle & Cooke three, Alexander & Baldwin five, C. Brewer ten, and Theo. H. Davies fourteen. *Hawaii Business* in a 1984 cover story entitled "Goodbye Big Five" pointed out that their 1982 earnings still accounted for a significant proportion of the gross state product—10%.[36]

Thus on the local scene, with all their land, money, statewide apparatus and depth of experience, the Big Five, even if they had to work with union leaders, people with political ties to the ruling Democrats, and a myriad of government agencies to implement programs, still had resources that counted heavily in the making of Hawaii's fundamental business and government decisions. They were still forces to be reckoned with.

7

ORGANIZED CRIME

Most institutions, social groups and individuals that weighed heavily in the power structure in the Democratic years were readily visible and easily identifiable.

No one could doubt, for example, the stature and influence of the ILWU, or Amfac, or the veterans of the 442d Regiment, or people such as Matsuo Takabuki or George Ariyoshi.

One group, however, that figured in the power structure did so in a shadowy and indeterminate way—the men who ran organized crime in Hawaii.

Organized crime, by nature secretive and shrouded in a certain mystique, is difficult to study, in the Islands or anywhere else.

Greatly complicating the effort to assign a proper weight to organized crime in Hawaii have been unproven allegations, whispered for years and then made public from 1977 on, that a close associate of both of Hawaii's Democratic governors was the leader of organized crime in the Islands.

In the end, the power position to be accorded organized crime in Hawaii, including power concerning land in the 1970s and into the 1980s, depended heavily on whether that friend of John Burns and George Ariyoshi, Larry E. Mehau, was or was not directing organized crime.

*　*　*

"Organized crime," as the term is generally used by law enforcement officials and the media, did not emerge in Hawaii until the early 1960s, according to a 1978 report by the Hawaii Crime Commission.[1]

Activities which typically formed the basis of criminal syndicates in the US had flourished in Hawaii since the arrival of westerners early in the nineteenth century. But for more than a hundred years this apparently led to no organized crime as such.

In part this was because until the mid-1940s, two of the most important "vices" on which organized crime is often based, prostitution and gambling, were either legal or tolerated in Hawaii.

Then toward the end of World War II prostitution was criminalized. And after the war, according to the Crime Commission, law enforcement authorities began to take a dim view of gambling.

The running of these and other illegal operations in Hawaii was small-time and decentralized until the early 1960s. At about that time, according to the Crime Commission, a local-Korean gang successfully began to extort a number of gambling game operators on Oahu, marking the inception of organized crime in Hawaii.

Although it is unclear why organized crime made its appearance at that time, several law enforcement officials interviewed for this book speculated that Hawaii in the early 1960s had reached a critical mass in terms of money available for the taking. With the early boom years of tourism and the military buildup there was enough money in "vice"—prostitution, extortion, fencing of stolen goods, and especially gambling—to make it financially worthwhile for criminals to organize.

By most accounts, Hawaii organized crime was always far less formal and structured than its mainland counterpart. The Crime Commission wrote that "on the Mainland it is clear that the so-called Mafia organizations, whether Sicilian, Mexican or Black, have developed into sophisticated entities with many of the complex . . . divisions of labor with which a corporation is endowed. Highly skilled and specialized persons perform duties full-time. There are clear and definite lines of authority and communication. The organizations are ongoing and likely to endure the death of the leaders. The individuals within their ranks may total hundreds for each family . . ." By contrast, "the visible street-level criminal organizations in Hawaii are crude. The core of each group may consist of no more than three to twelve individuals who self-consciously feel themselves as part of an ongoing conspiracy. Compared to mainland models, there is a notable lack of sophistication and complexity in their structures."[2]

The differences appeared to result from several things. Among these were Hawaii's relative smallness, distance from the mainland, and insularity, all resulting, perhaps, in smaller and less sophisticated organizations. There was also the great personal familiarity among people born in Hawaii that could lead to informality in dealings, with less need to articulate relationships, understandings, and so on. In addition, at least in the early years, there was not so much money at stake in Hawaii as compared with big mainland cities, perhaps leading to less emphasis on professionalism in criminal organizing.

Hawaii's first "organized" criminal, according to various law enforcement authorities, was a Korean named George S. B. "Yobo" or "Chungie" Chung. The Crime Commission wrote that about 1962, as head of a gang called the "*Pakes*" or "Orientals," he "began to extort professional gamblers on Oahu who sponsored gambling events."[3] ("*Pake*" is a Hawaiian-pidgin-English word for "Chinese," said to be a bastardization of Cantonese words meaning "uncle.")

Through the 1960s organized crime was headed by local-Asians, and then reportedly by a Samoan, Alema Leota.

A major turning point came in 1969, when a group of Hawaiians under

Wilford K. "Nappy" Pulawa became the first to organize criminal enterprises statewide.

Pulawa was jailed in 1975 for tax evasion. After his imprisonment, there was no clearly identified single statewide leader.

At about the time Pulawa made his bid, his organization was called various things, according to the later court testimony of one of its members, Roy R. Ryder Sr.: "The Family," "The People," "The Company."[4] But also about this time, according to *Honolulu Advertiser* reporter Gene Hunter, the *Advertiser* applied the name "The Syndicate," a term then widely in use on the mainland for crime groups. The name caught on and stuck, even after Pulawa's imprisonment when there was no obvious single statewide organization.

Into exactly how many spheres of life in Hawaii the syndicate spread was unclear, though there was evidence of activity at various times in the entertainment field, among commercial fishermen, in organized labor, in Hawaiian cultural and rights groups, and in land.

*   *   *

Regarding organized crime, land, and development, the following made its way onto the public record:

Admitted crime leader Henry W. Huihui was, during the 1970s, an employee and at times officer of an electrical workers' union, the International Brotherhood of Electrical Workers (IBEW), Local 1186. Much of the members' work was construction-related. For a time Huihui was also secretary-treasurer of the Honolulu Building and Construction Trades Council. In pleading guilty in 1984 to a variety of crimes, he admitted to having worked an extortion racket on a number of building contractors.[5]

Syndicate leaders often invested or attempted to invest in land and development in Hawaii, reportedly to put illegally obtained money to work. For example, Huihui and several associates, including members of the Carpenters Union, Local 745, in 1977 set up nine businesses. *Honolulu Star-Bulletin* reporter Jim McCoy wrote that these were "'dummy' corporations to funnel money made from gambling and other activities into seemingly legitimate ventures." Four of the nine were development-related: Madonna Development Inc.; Sophisticated Rental Inc. (rental of construction equipment); Cliff Towers Inc. (real estate); Sanzo Inc. (land development). These businesses never got off the ground, according to the lawyer who incorporated them, Ralph F. "Munro" Matsuura, former Honolulu Liquor Commission chairman. He told McCoy that they became inactive before even starting because of adverse publicity surrounding their creation.[6]

During Nappy Pulawa's tax trials in 1974 and 1975, there was testimony that he had taken illegally earned money and invested in a variety of real estate projects.[7] These included some small parcels of land in California City, in the Mojave Desert in California—a "nice place," as prosecution witness Roy Ryder described it, with "a golf course and everything." Also, a company called Pacific Development Co. was formed. It allegedly made a $25,000 down payment on the Grand Hotel near Disneyland. The Grand Hotel deal was to provide credential for a bigger deal in Honolulu real estate, involving the Forbidden City nightclub near the corner of Kapiolani Blvd. and Kalakaua Ave. The first step was to buy the lease of Forbidden City for $98,000 and rename it Club Blue Lei. The plan apparently was to use its lot and an adjacent lot to erect the Pacific Monarch Center, an $8.5 million restaurant-nightclub, seating 1,500, along the lines of Caesar's Palace in Las Vegas, with a private athletic club, office space, and a full recording studio.

In addition, there was testimony that in rural Oahu, a $20,000 down payment was made on the approximately 15-acre, $1.3 million-dollar Cooper Ranch at Hauula. In addition it was testified that a syndicate-controlled development company was formed to buy land around Cooper Ranch.

In addition there was testimony that a syndicate front company, Akamai Development Inc., about 1971-1972 bought some $42,000 worth of real estate. The company principals were Henry Huihui and a former speaker of the territorial House of Representatives, Charles E. Kauhane. Kauhane testified that Huihui regularly met him in a bank parking lot with $5,000 to $6,000 cash in a paper bag. Kauhane bought cashiers' checks with the cash, then made payments on the real property. (Honolulu Mayor Frank Fasi in 1973 nominated Kauhane to the Honolulu Police Commission. At a hearing on the nomination Kauhane was questioned about allegations that he had a close relationship with Nappy Pulawa. The City Council declined to confirm him.)[8]

According to the testimony of Pulawa and others involved, none of the real estate deals prospered. Indeed, almost none were completed, except possibly the one involving Kauhane, and the purchase of a pool hall in rural Oahu. In several cases down payments were forfeited.

Pulawa said on the stand that he knew nothing about buying real estate—that others involved, including Sherwin K. "Sharkey" Fellezs, handled everything, and that a great deal of money was lost. Pulawa claimed that Fellezs took much of the money with him when he turned state's evidence and went into hiding under the federal witness protection program.

What Pulawa and his family wound up with in the way of real property assets, by their own reckoning in court, was no more than a few house lots in the Mojave Desert.

The Pulawas bought their first lot sight unseen, after a slide presentation, for $100 down and easy terms. Later there was what was described as an "improved" sales presentation, with a flight to the mainland for the Pulawas and other buyers to inspect more properties for sale. As the salesman said in testimony at Pulawa's trial, if you can sell a lot to someone, and then they see activity in the development, maybe they will buy another.

Pulawa said it was his first trip to the mainland. He said he traveled free, a favor from a gambler for whom he had once done a favor. The Pulawas wound up eventually owning three lots in the desert, Pulawa's wife Evelyn testified. All were paid for in cash, partly borrowed, she said. Pulawa rather than his wife was assumed to be the breadwinner responsible for making payments, and so he had to have his life insured. But according to the Pulawas, by the time of the third purchase in 1971 Hawaiian Life Insurance Co. would no longer insure him. The purpose of the purchases, according to Mrs. Pulawa, was an investment to help pay for their children's education, but one of the lots shortly had to be sold to meet Pulawa's legal expenses.

It is worth noting that by the Pulawas' account, they were buying $100-down speculative lots in exactly the same way as other small Hawaii buyers in the thousands were buying such lots in those years. The Pulawas bought in California. Much closer to home, similar cheap lots were being sold by the thousands and by identical methods to other real-estate amateurs—on the lava fields of the Big Island. And if the Pulawas had found it suited them to buy locally, in Puna, rather than out-of-state in the Mojave Desert, they might very well have made a better paper profit on their investment.

* * *

Whatever Nappy Pulawa's actual record was as a real estate investor, certainly he and others in organized crime covered a lot of territory on Oahu and elsewhere in the course of conducting their business; and in doing so they made use of any number of places constructed during Hawaii's real estate boom. Business meetings of reputed syndicate members were held not only on public property in Honolulu at Sand Island, Ala Moana Park, Farrington High School, Kaneohe Bay, in a Maunakea Street parking lot, on Punchbowl, in the Chinese cemetery at Pauoa, and in the horse stables just before the start of the Kamehameha Day parade, but also at a private home in Keolu Hills, in various coffee shops in Kaimuki, cocktail bars around Ala Moana and at Ala Moana Center itself, a bar in Kailua named Biggie's Nut Shell, the Dunes nightclub on Nimitz Highway, the Hauula Shopping Center, the Ranch Inn, the Ala Wai Manor, the Waikiki Beach-comber Hotel, the Hale Makai Hotel, Kapiolani Towers, Sunset Towers, and at the Kaanapali Beach Hotel on Maui. According to testimony at his trials, Pulawa had $10,000 in protection money brought to him each week, to be counted out on a bed at an apartment he had on the thirty-fourth floor of the Contessa in Moiliili (the lease was under another person's name). And testimony was also given that in an apartment at the Woodrose in the Kapiolani district, also leased under another name, those who failed to meet payments or other obligations were beaten.

* * *

On Maui, two men who allegedly ran large-scale illegal gambling and were reputed syndicate leaders—Yujiro "Tani" Matsuoka and Takeo Yamauchi—and one who helped run gambling—Stanley T. "Banjo"

Tamura—invested in real estate, sometimes in association with high government officials.

The evidence for this involvement comes mainly from the court probate files of Matsuoka and Tamura, who were murdered in the mid-1970s.[9]

Tamura, a Maui County employee since 1951, was for many years chief teller for the Maui County Finance Department. He was reputed to have simultaneously been one of the island's chief organizers of illegal sports betting. Reportedly he ran betting operations from his county office. A man who was a high-ranking Maui police officer during the late 1960s and much of the 1970s said in an interview for this book that it was "known [Tamura] was running 6-5 in the county building." ("6-5" refers to betting in multiples of six and five. On a $5 bet a winner receives $5, a loser pays $6.) In 1962 Tamura and another man were federally indicted for using the mail to operate a football pool. Tamura pled no contest. In 1969 he was one of three arrested on state charges of running an island-wide sports betting operation. Charges against all three men were dismissed after a prosecution witness refused to testify.[10]

Tamura was murdered in 1975. He was found in his home in Wailuku, dead from multiple stab wounds. As of the mid-1980s the crime remained officially unsolved.[11]

Police believed the killing was syndicate-related, possibly an execution for not paying off sufficiently to an Oahu syndicate group or not meeting some other kind of obligation. Police also wondered if the crime was related to some aspect of Tamura's personal life having nothing to do with gambling, though on balance they believed his role in helping to run gambling on Maui was somehow central to his death. In various news media reports it was speculated that the killing was part of an intra-organized crime struggle for control of gambling on Maui.[12]

Matsuoka, a former tailor who became a professional gambler, was referred to in various criminal proceedings in the 1970s as either the number one or the number two man in running organized crime on Maui. When Nappy Pulawa was being tried in 1974, he called Matsuoka "the Maui boss" for the syndicate, who served as a receiver of gambling and protection money. Matsuoka was found shot to death in a canefield in 1978. This crime also remained officially unsolved as of the mid-1980s.[13]

As with Tamura, Maui police believed Matsuoka was executed for not meeting some kind of syndicate-related obligation. Also, as with Tamura, there was media speculation that Matsuoka might have fallen victim to a syndicate power struggle.[14]

After Matsuoka's death, FBI agents interviewed Takeo Yamauchi. He reportedly told them Matsuoka had been the "boss" of gambling on Maui. But the better estimate, according to law enforcement authorities, was that in fact Yamauchi was the boss.[15]

The special agent in charge of US Customs in Honolulu, H. Ezra Wolff, stated in a deposition in 1972 that, as of 1970, Yamauchi was "designated as the number one man on Maui in connection with organized gambling." Matsuoka was number two. Both were "connected with the organized crime group in Honolulu."[16] A high-ranking Maui police officer during this period, who was interviewed for this book, echoed Wolff's appraisal. And *Honolulu Advertiser* reporters Walter Wright and James Dooley wrote in 1978 that Yamauchi was "described by authorities as Maui's most powerful organized crime figure." They also wrote that Yamauchi was "allied with one, possibly two, Honolulu organized crime groups headed by individuals who formerly worked under now-deposed syndicate boss Wilford 'Nappy' Pulawa."[17]

Also in 1978, in a Las Vegas gaming authority proceeding, a similar appraisal of Yamauchi was made. At issue was the application of Irving "Ash" Resnick to direct casino operations in the Aladdin Hotel. The Nevada Gaming Board turned Resnick down. According to United Press International the decision was based in part on allegations that Resnick "associated with undesirables in organized labor and with Hawaii underworld figures, including Takeo Yamauchi, described by authorities here [Las Vegas] as Maui's most powerful organized crime figure." (Resnick's application was later granted by a higher commission. Included in testimony on this occasion were favorable letters about Resnick from Hawaii State Sen. Duke T. Kawasaki, Honolulu Mayor Frank F. Fasi, and Gov. George R. Ariyoshi.)[18]

In 1979 Yamauchi was tried in federal court on extortion charges, related to his allegedly running gambling on Maui. He was acquitted. During the trial he testified, according to the *Honolulu Advertiser*, that "he ran the administrative end of 6-5 gambling in association with Stanley 'Banjo' Tamura in the 1960s;" but "with investments in several Maui condominium projects at stake, Yamauchi said, he had heeded the warnings of partners and given up illegal gambling, except as a regular player or bettor himself." The paper also wrote that "Yamauchi admits ... [he] still associates with organized crime figures from Hawaii and Japan."[19]

An attempt was made to interview Yamauchi for this book. He declined, saying only that news stories about him over the years had been "all bullshit," and that he did not "know anything about gambling."

Yamauchi, Tamura, and Matsuoka, besides allegedly running organized crime on Maui, all had legitimate business investments as well, including in real estate. Sometimes they invested together.

Research for this book indicated that over the years Yamauchi and his wife held a number of real estate interests. There were never allegations, however, that these investments were made possible by illegally obtained money. In any case, the investments, were: a share in Pukalani Terrace Landco, a *hui* that had been developing a large residential community in Maui's Pukalani since the mid-1960s; a share in Haake First Hui, organized by then-Maui Police Captain Richard H. Haake; a vice-presidency in and partial ownership of Maui Shiraishi Inc., a general contracting firm; a share in Club 10, a partnership which bought and renovated an old chop suey house in Wailuku, Maui; plus units in the Lahaina Residential Condominium, the Maui Kai, and the Kahana Sunset, an 80-unit resort condominium in west Maui. In addition, Yamauchi's wife was a general partner of McGowan-Mahoe Development Co., which built the Kahana Sunset. She was also a partner in Kahana-Lahaina Asociates and in LCW Hui.

When Tamura's estate was going through probate after his murder, both Yamauchi and Matsuoka stepped forward to claim partial interests in some of his property holdings. Evidently Yamauchi and Matsuoka had at times invested through Tamura. Yamauchi claimed and got one half of Tamura's interest in Haake First Hui. Matsuoka claimed and got half of Tamura's stock in Golden Palace Inc.[20] All three men invested in Club 10, the *hui* formed to renovate the chop suey house. According to the Club 10 accountant, Sadao Kon, in an interview for this book, the restaurant was turned into four small apartments and two offices; Kon said the venture lost money. Matsuoka and Tamura also each invested in Kaanapali Hui and in a partnership called M. Yokouchi & D.Y.S. Kong *et al*, though here it is unclear whether the two men invested together or as separate individuals.

Tamura, Matsuoka, and Yamauchi not only invested individually and with each other but with a variety of other people, including several high public officials.

Tamura was closely associated with the Democratic Party establishment. Indeed since the 1950s he had been active in electoral politics on Maui, working with mainstream Burns Democrats. For example, when Burns chose Kenneth F. Brown as his running mate in 1966, Tamura was named one of Brown's two campaign coordinators on Maui.

In his known real estate investments, Tamura was also closely affiliated with Burns Democrats. Although others involved may not have been aware of it, he held shares in International Development Co. and Heeia Development Co., two very large *huis* whose memberships were heavily mainstream Democrats. A principal organizer of IDCo. was Clarence T.C. Ching, who was John Burns' chief campaign fundraiser in the 1960s. One of Heeia Development's most visible founders was Democratic politician Mitsuyuki Kido. A list of the known investors in these two ventures read like a Who's Who of the Democratic Party. Another partnership in which Tamura invested, Waipao Joint Venture, contained a fair number of public officials from Maui, as did Valley Isle Realty which, according to Tamura's probate, was handling several real estate transactions for him at the time of his death.

A prominent Maui political figure associated in land investing with Tamura was Nadao Yoshinaga. Yoshinaga was for many years influential in the Legislature as a representative and senator from Maui, and then as a senator from Waipahu on Oahu. A real estate broker beginning in 1959, Yoshinaga was himself active in real estate dealings. According to Tamura's probate, Tamura held a 7% interest in a *hui* called Mieko Yoshinaga *et al.* (Mieko was Nadao's wife.) Mieko and Tamura also held in their names 1959-1966 a 25-acre parcel of land on Maui.

Yoshinaga was contacted twice for this book, both times briefly and on limited points. He declined what would have been a wide-ranging interview which was to have included questions on Tamura.

Haake First Hui, in which Tamura and Yamauchi had shares, was organized by Maui Police Captain Richard H. Haake. The *hui* was apparently never registered with the state office in charge of the registration of businesses operating in Hawaii, though neither was it altogether clear whether by law the group ought to have registered.

Haake was a respected man on Maui. A career police officer, in 1966 he was also elected president of the Maui chapter of the Hawaii Government Employees Association, though he resigned the post a year later. During Edward J. Hitchcock's brief tenure as Maui's police chief in the late 1960s, Haake was reportedly in line to become chief upon Hitchcock's retirement. Hitchcock was, however, fired by the Police Commission in 1969, which apparently adversely affected Haake's career. At the time of Tamura's death in 1975, Haake held the rank of captain.

In an interview for this book Haake acknowledged that he was aware of Tamura's investment but said he knew nothing of Yamauchi's. Haake also indicated that he was in general aware of Tamura's illegal gambling activities but stressed that the basis of the two men investing together was purely friendship.

Tamura's probate also revealed that a man who at the time of Tamura's death was a circuit court judge on Maui, S. George Fukuoka, was managing an investment for him in Heeia Development Co. Two of the *hui's* organizers, George M. Hasegawa and Sen. Mitsuyuki Kido, were both originally from Maui, and consequently so were many of the investors. Although Heeia Development was duly registered with the state, it contained several sub-*huis* that were not. Fukuoka and Tamura were investors in one of the unregistered sub-*huis*.

In an interview Fukuoka explained that he and Tamura had gotten to be friends in the 1950s, while working together to vitalize the Democratic Party on Maui. Fukuoka also said that he and Tamura had been part of other *huis* in the past. In addition Fukuoka, before becoming a judge, had done legal work for Tamura. In 1964, for example, when Fukuoka was a state senator, he represented Tamura as an attorney in the matter of a land purchase, according to a copy of a letter on file in Tamura's probate. As did everyone who was interviewed concerning Tamura, Fukuoka said he had been a kind and gentle person, whose death came as a terrible shock. Fukuoka in addition acknowledged that he was aware of Tamura's involvement with gambling, though only in a general way.

Thus, on the public record, the composite picture of Tamura's land and real estate dealings showed him investing in land and real estate *huis* with the following members of the new establishment from Maui: two leading state legislators, one of whom later became a judge; and a police captain.

Two other public figures had business relationships not only with Tamura, but also with Yamauchi and Matsuoka. One was Walter T. Shimoda, a Maui district court magistrate 1960-1971. The other was Masaru "Pundy" Yokouchi, who was John Burns' chief campaign organizer on Maui in Burns' three successful runs for governor, and Burns' chief representative on the island. In addition, Burns in 1966 appointed Yokouchi the first chairman of the State Foundation on Culture and the Arts, a position he held till 1978. (Shimoda as a private attorney at times did legal work for Yokouchi's *huis*, including the highly controversial Nukolii *hui*.)

Yokouchi's ties with Tamura, Yamauchi and Matsuoka were but one part of an extremely varied network of people with whom Yokouchi worked and invested over the years. On Maui there were few with connections to match Yokouchi's.

Tamura's investments in *huis* managed by Yokouchi included a 2% interest in M. Yokouchi & D.Y.S. Kong; a share in a 44-acre parcel in Alaska bought in 1973; and an interest in H. Fujitomo Hui, a registered sub-*hui* within Waipao Joint Venture, which bought and sold the 16 acres on which the Makena Surf condominium was later built. Tamura's probate also indicated that at the time of his death, Yokouchi's Valley Isle Realty was handling sales of property for him in Kula Meadows, also another parcel called the "Chong property," and property held by the T. Shibano Hui. In addition, Tamura had once been a co-trustee of a *hui* in which Yokouchi invested, that in 1969 bought and sold a 130-acre parcel in Kula, Maui.

Yokouchi indicated in several interviews for this book that he was merely acquainted with Matsuoka. Yokouchi did, in 1969, sell Matsuoka the Yokouchis' old home in Wailuku when the Yokouchis were moving to Wailuku Heights. Yokouchi said that Matsuoka contacted him through a mutual acquaintance to initiate the transaction, an indication that the two men were not particularly close.

Yokouchi also said that in the mid-1970s he agreed to help Yamauchi organize a small car rental business, Continental U-Drive. Yokouchi explained that Yamauchi wanted some legitimate business that his daughter could put down on forms she occasionally had to fill out that asked her to list her father's occupation.

Walter Shimoda's judgeship was part-time, and he was allowed to also practice law. In 1968, while a judge, Shimoda incorporated a travel business, Aloha Travel Service Inc., of which Matsuoka was an officer.

After leaving the bench Shimoda continued to practice law. He represented Tamura's estate in probate proceedings. In 1977 he incorporated a small business for Yamauchi, KY Corp., whose purpose was auto repairs.

In an interview for this book, Shimoda explained that he and many other Maui-born people who became prominent in recent decades, whether in fields legitimate or illegal, grew up in small, close-knit plantation communities. He said most were "everyday kind of people," that there was "very little social stratification" separating them, and that strong ties developed, persisting to this day, regardless of the different roads later traveled in life.

Shimoda said he came to know Tamura personally, but knew "very little" about his gambling activities. At some point he also became acquainted with Yamauchi. He said that he was aware of Yamauchi's reputation as a gambler. "From all outward appearances," Shimoda said, Yamauchi was "a hell of a nice guy."

Asked if he thought he ought not associate with people who were reputedly connected to the state's organized crime syndicate, Shimoda said that, in view of the personal roots he shared with these men, "even if 30 years go by or 40 years go by, how can you dissociate yourself?" "Other than in official duties [as a judge] I can't see dissociating myself. I don't care what they did."

Longtime Maui planning commissioner and insurance man Kazuo Kage in an interview expressed thoughts similar to Shimoda's. Kage, like many Hawaii residents, considered gambling relatively harmless, and thus attached no stigma to those who ran it. He said of Yamauchi, Matsuoka and Tamura: "They're my friends." Furthermore, Kage said, he "would rather have them as my friends than the president of A&B," meaning Alexander & Baldwin, one of Maui's largest landowners and a major part of the old establishment that for decades held down the Islands' non-*haoles*.

What all this demonstrated was that alongside those who, like Walter Shimoda, Nadao Yoshinaga and Masaru Yokouchi, grew up in humble surroundings and moved on to become leaders of the new Democratic establishment, future professional gamblers were growing up and moving up at a time when organized crime was also coming into being in Hawaii.

Even as late as the mid-1980s, the known involvement of organized crime in real estate by no means added up to a controlling interest—nothing remotely like it.

But, as in other areas of Island life, a syndicate presence in land in the Democratic years was a sign of the times in the modern history of Hawaii.

*   *   *

Conventional wisdom holds organized crime to be a social cancer, with its extortion of legitimate businessmen, trafficking in drugs, and syndicate-related murders.

Yet in the Islands, where illegal gambling was the economic base of organized crime, great numbers of otherwise respectable people participated in unlawful gaming—betting on sports events, cockfights, cards, dice, monte.

In doing so they simply did not connect betting on the University of Hawaii Rainbows or the Los Angeles Rams with the bodies of syndicate-murder victims buried in the sand at Mokuleia and Maili.

Various law enforcement officials interviewed for this book asserted that Hawaii was one of the "gamblingest" states in the nation.

It was certainly the case that Hawaii's amateur gamblers came from all walks of life, including political and business leaders.

The following stories give an indication of the extent of illegal gambling and local attitudes toward it:

In 1969 a Big Island reporter for the *Honolulu Advertiser* wondered in print: "Is the Hawaii County Building still the place to pick up the football pool slips in Hilo, or has the publicity given to recent gambling sentences helped to cut into the operation?"[21]

On Kauai, police on December 22 1978 raided for the first time ever the gambling game at the annual Christmas party in the County Council offices. Following the raid the *Honolulu Advertiser's* Kauai reporter, Jan TenBruggencate, wrote that "gambling has been a popular pastime here for years, and it has enjoyed the unspoken approval of the powers that control the island." Witness the fact, he went on, that "a number of politicians of note over the years have been seen at gambling affairs—the year-end ones at contractors' parties, the ones that have been started at meetings of government officials like the Hawaii State Association of Counties. On occasions in fact, there have been gambling games in county buildings."[22]

Those prosecuted on Maui over the years on various gambling charges included: Edwin K. Wasano in 1963, an ILWU business agent and chairman of the County Civil Service Commission; Richard I.C. Caldito Sr. in 1963, then between terms on the Board of Supervisors; Charles Allen Jr. in 1968, then president of the Maui Junior Chamber of Commerce; Police Officer Francis M. Kahoohalahala in 1981, whose case was on appeal as of early 1985; Joseph G. Kealoha Jr. in 1969, who later became Maui's elected Office of Hawaiian Affairs trustee; County Civil Defense Coordinator Manuel K. Oishi in 1969, though charges were dismissed after a prosecution witness declined to testify; and Maui member of the Land Use Commission Shinsei Miyasato in 1978, though his charges were also dismissed, based on a procedural error by the prosecution.[23]

In December 1981, 12 people were arrested on Maui for allegedly running a sports gambling operation. Two were Kenneth Yamanaka, a Finance Department accountant, and Donald T. Fujii, a Finance Department buyer. The two pled guilty in 1983 to illegally possessing gambling records. Sports betting paper was seized from Finance Department offices in connection with their arrests.[24]

As indicated by this last case, the public record shows that, from the early days of "Banjo" Tamura on, county Finance Department offices on Maui had been used for organized illegal gambling for the better part of two decades.

Indeed the practice of county finance department personnel helping to run illegal gambling in Hawaii in these years was apparently not unique to Maui. On the Big Island, in the 1981 trial of a bail bondsman on gambling and extortion charges, prosecution witness Randall Kaupu testified that Big Island Finance Department accountant Norio "Mungo" Kagimoto was a gambling promoter whose area covered South Hilo.[25]

A Maui deputy prosecutor who handled the 1981 Finance Department gambling cases observed that there was perhaps a logical tie between finance work and keeping sports betting records. Both required "fairly meticulous record keeping" and conscientious attention to detail.[26]

* * *

As remarked earlier, Hawaii, even in the boom years, even in the early 1980s when the total population reached a million, always functioned as a small place.

This could lead to personal associations that might seem surprising to people not born in the Islands.

Take Roosevelt High School in Honolulu in 1952. The varsity and junior varsity football squads of that year included Wilford K. Pulawa, Roy R. Ryder, Sherwin K. "Sharkey" Fellezs, Dante K. Carpenter, Arthur Hoke, Spencer K. Schutte and Larry D. Price. Other classmates of Pulawa, not on the football teams, included Danny Kaleikini and Matthew S.K. Pyun Jr.[27]

Pulawa, as mentioned, went on to head the Hawaii syndicate from about 1969 to 1975. He was in federal prison 1975-1984. Ryder became a gunman and admitted killer, who eventually turned prosecution witness; his testimony in 1975 was instrumental in convicting Pulawa. Fellezs became an entertainer. During Pulawa's trials Fellezs testified that he served as a front for several of Pulawa's real estate investments. Carpenter became a successful politician on the Big Island, elected to the County Council and State Senate; in 1984 he was elected Big Island mayor. Arthur Hoke became a police captain on the Big Island. Schutte became a Honolulu policeman and later a Big Island rancher and councilman. Price became a celebrity in various ways, as coach of the University of Hawaii football team, then a reporter for KITV television and an announcer on K-59 radio. Kaleikini became an extremely successful entertainer, and Pyun an accomplished lawyer and part-time state district court judge.

Counciiman Schutte was asked for this book about any personal relationship he and Pulawa might have, going back to their years on the football team at Roosevelt. Schutte said the two were "very close in school," that Pulawa "was a good guy" and "good athlete," also that there was "no real indication" in those days of the path Pulawa would take later in life. And, Schutte said, regardless of what Pulawa later did, the two had "always been friends," and that Schutte was always glad to see him.

Schutte also indicated sympathy with views he said Pulawa had expressed to him, to the effect that most syndicate killings should not be taken too seriously by the public because "we only kill each other," and that Hawaii's real crime problem involved men who wear "white collars"—business executives, for example. According to Schutte, Pulawa used to say that there were "many more crooks in white collars" than among ordinary working people.

An attempt was made for this book to reach Pulawa through his attorney as of the mid-1980s, Hayden F. Burgess, but Burgess said Pulawa declined.

The cases of Kaleikini and Pyun appear to illustrate how school friendships might lead to later associations that some might find questionable.

In Kaleikini's case, according to Sharkey Fellezs' testimony in the Pulawa trials, it was a friendship formed at the University of Hawaii with Fellezs.

When Pulawa was putting together his Forbidden City real estate deal in 1972-1973, he approached Kaleikini through Fellezs to serve as a front. The project was to emphasize entertainment, and Kaleikini's involvement would lend an appearance of substance and legitimacy.

During Pulawa's second tax trial, Fellezs testified that, "Danny and I being [university] fraternity brothers," he was the best person to approach Kaleikini. Fellezs said that "Nappy said fine." Fellezs then arranged for the three (and one or two others) to meet at the Waikiki Beachcomber Hotel.

Fellezs went on: "When Danny came up, I explained the whole project to Danny. We didn't need his money, $35,000, because we had any amount of money that we needed already ... All we wanted to do was laundry the money. Rinse our money out ... All we needed was Danny to come in and be a front. We would give him back his money. On top of that we would give him stock in Pacific Monarch [the front corporation]. In fact I made him an officer."

Keleikini did not remain an officer for long, however. Fellezs said that after the meeting Kaleikini decided to pull out. Fellezs said that he then drafted a letter of resignation for Kaleikini, which Kaleikini signed.

An attempt was made to interview Kaleikini for this book about Pacific Monarch. The above events were related to his secretary. Through her Kaleikini declined the interview, though he said the description of events was generally accurate.

Matthew Pyun, like Kaleikini, went from Roosevelt High School to the University of Hawaii, then to law school on the mainland, then through a series of jobs typical of lawyers just starting out: he was a federal district court clerk, a deputy Honolulu city attorney, and he worked for Legal Aid.

Later, as a private attorney, he became noted for effective criminal defense work. One of his clients was Takeo Yamauchi of Maui, tried and acquitted on extortion charges in 1978-1979. Pyun was also lead counsel for Harry C.C. Chung in a highly political case in 1977. Chung and his co-defendant, Honolulu Mayor Frank Fasi, were charged with bribery in connection with a major city urban renewal project. The case was dismissed when the chief prosecution witness refused to testify.[28]

In 1975 Pyun successfully defended a Waianae dairyman accused of paying for the murder of State Sen. Larry N. Kuriyama in 1970, one of the most notorious crimes in the history of contemporary Hawaii (and one which some observers believe was real estate-related).[29]

Pyun also represented Nappy Pulawa in pre and post-trial matters in connection with tax charges in the mid-1970s. In 1979 Pyun obtained an acquittal for Pulawa after Pulawa and four others were charged with kidnapping and murdering two gambling figures in 1970.[30]

During Pulawa's first tax trial, Sharkey Fellezs testified that Pyun was for a time an officer of Pacific Monarch Corp., the company later allegedly used by Pulawa as a front for the Forbidden City project. According to trial testimony Pyun was a vice-president, but he resigned, to be succeeded by Kaleikini, who also shortly thereafter resigned, all before the Forbidden City purchase actually took place.

During that trial Roy Ryder also testified regarding Pyun: "We're good friends."

Pyun in 1970 incorporated Professional People Inc., whose initial officers and directors were three of Pulawa's reputed strongarm men: Henry Huihui, Alvin G. Kaohu, and Robert "Bobby" Wilson. The company bought a pool hall in Hauula on Oahu's north shore with syndicate money, according to testimony in both of Pulawa's tax trials.

Because of these and other alleged associations of Pyun with syndicate figures, a federal Organized Crime Strike Force attorney in 1984 moved to have Pyun, who by then was also a part-time state judge, barred from representing a client in an organized crime case. Pyun denied the charges. The motion failed.[31]

An attempt was made to interview Pyun for this book; a telephone call to his office was not returned.

                              *   *   *

During Pulawa's tax trials there was testimony that some noted local entertainers were friends of Pulawa's and others implicated in organized crime. Roy Ryder, for example, testified that on at least one occasion a syndicate meeting was held in the Waikiki apartment of Donald T.L. Ho—entertainer Don Ho. Ho told a reporter, though, that he had "nothing to do with the underworld." He said the association went no further than the fact that the reputed syndicate leaders "are friends of mine from before," and that therefore his "doors are always open" to them.[32]

However, the man who at the time was vice-president of Ho's theatrical productions company, Ho-Brown Productions Inc., was reputed to have had long-standing ties to mainland organized crime:

Marcus Lipsky was born in Kiev, Russia, in 1905 and raised in Chicago. While he was an officer in Ho's firm he lived in Beverly Hills, California. According to US Senate testimony in 1958, Lipsky had been an associate of Al Capone's in Chicago in the 1930s. In the early 1940s Lipsky was said to have represented Chicago mobster Frank Nitti in an unsuccessful attempt to take over gambling interests in Dallas. In Senate testimony in general, Lipsky was identified as "one of the well-known hoodlums in Chicago" in those years.

Lipsky was also said to have associated from the 1930s on with known *Cosa Nostra* members in various businesses that dealt in dairy products. From 1947 to 1969 he was board chairman and then president of Reddi-

Wip Inc. One of the company's employees for at least part of that time was reputed Los Angeles mob lieutenant Angelo Polizzi.

Investigative writer Tom Renner of *Newsday* wrote that about 1969, "Lipsky decided on semiretirement and the life of a respectable philanthropist with major entertainment ties."

In 1970 Lipsky appeared in publicly filed business records in Hawaii as an officer of Donho Inc., which in 1971 changed its name to Ho-Brown Productions. Lipsky remained an officer through 1975.

Donho Inc. took over the lease of the Forbidden City in 1967. Whether the company had any interest in the property at the time of the Pulawa/Pacific Monarch approach there, or at the time Lipsky became an officer of Donho, is not shown on the public record.

Reportedly it was Larry Mehau who ended Lipsky's participation in Ho's company. A *Los Angeles Times* reporter, citing unnamed sources, wrote in 1979 that "Mehau helped extricate Ho from 'financial problems' with Lipsky and a Los Angeles attorney, and that Lipsky and Ho no longer have any business relationship." He also wrote that Ho said that about this time, Mehau was becoming a business advisor to him: "He helps me in making deals. He's like a big brother to me."[33] A company was incorporated in 1976 as a successor to Ho-Brown Productions. Lipsky was no longer listed as an officer. Mehau was, as a vice-president.

Lipsky had died by the time research for this book was undertaken. Attempts were made to interview both Ho and Mehau. Ho did not answer a letter sent to his office; Mehau did not return phone calls to his office and his home.

*   *   *

Gunman Roy Ryder testified in Nappy Pulawa's tax trial in 1975 that part of the Pulawa syndicate's bid for statewide control of organized crime in 1969 was to make ethnic Hawaiians supreme.

Local-Asians then reportedly ran most of the gambling, which provided the bulk of organized crime's revenue. Ryder testified: "Oh, we planned to make things good for the state of Hawaii, to help our own Hawaiian people. You know, we're going to get organization. All the Orientals had everything for all the years. Now we're going to take for our people and make everything good."[34]

Take over they did, killing a number of people in the process, according to Ryder.

After the takeover, according to Sharkey Fellezs, Nappy Pulawa, while eating out in a Honolulu restaurant in 1972, asked a professional sketch artist "to draw his picture and put a helmet on his head like Kamehameha."[35]

Even though after Pulawa's imprisonment in 1975 there was no single visible leader in control at the level on which Pulawa had functioned, still most of the reputed top leaders were Hawaiian and part-Hawaiian, in particular Henry Huihui and Alvin Kaohu.

The rise of Hawaiians to leadership of organized crime occurred at the same time as the Hawaiian political and cultural revival movements, the "Hawaiian renaissance" that began in the late 1960s and early 1970s.

Hawaiians were landless in their native land, and excluded from most seats of legitimate power. Often deeply alienated from a system that promoted individualism and competitiveness in contrast to the Hawaiian emphasis on sharing and cooperation, Hawaiians were present in large numbers in the statistics of school dropouts, and they showed up disproportionately in other indexes of social breakdown—as prison inmates, for example.[36]

As a Polynesian people in a population otherwise Asian and Caucasian, Hawaiians were also on the whole physically larger and more powerful than most others in Hawaii.

This combination of deep alienation and physical strength, in a reservoir of disadvantaged people that produced many of the Islands' street criminals, made Hawaiian strong-arm men like Pulawa, Huihui and their followers naturals for building criminal organizations that could bid for leadership of Hawaii's underworld.

At the same time, while running the syndicate, men like Pulawa reportedly retained concerns for and ties with the Hawaiian communities that produced them.

Sharkey Fellezs, testifying in 1974, said he ran a business through Pacific Monarch that hired Hawaiian high school students, and Pulawa liked this: "Mr. Pulawa came down, he liked what was happening and we used to sit down for hours and we used to talk and he used to tell me all about this Hawaiiana thing that he was very interested in . . . that would help our kids work."[37]

The Forbidden City real estate deal included, as mentioned, running a nightclub on the property that was to emphasize Hawaiian musical talent.

Huihui told a reporter in 1978 that he first became acquainted with Pulawa about 1970 over concerns they shared about a land issue in Kalama Valley, Oahu, that had a good deal to do with Hawaiians.[38]

Bishop Estate owned the valley, and about 40 mostly low-income Hawaii-born families, including a number of Hawaiians, were being evicted to make way for a moderately expensive residential subdivision and golf course.[39]

A group of mostly young people of various ethnic backgrounds joined to oppose the evictions and development in Kalama, raising issues similar to those current in the more radical sectors of the mainland civil rights and anti-war movements, which were then going strong, as was a youth culture which had a marked anti-establishment aspect.

An organization came into being, named Kokua Kalama and then renamed Kokua Hawaii, to lead the resistance in the valley. *Haoles* were excluded. The leadership became Hawaiian.[40]

Eventually all valley residents moved out except one, a pig farmer named George Santos. Santos and about 30 Kokua Hawaii members were then arrested. The valley was later developed as planned.

In 1978 a reporter who interviewed Huihui wrote that he "said he met Nappy Pulawa ... during the Kalama Valley struggle." By various other accounts the two had been working together for about a year already. In any case, Huihui said "I involved myself with Nappy Pulawa [at the time] because of the Hawaiian cultural revival" movement.[41]

Former Kokua Hawaii members interviewed for this book said that they recalled no contact with either Pulawa or Huihui during the struggle. Furthermore there is no evidence linking Pulawa and Huihui to any events in or concerning the valley.

Four Kokua members did say, though, that men they took to be syndicate-connected several times offered them guns for the defense of the valley.

The members said that on one occasion while Kokua Hawaii was occupying the valley and was anticipating a confrontation with police, a man or several men drove into the valley, opened the trunk of their car, showed Kokua Hawaii members what one said was "an arsenal" inside, and offered the weapons to the activists.

On another occasion, while Kokua Hawaii was meeting at the Off Center Coffee House near the University of Hawaii Manoa campus, two Kokua leaders took a ride with a couple of men who offered them weapons and use of a printing press. On this occasion no weapons were displayed.

The Kokua Hawaii members said they declined all such offers.

When police made arrests, the Kokua Hawaii members resisted only by sitting on top of George Santos' house, requiring police to carry them down and into police vehicles.[42]

It is impossible to know with certainty whether these offers were coming from men actively involved with organized crime in Hawaii, although there is that appearance. And even if it is assumed those making the offers were somehow syndicate-connected, there is then a question of whether the offers represented some kind of policy decision by syndicate leaders, or whether these were simply rank-and-file organized crime members independently wanting to help causes they sympathized with.

Nevertheless the fact of such offers would not be altogether surprising, given a kind of Hawaiian nationalist ideology that permeated the Hawaiian part of the syndicate.

The Hawaii Crime Commission believed there was some sort of racial or nationalist feeling among some elements of organized crime in Hawaii, but perceived it as a case of "native localism" more than race. "Though race is a factor in the composition of individual gangs, there is a far stronger current of 'native localism' from which caucasians and, to some degree, those of the 'Japanese establishment' are ultimately excluded from consideration."[43]

Whether grounded in localism or race, the ideology was that of an underclass group with a hatred of the legitimate sectors of the establishment, that tended to justify criminal activities.

As the Commission also wrote, the merging of gangsterism and localism was not a feature unique to Hawaii. "Examine any other organized crime movement—the Sicilian Cosa Nostra, the Mexican Mafia, the Japanese Yakuza, the Chinese Triads, the Black Mafia—and there will be found an intense dislike or hatred of outsiders, combined with conscious and demonstrative loyalty to their 'own people,' which appears to justify in their minds a callousness toward established law and morality. In Hawaii, such a situation is manifested in the organized crime figures' persistent interest in ethnic social clubs and political movements."[44]

In addition to the examples cited above, Henry Huihui during the early 1980s attended meetings of the Protect Kahoolawe Ohana, a primarily Hawaiian group formed to stop the island of Kahoolawe being used for bombing practice by the US military. Hawaii's foremost identified contract killer of the 1970s and early 1980s, part-Hawaiian Ronald K. Ching, made at least one trip to Kahoolawe, as part of a group who visited the island to show it respect and to demonstrate opposition to the bombings.[45]

Reputed syndicate strong-arm man Bobby Wilson during the 1970s headed a Hawaiian canoe club in Hanalei, Kauai. Nappy Pulawa's attorney as of 1984, Hayden F. Burgess, was a trustee for the Office of Hawaiian Affairs. In an interview for this book Burgess said that Pulawa had often contributed money to the support of Hawaiian canoe racing and Hawaiian music concerts. Others interviewed said that syndicate-connected men at times contributed money to Hawaiian canoe clubs and Hawaiian nationalist causes.

Pulawa once, on trial for murder, told the judge that he refused to submit to the jurisdiction of the court because he was a Hawaiian, and the court was an appendage of a government established by those who in 1893 overthrew the duly-established Hawaiian monarchy.[46]

While in prison 1975-1984 Pulawa wrote several essays and articles on Hawaiian nationalism. In one he attacked "the process of being assimilated into the mainland culture of the United States [as] merely a continuation of the process of thievery, initiated from our earliest days of foreign immigration. It's all take, take, take, with very little give. Hawaiians became displaced persons in their *own* homeland. It's intolerable."[47]

Concretely, what the overall role of organized crime was in the various aspects of the Hawaiian renaissance would be impossible to assess accurately. The syndicate was certainly not the leading force. Regardless of any actual or apparent offers of money or help from organized crime, various parts of the renaissance had their own autonomy, including the broadly based Hawaiian land rights movement. It would not be remotely sensible to assert that Hawaiian activism in relation to land was "controlled" by organized crime, any more than it would make sense to assert that that organized crime in some way "controlled" canoe racing.

But, even on the limited evidence available, a presence was indicated.

*   *   *

In writing about organized crime in Hawaii, a given topic must often be left hanging, the full picture unclear. As of early 1985 the greatest enigma of all remained: what was Larry Mehau vis-a-vis the syndicate?

Gov. Burns in 1970 appointed Mehau to the powerful State Board of Land & Natural Resources (BLNR). At about the same time, George Ariyoshi launched his first campaign for a statewide office, lieutenant governor, and he named Mehau his statewide coordinator. In an interview for this book, Ariyoshi said that he and Mehau first met and became friends when Ariyoshi, in his first year or so out of law school, occasionally represented petty criminals whom Mehau—then a policeman—had arrested. In Ariyoshi's races for governor Mehau played a major role, though without formal title. Ariyoshi in 1974 reappointed him to a second BLNR term, which ended in late 1977.

There were two camps of opinion apparently believing with equal certainty that Mehau was or was not the top man in organized crime in Hawaii.

One state judge who had overseen some criminal proceedings relating to organized crime in the late 1970s and early 1980s was fond of telling a reporter that Mehau was either the most maligned or the guiltiest man in the Hawaiian Islands.

To illustrate how widely opinion diverged on Mehau, consider the following:

In February 1977, KHON-TV reporter Scott Shirai aired a story following up on a heroin bust the previous summer, and reporting the conviction of most of those arrested. Quoting unnamed "reliable sources," Shirai said there were several prominent Hawaii residents who were members of the heroin ring who had not yet been arrested or publicly named.

He said one was "a member of a state board—the so-called 'godfather' of the operation. Several meetings were held between this State board member with those arrested in the bust, sometimes at the apartment of a well-known Waikiki entertainer. One of those arrested worked for this entertainer and was also directed to act as a bodyguard for a candidate for statewide office in last year's election. That candidate was also seen publicly with at least one of those arrested."[48]

Then, in June, a small newspaper on Maui picked up the ball on the "godfather" question raised by Shirai. The *Valley Isle* created a major uproar by publishing several stories claiming Larry Mehau was the "godfather" of all organized crime in Hawaii. Mehau subsequently sued the paper for libel, as he did a number of other media organizations that republished the allegations, as well as several individuals, including Shirai.

During the furor two Republican politicians, Kinau B. Kamalii and D.G. "Andy" Anderson (both, incidentally, of Hawaiian background), met with the then-chief of the Honolulu Police Department, Francis A. Keala (also of Hawaiian background), to ask him whether, in his opinion, Mehau was a syndicate godfather.

Anderson and Kamalii, talking to reporters later, could agree about Keala's more concrete statements concerning Mehau and organized crime.

To quote Anderson: "He [Keala] described Larry's position this way: He said that whenever there's a gang war or fighting between factions and they want to talk it over, they call Larry and ask him to arrange a truce. He is used as a mediator. I understand, too, that even the police have on occasions asked him to intercede and bring peace to some situations."

But Anderson and Kamalii diverged radically on what this might mean.

Anderson's understanding was that Mehau was performing a sort of public service by mediating syndicate problems, and that this in no way made Mehau a godfather. Anderson also said that "the chief said Larry was nowhere involved in gambling, pimping, heroin, drugs or anything else as far as the police know."

Kamalii, on the other hand, also leaving the meeting "with the impression that Larry Mehau was a peacemaker of the underworld," asked rhetorically: "If that isn't aiding and abetting the underworld, what is? What is a godfather?"[49]

For statements like these Kamalii was sued in 1977 by Mehau, who simultaneously sued a host of news media organizations and several other individuals. Most media defendants successfully sought dismissal on grounds that they were merely republishing statements made by the *Valley Isle*. KHON-TV on behalf of itself and its reporter, Shirai, settled out of court with Mehau in 1978 for $42,500. In early 1985 Mehau dropped his case against all remaining defendants except one, United Press International. Mehau's attorney explained that of those remaining in the case, only UPI had sufficient assets to be worth proceeding against.[50]

Whatever Mehau was or was not in organized crime circles, one thing he indisputably *was* was an influential man among the modern establishment. Take as an example those who attended his daughter's wedding in 1980. Guests at the reception, numbering over 3,000, included Gov. Ariyoshi; the wife and a son of the late Gov. Burns; US Rep. Daniel K. Akaka; banker K.J. Luke; Republican State Sen. Wadsworth Y.H. Yee; Democratic State Sen. Duke T. Kawasaki; comedian Andy Bumatai; former House speaker Tadao Beppu; ILWU Regional Director Thomas Trask; Hotel Workers and Teamsters local head Arthur A. Rutledge; Bishop Estate trustee Myron B. "Pinky" Thompson; the president of Caesar's hotel at Lake Tahoe; and State Agriculture Board Chairman John Farias Jr. At the reception Mehau was photographed with television actor Jim Nabors, who said of the crowd of guests and mountains of food and presents: "I've never seen anything like it."[51]

Mehau's reputation was made as a policeman. He served on the Big Island force 1951-1953, then switched to the Honolulu force. Assigned eventually to vice units, he compiled an outstanding record in arresting gamblers. During an 11-month period in the late 1950s, the gambling squad he led raided 485 games and made 4,162 arrests.[52]

This kind of record was in part due to Mehau's impressive physical power. Over the years he was described as weighing between 250 and 300 pounds. During his later years as a policeman he was an amateur sumo wrestling champion. He once, according to the *Honolulu Star-Bulletin*, "smashed his fist through the windshield of an automobile in a zealous attempt to catch a criminal who had locked himself in the car."[53] During a martial arts demonstration in 1957 Mehau broke bricks with karate chops. He then attempted to break two at a time, taped together. But, as a reporter wrote, "they wouldn't break cleanly. All they did was crumble. Sgt. Mehau, determined man, kept smacking them until spectators' stomachs began turning over and Deputy Chief Arthur Tarbell made him stop." At the same demonstration, Mehau suspended himself between two chairs. Three officers placed a 300-pound rock on his stomach. "An assistant battered at the rock with a nine-pound sledge hammer. Sgt. Mehau didn't even grunt. After several sharp blows, the rock broke in two. Sgt. Mehau walked away unharmed. He didn't even stagger a bit."[54]

Mehau was intelligent as well as strong. By 1960 he had the job of guarding dignitaries visiting Hawaii, including Vice President Richard M. Nixon, Madame Chiang Kai Shek, German Chancellor Konrad Adenauer, the kings of Nepal and Thailand, and Korean leader Synghman Rhee.

Once during one of these visits a reporter quipped: "Police Sgt. Larry Mehau knows his place. It's close to princes and presidents, premiers, kings and queens."[55]

This was a moderately prophetic statement.

Mehau in 1963 retired from the Honolulu Police Department and moved to the Big Island, where he took up ranching on 300 acres of Hawaiian Homes land in Waimea. He also bought into a small security guard company. And he became active in Democratic Party politics.

During his years as a policeman, particularly serving with vice units, Mehau made the acquaintance of much of Hawaii's underworld. At some point following his retirement from the force, rumors began to circulate that through these acquaintances, plus his political ties, plus his own exceptional physical power, Mehau had become a kind of godfather of organized crime in Hawaii.

The rumor first circulated on the streets, then began to be whispered to reporters by opponents of the Burns-Ariyoshi political organization. The *Valley Isle* in 1977 made it public.

Finally, the rumor turned into an allegation reportedly made by an admitted syndicate contract murderer who in 1984 turned government witness. Mehau's lawyer told reporters that Ronald Ching, in admitting to a large number of murders, had implicated Mehau in some of them.[56]

Over the years Mehau acknowledged that he had rapport with the publicly identified leaders of organized crime in Hawaii. The *Los Angeles Times* reporter who interviewed him in 1979, quoted him as saying, as Honolulu Police Chief Keala had said two years earlier, that he was called on from time to time to help settle disputes between rival gangs. Often it was the police who asked for his intercession, Mehau added.[57]

But Mehau and others steadfastly denied that his involvement went any further, a denial bolstered by the fact that vigorous criminal investigations from about 1978 till 1980 by three separate law enforcement agencies, coordinated by the federal Organized Crime Strike Force and including a hearing of evidence by an investigative grand jury, resulted in no charges being brought.

As with what Mehau told the *Los Angeles Times*, the criminal investigators and prosecutors found that Mehau had underworld associates, but apparently no underworld activities *per se*. *Honolulu Advertiser* reporter James Dooley wrote: "Investigators found Mehau to have created a remarkable network of personal ties with rich and powerful figures of high and low repute throughout Hawaii and the Pacific Basin." But, as Dooley added, "personal associations are hardly ground for prosecution . . ."

Far from dispelling the suspicions harbored by some, the investigations, as Dooley wrote, "if anything . . . may have served merely to broaden the mystique which has built up around the physically imposing Mehau since he began to make a name for himself as a tough, no-nonsense cop in the 1950s."[58]

If questions lingered, however fairly or unfairly, about Larry Mehau as some kind of organized crime godfather, this was true of organized crime in general. The local syndicate was like a guerrilla force of unknown strength. It was known to be out there, a factor to be reckoned with in the equation of modern Hawaii. But how big it really was, what territories it controlled, what high ground it might be seeking to occupy—these were things that few or none outside of organized crime knew. And as of early 1985 no highly placed organized criminal had spoken comprehensively on the public record.

8

HAWAII: SUBDIVIDING LAVA FIELDS

HAWAII'S real estate boom was brought to the Big Island in 1958 by two mainland businessmen from Denver, Colorado.

Glen I. Payton and David F. O'Keefe organized a Hawaii corporation called Tropic Estates Ltd., which included several local-Asians among its members. In 1958 Tropic Estates bought 12,000 acres of land between Kurtistown and Mountain View in Puna from Big Island Democratic politician and businessman Robert M. Yamada. The land was cut up into 4,000 lots which were put on the market for $500-$1,000 with terms as low as $150 down and $8 a month. The project was named Hawaiian Acres. The lots sold spectacularly well.[1]

The effect of this success was electrifying. A Big Island subdividing boom was on. For the next nine years new large-scale subdivisions were approved one after the other by Hawaii County.

There was substantial development of other kinds all over the Big Island then and later that had counterparts elsewhere in the Islands: resort hotels at Hilo, with an international-size airstrip to serve them; heavy hotel and condominium building at Kailua-Kona; and an ambitious attempt, spearheaded by Gov. Burns, to transform the whole northern stretch of the west coast into a regional resort complex, making it, in Burns' words, a "Gold Coast."[2]

But the developments unique to the Big Island were in the mold of the one in Puna that set off the boom: sizable acreage in remote areas, of little or no real economic use value, subdivided into house lots on which practically no one ever actually built homes.

Only on the Big Island was there so much empty space that had no foreseeable economic use. Thus nowhere else were there speculative subdivisions.

Most of the really big subdivisions of this sort were done in the vast, sparsely populated southeast and southern districts of the island, in Puna, Ka'u, and South Kona.

By the time the Big Island boom came to a halt in the mid-1970s, something like 80,000 lots of this kind had been created—on an island whose population at the time was somewhat less than 80,000.

* * *

Participation by local people in this subdividing boom was remarkable. Probably one Big Island family in four put money into a lot in one of these subdivisions.[3]

But even with such heavy participation, Big Islanders bought fewer than 12% of the roughly 65,000 lots sold by 1975.[4] This meant that the rest of the buyers were outsiders—some 35% from Oahu, and most of the rest from the US mainland. And this in turn meant that a nationwide phenomenon had made its way to the Big Island.

The post-World War II middle class of the United States in the national boom years of the late 1950s and 1960s had money to spend, and they also had increased leisure time. It was now within the financial reach of a great number of people to spend this time in vacation and retirement communities. In the country's sunnier states developers stepped in to make possible a logical next move: actually investing in vacation and retirement real estate. By the mid-1970s, one American family in 12 owned a piece of this sort of land.[5]

There were, to be sure, serious developers and serious buyers on the mainland. Over the boom years millions nationwide bought lots in planned communities that evolved more or less as promised.

But at the same time among both developers and buyers there were also speculators—meaning that millions bought into subdivisions which 25 and 30 years later remained largely vacant and without even minimal site improvements.

Most Big Island subdivisions of the boom years in the Puna, Ka'u and South Kona districts fell into the speculative category.

The distinction between investment and speculation made no difference to most people on the Big Island, at least in the early years of the boom. Overall the lots appreciated in value, meaning that many Big Island families did well, at least in terms of paper gains. And Hawaii County did well too, at least on the face of things. Right from the first boom year, the county's revenues increased because these subdivisions came onto the tax rolls.

In the middle of that euphoric first twelve months, the *Hilo Tribune-Herald* editorialized: "This newspaper goes along with the optimists, confident that the eager buying of land, much of it sight unseen, means that the Big Island is finally coming into its own, and that we are on the threshold of development that has kept Oahu singing with prosperity . . . Here on the Big Island we don't much care what brings them in as long as they come and as long as they buy . . . "[6]

*   *   *

Not everyone on the Big Island liked the new speculative subdivisions. As early as 1960, Hawaii County Planning Director Hiroshi Kasamoto called the existing subdivision ordinance "a bad law." He wanted to "control development and stop speculation."[7] County Attorney Yoshito Tanaka in the same year described the situation simply as "a mess."[8]

The ramifications of speculative subdividing on the Big Island went beyond the county, affecting attitudes to development statewide. In fact this sudden rush to subdivide on Hawaii generated part of the momentum for the statewide Land Use Law of 1961. Big Island subdivisions were springing up wherever developers could acquire large parcels cheaply. Usually this was far from established population and employment centers, and the parcels were not necessarily near each other. Puna alone was the size of the entire island of Oahu. The projects were thus dotting remote, huge districts. The Land Use Law's preamble decried "scattered subdivisions with expensive, yet reduced, public services"—exactly what was appearing all over the south and southeast parts of the Big Island.

Once the law was in place, the Land Use Commission it brought into being tried to close a crucial loophole allowing the creation of speculative and urban-type subdivisions on agricultural land. The LUC adopted a rule forbidding the subdivision of land in the agricultural district—where most of the speculative subdivisions were—into lots smaller than five acres, on the argument that even subdivided lots on agricultural land ought to be used for *bona fide* farming, and most viable farms demanded at least five acres.

But the state attorney general ruled the LUC out of bounds. He said agricultural lot sizes were the jurisdiction of the counties.[9] Counties were thus allowed to continue setting minimum sizes in the agricultural district. And Hawaii County was happy to allow lot sizes well under five acres, in fact all the way down to about one-sixth of one acre. (Not till 1969 was a uniform statewide minimum set by the Legislature—one acre.)[10]

Evidence of Hawaii County's real attitude in the early boom years toward controlling or restricting development in general could be seen in a Big Island Planning Commission move in 1962 on the eve of the effective date of the Land Use Law, when on a single day 42 new subdivisions involving 3,500 lots were approved, "in order to beat the [Land Use] law deadline," according to the *Honolulu Star-Bulletin*.[11]

Beyond that, state legislators from the Big Island were active in attempts to actually get rid of the Land Use Law, which had created a step in the construction approval process that many in the business disliked. In 1963, only two years after the law was adopted, a Senate bill for repeal was introduced. Four of the nine introducers were Big Islanders. A second attempt at repeal followed the next year, when the Senate Lands Committee unanimously reported out a bill that would have done away with the Land Use Law. The committee report called it a "barrier to economic development."[12] Three of the committee's eight members were from the Big Island, including the chairman, Kazuhisa Abe.

In short, on the Big Island there was both political muscle and substantial public backing in favor of large-scale, virtually unrestricted development, and this continued to be so for several years.

* * *

How were these Big Island subdivisions promoted and sold? Who were the sales campaigns aimed at? What did the buyers think they were getting? And what did they actually get?

"Along the southern shores of the Big Island, Hawaii, largest of the Hawaiian chain," read a brochure for one typical development, "lies the historic and legendary lands of Kalapana. This is the setting for Royal Gardens, a fertile area directly adjacent to the Hawaii Volcano National Park with its spectacular attractions, yet only walking distance away from lovely beach and shore areas. Royal Gardens lots are all one acre in size, making it possible for the owners to have a small orchard or truck garden, or a magnificent garden, as well as a home and a haven for retirement."[13]

Royal Gardens started selling its one-acre lots in the early 1960s for $995—only $100 down and $15 a month, plus 6% interest on the unpaid balance. The development was widely and heavily promoted, locally and on the mainland. For example, in 1961 a Royal Gardens lot was given away as a prize to ABC-TV's Queen For A Day, plus a trip to visit the place.[14]

This was in the world-famous tropical paradise of Hawaii, now the fiftieth state of the Union, only five hours by commercial jet from the West Coast. The price seemed amazingly low.

At Royal Gardens and elsewhere on the Big Island, people by the thousands, by the scores of thousands, were ready to buy—and even to buy from a distance. A sizable majority, in fact, bought sight unseen: well over half, perhaps as many as two-thirds.[15]

Here there was a loud echo of the classic American story of speculative land development, going back far beyond the Hawaii boom, back to the mainland, back to the original boom in subdivided vacation or retirement house lots—Florida in the 1920s.

The formula as perfected in Florida went like this: acquire cheap raw land with little or no economic use value, even waste land. Subdivide it with little or no site improvement. Promote it heavily nationwide. Advertise in terms that make the house lots sound simultaneously like a place to be enjoyed on vacation, a haven for old age, a prudent investment, and an exciting bit of speculation offering quick return. And sell sight unseen if possible, to first-time buyers if possible—in other words to real estate amateurs.[16]

Florida was worth millions to developers. And from then on, between the 1920s on the mainland and the 1960s on the Big Island, any number of similar developments were floated, especially in states with a high number of sunny days per year.

One characteristic common to many of these subdivisions was that they were located on land that had virtually no productive value, remote, often essentially waste land, sometimes totally unlivable.[17] In Florida, so intense was the speculation—and so frequent the fraud—that a purchaser who had bought a lot through the mail, sight unseen, might arrive to take a first look at his "beachfront" real estate and find that it was even closer to the sea than he would ever have dreamed possible, actually underwater at high tide.

The Big Island version of a Florida development was a subdivision laid out on volcanic lava.

Royal Gardens was an example of this. It covered part of the old Hawaiian *ahupua'a* of Pulama, which made a kind of boundary from the mountains to the sea between the habitable areas of Puna and the uninhabitable lava fields of Kilauea Volcano.

The land of Royal Gardens was about 40% covered with *a'a*. *A'a* was defined by the US Soil Conservation Service as loose lava rocks, "rough and broken . . . a mass of clinkery, hard, glassy, sharp pieces [of lava] in tumbled heaps." About 20% was *pahoehoe*, solid thick sheets of lava, hard and smooth-surfaced, with "no soil covering," usually "bare of vegetation" except for mosses at lower elevations, and scrub bushes and trees growing in cracks higher up. The remaining 40% was *opihikao*, "extremely rocky muck," with *pahoehoe* underneath. Water was chronically scarce—no streams, just a few widely scattered waterholes.[18]

When a private property system was introduced in the Hawaiian kingdom in mid-nineteenth century, the area became the property of the king. It had no great value because it had no real usefulness. In 1864 1,179 acres of what later became Royal Gardens were sold by the government for $110.50; and in 1894 the balance of 628 of the future subdivision's 1,807 acres were sold for $680. Early in the twentieth century a Portuguese rancher put some of the land to extremely limited pasture use. But a trust company officer who later helped administer the rancher's estate said the land had essentially "no value for pasturage . . . I doubt a cow could walk far enough in a day to get enough to eat."[19] In loose *a'a* Hawaiians used to grow sweet potatoes. As well, some kinds of fruit trees, like papaya, and ornamentals like the Hawaiian Christmas berry, could grow. Overall, though, the Soil Conservation Service gave *a'a* the lowest possible soil productivity rating. *Opihikao* contained some organic matter, but the SCS classified it as having "very severe limitations that make [it] unsuitable to cultivation."[20] On *pahoehoe* nothing would grow, except in the cracks, though it was possible to use a bulldozer to rip up *pahoehoe* and then plant it as if it was *a'a*. One thing was certain—there were never "royal gardens" on the land that became Royal Gardens. There never could have been. And in the twentieth century, to have a truck garden or a "magnificent" home garden of the kind the brochures talked about, a lot owner would have to catch his own water, possibly haul in his own soil, and anyway use chemical fertilizer.

All this was so because Royal Gardens was on volcano land, recent lava. A brochure described the development as being "directly adjacent to Hawaii Volcano National Park with its spectacular attractions."[21] Another way of putting this would be to say that Royal Gardens was only 12 miles to the east-southeast of an active volcano, Kilauea.

Kilauea's east rift zone stretched from the volcano's crater to about 30

miles northeastward to Kapoho, passing about a mile-and-a-half from the
rear of the Royal Gardens subdivision.

The US Geological Survey in 1974 rated all areas of the Big Island for
vulnerability to volcanic hazard. According to the USGS, Kilauea and its rift
zones "must be expected to erupt repeatedly in the future," and "all areas
downslope from volcanic vents should be considered vulnerable to eventual
burial by lava flows."[22] From 1955 the east rift zone had been the source of
most of the Big Island's volcanic activity. There were several major eruptions
within the zone, sending lava flows downslope toward the sea. In 1960 a lava
flow covered much of Kapoho, destroying the village of that name. In 1977 an
eruption nearly destroyed the village of Kalapana, about three miles northeast along the coast from Royal Gardens, and at one point it seemed as if
Royal Gardens itself might be covered with lava. Then, in 1983, 1984, and
1985, a total of seven lava flows entered Royal Gardens, destroying altogether
22 homes, or about one in three of all residences so far built in the subdivision.[23]

Associated with volcanic activity was earthquake risk. Royal Gardens lay
entirely within the Hilina Fault Zone, an area that the USGS said was especially prone to surface ruptures because of land movement within the fault.

Here again there was a repetition of the pattern of large-scale speculative
subdivision on the mainland, where often it was natural hazards that made
subdivision areas wastelands from an economic standpoint. When the authors of a multi-volume national study of rural speculative subdivisions like
those on the Big Island selected 10 mainland projects as case studies, they
found that seven out of the 10 "subdivided and allowed building on highly
hazardous land—near an earthquake fault, within the 100-year floodplain,
and on very steep slopes."[24] This was true for the Big Island. Not just Royal
Gardens but a majority of the Big Island's speculative subdivision lots—as
many as 60%—lay within USGS "high risk" or "highest risk" zones.[25]

Beginning in 1971 the US Department of Housing and Urban Development refused to insure residential mortgages in the east rift zone and downslope from it, and in most areas at risk from eruptions of Mauna Loa flowing south and west—meaning that 60% of speculative subdivision lots on
the Big Island were excluded from coverage.

* * *

Did lot buyers know what they were getting?

Most of them really did not, at least at Royal Gardens, where at the time
of purchase, according to a sample survey done for this book, some 72%
believed their lot had fertile soil, and 69% did not know their lot was in a
zone of serious volcanic hazard.

In the developer's public offering statements (required by state law since

1968), there was no discussion of hazard until sale began in late 1972 of Unit V of the subdivision.[26]

And in none of the Royal Gardens sales brochures on file with the Hawaii County Planning Department and the State Department of Commerce and Consumer Affairs (DCCA) was there any mention of volcanic hazard. In general these were the two government agencies most responsible for regulating development and sale of Royal Gardens and the two with which the buying public would have had the most contact.

There were other omissions as well in the Royal Gardens promotional material:

Lots in the subdivision were being sold with no water lines, no power, and no sewerage. Some roads were county standard, some were not. When the Hawaii County Planning Commission in 1960 granted Royal Gardens preliminary subdivision approval, this condition was imposed: "Subdivider shall notify buyers of land in this subdivision about the use of oil-treated surface for roads [these were sub-standard roads that the County would allow to be built but not permit to be turned over to the County for maintenance at public expense] and the present lack of water and sewer systems and the lack of electrical power. All advertising shall call attention to the above-mentioned modification of standards and the lack of facilities."[27]

Although public offering statements in general noted these deficiencies, no advertisement for Royal Gardens on file with the Big Island Planning Department or DCCA pointed them out.

Royal Gardens was not alone in such matters. More than once during the boom years, Big Island subdivisions which advertised nationwide were banned for sale in California, either because they were not registered there as required by California state law or because their sales brochures were found to be deceptive, suggesting that the developments had government-standard roads and other improvements when in fact they did not.[28]

Yet the Big Island subdivisions kept on advertising and kept on selling without county-standard roads, water, or utilities, or even easy access to beaches. Though the Royal Gardens brochures talked about being "only walking distance away from lovely beach and shore areas,"[29] in fact the average Royal Gardens lot was one or two miles from the sea, usually along hot, dusty roads, and a six-mile drive from the nearest sand beach at Kalapana. A Bishop Museum study done in 1959, just as the Big Island subdivision boom was getting under way, described the coast nearest to Royal Gardens as a "shoreline of low, black, lava cliffs, battered continuously by windward waves . . . This coast bears witness to the great volcanic forces underlaying it through numerous earthquake-opened fissures, and to the violence of tidal waves through huge blocks of lava which have been ripped from the ocean cliffs and hurled inland."[30]

To those with some sophistication in real estate, the overall effect was strange, almost hallucinatory. As financial columnist Sylvia Porter wrote after touring several subdivisions in 1961: "I spent a day destroying a pair of shoes walking over these lava 'developments,' taking pictures to remind myself that they had no irrigation, no roads, no essential utilities, no beaches, no buildings—nothing except lava."[31]

If there was some distance between Royal Gardens and the beach, and some distance between the advertising brochures and reality, there was also some distance between what Royal Gardens was supposed to do under county law and what the developers actually did.

For example, lots were sold in the second increment for three years without county permission. The County Planning Department staff wrote in 1966 that "the subdivider sold lots to individuals within Unit II of Royal Gardens Subdivision which was declared null and void by the Commission in October, 1963, and any sale transaction within this unit is considered illegal."[32] In other ways there were indications that the emphasis was so strictly on mass selling of purely investment or speculative real estate that rational quality control procedures were not initially adopted:

After the experience of the first few years of the boom, subdividers were required to post a performance bond on their promise to build site improvements. Usually these improvements were nothing more than roads, and substandard at that. But even so, in the case of Royal Gardens, the County for years was prepared to accept a letter of credit from an affiliate of the subdivider, rather than requiring an actual bond from an unaffiliated company.

This practice was not halted until 1973, following a memo from the County Department of Public Works: "Letters of credit should generally not be accepted in lieu of a performance bond because the future worth of the letter of credit is tied directly to the applicant's financial stability. In order to avoid such problems, we recommend that performance bonds insured by a financial institution not connected with the applicant be required."[33]

*   *   *

With all this as background, what was the connection on the Big Island between speculative subdividing and politics?

The public record shows that if a large number of Big Island families were buying lots, their political leaders were heavily involved in creating those lots for sale.

Most of the island's most influential legislators of the 1960s and 1970s were involved with companies doing speculative subdivisions, as partners, corporate officers, shareholders or attorneys.

Included were Democrats Kazuhisa Abe, who became Senate president and later an associate supreme court justice, who as a corporate officer helped direct the creation of Orchid Land Estates and Vacationland Hawaii; Nelson K. Doi, also a Senate president who later became a circuit court judge and then lieutenant governor, who served as the attorney for Glenwood Subdivision and for Kalapana Corporation, which bought and sold land that later became Kalapana Vacation Lots; and Jack K. Suwa, who for much of the 1970s chaired the powerful House Finance Committee, and who was a shareholder in Kalapana Corporation, also a limited partner in Vacationland Associates, the developer of Vacationland Hawaii.

Other Democratic politicians involved were former senator William J. Nobriga as the developer of Aloha Estates; Stanley I. Hara, a Democratic representative and later a senator, who as a corporate officer and partner was involved with Orchid Land Estates and Vacationland Hawaii; and Robert M. Yamada, Democratic member of the Board of Supervisors, County Council, and Planning Commission, who in 1958 sold the 12,000 acres that became the first such subdivision, and who as a developer or road building contractor took part in the creation of a 413-lot project near Kalapana Beach, of Eden Roc, Hawaiian Ocean View Estates, and of a subdivision called Hawaiian Parks, Beaches and Shores.

Another prominent member of the Big Island Democratic establishment, though not a politician, who was a partner in Vacationland Associates and a shareholder in Kalapana Corp., was Yoshio Yanagawa. From 1960 through 1966 he worked for county and state urban renewal and housing agencies, and in 1966 was appointed executive director of the state's Hawaii Housing Authority.

One Big Island Republican involved was Sen. William H. Hill's protege, Richard Henderson, as a director of a company developing Kapoho Beach Lots. (Henderson became a senator himself in 1970.)

Henderson also was president of The Realty Investment Co. Ltd., which in 1969 petitioned the Land Use Commission for the redistricting to urban of 428 acres of what ultimately was to be a 6,000-acre resort-residential complex in the Kapoho area of Puna. Bishop Estate trustee and former Republican senator Richard J. Lyman Jr. was president of the Kapoho Land & Development Co. which owned the land involved in the petition.

The LUC staff believed the project to be essentially one more Puna land sale scheme, and wrote in recommending denial: "Approval of this petition would contribute to the already scattered residential developments which are so evident in the Puna District and would therefore be contrary to the intents and purposes of the Land Use Law."[34] (This LUC application was surely one of the most extreme ever filed. The petitioners' planning consultant wrote that the project's "major tourist attractions include ... the 1960 lava cone and surrounding lava field providing visitors with an opportunity to experience the awesome forces of nature."[35] Indeed. The project would sit directly on top of an active volcanic rift zone. About half of the total project area had been inundated by eruptions in 1955 and 1960. More eruptions were almost certain to come, making it likely that residents would experience the awesome forces of nature at very close quarters, for instance in their front yard. The application was supported by the Big Island Planning Commission and the island's two Land Use Commission members. It was turned down.)

Political figures from Oahu also invested in Big Island speculative subdivisions. Republican US Sen. Hiram L. Fong's Finance Realty Co. was the developer of Fern Forest Vacation Estates and Royal Hawaiian Estates. Democratic State Rep. Robert C. Oshiro (later a leading campaign coordinator for Gov. Burns and a confidant of Gov. Ariyoshi) was one of the attorneys for Kalapana Corporation. Republican legislator Ralph K. Ajifu, first chairman of the Land Use Commission, invested in Milolii Syndicate.

Kauai Republican politician Clinton Shiraishi also invested in Milolii Syndicate.

As for the company that developed Royal Gardens, the following table (Table 16) shows that investors included several state legislators, among them future Gov. George Ariyoshi, who obtained his partnership share in trade for drafting the partnership registration statement. Another investor was the wife of an associate justice of the Hawaii Supreme Court. The parents of County Supervisor Herbert T. Matayoshi, who later became the island's mayor, invested, as did university agricultural extension agent Yukio Kitagawa, who later became deputy director of the State Department of Agriculture and chairman of the Honolulu Planning Commission. The attorneys who represented Royal Gardens before county agencies included the law firm of State Sen. John T. Ushijima and an attorney who was simultane-

---

TABLE 16

PUBLIC OFFICIALS, PUBLIC EMPLOYEES AND FAMILY MEMBERS INVOLVED WITH ROYAL GARDENS AS INVESTORS, ATTORNEYS, CONSULTANTS

Note: Governmental position is as of the time of the work on behalf of Royal Gardens or during the period that the investment was held.

ARIYOSHI, GEORGE R. State senator, lieutenant governor. Attorney who drafted partnership registration statement in part for share as limited partner.

HIROTA, SAM O. Former deputy director State Dept. of Transportation. Engineering consultant.

INABA, ALBERT Y. Principal Molokai High and Intermediate School. Limited partner.

INABA, YOSHIO. Former Hawaii County chief engineer. Engineering consultant.

ISHIMOTO, ARTHUR U. Hawaii National Guard staff supervisor, later state adjutant general. Limited partner.

KITAGAWA, YUKIO. Assistant extension agent, University of Hawaii Agricultural Extension Service. Limited partner.

KUSHI, MASANORI. District court magistrate. Attorney.

MATAYOSHI, MIDORI and ZENKO. Parents of County supervisor and then councilman Herbert T. Matayoshi. Limited partners.

MIZUHA, MRS. JACK H. Wife of Supreme Court justice. Limited partner.

NAKASHIMA, SUMIO. Former Territorial representative, district court magistrate. Limited partner, attorney.

USHIJIMA, JOHN T. State senator. Law firm represented company before Hawaii County government.

Sources: Hawaii County Planning Department files on Royal Gardens; Gwenfread E. Allen, ed., *Men and Women of Hawaii: A Biographical Directory of Noteworthy Men and Women of Hawaii* (Honolulu, 1966); Betty F. Buker, ed., *Men and Women of Hawaii 1972: A Biographical Directory of Noteworthy Men and Women of Hawaii* (Honolulu, 1972); Department of Commerce and Consumer Affairs, Business Registration Division; State of Hawaii, Legislative Reference Bureau, *Directory of State, County and Federal Officials: Supplement to Guide to Government in Hawaii* (published occasionally, most recently annually); Chamber of Commerce of Hawaii, *Who's Who in Government State of Hawaii* (various years); Hawaii State Archives; miscellaneous references in newspapers and periodicals.

---

ously a part-time judge. Engineering consultants included the former chief of the Hawaii County Department of Public Works, and a former deputy director of the State Department of Transportation.

As mentioned, lava flows entered Royal Gardens beginning in 1983 and destroyed 22 homes. With this in mind, it is ironic to note that among those who invested in Royal Gardens in the 1960s were several people connected directly or indirectly, then or later, with government response to natural disasters such as volcanic eruptions.

Investor Arthur Ishimoto was in 1983 state director of civil defense. Engineering consultant Yoshio Inaba had approved Royal Gardens creation as county engineer. As county engineer he also had some responsibility for Big Island civil defense plans and operations. One of Royal Gardens' lawyers, George Ariyoshi, was the state's chief executive when the volcano erupted. The son of two other investors, the Matayoshis, was the Big Island's chief executive in 1983. Thus, in a small way, these people in the early 1960s helped to bring into existence a subdivision in a US Geological Survey high-risk zone that was repeatedly hit by lava beginning in 1983, requiring repeated evacuations and continual civil defense help. This is not to say that these people acted cynically in putting their money into or working on Royal Gardens—it was just that back at the start of the Big Island boom most of those involved, all the way from individual investors to the government bodies that approved such subdivisions, had their eye on real estate profits rather than natural hazards.

* * *

Besides natural hazards, also ignored in at least one Big Island speculative subdivision were native Hawaiians:

Developer Norman Inaba had a project in South Kona called Milolii Beach Lots Subdivision, for which Sen. George Ariyoshi prepared the partnership papers as he had for Royal Gardens. As with Royal Gardens, Ariyoshi took as his fee a limited partnership interest worth $1,000.

Abutting the subdivision on the north was a lava flow that in 1926 wiped out the Hawaiian fishing village of Hoopuloa. The residents of the village who chose to remain in the immediate area moved into another tiny village, on territorial government land a little to the south.

This village was called Milolii. It still existed in the 1980s, home to 60–70 people, mostly Hawaiian and part-Hawaiian. It was the only such fishing village left in the Hawaiian Islands.

From the 1926 destruction of Hoopuloa until 1982 there were ongoing efforts to give the residents of Milolii some kind of secure land tenure, in recognition of the uniqueness of their community. Finally in 1982 the Legislature passed a law which the governor signed, creating a subdivision with long-term leases available for the residents.

Norman Inaba in 1960 bought from Onomea Ranch Ltd. 423 acres between Milolii Village and the 1926 lava flow. Remote from existing population and employment centers, very hot, with little rainfall, almost totally covered in lava, with virtually no soil, and down about 1,200 feet in elevation from the government access road, the land was nearly worthless as far as Onomea was concerned. Inaba thus had to pay only about $137,000. He then cut it up into about 1,000 lots, provided virtually no site improvements, and sold at prices which research for this book suggests brought a gross return of some $3.5 million.

When Inaba started out he announced that Milolii was to be an "exclusive subdivision for retired military officers."[36] In the first four months on the market some 30% of the lots were sold, most of them presumably to active duty officers, since a community association formed shortly thereafter was headed entirely by active duty officers. (The association secretary-treasurer was Gen. Robert Lee Scott, author of *God Is My Co-Pilot*.)[37]

In his early public statements Inaba also said there would eventually be a beach club and a 60-acre park.[38]

As with the Royal Gardens sales brochures, which said the subdivision was "only walking distance away from [a] lovely beach," there was a problem with the beach at Milolii. Despite the subdivision's name there was no real beach, only a gravelly shoreline area directly in front of the Hawaiian fishing village, which also had the only good boat launching place in the area.

Inaba's 1,000-lot subdivision had in the mid-1980s only a 2% buildout rate—15-20 houses, several of which looked like weekend homes.[39] The military retirement community never materialized. Nor did the beach club. Nor did the park. In an exceedingly hot and dry area, with non-county standard roads, no phone service nor electricity, and with the need during much of the year of having to haul potable water, not to mention oneself, down a steepish mountain side to a lava homesite, there seemed little likelihood of many people ever living there.

How could a reasonable balance sheet be drawn up between Inaba's development at Milolii and the Hawaiian village?

On the one hand, had Inaba's promises materialized—1,000 house lots occupied by retired military people abutting 60-70 Hawaiians—the subdivision could well have obliterated the last Hawaiian village of its kind, meaning that this kind of life would have become extinct.

On the other hand, all the subdivision ever amounted to was a set of streets laid out in perfect grid patterns on a baking lava field and a sales strategy that yielded the developer a gross profit in the millions of dollars.

* * *

In the rush to subdivide places like Milolii, it was not only the interests of native Hawaiians that were ignored but also the spirit of the State Land Use Law of 1961.

The law specifically attacked the Milolii kind of subdivision. Yet the attorney who prepared the subdivision's partnership registration papers, in payment for which he received a *hui* share, was George Ariyoshi, a state senator who had voted in favor of the law. One of the *hui*'s limited partners, Ralph K. Ajifu, had before investing served for a year as the first chairman of the Land Use Commission. In an interview for this book Ajifu said he believed then and now that Milolii was a proper place for a residential subdivision and its existence was not contrary to the Land Use Law, because the land had no agricultural value nor any viable economic use other than to be subdivided.

* * *

Norman Inaba, who brought Milolii Beach Lots Subdivision and Royal Gardens into existence, was among the biggest of Hawaii County's developers. In 1964 the *Honolulu Star-Bulletin* described him as "the Big Island's most diversified if not biggest subdivider with nine developments around the island covering some 7,000 acres."[40]

Just as on other islands where strong family/business/political interconnections grew up in the Democratic years, so on the Big Island Norman Inaba and his immediate family interlocked with the Democratic leadership, and with investors from outside the mainstream Democratic ranks as well.

Inaba, for example, was a limited partner in the Kona Highlands Development Co., registered with the state in 1968 to undertake a 250-lot project in Kalaoa, Kona. Unlike most Puna-Kaʻu-South Kona subdivisions, this one had county standard roads and conventional utilities. Partners with government positions held at various times during the life of the venture were:

Sen. John T. Ushijima; former Supervisor Richard M. Jitchaku, who was also an aide to Ushijima; the chief of the State Department of Taxation for the Big Island, Sanford Y. Yanagi; Honolulu Police Commissioner William C. H. Chung, whose brother was the chief fundraiser for Honolulu Mayor Frank F. Fasi; the number two man in the county corporation counsel office, George S. Yuda; and District Court Magistrate Roy K. Nakamoto.

Inaba also invested in real estate through his Great Hawaiian Realty with Republican Richard Henderson's Realty Investment Co., to form Leilani Estates Inc.

Inaba's family was deeply involved in government. One brother, Yoshio, was chief of the Hawaii County Department of Public Works 1953–1963. Goro, another brother, was Kona District representative on the State Land Use Commission 1963–1973. A third brother, Minoru, an educator for much of his adult life, served in the State House 1969–1972, then again 1975–1980. A fourth brother, Albert, was a public school principal, and a civic and political leader on Molokai for nearly 30 years.

At times the brothers worked together. After Yoshio, the engineer, retired from government, he did consultancy work for Norman. Minoru, after retiring from the Department of Education but while he was in the Legislature, worked for one of Norman's development company affiliates. Albert, the public school principal, invested in the Royal Gardens *hui.* Land Use Commissioner Goro was once sold a lot in Milolii at a low price—$500— when buyers of comparable lots were paying several thousand.

At times the Inabas' public and private activities overlapped. Yoshio twice 1959–1960 was found to be in conflict-of-interest situations for drawing up subdivision plans as a private engineer that he then approved as county engineer. Goro three times as a land use commissioner, once in 1969 and twice in 1971, voted to approve redistricting applications in which Yoshio was involved as a private engineer. In one case Goro made a disclosure of interest, in the other two he did not. (In all probability Goro's votes did not violate the state ethics law. In general to be in conflict a commissioner had to vote on matters directly affecting his or her own financial interests, or those of a spouse or dependent child.)

The Inaba family, from about the time of statehood, had a close working relationship with George Ariyoshi, a rising Democratic politician, a legislator 1955-1970, and thereafter lieutenant governor and a three-term governor. Ariyoshi in 1960 represented Norman Inaba before the State Board of Agriculture and Forestry on a forest reserve matter in connection with Inaba's Hilolani Acres (now Kaumana City). In 1963-1964, as mentioned, Ariyoshi drafted for Norman the partnership registration statements for Royal Gardens and Milolii Syndicate. Norman's son Rodney worked for Ariyoshi in the Legislature 1966-1967, first as a committee clerk and then as a research assistant. About this time Ariyoshi's law firm handled for Rodney the registration of Great Hawaiian Realty Inc. with the State Department of

Regulatory Agencies. In 1969 Ariyoshi was the attorney for the construction of the Waikiki Gateway Hotel, one of whose developers was Rodney Inaba. In 1981 Norman Inaba on behalf of Milolii Syndicate contributed $500 to Ariyoshi's re-election campaign.

Norman Inaba was thus solidly part of Hawaii's power structure in the Democratic years. He was known and trusted, someone to be accommodated. His dealings with government were normally smooth. For example, when in 1972 he filed a subdivision registration statement for an increment of Royal Gardens, a mid-level official in the State Department of Regulatory Agencies wrote in an intra-office memo: "Norman Inaba has done a good job of filing papers and gave us no problem all these years. This new increment is like the previous ones. (I haven't seen any documents, but they should be in order.) They just filed yesterday. But can you give a fast look. Let's try to accommodate them. Let's give them the approval as of today."[41]

*   *   *

Without question there was money for Big Island developers in speculative subdivisions.

Norman Inaba's Royal Gardens was 1,807 acres, bought in 1961 from Bishop Trust Co. for $200,000, as determined from the tax he paid at the time of conveyance. In a prospectus Inaba gave to potential *hui* investors in 1961, he estimated that total costs to subdivide and sell would be $940,000.[42] Of the approximately 1,500 lots, 90% were sold by the mid-1980s, according to a realtor associated with the project. The realtor also said that prices ranged from $1,000 in the early 1960s to $16,000 in the late 1970s and early 1980s. He believed that an average price was probably $12,000, meaning a gross return of something like $16.2 million. Inaba's net was never made public, though presumably it was substantial, since there were so few site improvement costs.

As mentioned, land for the Milolii Beach Lots Subdivision cost Inaba about $137,000 in 1960. Most of the 1,000 lots, only minimally developed, were sold by the end of the 1960s, for a gross return of an estimated $3.5 million.

As for buyers of individual lots, probably the great majority showed a paper gain. On the Big Island most first buyers were able to resell if they wanted to, by contrast with some speculative subdivisions on the mainland where first buyers got stuck. On the other hand, in later years the rate of appreciation was less (in some cases considerably less) than the rate on properties with an immediate and actual use value as well as just an investment or speculative value—for example a house and lot in Oahu's Manoa Valley.

But if there was price appreciation, as there was on residential property throughout Hawaii, still, in the matter of actual construction on individual lots, a strange picture emerged:

In 1975, after the subdividing boom had come and gone, 97.5% of all lots in Puna in subdivisions of 100 or more lots were still vacant. By the end of 1983, a quarter-century after the start of the boom, no more than about 5% of lots held residences.[43]

So whatever the Big Island boom was about, it really was not about actually providing homes.

It was not even about developing subdivisions fully. After all those years, many subdivisions still did not have adequate roads and functioning utilities.

Perhaps, in an ironic sense, it was best that the subdivisions never did fill up beyond radically low levels, because what would have happened if they became even so much as 25% full in, say, 30 years? What would the costs have been to the county and the state governments to provide normal public services to these home owners, living so far from existing population centers and not even close to each other?

So appalling was this fiscal prospect that consultants to the Land Use Commission wrote in 1963 that "when the provision and maintenance of public facilities and services are requested and demanded by property owners in these subdivisions ... both the solvency of the investment and the government are threatened."[44]

This view was supported by University of Hawaii Land Study Bureau researchers, who wrote two years later: "The people of the county can only hope that these and subsequent developments in the area do not have sufficient construction activity to necessitate the provision of normal urban services, for the costs of their installation and operation would be a fantastic burden for the county to assume."[45]

In the late 1960s Big Island Planning Director Raymond Suefuji said that it would actually be cheaper for the County to buy up all those scores of thousands of vacant lots to forestall any more house-building than it would be to face the financial disaster of having to service a significant percentage of them some day.[46]

*   *   *

For nine years, 1958–1966, Hawaii County routinely approved speculative subdivisions. And development of subdivisions approved during that period continued into the 1970s. Reform was a long, hard-fought process. It took a rising tide of alarm over how to finance services if people should ever come in large numbers to live on their lots; a threat from the County Planning Commission to void a large subdivision because the developer for years had refused to meet his road-building schedule; weeds growing in many roads because maintenance arrangements did not function; embarrassment over sales injunctions issued in California; and a federal land fraud prosecution involving the owners of one Big Island project.[47] It was principally the efforts of then-County Planning Director Suefuji in rewriting the county subdivision ordinance that choked off the creation of new speculative developments.

The new ordinance shifted approval of subdivisions away from the County Planning and Traffic Commission to the Planning Director. Where it had been a simple matter for the Commission to grant variances from the road paving requirements, it was now made mandatory for the director to require paving, and it was made very difficult for the commission to override him. Where water lines had not been required if a subdivision was more than 1,500 feet from a county line, now water lines were mandatory wherever the subdivision might be. The director enforced this provision, and here again variances were made extremely difficult. The new ordinance also forced subdivisions to conform to county zoning and the county general plan. If county land use maps did not show a certain area for residential use, then a residential-type subdivision there would be disallowed.

Suefuji's ordinance was eventually adopted by the County Board of Supervisors in December 1966.[48]

The era of ever-expanding Big Island speculative subdivisions, with substandard roads, without water or electricity, below a volcano, in the middle of a lava field, without houses, had come to an end.

* * *

In the mid-1980s, those boom-time subdivisions were a kind of spectacle the Big Island possessed, along with active volcanic craters, snowcapped volcanic peaks, papaya trees growing in lava, and the simple vastness of the island compared to the rest of the state. If they wanted to, tourists on their way from Hilo to Volcano National Park could wander along rutted roads laid out in perfect grid patterns regardless of the landscape, looking at dilapidated street signs in semi-wilderness, aware of the strangeness of being in a lava field, and seeing, every once in a great while, a house.

The few tourists who actually did venture into a Puna subdivision, particularly those farthest from the county seat of Hilo, might also encounter something else: a close, sometimes hostile scrutiny from people living there.

Beginning in the mid-1970s and continuing into the 1980s, many Big Island speculative subdivisions came to have as their major economic use something no one could have foreseen at the time of their creation: the criminal activity of growing marijuana.

Marijuana being an illegal crop, its total value never turned up in the state's economic data book. Still, by all sorts of accounts, it had come to be very big business in Puna and other districts of the Big Island, as in the state at large. Most estimates of the early 1980s ranked marijuana as the Islands' third largest revenue producer, behind only tourism and military spending—but as big as sugar and pineapple combined. *Newsweek* in October 1982 wrote that the Hawaii marijuana business "by most estimates . . : now tops half a billion dollars annually." In 1982 sugar was worth $352 million and pineapple $206 million. In October 1984 the state attorney general estimated that the annual marijuana crop value was $3 billion, about the highest estimate so far. If accurate this would probably make marijuana Hawaii's number two industry in annual revenues.[49]

The Big Island, with all those remote places for growers to hide their operations, was the state's marijuana capital. Extrapolating from the amount of marijuana seized by law enforcement officers county by county, in 1982–1983 the Big Island accounted for about two-thirds of the state's crop. Moreover, by one reliable estimate, marijuana by the early 1980s had become the Big Island's single largest industry. *Hawaii Business* in 1982 estimated the value of the Big Island's 1981 crop at $300–$500 million, as against revenues for Big Island tourism in 1981 of $180 million and $160 million for lawful agriculture.[50]

If the Big Island was Hawaii's marijuana headquarters, then the speculative subdivisions of Puna were the center of the center. Extrapolating from Big Island police estimates on the percentage of the Big Island crop grown in Puna, and from amounts of marijuana seized county by county, Puna in 1982–1983 accounted for about 40% of the total state crop.[51] According to police most of this was grown by people living in the subdivisions.

The creation of speculative Puna subdivisions required dirt-cheap land in large parcels, to attract amateur first-time buyers on a mass scale. This in turn meant the subdivisions were relatively cheap residential areas to move to, a fact of importance to prospective marijuana growers who were often young mainlanders with relatively little capital. In fact, moving in might even be free. So little did the average Puna absentee owner care about his lot, aside from its appreciation value, that there were occasional squatters—people who just appeared on a lot and lived there without benefit of the law.

As noted, speculative subdivisions commonly existed only in places far from other people and jobs, on land usually valueless for other purposes, waste land or even hazardous. In other words, places where ordinary people would not really want to live and where indeed few built homes.

All this was desirable to marijuana growers. They needed to be as nearly invisible as possible, they liked to have very few other people in the vicinity, and they needed to know by sight everyone else who had business being in a certain place. And they liked to be able to shift around if they had to. Puna had the remote spaces for this. With an area as big as Oahu, Puna in 1980 had a population only 1.5% of Oahu's.

Athough beginning in the late 1970s there was police pressure on marijuana growers, mostly in the form of crop seizures but with occasional arrests, the main response into the mid-1980s was simply to move the principal cultivation areas away from growers' dwellings and deeper into Puna's empty spaces.

In 1978 a Big Island realtor placed a general advertisement in a drug culture magazine called *High Times*. Noting that two and three-acre lots in Puna could be had for as low as $1,500, the advertisement said: "Yes, Hawaii's Gold Rush is not only in its smoke, but also in its land. On the Big Island [Hawaii], which has gained international fame for its sacred herbs, fantastic land values are still available, but for how long?" "Think," the ad prodded, "what land prices will do when legalization occurs."

With the discreet buyer in mind, the ad also said that sellers would finance "with no questions asked," and there would be "total confidentiality on your purchase."[52]

Among the consequences of the ad were telephoned death threats to the realtor. In an interview for this book, he said he assumed the calls came from marijuana growers who did not want more people in Puna.

9

MAUI: DEVELOPING KIHEI

OF all the outer islands, Maui saw the most urban development.

American Factors (later Amfac) led off, with the first big destination resort anywhere in the outer islands, Kaanapali in west Maui. Publicly announced in 1957, the first hotel groundbreaking was in the early 1960s.

In those years, the plantation-based economy of west Maui was chronically depressed, and in 1962 the old Baldwin Packers pineapple cannery in Lahaina closed—west Maui's only cannery in the region's only town of any size.

Part of Kaanapali went up on sugar land, an early example of the Big Five switch from plantation agriculture to exploiting the new business of tourism, from conservative land holding to intensive land development.

Kaanapali was developed on lands of the Pioneer Mill Co., as of 1960 a 24,454-acre plantation which American Factors' predecessor firm, H. Hackfeld & Co., started servicing in the nineteenth century. Hackfeld began a takeover of Pioneer with a foreclosure on a half interest in 1885. Thereafter Hackfeld and American Factors increased ownership, until in 1961 American Factors came to own Pioneer 100%.[1]

Kaanapali was good territory for a big tourist development. The west Maui mountains shielded the area from clouds, heavy rain and strong trade winds. The climate therefore was perennially sunny, and not especially windy though usually with a slight breeze. The mountains made a dramatic visual backdrop, too, rising up close inland out of vistas of green sugar cane. American Factors had two-and-a-half miles of ocean frontage at Kaanapali, with a good deal of white sand beach. Directly across the water the island of Lanai could be seen; across the water to the north Molokai was usually visible, too. And a few miles to the south was the nineteenth-century whaling port of Lahaina, the only old-style town of its kind and size anywhere in the Hawaiian Islands.

A fine climate, excellent beaches, beautiful vistas, and the unique tourist attraction of Lahaina—capitalizing on all this, Amfac built Hawaii's first fully integrated destination resort, master-planned for optimal land use and visual effect.

Kaanapali turned out to be an idea whose time had come. After a slow start, it took off and kept on growing. In the early 1970s an Amfac executive said of Kaanapali: "From now on, it is nothing but a money machine."[2] At that point there were about 325 developed acres. By the mid-1980s there were 600.[3] Measured by the number of hotel and condominium units in place, Kaanapali was the largest project of its kind in the Islands—and the greatest continuing financial success.

And Kaanapali had a value beyond the huge boost it gave to the strictly local economy of the district. It became a growth generator for the entire island of Maui.

*   *   *

With the benefit of hindsight, it is possible to theorize as to why Maui was developed more rapidly than the other outer islands.

In the first place, from early on, Maui was heavily promoted by American Factors in the company's promotion of Kaanapali.

To the extent that Maui took off because Amfac chose early to get into tourism and did it relatively well, there is this related fact: of the two destination resort sites that American Factors owned on the eve of Hawaii's development boom—the other was the Princeville Ranch on Kauai's north shore—Kaanapali was where Amfac chose to start. Amfac did at least one feasibility study on Princeville, and for a time reportedly considered developing it itself, in addition to doing Kaanapali. Then in 1968 Amfac sold the ranch to an oil company, which in the 1970s initiated a major resort there.[4] Partly for having started earlier, though for other and probably more important reasons as well, Kaanapali after its first 10 years was far ahead of the Princeville resort after its first decade, in terms of such things as hotel and condominium units built and number of tourists who were staying there.

Then, to some people Maui had a particular beauty. A tourist driving through central Maui could see the massive extinct volcano of Haleakala, rising up from the floor of the central Maui plain on the east side. Looking down from Haleakala there were sweeping views of central Maui and the east Maui mountains. Looking or walking inside the crater one saw a place that resembled the surface of the moon. As mentioned, Maui had the unique attraction of Lahaina. All along the west coast of Maui, from Maui Land and Pineapple Co.'s Kapalua resort in the extreme north to Seibu's resort in Makena, one could usually see offshore islands, a feature none of the other major Hawaiian islands really had. And running much of the length of that coast were good white sand beaches; in terms of beach area Maui was roughly comparable to Kauai, but far surpassed the Big Island.

Then too, Maui was far enough away from big-city Honolulu but not too far; not as far, say, as Kona, the sunny but remote western coast of the Big Island. Maui was neither too big nor too small, not so big as the Big Island with its sometimes long and tiresome drives from places like Kilauea Volcano to Kona's sun, yet larger than Molokai, where some tourists got bored because there was so little room to drive around. Also, Maui had a road through its center that made for relatively easy access to its major tourist attractions; Kauai had only a road along its perimeter and which did not encircle the island, and the road through the middle of the Big Island was long and sometimes treacherous.

Finally, Maui's power structure was small and stable throughout the boom years, and those who ran the island's politics were united in wanting rapid and extensive development, just as much as Amfac did, or, in their turn, the other large landowners with lands that had resort potential. At the same time, there were few opponents of development compared with, say, Oahu and Kauai.

The result was that, just in terms of resort condominiums, Maui by the early 1980s had three to four times as many as all the other outer islands combined.[5]

* * *

About half of Maui's condominiums came to be built on the lower half of the island's west coast, from Maalaea to Makena, a stretch called Kihei after its main town. In the early 1980s the Kihei coast held some 8,000 condominium units.[6]

Like west Maui, Kihei was sunny and had good beaches, though Kihei was far windier. Kihei sat to the south of an open area between the mountains of east and west Maui, and this opening formed a kind of funnel for the trade winds that came out of the northeast.

Just as Amfac planned and built a big destination resort at Kaanapali, so Alexander & Baldwin in joint venture with Northwestern Mutual Life Insurance Co. developed Wailea in Kihei. As of 1970 Wailea accounted for nearly half of all "lands zoned for urban use in the Kihei planning area," according to a study done for the county.[7] And south of Wailea, a big Japanese firm, Seibu Group Enterprises, in the mid-1970s started a resort on half of 1,000 acres it owned at Makena, more or less the end of the road along the Kihei coast.

But what set Kihei apart from west Maui from the start of the development boom was that while most of the prime development land in west Maui was in the hands of no more than two large landowners, in Kihei, even after the major owners were accounted for, there was still a great deal in the hands of numerous small owners.

Early in the century the territorial government developed the large-lot, fee-simple Kamaole Homesteads in Kihei, where initially many Hawaiians lived. In 1940 the territorial land commissioner auctioned off half-acre lots on the ocean at Kamaole. Then, long before a boom could have been imagined, when Kihei was an economic wasteland with no plantation agriculture, A&B sold off in small parcels a good deal of land in Maalaea: that is, north Kihei. All of these areas in the 1970s came to be sites for heavy development of resort condominiums and a handful of hotels, built by many small local and mainland companies.[8]

In the end all kinds of small as well as diverse landholdings at Kihei were put under heavy development. Condominiums were built on what used to be a Maui Pineapple Co. employees' park, on Hawaiian Homes Commission land, on land that once belonged to the Roman Catholic Church, and on territorial homesteaders' land.

Like Kaanapali, Kihei had a master plan. Unlike Kaanapali, the Kihei master plan did not work.

It was a plan produced by the County on the eve of the Kihei development boom. In it were strong words about what was good for Kihei: "Since the ocean vistas throughout this entire planning area are its most important natural asset, it is imperative that these views be preserved wherever possible." And: "Continuous, high-density lateral coastal sprawl forming a barrier between the ocean and the land must be discouraged."[9]

The County did not get what it said it wanted at Kihei. On the contrary. Kihei promptly became the outer islands' outstanding example of continuous, high-density lateral coastal sprawl, with a barrier of close-set moderately high-rise condominiums and hotels blocking off the ocean view.

Occasionally people stood up for Kihei. For example, in 1983 there was Toshio Ishikawa, the county planning director. A reporter wrote that Ishikawa "defends the urban planning in Kihei, noting the community has developed better than many other areas, including southern California. He points out that beach accesses and public amenities are given more attention here."[10]

Yet it was hard to find people who liked the look of developed Kihei. Certainly many planners did not. Neither did people in the real estate business, even if they made good money there; many of them said privately that Kihei had a disgraceful appearance.

What happened at Kihei was that, despite the existence of a master plan, most of the 100 projects that produced the 8,000 condominium units were carried out individually, not as part of a comprehensive resort development. Each developer went his own way in terms of design, each maximizing his project's size, each going for as much ocean view as he could get. The result was a jumble of buildings that crowded their own lots and crowded both sides of the county road that ran along the water.

The effect was even once criticized by a travel writer and a local three-dot newspaper columnist—people not noted for being negative about Hawaii's tourist and resort development business. In 1975 a *Honolulu Advertiser* columnist picked up a mainland reference to Kihei and had fun with it: "[R]espected travel writer Jerry Hulse has an inaccurate view of Maui that ran as the top story in the *Chicago Sun-Times* travel section. Writes Hulse, 'Along the Kahei Coastline certain condominiums can best be described as monuments to obscenity. Not even their romantic names can disguise the disregard for the surrounding landscape. They seem joined together in a contest of bad taste.'" The *Advertiser* writer said that "the inaccuracy in all that is the misspelling of Kihei."[11]

* * *

Part of why Kihei came to look ugly to most people was that virtually the full spectrum of Hawaii's power structure, and especially Maui's political leaders, took part in speculating in and developing the region. This left little room for truly independent governmental decisions, of the kind that might have made developers take seriously the county's Kihei plan.

It is important to understand that the great majority of people investing or building in Kihei were not in government. Rather, the significant fact regarding public officials' private involvement with Kihei is that so many in government were among the large number of investors and developers.

Research was done for this book to see how many people in politics and government had a financial interest in Kihei as investors, corporate officers, members of partnerships, lawyers, consultants, and so on.

The results, set out in the following table (Table 17) showed fully 88 people who during or prior to their private involvement with Kihei were also government officials or employees, in most cases relatively high-ranking. Some 30% were from other islands, mainly Oahu; about 70% were from Maui. Of the 88, 74% were in office at the time they became involved at Kihei.

────────────── TABLE 17 ──────────────

PUBLIC OFFICIALS INVOLVED IN PRIVATE CAPACITIES WITH THE
DEVELOPMENT OF THE KIHEI COAST

ACOBA, RAFAEL. Maui Police Pension Board, State Crime Commission. In office: Partner Kihei Maui II.

AIONA, ABRAHAM. Maui Council. In office: Partner Tara Hui, which 1977 bought, 1981 sold lot Kaiola Subdivision.

AJIFU, RALPH K. House, Senate from Oahu. In office: Partner Wailea Ekahi II Apt. 23-D.

ALAMEDA, FRANK A. Territorial tax assessor on Maui. While holding that position: One of 2 partners subdividing 26 acres 1956 Kaonoulu Beach into single-family lots.

AMARAL, ALVIN T. House, Maui Council. In office: Realtor Amaral-Cole Realtors representing several sellers Kihei oceanfront lots; partner Tara Hui; partner Wailea Ekahi II Apt. 23-D.

ANDREWS, LOIS M. Maui Police Pension Board, Police Commission. In office: Partner Makena 700 selling 700 acres Makena.

ANDREWS, MARK J. House from Maui. In office: 1/2 interest lot Ilima Houselots.

ANSAI, TOSHIO. Maui Board of Supervisors and Council, Senate. In office: Partner Makena Beach Investors; owner unit Wailea Ekolu; partner Tara Hui; owner section of land on which Maalaea Kai later built.

BARLOW, A. WILLIAM. US Attorney. After office: Officer La Ronde Restaurants which owned lot on which Hale Pau Hana later built.

BEPPU, HIROSHI. Maui Liquor Control Adjudication Board. In office: Member several huis with interests Kihei coast, including Kihei-Davis, Murata Hui.

CALDITO, RICHARD I. C. SR. Maui Board of Supervisors. After office: Partner Kihei Maui II.

CAMERON, COLIN C. Maui County Liquor Control Adjudication Board. In office: Owner 12-acre parcel on which Kamaole Beach Terrace later built.

CHING, CLARENCE T. C. Chief campaign fundraiser John Burns' 1962 governor's race. While holding that position: V-P Loyalty Enterprises Ltd. which 1962 obtained from LUC redistricting 830 acres Kihei, agricultural to urban.

CHUCK, WALTER G. House and Senate clerk, Honolulu district court magistrate. After office: Director Crown Corp. which co-developed Kihei Kai Nani.

CRAVALHO, ELMER F. Mayor of Maui. In office: Shareholder MDG Supply Inc. which bought/sold parcel on which Maui Vista later built; bought/sold part-interest in group Kihei parcels.

CROCKETT, WENDELL F. Territorial Senate, Maui Board of Supervisors, Circuit Court judge, chairman Maui County Republican Party. In office: part-owner land on which Milowai later built. After office: As attorney he or his firm represented developers of numerous condominiums, including Maalaea Kai, Maalaea Surf, Koa Lagoon, Kihei Park Shore, Puuhala Apts., and Hale Hui Kai.

CROCKETT, WILLIAM F. Member two Maui Charter Commissions. After office: As attorney he or his firm represented investors in and developers of numerous condominiums, including Kihei Villa, Kamaole Beach Royale, Hale Hui Kai, and Royal Mauian.

FELIX, JOHN F. Aide to Gov. William F. Quinn. After office: President La Ronde Restaurants Inc. which bought/sold lot on which Hale Pau Hana later built.

FREITAS, ANDREW S. Maui Deputy police chief. While holding that position: One of 2 partners subdividing 26 acres 1956 Kaonoulu Beach into single-family lots.

FUJIYAMA, WALLACE S. University of Hawaii Board of Regents. In office: Attorney Seibu Group Enterprises' Hawaii subsidiary before Maui Planning Commission for hotel Makena.

FUKUDA, ROBERT K. House from Oahu, US Attorney. After office: Attorney Kihei Kai Nani.

FUKUOKA, S. GEORGE. Maui Board of Supervisors, Senate, Circuit Court Judge. In office: Partner Upten; partner Kam 5; partner Waipao Joint Venture which bought/sold land on which Makena Surf later built; part-owner at various times parcels on which were later built Menehune Shores, Kihei Kai Nani, Kihei Akahi, Keawakapu.

FURUTANI, GORDAN Y. Exec. officer LUC. While holding that position: Owner 1/2 interest unit Maui Vista.

HAAKE, ALVIN M. Maui Circuit Court probation officer. While holding that position: Part-owner at various times several parcels Kihei, including land on which Maui Villa later built.

HAAKE, RICHARD H. Maui Police captain. While holding that position: Part owner at various times several parcels Kihei, including land on which Maui Villa later built.

HARADA, WALTER M. House. After office: Developer The Kihei.

HAYASHI, RALPH M. Director Maui Dept. of Public Works. Engineering consultant for Makena Surf before LUC 1978, later as county public works director reviewed and approved Makena Surf matters.

HEEN, ERNEST N. JR. House. In office: Part-owner parcel on which Royal Mauian later built.

HEFTEL, CECIL. US Congress. In office: He and Heftel Broadcasting Corp. were 97% owners 154-acre parcel Kamaole 1977–78.

HIRANAGA, TOM T. University of Hawaii Board of Regents; manager Maui office State Employment Service. In office: Partner Waipao Joint Venture which bought/sold land on which Makena Surf later built.

HONG, WILLIAM K. Maui Planning and Traffic Commission; Board of Adjustment and Appeals. In office: Part-owner 29-acre parcel Kihei.

HOUGHTAILING, GEORGE K. Honolulu planning director, consultant to Maui Planning and Traffic Commission on Kihei master plan. After office: Consultant Loyalty Enterprises Ltd. which 1962 got LUC redistricting agricultural to urban 830 acres Kihei.

IGE, EDWIN T. Maui Police Commission. In office: Partner Portland Alii Oregon Ltd. which developed Maalaea Surf; owner parcel on which Koa Lagoon later built; family owned parcel on which Koa Resort later built.

ING, LAWRENCE N.C. Asst. US Magistrate, Maui member Hawaii Housing Authority. Before and in office: As attorney involved with numerous condominium projects Kihei, including the Leinaala, Moana, White Sea Terrace, Na Holokai, The Gardens; as investor held interests in parcels on which were later built Waipuilani, Maui Villa, Princess Iolani, Kihei Alii Kai.

IZUMI, JAMES M. Maui County Personnel Director. Partner Waipao Joint Venture which bought/sold land on which Makena Surf later built; owned unit Maui Vista.

JANSSEN, ARMOND. Principal Lanai High and Elementary School. In office: Sold 3.5 acres.

JENNINGS, WILLIS C. LUC. After office: President C-V Land Corp. which 1962 got LUC redistricting agricultural to urban 10 acres Makena.

KAGE, KAZUO. Maui Planning Commission. In office: Partner Puuhala Assocs. which developed Puuhala Apts.; partner Waipao Joint Venture which bought/sold land on which Makena Surf later built.

KAMAKA, HIRAM K. House, State finance director. After office: Attorney for 1976–77 unsuccessful LUC redistricting agricultural to urban 85 acres.

KEALOHA, JOSEPH G. JR. Maui trustee Office of Hawaiian Affairs. Before office: Partner Waipuilani Hui Assocs. which built Waipuilani; member of company that built Leinaala. In office: Realtor representing sellers several oceanfront lots Kihei.

KIDO, MITSUYUKI. Senate. In office: Partner Maui Meadows Development Co. which 1965–66 got LUC redistricting agricultural to urban 40 acres Kihei.

KIDWELL, ALLAN B. Hawaii Housing Authority. In office: Partner Makena Beach Investors.

KIMURA, MANABU. Deputy director Maui Dept. of Personnel Services. In office: Partner Waipao Joint Venture which bought/sold land on which Makena Surf later built; half-interest in unit in Maui Vista.

KON, SADAO. Maui member Public Utilities Commission. In office: Part-owner 25-acre parcel Kihei; part-owner of land on which Menehune Shores later built.

KONG, DAVID Y.S. Maui Council. In office: Partner Seaside Developers which developed Kihei Surfside; director Surfside Vacation Club Inc., organized to sell time shares Kihei Surfside.

LANGA, SANFORD J. Assistant US Attorney, Chairman Republican Party on Maui. After office: As attorney he or his firm represented developers or investors involved with numerous condominium projects, including Keokea Beach, Auhana Kuleana, Kalama Villa, Bay Vista Apts., Kamaole One.

LUNA, B. MARTIN. Maui member Hawaii Housing Authority, Chairman Democratic Party on Maui. In office: As attorney he or his firm represented developers/investors numerous condominium projects, including Maalaea Yacht Marina, Waiohuli Beach Hale, Haleakala Shores, Island Surf; part-owner parcel on which Princess Iolani later built; part-owner parcel on which Kihei Alii Kai later built.

MACHIDA, GERALD K. House, Senate from Maui. In office: 1/2 interest lot Kamaole.

MATSUI, YOSHIKAZU "ZUKE." Maui Planning Commission, deputy planning director. In office: Partner Waipao Joint Venture which bought/sold land on which Makena Surf later built.

McCLUNG, DAVID C. House, Senate. After office: Partner Leialoha Assocs. which developed Leialoha Subdivision; partner Maui Waiohuli Assocs. which developed 42-lot Waiohuli subdivision.

MEDINA, RICARDO. Maui Council. In office: Partner Tara Hui.

MIYAHIRA, WINSTON S. Director Dept. of Liquor Control. In office: Partner Waipao Joint Venture which bought/sold land on which Makena Surf later built.

MOLINA, MANUEL S. Maui Council. In office: Partner Tara Hui.

MORISAKI, LANNY H. Maui Council. Partner Waipao Joint Venture which bought/sold land on which Makena Surf later built (Morisaki son initially partner, but subsequently turned over interest to Lanny).

NAKAMURA, HOWARD K. Maui planning director, managing director. Between office: Consultant for Makena Surf, appearing before Maui Council and LUC.

NAKASHIMA, SUMIO. House from Big Island, district court magistrate. After office: Part-owner part of land on which Menehune Shores later built.

OGATA, THOMAS S. Senate. In office: Attorney 1962 before Maui Traffic and Planning Commission to rezone land abutting Fort Vancouver.

OHASHI, GWEN Y. Director Maui Office of Council Services. In office: Owned half-interest in time-share condominium unit Kihei.

OTA, CHARLES S. Maui Council, Maui Planning Commission. In office: Partner Waipao Joint Venture which bought/sold land on which Makena Surf later built.

ROMME, MARVIN P. Maui Planning Commission. Before office: Investor miscellaneous lots Kihei, including land on which Kihei Kai Nani later built. In office: Partner Seaside Developers, which developed Kihei Surfside; director Surfside Vacation Club Inc., organized to sell time shares Kihei Surfside; partner Waipao Joint Venture which bought/sold land on which Makena Surf later built.

SAITO, NORMAN M. Manager, chief engineer Maui Water Dept. After office: Engineering consultant for Makena Surf before Land Use Commission.

SAKAI, HIROSHI. Chief clerk/counsel several key legislative committees. After office: Attorney Leisure Industries Inc. which owned part of land on which Maui Sunset later built; attorney for developer Kihei Surfside.

SHIBANO, TOM T. University of Hawaii Board of Regents. In office: Partner Puuhala Assocs. which developed Puuhala Apts.; partner Waipao Joint Venture which bought/sold land on which Makena Surf later built; part-owner part of land on which The Gardens later built; part-owner lot on which Kihei Bay Surf I later built.

SHIMODA, WALTER T. District court magistrate. After office: Attorney Makena Surf.

SODETANI, DOUGLAS R. Maui Planning and Traffic Commission, Maui Charter Commission, State Real Estate Commission, State Civil Service Commission. In office: Officer Maui Realty Co. Inc. which represented buyers/sellers Kihei; part-owner lot on which Island Surf later built.

SOUZA, MANUEL R. Maui Police Commission. After office: Owner lot on which Beachside later built.

TAGAWA, TOM T. Maui Board of Supervisors. After office: Partner Kihei First which owned land on which Kauhale Makai later built.

TAKEYAMA, ROY Y. Secretary to University of Hawaii Board of Regents. In office: Attorney Makena Surf before Maui Council and LUC.

TAKITANI, HENRY T. House, Senate. Before office: Part-owner 6-acre parcel Kihei. In office: Part-owner 129-acre parcel Kihei.

TAM, EDWARD F. Maui County chairman. In office: Partner Kihei Land Co.

TAMURA, STANLEY T. "BANJO." Chief Teller, Maui County Finance Dept. In office: Partner Waipao Joint Venture which bought/sold land on which Makena Surf later built.

TOKUNAGA, DONALD H. Maui Member Hawaii Housing Authority. Before office: Part-owner land on which Kamaole Beach Terrace later built. In office: President Maui Realty Co. Inc. which handled sales Kihei. After office: Maui Realty was partner Wailea Hui.

TSUKIYAMA, TED T. Chairman Hawaii Employment Relations Board, Labor and Industrial Appeals Board. After office: Officer Develco Corp. when developed Kanai A Nalu.

UEOKA, MEYER M. House from Maui, Board of Education, district court magistrate. In office: As investor and attorney he or his firm involved with many parcels Kihei on which condominiums built and with condominiums themselves, including Maui Vista, Mana Kai, Haleakala Shores, Kihei Garden Estates, Island Surf, Kihei Alii Kai; also director David P. Ting & Sons Inc., which was owner/developer Maalaea Yacht Marina; director Kihei Properties Inc. (owner) and Kauhale Makai Inc. (developer) of Kauhale Makai.

UNEMORI, WARREN S. Engineer Maui County Dept. of Public Works, State Dept. of Transportation. After holding those positions: Engineering consultant to Maui 100 Partners which 1980 got LUC redistricting 94.5 acres agricultural to urban Kihei.

USHIJIMA, JOHN T. Senate from Big Island. In office: Part-owner lot on which Leinaala later built.

WAKATSUKI, JAMES H. House from Oahu. In office: Attorney for Kalama Terrace.

WIRTZ, CABLE A. Circuit Court Judge, Hawaii Supreme Court. In office: Owner land on which Polo Beach later built.

WONG, DICK YIN. Judge State Tax Appeal Court. In office: Part-owner of part of land on which Laule A Resort later built; part-owner 9-acre parcel Kihei.

WONG, GORDON Y. H. Director Dept. of Taxation. Before office: Partner Waipuilani Hui Assocs. which developed Waipuilani condominium.

WONG, WILLIAM C.N. Industrial Accidents Board. In office: Part-owner land on which Kihei Park Shore later built; part-owner part of land on which Hale Kamaole later built.

YAMAMURA, TANJI. Maui member LUC. In office: Partner Makena 700 which bought/sold 700 acres Makena.

YAMAGUCHI, YONETO. Maui Board of Supervisors. In office: Officer MDG Supply Inc. which bought/sold parcel on which Maui Vista later built; bought/sold part-interest in group parcels Makena.

YANAGI, WALLACE. Deputy administrator and then administrator Maui Memorial Hospital. In office: Partner Waipao Joint Venture which bought/sold land on which Makena Surf later built.

YANAI, EDWARD K. LUC. In office: Part-owner unit Maui Vista.

YEE, WADSWORTH Y.H. House, Senate. In office: Officer Polynesian Shores Inc. which was co-developer Maalaea Mermaid; Yee also part-owner land on which Maalaea Mermaid built; part-owner part of land on which Laule A Resort later built.

YOKOUCHI, MASARU "PUNDY." Gov. Burns' representative on Maui, Chairman State Foundation on Culture and Arts. In office: Number investments including in land on which were later built Kihei Akahi and Kihei Kai Nani; managing partner Waipao Joint Venture which bought/sold land on which Makena Surf later built; partner Seaside Developers which developed Kihei Surfside.

YOSHINAGA, NADAO. House from Maui, Senate from Maui then Oahu. In office: Officer Valley Isle Realty Inc. which was involved various transactions Kihei; wife part-owner 24-acre parcel Kihei.

Sources: County of Maui, Department of Finance, Property Tax Division; City and County of Honolulu, Finance Department, Real Property Assessment Division; State of Hawaii, Bureau of Conveyances; Gwenfread E. Allen, ed., *Men and Women of Hawaii: A Biographical Directory of Noteworthy Men and Women of Hawaii* (Honolulu, 1966); Betty F. Buker, ed., *Men and Women of Hawaii 1972: A Biographical Directory of Noteworthy Men and Women of Hawaii* (Honolulu, 1972); Department of Commerce and Consumer Affairs, Business Registration Division; State of Hawaii, Legislative Reference Bureau, *Directory of State, County and Federal Officials: Supplement to Guide to Government in Hawaii* (published occasionally, most recently annually); Chamber of Commerce of Hawaii, *Who's Who in Government State of Hawaii* (various years); miscellaneous state and county public officials' personal financial disclosure statements, on file with State Ethics Commission and offices of Maui County Clerk; State of Hawaii, Land Use Commission, miscellaneous files; Hawaii State Archives; files of Maui County Planning Department; miscellaneous references in newspapers and periodicals.

With so many public officials taking part in developing Kihei, perhaps it was inevitable that on a number of occasions they took official actions that directly or indirectly benefited their private interests or those of their relatives and associates.

So voluminous and many-layered were investments and developments at Kihei that this could occur unknowingly; though just as readily, whether deliberately or unconsciously, access to official information might be turned to private advantage.

What this extensive intertwining of public and private interests and actions also indicated, among other things, was that virtually all public officials believed that heavy development was good for Maui, and that it was legitimate for anyone who could afford it to take part, whether or not he happened to be in public office at the time.

It should be noted that, in general, research for this book indicated that whether or not a mayor or a councilman or a land use commissioner had a private real estate investment in Kihei (or anywhere else, for that matter), there were usually good and sufficient public reasons for the official action they took in favor of development.

But just the same it is noteworthy that they generally decided in favor of developing Kihei. Their investments, as an expression of their wish to get ahead, and their belief in the correctness of development, combined to speed up construction.

As mentioned, the full range of the political establishment of the Democratic years took part. To begin at the level of the office of mayor and the predecessor office, chairman of the Board of Supervisors:

Chairman Edward F. Tam obtained a personal financial interest in Kihei land about a month before the Board in 1960 passed on final reading a county master plan for Kihei. Tam bought a share in the Kihei Land Co., which was buying a 41-acre parcel in central Kihei. For whatever reason, Tam did not vote on final reading. The *hui's* land was not given an intensive development classification by the plan.

Tam's successor, Elmer F. Cravalho, who was chairman and mayor throughout the boom years, indirectly acquired interests in prime land at Kihei, again at a time when the County was finalizing a Kihei master plan. This time the lands were zoned for intensive use.

When Cravalho was first elected chairman in 1967, he was general manager of MDG Supply Inc. and owned 15% of the company. When elected he resigned as manager and announced he was turning over decisions regarding his stock to his attorney.

Less than two months before final County Planning Commission action on the Kihei Civic Development Plan in 1969, MDG bought for $509,000 an 8.8-acre parcel in Kihei. MDG about the same time bought for $162,000 a 14% interest in a group of oceanfront parcels at Makena that totalled 9.7 acres. The Kihei plan, which Cravalho signed into law some months after the two purchases, designated all of MDG's land for resort-type uses. Whether Cravalho was aware at the time that MDG had made these acquisitions is unclear. In an interview for this book he said that the holdings would have had no bearing on what his administration did on the plans. In any case, MDG late in 1973 sold the Kihei land to a developer for $1,536,800. The Maui Vista, a 280-unit condominium, was later built on this parcel. In 1974 the Makena interest was sold for $350,000.

Cravalho's successor, Hannibal M. Tavares, at the time he ran for mayor was an officer of Alexander & Baldwin, co-developer of the Wailea resort at Kihei.

Other public officeholders took both public and private action in the early Kihei years. In 1959 S. George Fukuoka was a Democratic senator from Maui serving in the last territorial Legislature, where he chaired the Ways and Means Committee. As such he helped oversee preparation of the budget that session, which provided $579,000 for a major new water system for Kihei. Fukuoka was also one of the managers of a *hui* that, at a time early in the 1959 legislative session, bought a 3.5-acre parcel near the ocean in Kihei from Armond J. Janssen, the principal of the only public school on Lanai. The *hui* sold the land in 1968, and in the mid-1970s the Menehune Shores condominium was built there.

US Sen. Hiram L. Fong in 1960 proposed an amendment to the then-pending federal Rivers and Harbors Bill, to study the feasibility of constructing a deep-water harbor at Maalaea, in north Kihei. Simultaneously four men who were executives or directors in Fong's real estate and finance companies were selling a parcel of land that fronted Maalaea Bay. Since 1959 two of these men had also owned 1/4-interests each in a 3-acre parcel down the coast, which they sold in 1962.

Several men who worked on county master plans for the Kihei area subsequently worked for private interests in developing the area. For example, former Honolulu planning director George K. Houghtailing in 1959–1960 produced Maui County's first Kihei master plan. In 1962 he represented before the Land Use Commission a successful application to redistrict 830 acres to urban in Kihei. In 1963 he represented before the Maui Planning and Traffic Commission C-V Land Corp. (whose president was former land use commissioner Willis C. Jennings) which hoped to develop 10 acres at Makena. Howard K. Nakamura, Maui County planning director 1969–1975, in 1978–1979 represented the developers of the Makena Surf condominium before the County Council and State Land Use Commission.

Conversely it happened that those who developed Kihei later took part in county planning work for Kihei. Mayor Cravalho in 1968 appointed Andrew S. Freitas chairman of the citizens advisory committee for the Kihei Civic Development Plan. In the late 1950s Freitas had been a co-developer of a 26-acre residential subdivision in Kihei.

*   *   *

An example of how diverse the people were who developed Kihei, and how persistent their ties to government, can be seen in a capsule history of the ownership of the land under the Kamaole Beach Terrace condominium, and of its builders:

Since at least the 1930s the land was owned by a local Chinese-Hawaiian-Irish man, Alex B. Akina, who was born around the turn of the century and had lived in Kihei most or all of his life.

For years the Akinas were farmers; they were also fair-sized landowners in the area. Akina told a reporter in 1983 that his father bought about 100 acres in Kihei in the late nineteenth century. He said that he himself bought 60 acres in 1937.[12]

In 1957 Akina sold the land that was later to become the site of the Kamaole Beach Terrace. In an interview for this book, he said he did so because his wife had terminal cancer and he had a $55,000 hospital bill to pay.

His buyers were an orthodondist from Tacoma, Washington, and the man's local business partner and friend, Donald H. Tokunaga.

Tokunaga in those years was part of the rising group of Hawaii's *nisei*. His brother, Bernard, was then a territorial representative who later served 1967–1976 on the County Board of Supervisors and then Council. Donald Tokunaga in 1957 was manager of the then-small Maui Realty Co. An employee who later became an officer, Douglas R. Sodetani, was on the County Planning and Traffic Commission. Donald Tokunaga himself in the 1960s served as Maui's representative on the state Hawaii Housing Authority. Sodetani in the 1960s and 1970s was on the State Civil Service Commission and State Real Estate Commission. In 1978 Sodetani chaired Elmer Cravalho's re-election campaign.

In 1961, Tokunaga and the orthodontist sold to Stephen F. Predy, one of the first Canadians to take an interest in Kihei from the standpoint of investment or development; starting in the 1970s there was a flood of Canadians buying in and visiting the area.

From 1969 to 1972 the parcel was owned by Colin C. Cameron and his mother. The Camerons were a branch of the Baldwin family, and major shareholders in Alexander & Baldwin; in 1969 they traded in their shares in the company and carved out an independent business, Maui Land and Pine-apple Co.

In 1973 Walter C. Witte bought the land. A builder out of Tacoma, Witte in the 1970s established himself as the most prolific condominium builder in Kihei. He built the Kamaole Beach Terrace with a *hui*, most of its members Canadians.

The *hui* had several lawyers with excellent political connections—something typical in the development business in Hawaii. For a shoreline management area permit in 1979, Witte used B. Martin Luna of Ueoka and Luna. Luna was active in the Democratic Party on Maui. During most of the 1970s he was Maui's member of the Hawaii Housing Authority. The magazine *Hawaii Business* in 1983 listed both Luna and his partner, Meyer Ueoka, as among the island's 20 most influential people. Of Ueoka *Hawaii Business* wrote: "Ueoka has long served as [Mayor] Elmer Cravalho's personal attorney, and many judges, politicians and prominent attorneys have at one time or another worked for or with Ueoka's firm. Ueoka himself has been a deputy county attorney, magistrate, constitutional convention delegate, and state representative, and presently sits on the state board of education as chairman of the budget and finance committee." The magazine also wrote that "mostly because of their political clout, Ueoka and Luna became the favorite of resort developers who needed help securing permit approvals and clearing other county hurdles."[13]

*   *   *

Compared to most other islands, Maui had few cases of anti-development protest.

When there were objections, generally they came from recently-arrived *haoles*—people of little or no political consequence who could be and were for the most part ignored by state and county government.

One reason for the lack of local protest against development on Maui was that, unlike Oahu and Kauai, no Maui development involved the evictions of whole communities with no acceptable relocation plan.

For example, as mentioned, Maui Land & Pineapple Co. and the ILWU were able to agree on relocating into new homes workers who lived in the middle of ML&P's planned Kapalua resort. Thus an old camp was closed and then destroyed without a protest.

Maui had no situations like Kalama Valley in east Oahu 1970–1971; Ota Camp at Waipahu on Oahu 1972–1973; Niumalu and Nawiliwili on Kauai beginning in 1972 and running through much of the 1970s; and Waiahole and Waikane valleys on Oahu's north shore in the mid-1970s. These were cases where large portions of local communities, or even entire communities, were being told they had to move out, with nowhere to go, usually to make way for more expensive residential developments.

Likewise Maui lacked the social cohesion and environmental conservatism of the tiny population of Molokai, the large Hawaiian segment of it in particular. Big projects proposed on Molokai in the mid-1970s and later would not have evicted anyone. But still, the Hawaiian communities especially resented the intrusion of condominiums and other developments into places they had always regarded as their own. Some of the sharpest anti-development objections anywhere in Hawaii were voiced on Molokai in the late 1970s and early 1980s.

The two Maui projects that drew the most fire were the 1,000-acre Seibu Group Enterprises resort planned at the southern end of the road along the Kihei coast, and the 184-unit Makena Surf condominium, on oceanfront land just in front of the north end of the Seibu project.

Seibu in 1973 bought its land from Ulupalakua Ranch, and in 1974 asked the Land Use Commission for urban districting. The Makena Surf developer went to the LUC in 1978. Both applications occasioned some outcries against development of then-remote Makena, the last substantially undeveloped stretch of the entire Kihei coast. A rallying cry of opponents had to do with the fact that Makena held two popular beaches: tiny Chang's Beach, near the site of the Makena Surf, frequented by locals; and Big Beach, fronting the Seibu land, used more by *haoles*. Big Beach was where young counter-culture mainlanders often camped and sunbathed naked in the late 1960s and early 1970s, something that both put Big Beach on the map and perturbed many locals.

As mentioned, those who objected were mostly mainland *haoles*, and not necessarily *haoles* with money. They could be and largely were ignored by the largely *nisei* political establishment on Maui and in the state government, that generally approved all Seibu and Makena Surf applications.

*   *   *

Part of the reason why government rolled so readily over these anti-development protests was that a rather large number of high-ranking public officials, including several with land use authority, were personally involved with Seibu and Makena Surf.

Once again there were good reasons of public policy, widely accepted on Maui, why those projects should advance. Once again, the investments and consulting and legal work by then-current and former public officials were to a great extent expressions of a general belief that developing Makena was both inevitable and good. But the heavy participation by people in key positions in government also helped ensure that the forward momentum of development would not be braked by protesters.

The Seibu project acted as a sort of southern anchor for resort development along the Kihei Coast, and as a growth generator for the Makena area. This could be seen with tangibles such as bringing a water line and a good road into the area and building resort amenities such as a golf course, also with intangibles—putting Makena on the tourist map, giving the area international visibility.

Fresh water was especially important. Makena was desirable to tourists because it was regularly sunny. This meant that it was also dry; water had to be brought in.

At about the time in 1973 that Seibu bought its Makena property, Mayor Cravalho said that he initiated discussions with several major landowners/developers, including Seibu, to have them participate in financing a new water source and transmission line, primarily to serve the Kihei coast. An agreement was announced in 1974. Most of the cost of these facilities was to be met by three large developers, including Seibu, with some of the money they fronted to be refunded later out of income generated by operating the new facilities. Other, smaller developers in the Kihei area were also to be allowed to use the system. The project was eventually built, and in 1985 extension of the line as far as the Seibu boundary was completed. The sizing of the line, and the volume and pressure of the flow through it, were such that most or all Makena properties with development potential, in addition to Seibu's, could have water. If dictated to an extent by self-interest, and mandated by Mayor Cravalho, still this was a major contribution on Seibu's part for the benefit of smaller landowners and developers in the Seibu area.[14]

Seibu also helped pay for what was to be the first paved road into Makena. The company paid 11.5% of the cost. Three other landowners in the general area paid the rest. Unlike the arrangement on the water, there was to be no reimbursement on the road expense.[15]

As mentioned, the Seibu resort in general would be a growth generator for Makena. Seibu's promotional activities would give the area international visibility. Such things as its golf course or courses, and the dining facilities in its hotels, would be big pluses for companies planning projects in Makena too small to include such things.

In an interview for this book, Elmer Cravalho said he endorsed the Seibu plan as mayor when it was first presented to him about 1973. That year, as mentioned, he said that he also initiated discussions involving Seibu concerning a major new water supply for the Kihei coast. Also as mentioned, in 1969 MDG Supply Inc., in which Cravalho held a 15% interest, bought a 14.5% interest in 9.7 acres of beachfront at Makena. This land was just past the end of the then-developed parts of Kihei, beginning where an unpaved road started into Makena. The water agreement involving Seibu would bring a water line past the MDG land, running down to the Seibu property. It would also help ensure that the whole Seibu resort would go forward, thus helping to pay for a paved road past the MDG property, and bringing the full range of resort amenities into Makena. MDG, having bought in 1973 for $162,000, sold in 1974 for $350,000, about the time that an agreement in principle was apparently being reached on the water agreement.

Cravalho said MDG's investment had no bearing on his official work on the water agreement. And indeed there is no evidence that without his MDG investment Cravalho would have acted differently regarding the water agreement.

The Seibu property was purchased from Ulupalakua Ranch in 1973. The ranch had initially listed the land for sale through one realtor, but when that firm proved unsuccessful, Masaru Yokouchi of Valley Isle Realty got the listing. He found a buyer in Seibu and brokered the sale on behalf of the ranch. Afterwards he became a consultant to Seibu on Maui. As such, when Seibu's Land Use Commission application was pending in 1974, Yokouchi contacted members of the LUC and asked that they meet privately with Seibu representatives.

Given his years in politics and his position as the governor's chief aide on Maui, Yokouchi was personally acquainted with several LUC members. The Maui member, Tanji Yamamura, was on the Commission because Yokouchi nominated him to the governor. Yamamura, an independent pineapple grower, was appointed in 1969 after Yokouchi was directed by the governor's office to recommend someone from Maui who was a farmer. In an interview for this book, Yokouchi said he did not know Yamamura at the time, and came up with his name by asking for suggestions from farmers' organizations. Concerning the Seibu application, Yokouchi said he asked Yamamura to meet privately with Seibu representatives to hear their case, and that Yamamura did so. For whatever reasons, Yamamura subsequently voted in favor of Seibu, which got urban districting for 500 acres.

Yamamura at the time was also a member of a *hui* named Makena 700, which had purchased 670 acres from Ulupalakua Ranch in 1971 for $1.8 million. The parcel sat inland between Wailea and what later became the Seibu resort area. In 1973 the *hui* resold to a Japanese firm, Taiyo Fudosan Kogyo Co., for $6.2 million. Yamamura's voting for Seibu in 1974 tended to enhance the overall growth potential of the region to the benefit of the *hui's* buyer, which indirectly helped ensure that Taiyo Fudosan would pay Makena 700 in full, which it apparently did in 1976.

For this book, an attempt was made to interview Yamamura on Seibu and other matters. He declined.

The relatively small Makena Surf project—using about 16 acres as compared with Seibu's 1,000—stood to benefit from what Seibu did (although Makena Surf had to contribute 20.5% of the road cost). Makena Surf also had some politically well-connected people involved.

The site of Makena Surf was purchased in 1970 by a group of five connected, unregistered partnerships, collectively called Waipao Joint Venture. They bought the land for $1.6 million on agreement of sale from Ulupalakua Ranch, and in turn resold it in 1977 to a developer for about $6 million via a sub-agreement. The sub-agreement was still being paid off into the early 1980s.

To an extent the success of the *huis'* investment depended on Seibu going forward. Thus, to a degree, official action that forwarded Seibu also tended to aid Makena Surf.

Councilman Lanny H. Morisaki's son, and then Morisaki himself by taking over his son's investment, were members of the *huis* that profited by selling the Makena Surf land, as were four Planning Department officials: Charles S. Ota, Yoshikazu Matsui, Kazuo Kage, and Marvin P. Romme. On a number of occasions they took official action in favor of Seibu that had the unavoidable consequence of protecting or enhancing their investments at Makena Surf.

In 1974 Planning Commissioners Kage, Matsui and Ota voted to recommend that the Land Use Commission redistrict Seibu's land. Kage and Matsui in 1975 voted to accept Seibu's environmental impact statement. That year as well, Matsui, now as deputy planning director, helped process a new county master plan for the Kihei-Makena region, that included various urban designations for Seibu's land. Councilman Morisaki voted to approve the plan. In 1978 Matsui participated in processing a shoreline management area (SMA) application filed by Seibu in connection with a golf course. Planning Commissioner Romme voted to approve, as he did the golf clubhouse in 1979 and an extension of the SMA in 1980.[16]

Several of these five also took official actions that bore more directly on Makena Surf. When Councilman Morisaki voted to approve the new county regional plan for Kihei and Makena, he was voting for a plan that included a resort designation for the Waipao Joint Venture property, then being held by the *huis* in hope of a resale, which took place in 1977. The Maui planning director in 1980 told a reporter that Matsui, as his deputy, had participated in Planning Department review of the proposed Makena Surf rezoning in about 1979.[17]

Morisaki in 1975 voted to approve $200,000 in county funds for a road past the Waipao Joint Venture property. Councilman Toshio A. Ansai voted for that appropriation as well. The year before, a then-unregistered partnership, Makena Beach Investors, bought an eight-acre parcel on the shoreline in Makena. The Toshio A. Ansai Trust invested $10,000 in the venture, with Ansai and his daughter as trustees. A new public road would facilitate access into the area where the Makena Beach Investors property was located.[18]

Councilman Ansai also in 1975 voted for the Kihei-Makena master plan, that included a residential classification for the Makena Beach Investors land.[19]

Although these decision-makers usually voted to approve Seibu and Waipao matters, there was at least one time when one did not. Planning Commissioner Ota in 1975 voted "no" on the Kihei-Makena plan.[20]

Also, when the official matter at hand related exclusively to property in which decision-makers had interests, they generally abstained from voting. Planning Commissioner Romme did so in 1980 regarding Makena Surf. In 1979 Councilmen David Y. S. Kong and Gordon S. Miyaki abstained from voting on rezoning the Makena Surf land. They were both realtors with Valley Isle Realty, which was to handle sales of Makena Surf units.[21]

But just the same, the indirect ties of decision-makers who did rule were persistent and strong, whether these people were councilmen, planning commissioners, or judges. For example, at the time of the Council rezoning of Makena Surf in 1979, Robert H. Nakasone was council chairman. Since 1977 his wife and Councilman Miyaki's wife had been listed as two of the five investors in a general partnership, Kula-Lahaina Partners. Also, Planning Commissioner Kage until 1976 was the Maui branch manager of First Insurance Co. of Hawaii Ltd. In an interview he said that from the time Seibu arrived in Hawaii in about 1973, First Insurance handled part or all of Seibu's local insurance needs. Kage also said that he personally took no part in insurance work affecting Seibu, that it was all done in First Insurance's main office in Honolulu. Opponents of Makena Surf at one point filed suit to block the project. One of Maui's two circuit court judges, S. George Fukuoka, was an investor in Waipao Joint Venture. The other judge, Kase Higa, thus heard the case. Higa at the time was an investor in a *hui* organized by the same man who organized Waipao, Masaru Yokouchi. Also in Waipao was the husband of the woman who was the circuit court clerk for the Makena Surf proceedings, Ethel M. Miyahira.

In other ways as well the Waipao/Makena Surf project had ties to government:

Former district court magistrate Walter T. Shimoda was the project's attorney before the Council. An engineering firm run by former chief engineer and manager of the county's Water Department, Norman M. Saito, was a consultant. This firm, in addition, at one point had an employee, Ralph M. Hayashi, who worked on the project, testified for it before the LUC, and subsequently became director of the county's Public Works Department. In that capacity he handled matters concerning Makena Surf. The project's attorney before the LUC, Roy Y. Takeyama, used to be the LUC's own attorney. As mentioned, former county planning director Howard K. Nakamura represented Makena Surf before the LUC in 1978 and the County Council in 1979.[22]

The Seibu and Makena Surf projects had equally important economic dimensions, and these were of considerable importance to decision-makers. For example, a Seibu attorney told the Land Use Commission in 1974 that, based on studies by an economic consultant, the development, if fully built out, would involve the expenditure on Maui of $235 million, create 4,050 jobs, and involve a cost-benefit ratio of governmental receipts to expenditures of three to one.[23]

The Makena Surf would bring public benefits, though on a smaller scale, creating fewer jobs and releasing less money into the Maui economy. At the time of the Makena Surf rezoning, the county planning staff wrote that "since the project will be a residential condominium project versus a hotel operation, it would appear that minimal direct employment opportunities would be created, beyond job opportunities during the project's construction phase."[24]

Overall, opponents of Makena Surf and Seibu fought a losing and possibly futile battle. In 1980 the *Honolulu Advertiser* reporter on Maui, Edwin I.

Tanji, attended a Planning Commission hearing on Makena Surf. He noted that of 25 who testified, 23 spoke against the project, but the matter was approved. Tanji concluded that "if a Maui Planning Commission decision on the Makena Surf condominium project is typical, public testimony in contested case hearings before the commission means nothing."[25]

Upon further investigation, Tanji wrote that one commissioner told him that even prior to the hearing, "the commission had directed deputy corporation counsel Sonia Faust to prepare documents to approve the project during an informal meeting."[26]

* * *

Maui, with the heaviest development of any of the outer islands, also may have had the heaviest involvement by the politically well-connected.

A shorthand way of summing up the importance of real estate in political life on Maui is simply to look at how many people elected to the Board of Supervisors and Council had realtors' licenses or interests in realty firms.

Maui County included three populated islands—Maui itself, plus Molokai and Lanai. Throughout the Democratic years virtually all of the real estate investment, development and sales activity that took place in Maui County occurred on the island of Maui. To examine the extent to which serving as a supervisor or councilperson overlapped with holding a realtor's license or an interest in a realty firm, it seemed most to the point to study only those officeholders who were residents of Maui. (See Table 18.)

Taking just those 31 members of the Board of Supervisors and later the County Council who lived on Maui and served between 1960–1984, 10, or 32%, simultaneously held a salesman's or broker's license or an interest in a real estate sales company. Three others obtained licenses after leaving office—right after leaving, in the case of two. A fourth had been a broker for 11 years but gave up his license seven years before becoming a councilman. He also was a past president of a realty company. Adding these four to the others, there was a grand total of 14, meaning that 45% of all supervisors and council members resident on Maui had at some time in their lives held licenses to sell real estate or interests in realty businesses.

Of the Maui residents on the Council elected in 1982, 43% either had licenses then or held one previously. In the general adult population of the island of Maui at the time, a maximum of some 7% held real estate licenses. Clearly Maui supervisors and council members as a group were extremely active in real estate. Moreover, given that by most accounts the weightiest job of supervisors and councilpersons in the period studied was regulating land use, this was a figure of some consequence.

There is a story within this story:

Of the 14 supervisors and council members who at various times had an affiliation with real estate sales, five were at one time or another with Valley Isle Realty, Masaru Yokouchi's firm: Fukuoka, Morisaki, Miyaki, Kong, and Ota. Yokouchi was Gov. Burns' chief campaign organizer and representative

─────────────────── TABLE 18 ───────────────────

ALL MAUI COUNTY SUPERVISORS AND COUNCIL MEMBERS 1960–1984 WHO WERE RESIDENTS OF ISLAND OF MAUI

Note: All supervisors and council members who were residents of island of Maui during this period are listed. Those with real estate licenses or interests in realty firms are so indicated. Years in parentheses are those of actual service on the Board or Council, including where start of service predated 1960.

ANSAI, TOSHIO A. (1935–1942, 1959–1962, 1975–1982)

TAM, EDWARD F. (1943–1966): salesman 1927–1948

TAGAWA, THOMAS T. (1953–1964): broker 1960–1973

FUKUOKA, S. GEORGE. (1955–1956, 1965–1966): secretary, director Valley Isle Realty 1960, director 1965–1971, shareholder 1960–1968 and possibly beyond

MOLINA, MANUEL S. (1955–1958, 1963–1970, 1973–1978)

KOBAYASHI, HARRY N. (1956–1962, 1971–1976)

CALDITO, RICHARD I.C. SR. (1957–1962, 1964–1972): salesman 1965–1979

CROCKETT, WENDELL F. (1959, 1963–1964)

MEYER, MARCO M. (1959–1974): salesman 1975–1979

MORISAKI, LANNY H. (1959–1976): director Valley Isle Realty 1960–1971, shareholder 1960–1968 and possibly beyond

BULGO, JOSEPH E. (1963–1966, 1969–1976)

TAVARES, WILFRED M. (1966–1968)

TOKUNAGA, BERNARD H. (1967–1976)

YAMAGUCHI, YONETO (1967–1973)

YAMAGUCHI, DORIS K. (1973–1976)

AIONA, ABRAHAM (1977–1984): salesman 1951–

AMARAL, ALVIN T. (1977–1978): salesman then broker 1972–

MEDINA, RICARDO (1977–1978, 1981–1984)

NAKASONE, ROBERT H. (1977–1982)

NEMOTO, CALVIN S. (1977–1978): salesman 1979–1982

MIYAKI, GORDON S. (1978): salesman then broker 1975–

ACOBA, MARIANO M. (1978–1980)

BARR, ALLEN W. (1979–1982)

KONG, DAVID Y. S. (1979–1980): salesman 1970–

KONDO, RONALD Y. (1979): salesman then broker 1973–

VAIL, JOHN T. (1979–1980)

KIHUNE, HOWARD S. (1981–1984): salesman 1979–

NISHIKI, WAYNE K. (1981–1984)

LIU, ELIZABETH E. (1983–1984)

OTA, CHARLES S. (1983–1984): broker 1964–1975; officer, director Valley Isle Realty 1961–1969, shareholder 1961–1968 and possibly beyond

SANTOS, VELMA M. (1983–1984)

Sources: List of Maui County supervisors and council members 1904–1983, provided by Maui County Clerk's office; State of Hawaii, Department of Commerce and Consumer Affairs, Real Estate Commission.

---

on Maui beginning in 1962. Founded in 1960, Valley Isle throughout its existence had as its officers, directors and shareholders, a preponderance of Burns Democrat officeholders and men in politics.

Valley Isle was one of a number of organizations on Maui with a concentration of politically successful men in the Democratic years. Maui was a small community where power and influence were closely held, with a relatively few organizations accounting for a disproportionately large percentage of those who were politically influential in this period: the ILWU; Alexander & Baldwin, which was Maui's largest landowner; the Democratic Party; and the various law firms in which Meyer Ueoka was a partner.

* * *

To return in conclusion to the case of the development of Kihei: all kinds of people got in on it. Looking at the entire coast from Maalaea to Makena, almost everybody who was anybody in the new power structure took part, everybody from mayors of Maui to men who ran illegal gambling on the island, from small local-Japanese contractors to one of Japan's biggest corporations, from the old Big Five firm of Alexander & Baldwin to the leaders of the Democratic Party.

Nowhere else on the outer islands were so many relatively small parcels of land available for sale in an area so desirable for development.

The fact that Kihei had room for "small" people to get in on development alongside the big names might have been a factor in heavy support by county and state government for growth at Kihei. This was good Democratic thinking in the 1960s and onwards—promoting land development as a way to prosperity and influence for new groups of people in Hawaii society. That is to say, like so many strategic decisions about land in the Democratic years, the way Kihei was encouraged to develop might have had a socio-political element.

One of the costs might have been a planning disaster. But whatever Kihei turned out to look like, the place was a financial bonanza for many in the locally-born middle class. They could not develop destination resorts. They did not have the land or the money. But they could invest in a small condominium project at Kihei, just as on Oahu people like them could invest in apartments at Salt Lake. It was their way to climb in the world.

This was the balance sheet on Kihei—it might have been badly handled from a planning point of view, but it was well timed and profitable for a great many local people in the Democratic years. One of Maui's major political figures, looking at both sides of the balance sheet, once described Kihei as a "necessary evil."[27]

10

OAHU: SALT LAKE

WHEN in the mid-nineteenth century the Hawaiian traditional land system was remade into one of private property, the chiefs of the ruling Kamehameha line took for themselves the *ahupua'a* or land division of Moanalua to the west of Honolulu.

Two valleys inland contained favorite resting and feasting places. There was also an extinct volcanic crater, with a body of water inside which the Hawaiians called *aliapa'akai*, salt-encrusted. This became known by *haoles* as Salt Lake.

According to written reports by westerners in the nineteenth century, the lake was spring-fed with augmentation from rainfall. The ground nearby was heavy with salt, and the lake bottom and shoreline were loaded with salt crystals, especially in dry seasons when the water level was low. Two English missionaries who visited Salt Lake in 1822 wrote that "plants, sticks, and tufts of grass, scattered on the beach, are . . . delicately frosted with spangles of salt. Here and there distinct masses of the same, attached to the rocks, consist of large cubes, regularly crystallized and very beautiful."[1] They believed the salt that nature produced here to be "of the finest grain."[2] Another westerner who once visited the lake thought it "the principal natural curiosity that this island affords."[3]

Hawaiians gathered the salt; then in the nineteenth century it became a commodity, sold to western sea captains and others.

As with Hawaii's fragrant sandalwood trees, so popular in China for making incense, commercial exploitation of the salt apparently caused rapid depletion. By mid-nineteenth century the salt deposits were no longer being mentioned by people writing about the Moanalua area.

In 1884 the Princess Bernice Pauahi Bishop died. She was the Kamehameha chief to whom Moanalua had descended. In her will the *ahupua'a* of Moanalua—some 9,405 acres—went to a *haole* banker, Samuel M. Damon, the business partner of the princess' *haole* husband, Charles R. Bishop.

At about the end of the century Damon leased land around the lake to a sugar plantation. Runoff from the cane fields silted up the lake, by some later accounts plugging the salt spring. In any event, in 1910 the plantation had an artesian well dug nearby that supplied a large amount of fresh water. The water was dumped into the lake to provide a steady source for irrigation. For whatever reason, the lake no longer produced salt.[4]

Upon Damon's death in 1924, Moanalua and Salt Lake were placed in trust for his heirs until the last of his grandchildren should die, at which time all the property in the estate would be divided among the heirs.

* * *

The Damon Estate trustees in about the early 1950s decided that urbanization of much of the Moanalua-Salt Lake lands would be appropriate. Initially they wanted to do it themselves. Then about 1954 they decided to include in the effort two rising local-Chinese businessmen, Kan Jung Luke and Clarence T.C. Ching, as heads of a *hui* to lease large tracts and oversee development.

Ching and Luke were both in their early forties at the time. Luke was a graduate of Harvard Business School. Since his early twenties he had been lecturing in business at the University of Hawaii. Ching was a graduate of St. Louis College in Honolulu. For several years he had been part-owner of a small grocery store located on Damon land, in an area called Damon Tract, not far from the Honolulu airport.

The leasing plan was dropped in 1956. Instead the estate sold the 233-acre Damon Tract by agreement of sale to Luke and a business partner, and the next year a 1,074-acre tract that included Salt Lake and Moanalua's two valleys was in effect sold to a partnership whose principal organizer was Ching.

* * *

Why did the Damon Estate trustees sell?

They sold because, as the 1950s wore on, developing the land themselves looked increasingly burdensome.

For one thing, in Damon Tract they had some 4,000 people living as tenants. "Many had the squatter-type of home built in the time of the depression," according to Damon trustee Herman V. Von Holt in a newspaper interview in 1958. This housing was substandard; the trustees wanted it to go.

But many Damon Tract tenants feared they would not be able to afford to move back in at the high rents that they believed would follow redevelopment. So when the estate presented its proposal to the City Planning Commission, the tenants protested. According to Von Holt, "we immediately ran into a hornet's nest of opposition from the tenants." Indeed at one point they staged a protest march on Iolani Palace. Reportedly because of these protests the Planning Commission balked at the Damon plan.

At the same time the territorial government was planning to condemn some of the land to expand the Honolulu airport, gearing up for the jet age.

Here was a real squeeze. The Damon trustees, who were having trouble getting rid of their tenants and thus upgrading the value of their property, thought that in a condemnation case the value of the land would be set, at least in part, according to the low lease rents being paid by tenants in ramshackle houses.

"So, to sum up," Von Holt said, "we faced a very decided risk of having the land condemned on the basis of how much income we were getting. Secondly, we couldn't subdivide. And third, we were facing tremendous agitation against the big estates. There was talk in the Legislature of enacting the Maryland law—a law that says a tenant can buy the land he occupies . . ."[5]

Now, inclined to sell and be rid of all these problems, the Damon trustees faced an unpleasant federal tax reality. Briefly, if Damon tried to sell house lots to a mass of individuals, the income would be taxed at so-called "ordinary income" levels, which according to Von Holt meant a tax rate of 90%. If on the other hand Damon simply sold in one or two large chunks, the tax would have been at capital gains rates—25%, according to Von Holt.

No matter who developed Damon Estate land, the estate's beneficiaries would make money and the estate's trustees would get a percentage. Why take so many risks and suffer all these headaches and expenses when a mere passive involvement, first leasing to a developer and then selling, would bring an adequate return?

People like Ching and Luke, for their part, were not big landowners, with thousands of acres to rely on. They could only get in on the incipient land boom by developing.

Also, people like Ching and Luke had the political connections to tackle involved governmental problems. For example, Luke's attorney was Chuck Mau, one of the founders of the post-World War II Democratic Party. Luke and Ching also brought in as an investor Mitsuyuki Kido, another Democratic founder.

The Democrats already controlled the territorial Legislature and the Honolulu Board of Supervisors. Whether or not anyone in the mid-1950s could see how complete the Democratic takeover would be by the mid-1960s, still it seemed likely that the rise had a way to go before peaking. Men like Ching and Luke could take part in that rise.

So the estate sold rather than holding. The 233-acre Damon Tract was disposed of in 1956 for $4.5 million to Loyalty Investments, a *hui* that Luke headed. This was followed by the sale in 1957 of 1,074 acres, including most of the buildable parts of Moanalua and Salt Lake, for $10 million. This latter sale was through Territorial Investors to a company Ching essentially headed, International Development Co.

Luke later in 1956 spun off 25 acres of Damon Tract for $1.65 million to another company whose principals were local-Chinese. In 1958 for $4.95 million the territorial government bought 67 acres from his group for expansion of the airport. Thus of the 233 acres Luke bought in 1956, he now had 141 left and had profited $2.1 million.

These deals established Luke as a major figure in the Hawaii real estate business. And in a way as concretely as the 1954 general elections, these transactions told the old money of Hawaii that local-Asian businessmen were growing up in their midst with certain capabilities and with a drive that men like the trustees of the great estates simply had to acknowledge. If the Damon trustees did not want the headaches and preferred to sell, Luke and Ching were ready to buy, with the expectation that hard work, intelligence, political connections, and the likelihood of substantial profits would take care of the headaches.

* * *

In the mid-1960s Clarence Ching's International Development Co. (IDCo) obtained state government permission to fill most of Salt Lake for a golf course. By the end of 1975 only 35 of the lake's 260 or so acres of surface water remained, and on the land around it residential development had taken place.

Development began at a time when there was a great need for fee simple housing in Hawaii. Moanalua and Salt Lake provided thousands of fee simple house lots and condominium units, at prices affordable by many ordinary middle-class and even some working-class families.

It was a very large development, carried out right at the high point of the boom, just at the growing point of population, as the center of population was moving west away from downtown Honolulu toward central Oahu. It was part of tract housing culture, freeway culture, condominium culture, part of the overall urbanizing and suburbanizing of Hawaii. The *hui* that developed Moanalua and Salt Lake was composed of literally hundreds of middle-class local-Asians, many of them investing no more than a few hundred or a few thousand dollars, a few of them putting in much, much more. The whole experience was part of the upward mobility of everyone concerned: developers, investors, and home-buyers.

* * *

As mentioned, the most active and influential member of IDCo was Clarence Ching.

Ching was a close associate of John Burns. They had done each other favors, going back to the time of statehood for Hawaii.

After Burns, Hawaii's delegate to Congress 1957-1959, ran for the governorship of the new state in 1959 and lost, he was low on funds. According to a Ching associate, Ching at that point offered Burns a fee for what Burns had already done in helping to get a federal charter for Ching's Hawaii National Bank.

The bank, among its other functions, was to be something of an outgrowth of and adjunct to the Moanalua-Salt Lake development.

By the account of a Ching associate, Ching had applied for a federal charter in 1959, in the closing days of Burns' last term as delegate. Ching believed that Hawaii's two big *haole* banks were attempting to obstruct the application. He asked Burns for help. Burns was close to US Senate Majority Leader Lyndon B. Johnson. In the summer following the end of his delegateship Burns approached Johnson. Johnson reportedly used his influence, and Hawaii National got its charter. Total processing time was nine months—"exceptionally fast action," according to the *Honolulu Star-Bulletin.*[6]

Ching offered Burns payment for his help. Burns declined, saying, according to the Ching associate: "You keep that money and give Merchant St. hell."

Ching and Burns stayed close through the 1960s, with Ching functioning in these years as Burns' principal fundraiser. This was a very influential position, particularly in the days before public reporting of campaign contributions became law. The man who knew where contributions came from, large and small, would also know who was and was not deserving of patronage.

*   *   *

Two years into Burns' governorship, Ching was getting ready to start developing Salt Lake.

In 1964, with little or no opposition, IDCo got approval from the Land Use Commission to fill 63 acres of the lake itself.

Then in 1966 IDCo went to the Land Board with a proposal to fill most of the rest of the lake. This time the developers ran into opposition.

The principal occasion was a public hearing held in August 1966.

IDCo's proposal was for a golf course, on 190 acres of fill land to be created out of the lake.

The Land Board, appointed by Gov. Burns, had jurisdiction over what were called "permitted uses" in the conservation district. Salt Lake was in the conservation district. A golf course was a permitted use.

A sizable argument built up over the IDCo proposal, in fact one of the biggest environmental/developmental disputes thus far in postwar Hawaii. (The only one to match or exceed it in the 1960s was over high-rises around Diamond Head.)

Debate at the public hearing and afterwards was heated. Everything came down to a single simple point: was it a good idea to fill Salt Lake and make a golf course out of it?

Along the way the history, the present condition and the future prospects of the lake were reviewed and disputed. Was Salt Lake in fact natural or artificial? Had it once been a nice place? Was it a nice place now? If it was a nice place now, was it nicer than a golf course would be? Nicer for whom? Was it desirable, and was it financially feasible, to preserve and even upgrade Salt Lake for calm-water recreation for people, and as a habitat for fish and native Hawaiian birds? What was fish and bird habitat worth anyway, against the benefits of development?

The debate got even more philosophical. The question of whether Salt

Lake was natural or artificial was held to be important. If the lake was artificial, then filling it would be no crime against nature, since what man had made he could do away with. On the other hand, if Salt Lake was natural, then it would occupy a higher plane in the overall scheme of things.

The lake was certainly natural to begin with. It existed in the shallow crater of an extinct volcano, and it was spring-fed. The two English missionaries who visited the lake in 1822 wrote that near the lake "there is a salt spring bubbling up into a basin a yard in diameter, running into the lake."[7]

By the turn of the twentieth century, when sugar was being grown around the lake, silt runoff from the plantation had reportedly plugged the source of the spring water. In 1910 an artesian well was drilled to fill the lake with fresh water, and a drainage tunnel was dug to carry excess water away into Moanalua Stream. By 1927, according to Lincoln L. McCandless, who drilled the well, "the fresh water has washed the salt away and Salt Lake is fresh today."[8] It was also now artificial.

By the mid-1960s the water quality was poor and getting worse, due mainly to development activity. The military since about the 1950s had been dumping sewage effluent into the lake from its housing in nearby Aliamanu Crater. In 1964 the Land Use Commission had given IDCo permission to fill 63 acres for urban development. By the time of the 1966 hearing on the golf course, 41 of those 63 acres had been filled, causing siltation and the washing of debris into the remaining lake area. Heavy grading had been going on along the shore for more than a year, causing more siltation and debris. In September 1965 IDCo had shut off the artesian well that supplied over 90% of the water. The lake level went down five or six feet and the water stagnated. As of the 1966 golf course hearing, according to State Health Department director Dr. Leo Bernstein, there was "a heavy green scum" on the surface that "has caused the death of large numbers of fish which in turn created an odor nuisance and a difficult disposal problem." There was also "heavy mosquito breeding on low-lying shore land" that had created a "significant mosquito problem for residents of an adjacent military housing area." Bernstein predicted that silt and debris would continue to pile up in the lake, making the water "turbid, dirty, and colored and unsuitable for swimming."[9]

Whatever Salt Lake might have been a hundred years before, by these accounts it hardly sounded like a place worth saving now. On the other hand just how much it had deteriorated depended on who was looking at it. *Honolulu Star-Bulletin* reporter Tom Coffman visited Salt Lake in 1973 after yet further decline. He wrote: "For my part, still somewhat believing officialdom, I expected to find a 'dead lake,' without really knowing what the phrase meant. But [I] found life all around," including shrimp, minnows, ducks and Hawaiian coots. "By resorting to the standards of common sense, one can report that Salt Lake is a lake. It is a lake and not a large mud puddle, as it has been portrayed to be."[10]

* * *

In the Salt Lake controversy, as so often in Hawaii in the Democratic years, choosing up sides on a development issue turned out to be choosing up ethnic sides as well.

Indeed if a being from outer space had walked into that Land Board hearing in August 1966, he might almost have concluded that someone had color-coded the two sides.

With very few exceptions, the opponents of filling the lake were *haole*. And beyond that they were middle and upper-class *haole*. They were the Conservation Council of Hawaii, the Audubon Society, the Outdoor Circle, the Garden Club, the League of Women Voters. Their money allowed them the luxury of, and their education and experience of mainland environmental degradation opened their eyes to, seeing a need to preserve Salt Lake, even if this meant forgoing some economic development.

These middle-class *haole* conservationists did have one or two somewhat surprising allies on this occasion: the Oahu Development Conference and the ILWU. The ODC was made up primarily of executives of large *haole* businesses, but took a conservationist stance here. The ILWU was in its planning-awareness phase, and the union spokesman on such matters, Eddie Tangen, voiced opposition to "a proposal to destroy a natural lake."[11]

Also against filling were some few Hawaiians, representatives of Hawaiian civic clubs. Their conservationism was as much cultural and social as environmental—a general wish not to see the past buried.

On the other side, favoring the fill—that is, favoring the golf course, and beyond that favoring heavy development at Salt Lake and Moanalua generally—were any number of locally born Asians. And practically no *haoles*—because practically no *haoles* were in on the *huis* formed to develop Salt Lake, and as yet few had bought house lots in the area.

IDCo's principals were mostly local-Chinese. As well, though this was not publicly known at the time, IDCo had numerous sub-companies, many of whose members were local-Japanese. Indeed all the large land sales involving Damon Estate lands in Moanalua were to companies organized by Chinese or Japanese. IDCo's attorneys, and most of their professional and technical consultants, were local-Asian. So were most of their lot buyers. A petition favoring the fill was submitted to the Land Board, signed by 243 buyers, and almost every name was Japanese or Chinese.

On the one side at the Land Board hearing, then, were mainly middle-class *haoles*, hardly any of whom lived anywhere near Salt Lake, pleading for the lake to be preserved, on respectable middle-class conservationist grounds. They argued that Salt Lake was Hawaii's only natural lake of any size, that it had historical value, that it once had recreational value and could again, that it was important for threatened Hawaiian bird life—and that if Oahu needed another golf course, well, build one on existing land somewhere else.

These arguments, and those who advanced them, together with ethnic-Hawaiian pleadings for the past, carried little or no economic or political weight in Hawaii in 1966.

Those in favor of the fill argued that maintaining the lake would be prohibitively expensive, that more golf courses were needed, and that a golf course would enhance the surrounding residential development far more than a lake which was polluted, an eyesore, a health hazard, and no longer a natural lake anyway.

These pro-fill arguments had no more or less weight than the anti-fill arguments. But those who put the pro-fill case definitely had political weight.

Favoring the fill were golfing clubs, tourist industry executives, a Damon Estate spokesman, the overwhelming majority of IDCo house lot buyers, as well as any number of politically well-connected Democrats who either had apartment-zoned lots by the lake or were investors in IDCo or its subcompanies.

In fact the fill had powerful support all the way up to Gov. Burns, who minimized the idea that Salt Lake would be destroyed. "I believe," he said, "there is no intent to 'destroy' Salt Lake, but rather to set off a part of it through the construction of a golf course which makes some use of it in a manner that would enhance its beauty."[12]

IDCo got unanimous approval from the Land Board to fill in most of the lake for its golf course.[13]

Among those voting "yes" was the ILWU member of the Board, Tai Sun Yang, even though Eddie Tangen, speaking for the union, had been against the fill. Tangen explained afterwards that Yang was instructed to vote as he did because the union believed there were no other votes against, and "there was no point in dissenting."[14]

* * *

To pursue for a moment IDCo's real intentions concerning the lake and the golf course, what the company said and what it did were at times inconsistent.

A comparison of utterances and events could lead to the conclusion that IDCo might say something because it would be acceptable to government and the public, and then do something altogether different if another option later looked more profitable.

In fairness, these shifts might have been related to changed circumstances between proposal and implementation stages. But however it was that shifts occurred, after a while it became hard to believe every word IDCo said.

For example, in 1964, when IDCo's engineer asked the Land Use Commission for urban districting for part of the lake so that it could be filled, he described Salt Lake as "the only natural lake in Hawaii"—the approach at that time being to describe how good it would be to build a "lovely residential area" around a basically intact natural lake. But then, beginning in 1965, when the plan for a golf course involving fill at Salt Lake was first announced, IDCo spokesmen consistently maintained the lake was not natural but artificial. A reporter who attended the Land Board hearing in 1966 wrote that "geological evidence was offered from [IDCo] engineers to show that Salt Lake is an artificial one." IDCo's approach now was that it was less serious to eradicate an artificial lake than a natural one.[15]

Along similar lines, when IDCo in 1965 obtained a major zoning amendment from the City Council, plans showed the lake being retained. One week after the rezoning, the fill plan was announced. Clarence Ching came back to the Council and apologized for what he said was a "communications problem."[16]

When in 1965 the golf course idea was first made public, it was on the basis that more golf courses were needed on Oahu. Gov. Burns agreed. In 1966 the petition to the Land Board by the 243 IDCo lot buyers spoke of the "demanding need within the City & County for additional golf courses and golfing facilities." The Board also got letters from a number of local-Japanese and Chinese golf clubs, and tourist industry executives, all saying Oahu was short of courses.

In other words, IDCo got what it wanted in 1966—permission to fill most of Salt Lake—at least partly on the basis that an increase in golf courses was needed on Oahu.

Yet in the years immediately following, IDCo made development proposals that would have led to no net increases in golf courses on Oahu. IDCo approached two private golf clubs in the Honolulu area, Waialae Country Club and Oahu Country Club, with the idea that a trade of land might be worked out. IDCo would develop a course and clubhouse at Salt Lake, then trade it for one of the existing clubs, which IDCo would then redevelop as a residential area (assuming permission from government agencies to do this). In other words, no more golf courses, just more development. None of this actually happened, but it was not for want of IDCo's trying.[17]

As to the Salt Lake course, IDCo in its 1966 application said the course would be open for play in 1968. The course did not open until 1977.

IDCo said the course would be 27 holes. Years before it was built, though, there were rumors that IDCo, having got enough acreage zoned to accommodate the 27-hole course, would renege and ask that nine holes' worth be rezoned for urban use. An IDCo attorney "took exception" to these rumors. But something like that in fact happened. In 1972 IDCo made an application for urban districting for an additional 30 acres of apartment development, partly on golf course land. But by that time IDCo was not planning 27 holes anyway. The course that ultimately opened in 1977 was 18 holes and no more.[18]

As for who could play on the planned golf course, IDCo's 1966 application to the Land Board spoke of it as "semi-public," meaning that there would be some private memberships, but the public would be allowed to play too, for a fee. An IDCo attorney said the course would be "so operated as to encourage public playing." But by the time the eventual 18-hole course opened for play in 1977, the area had been sold by IDCo to a company that operated it as the Honolulu International Country Club, on a membership basis, making no mention of public play. IDCo's position was that in negotiating the sale of the course, it had been agreed that members of the immediate area's community association (that is, some few members of the public but by no means all of the public) could play for a fee. The Honolulu International Country Club, though, allowed non-members to play only during slow times, and only with the permission on each occasion of a club committee chairman. According to research done for this book, seldom did community association members actually play golf at Salt Lake.[19]

* * *

What went on at the Land Board hearing in August 1966 was not just about a golf course or even about a golf course and a lake. It was really about a major land development, which meant that it was political, intensely so.

Given the makeup of IDCo, the composition of Democratic Party leadership, and the real estate market of the mid-1960s, it would be difficult to imagine such a decision at that time going against the developer.

Apart from Clarence Ching himself, politically well-connected investors in IDCo at the time the Land Board issued the fill permit included: Dr. Nobuichi Masunaga, a sitting member of the Land Board; State Sen. Mitsuyuki Kido; House Vice-Speaker Tadao Beppu, who in 1967 became speaker; former territorial judge and city supervisor Chuck Mau; Wilfred M. Oka, former Democratic Party activist and, beginning in 1969, a City Parks & Recreation Department employee; long-time Burns intimate and Democratic Party figure Michael N. Tokunaga, in 1966 Deputy Director of the State Department of Regulatory Agencies; City Information and Complaints Officer Brian L. Casey, later a city councilman; State Board of Education Chairman Edwin H. Honda; Maui County Finance Department teller Stanley T. "Banjo" Tamura; plus a large number of other Maui government officials.

When Ching's IDCo came to develop Salt Lake, among the investors in apartment-zoned lots, most of them first purchasers from IDCo, were many people either prominent in Democratic politics or close to those who were: Chuck Mau; City Council leader Matsuo Takabuki as a one-third owner of Tropicana Investments Inc.; Takabuki's secretary, Edith M. Hasegawa; Councilman Clesson Y. Chikasuye's father Oen, half of whose investment he later gave to Clesson; Councilman Chikasuye's secretary Mildred M. Nakamura (who said in an interview for this book that her name appeared only as a front for others whom she declined to name); Councilman George M. Koga, who bought two lots through a junior member of his law firm, Wilfred H.C. Youth (Koga resold these lots; he also bought in his own name a cluster of six lots on which he put up an apartment building); Deputy City Clerk Wilbert S. Holck, who in 1974 became a councilman; Gov.

Burns' daughter and son-in-law, Mary Beth and Harry J. Statts Jr.; former Honolulu planning commissioner Stanley T. Himeno; City Zoning Board of Appeals member Henry C.H. Chun Hoon, also a former city planning commissioner; Honolulu District Court Magistrate Jon J. Chinen as secretary and director of K&H Inc.; Wilfred M. Oka; Deputy State Attorney General Wallace S.J. Ching, who was Clarence's son; and State Finance Director Andrew T.F. Ing, who served as John Burns' lieutenant governor in 1966 and before that had been an executive in several firms affiliated with the Moanalua and Salt Lake developers—Loyalty Enterprises, Loyalty Mortgage Co., Loyalty Insurance Agency, and Hawaii National Bank.

Ing was in a particularly strong position to aid Ching's enterprises. As state finance director, Ing deposited large sums of public money in Hawaii National, giving that bank, though it was the smallest in Hawaii as measured by assets, by far the highest percentage of state deposits to assets—18.7%, as against the 4.4% of the largest bank, Bank of Hawaii—according to a state legislative auditor's report in 1969.[20]

Why should Hawaii National be favored so heavily with the deposit of state money? The auditor was critical of this. Ing's response had everything to do with the coming to power of the Democrats. He said that before the time of John Burns as governor, the two big banks, meaning Republican banks, *haole* banks—Bank of Hawaii and what by 1969 was called First Hawaiian Bank—got 80% of state deposits. The small banks, meaning new banks founded by local-Asians, got only the remaining 20%.[21]

As with so many other areas of life, the coming to power of the Democrats overturned that old arrangement. This meant that the smaller man, the new man, the man who might not have been *haole*, the man who might not have gotten good treatment when he went to one of the old banks for a loan, now had a chance to get ahead. These were some of the broad social and political underpinnings of Ing's deposit ratios.

Clarence Ching, getting ahead, had found it useful, indeed necessary, to participate in founding a bank. And his was the bank that the State now favored heavily when it was putting its money at deposit. However one viewed the wisdom of a state deposit policy of this kind, what it led to was the creation of yet another thread in the ties that bound together government and the developers of Salt Lake.

More of these threads continued to be woven into the early 1970s, when investors in Salt Lake apartment lots included: Wallace T. Yanagi, then deputy director of the state-owned Maui Memorial Hospital; former Honolulu deputy city planning director Wallace S.W. Kim, who in the early 1970s was a planner with the State Department of Land and Natural Resources; Honolulu Board of Water Supply Chairman John H. Felix as a partner in Monte Vista Development Co.; former city planning director George K. Houghtailing as a director of Reliance Industries Inc.; and Honolulu Mayor Frank F. Fasi's chief fundraiser, Harry C.C. Chung, as a partner in Lakeview Gardens Associates.

When people bought apartment lots from IDCo, they signed agreements of sale that included this stipulation: "Purchaser does hereby consent to and approve such [golf course] development of said Salt Lake [and promises] to abstain from registering and/or making, directly or indirectly, any protest, objection or complaint."

In effect, these apartment lot buyers were legally bound to support the filling of Salt Lake.

While many were perhaps unaware of this stipulation or had not thought through its implications, it nevertheless expressed a fundamental reality in the relationship of the state and city governments to Salt Lake—that is, government leaders were so thoroughly tied up with IDCo that obstruction of IDCo's overall plans was all but unimaginable.

Whether or not filling the lake was a good idea was a matter of judgment. Whether or not all these politically well-placed apartment lot buyers were likely to have a detached opinion on the subject was quite another question.

* * *

Clarence Ching was thoroughly a part of Hawaii's new establishment, and in his circle of associates were men who counted heavily in making his Salt Lake plans a reality.

For example, as one of his business interests, Ching sat on the board of Aloha Airlines, successor to an inter-island airline organized just after World War II by local-Asians to challenge the predominantly *haole*-owned Hawaiian Airlines. Here again there was a Salt Lake connection. Besides Ching, Aloha's directors in 1966 included Kenneth F.C. Char, Clesson Y. Chikasuye, K.J. Luke, and Mitsuyuki Kido. Char was the Honolulu planning commissioner who in August 1966 moved that the Commission recommend that the City Council approve a new master plan for Salt Lake as proposed by IDCo. Chikasuye as a city councilman voted in December 1966 to approve the plan. The plan's applicant before the Council was Loyalty Enterprises Ltd., of which Luke was president and Ching executive vice-president and treasurer. The ultimate developer would be IDCo, of which Ching was a general partner and Kido a limited partner.

* * *

One particular case involving multiple public-private sector crossovers in the development of Moanalua and Salt Lake was that of the Kido brothers, Mitsuyuki and Sunao.

Mitsuyuki was one of the original major investors in IDCo. As a limited partner in 1957 he subscribed to $328,000 of the company's value. Much of this he sold in turn to members of an IDCo sub-company, a company within a company, which he organized and managed. This sub-company was never registered with territorial or state agencies, making it impossible to know who all its members were.

As a state senator 1963-1966, Mitsuyuki voted to confirm the nominations of most of the Land Board members who in 1966 voted to allow the filling of Salt Lake. (The one board member who abstained from voting, Dr. Nobuichi Masunaga, did so because he had an investment in IDCo through Mitsuyuki's sub-company.)

Furthermore Mitsuyuki in 1966 was chairman of the Senate Oahu Select Committee, which made recommendations on the distribution of state capital improvements money for Oahu. Funds appropriated that year included a number of items that would speed the development of Salt Lake and Moanalua. There were funds for master planning and land acquisition for a new high school to be located in Salt Lake. The state portion of matching state-federal funds was appropriated for a freeway interchange at Puuloa and Moanalua roads, which many later Salt Lake residents used on their way into town. There was $460,000 in aid to the Honolulu city government to build a Salt Lake Boulevard bridge.

There was also appropriated $1.8 million for construction of the first increment of Moanalua Intermediate School, which would serve the single-family home development on the mountain side of Moanalua Road.

As to Mitsuyuki's brother, according to James P. Ferry, when governor-elect Burns in 1962 chose Ferry as chairman of the State Land Board, Ferry asked Burns to appoint Sunao Kido as his deputy. Ferry had business experience, Sunao had a background in personnel work. Ferry believed they would make a good team, and indeed Ferry later said he was very pleased with the quality of their work together.

Ferry said in addition that Burns expressed some concern to him about the propriety of appointing the brother of a prominent developer as the first deputy to the chairman of a state board that existed in part to rule on development.[22] (In fact Sunao was not only brother to Mitsuyuki. He also invested in some of Mitsuyuki's development *huis*, most notably Heeia Development Co. Sunao also had a license to sell real estate, as did Ferry.) Despite Burns' reported concerns, he made the appointment. And when in 1968 Ferry left the Land Board, Burns appointed Sunao as his successor. Sunao held the post until 1974.

In his capacity as deputy director in 1966, Sunao was active in the processing of the IDCo fill application, which involved his brother as a major investor. The staff report recommending that the Board approve the fill bore the words at the bottom: "Recommended for approval: Sunao Kido for Jim P. Ferry, Chairman."[23] In 1972, as Land Board chairman, Sunao reviewed and approved IDCo grading plans for the filling of Salt Lake. Over the years, most of the correspondence and staff memos regarding the IDCo fill and golf course were directed to and signed by Sunao; in fact, during all the years he was with the Land Board, hardly any other ranking staff member's name appeared in the IDCo file. And when in 1973 the State House Committee on Environmental Protection asked Sunao about reopening the question of whether to fill the lake, he said he found "no compelling reason" to do so.[24]

There were indications that in Sunao's time at the Land Board, he and other staff members took actions intended to promote IDCo's public image in the Salt Lake issue. For example, just before the 1966 Land Board hearing on the fill, Sunao wrote a memo to a subordinate about a letter received from a United Airlines executive supporting the fill. Sunao's memo read: "Paul. Please have this at the public hearing. Jim [Ferry] thought that maybe this should be read into the record."[25]

Paul was Paul Tajima, a planner in the Department of Land and Natural Resources. At about the same time, Tajima wrote a memo to Sunao that a man known to oppose the fill had charged IDCo with illegal grading and filling around the lake. Tajima suggested that Sunao have IDCo write the Land Board a letter stating that IDCo was investigating possible violations and would take any needed corrective actions.[26]

The question arises: why were Land Board staff members concerned to help IDCo make its case at the public hearing, rather than leaving IDCo to make its own case, as most other applicants did? IDCo was certainly not short of attorneys and consultants to argue in its behalf. And if there were serious suggestions from a member of the public that IDCo was grading and filling illegally, why did not the Land Board staff investigate, rather than suggesting a way for IDCo to respond?

The answer is that, broadly speaking, the government was anything but detached in the Salt Lake case. There was little or no difference between the general and particular interests of a number of government leaders who sat in judgment on Salt Lake matters, and the developers themselves.

It is possible that all the Kido brothers' public-private interest overlaps made no difference to how they approached their governmental responsibilities. Both of them publicly maintained that this was so, and that they never discussed between themselves the connections between Sunao's official duties and Mitsuyuki's development projects. Further, as Sunao said in an interview for this book, when IDCo's fill appplication was before the Land Board in 1966, he was but the deputy director. As such he had no vote, and he had a boss over him. He also said that such actions as he took were generally "ministerial," by which he meant that he had no discretionary leeway or independent force. Against this it might be argued that Sunao was acting in a highly discretionary way when in 1973 he recommended that the Legislature not reopen the question of whether to fill the lake, despite growing public sentiment to the contrary. Yet again, though, given the general support within government for IDCo at Salt Lake, even if Sunao had opposed the fill it would probably have been approved anyway.

* * *

The Kidos were at the center of mainstream Democratic politics. Joining them in an interest in Salt Lake were other men from all manner of leadership positions within the Democratic power structure.

George Ariyoshi throughout the 1960s invested in IDCo-developed lots in Moanalua Valley and Moanalua Gardens. Ariyoshi by himself bought a house lot in Moanalua Gardens in 1960, and resold it two years later as a still vacant lot. With his law partner, part-time judge Russell K. Kono, Ariyoshi bought the first four lots at the entrance to Moanalua Valley and built houses on them. Two of these houses and lots were resold within two years; the other two were held and used as rentals. In 1966 Ariyoshi and Kono bought a lot on the east side of Moanalua Valley, built a house, and sold the package in 1968.

Ariyoshi's younger brother James worked 1963-1968 for Hawaii National, the bank founded by Clarence Ching and others in part to support the development of Salt Lake and Moanalua.

Daniel K. Ainoa was a director of Reliance Industries Inc. which invested in two apartment-zoned lots 1971-1972. Ainoa in 1933 had been a co-founder of the Hawaii Government Employees Association (HGEA), and had been this powerful union's executive director 1965-1969.

Stanley Tamura, reputed to be one of those who ran illegal gambling on Maui, who was murdered in 1975 apparently in connection with gambling activities, was an investor in IDCo.

Even individuals considered by some to be political radicals invested. Wilfred M. Oka was not only a purchaser of apartment land but a member of IDCo. Oka, long active with the Democratic Party, in the 1950s wrote for the left-wing *Honolulu Record*. He was investigated by the House Un-American Activities Committee in the McCarthy era, and was one of the Reluctant 39, so-called because they took the Fifth Amendment rather than testify before the committee on communism in Hawaii.[27]

Harry C.C. Chung, an associate of Democratic dissident Frank F. Fasi, who was elected mayor of Honolulu in 1968, for years was Fasi's chief fundraiser, and was a member of a *hui* that owned the Lakeview Gardens condominium in Salt Lake. Another apartment developer at Salt Lake was former state senator Vincent H. Yano, co-developer of the 44-unit Lakeview Sands. Yano ran for lieutenant governor in 1970, with gubernatorial candidate Tom Gill, the leading liberal Democrat, head to head against the Burns-Ariyoshi ticket.

As was the case everywhere in Hawaii, at times political lines were crossed when Salt Lake *huis* were formed. For example, John H. Felix, who was a limited partner in Monte Vista Development Co., had in the early 1960s been an aide to Republican Gov. William F. Quinn. At the time of the Monte Vista transaction, Felix was chairman of the Honolulu Board of Water Supply, having been appointed by Mayor Frank Fasi. Other members of Monte Vista were mainline Democrats Mitsuyuki Kido and Chuck Mau.

* * *

Another sub-set of connections arose with city planning commissioners who voted to approve apartment zoning for Salt Lake, and later acquired a financial interest in the development. Commissioner Stanley T. Himeno in

December 1964 seconded a motion to approve large-acreage apartment zoning around the lake. A year later he was among the first to buy into this acreage.

Commissioner Henry C.H. Chun Hoon in 1957 voted on a master plan for Salt Lake that included 40 acres for apartments. With a business partner in 1966 he bought two apartment-zoned lots within this area. At the time of purchase he was a member of the city's Zoning Board of Appeals.

* * *

There was also the matter of former government officials and employees representing Moanalua and Salt Lake developers before government agencies.

One of the first times the developers applied to the City for a major zoning change was 1957. Their planning consultant was George K. Houghtailing, who until the year before had been city planning director. His former deputy was now director; as such he reviewed the rezoning proposal. Former land use commissioner Franklin Y.K. Sunn in 1964 as an engineering consultant represented IDCo before the Land Use Commission in successfully urging urban districting for 63 acres of lake surface. Throughout the 1960s former city deputy corporation counsel Donald K. Iwai represented IDCo before the City and the State Land Board. When the idea of a golf course was first announced in 1965, it was also announced that a former director of the State Department of Transportation, Timothy Ho, would be the project coordinator. Former city planning director Frederick K.F. Lee represented IDCo before the LUC in 1972, at which time former land use commissioner Sunn's firm was still IDCo's engineering consultant.

* * *

As for actual sitting councilmen, a number of times in the late 1960s and early 1970s George Koga, Clesson Chikasuye and Matsuo Takabuki voted on master development plans for Salt Lake that included land owned by themselves, their secretaries, and Chikasuye's father. They also voted for capital improvements and other zoning matters that had the effect of enhancing their investments.

Never during these votes were the investments disclosed. It is not clear, though, whether these councilmen were required to disclose. Year in and year out the only certainty with regard to what councilmen were bound to disclose had to do with cases where there was an interest in a business or piece of property that was the only item before them at the time—for example, owning a single lot which alone was up for rezoning.[28]

In the Salt Lake cases, there were always many others who stood to benefit in addition to one or another councilman; also, in the case of secretaries and relatives, the councilman's interest was yet one more step removed.

In any event, Takabuki three times 1966-1967 voted for master plans for Salt Lake that included his secretary's lots, and in 1968 voted for CIP money for Salt Lake Boulevard while he had his own investment.

Chikasuye three times 1966-1967 voted for Salt Lake master plans that included his secretary's lots, and on several occasions 1968-1974 voted on CIP matters affecting the property listed first in his father's name, and starting 1970 in his own name as a 50% owner.

Koga in 1966 voted twice on master plans that included two lots he owned. In 1967 he voted once on another master plan that included one of these lots. In 1971 he voted on zoning for a neighborhood shopping center that enhanced the value of a cluster of six lots he owned at the time. And in 1972, while he still owned these six lots, he voted for more CIP money for Salt Lake Boulevard.

Koga, in fact, apparently bought his first two lots the same day that he voted for a bill to reshuffle the zoning of the part of Salt Lake that contained them, although the bill actually decreased the density in and around where he bought. The Council on December 21 1965 voted on final reading for a bill that reorganized the zoning in Salt Lake's primary apartment district. That same day a junior associate in Koga's law firm, Wilfred H.C. Youth, signed agreements of sale in his own name for two of the apartment-zoned lots. About a week later Youth transferred the lots to Koga's name. As indicated by state conveyance tax records, apparently no money actually changed hands between Youth and Koga in this second transation, meaning that it was probably Koga's money involved in Youth's purchase on December 21.

In 1972 *Honolulu Star-Bulletin* reporter Tom Coffman found that Koga and Chikasuye had interests in IDCo apartment lots at Salt Lake. IDCo that year had an application before the State Land Use Commission to add 30 more urban-district acres to the overall project. If the LUC approved, then IDCo would have to come to the Council for city zoning. Coffman asked the two councilmen what they would do in that event.

Chikasuye said he would seek an opinion from the city attorney. Koga said he would publicly announce a conflict of interest, would probably consult the City Ethics Commission, and might not vote.[29]

As it turned out the LUC denied the application, so the matter never came before the Council.

The ethics question being discussed was whether the two councilmen should vote on an item involving a company from which they (and in Chikasuye's case a relative) had bought property in the past.

What neither councilman told Coffman, however, was that each of them had already on several occasions voted on bills affecting their own investments in Salt Lake.

In 1974, two years after the *Star-Bulletin* interview was published, Koga was faced on the Council with exactly the situation Coffman had put to him. IDCo was before the Council with an application to rezone some Salt Lake land from residential to apartment. Koga voted in favor. There is no indication of him consulting the City Ethics Commission prior to the vote.

Koga did on one occasion file a written disclosure of interest during a Council discussion of Salt Lake. This was apparently the sole occasion when he did so over Salt Lake; it was also an instance which apparently did not involve a vote of any kind.[30]

In 1978 Walter Wright of the *Honolulu Advertiser* looked into another aspect of Koga's Salt Lake investments, and came away wondering if Koga had gotten a preferential deal from the Hawaii Housing Authority (HHA). He wrote that Koga in 1968 had signed an unrecorded option agreement for six abutting apartment-zoned lots. In 1971 he bought the lots. He put up an apartment building, Lakeside Manor, and entered into a rental agreement with the US military covering most of the units. When he lost this agreement in 1975, Koga sold Lakeside Manor to HHA, for a before-tax profit of about $700,000. A year and a half later, Wright's story continued, "HHA still had 30 of the Lakeside Manor units [about one-third] for sale, after it poured another $660,000 into a sales program. In their own defense, HHA officials pointed out that many private developers had lost their shirts on similar condominiums in the previous two years; Councilman Koga was not among them."[31]

It might be noted that another councilman with Salt Lake interests, Brian L. Casey, on several occasions just before voting on IDCo matters disclosed his interest in the company. He then voted each time in favor of IDCo. And once, in 1971, Councilman Chikasuye voted against a bill that apparently would have enhanced the value of his investment at Salt Lake by allowing construction of the Salt Lake Shopping Center.

Still on the matter of disclosure of interest, a Land Board member, Dr. Nobuichi Masunaga, in 1966 both disclosed his interest and abstained from voting on the question of a fill permit for Salt Lake.

*   *   *

To what extent did investments by public officials in Salt Lake create potential obligations to Clarence Ching?

Apparently to some extent. The case of Wilbert S. "Sandy" Holck appeared to illustrate this:

In the mid-to-late 1960s Holck was a deputy city clerk. In an interview for this book he said that this job did not pay that well. He also said that he had some outside income, but not much. He and his wife had bought a house a few years before and were struggling to pay it off. Then another city official suggested to Holck that he might invest in Salt Lake. The arrangement was that Holck would buy two apartment lots, hold them long enough to get capital gains treatment by the Internal Revenue Service, and then IDCo would sell them for him. Holck said he never looked at the land, never even knew exactly where it was, just that it was in Salt Lake. IDCo took care of everything. Holck made a pre-tax profit of about $15,000. In an interview Holck said: "I guess I got taken care of."

A case similar to Holck's was that of Gov. Burns' daughter Mary Beth and her husband, Harry J. Statts Jr.:

Statts in 1965 was on an apprentice electrician's salary. He and his wife had just bought a home in Kailua and were struggling to make payments. Nevertheless, that same year they bought from Clarence Ching at Salt Lake a half-acre with a lake view, in two equal-sized lots, at $42,500 apiece. In an interview for this book Statts said that IDCo looked after the conveyancing, and asked only minimal payment from the Statts on agreements of sale they had signed. A little more than six months later, the lots were resold to Tajiri Supply Inc., with IDCo handling the transaction for the Statts, whose pre-tax profit was $30,000. Because they had held the land just long enough to warrant capital gains treatment, 50% of this was not federally taxable. Statts said he and his wife used some of this profit to repay a private family loan from John Burns.

Statts said that in taking care of him and his wife, "in essence Ching was repaying the Old Man [Burns] for something, or making a down payment" on a future political debt. Also, taking care of the governor by taking care of his daughter and son-in-law was more palatable than simply giving Burns money. "It would be less obvious if you went through the son-in-law. It would be less upsetting to the public."

*   *   *

Right down to the 1980s Salt Lake continued to provide opportunities to do favors in the political arena, as indicated by the case of Democratic Sen. Richard S.H. Wong and the Lakeside Plaza:

Lakeside Plaza was an 8-story, 40-unit condominium on a half-acre of land on Ala Lilikoi St. near the Salt Lake Shopping Center. Its builders and unit buyers were heavily mainstream Democrats or companies and people associated with the Democrats. A number of individuals were from Maui.

The project was constructed 1973-1974 by the then-deputy administrator of the state-owned Maui Memorial Hospital, Wallace T. Yanagi. (Yanagi in 1975 rose to be chief administrator. When he retired he went to work for Masaru Yokouchi's Valley Isle Realty Inc.)

Yanagi bought the land from IDCo in 1973. As was common at Salt Lake, Yanagi also contracted with IDCo-related Dynamic Industries Corporation to put up the building, and with Loyalty Enterprises Ltd. to manage it once built.

Lakeside Plaza's attorney as it was being planned was Francis M. Izumi, who had been a deputy Maui County attorney and later a deputy state attorney general assigned to the State Land Board. Izumi's law partner, Tamotsu Tanaka, invested in a unit. So did Izumi's brother James, who at the time was Director of Maui County Department of Personnel Services.

Maui Planning Commissioner Yoshikazu "Zuke" Matsui bought a half-interest in a unit. His brother Sajiro Matsui, who was in the vending machine business, bought a half-interest in another unit.

Other investors in Lakeside Plaza units included Maui County Councilman Lanny H. Morisaki; the immediate family of former state senator Nadao Yoshinaga (Yoshinaga represented Maui in the Legislature 1955-1966 and Waipahu on Oahu thereafter); the Maui Division Director of the ILWU, Thomas S. Yagi; singer Nephi Hanneman, who frequently provided entertainment at Democratic Party election rallies, including those of Gov. Ariyoshi and Sen. Wong; and a business associate and personal friend of Gov. Ariyoshi, Francis H. Yamada.

Another investor was Michael T. Suzuki, an architect sometimes retained to design buildings in which the Ariyoshis or their close associates such as Yamada were involved. For example, in the late 1960s Suzuki designed a condominium called The Coronet, near the Honolulu Academy of Arts. James Ariyoshi was a member of the project's development company. George Ariyoshi was the building's attorney. Both James and George bought units. Suzuki also in the early 1970s designed a west Maui condominium, the Kahana Sunset. One of the development company's principals was Francis Yamada. The law firm of which George Ariyoshi was then senior partner did legal work for the project's development company. Simultaneously Suzuki was among a handful of architects, most of them close associates of leading Democrats and most of them local-Japanese, who got a large share of the state's non-bid architectural contracts.

In 1974 Masaru Yokouchi bought Apt. 501 of the Lakeside Plaza from Wallace Yanagi. In 1981 he resold it.

There is a question as to whom.

Yokouchi said in several interviews for this book that he believed he was selling it to Sen. Wong. By Yokouchi's account, he negotiated the sale through an attorney, whom he always understood to be representing Wong.

A Democrat, Wong had been a member of the House 1966-1974, a senator since then, and president of the Senate since 1979. He was often identified in his earlier years as an independent, or a spokesman for liberals and dissidents.

For many years Wong's principal income was his legislator's salary. In 1979 he began to make small real estate investments and to work for real estate and development firms. In 1980 he got a real estate salesman's license.

In an interview for this book, Wong said that Yokouchi misunderstood, that the sale was actually to his uncle, Chu Ung Wong. Indeed on January 19 1981 Chu Ung Wong signed an agreement of sale for the unit. Yokouchi signed January 29, and the agreement was later recorded in the state Bureau of Conveyances. It indicates that the conveyance was to C.U.W. Corp., whose president and sole stockholder was Chu Ung Wong. (At the time the company's vice-president and secretary was nurseryman Sidney G.U. Goo, appointed by Gov. Ariyoshi in 1981 to the State Board of Agriculture.)

However there was another agreement of sale covering the same unit, this one signed by Sen. Wong on January 14 but apparently never recorded.

It was not possible to ascertain who else signed this earlier agreement. Yokouchi said he did not recall signing two agreements of sale for the same unit, but said it was possible he had forgotten that he had done so.

In an interview Wong said the reason he signed one of the agreements of sale was that he held a power of attorney for his uncle. Sen. Wong did not explain, however, why if this were so his uncle signed the second agreement on his own, nor why apparently only the agreement signed by his uncle was publicly recorded.

Whomever Yokouchi sold to, he did so at an apparent discount of at least $25,000.

As Table 19 indicates, Yokouchi sold for $52,000. For the previous three months all other reported sales in Lakeside Plaza had been for no less than $70,000; the two most recent were for about $72,000. The only other sales that occurred for two-thirds of a year after the Yokouchi sale were for about $73,000 each.

———————————————— **TABLE 19** ————————————————

LAKESIDE PLAZA ALL SALES OF UNITS FROM OCTOBER 1980 TO SEPTEMBER 1981

Note: The nine sales listed are all the sales which took place for units in this building between October 1980 and September 1981, as indicated by City and County of Honolulu real property tax records and documents on file with the State Bureau of Conveyances. The project developer retained the fee-simple interest in the land, hence this is a leasehold condominium. The figures on downpayments, time in which to pay off the balance owed, and percent interest to be paid on balance owed, came from conveyance documents. Some documents did not reveal these terms; in such cases these terms do not appear on the table. Nevertheless for all sales a state conveyance tax was paid; the amount of this tax is a matter of public record and provides a usually reliable indication of sale price when the actual conveyance documents do not provide the sale price. All conveyances were agreements of sale or sub-agreements of sale. In computing the average downpayment for all sales other than that to Wong, the sale of apartment 305 was left out. Although the total purchase price of this unit at about $73,000 was in line with most other sales and therefore comparable in that respect, still the $45,000 downpayment was atypical, as was the 8.75% interest rate, which likewise was omitted from computations as to average interest rates charged on unpaid balances, and the ten years in which to pay the balance, which also was left out.

SALE DATE	UNIT	PRICE	DOWNPAYMENT	TIME TO PAY BALANCE	INTEREST ON BALANCE
10-24-80	606	$70,000	$28,000	4 years	11.5%
11-14-80	802	$70,000			
11-19-80	603	$70,000	$10,000	3 years	11.8%
12-12-80	303	$70,000			
12-22-80	706	$72,000	$12,000	3 years	11.5%
1-15-81	705	$71,900	$17,000	3 years	11%
1-29-81	501	$52,000	$ 5,000	1 year	10%
3-30-81	604	$73,000			
9-9-81	305	$73,470	$45,000	10 years	8.75%

Furthermore, Yokouchi agreed to accept a $5,000 down payment at a time when all other known down payments in Lakeside Plaza sales were averaging nearly $17,000. Finally, Yokouchi accepted an interest rate of 10% on the unpaid balance, at a time when rates in all other known sales in the building averaged 11.5%. Conservatively, Yokouchi's buyer saved $25,000 by all of these arrangements.

The only major term in the Yokouchi sale that could have been considered unfavorable to the buyer had to do with the amount of time which the buyer was given to pay the balance owing after the down payment. The Yokouchi sale and all comparable Lakeside Plaza sales involved agreements or sub-agreements of sale, in which a large portion of the sale price was to be paid by the buyer at the end of the agreement period in one lump sum, called a "balloon payment." In such cases initial finance for the buyer was provided by the seller rather than, say, by a bank, until the end of the agreement, when the buyer normally went to a conventional lending institution to obtain financing for the balloon payment.

By the terms of the publicly recorded agreement of sale, Yokouchi's buyer was given only one year to make his balloon payment, as against about three years in most of the other sales. At the time of the Yokouchi sale, interest rates on conventional loans were high and it appeared that they would remain so. Thus, to have only one year to make the balloon payment seemed like a disadvantage.

But the balloon payment was not made within a year. Indeed four years later, in early 1985, it still had not been made, according to both Yokouchi and Sen. Wong.

Yokouchi said the reason for all of these favorable terms was that he believed that he was selling to Sen. Wong. Wong was an old friend, and Yokouchi had been told by a mutual friend that Wong was then low on funds. Yokouchi said that prior to 1981, Sen. Wong was living in the unit as his tenant, though paying only a nominal rent. Yokouchi said that at some point the mutual friend suggested that Yokouchi sell the unit to Wong at a discount.

Yokouchi said he was agreeable to helping Wong out, and so negotiated the sale of the unit through a lawyer whom he took to be representing Wong.

Yokouchi said that neither he nor anyone representing him checked to see how sale prices were running in the Lakeside Plaza at the time, so he had no clear idea of the current market value of his unit. He said the lawyer with whom he negotiated said that sales were running between $60,000 and $70,000, and then, on behalf of his client, offered Yokouchi $50,000. Yokouchi said that a price in the neighborhood of $50,000 would represent a satisfactory profit over what he paid in 1974—about $39,000. Also, since Yokouchi was a real estate broker, he could broker the sale himself, saving about $3,000 in a commission that the seller would normally pay to a broker; Yokouchi felt he could pass this savings along to Wong. Since Yokouchi was agreeable to helping out Sen. Wong, he settled with the lawyer on

$52,000. Along with the other terms this was an apparent discount of at least $25,000.

In an interview Sen. Wong said he did not think the discount was as large as that, but said "I have no idea" what the actual amount was.

Whatever the discount, Sen. Wong said that Yokouchi gave it as a favor to him and not to his uncle.

Although Wong also said that the sale "definitely benefits me," he said it did so only because he got to live in the unit, and not because he profited financially—"it's not my money that's in it."

Both Wong and Yokouchi said in addition that Yokouchi never asked Wong a political favor in return. They both said that they never did any private business together, either.

Yokouchi has said that many times in his business career he helped out friends who were in difficult financial straits, most of whom were not in politics and were in no way influential. Several other people interviewed corroborated this; Yokouchi was reputed to be very generous, and in addition throughout his adult life had spent a great deal of time doing volunteer work in the areas of sports, the arts, and vocational rehabilitation.

For Yokouchi, giving Sen. Wong a break on a condominium unit was another act of generosity. What it also represented was another strand in a network of ties connecting persons prominent in land and politics in Hawaii's Democratic years.

*   *   *

After the 1966 Land Board decision allowing IDCo to fill much of Salt Lake, the next time IDCo went before a government agency on a major question was 1972-1973, asking the Land Use Commission for 30 more acres for apartments along Salt Lake's western shore.

Between 1966 and 1972, opposition to development in Hawaii had increased markedly among some sections of the community, becoming linked on the one hand with the nationwide environmental movement of those years and on the other with specifically locally-based community movements.

In hearings before the LUC in 1972, IDCo ran into a firestorm of opposition, mostly organized by young people, who booed IDCo speakers and stood up and yelled at LUC members. IDCo was accused of "lying and deceit" for indicating to the LUC in 1964 and the City Council in 1965 that the lake would be retained, and then applying in 1966 for a permit to fill it. Clarence Ching's relationship to Gov. Burns was pointed out, as were Ching's campaign contributions to Honolulu Mayor Frank Fasi. Angry statements were made that politicians manipulated governmental decisions to enhance Ching's profits. Speakers urged not only that the latest rezoning application be denied, but that the 1966 decision to fill the lake be rolled back.[32]

Not only the young and radical were opposed to what IDCo had done and wanted to do at Salt Lake. Now the LUC professional staff also went on the public record opposing more apartments, arguing that "the areas pres- ently developed by petitioner, particularly the high-rise apartment areas, already give the impression that desirable densities may be exceeded when the Lakeside project is ultimately completed."[33] The City Planning Com- mission also recommended denial.

Within the Salt Lake community itself there was now substantial opposi- tion to more development. In 1966 the bulk of Salt Lake lot buyers sup- ported the filling of the lake and IDCo's overall development plan. On the eve of the 1973 LUC decision, the Lakeside Community Association re- versed a previous endorsement of the proposed new rezoning. This hap- pened despite the fact that a host of minor establishment figures, most of them local-Asian, supported the IDCo proposal, including past community association officers, the local elementary school principal, the president of the PTA, a Boy Scout troop master, and the coach of a boys' baseball team.

The LUC unanimously denied IDCo's petition.

In the area of government decisions it was the first serious reversal IDCo had experienced at Salt Lake.

But there were still large areas of already-zoned land to build on at Salt Lake, much of the lake still be filled in, and the golf course to be built. These things went ahead.

* * *

By the early 1980s most of the lake had been filled. Most of the native Hawaiian birds were gone, replaced by species able to adapt to an urban environment: mynahs, cardinals, doves, sparrows. Members of the Hono- lulu International Country Club, including businessmen from Japan, played on the golf course. The club employed about 150 local people.

Most of IDCo's urban development had gone in. Though there were a number of relatively expensive condominiums by the lake, the apartment district overall was considered something of an underclass area by many better-off people who lived elsewhere. This was because quite a few resi- dents were military, or low-income families in buildings purchased by the Hawaii Housing Authority, or young local families who could not afford anything else.

The Damons, following their large land sales in the late 1950s and 1960s, had passed from active participation in the scene, but still collected large amounts of money from the estate. Damon Estate derived a good deal of its continuing income from leasing about 220 acres of industrial land in the general Salt Lake area to various businesses, and from securities, including its 23% ownership of First Hawaiian Bank. The estate also owned a ranch on the Big Island and one in California. In 1979 each of the estate's five trustees was paid about $154,000. There were then 13 estate beneficiaries dividing eight full shares of estate income, with five beneficiaries receiving a full share each, and the other eight beneficiaries dividing the balance. In 1979 the holder of a full share received about $1 million.[34]

Also collecting income were the many owners of IDCo, most of whom were not listed in any public record.

Then there was Clarence Ching. He made a fortune out of real estate in the Democratic years, and a large part of this must have been made at Salt Lake. He was a man much honored and respected by his peers in his day. He had risen by hard work and intelligence from humble beginnings on Kauai. While he was making his money he was doing other things in the community as well. For example, at the very time he was developing Salt Lake, he founded a non-profit corporation that undertook development of the 822-unit Kukui Gardens urban renewal project in Honolulu's Chinatown, built for low-income people, reportedly at no personal profit to Ching.[35]

By the early 1970s, however, his name had become less respected by many people. In 1973 *Honolulu Advertiser* reporter Bob Krauss wrote: "I asked four people what comes to mind at the mention of Clarence Ching. They answered: 'Salt Lake ... rip off ... political connections ... shady deals.'"[36]

*   *   *

Taking a broader view, it might be said that Ching, like any number of others, could be seen moving with a strong current of contemporary Hawaii history that brought together prominent Democrats, land developers, and family members, among other people, in the urbanization of the Islands. The prime movers in this process believed in the rightness and soundness of what they were doing, both in politics and business. In promoting or approving IDCo's Salt Lake development, they saw themselves as helping at one and the same time the former underdogs of life in Hawaii, society in general by stimulating the economy, and themselves. For a well-connected Democrat to refrain from acting because, for example, a family member or an associate might directly benefit would be making a mountain out of a molehill. Better by far to make a high-rise development and a golf course out of a lake.

11

KAUAI: NUKOLII

In the fall of 1974 a land use commissioner and a reporter were having a talk about the Kauai phase of a statewide review that the Commission was just winding up.

As the Land Use Law was then written, the State Land Use Commission (LUC) was required every five years to conduct such a study, and then rewrite rules and redistrict lands where appropriate.

That year there had been a great deal of media and public attention on the review. A rising environmental consciousness in the Islands had collided with the largest group of major development plans to be considered at one time in the history of Hawaii. Hearings had been the lengthiest the LUC had ever experienced, at times punctuated by disruptions, and a whole set of community organizations had come into existence specifically to protest particular developments at LUC hearings.

Statewide a total of 228 separate items had been considered, including some proposals by the LUC itself, which in general were to downzone certain lands into agricultural or conservation districts.

On Kauai attention had been focused on major resort plans for Hanalei, Kilauea, Poipu and Mahaulepu, covering altogether more than 3,000 acres and likely to have great impacts on economic growth and the natural environment. In addition, in places like Wailua Homesteads and Kalaheo, there were proposals for what on Kauai would have been medium to large-sized residential projects.

Most of the conversation that passed between the reporter and the land use commissioner concerned the large resort plans.

At one point, though, the commissioner made a passing reference to a small resort planned for just north of Lihue. He said something like: "Say, you know that area that's proposed for urban by the beach at Hanamaulu? There's this powerful guy from Maui involved in it and it's going to pass."

The reporter thought this was an interesting piece of intelligence. But then, he had almost no idea where the place was, or even if it had a name. In any case, it was only indicated by LUC records to be 66 acres, much too small to care about.

A month or two before this discussion the Commission had denied the largest resort proposed for Kauai at the time, at Mahaulepu. In December, at the end of its review, the LUC turned down all the other major resort proposals for the island.

The 66-acre Hanamaulu project passed, however.

* * *

Ten years later the mayor of Kauai was being interviewed about the same place.

He seemed bewildered, as did many people by 1984, by the size and intensity of a conflict that had begun three years after the LUC decision, over the planned resort.

The mayor pointed out to the interviewer that "no one knew where Gettysburg was till they had the battle there."

It was the same for those 66 acres, later revised in government land use records to 60 acres, now known to everyone by a Hawaiian name—Nukolii.

* * *

Nukolii.

Before 1977 it did not exist by name for most people.

Back then you could ask most Kauai residents where Nukolii was—even those who had lived on the island their whole lives—and they would not know.

The 1974 edition of the authoritative *Place Names of Hawaii*, by Mary K. Pukui, Samuel H. Elbert and Esther T. Mookini, contained about 4,000 entries. Nukolii was not one of them.

The word nevertheless was an apparently now-obscure, old Hawaiian place name.

The Lihue Plantation Co. owned the area from sometime in the nineteenth century. About 1900 the company had a map prepared of all its holdings in the Lihue-Hanamaulu area. The work was done by M. D. Monsarrat, a leading Hawaii surveyor and map maker.

Apparently some or even much of what became a resort in the 1980s was indicated on Monsarrat's map to have been a marsh. Just to the south of where the resort went was a fenced-off area of about five acres. Perhaps this was a small pasture, a precursor of the dairy that was operated in the area later in the twentieth century. At about where in the early 1980s a Hilton hotel was going up, there is written "Nukoli."[1]

Whether the correct spelling and pronunciation of the word involved one "i" or two is now apparently lost, as is whatever the word might have meant, however said or written.

For the few who knew the area in the years just before Nukolii became a political battleground, it was called the old Hanamaulu or Nukolii Dairy, referring to an 11-acre operation that passed out of existence in the late 1960s. During World War II there had been a marine camp nearby, some remains of which existed into the 1980s. At some point the state and county governments established baseyards in the general area. They too were still there into the 1980s, to the north of the resort site, separated from it by a line of ironwood trees and a small stream or ditch.

Just to the north of the baseyards was the county's Wailua Golf Course. Immediately to the south of Nukolii was the plantation community of Hanamaulu. Slightly to the south of that was the county seat of Lihue.

Although for years a plantation owned Nukolii, although sugar cane had long grown just inland from it, and although state and county land use maps since the early 1960s had designated the general area agricultural, still at Nukolii itself the soil was sandy and of virtually no farming value. The University of Hawaii's Land Study Bureau (LSB), using an agricultural suitability scale from "A" to "E" with "E" the worst, rated Nukolii "D." Translated that meant "poor."[2] Furthermore, after the LSB determination and for a few years after the dairy closed, there was an open pit sand and coral-mining operation at Nukolii, further lessening whatever agricultural value the land might have had. Throughout, farming would have been hampered by hard onshore winds that blew much of the year. By the time the resort plan became controversial, there was only the occasional horse or cow grazing at Nukolii.

If Nukolii by the 1970s did not recommend itself for agriculture, it was also to some extent an unlikely resort location.

When in 1978 a developer petitioned the County for hotel zoning, the developer's attorney wrote that the project would need windbreaks since most of the year direct onshore tradewinds blew at between 13 and 24 miles an hour. Indeed so strong and constant were these winds that ironwood trees along Nukolii's shore reached only very small heights and were permanently bent in an inland direction—a sort of natural *bonsai* effect.

The attorney also wrote that "for a good part of the year, rough waters with strong currents, including rip tides and undertow, are common occurrences. Swimming during these periods will not be advised, but discouraged."[3]

Moreover there was a reef close in along the entire Nukolii shore, so that even during the periods when the ocean was calm, Nukolii was still very undesirable for swimming.

In 1972 an appraiser for the landowner took note of these natural features, also of the nearness of the baseyards and the fact that at that time Nukolii's land use classifications permitted essentially no development. He believed, despite all this, that Nukolii ought to be considered an eventual resort site, but that its value as such should be reduced by 25% "by reason of the foregoing elements of inferiority."[4]

If inferior as a resort location compared to, say, Poipu, still there were things about Nukolii that definitely recommended resort use. The area had wonderful views of coastal mountains to both the north and south. Nukolii was quite near Kauai's main airport, also to places for shopping and entertainment. As mentioned, a public golf course was right next door. Kauai, like most Hawaiian islands, was impossible to drive completely around. For tourists wanting to see as much of the island as possible Nukolii would be a good place to stay, since it was roughly equidistant from where the main road ended going in either direction.

Also, all of the roughness of the natural environment at Nukolii had another side to it—it could cause a feeling of great distance from cities like Los Angeles and Tokyo. Nukolii was a place where even if a person was blown around a bit, he or she could feel far away and alone, and still inside.

* * *

Nukolii's owner in 1972 had the place appraised in preparation for offering it for sale.

A sale did occur not long after, in 1973 and 1974 in two segments, setting in motion a complex chain of events that became, as the *Honolulu Advertiser*'s Kauai reporter wrote in 1984, "the most wrenching political issue in Kauai's history."[5]

If the sale had significant effects it also had had important causes; it not only pushed events forward but had in turn been stimulated by others.

As mentioned, Lihue Plantation had owned Nukolii since sometime in the nineteenth century.

Since the latter part of that century the predecessor to the Big Five firm of Amfac had been agent for the plantation. With most Hawaii sugar companies their agents eventually came to substantially or entirely own them; this was so with Lihue Plantation. Thus it was Amfac, in essence, that owned and sold Nukolii in 1973 and 1974.

In Hawaii's Republican years Amfac and the other large owners seldom sold land. Entering the early post-World War II years they slowly began to. A decade later the pace picked up with the start of the Islands' land boom. At Amfac, following the ascent to its presidency in 1967 of Henry A. Walker Jr., there began a sustained sales program, the first large one being to an oil company in 1968—all but 50 of the 11,000-acre Princeville Ranch on Kauai's north shore.

Now in a much more dynamic business age, Amfac was selling for such reasons as to help finance diversification and expansion onto the US mainland. At times as well the company now sold to bolster earnings when one or another of its lines of business faltered. To a degree all of these reasons were related to efforts to avoid an unfriendly takeover.

In 1973, the year Nukolii was sold, Amfac's retail operations were suffering, and Walker reportedly believed he needed cash to compensate.

Since the nineteenth century, Amfac and its predecessor had had one of Hawaii's most successful department stores, called Liberty House since the end of World War I. The expansion that followed Walker's becoming president tended to be by way of acquiring mainland companies that were in areas of business with which Amfac was already familiar. Thus in 1969 Amfac bought two high quality department store chains that had locations throughout western American states: Joseph Magnin Co. Inc. and Rhodes Western.

Where Amfac's Retail Division in 1968 had accounted for but 16% of the company's revenues, in 1970 the figure stood at 42%. By then renamed the Retail Group, it now contributed "more than any other Company group to Amfac's revenues and net income," according to the company's 1970 annual report to stockholders.

Despite this impressive growth, the report also said that "during much of 1970, Joseph Magnin sustained a decline in business, owing in part to the general decline in U.S. retail activity and in part to the fashion controversy over whether and by how much women's skirt lengths should drop."

Problems continued through 1971 and 1972, and the next year as well was a bad one for the Retail Group. That year's annual report said that "Amfac did not quite meet its goal for increased earnings per primary share in 1973. One factor which kept the Company from reaching its target . . . was the inability of its continental US retail stores to perform anywhere near expectations."

Amfac attributed much of the difficulty now to general distress in the US retail clothing business. This was said to be due to a number of national and world problems—things like price controls, energy shortages, rising interest rates, and so on.

Real estate sales in Hawaii were stepped up in 1973, reportedly to compensate for this downturn in retailing. Thus as a consequence of, first, the inability of American women and/or fashion designers to decide how much leg to expose, and then of general economic problems in the US and in other countries, Nukolii was put on the block. It was sold in two increments in June 1973 and January 1974 for a combined total of $1.2 million.

Nukolii's buyer was Masaru Yokouchi of Maui. Upon negotiating the purchase he in turn organized a large limited partnership, or *hui*, that became the actual buyer/owner.

Yokouchi said in an interview for this book that he initially learned that Nukolii might be for sale when he heard that Angel Maehara, once an aide to former Honolulu Mayor Neal S. Blaisdell, had an option on a parcel of Amfac land in the Hanamaulu area. Yokouchi at first thought the option pertained to Nukolii. As it turned out it was for land in Hanamaulu Valley. (Maehara did not exercise his option.)

Once Yokouchi expressed interest in looking at some of Amfac's land on Kauai, he said he was shown not only Nukolii, but also Ninini Point just outside of Lihue, and an approximately 360-acre area in Moloaa, a fairly undeveloped region well along the road to Kauai's remote north shore.

At about the same time in mid-1973 that Yokouchi negotiated for Nukolii, Amfac was selling most of its prime commercial property in Lihue, including the Lihue Shopping Center, to wealthy businessman Harry Weinberg, who at the time also bought some light-industrial property in Lihue from Amfac.

By various measures the Weinberg sales appeared back then to have been much more significant than that to Yokouchi. For one, of all the Amfac sales of real estate on Kauai in and around this time, those to Weinberg involved by far the most money. For the Lihue Shopping Center alone Weinberg paid nearly three times what Yokouchi paid for Nukolii. As an index of perceptions of which of the Amfac sales mattered most at the time, there was the fact that Kauai newspeople paid vastly greater attention to the Weinberg sales than to the Yokouchi sale.

As indicated, in some respects Amfac had been under economic pressure to sell off assets like Nukolii. This was a general pressure, though, not specific to Nukolii; it could just as easily have led to the sale of, say, Ninini Point instead. Nukolii's buyers, on the other hand, would be under much greater pressure to get something done with the area.

Amfac, for example, had owned the land for many years and therefore was not having to repay a loan on it. Furthermore Nukolii's real property tax costs to Amfac were not onerous—as of the early 1970s about $1,000 a year. The company of course owned a great deal of other land; to an extent it had the choice of holding onto Nukolii for an indefinite period, waiting for a favorable moment to sell or attempt to build.

The economics of the Yokouchi *hui* involvement, on the other hand, dictated a different orientation. Given the sale price and the effect it would have on assessed value as assigned by the State Department of Taxation, real property taxes were going to rise once the sale became known to state assessors. Indeed a newspaper story in April 1974 about the sale to Yokouchi, plus the LUC redistricting in December 1974, led an assessor to value the site as a potential resort beginning in 1975, rather than as agricultural land. Thus, whereas assessed value was $77,000 in 1973 and 1974, this jumped to nearly $2 million in 1975. This meant that the tax bill would have been just over $1,000 in 1974; it would have gone to about $32,000 in 1975. Also, the *hui* was made up of mostly middle-class people who collectively had to make regular payments to Amfac as well as pay property taxes that were about to go up. With Nukolii they were speculators, not builders; they made their payments in the hope of a resale at a profit. And, in fact, after owning for only about two-thirds of a year, and before the jump in real property tax assessment, the *hui* was able to resell, to a Hawaii subsidiary of Pacific Standard Life Insurance Co., based in Davis, California. Having bought for $1.2 million the *hui* resold for $5.25 million.

Pacific Standard indicated it wanted to build. Also, the price the company paid was essentially for developable land at a time when the land had no urban-type zoning whatsoever. Pacific Standard thus had great need to push forward on rezoning. A buyer in 1980 of the portion of Nukolii that by then was fully zoned was a developer who paid a price that one would only pay for a resort site. The economics of the developer's situation impelled it to attempt to build.

So, beginning in 1973, the shifts in ownership created, from then on, a degree of unyielding pressure on the government land use approval process, pressure that might not have been there had Amfac remained the owner.

That Amfac might not have needed to move as quickly or push as hard as the *hui* or Pacific Standard was indicated by Amfac's behavior vis-a-vis two other potential resort sites which it owned in the general Lihue area:

During 1975 and 1976 the Kauai County Planning Department worked on a regional development plan for the Lihue area.[6] Called the Lihue Development Plan (LDP) it was in essence a refinement for that area of the county's 1970 general plan.

Those preparing the LDP initially considered for resort use some Amfac land at the northwest corner of Hanamaulu Bay.

While the LDP was underway the company decided to ask that Hanamaulu be withdrawn from consideration, which it was. Reportedly Amfac thought that, of various potential resort sites it owned in the general region, this one was of relatively poor quality. For one thing, the beach area that its visitors would go to faced east and had moderately high ground behind it, meaning that it shaded up early in the day. Marshlands in nearby Hanamaulu Valley produced a lot of mosquitoes—not a plus for a resort. As well the site had drainage problems, and its ability to expand much beyond a first increment was restricted by the existence of a fair amount of housing in the area.

All of these factors would probably have been noted by any owner of this property. But an owner in the position of either the *hui* or Pacific Standard would have had a much harder time suggesting that it not be rezoned.

Amfac also owned a potential resort site at Ninini Point, near the Kauai Surf Hotel, for which the company had been trying to obtain resort zoning on and off since at least the late 1960s. Delays had principally to do with waiting for the State Department of Transportation to realign the runway at the nearby Lihue Airport. Amfac did not even succeed in getting urban districting for Ninini until 1983. Again it is reasonable to assume that an investment *hui*, or a developer in Pacific Standard's shoes in Nukolii, would have had much more trouble being so patient.

Regardless of what might have been, Amfac sold Nukolii and the *hui* resold, touching off a long and spectacular chain of events.

*   *   *

In early 1977 the Kauai Planning Commission finished with the Lihue Development Plan (LDP) and sent it on to the County Council.

Nukolii was within the LDP planning area.

In the overall regulation of land use on Kauai, three highly discretionary decisions were normally pivotal in deciding whether a resort would eventually be allowed at a place like Nukolii.

They were, first, land use districting, a function of the State Land Use Commission; and second and third, establishing the county general plan classification and county zoning, both of which were primarily up to the County Council. (The Planning Commission was merely advisory on these matters. The mayor had veto power over Council decisions on both general plan and zoning items by the time Nukolii started making its way through the county, but with a two-thirds majority the Council could override the mayor.)

Nukolii in 1974 had been given urban districting by the LUC. The next hurdle was the Lihue Development Plan, since the LDP would in effect be the county general plan for the Lihue area.

The LDP as approved by the Planning Commission, and thus as things stood when it reached the Council, contained a resort classification for Nukolii.

There had been a 15-member citizens advisory committee (CAC) chosen by the Planning Commission to make input on the LDP at the Planning Department stage, meaning essentially during 1975 and 1976.

The CAC was a cross section of people living and/or working in the general Lihue area. Research for this book indicated that a majority of the CAC either did not support, or may even have opposed, a resort at Nukolii. Nevertheless they had their minds changed or their objections overridden by the LDP's consultants and/or by the Planning Commission, both of which favored a resort.

This early difference of opinion and its resolution occurred politely and quietly; a faint sign of things to come, not only with respect to a coming major public dispute over Nukolii, but also, when all the dust settled a decade later, as to final outcome.

At a meeting in 1975 apparently attended by 12 CAC members, a vote was conducted by the consultants on which of four possible sites, if any, in the Lihue area might be advisable for resort development. The four were, moving from south to north: Ninini Point; the northwest corner of Hanamaulu Bay; Nukolii; and the Lydgate Park/Kauai Resort Hotel area, near where the Wailua River flowed into the sea.

Ninini got zero votes, Hanamaulu seven, Nukolii two and Lydgate three.

Of the four sites, two ultimately got resort designations in the final LDP: Ninini and Nukolii.[7]

It is something of an irony that the two locations that were not finally classified resort got a combined 83% of the CAC votes, while the two that were made resort got only 17%.

How this happened is not altogether clear, but appears to be as follows:

Following the vote there was apparently only one CAC meeting at which there was active discussion of whether to classify any vacant lands in the Lihue region for resort use.

According to the minutes, one of the consultant companies' planners, Richard Senelly, pointed out that the CAC had early on opted for a certain overall population and economic growth rate for the area. He explained that for that growth to occur "resort development [in general] *must* happen."[8] The question thus was not whether new lands would be designated resort, but which lands.

At some point the Hanamaulu Bay option was withdrawn at Amfac's request. Perhaps it had happened by the time of this meeting in that there was no reference to Hanamaulu in the minutes. (On the other hand there was also no discussion of Ninini, and Ninini was definitely still in the running.) In any case, according to the minutes, discussion was limited to Nukolii and Lydgate.

As reflected in the minutes, the thrust of Senelly's argument was for Nukolii and against Lydgate. He pointed out that development of Nukolii would provide the kind of growth stimulator for Lihue that the CAC indicated it wanted. Lydgate, on the other hand, was actually much nearer the Wailua-Kapaa area, the urban region to the north of Lihue, and would really have much more impact on and benefit for that area than on Lihue.

After Senelly spoke several CAC members reacted. Apparently all CAC people who did so said they opposed making Nukolii a resort. There is no record of anyone speaking in favor of developing Nukolii. The minutes say: "Discussion followed on the reason committee members were against resort use at Nukolii. One member felt that there are areas already zoned for resort uses which are available and believed that hotel development should go to these zoned areas. Another member felt that by developing a hotel in such an isolated area, the ancillary services accompanying such a hotel detracts from the commercial activities in Lihue rather than complement them."[9]

Taken together the voting and the above minutes would appear to indicate either CAC non-support for a resort at Nukolii, or even opposition.

On the other hand, there is the fact that on several later occasions when the CAC was polled on all land use changes being proposed by the Planning Commission and consultants, one of which would designate Nukolii for resort use, there is no record of anyone objecting.

Also, one must wonder how the voting would have gone if the Hanamaulu site that got seven votes—58% of the total—had not been an option at the time of the vote. On the ground, the area was not that close to Nukolii—about half a mile. On the map that the CAC members viewed when voting, the two areas appeared to be fairly close. If not wanting more resort development at Ninini and Lydgate was part of what motivated those who voted for Hanamaulu—and development proposals for both Ninini and Lydgate had been controversial in the recent past—then, if there had been no Hanamaulu option and if CAC members felt they had to vote for at least one place, Nukolii would have been the obvious next best choice.

Also, some of the things that initially made Nukolii controversial might have made development of Hanamaulu even more controversial. Most especially, the shoreline area to which guests at a Hanamaulu resort would probably have gone would have been the beach at Hanamaulu Bay, a place more heavily used by local people than Nukolii. Also, although Nukolii had long had agricultural classifications on state and county land use maps, it was in fact of no current farming value. Hanamaulu, on the other hand, would have taken sugar cane land then in actual use. From at least the time of the drafting of the State Land Use Law in 1961, a major—at times paramount— concern of all types of people analyzing the pros and cons of particular developments was whether usable farmland would be lost.

On balance, though, given what the CAC actually did with what it actually had to go on, and given what several committee members said regarding Nukolii, the record of the CAC was one of latent non-support for or even opposition toward development there. But as mentioned, apparently these feelings were weakly held and easily overridden or minds changed by consultants and the Planning Commission who, on grounds of recognized planning principles, saw value to the community in allowing a resort at Nukolii.

*   *   *

In the contemporary world it was not only residents of great metropolises that sought the peace of places like Nukolii, but Kauai residents as well.

For years local Kauai people, especially from Lihue, Hanamaulu, Wailua and Kapaa, had in small numbers gone surf casting and camping at Nukolii. They set nets just beyond the reef or cast hand-held nets inside of it. People dove for fish and lobsters; they picked squid, small crabs and *limu* (seaweed) from the reef. The reef had a surf break that surfers used. Nukolii was barren and flat, without trees or utility poles, and sometimes model airplane enthusiasts flew planes there on weekends. Motorcyclists drove along rutted dirt roads that criss-crossed the area. When jogging became the thing to do, joggers started to go to Nukolii, too.

It was this local use of Nukolii that in 1977 provided an initial base of opposition to development. But local use alone could probably never have produced opposition on the scale that eventually arose.

Kauai starting about 1969 had produced, as compared with the size of the island's population, as large and successful an environmental and anti-eviction movement as any in the state.

Exactly why this was so is unclear. Nevertheless one can notice several things that might explain it:

For one, unlike Oahu and Maui, no destination resort or major resort area was established on Kauai until after a vigorous environmental movement took hold. For the most part the movement had begun on Oahu and spilled over onto Kauai, taking on Kauai's major resort plans more or less from the start. This meant that opposition occurred before what eventually became the island's major resorts had much chance to develop sympathetic constituencies and dependency relationships—unlike what happened, for example, in the Kaanapali area of Maui.

Part of why Kauai started late in the destination resort business may have been because the Big Five firm that owned one of Kauai's major sites (Amfac, which owned the Princeville Ranch), also owned a much better one on Maui, at Kaanapali. Amfac began master-planning Kaanapali in the 1950s, and actual construction was underway in the very early 1960s. During those years the company also considered a resort at Princeville, but held the plans in abeyance. Amfac then decided to focus exclusively on Kaanapali, and in 1968 sold most of Princeville to an oil company. To the extent that Amfac's decision to build on Maui was based on a wish to get into the resort business at whatever was the best site the company had, Maui may have gotten a head start on Kauai, one which got Maui way down the resort development road before there existed many critics of urbanization in the Islands. Then again, Kauai may have lagged behind Maui because tourists may have thought Maui prettier or more interesting.

Another factor which is conceivably substantial but hard to gauge has to do with power structures. Specifically, Maui from the late 1950s through the end of the land boom in the mid-1970s had a far smaller and more stable structure. The Kauai County government, for example, from the late 1950s through the late 1970s, had six different elected chief executives. Maui, on the other hand, had only two all the way from 1949 to 1979: Edward F. Tam (1949–1966) and Elmer F. Cravalho (1967–1979). Moreover Cravalho, who was mayor during the years of greatest construction and greatest criticism of construction elsewhere in Hawaii, was a harsh disciplinarian whom many were disinclined to oppose on any issue.

Maui may have had more forceful leaders, period. Besides Cravalho there was Nadao Yoshinaga, who was born on Maui and represented Maui in the Legislature 1955–1966 (at which time, because of a reapportionment of the Legislature, he moved to leeward Oahu and ran successfully for the Senate there). Yoshinaga was one of the strongest and most accomplished leaders in all Hawaii during his years in politics, which ended in the mid-1970s, and he really had no counterpart on Kauai. During this period there were politicians of great distinction who had been born on Kauai, such as Spark M. Matsunaga and Sakae Takahashi, but they all left the island early and never represented Kauai as such in office.

Throughout the Democratic years the ILWU was a major power on the outer islands. From 1952–1983, Maui had but one director for the county's ILWU division, Thomas S. Yagi. Kauai during this time frame had at least half a dozen division directors. Also, Yagi throughout was a close supporter of Cravalho; with the Kauai division directors, some were close to the county's chief executive, some were not.

Gov. John Burns' chief aide on Maui, Masaru Yokouchi, was a close personal friend of Yagi and long a supporter of Cravalho too. Cravalho in turn, while a legislator had been aligned with Burns. Yokouchi was the man who bought Nukolii from Amfac, and in general was active in land investment and development. Yokouchi in effect helped bind together the Burns and ILWU and development segments of the power structure on Maui.

Yokouchi's counterpart on Kauai, Turk Tokita, rarely in a private capacity had anything to do with land.

Overall Maui compared to Kauai had a relatively small, compact, and enduring political/organized labor power structure, one that was altogether in support of rapid development. This meant there was less room on Maui than on Kauai for the emergence of serious alternative views on the subject of development.

Then too, Kauai's major newspaper throughout this period, *The Garden Island*, had an editor who more than perhaps any editor or news director in the state encouraged ordinary people to bring to the paper such things as their groups' announcements and their personal complaints about government. She also opposed quite a few developments. Everyday kind of Kauai people fighting mass evictions and/or development thus had a ready means of mass communication not possessed by such people on any other island.

Some people, in reflecting on how Kauai developed such strong anti-development populism, talk of a singular independence on the part of Kauai people, something that, it is occasionally argued, traces back to the fact that of all the Hawaiian Islands, Kauai was the only one never physically taken by the Hawaiian king who conquered the other islands.

One factor in all this that is less speculative is that in the fall of 1972, before much construction had taken place on Kauai, a medium-sized landowner/landlord attempted to evict a lot of its old-time tenants to make way for a resort.[10] Most of these people were working-class. This move had major repercussions, greatly stimulating the then-small environmental movement around the island. No evictions of this sort happened on Maui, nor anywhere else in the state except Oahu, for that matter.

The Kauai movement had begun with a few scattered protests over relatively small development proposals for scenic coastal areas like Hanalei and Poipu.

Of these early skirmishes, that over Poipu in about 1969–1970 was apparently the largest. At issue was whether the county government, in expanding a beach park, should condemn a lot that was leased to a major hotel corporation, Island Holidays Ltd., which wanted to use the parcel to expand its Waiohai Hotel. (At about this time Amfac bought Island Holidays.) At one point Kauai Community College students collected about 5,000 signatures on a petition favoring acquisition. Eventually the county bought the lot.[11]

Things on Kauai got underway in real earnest when about 20 families, tenants of Kanoa Estate Inc., living in the old communities of Niumalu and Nawiliwili near Nawiliwili Harbor, got eviction notices in the fall of 1972. The balance of Kanoa's tenants in the area—about 20 more families—feared they would be next. All 40 or so banded together to oppose evictions and pressure government officials with control over land use to disallow the intensive development plans that Kanoa and its developers had for the area.[12]

The Niumalu-Nawiliwili Tenants Association (NNTA) around Christmas 1972 put on the first political demonstration that Kauai had seen for many years. About 100 sign-carrying people, virtually all local adult residents of Niumalu and Nawiliwili, staged a short march to the County Building in Lihue.[13] One had to look back to the decade after World War II when the ILWU was fighting to establish itself on Kauai to find parallel actions that, for Kauai, were as radical.

The NNTA late in 1973 turned out the largest crowd Kauai had ever seen attend a public hearing on a land use question—about 200 people. In preparation for this County Planning Commission hearing, the organization obtained signatures on a petition amounting to about 20% of Kauai's adults. Moreover the NNTA chief spokesman, Stanford H. Achi, in essence ran a good portion of the hearing by being allowed to handle introductions of NNTA speakers in an order that his organization had worked out. These speakers were mostly local working-class residents of Niumalu and Nawiliwili—the kind of people who seldom aired their thoughts in public on a major community issue. Their testimony took up most of the meeting. The subject of the hearing was a county consultant's report recommending a resort in Niumalu.[14] The County eventually shelved the report. Thereafter neither state nor county ever rezoned land in Niumalu or Nawiliwili over the objections of the NNTA.

In the early and mid-1970s the activities of the NNTA became a training ground and model for other local people on Kauai who opposed urbanization of areas with which they were concerned for whatever reasons.

Significantly for what was coming over Nukolii, the depth of the NNTA's opposition to evictions was to be tested in the spring of 1977, only a few weeks before a developer first unveiled resort plans for Nukolii.

* * *

Most of Kanoa Estate's several hundred acres in Niumalu and Nawiliwili had state and county land use designations that allowed little or no development. As indicated the NNTA worked hard to keep it that way. A result, as intended, was that the NNTA was able to forestall evictions in these areas since the landlord had no really profitable alternative to renting to the tenants.

One approximately 14-acre parcel on a hillside in Nawiliwili, however, had long had multi-family zoning, and Kanoa in 1974 sold it to a development group based in Honolulu.

Once the fact of the sale and a subsequent condominium development plan became known to the NNTA, the organization sought to have the County downzone the land to prevent development. Failing in that, the group dug in behind a dwindling number of what had originally been about 10 tenant families. Tenants of both Niumalu and Nawiliwili plus outside supporters announced that they would get arrested if necessary to underline their opposition to the eviction of low and middle income local families, who were being displaced for what the NNTA believed would be high-priced condominiums.[15]

In the late spring of 1977 things came to a head in such a way as to generate the most highly-charged atmosphere Kauai had yet seen over a development question.

For one thing, the developer initially was to have been an entity called Nawiliwili Joint Venture (NJV), which was a partnership of two small Oahu-based corporations: Bishop Development Inc., which had bought the 14 acres from Kanoa in 1974, and Read Development Inc. (This Bishop had no relationship to or affiliation with the founders of the Bishop Estate, or with Bishop Insurance, or with a major Hawaii bank that for years bore the name Bishop, which today is First Hawaiian Bank.)

As of 1976 a Honolulu contractor named Stanley T. Ota was an officer and roughly half-owner of Bishop. In September of that year he was arrested along with five others in a major heroin bust on Oahu. When arrested Ota had about $250,000 worth of heroin in his car, according to the federal Drug Enforcement Administration agent-in-charge in Honolulu, John Y. Y. Lee, who also said that those picked up were central to Hawaii organized crime heroin operations.[16] Then, several months after his arrest, Ota was found murdered in a housing construction site at Aliamanu on Oahu.[17]

Adding to a suspicion that there might have been some general organized crime involvement with NJV was the fact that a man who was to be a minor contractor on the Nawiliwili project, Louis K. Rego, was reputed by law enforcement authorities to be a chief organizer of illegal gambling on Kauai.

The Hawaii Crime Commission in a report published in 1978, *Organized Crime In Hawaii*, wrote that Rego in the early to mid-1970s, together with another man, "established a profit-sharing relationship from gambling games [on Kauai] and levied collection on a number of gambling events not organized by them."[18] The man with whom Rego allegedly controlled these gambling interests was Fendel P. "Ding" Oclit, who also worked for a time for Rego's contracting firm. According to Honolulu police Oclit had formerly been a gunman for, first, Francis L. Burke and then Harold K. "Biggie" Chan, two Oahu syndicate leaders who were murdered in 1970 and 1972 respectively, some time after which Oclit came to Kauai.[19]

Subsequent to the Crime Commission's study, attorneys for both Rego and Oclit denied the report's allegations or disputed their thrust.[20]

In late April 1977, about the time that the NJV-NNTA conflict was climaxing, the home of the NNTA leader directly in charge in Nawiliwili, Edward Panui Jr., burned to the ground.

The county fire inspector said that he "couldn't find the cause." Tenants and supporters, however, believed the cause was arson. They said neighbors had heard a sound like an explosion at the start of the fire; that there was a fresh trail through tall grass and bushes behind the house, leading to a seldom-used road nearby which could allow an altogether unnoticed exit from the general area; and that it was singular that the fire involved the NNTA's chief leader in that particular fight.[21]

There were also things about the timing of the fire that were noteworthy. For one it occurred while no one was home. For another it came not long after NJV had lost a round in court that set back its eviction timetable considerably; immediately after the fire, NJV obtained a court order barring Panui from rebuilding, effectively evicting him in far less time than it appeared it was going to take. Next, at the time of the fire a notice of foreclosure was pending against the project, filed by NJV's lender, so NJV was under considerable pressure to get moving on construction. Finally, about a week after the fire, the NNTA reported that a shed in Niumalu housing its files on NJV had been broken into and all the files stolen.

About a week after the fire, a completely unrelated event increased considerably the fears of violence that were growing among people opposing NJV. In early May the Hawaii leader of the Inland Boatmen's Union, Josiah Lii, was gunned down outside his office in downtown Honolulu.[22] At the time the killing was perceived by many who learned of it only through the media, as a case of an honest union leader unsuccessfully resisting an attempted intrusion by Hawaii's crime syndicate into his union's affairs. Whatever led to Lii's killing, the murder had a profound effect on the overall leader of the NNTA, Stanford Achi. In light of what was known or believed by the tenants about the involvement of the syndicate in the overall situation in Nawiliwili, and in view of what the tenants believed to be the cause of Panui's house burning, Lii's murder became further evidence to Achi that community leaders who fought the project were risking their lives.

By this time the situation was evolving to where police might be sent in to arrest those who refused to get off the NJV land. The chief of police told reporters that 25 officers were being trained in "crowd control."[23] Essentially they were practicing how to arrest a large group of people.

The mayor had been receiving phone calls about the overall situation, a few of which, he said, "intimated that violence would occur."[24]

A county department head reportedly told others in the county that police officers entering the property might be shot at.

The tenants and supporters in fact had no weapons, but were organizing to passively resist arrest. CB radios were just coming into popular use on Kauai. A network of people equipped with these and with walkie-talkies was organized to watch all approaches to the property. This communications net was linked to a telephone tree so that as many as possible who wanted to be arrested could be there if the time came.

As it turned out, when things were coming to a head, the tenants and NJV reached an agreement.

Stanford Achi believed there were insufficient people willing to be arrested in order to make a real stand—there were about 60—and he declined to force the issue to the point of confrontation with police. The result was that the two tenant families still on the land were each given a free lot on what would have been throw-away land owned by NJV, left over after the condominium project. A small church abutting the land where the two families were to relocate was given in fee simple the land that it had been renting from NJV. In exchange the NNTA dropped its opposition to the development, which eventually was undertaken by an entity other than NJV since NJV's lender in the end completed its foreclosure. The Banyan Harbor Resort condominiums were built on the site, not far from the Kauai Surf Hotel and overlooking Kalapaki Bay.[25]

In the end, it was never established why Panui's house burned, nor was there any known evidence linking Louis Rego, Ding Oclit or anyone in NJV with the fire or with the theft of the NNTA files.

*　*　*

If the Nawiliwili fight was finally settled peacefully, with more or less everyone getting something, still it left a large residue of ordinary people who had been highly politicized; who looked at developers with deep antagonism; and who were resentful toward public officials for having declined to downzone land in order to take some pressure off the tenants.

Furthermore, a number of the younger NNTA members and supporters had not wanted to settle with NJV. Nor had they had much chance to argue their position—a frustrating situation. Some later welcomed a chance to take part in opposing a resort at Nukolii, where it appeared there would not exist the factors that made for compromise in Nawiliwili, and where they could have more say.

Nawiliwili thus to an extent spilled over onto Nukolii, a fact reinforced by geography.

Nawiliwili and Nukolii were in roughly the same part of Kauai—about four miles apart on a straight line—and several young local people who were either members or close supporters of the NNTA also used Nukolii for surfing and fishing. A part-Hawaiian couple, Keoni and Laola Lake, originally from Oahu and now living in Niumalu as Kanoa Estate tenants, surfed at Nukolii, as did Lihue Plantation employee Eric T. Kato. Kato's grandmother and aunt had made up one of the two Nawiliwili households to hang on to the end, and Kato was deeply involved in the whole NNTA effort on their behalf. Another LP employee, James E. Nishida Jr., had been off and on a supporter of the NNTA since its formation, and also was heavily involved with the Nawiliwili situation. Nishida had fished at Nukolii since he was a small boy. Nishida, Kato, and the Lakes were among the founding members of the group that opposed development at Nukolii. Several others were NNTA activists.

This was not altogether a case of a spillover from one community-organizing effort to another, however; several of those most central to starting the opposition to construction at Nukolii had had no involvement with Nawiliwili nor with anyplace else. These were mostly people like Allen Perreira—young local residents of Hanamaulu, the community nearest Nukolii, who made use of the area for things like surfing and fishing.

*　*　*

If Nawiliwili provided some of the direct impetus to the initial campaign to oppose construction at Nukolii, there were also more general factors at work.

By this time on Kauai there was an approximately seven-year-old environmental movement that had stirred people in many parts of the island. The movement involved a probably greater proportion of locally-born people than had been the case on any other island; it had a not bad win/loss record, now had a certain amount of depth and expertise, and in the spring of 1977 was seeing activity in various parts of Kauai.

At a recent hearing in Hanalei, several in the crowd had shouted at a State Department of Transportation official who was proposing to widen bridges across streams along the remote north shore. The widening would conceivably lead to more tourist visits and more development.[26]

On behalf of a group of longtime tenants living in the Rice Camp area of Lihue, a spokesman at a County Council hearing strenuously objected to a proposed high density residential designation on the county general plan, saying it would lead to evictions.[27]

The NNTA at the time was also busy on another front, opposing a similar designation for an old graveyard in Nawiliwili. Along the south shore of Kauai a group was just winding up an unsuccessful effort to halt a 457-acre resort at Poipu.[28] In addition a locally-born environmental and community activist, JoAnn A. Yukimura, who grew up about a mile from Nukolii and who worked closely with the NNTA in the Nawiliwili fight, had been elected to the Council in 1976. In that general election, she had received the greatest number of votes of any candidate running for any office on Kauai. Following the election she was named chairperson of the Council's planning committee. From the platform of her Council seat and her chairmanship, Yukimura was a frequent critic of most of the major developments planned for Kauai at the time, including Nukolii; and in doing this she got a great deal of coverage by local news media, which helped to further stimulate and galvanize opposition to many construction projects.[29]

There were other important socio-economic dimensions to the stage that was being set for Nukolii. In 1977 Kauai's unemployment figure stood at 6.5%; by American standards not a worrisome rate. Moreover it was the lowest for Kauai since 1971. Kauai hotel occupancy in 1977 stood at 80.6%. Tourist industry analysts hold that the break-even rate for Hawaii hotels was in the area of 70%-75%, so 80.6% was moderately healthy. Furthermore the Kauai rate had been rising almost steadily since 1970, when it had stood at 58%.[30]

The one cloud in the economic sky had to do with sugar, the other of Kauai's two economic props. Congress had allowed the Sugar Act to expire in 1974. Wildly rising prices followed for the rest of that year, with ILWU members in the Hawaii sugar industry each getting a $1,000 bonus that Christmas.[31] But without the act's price stabilization mechanism the price could decline, too, and in 1975 it started to. For this and other reasons the

Hawaii industry in 1977 had one of its worst years ever in terms of profitability. The real depth of the sugar industry's problems, however, was not so apparent in 1977.

In 1977 the economic backdrop to the question of whether to build at Nukolii was thus felt to be a moderately healthy one.

At the same time Kauai was seeing a rise in construction, leading to a loss of some of the island's natural beauty, plus an influx of mainland *haoles*, all of which was agitating a good number of long-time Kauai residents.

The island's population had grown only 7% during the entire decade of the 1960s. Between 1970 and 1977 it grew at twice that rate. Many of the new residents of the 1970s were mainland *haoles*. A fair number of these were young, had long hair, by Kauai standards were disheveled in personal appearance, and had few qualms about living off welfare rather than working. It was these "hippies" who either first brought drugs like marijuana and LSD to Kauai or popularized their use, and who first in large numbers gathered and ate the "magic mushrooms" that grew best in cow manure. Some local young people now began to use these drugs, too. All this disgusted and infuriated most local people. At times it led to physical attacks on *haoles*.[32] It also created a reservoir of antipathy toward development, since development to an extent was equated with the *haole* influx, and at a time when Kauai's economy allowed a large number of people the luxury of opposing development.

Now enter Nukolii.

* * *

The County Council held a hearing on the Lihue Development Plan in June 1977. At the hearing a Kauai attorney, Walton D. Y. Hong, announced on behalf of Pacific Standard Life that the company had purchased Nukolii and planned a 1,500-room/three-hotel resort there.

In 1974 Nukolii represented only a fraction of what the Land Use Commission then had under consideration. In 1977 it was not only almost the sole major project on the agenda of a body that was deciding land use matters, but, if approved as proposed, it would have meant an increase of about 40% in Kauai's hotel room count. With this reversal in the scale of things; with Nawiliwili substantially settled, thus freeing up the time of activists involved there; and with an actual project to look at for the first time, Nukolii suddenly became an area of contention between pro and anti-growth forces on a scale that was new for Kauai.

During the first few years of environmental activism on Kauai, those opposing developments were in turn usually opposed only by the developer himself, plus the occasional realtor or merchant whose business led them to see value in the project under consideration. Mainly starting with Nukolii that changed.

At a public hearing on Nukolii before the Council in July 1977, a force of carpenters attended to support the project. This was the first time that construction workers had showed up *en masse* at a land use hearing on Kauai. Their presence led Walton Hong to say: "I feel tonight is a turning point. This is the first time we have had the silent majority come out to speak for something. They have let it be known there are two sides to the coin."

Their pension fund three weeks earlier had acquired a passive interest in the Nukolii land, though Carpenters Union officials later interviewed for this book said that had nothing to do with union support for the project.

From a legal standpoint, what in essence was involved with the Carpenters' purchase was this: Amfac in 1973 and 1974 had sold to Masaru Yokouchi the two parcels that then comprised the potential resort portion of Nukolii. The transaction was by two agreements of sale. Yokouchi in turn organized a *hui* that in effect became the agreements-of-sale buyer. The *hui* about two-thirds of a year later resold by sub-agreement to Pacific Standard. Thus as of the resale there was a chain of three entities on the title: Amfac, next the *hui*, next Pacific Standard. Money flowed up the chain according to the terms of the various agreements of sale. What the Carpenters did was replace Amfac in the chain. Their doing this had no bearing on the already-fixed rights of others down the chain. In 1980 the Knickerbocker Life Insurance Co. of Ohio bought out the Carpenters.[33]

At the Council hearing to which the carpenters came in force, an equally large group of opponents were present. A number of the carpenters had been drinking; for that or other reasons they were verbally abusive of opponents, at times interrupting their testimony.[34]

The Council eventually approved the LDP with a resort designation for Nukolii. The project still needed complementary zoning, and both sides organized for and testified at a hearing on this in 1978.

In late 1978 or early 1979 the Council member who was to be the swing vote on zoning said that he received threats by mail and by phone to the effect that if he voted in favor of the resort, he would be shot. He voted in favor nonetheless, in front of a large crowd of both supporters and opponents of development, making approval possible by a one-vote margin. The mayor then signed the Nukolii resort zoning bill into law.[35]

Pacific Standard had believed it necessary to scale down the project in order to get zoning. In any case, as approved by the Council in 1979, the development was about one-third the size of the original proposal: a 350-room hotel and 150 condominium units, on but 25 of the area's 60 acres.

Following rezoning, opponents organized themselves into the Committee to Save Nukolii (CSN) and, using a county charter provision, conducted a petition drive for a referendum to overturn the zoning.[36]

For a referendum, the Kauai County charter required as a preliminary matter that a petition calling for a referendum be signed by at least 20% of the number of people registered to vote in the last general election. Once sufficient signatures were obtained and that fact was verified by the county clerk, then the Council could either approve the subject matter of the petition right then and there, order a special election, or put the issue on the ballot in the next general election.

On a petition to downzone Nukolii, sufficient signatures were gathered, as verified by the clerk in January 1980, and the Council opted to put the issue on the November 1980 general election ballot.[37]

CSN then filed three court actions over the next half year, in an attempt to slow the project. The first appealed a County Planning Commission decision to grant two permits that the project required. The second was a lawsuit to attempt to halt the County's whole processing of the project pending the outcome of the referendum. The third alleged that faulty procedures had been followed in obtaining State Health Department approval for the project's sewage system. All three actions failed.[38]

As mentioned, the county charter provided that referenda elections could, at the discretion of the Council, either be held along with general elections or as special elections. When in February 1980 the Council placed the Nukolii question on that fall's general election ballot, there had been little or no discussion of the possibility of a special election. The CSN petition asked that the Council consider, as one alternative, holding a special election on Nukolii; but CSN, believing it unlikely that a Council with a majority in support of developing Nukolii would actually do this, apparently went no further than raising the possibility. Now, in the spring of 1980, Council members who opposed a resort at Nukolii proposed that the referendum be held as a special election during that September's primary. They believed that the developer was racing to complete as much of the project as possible before the general election, and that should some as-yet-undetermined amount of work be completed before the vote, then the developer might acquire vested rights to continue irrespective of what happened at the polls.[39]

Council member JoAnn Yukimura argued that putting Nukolii on the primary ballot would cost the same as putting it on the general ballot. She also said that people should have a chance to vote on downzoning before the developer's rights might become vested. Council Chairman Robert K. Yotsuda counterargued that there was "express language of the County Charter ... that those persons whose rights are subject to a referendum be given the opportunity to obtain vested rights before an election is held."[40]

The effort to advance the election date was defeated by the same 4–3 margin as the zoning had been approved.

* * *

That August, Pacific Standard and a Seattle architect with which it had gone into partnership regarding Nukolii, sold their interests in the 25 acres that had resort zoning, retaining the balance of 35 acres. The buyer, Hasegawa Komuten (USA) Inc., kept the shell of the business entity with which Pacific Standard and the architect were building the project, a limited partnership called Graham Beach Partners (GBP). The developer thus continued to be called Graham Beach Partners in the media, even though, according to a GBP attorney, Hasegawa really was now in it all alone.

Hasegawa was a Hawaii subsidiary of a one-billion-dollar Japan company that mass-produced condominiums in Japan. The *Honolulu Star-Bulletin* wrote in September that the parent company was then annually accounting for about 20% of all condominiums built and sold in Japan, and that the next largest builder had only 4% of the market.[41]

Hasegawa Komuten (USA) had been in Hawaii since 1973. It was a well-run and successful builder of resort and residential condominiums on three islands. That September of 1980 the company was dedicating its own eight-story office building in downtown Honolulu. At the time, Takehiko Hasegawa, the founder and chairman of the parent company, said that at least nine more condominium projects were planned for Hawaii.[42]

Hasegawa decided to buy Nukolii's 25 zoned acres on the strength, among other things, of opinion letters from several attorneys that the project's rights had already vested, also based on Kauai County's apparent endorsement of that position.[43] However wise or unwise a business decision it was to get into Nukolii, still the fact of so wealthy and apparently stable a corporation becoming the developer gave to the project resources and staying power that Pacific Standard and its partner probably did not possess.

* * *

A month before the 1980 election the baseyard of the project's general contractor was broken into. Fuel and hydraulic hoses were cut on three machines. Fuel tanks were filled with sand. Some tires were punctured and crank cases damaged.[44]

Leading up to the election, both sides campaigned intensely, with the issue of development at Nukolii spilling over into other elections as well.

The developer in August had obtained building permits for the condominiums and immediately began construction. A permit was still needed for the hotel, however. In working to obtain the hotel permit, Hasegawa to an extent was proceeding at ordinary speed for normal business reasons, to an extent racing to get it before the election, on the theory that having the permit before the vote would help vest the right to build the hotel.

Hasegawa got the hotel permit. The County issued the hotel building permit on the afternoon of the day before the election.[45]

In an interview for this book, Michael J. Belles, who in 1980 was a deputy county attorney assigned to Nukolii, said he believed it would have been his recommendation that had the permit not been obtained before the vote, and had the vote been to downzone, that the permit should not be issued.

Whether this would have meant that the hotel would never have been built is a matter of opinion; though given what happened in court three months later, the hotel would probably have gotten a court-ordered building permit had the County not issued one when it did.

Regardless of the long-term effect of issuing the hotel permit just before the 1980 election, issuance was powerful evidence to opponents of building at Nukolii that county government was hand-in-glove with the developer. It was part of what led the editor of *The Garden Island* to write: "The people of Kauai are obviously the victims of a well-organized conspiracy to circumvent their wishes."[46]

* * *

Events were now homing in on the election process from several directions.

A week before the vote, the *Honolulu Advertiser* ran a lengthy story by investigative reporter James Dooley that added a large note of scandal to the already highly-charged issue.[47]

The article was the first published report that there was a Masaru Yokouchi *hui* with an interest in Nukolii; that several high-ranking public officials were in it; that the Nukolii conveyance documents had not been publicly recorded until about four years after the fact; that even then the documents did not indicate that a *hui* was involved or even that Yokouchi was involved; and that on behalf of the *hui*, which operated more or less like a limited partnership, no partnership registration papers had ever been filed with the state agency in charge of registration, even though at the time the *hui* was organized, one of its investors was the director of that agency.

In the post-Watergate era, these facts alone would have raised eyebrows. There was more, however.

Yokouchi paid Amfac $1.2 million. Two-thirds of a year later, after no intervening rezoning and not long before LUC redistricting, Pacific Standard's local subsidiary paid $5.25 million.

Also, Dooley determined that the Amfac executive who handled the early stages of negotiating the sale, C. Earl Stoner Jr., later joined the *hui*. Dooley wrote that when he confronted Stoner with this fact, Stoner denied it, then later admitted it. Dooley also wrote that Stoner had apparently misled the LUC in 1974 by indicating that Amfac still owned the land and was planning a resort there, when in fact, as Stoner knew, the land had already been sold.

With these added facts it all started to look sinister to many people. Many thought that the price Yokouchi paid had been rigged low by a secret side deal with Stoner, whereby Stoner would get to invest in the *hui* as his payoff. Furthermore, many readers made the simultaneous assumption that Pacific Standard paid too much. This was because Pacific Standard was believed to have paid extra to get politically well-connected *hui* members to use insider-influence to obtain LUC approval, also to later help with Kauai County approvals.

In the political environment of Kauai, where Nukolii had been a hot issue for three years running, and where many people were openly suspicious of public officials anyway, Dooley's story hit a tremendous nerve.

In interviews for this book Stoner, Yokouchi, and the then-president of Pacific Standard, Clifford N. Gamble, all said in essence that Dooley's story consisted of a set of facts which taken together were highly damaging, but that each individual fact had an innocent or innocuous explanation. Stoner also said there was at least one significant error.

In the first place, evidence was offered that the price Yokouchi paid Amfac was fair to Amfac. Stoner gave the authors of this book an appraisal of Nukolii done for Amfac in 1972 by an independent appraiser, Quinton L. Butler of General Appraisal. In it Butler recommended a sale price of $1.2 million as of late November 1972. This was exactly the price offered to and agreed to by Yokouchi six months later. Also, Stoner said that although he handled negotiations with Yokouchi in the early stages, past a certain point the matter was handled by a superior, and ultimately it was reviewed and approved by the Amfac board of directors. According to a statement made to the news media by Amfac in early 1981, an investigative committee of three Amfac directors, "who were not affiliated with the company in any way at the time of the [sale]," reviewed it following the Dooley story, and found that what Yokouchi paid was "fair to the company."[48]

Stoner, Yokouchi and Gamble all pointed out how a markup like that paid by the Pacific Standard subsidiary was not at all unusual in Hawaii during the 1960s and 1970s. As evidence, Yokouchi pointed to any number of oceanfront parcels of land he knew of on Maui that had changed hands over the years at continually escalating prices. There was, for example, a parcel in Kealia, along the Kihei coast, slightly larger than an acre, that changed hands three times between 1954 and 1978. In 1954 it sold for $3,800. In 1963 it resold for just over $100,000. In 1978 it was leased on a long-term basis for one and a quarter million dollars.

Gamble also said that, from his standpoint, it was an "arms-length transaction," and that he "didn't know the people" in the *hui*, thus he was not even thinking about attempting to make use of whatever political influence they might have. Gamble said in addition that he "hadn't the slightest idea" what Yokouchi had paid Amfac, nor did he care, that he only was looking at what might be a fair open market price as of mid-1974.

Yokouchi said that the *hui* was organized by putting the word out to friends that a *hui* was being formed. Of the roughly 50 people who then invested, he said the fact that several were in politics and government was simply a reflection of his having been politically active for many years, thus having friends in that area of life.

Yokouchi also said that if the group had been assembled with an eye toward exercising political influence over the government land use process, there should have been Kauai officials included, in that most of Nukolii's approvals would have to come at the Kauai County level. But there were no Kauai people known to be in the *hui*.

* * *

On the other hand there were people prominent in politics on Kauai who joined another not-publicly-registered Yokouchi *hui* that by another initially unrecorded agreement of sale bought another Kauai parcel from Amfac, after the Nukolii sale to Yokouchi. This was "the other half of Nukolii," as some people saw it, though no evidence ever surfaced that the Kauai politicians and government people in this latter *hui* were included to help pave the way for county approvals of Nukolii.

This other *hui* was Kauai Ventures. In 1975 Yokouchi entered into an agreement with Amfac to buy 17 acres in Lihue. A friend of his on Kauai then organized a *hui* that became the actual buyer/owner. The existence of Kauai Ventures became known when it publicly registered with the State Department of Regulatory Agencies (DRA) in 1981. Registration resulted from a James Dooley series on unregistered *huis* that prompted the DRA to ask for the registration of many then-unregistered passive land investment groups. The first that the general public knew of Kauai Ventures came through a Dooley story.[49]

Included in Kauai Ventures were Kauai Rep. Richard A. Kawakami, who told Dooley that actually it had been his sister who invested, and that he took over her share in 1978; Paul Shinseki, campaign manager for Kauai Sen. George H. Toyofuku; Kauai County Personnel Director Herbert T. Doi; Valentine K. Hataishi, executive secretary of the county Liquor Control Commission; the wife of the late Kauai mayor Francis M. F. Ching; Samuel S. Lee, state land agent on Kauai; and Masao Seto, who was a former county supervisor and finance director, who later became a county public information officer and then member of the Liquor Control Commission.

In an interview for this book, Yokouchi said that he opened this *hui* to Kauai people after a Kauai realtor who was a personal friend complained that no Kauai people were notified about Nukolii when that *hui* was being organized. Yokouchi said, however, that opening Kauai Ventures to Kauai people had nothing to do with attempting to smooth the way for Nukolii at the county level. He also said he had no knowledge of nor control over who invested in Kauai Ventures; thus it was not an attempt on his part to buy political influence on Kauai.

As it turned out, the Kauai Ventures investment did very poorly.

Yokouchi also said that only once did he attempt to talk to a Kauai County decision-maker regarding Nukolii, when at one point, probably in 1978, he attempted to talk with then-Kauai Councilman Edward L. Sarita about Nukolii.

Sarita in 1973 had been employed by the division or subsidiary of Amfac that handled the sale of Nukolii to Yokouchi. Yokouchi said in an interview that when he went to Kauai in 1973 to look at properties, including Nukolii, Sarita was the person or one of the people who took him to see Nukolii. In Yokouchi's opinion, Sarita knew that Yokouchi as well as Amfac itself considered Nukolii as logical for a resort. As a councilman, however, Sarita generally voted against resort classifications for Nukolii. It was at a point when Sarita was about to do so that Yokouchi said he called Sarita. But Yokouchi said Sarita declined to discuss the issue, saying it would be unethical for him to discuss Nukolii with him. In an interview for this book, Sarita confirmed that he had declined to talk to Yokouchi about Nukolii for this reason.

* * *

Yokouchi said he did not register the Nukolii partnership with DRA because he believed the registration requirement did not apply. This, he said, was because the group was one of passive investors and not actively engaged in business as such. Also, in those years, especially on the outer islands where investing was often handled informally and where people who invested together generally knew and trusted one another, many people did not think to do something so formal as register their group with a state office in Honolulu.

It was indeed an arguable legal point whether, based on publicly-known facts, *huis* such as Yokouchi's ought to have registered.

In the eyes of the law, if groups like the Nukolii or Kauai Ventures *huis* were any kind of conventional business organization, they were partnerships. This was because they were operated the way partnerships were; also for reasons of how they paid income taxes. If these *huis* were not partnerships, then they were *de facto* corporations. An ordinary corporation paid income taxes on profits, then, if the corporation distributed part of the profits to shareholders as dividends, the shareholders also paid taxes. The run-of-the-mill Hawaii land *hui*, on the other hand, simply allowed profits and losses to flow through the group to each individual. The group as a group did not pay income taxes; only the members did as individuals. This was how partnerships worked, too.

There was a Hawaii state statute which set out "Rules for determining the existence of a partnership," hence for determining whether an investment group had to register as such with the Department of Regulatory Agencies. Mainly what this law did was outline what a partnership was not; among other things, passive joint ownership of property, apparently regardless of how many people were joint owners on a single piece of property, was not an *ipso facto* determinant of the group being a partnership. Rather, to be a partnership, the group had to be actively in business somehow—by interpolation, the statute seemed to require that the group do something concrete and overt like attempt to rezone or build.

The Nukolii and Kauai Ventures *huis* were publicly claimed to be passive only; hence their organizers and lawyers said they were under no registration requirement.

In an interview for this book, the head of business registration for DRA in 1980, Russel S. Nagata, indicated that he too believed mere passive investment *huis* were generally under no requirement to register; that they first had to take some kind of action, like attempting to rezone the land they owned, before qualifying as a partnership in the eyes of Hawaii law. Nagata indicated that he was not sure whether the Nukolii *hui*, for example, was active or passive; but due to what he felt was adverse publicity generated by the Dooley stories, he suggested that all the apparently passive *huis* register anyway, which a number then did.

(His successor, however, Russel H. Yamashita, said in an interview for this book that in general he was not requiring *huis* to register unless, as Nagata said, they first engaged in some kind of actual activity other than simply buying, holding and reselling land. The requirement that a passive *hui* register had thus been a one-time thing, brought about by James Dooley.)

Unknown to Nagata, however, Yokouchi did indeed attempt to help get Nukolii rezoned—a step that may have triggered a requirement that the *hui* register. As mentioned, Yokouchi at one point attempted to persuade Kauai councilman Sarita to vote for development at Nukolii. Yokouchi in an interview said he could not remember when he called Sarita. Sarita in an interview, however, placed the event as late 1978—well before the registration issue was raised in the media. Moreover, in another interview Yokouchi also said that, while he could not be sure, he thought he might have informally lobbied land use commissioners regarding Nukolii in 1973 or 1974. At the time he was lobbying a number of commissioners anyway on behalf of a client, Seibu Group Enterprises, that had just bought 1,000 acres at Makena on Maui and was seeking LUC approval for a resort. In an interview Yokouchi said that it would have been like him, when seeing these commissioners, most of whom he knew well personally, to also put in a good word for Nukolii. On the other hand all commissioners interviewed on this subject said that Yokouchi had never talked to them about Nukolii.

In any event, Yokouchi also indicated that it never occurred to him that activities of this sort might have triggered a DRA registration requirement.

Of Dooley's writing that Stoner denied having been a Nukolii *hui* member when first interviewed but then admitting to membership in a follow-up interview, Stoner said that he did not lie. He said that Dooley in first talking with him inaccurately identified the *hui* as being headed by Maui attorney Walter T. Shimoda, as opposed to being headed by Yokouchi. (This occurred because the only publicly recorded title document indicating Amfac had sold Nukolii was an agreement of sale that listed Shimoda alone as the buyer. Shimoda was Yokouchi's lawyer and was serving as the *hui* trustee on the recorded agreement of sale.) Stoner said Dooley's so labeling the *hui* confused him, and that, in the second interview, when he realized which *hui* Dooley was referring to, he admitted to having a share.

Dooley, on the other hand, said in an interview for this book that he identified not only the *hui* as being headed by Shimoda, but also the land area which he believed the *hui* bought and resold. He said that the whole context of the interviews with Stoner had concerned the Nukolii land, so that no matter what name Dooley gave the *hui*, it was clear what was being discussed.

Stoner also told Dooley that he did not invest until after quitting his job at Amfac in 1975. But in interviews for this book, both Yokouchi and Stoner indicated that in fact Stoner bought his share before leaving. They said that Stoner was invited to invest in about 1973 or early 1974, and did so.

As mentioned, the record of the Land Use Commission hearing at which Stoner testified in 1974 regarding Nukolii indicated possible lying, as described by Dooley.

Nukolii had been sold twice by that point. In an interview for this book, Stoner said that he did not know of the resale until long after the hearing. He knew of the first sale, of course, since he personally helped negotiate it.

As reflected in LUC minutes, Stoner nevertheless told the LUC that Amfac had a resort plan for the site which at that stage was still "conceptual," but that "we are in a situation where we are going to have to begin to do some very involved engineering on that project." He guessed that in the resort that Amfac would build, "a majority of employees would be local people."[50]

Dooley asked Stoner why he said those things? Dooley wrote that Stoner replied that he thought it possible that Amfac was considering going into joint venture with whomever had bought Nukolii, although Stoner indicated this was only speculation on his part, in that he knew of no actual plans for a joint venture.

In an interview for this book, Stoner was also asked why he testified as he did. He made the above point. He also said that starting in late 1971 or early 1972, Amfac people had begun assembling data for presentations to the Land Use Commission during its 1974 statewide review. In 1971 or 1972 information was assembled and testimony prepared regarding Nukolii. When it came time for the Kauai hearing in 1974, Stoner said it was decided inside Amfac that he would testify on Nukolii as previously planned. In the interview Stoner declined to explain precisely why. He did say, though, that he did not consider he was lying in his testimony. He explained that since Yokouchi's group was buying by agreement of sale, therefore Amfac was still the fee simple owner and could legitimately represent the property before the LUC. Not saying that there was an agreement of sale in effect was not lying, "it was just not telling them [the commissioners] all the truth." In general he noted that there were various people participating in the hearings who were highly critical of major landowners and developers, leading to a situation where, he felt, "you tell what's required by law and you paint as pretty a picture as possible," but you went no further. Moreover, in those hearings there was a fair amount of inflammatory and exaggerated testimony by people opposing development, which did not create an atmosphere conducive to large landowners and developers making absolutely full disclosure on the public record.

Although Stoner declined to explain on the record why, according to him, it was decided inside Amfac that he should proceed with his testimony as though no one was buying Nukolii, research for this book indicated that this may have been related to the fact that the sale to Yokouchi had not yet been publicly recorded with the Bureau of Conveyances. Indeed recording did not occur until about four years after the transaction. According to a former Amfac executive familiar with Nukolii, Amfac may have been holding off on recording in part because executives did not want company books to reflect the sale immediately, due to how they wanted the company's earnings picture to look.

In an interview, Yokouchi said that he could not recall why there was no recording until after the fact, but said if he had been asked to hold off on recording for the above reason, he probably would have done so.

Interviews for this book were conducted with several others who were top Amfac executives at the time, whose duties might have put them in a position to know why recording did not immediately take place. One, Thomas R. d'Arcambal, said it was simply routine policy to not record until an agreement of sale was paid off, and that this was why the Nukolii agreements with Yokouchi were not immediately recorded.

On the other hand again, at the time a Nukolii agreement was recorded, it had not yet been fully paid off. (In 1973 Yokouchi signed an agreement of sale for part of Nukolii. The agreement contained an option on the other part, which he exercised in early 1974 by another agreement of sale. In 1977 a single agreement of sale from Amfac to Yokouchi's lawyer was publicly recorded, covering both parcels and transactions.)

(One comical element in all of this was that six months before the LUC hearing, the *Honolulu Advertiser* Kauai reporter had written that 35 of Nukolii's 60 acres had been sold to Yokouchi; also that in December 1973 Amfac had filed an application with the Kauai Planning Department to subdivide out of a much larger parcel what was to become the 60-acre resort site; and that a letter by an Amfac employee accompanying the application read, as paraphrased in the paper: "Amfac does not plan to develop the land and will leave it in pasture until sold."[51] The story was republished by other media on Kauai. Also, one land use commissioner listening to Stoner's testimony said in an interview for this book that he knew of Yokouchi's purchase at the time of the LUC hearing. And that commissioner also said that, to the best of his recollection, it had been the Maui commissioner who told him. Despite all the above, Stoner's testimony was not challenged by anyone who knew or might reasonably have suspected that he was being less than candid with the LUC.)

Whatever was the ultimate meaning of all this, what most readers thought they saw when they read Dooley's story were local public officials' selling an ability to influence the LUC to a mainland *haole* company; also that the sale price to the *hui* had been rigged low by a secret side deal with Stoner; plus consistent attempts to cover it all up. The picture in most people's minds was one of highly questionable dealings. It had a powerful effect on Kauai voters.

*   *   *

The economic backdrop to the 1980 election was favorable to an anti-development vote.

If Kauai's unemployment rate in 1977, the year opposition to building at Nukolii was first organized, was low at 6.5%, in 1980 it was an extremely low 4.2%. Although hotel occupancy was down from 80.6% to 69.6%, still the latter figure was more or less at the lower limits of breaking even, thus not necessarily a cause for overwhelming concern. Also, Hawaii sugar in 1980 sold for about the highest prices it had ever obtained, due to poor sugar crops elsewhere in the world in 1979 and 1980.[52]

*   *   *

By a 2–1 margin in the 1980 election Kauai voters rejected resort zoning for Nukolii. The councilman who in 1979 had provided the crucial fourth vote on Nukolii's zoning was defeated in a re-election bid, a loss he attributed to his Nukolii vote.[53]

Vandalism occurred again at the construction site, this time minor.[54]

Despite the vote Hasegawa continued to build, in the belief that its rights had vested.

The County administration took the position that the developer had proceeded so far into the project that indeed it had vested rights. The County declined to cancel the building permits.[55]

One of the Save Nukolii Committee supporters, as spokesman for a delegation, now made an emotional and angry appeal to the mayor, telling him to revoke the permits. Otherwise, he was reported in the media to have told the mayor, "Expect the worst. Maybe bloodshed."[56]

The mayor's administrative assistant said in a newspaper interview that about this time several death threats were made against the mayor in connection with Nukolii.[57]

In early December, 32 people who opposed development formed a human chain across an access road into the project in a civil disobedence action, an effort to dramatize their position that continued construction was illegal. They were all arrested. In the process a few were slightly roughed up by police. (Later, charges of obstruction were dropped against 31, in return for a plea of no contest by CSN, after which CSN was fined $350. The remaining defendant also had an obstruction charge dismissed, but then was tried and convicted on an assault charge, for allegedly having resisted arrest and biting two policemen. She was sentenced to 50 hours of community service work and a year on probation.)[58]

The county administration received assassination threats about the time of the January 1981 inauguration of elected county officials. The threats were believed to be connected with the mayor's continued support of a resort at Nukolii despite the outcome of the referendum. Inauguration ceremonies were nearly canceled. They then proceeded under tight security—a first for Kauai—with picketing by 150 opponents of development at Nukolii.[59]

A month later five people were arrested at the Lihue Airport while they were passing out to Japanese tourists leaflets opposing development at Nukolii. Charges of "unlawful picketing and public demonstration" were subsequently dropped.[60]

Then, by coincidence or not, on the night of the airport arrests the mayor's office was damaged by a small bomb. Nothing like this had ever happened on Kauai, and it was a great shock. The crime was never solved. But its target, timing, and the fact that another, although unexploded, bomb had been found at the Nukolii construction site not long before, all pointed to the motive being opposition to development at Nukolii.[61]

The next day a bomb threat was phoned in to the Kauai Surf Hotel, though there was no explosion, nor was any bomb found.[62]

*   *   *

The County had gone to circuit court on Kauai as soon as the election results were certified in order to obtain a determination as to whether the developer had a right to continue or not. The County took the position that indeed rights had vested. Two and a half months later, in February 1981, Judge Kei Hirano ruled that the developer, "having incurred substantial expenditures in reliance upon the existing zoning, did acquire vested rights to continue and complete the condominium and hotel project at Nukolii."[63]

CSN planned an appeal while construction continued.

CSN also now obtained representation by the senior attorney in one of the nation's most accomplished public interest law firms, Public Advocates Inc., based in San Francisco.[64]

As mentioned, despite voters having overwhelmingly rejected Nukolii's resort zoning in 1980, Mayor Malapit was dogged in his support of construction there. Then, in June 1981, he told reporters that, if the Council wanted to change the general plan from resort to agriculture on the 35 acres not being built upon, he would sign the bill. But when the Council early next year did pass such a bill, he vetoed it, though he was then overridden. (Subsequently, in 1984, when the County updated the general plan for the entire county, the 35 acres were again made resort.)[65]

Behavior of this kind made Malapit extremely unpopular, to say the least, among a large segment of voters on Kauai. Early in 1982 he told county officials that he would not stand for re-election that year. In the fall he attributed the cause to the Committee to Save Nukolii. He he told a reporter that "their [CSN] actions are the main reason why I, Eduardo E. Malapit, decided not to run for re-election in 1982."[66]

About this time Malapit's office was bombed again. The device was apparently similar to that used the first time.

Malapit told reporters that he believed the bombings were Nukolii-related. CSN took this as a defamatory insinuation and issued a statement: "The committee had nothing to do with either of the bombings and doesn't approve of them in any way."[67]

CSN had long said or insinuated that Malapit, government officials in the *hui* that bought and sold Nukolii in 1973–1974, the Amfac executive who negotiated the sale, the LUC, the Kauai circuit court judge who ruled in favor of the developer in 1980 and 1981, and so on, had connived, had favored the developer for political reasons, and/or were corrupt. In making statements like these they were also giving expression to what many ordinary people on Kauai believed, watching all this from the sidelines.

But charges like these infuriated Malapit, who on the occasion of the second bombing of his office turned the verbal tables. CSN members, he said, "are the champions of implicating all kinds of things. They implicated Amfac; they implicated our own judge; they even implicated me and my administration. Now when they are implicated, they get angry. They can dish it out but they can't take it."[68]

The bombings, however small their physical impact—the first caused an estimated $500 damage—had enormous political effects. The second explosion at the mayor's office came just two weeks before the 1982 primary election in which JoAnn Yukimura was running against Kauai Rep. Tony T. Kunimura for mayor. Yukimura had been associated with the opposition to development at Nukolii from the start. The bombings were widely believed to be the work of someone opposed to construction at Nukolii. To some extent in the popular mind, then, Yukimura looked as though she associated with extremists, and she believed this image hurt her politically. In any event, with 17,315 voting for mayor she lost by 853.

*   *   *

In October 1982 the Hawaii Supreme Court in a stunning decision overturned the Kauai circuit court decision. It was immensely gratifying to the Save Nukolii Committee and its supporters. It shocked Hasegawa, the County, and many business and political leaders, who were amazed that so many land use approvals could be obtained and money expended and then zoning canceled.

In general a referendum is a process whereby the electorate votes on a law; normally it is a question of whether to cancel an existing law. In the case of Nukolii the law at issue was an ordinance that zoned the 25 acres under construction for resort use.

The Kauai County Charter that established the referendum process used in the Nukolii case, also provided that "a referendum that nullifies an existing ordinance shall not affect any vested rights or any action taken or expenditure made up to the date of the referendum."[69]

In view of this provision, the developer had been attempting to get as much of the project completed as possible prior to the date of the referendum vote.

What shocked many who supported construction at Nukolii and who read the Supreme Court opinion, was that despite the apparently clear language of the charter quoted above, the court rejected "a literal interpretation" of those words, in that the effect of a literal "construction would be to grandfather all activities the referendum sought to prevent."

Rather than the date of the actual election, what the court keyed in on in terms of a pivotal event had to do with the fact that the referendum issue had been certified by the county clerk before the developer obtained its last county permit of a discretionary nature.

This was a special management area (SMA) use permit, having to do with development near the shoreline. In the Nukolii SMA application, the area at issue was a good portion of the project site. The Planning Commission ruled on SMA permits; although it seldom happened, in theory these permits could be denied and development prohibited altogether. In practice the Commission at most scaled down the size of projects when ruling on SMAs. Also, in awarding SMA permits, the Commission could attach conditions of a magnitude and variety that could affect the final location and appearance of a project; altogether unlike the very non-discretionary way that such things as county subdivision and building permit applications had to be handled.

"Because the government had not taken final discretionary action authorizing the Developers' project before the referendum was certified," the court ruled, therefore the developer had no guarantee that the resort could be completed regardless of the outcome of the election; and the vote then could and indeed did serve to cancel the resort zoning on 25 acres at Nukolii established by the Council in 1979.

The court also had harsh words for the race that it said the developer had engaged in, writing that "we are persuaded that the good-faith requirements of zoning estoppel are not demonstrated by the Developers here. The expenditures made toward commencing construction before the referendum vote were not only speculative but also fell short of good faith as manifestations of a race of diligence to undermine the referendum process."

For these and other reasons the Hawaii Supreme Court, among other things, directed the Kauai circuit court to "order revocation of the condominium and hotel building permits" and "to restrain any further construction on the Nukolii site."[70]

*　*　*

By now the condominiums had long been completed. But the hotel was only 30% finished. Construction on the hotel came to a halt, and Hasegawa faced the possible loss of what it said was a $50 million dollar investment.

Just after the Supreme Court decision, Gov. Ariyoshi's chief campaign organizer on Kauai, believing that public opinion was shifting in favor of construction at Nukolii, said he got the idea to do a second vote on Nukolii, in the form of an initiative. He later spearheaded formation of a group, Kauaians for Nukolii (KFN), to undertake a petition drive to certify an initiative item to re-establish Nukolii's resort zoning.[71] (Once certification occurred a successor group with essentially the same people took over, Kauaians For Nukolii Campaign Committee [KFNCC], to do the pre-election campaigning. The reason for the two organizations was the belief that the financial affairs of a legally separate group that dissolved itself at the time campaigning began would not have to be reported to the State Campaign Spending Commission. As it turned out both KFN and KFNCC filed, following a complaint by CSN. In this book for the sake of simplicity "KFN" will be used to designate both KFN and KFNCC, unless otherwise noted.)

A poll undertaken in early 1983 by an experienced opinion survey firm, paid for by the people who later founded KFN, discovered that indeed public sentiment had shifted.[72]

Hasegawa in about 1982 retained two additional Hawaii law firms: Cades Schutte Fleming & Wright, and Fujiyama Duffy & Fujiyama. Both contained some of the best legal talent in the Islands.[73] Cades was for on-the-record litigation in the person of Edward A. Jaffe; Fujiyama, in the person of Wallace S. Fujiyama, for strategizing and political lobbying.

The developer attempted to get the US Supreme Court to review the Hawaii Supreme Court decision.[74]

In a rare move the governor stepped in and had the state attorney general urge the high court to accept the case and reverse the Hawaii Supreme Court. Several national organizations affiliated with the construction industry also filed briefs urging reversal. The Supreme Court declined to take the case, however.[75]

The whole situation by now was getting national and even some international attention in development and financial circles, so remarkable and dangerous a precedent was it considered by many businessmen that a major construction project could be halted after government had allowed it to proceed so far.[76]

KFN was vigorous and well organized, and was riding a groundswell of public opinion favoring completion of the Nukolii resort. In the summer of 1983, in one-fifth the time it had taken CSN to gather its referendum petition signatures in 1979-1980, KFN gathered roughly double the CSN number.[77]

* * *

Where CSN failed to get Council approval for an early special election on its downzoning referendum, KFN was successful in urging the Council to schedule a special election on the question of restoring resort zoning. CSN's failure was due in large part to there being a majority on the Council in favor of a resort at Nukolii; holding the special election that CSN urged would conceivably have been disadvantageous to the developer. In large part KFN's success derived from KFN offering to pay the cost of a special election, by way of a $40,000 loan and a $10,000 donation to KFN from Hasegawa.[78] It was also significant that, as before, a majority of Council members favored the development.

The fact that former councilman Robert Yotsuda was chairman of KFN now brought charges of hypocrisy from CSN, since Yotsuda as council chairman had led the opposition to a special election the first time around.

On both occasions what was heavily at issue in deciding when the elections would take place was who would ultimately prevail.

The first time it had to do with vested rights. Those wanting an earlier date in 1980 argued that the less time the developer had to obtain permits and to build, the less likely that its rights would vest. Yotsuda in 1980 dismissed their point as insignificant. He wrote: "I personally have serious doubts whether such a limited period of forty-six days [between the primary and the general] would effectively deter or inhibit the landowner's ability to obtain vested rights before the proposed special election."[79] Although this was only speculation on his part at the time, as it turned out he was right. Neither the circuit court decision which held that rights had vested, nor the Supreme Court's reversal of this opinion, found that the date of the 1980 election had been determinative of anything.

The second time around the timing of the election was thought by both sides to matter in terms of voter participation rates and attitudes, thus ultimately how the vote would go. CSN argued, as their lawyers wrote in a court document filed after the second election, that a "lower voter turnout . . . traditionally accompanies a special election." Moreover, not only would fewer people vote, but they would do so "at a time of year when the economy on the island of Kauai was sluggish; it was off-season for the tourist industry and consequently people were unemployed; and generally, construction and development on the island had slowed."[80]

Now also Hasegawa, every day the project was stalled, was incurring expenses—interest charges, for example. In an interview for this book, a Hasegawa attorney estimated that if the KFN initiative question had gone on the 1984 general election ballot instead of the much earlier date that KFN was pushing for, this would have meant an additional $2.7 million in non-recoverable expenses of this kind.

The election was scheduled for February 1984.

Following the election CSN filed suit in federal court, seeking, among other things, a judgment that the way the special election issue was handled by the Council in 1980 and 1983 was unconstitutional; that the Council had violated CSN's right to equal protection under the law by denying CSN a special election but granting one to KFN. CSN claimed this happened because CSN was unable to pay the cost of a special election but KFN was, a matter of "discrimination based upon wealth," according to CSN.

Federal District Court Judge Harold M. Fong dismissed comparisons of the 1980 and 1983 Council decisions as attempting to compare apples and oranges. He wrote that when CSN "first submitted their petition in the beginning of 1980, they did not request a special election." In fact what they did was submit their petitions, which asked the Council either to schedule a special election or to place the Nukolii issue on that fall's general election ballot. CSN then apparently stood silent on urging one or the other course, and initially acquiesced in the Council's placing the issue on the general ballot.

Several months later, as mentioned, CSN attempted to switch the date of the Nukolii vote to that fall's primary. Fong wrote that this request "did not involve an actual petition for a special election, but merely a tardy request to shift a referendum question already on the general election ballot to the primary election ballot forty-six days earlier." KFN, on the other hand, from the start requested a special election.

Fong also pointed out that the Council's denial of the CSN special election request had nothing to do with election expenses. Scheduling the Nukolii vote for either the primary or the general would apparently have cost the County about the same amount of money. Thus it probably did not matter that CSN could not have offered to pay for the election.

Then, when the Council agreed to schedule a special election for KFN, Fong wrote, CSN had the opportunity to get on that ballot with an initiative item of its own, for which it was gathering signatures.

Fong concluded: "Based on the foregoing undisputed facts, the court . . . finds that there is insufficient relationship between the County Council's decisions in 1980 and 1983 to raise an issue of equal protection."

* * *

In preparation for the 1984 election, more money was reported spent as of election day than had ever been spent on a Kauai election—85% of it by KFN with 57% of KFN's money coming from the developer by way of loans and outright contributions, with most of the rest coming from businesses and individuals involved with the construction industry.[81]

By almost any standard, the money spent in the 1984 Nukolii initiative exceeded anything Kauai had ever seen. To take one measure—dollars spent by election winners per registered voter—KFN spent, as measured in 1980 dollars, $7.62. The next closest figure came from the 1980 mayoral primary. It was $4.20, as measured in 1980 dollars. Next after that was the 1982 mayoral primary in which, again counted in 1980 dollars, the winner spent $3.29 per registered voter.[82]

* * *

Part of KFN's large bankroll was spent on a clever use of a previously little-noticed 1981 change in the state's absentee balloting law.

As amended in 1981 the law allowed a person to obtain an absentee ballot simply on request, with no showing that, for example, he or she were ill, could not be physically present the day of the election, etc.

KFN mailed and handed out absentee ballot request forms to some 58% of Kauai's registered voters. The forms contained postcards addressed to KFN, on which were printed requests that the county clerk send absentee ballots to the voters who signed the cards. The cards were mailed to KFN, who upon receipt paid the postage. KFN then hand-carried the cards to the clerk's office. The clerk then mailed absentee ballots directly to voters.

KFN had several criteria for deciding who should be sent a ballot request form. First, everyone who signed the KFN initiative petition got one. This accounted for three-quarters of the 58%. Second, so also did everyone who had voted absentee in the last general election. The theory in mailing to these people—students away at school and shut-ins—was that by having been entirely or even somewhat removed from the swirl of events surrounding Nukolii, they might somehow have been less influenced by negative attitudes on Kauai toward the project. Also, in mailing to these people KFN included a campaign leaflet; in doing so KFN conceivably was able to reach them with its campaign material before CSN could. Finally, all registered voters with Japanese last names who had not fallen into one of the above two categories were probably sent forms, on the assumption, as verified by several KFN opinion polls, that in disproportionate numbers Japanese tended to favor completion of the project. Thus, ironically, several CSN leaders with Japanese last names received a KFN form in the mail.[83]

Whether KFN similarly targeted other ethnic groups is unclear, except that in several interviews for this book with KFN leaders, it was indicated that *haoles*, unless they had signed the KFN petition or had been absentee in 1982, were not sent forms. Again this decision would have been based on survey results showing that of all ethnic groups, *haoles* were most likely to oppose completing construction at Nukolii.

*   *   *

Many people in the course of the Nukolii conflict did newsworthy things, and the media generally took a keen interest in what went on.

At one point even, CBS-TV's *60 Minutes* came out to Kauai. A crew, including correspondent Ed Bradley, filmed the second Nukolii election and did interviews, though no story ever aired.

Hawaii media in varying degrees covered Nukolii as well of course. On Kauai there was *The Garden Island* newspaper, which had been coming out since 1902. It was joined in 1979 by the *Kauai Times*. Also covering Nukolii were Honolulu's two dailies, which each had a writer on Kauai, two AM radio stations located on the island, and occasionally a television station based in Honolulu, which might or might not send over a reporter and cameraperson.

Although it is impossible to be certain, for Kauai residents *The Garden Island* was probably the greatest single source of information about Nukolii. *The Garden Island* had far greater circulation on Kauai than the two Oahu-based papers combined. Published since practically the start of the twentieth century, it had a well-established readership that the *Kauai Times* had trouble shaking. Radio news had immediacy, but seldom provided the volume of detail that a newspaper could; nor could a radio news story be gone back to by a listener with the ease that a newspaper reader could later pick up his or her paper to re-read a story.

By ordinary journalistic standards in Hawaii, both *The Garden Island* and the *Kauai Times* were on occasion as much participants as dispassionate observers when it came to Nukolii. Arguably their behavior added to the intensity of it all; *The Garden Island*'s in particular, since apparently it was taken seriously by many more Kauai readers than the *Kauai Times*.

Much of what appeared in *The Garden Island* as hard news regarding Nukolii was handled in a straightforward and objective way. At the same time, on the whole there appeared to be more words in print in *The Garden Island* that were voiced by critics of building than by proponents.

As mentioned, since taking over as editor of *The Garden Island* in the late 1960s, Jean Holmes, a warm-hearted populist, had made it a strong policy to welcome ordinary people bringing their announcements to the paper and writing in their letters.

She and most or all of the others among *The Garden Island*'s editorial and writing staff strongly opposed development at Nukolii; they applauded the willingness of the everyday sort of people in CSN to take on big developers and the government, whom the editors and writers generally viewed as being in collusion to push construction at Nukolii against the wishes of many on Kauai.

Thus *The Garden Island* readily printed in full or quoted extensively from the numerous news statements issued by CSN. Indeed a CSN leader said that on occasion *Garden Island* staff encouraged CSN to write more. So close was the CSN-*Garden Island* relationship that frequently court documents prepared by CSN lawyers were written about in the paper before they were even filed in court or copies given to opposing attorneys.

If as a result of all this a great deal more anti-development words regarding Nukolii got printed in *The Garden Island* than in, say, the *Honolulu Advertiser*, Holmes maintained that, nevertheless, space would always be made for those being criticized to issue rebuttal statements, and that when ordinary news practice required, the other side was always contacted for comment.

Even so, the relative closeness between several on *The Garden Island* staff and CSN appeared to lead the paper at times into the rather uncritical printing of CSN propaganda.

*   *   *

The most remarkable instance of this involved a *Garden Island* reporter writing a story attacking an article written by another *Garden Island* reporter that, although essentially accurate, had reflected badly on CSN:

Following CSN's win in the Hawaii Supreme Court in the fall of 1982, CSN lawyers offered to Hasegawa lawyers to discuss settling the case, rather than fighting it out on remand to circuit court over whether the condominiums could stay and the hotel be completed, and over whether Hasegawa had to pay damages for now having resort structures on land that voters downzoned to agriculture.

An initial discussion was held in the office of Hasegawa's attorney on Kauai, Walton Hong, and about two days later there was a short standup meeting at the airport in Honolulu. According to attorneys for both sides who were interviewed for this book, the parameters of the talks, as suggested by CSN attorneys, were that the condominiums could stay and the hotel be completed, in exchange for a sum of money donated by Hasegawa to a community trust fund. The actual dollar figure or figures mentioned by CSN lawyers at the time—around $20 million—were rejected as too high. Thereafter, in about June 1983, CSN and Hasegawa lawyers met for several days in Honolulu to try to agree on a figure. No settlement was ever reached, however.

In late 1982 or early 1983 the *Honolulu Advertiser* reporter on Kauai had gotten a tip about the CSN offer. In April 1983 he corroborated it and included the information in a story.[84]

Garden Island reporter Julia Neal either saw the *Advertiser* article or was independently pursuing a tip of her own. She contacted an attorney representing the developer and two who represented CSN—one based in San Francisco and one on Kauai. Neal wrote a story essentially identical to the *Advertiser*'s, though lengthier.[85] Research for this book indicated that stories by the *Advertiser* and Neal were basically accurate.

The CSN attorney on Kauai, Linda B. Levy, caught tremendous criticism, however, from CSN members and supporters who had known nothing of a possible settlement. By their account, even if they had known they would not have approved. To them it was unthinkable to consider asking for money in exchange for dropping what they considered a matter of high principle. Some were also upset at the fact that CSN lead attorney Sidney M. Wolinsky was asking that his firm be given a percentage of any settlement money that might be obtained. This fee would go to support his firm's public interest legal work.

In addition there was a blackening of CSN's reputation among many in the general community, for what they saw as CSN literally selling out. Levy told the *Advertiser* after the story had broken that "she fears the public will come to distrust the Committee to Save Nukolii over the settlement issue."[86]

To lessen some of the criticism and, in Levy's eyes, to clarify things, she or another CSN member contacted a *Garden Island* reporter who was particularly sympathetic to CSN, William LeGro, about doing a story. A story resulted, apparently based only on statements by Levy.[87] Its headline read: "Save Nukoli'i Made No Offer." Its lead paragraph was: "The news reports that the Save Nukoli'i Committee is prepared to allow completion of the hotel at Nukoli'i in return for a cash settlement are 'false,' a Committee attorney told The Garden Island yesterday."

What made LeGro's story so remarkable was that the CSN lead attorney, Wolinsky, based in San Francisco, had just written a statement on the matter, part of which ran in the *Advertiser* two days before LeGro's piece, which read: "In order to avoid a lengthy trial as to damages, the Committee has made a fair and reasonable settlement offer to the developers."[88]

LeGro said later that he viewed his handling of the matter as a case of *The Garden Island* readily providing an outlet for a citizen group to air its views on a vital issue, as was the paper's strong policy. In this instance, however, because of a disinclination to closely scrutinize what the paper was being told, what got into print was a great distortion of fact.

* * *

Editor Holmes was away when LeGro's and Neal's articles ran. She said that upon returning she criticized both. Holmes said she was critical of Neal's story because it left the impression that the initial CSN offer and Hasegawa's rejection of it had been quite recent. The offer and rejection had taken place perhaps half a year before Neal's article, but it was not until far into her story that the reader saw that. Since many newspaper readers look only at an article's first few lines, Holmes said that a number of readers might have thought the events had just recently taken place. She said that a misleading impression of this kind violated one of the fundamental rules of news reporting—be precise as to the "when" of things.

In any event, while those who read Neal's story had to read on in order to learn precisely when the key events occurred, still, this had no bearing on what was the underlying accuracy of what she wrote.

* * *

There were other cases of arguable *de facto* bias in what *Garden Island* reporters wrote about Nukolii.

For example, on the eve of the 1984 initiative the paper ran a long article delving deeply into an aspect of a then two year-old incident that, when it first surfaced, had reflected badly on the developer:[89]

In 1981 Hasegawa applied to the State Board of Land and Natural Resources to demolish an old World War II bunker that was on conservation district land. In connection with this a BLNR employee talked with an attorney for Hasegawa about the status of the whole project. While talking, the BLNR person learned that the year before, the developer had subdivided the property in order to make separate lots for the hotel, the condominiums, and the 35 reserve acres. The subdivision lines ran perpendicular to the ocean, thus they ran into and part way through a strip of conservation district land that bordered the ocean. This in effect was a subdivision of conservation land; it should have been authorized by the Land Board prior to or in conjunction with the Kauai Planning Commission approving those parts of the subdivision lines that lay in urban district areas.

To put things right, it was agreed that Hasegawa would file an after-the-fact conservation district use application.

Once that was filed and while it was in progress, it was determined by the

Land Board that the siting of a now-constructed condominium building, plus some things like sprinklers, were partially or entirely inside the conservation district. That there was an illegal encroachment was a matter of opinion; it depended on which surveying method was used to establish the location of the shoreline. Apparently there was precedent for the approach used by the developer's surveyor. Nevertheless the Land Board ruled he was in error. For this Hasegawa was fined about $35,000 and ordered to apply to the Land Use Commission for urban districting for the land involved. Early in 1983 Hasegawa filed its LUC petition. A hearing was held that summer. Then, with the KFN initiative underway, the LUC withheld final action pending the result of the election. (About 10 months after the election the LUC approved the redistricting.) As of the time of the election and *The Garden Island* story, there had been no action on the issue for over half a year.

The newspaper story was a long analysis of how various surveyors viewed the question of establishing Nukolii's legal shoreline boundary.[90] Where the boundary was had to do with whether there had been illegal encroachment, if so how much, and possibly whether the encroachment had been deliberate. The subject is complex; the story was very difficult to follow. Summarizing it on the eve of the election had the arguably legitimate objective of reminding voters about an issue pertaining to the project that many might now be hazy on, if they ever understood it at all. On the other hand, there was no direct evidence that the whole episode had arisen from anything but an honest oversight regarding subdivision, and a simple difference of opinion regarding shoreline boundaries. Moreover, from Hasegawa's standpoint, this issue was one of the most negative and embarrassing things that could be written about at the time. The article had the appearance of an effort to discredit the development, thus to influence voters to vote against construction.

Another example of the feelings of a number of *Garden Island* writers came in a witty, Nukolii rendition of a game that resembled "Monopoly." In the summer of 1983, a *Garden Island* reporter developed "The Nukolii Game." Taking up a full page in the paper to present a game board and rules, it was a rather creative adaptation of a "Monopoly"-style game to what had been taking place on Kauai with respect to Nukolii.

Several supporters of development at Nukolii said they found the game offensive. It was not hard to see why. The first game rule listed by the reporter was: "Any number can play, but it's good to form a hui of influential friends with access to inside information and play as a team." The second rule read: "Object of game is to develop as much of Kaua'i as possible. When nobody can go anywhere or do anything without paying or being arrested for trespass, the game should be called."[91]

*   *   *

If *The Garden Island* leaned one way on the question of Nukolii, the *Kauai Times* leaned the other way.

Founded in 1979 by a group of local businessmen, most of whom were involved with some facet of land development, with perhaps the most noteworthy among them being Clinton Shiraishi, the paper was consciously set up as a pro-business alternative to *The Garden Island*.

In editorials and news reporting the *Times* took consistently pro-development-of-Nukolii positions, usually citing as the reason the need to improve Kauai's economy.

On occasion what appeared in the *Times* was shrill and heavy-handed. As mentioned, CSN's lead attorney was based in a San Francisco public-interest law firm. With reference to this fact and in a play on the words "Kauaians for Nukolii," in an editorial in early 1984 the *Kauai Times* editor/publisher wrote derisively of "Californians against Nukolii." Elsewhere in the editorial he indicated that they were outsider meddlers.[92] This despite the fact that the current developer of Nukolii was a company from Japan, and he himself had not lived on the island all that long.

Also around this time, there was a "special report" on conservation prepared "exclusively for Kauai Times" by a member of the Robinson family, owners of the island of Niihau and a large part of southwest Kauai. In an author's note prefacing Part IV of a series, Keith Robinson recounted how he had predicted to the *Kauai Times* editor that, following publication of his series, "environmentalists and perhaps some Hawaiian activists would go into a jibbering frenzy, and engage in all kinds of name-calling, vituperation, and personal abuse." Not to be outdone when it came to name-calling, Robinson in the body of the article went on to say that many environmentalists were "ecomaniacs" who were "little more than headline-hunting publicity hounds," who engaged in "constant trespassing" and in general "cause nothing except distrust, fear, instability, and chaos." In an earlier instalment, Robinson had called the environmental movement "little more than a howling mobocracy."[93]

On occasions the *Kauai Times* took shots at *The Garden Island* too. A *Times* editorial in mid-1983 said that "for years there has been no objective reporting in the local newspaper and commentary and opinion has been placed somewhere other than the editorial page where it belongs. The *Kauai Times* staff and management," on the other hand, "has no axe to grind with any one group . . ."[94]

By most accounts, though, Kauai's next-most-read newspaper, the *Honolulu Advertiser* with its outer-island edition, played it absolutely straight throughout the Nukolii controversy.

* * *

If in the key Nukolii years of 1977 and 1980 Kauai's economy was or appeared to be healthy enough that voters in large numbers could disregard the potential financial benefit to the community of a resort at Nukolii, by the time of the 1984 special election this was no longer so.

Sugar statewide by 1983 was in an extremely precarious condition. In 1981 the industry had lost about $100 million. In the early 1980s there were temporary shutdowns of plantations. Rumors ran wild that this and that plantation might permanently close. Amfac's Puna Sugar Co. on the Big Island announced that indeed it would close, and began doing so in 1982.[95]

Around Thanksgiving 1982, Hurricane Iwa devastated Kauai, creating a short-term economic disaster island-wide, leading to a much greater support for development in general.[96]

Kauai unemployment in 1983 was a moderately serious 7.7%. Hotel occupancy was a disastrous 57.2%. That both of these figures were in part related to the hurricane, the effects of which would probably pass eventually, was little immediate comfort to many on Kauai, who had not seen such bad economic times in years.

*　*　*

Another element of change on Kauai that was setting up the 1984 vote for a result different from 1980 had to do with ethnicity.

The overwhelming majority of people who made up the first organization that opposed a resort at Nukolii were Hawaii-born, lived somewhere in the general vicinity of Nukolii, and actually used the area for one purpose or another.

By the time of the 1984 vote the visible leadership, as well as the membership, of CSN was heavily mainland *haole*, whose reasons for being involved were more generally political, rather than, say, having surfed at Nukolii since childhood.

What had happened was that the place of battle had shifted from informal public hearings before the County Council to much more technical settings like courts or quasi-judicial hearings before the County Planning Commission. Also, with the CSN referendum petition drive, the social arena became the whole island. Now people with legal and research skills and more theoretical ideologies about government and development tended to displace people without these skills and whose focus was more that of preserving Nukolii for its intrinsic value to themselves, their families and friends. In short this tended to mean mainland *haoles* displaced locals.

The leadership of Kauaians For Nukolii, on the other hand, was overwhelmingly an ethnic cross-section of Kauai-born people, with some tendency toward a concentration of local-Asians.

Opinion surveys done for KFN by one of Hawaii's leading pollsters, Hawaii Opinion Inc., indicated that the ethnic makeup of KFN and CSN were rooted in Kauai's wider society. A poll done in September 1983 found that 64% of those surveyed wanted to see the hotel finished and only 26% were opposed. While 50% of those who had lived on Kauai three years or less said they supported completion, the figure rose to 70% for lifelong residents. Moreover, while 48% of *haoles* surveyed were found to endorse completion, 62% of Hawaiians did, and 74% of Japanese and 77% of Filipinos.[97]

Exactly where in sociological terms the newfound support for Nukolii had come from since 1980 is impossible to say, since apparently no similar polls were done prior to or just after the 1980 vote.

In any case, for whatever reasons and regardless of intentions, the conflict in the period just before the second election had become to an extent one of mainland *haoles* versus locals. Given the anti-*haole* feeling that had played some part in the initial organizing against the resort back in 1977, this was a major turn of events. Also, on an island that was still quite anti-*haole*, on which *haoles* in 1983 made up only some 30% of the population, the turn was of major consequence.

* * *

Voters in the 1984 special election reinstated Nukolii's resort zoning by a 58%-42% margin.[98]

KFN's use of absentee ballots played a role in this result.

In the election altogether 14,504 ballots were cast both for and against restoring resort zoning, both in person and absentee. Of these 4,680 were absentee, 82% of which favored restoring the zoning. Another way of looking at this was that 45% of all votes in favor of restoring the zoning were cast absentee, while only 14% of all votes against were. And while CSN won in terms of people who actually went to the polls—5,099 to 4,656—when the absentees were added in, KFN won 8,476 to 5,917.

Arguably, though, KFN would have won by at least a 52% to 48% margin even without massive reliance on absentee voting. Assuming that most who voted absentee were physically present on Kauai the day of the election and physically capable of going to the polls, both of which assumptions seem logical, and assuming those who voted absentee would have gone to the polls at the same rate that non-absentee voters did, then KFN would have won by about 52% to 48%. But it is probably incorrect to assume that those who voted absentee would have physically gone to the polls in the same proportion as the rest of Kauai voters. Those who voted absentee would, if forced to go to the polls, probably have gone in greater numbers, since their casting an absentee ballot indicated they wanted to vote on Nukolii. And since 82% of the absentee votes were cast in favor of the resort, 52% is probably a low figure for the percentage by which KFN would have won even without the absentee maneuver.

CSN made many bitter complaints about the absentee ballots. For one, CSN suggested that the ballots were highly susceptible to having been tampered with. In a Hawaii Supreme Court suit CSN wrote that the County administration, "who publicly and consistently took a partisan position in favor of the development . . . made the arrangements for thousands of already marked and voted absentee ballots, which altered the results of the election, to be kept in the Kauai County Courthouse for many nights unguarded and 'secured' only by ordinary small locks purchasable in any hardware store. The tie-in between local Kauai government and the development has always been close, heightening the opportunity for unfair or illegal election tactics. These factors, coupled with the absence of public confidence in the integrity of the local government process on Kauai, highlight the need for close judicial examination of the circumstances of this unique election and its numerous irregularities."[99]

CSN also attacked the fact that the cost of the special election was paid by the developer itself, although KFN later repaid Hasegawa the $40,000 loan. The expense of holding an election being borne by an interested party was something nearly or altogether unprecedented in the United States. CSN argued that it had dangerous implications.

The Hawaii Supreme Court rather quickly threw CSN's case out. The court wrote that the law at issue required "factual allegations to show that as a result of the alleged irregularities or irregularities, there was a difference in the election results sufficient to change the same." But, the court indicated, CSN had merely made conclusory allegations that failed to link claimed irregularities "to any quantity of votes cast."[100] By about a year later a federal case had also been thrown out. In dismissing part of the CSN federal lawsuit that asked that the 1984 special election be voided, Judge Harold Fong scolded CSN for not having filed suit before the election was held. What CSN had done was to wait to see if CSN could win the election. When it lost it then went to court. Fong wrote that "it was incumbent upon [CSN] to raise [its] concerns in this Court prior to the election."[101]

The State Supreme Court's 1982 decision had left up to the circuit court judge on Kauai the question of what to do about the fact that, in view of the Supreme Court's decision, the project had no legitimate building permits. Specifically concerning the condominiums, although the Supreme Court decision did not decide whether they should be torn down, the justices indicated that probably they should be allowed to stay. The court wrote in a footnote that the developer had not deliberately broken zoning laws, but rather had engaged in a race and lost. "We conclude that where, as in this case, a defendant does not intentionally violate underlying zoning," the rule should apply that the completed improvement be ordered removed only "if serious injury is being inflicted or will be inflicted." The opinion indicated that here there either was no injury or that it was not serious. The court suggested in the alternative that money damages might be more appropriate, "or the fashioning of other injunctive relief which might mitigate any harm caused by the offending structure." Conceivably an extensive tree and bush buffer could be planted on the seaward side of the condominiums so that they would not be readily visible from the beach.[102]

Regarding the hotel, since it was not completed, conceivably the developer would not be allowed to finish it. But as of the conclusion of the second vote, there was no longer any question about whether the condominiums would stay, nor whether the hotel would ultimately be finished.

In late 1984 the circuit court judge said he now had two alternatives: order that the project be removed, or order damages be paid to CSN. The judge decided that ordering the project torn down would be improper in view of the results of the second election, and that, since CSN had said it wanted no damages for itself, the case should be, and was, dismissed.[103]

CSN indicated it would appeal on the assertion that damages were owing for the time between the two elections in which condominiums and a partially-completed hotel stood on land not zoned for such buildings, with any such damages due not to CSN but to the County as the representative of the public on Kauai.

The County for its part had said, following the second election, that it wanted no damages, a stand that infuriated CSN, which saw this as another instance of government working hand-in-glove with the developer.

The County Attorney's position was that any damage payments would be for criminal violations of county codes—having a plumbing system in a building that for a period of time was a resort-type use in an agriculture zone. Prior to the 1984 election the County Attorney was prepared to attempt to exact damages in court on this basis. But since a majority of Kauai voters indicated in 1984 that they wanted the project to stay, therefore for the County to now assess or receive damages seemed to the County Attorney contrary to the general position of the electorate, especially since it was the County Attorney's view that the developer had not intentionally violated any law.[104]

* * *

What had produced such a conflict, one that for Hawaii was so large-scale?

What made this question doubly intriguing was that, throughout the previous quarter-century, all other places in Hawaii where people had squared off in big ways on environmental issues were locations like Diamond Head, the Hawaiian Islands' best-known landmark; Salt Lake, Hawaii's only lake of any size; Kalama Valley in east Oahu, an entire valley involving the eviction of tenants; Waiahole and Waikane valleys in windward Oahu, two entire valleys, both particularly beautiful and making significant contributions to local food production, and containing several hundred tenants; Niumalu and Nawiliwli, also two especially pretty valleys, involving historic sites and about 140 people as tenants; a highway project on Oahu generally called H-3, involving huge land areas and major recreational resources and historic sites, also the potential for a large increase in urbanization along the entire northern part of windward Oahu.

Even many controversies of lesser intensity than Nukolii involved far greater land areas and more significant natural resources: the question about whether to develop geothermal energy in large tracts along the east rift zone of Kilauea Volcano on the Big Island; whether to allow Japan's Seibu Group Enterprises to build a major resort in Maui's remote Makena area; whether to allow condominiums in front of Molokai's Kawakiu Bay.

Several kinds of things made Nukolii the huge battleground that it became. Among these were simple accidents, coincidences, fortuitous events.

For example, the abrupt end of the fight in Nawiliwili intersected with the County Council starting to process the Lihue Development Plan. Environmental activists as well as ordinary people who had seldom if ever been involved in opposing development were primed for a fight. And there was at that time such a sense of commitment on the part of community and environmental activists on Kauai that, once started in on Nukolii, disengagement was unlikely.

Also, the investigative work undertaken by *Honolulu Advertiser* reporter James Dooley initially had nothing to do with Nukolii, but coincidentally wound its way around to Nukolii on the eve of the 1980 referendum vote—with tremendous effect.

Dooley's work started with his seeing trucks connected to a Hawaii Housing Authority project regularly pass his house in Kuliouou in east Oahu. Wondering about and then researching the development led indirectly to his discovery, through examination of a probate file generated by an apparent syndicate murder, of an unregistered land *hui* organized on Maui, one that involved several public officials or people influential in politics.

As a result a series on unregistered *huis* ran in the spring before the 1980 Nukolii referendum vote.[105] The series led to an anonymous telephone tip about a similar *hui* involved in Nukolii. After sporadic research sandwiched between other work, this led Dooley to a story about such a Nukolii *hui*, a story that was completed and ready just before the 1980 general election.[106]

There were coincidences of an economic sort that also made themselves felt. Most importantly, in the early 1980s there was a serious economic downturn statewide, leading to many people becoming more concerned about the health of business in Hawaii. During this came the Hawaii Supreme Court's October 1982 Nukolii decision that shocked the state's business community, and led to dire predictions by many businesspeople and public officials about the decision's impact on the Islands' economy. A few weeks later Kauai was ravaged by Hurricane Iwa, which created short-term economic devastation on the island, leading to many people looking much more favorably on development in general. All this was followed, in January 1983, by a business magazine with national circulation saying that Hawaii businesspeople had long considered the Islands to have a particularly anti-business atmosphere.[107] The public airing of this view at long last tended to spur Hawaii businesspeople into action on various fronts. As they now spoke out, the Hawaii Supreme Court's Nukolii decision became perhaps their number one example of how difficult and dangerous a place Hawaii had become in which to do business.

*   *   *

Something else that made the fight over Nukolii large and intense was the fact that elements from across virtually the entire spectrum of powerful organizations in Hawaii were ranged in favor of development. Persons and organizations with a great deal of money, connections, pride and know-how were directly involved. Some were willing and able to go the limit to win, which helped escalate the whole controversy to heights previously unknown on Kauai, and seldom seen elsewhere in Hawaii for that matter.

Moreover these establishment elements weighed in at a time when Hawai'i's era of liberalism in the area of land use was in steep decline, meaning that more conservative and pro-business views were on the rise with respect to development. In general the "environmentalist years" were slipping into the past. In the public arena pro-development forces were asserting themselves boldly and on a large scale against anti-development groups. And because the Kauai county charter had referendum and initiative provisions that could be used on zoning matters, the public arena for Nukolii became not just public hearings and media statements, but the electorate itself, directly.

There were other important political dimensions to Nukolii:

To a remarkable extent persons somehow involved with the sale or development of Nukolii were part of the core of the Islands' political power structure, and to a remarkable extent political influence played or to some appeared to play a role. And given that the opposition to development was made up of many of the elements that in turn comprised the opposition to the Democratic establishment statewide, this made Nukolii a microcosm of larger forces evolving and clashing within Hawai'i's society overall. The fact of Nukolii being a struggle within a struggle heightened its intensity.

Regarding mainstream Democrats being involved with Nukolii, there was in the first place the matter of Amfac in 1973 agreeing to sell the land to Masaru Yokouchi.

Yokouchi was that "powerful guy from Maui" that the land use commissioner told the reporter about in 1974. Because of his influential role in politics, together with a combination of luck and astuteness in real estate investing and developing, and because of a reputation for a particularly fair and generous way of treating others, Yokouchi was one of the most sought-after and best-connected people in Hawaii in the Democratic years. His close friends or associates in business included John Burns, state legislators, Hawaii's foremost artists, judges, the reputed head of organized crime on Maui, members of Hawaii's old *haole* monied class, and union leaders, as well as a host of ordinary people. Also, Yokouchi was associated in a small retail clothing business with former congresswoman and ambassador Clare Booth Luce. For a period of time Yokouchi sat on the eight-member board of directors of Pacific Aquaculture Corporation with Harry C.C. Chung, chief campaign fundraiser for Frank Fasi, an arch rival of the Democratic faction with which Yokouchi was associated.

Yokouchi, as detailed earlier in this book, had been able to help Amfac settle some community and labor problems in west Maui in the late 1960s. Six times in the years ahead when Amfac had land for sale the company sold to him. By Yokouchi's own account, five of those cases were indirect results of his work for Amfac; Amfac was grateful for his help, considered him someone worth cultivating on a long-term basis, and thus someone to whom the company would sell to when it had land for sale.

One of the five was Nukolii.

Once Yokouchi had negotiated the Nukolii purchase, he organized a *hui* that became the actual owner. The *hui* was made up mostly of friends of his, or friends of friends. Most were ordinary local-Asian middle and even some working-class people from Maui. For example, Yokouchi said that several carpenters who had once worked on the Yokouchis' house, when the family lived in Wailuku, were invited to invest.

Because Yokouchi had been in politics for many years he had many friends in the political arena. When word went out about Nukolii it went out to these political friends as well as to non-political ones.

Thus Nukolii investors included people like the family of Nadao Yoshinaga. Yoshinaga and Yokouchi were very close; they were two of the top leaders of the "Democratic revolution" on Maui. Two of Gov. John Burns' children also acquired shares in Yokouchi's Nukolii *hui*, though one of these shares had actually been donated by Yokouchi in trust as financial assistance for Burns' daughter and son-in-law to raise a three-year-old physically handicapped boy they adopted in Japan.

Others in politics or government who in 1973 invested in the Nukolii *hui* were Kase Higa, then a district court judge on Maui; Edwin H. Honda, director of the State Department of Regulatory Agencies; John E. S. Kim, a former Republican Party official; Wallace T. Yanagi, deputy administrator of the state's Maui Memorial Hospital; Yoshikazu "Zuke" Matsui, a Maui planning commissioner; Lanny H. Morisaki, a Maui councilman; and Charles S. Ota, Maui member of the University of Hawaii's Board of Regents.

Thomas S. Yagi, ILWU division director for Maui County, was also a member of the Nukolii *hui*.

The person with whom Yokouchi negotiated the resale was Daniel R. Matsukage, then president of Real Estate Finance Corp. (REFC), a Hawaii subsidiary of Pacific Standard Life Insurance Co. Matsukage was thoroughly a part of the Democratic Party establishment. For example, Matsukage, George Ariyoshi, George's younger brother, plus one other man in the mid-1960s built and then sold a small apartment building near Queen's Hospital in Honolulu.

An officer of REFC as of the time of purchase of Nukolii was University of Hawaii Regent Wallace S. Fujiyama. Later Fujiyama's life touched Nukolii in another way, though not until the early 1980s. This was when as an attorney, in 1982, Fujiyama was retained by Hasegawa Komuten to help solve its Nukolii problems.[108] Fujiyama came to occupy a senior strategist position in all that followed.

Fujiyama was one of Hawaii's most accomplished lawyers and an extremely intelligent man, whose services in this case were sought in part, as he indicated in an interview for this book, because of his also being well-connected politically. In the interview he said his entree with decision-makers did not allow him to manipulate things, nor would he. Rather it guaranteed that when he wanted to see someone he could, and that person—the governor, perhaps—would be inclined to believe what Fujiyama said.

Fujiyama started out his adult life as a Republican. In the late 1950s he was Oahu County chairman of the Young Republicans. By his own account, Fujiyama soured on the Republicans in 1962 for not making him a delegate to the Republican National Convention. Thereafter his affiliations ran more in the direction of Hawaii's Democrats, and Gov. Burns nominated him and the State Senate in 1974 confirmed him as a university regent.

Fujiyama was a particularly well-connected man. Over the years, for example, he was associated in various sports and business activities with David K. Trask Jr., executive director 1969–1981 of one of Hawaii's largest unions, the Hawaii Government Employees Association, Local 152 (HGEA). Both in 1975 were to be officers of a proposed new savings and loan company, Community Savings and Loan Association, though the venture failed to get off the ground.[109]

Honolulu Star-Bulletin reporter John Christensen wrote of Fujiyama in 1978: "He is . . . an important figure in the smoke-filled rooms. He has the governor's ear if he wants it, has lobbied often and successfully in the legislature, and has clients, friends and acquaintances who account for a lot of clout in the state."[110]

To another writer Fujiyama once said that George Ariyoshi was "a classmate of mine" and that "obviously I have close relations with the present governor [Ariyoshi]."[111] In an interview for this book, Fujiyama said that he and Ariyoshi attended the same Japanese language school as small boys. Fujiyama noted that he and Ariyoshi also attended McKinley High School in Honolulu at the same time. (They were not technically in the same class at McKinley—Fujiyama graduated in 1943, Ariyoshi in 1944.)

Several times in 1982 there were newspaper accounts of Fujiyama being included in small gatherings, part social, part business, that included Ariyoshi and other close friends and associates of Ariyoshi. For example Fujiyama was reported to be leading a small party that included the Ariyoshis on a trip to an outer island—aboard Mid Pacific Airlines, of which Fujiyama was a corporate director.[112]

Also as of 1982 Fujiyama was the attorney for Y. Hata & Co. Ltd., a food wholesaling business, one of whose vice-presidents, Frank J. Hata, was a principal fundraiser for Ariyoshi, also for Eileen R. Anderson, Ariyoshi's former budget director who ran for and won the Honolulu mayor's office in 1980. (She lost a re-election bid in 1984.)

Fujiyama was president of the Hawaii Bar Association in 1973. In 1981, one of President Ronald Reagan's top advisors, Edwin Meese III, was the featured speaker at a dinner honoring Fujiyama in Honolulu. Honolulu newspapers variously described Meese as a "friend" and a "close friend" of Fujiyama.[113] The dinner was a fundraiser, the proceeds from which went to the University of Hawaii law school, which Fujiyama had been instrumental in founding. In the early 1980s a major corporate client of Fujiyama, Duty Free Shoppers Ltd., on whose behalf Fujiyama in 1982 had helped persuade the Legislature to grant an exclusive franchise to sell duty-free goods at Honolulu International Airport, funded the Wallace S. Fujiyama Distinguished Visiting Professor of Law chair at the law school.

*   *   *

For a while former Democratic state Sen. Francis A. Wong also did legal work for the Nukolii developer.

Another lawyer who initially represented Pacific Standard regarding Nukolii, and who later was one of many representing Hasegawa, was Walton D. Y. Hong. Hong was a former deputy state attorney general who had been assigned to the Land Use Commission during part of his state tenure. Hong was also reputed to be a particularly energetic and competent attorney.

In a very small place like Kauai, another aspect of Walton Hong's practice illustrated how small Kauai's power structure was. Hong's law partner was George M. Masuoka. As of, for example, the time in early 1981 that Circuit Court Judge Kei Hirano ruled that Hasegawa had vested rights to proceed, Masuoka's father, Shinichi, was Hirano's bailiff. George Masuoka at the time was a *per diem* district court judge, making him and Hirano the only or among the only judges on the island, working out of the same small courthouse in Lihue.

Hirano himself was a study in law and local politics. Born on Kauai in 1930, he grew up on the island, got a university degree in Honolulu and a law degree on the mainland. His first job after law school was in 1959–1960 as a clerk at the Hawaii Supreme Court. Thereafter and on through his years as a judge, every job Hirano obtained was also a governmental position, either directly or indirectly a political appointment. This had partly to do with political activity on his part; during the mid-1950s, and especially throughout the 1960s, Hirano was active in electoral politics on Kauai as a Democratic Party campaign organizer. Hirano declined to be interviewed for this book. However, a man who was a key Democratic Party leader on Kauai during this period said in an interview that Hirano "was active in Democratic Party activities." He said Hirano worked for such Democratic candidates as John Burns and Spark Matsunaga; moreover he also said that the Matsunaga and Hirano families were close, having come from the same part of Kauai.

In addition he said that when William S. Richardson was Burns' running mate in 1962, Hirano was one of Richardson's key campaign organizers on Kauai. For whatever reason, about ten years later, while Hirano was Kauai county attorney, Richardson appointed him Kauai's only state district court judge. This was at the time in 1971 when Hawaii's old district court system was abolished, with its many part-time magistrates, and a consolidated system set up, staffed mainly with full-time judges. Later George Ariyoshi appointed Hirano as Kauai's only circuit court judge. The Democratic Party leader interviewed regarding Hirano said that once Hirano was appointed a judge, he totally divorced himself from politics, and was a particularly ethical and conscientious judge.

The fact of the Hirano-Richardson association provided one large irony: it was Richardson who, as one of his last acts as Chief Justice of the state Supreme Court in 1982, authored the court's Nukolii opinion, reversing Hirano.[114]

The Richardson opinion pointed to yet another high public official, an appointee of Gov. Ariyoshi to the Hawaii Supreme Court, with a connection to Nukolii: Justice Edward H. Nakamura, as indicated in the decision, had declined to take part in deliberations. Conceivably this was because, prior to Nakamura's Supreme Court appointment, he purchased and now still owned a share in Masaru Yokouchi's Nukolii *hui.*

* * *

Most members of Kauaians For Nukolii and its successor organization, KFNCC, were locally born professionals and business people. Several others had held public office. They were Tad T. Miura Sr., a former mayoral aide and former county clerk, who was a KFN assistant treasurer and KFNCC treasurer; Robert K. Yotsuda, a former Kauai councilman who had been council chairman in 1979 and 1980, who was the KFN chairman and a KFNCC director; Turk Tokita, who from 1957–1982 was an aide to the County Board of Supervisors and then Council, and who from 1954–1984 organized election campaigns on Kauai for John Burns and George Ariyoshi; Burt K. Tsuchiya, a former county councilman and council chairman who later served on the University Board of Regents; Wallace G. Rezentes, a former county finance director, who was a KFN subcommittee chairman; and R. Barbara Daly, a former county public information officer, who was KFN's executive director. Another KFN member was Clarence "Gadget" Takashima, recently retired as head of the HGEA on Kauai.

Tokita was particularly central to the KFN effort and to Democratic Party politics on Kauai. A 442d veteran who in 1954 became John Burns' chief campaign organizer on Kauai, Tokita was thus the counterpart of Masaru Yokouchi on Maui. As mentioned Tokita also served in that capacity for George Ariyoshi.

In an interview for this book, Tokita said that it was he who first got the idea for a second election, right after the 1982 Hawaii Supreme Court decision on Nukolii, which came in the closing days of that year's gubernatorial election campaign. (Wallace Fujiyama said that he too independently concluded there ought to be a second election.)

Tokita said that he then involved or talked over the idea with others who were central to the Ariyoshi organization.

As mentioned, Tokita was coordinating the Ariyoshi campaign on Kauai. Former Ariyoshi aide Gary Caulfield was a statewide campaign co-chairman, whose duties covered the outer islands. He and Tokita were in regular contact during the 1982 campaign.

According to Tokita, at one point just after the campaign he mentioned the election idea to Caulfield, who said he would help. Indeed it was Caulfield who later proposed the absentee balloting plan that KFN relied on so extensively.

Tokita said that he also raised the idea of a second election with Robert C. Oshiro, a key Ariyoshi campaign strategist, who also said he would help, though according to Tokita Oshiro was never called upon by KFN. Tokita did say that Oshiro, in one conversation, reflected on a recent unsuccessful experience Oshiro had had in working for Amfac on Oahu, in trying to organize grassroots support for Amfac's garbage-to-energy plant idea when the project was proposed for Waipahu. Tokita said that Oshiro stressed to him the importance of thorough organization.

To handle advertising and opinion polling KFN retained Starr Seigle McCombs Inc., which in turn brought in Hawaii Opinion Inc. for polling. The Starr board chairman and chief executive officer, John M. Seigle, had been since 1970 the chief paid advertising consultant to most or all of the Burns and Ariyoshi campaigns.

*   *   *

Ariyoshi himself several times played or was reported to have played important parts in forwarding development at Nukolii.

If it actually happened, probably the most pivotal was Ariyoshi helping in 1979 to reverse Kauai councilman Stanley L. Baptiste's 1978 election promise to oppose construction at Nukolii. Baptiste's switch made possible a 4-3 Council rezoning vote in early 1979.

As of the 1978 election, and as of the first occasion on which Baptiste voted, at which time he voted "no," the project was to have been 60 acres and three hotels totalling 1,500 rooms.

But faced with the probability that the Council would not support a development of that size, the developer began to make concessions. Most importantly the project was scaled down to 25 acres and to one 350-room hotel and 150 condominium units. This not only meant fewer units but a potentially less profitable mix of units; having all hotel rooms would have made for a more efficient overall operation, for greater economies of scale.

The developer also made public interest concessions. It offered to build and maintain at its own expense an access road into the beach at Nukolii, also a parking area, pavilion and barbecue pits, all for public use. The developer in addition agreed to pay the entire cost—almost $2 million—of a new well and water line. The sizing of the system was far greater than Nukolii's projected needs, and the line ran for several miles along the coast of east Kauai; in essence the developer was making a major contribution to future water supply throughout this region.[115] (At some point Pacific Standard and its partner based in Seattle, also agreed to a design concession that Hase-

gawa executives found offensive when their company took over the project
in 1980. Hasegawa attorney Edward Jaffe said in an interview for this book
that, to Hasegawa, the roof design used on the condominiums, which he
said was requested by the Kauai Planning Department or Commission and
was ultimately used, closely resembled that of a building a mile up the road,
the Kauai Community Correctional Center—the jail.)

In an interview for this book Baptiste recounted how, immediately following his being elected a councilman in the fall of 1978, he was made chairman of the Council Finance Committee. Baptiste explained that in that role
he became acutely aware of what he saw as the County's need to expand its
tax base—that is, to encourage the creation of additional taxable real estate.
Baptiste said that by his calculations, the real property tax revenues that
even the 25-acre Nukolii development would generate would be equal to
what 1,200 homes on Kauai accounted for; and the homes, in turn, required
far more county money for servicing than did a resort. Baptiste said that
this new awareness of his, plus the Nukolii developer's public interest concessions and its scaling down of the project, all began to change his mind
about where he stood.

Baptiste also said that while he was having his change of heart, he met with
Gov. Ariyoshi in Baptiste's capacity as Finance Chairman. In a discussion that
he said he and the governor had on Kauai County finances and the role of
state moneys in supporting the county, Baptiste said that Ariyoshi encouraged him to vote "yes" on Nukolii's zoning. Baptiste said that Ariyoshi indicated it was the fiscally responsible thing to do, to make an effort for Kauai to
be more self-reliant financially, rather than depending on the state so much.

Baptiste said that while Ariyoshi's encouragement played a role in his decision ultimately to vote for Nukolii, Ariyoshi's input was not decisive. According to Baptiste it was the scaling down of the project, the public interest concessions, and the need to expand Kauai's tax base that made up his mind.

In the months following the Council's Nukolii vote, Baptiste said that
Kauai's legislative delegation unsuccessfully attempted to persuade Ariyoshi to release already-appropriated state money for a neighborhood center
for Kalaheo. Baptiste said that he then asked Ariyoshi to release the money
and the governor did so.

According to Baptiste, when he talked to Ariyoshi about the neighborhood center there was no discussion of Nukolii. Still, Baptiste attributed
what he regarded as his success in this matter to Ariyoshi's wanting to reward and support him for casting the decisive Nukolii vote in the face of a
great deal of public opposition and even hostility.

George H. Toyofuku, at the time Kauai's only senator, confirmed Baptiste's story, although like Baptiste, he said he really did not know what
changed the governor's mind regarding Kalaheo.

Ariyoshi, asked via a letter by an author of this book to comment on Baptiste's story, said orally through his press aide that he could not recall even
meeting with Baptiste, much less discussing Nukolii. Ariyoshi also said that

in general Baptiste's story was "totally inaccurate" in that Ariyoshi throughout his life in government never engaged in the even implicit *quid pro quo*
arrangements that Baptiste described. Regarding Kalaheo, Ariyoshi said
that at the Kauai County level he spoke only with then-mayor Malapit about
the neighborhood center.

In the next election, that of 1980, in which Kauai voters by a 2-1 margin
withdrew Nukolii's resort zoning, Baptiste failed to get re-elected. He and
most others attributed his loss to his Nukolii vote in 1979. In an interview
for this book Baptiste said he felt "bitter" about his loss since he had tried to
do the principled thing and got rejected for it.

*   *   *

Another reported instance of Ariyoshi playing a part in Nukolii came in
the days just after the Hawaii Supreme Court's 1982 decision. One of Hasegawa's attorneys said in an interview for this book that Ariyoshi asked the
executive in charge of Hasegawa in Hawaii, Osamu Kaneko, to come to the
governor's office. The attorney said that Ariyoshi expressed sympathy to
Kaneko, and suggested a legal strategy to him. The strategy was similar to
what several Big Five firms were then using with some apparent success, in
attacking a Hawaii Supreme Court decision on water rights that held that
stream waters in the Islands belonged to the state government.

Another instance of Gov. Ariyoshi supporting a resort at Nukolii was in
having his attorney general in 1983 urge the US Supreme Court to review the
Hawaii Supreme Court decision on Nukolii and overturn it. This was truly
unusual. Ariyoshi said it was necessary, however, in that the impediments that
the Nukolii developer was experiencing were unfair since the developer had
proceeded so far before the Hawaii Supreme Court called a halt, and that the
whole thing was giving Hawaii a black eye in business circles around the
world.[116] The high court declined to take the case, however.

Then, some four months before the second vote, Ariyoshi's director of the
Department of Planning and Economic Development, Kent M. Keith, gave a
speech to a Kauai Rotary Club urging the restoration of resort zoning. Keith
delivered one of the most detailed arguments for allowing completion of the
resort at Nukolii that had been heard throughout the entire controversy. In it
he quoted Dr. Thomas Hitch, senior economist for First Hawaiian Bank, who
had recently said that "Hawaii has always been a capital-short area in which
most economic growth has had to be financed by capital from other places.
The [Hawaii Supreme Court] Nukolii decision threatens to dry up that source
of capital [because of the great fear it has put in investors that Hawaii government may halt a project once it has given it permission to start], and that is
why I say it is the worst thing that has happened to the Hawaiian economy in
all my years here."[117]

*   *   *

What did all this involvement mean?

To CSN as well as to many onlookers it was evidence of a massive conspiracy that involved, among other things, high public officials cynically enrich-

ing themselves in possibly illegal or unethical ways, off a project that was extremely unpopular in the affected community.

It certainly was a remarkable constellation of top-level Democrats—in one way or another linking the courts, the governor's office, the Land Use Commission, among others, with people and companies seeking to develop Nukolii.

On the other hand, to people like Ariyoshi, Yokouchi and Tokita it was no conspiracy at all, nor was there anything underhanded or unprincipled in what any of them did.

Yokouchi said in interviews for this book, for example, that the Nukolii *hui* was organized essentially from among his friends, and that, as explained, it just happened that he had friends in politics and government who got word of the possibility of investing. Yokouchi has said repeatedly that the presence of "political" people in his *hui* had nothing to do with his supposed attempts to "wire in" government land use approvals. Indeed extensive research for this book turned up no evidence that contradicted Yokouchi on this point.

Tokita, for his part, said that it was solely his idea to do a second election, and that though he told Gov. Ariyoshi about it, he did so merely as a courtesy. Tokita also said that Ariyoshi replied that he would be staying clear of KFN.

Tokita had been animated by high ideals all of his adult life and saw his KFN work as in the same vein. The son of a handyman for a plantation manager, Tokita fought with the 442nd, and at school on the mainland after the war he was exposed to ideas of social justice for the have-nots. When he came back to Hawaii he gravitated toward Democratic politics, and played an important part in the "Democratic revolution" on Kauai.

Although a great deal of what this movement was about was expanding economic opportunities for local-Asians, Tokita was not in it for the money for himself. From 1957 to 1982 his salaried work was for the Kauai Board of Supervisors and then County Council, jobs which never paid much, and from which he had to take two-month unpaid leaves each time there was a Burns or Ariyoshi campaign to manage.

Tokita was not a Masaru Yokouchi in terms of land investment and development. His private investments in land were small and few. One that he did make, though, ironically played an indirect role in stimulating the anti-eviction and environmental wave on Kauai that broke upon Nukolii with such force beginning in 1977:

A small land development corporation, MSW Ltd., was set up in 1970 with Tokita a director and 10% owner. The other officers and directors were former Kauai land use commissioner Shiro "Sally" Nishimura, former Sen. Mitsuyuki Kido, and realtor/developer Walter S. S. Zane.

Zane held an option on Kanoa Estate lands in Niumalu, and MSW was to build a resort there if county approval could be obtained. The airing of a Zane or MSW development plan at a public hearing in 1971 toward the close of making Kauai's general plan, was the first occasion on which Stanford

Achi, who came to lead the Niumalu-Nawiliwili Tenants Association, spoke publicly against intensive development in Niumalu.[118]

The County Council declined to give Niumalu lands a resort category. Zane allowed the option to lapse; MSW was dissolved.

Kanoa did not give up, though. As a result the NNTA was formed and it spurred activism on Kauai to rather great heights. A decade later Achi was a key leader of those 32 people arrested for blocking access to Nukolii after Mayor Malapit refused to cancel building permits following the 1980 referendum.

When Nukolii became highly controversial, Tokita saw it as a case of mostly outsiders—mainland *haoles* in effect—trying to force longtime local residents who genuinely desired economic growth to cut themselves short in this respect, in order to preserve Kauai for the edification of the outsiders. As mentioned there were opinion survey results that tended to underpin Tokita's view that it was mainlanders versus locals.

For Tokita, then, his work on behalf of furthering development at Nukolii was but a continuation of much of his life work, of expanding economic opportunities for Hawaii's locally born people.

There were, of course, differences between when he started out doing this in the early 1950s and when he spark-plugged KFN in 1983. One big change was that by 1983 Tokita had access to considerable resources that the fledgling post-World War II Democrats did not have, resources that went a certain distance toward making sure that the numbers on election day came out the way the pre-election polls looked.

*   *   *

What also helped hyperinflate Nukolii was the fact that a number of rising liberal politicians on Kauai, most of them young, who actively opposed construction at Nukolii, wove their opposition into their election campaigns. Several won seats on the County Council; and indeed during Nukolii's years as a controversial issue, the Kauai Council had more land use liberals serving than any other elected body in the Islands. This included Jeremy Harris, Council chairman 1981–1982. When first elected in 1980 Harris was 29 years old.

First of this group to appear was JoAnn Yukimura, who served on the Council 1977–1980, and twice ran unsuccessfully for mayor, in 1980 and 1982.

During her first two-year term, which saw the first announcement of an actual development plan for Nukolii, Yukimura chaired the Council Planning Committee.

And in somewhat the same way that Walton Hong had his ties to the Land Use Commission and to Judge Hirano, Yukimura had hers to Nukolii. She had grown up near there. When she was very small her parents used to take her and their other children to Nukolii to play. Much later, while home on summer vacation from Stanford University where she was an under-

graduate, Yukimura used to jog at Nukolii, or just go down there to be still
and to think. In a place as small as Kauai, where everyone's life was so inter-
woven with everyone else's, where local political issues had enormous immediacy, and where an issue like Nukolii was closely followed by the local media, *The Garden Island* especially, personal connections to Nukolii by people
like Walton Hong and JoAnn Yukimura affected many other people rapidly
and considerably.

★ ★ ★

For CSN lead attorney Sidney Wolinsky, the "political" nature of much of
the backing for developing Nukolii translated into a conviction that the project had gotten preferential treatment from virtually every government official and agency along the entire government approval route. In mid-1983
Wolinsky said that the developers "seem to have the permit process well-
greased."[119]

Did they?

Though there were notable exceptions, throughout the Nukolii case the
developer prevailed in most cases where there were government officials
and agencies reviewing applications, ruling on lawsuits, or taking public
stands on one or another issue.

To be sure, there were always good and sufficient reasons for whatever
was done by the government—be it land use districting, entering a resort
classification in the Lihue Development Plan, rezoning, issuing building
permits, dismissing lawsuits, refusing to cancel building permits, etc.

But one case seemed strongly, on the face of things, to be an instance of
government giving preferential treatment to the Nukolii developer. This
was when the Building Division of the County Department of Public Works
issued the Nukolii hotel building permit early in the afternoon of the day
before the 1980 election.

Permits for the condominiums had been issued three months earlier—
well before the election. Issuance of the hotel permit, though, was going to
go down to the wire. If the developer had the permit before the vote, arguably it could not be revoked. But if the permit were not in a position to be
issued until after the vote, and if the vote was to downzone, then conceivably
the County would refuse to hand over a permit.

In an interview for this book, the man who in 1980 was the deputy county
attorney assigned to Nukolii, Michael Belles, said that while the question
was academic, nevertheless he believed that had the permit not been issued
before the election, that it would have been his advice to not issue it afterwards, since in that event the permit would have been for a hotel in
agriculture-zoned land.

As it turned out in real life, the County administration took the position
that since the permit was issued before the election, therefore the County
could not revoke it.

What difference it made in the long run whether or not the County issued the permit before the election is of course speculative; very likely, though, it would have made little difference. Three months after the election, Judge Hirano held that the referendum came too late to cancel the zoning; the developer's rights had vested and the project could continue. In so ruling he indicated that the issuance of the hotel building permit on the eve of the election had no bearing on his decision. He wrote that "the vesting occurred prior to the issuance of the condominium building permits,"[120] which had been back in August. If at the time Hirano ruled, the County was withholding a building permit for the hotel, very likely the developer would have obtained an order from him compelling the County to issue one. And in the long run, such a delay would probably have had no major impact on other significant events that were coming.

*   *   *

But of course no one knew how Judge Hirano was going to rule until he did. So in the months before the 1980 referendum, it made strong good sense for Hasegawa to get that hotel building permit before the balloting, just in case having it in hand would help later in making its vesting case in court. It is therefore worthwhile to inquire into the circumstances surrounding the issuance of the permit, as a rough test of how impartial the government was in the entire Nukolii matter.

At the start of such an inquiry, it is very important to note that the developer had applied for the hotel permit far enough in advance that in the normal course of events, the County would probably have been in a position to issue a permit roughly in early November—in other words, about the time of the election.

An indication that processing time for the Nukolii hotel permit was about normal comes through a comparison with the time it took to issue the permit for the Waiohai Hotel in Poipu about a year earlier. The Nukolii permit took just about exactly three months to process. The Waiohai permit, which was for a project about 45% larger as measured by square footage of floor area, took about three and a half months.[121]

Besides the Waiohai being larger and thus perhaps more complicated to review, the Waiohai application was apparently left by the builder to be passed around from one county and state agency to another as each signed off, rather than, as is permissible and as was done in the Nukolii case, the developer himself hand-carrying the permit around for signatures once everybody who had to sign was ready to.

The Nukolii developer showed great diligence in doing things like carefully learning and conforming to procedures, and then hand-carrying the permit around up to the last moment. Certainly this in itself was an important element in getting the permit issued in time.

Interviews were conducted for this book with 14 county and state employees who: personally reviewed an aspect of the Nukolii hotel building permit application; were in a supervisory position vis-a-vis something relating to the permit; were in a supervisory position at the time of the interview, though not at the time of the permit processing, but who now spoke for subordinates who had worked on the application; or reviewed legal aspects of the situation. (Because several of those interviewed asked that their identities be withheld, as a general matter none of the names of the 14 are given here.) Also interviewed was one of the developer's consultants, making 15 in all.

All 15 said that the builder had met all applicable laws and standards, thus the permit deserved to be issued. Also, most of the government people said that their processing time was altogether normal and in no way speeded up.

Moreover, men who signed the permit on behalf of three county departments said that they were in a position to sign off long before they were actually asked to. They also said that they did their work at altogether normal speeds.

Several of the government employees interviewed said they thought that, if there was anything unusual about processing time in the case of the Nukolii hotel building permit, it was that it may have been longer than normal, that there may have been a slowdown. None of those who said this also said that they themselves had gone slower than usual, though.

On the other hand, three who directly handled the permit indicated in interviews that to an extent they deliberately speeded up their work. In one case the speedup was with the intent of accomodating the developer's consultant, in two others it was specifically to see that the election deadline was met. Also, one person in a supervisory position vis-a-vis the permit said he believed there was a speedup to meet the election deadline, but said he had no evidence to support his belief. "My personal opinion," he said, "has always been that it was too much of a coincidence, but I don't have any evidence to substantiate that." He added that there might be no physical evidence with which to check whether his belief was accurate, in that, he speculated, any artificial speedup could have been a matter of extra tight coordination by all concerned, simply over the phone.

Whether and however any speedups might have occurred, there is no indication of their having been mentioned to the Kauai County Attorney's office, which played a central role in advising all county agencies involved, and in speaking on behalf of the county to the media on this matter. Thus then-deputy county attorney Belles said, and ever after maintained with all sincerity, that issuance of the hotel building permit the day before the 1980 election was not, on the part of the County, a deliberate attempt to undermine the referendum process.

* * *

One who said that to a degree he speeded up to meet the election deadline said that "it wasn't done consciously."

He was then asked if he thought that one element in his attitude toward Nukolii at the time was that he knew that his superiors supported the project, that if the permit were not issued before the election then the hotel might never be built, and that therefore he ought to make sure to get his work done in time for the election.

He answered: "I'm sure that was the situation." He also said: "I'm sure that's the correct assumption for all agencies."

Asked what bearing the County administration's strong support for the project had on the overall timing of the issuance of the permit, he said he believed that "without it this wouldn't have flown."

This person's words were repeated in capsule form to another of the government people interviewed, who indicated that he, too, to a degree sped up to meet the election deadline. The second indicated that he agreed with the analysis by the first. The second also added, rhetorically: "I just wonder if there was no deadline if it would have gone through the way it did?"

The man who said that he deliberately sped up to accommodate a consultant was a State Health Department employee who took part in reviewing the project's sewage system. He said that for his office such a speedup was not unusual. He explained that when his schedule allowed and a builder or builder's consultant requested a speedup, it was his office's practice to be accommodating.

The Nukolii developer's consultant firm working with the Health Department on the sewage system, Belt Collins & Associates, had its offices in Honolulu literally right across the street in Kakaako from the Health Department offices involved. This made for ready access to the offices by the Belt Collins engineer working on sewage disposal for Nukolii.

Of Belt Collins the department employee said: "They're our classmates, our friends." He also said that in the past he had reviewed plans that were handled by the particular Belt Collins employee handling the Nukolii plans, that he knew him and liked him. He said the consultant explained that the situation was urgent and why. The Health Department employee said he took the position that whether the deadline was met or not was the consultant's concern and not his, but that he would do everything reasonable and possible to speed up in order to help out the consultant.

The speedup included things like this:

In response to a verbal question from the consultant, the employee told the consultant that a letter was being drafted to the consultant. The employee verbally outlined its contents. The consultant then hand-carried in a reply before the Health Department letter was even sent.

In addition, particularly near the end when time was of the essence and when various pieces of correspondence had to circulate in sequence, each triggering the next, the Health Department employee said that the fact and contents of most or all correspondence were probably telephoned to the receiver in advance of actual physical delivery, and that delivery was probably often by hand, even when going interisland.

For example, on October 29 1980, Kauai Planning Director Brian K. Nishimoto wrote a letter to a deputy director of the Health Department in Honolulu, advising him that, given the type of sewage system the developer now proposed, there was no need for an additional shoreline special management area permit for the project. Nishimoto had once determined that a different system would have required such a permit. On that basis the Health Department had withdrawn its own previously-granted approval for that system. Now the department was refusing to act on the then-current proposal until Nishimoto assured the Department in writing that no further shoreline permit was needed.

The same day Nishimoto's letter was dated, it was hand-carried to the office in Honolulu to which it was addressed. Hand-written on the top of the letter was "hand delivered by Davis" (Michael W. Davis, Nukolii's development manager).[122]

According to a Health Department route slip also dated that same day, the letter was transmitted to two Health Department employees assigned to review technical aspects of the proposed sewage system.[123]

Later on the same day one of the employees telephoned the consultant, according to a Health Department file memo, "and informed [him] that the injection well submitted did not conform to our regulations." A letter from the consultant to the employee, rectifying the problem, was dated that same day. A Health Department notation on the top of the letter indicates it was received the next day, October 30.[124]

The day after that, October 31, the Health Department division chief for Environmental Protection and Health Services signed a letter to the department's Kauai office. The letter indicated that Health Department people in Honolulu had completed their review, and it was now alright for the Environmental Health Services section of the Kauai office to sign off on the hotel building permit.[125]

October 31 was a Friday. The deadline for getting the permit before the election was the following Monday.

A department employee in Honolulu said in an interview that while he could not be certain, most likely someone phoned over to the Kauai office the fact of the October 31 letter. He said it was also possible that the man in charge of Environmental Health on Kauai initiated the call. This man "was calling quite often" about the Nukolii matter, the Honolulu Health Department employee said. In any case, he said, someone probably hand-carried the letter to Kauai.

Then, on Monday, a Kauai Health Department employee signed the building permit, which the county Building Division then issued that afternoon, a few hours before the election deadline.

As mentioned, the Health Department employee in Honolulu stressed that steps like these had been taken on behalf of other projects in the past, when agency time allowed and the builder or its consultant requested a speedup and gave a legitimate reason for one.

He also explained that the Nukolii developer was fortunate that it requested a speedup at what was a slack period for the Health Department people who were charged with the technical review of the project's sewage system.

At the same time there had apparently never been a case like Nukolii, where there was not only one side directly asking for a speedup, but another that obviously would have preferred a slowdown.

The employee was asked if he thought such a situation argued for simply processing at normal speed, which in this case would likely have meant not issuing a hotel building permit before the election? He answered in effect that CSN never directly asked for a slowdown, thus he never addressed the question. He said that although CSN made inquiries with his agency, that CSN "seemed more concerned with proper procedures" than with anything else, and "at no time did they ask us to do anything" bearing on processing time.

The three government employees who said they speeded up all said they had not been instructed to do so by superiors; research for this book did not turn up any contrary evidence.

What then may have happened was that, by the natural operation of the system, a highly controversial development that had strong support from the Democratic political/governmental establishment was nudged over the finish line by subordinates a little ahead of schedule, on the assumption that otherwise it might never have made it. It appears to be a small example, with consequences that at the time were thought potentially very great, of government's attitude, when push came to shove, toward proponents and opponents of land development in Hawaii's Democratic years.

*   *   *

If the hotel permit got extra help from lower-echelon government employees, people higher up in politics and government had been helping Nukolii along in other areas as well, making use of contacts built up over the years, of personal relationships that arose from serving on the same government boards, working in the same law firm, and so on.

For example: in response to the KFN petition drive in 1983, CSN began circulating yet another petition, this one an initiative to require that if the hotel at Nukolii was completed, then for 10 years 10% of its gross revenues would be contributed to a community trust fund. The fund would be used to finance environmental protection, housing, job training, and scholarships.

In an interview for this book, a Hasegawa attorney, Edward Jaffe, said he believed the effect of such a tax would be to kill the project. He also believed it was unconstitutional to impose what, by all appearances, was a tax that would fall on only one hotel on Kauai, indeed in all Hawaii.

To bolster his position, Jaffe said, he contacted Kent Keith, Director of the State Department of Planning and Economic Development, whom Jaffe said he knew from when he and Keith worked in the same law firm, Cades Schutte Fleming and Wright. Jaffe said that he asked Keith to ask the state attorney general to issue a legal opinion on the CSN plan. Jaffe said that Keith did so. The resulting opinion called the CSN idea "constitutionally impermissible."

When Hasegawa's lawyers were preparing to ask or had just asked that the US Supreme Court review and reverse the Hawaii Supreme Court's 1982 Nukolii decision, another Hasegawa lawyer, Wallace Fujiyama, said that he went to see the state attorney general about supporting the Hasegawa effort in the US Supreme Court. In an interview for this book, Fujiyama indicated that he knew then-State Attorney General Tany S. Hong well, that they shared a mutual respect. Fujiyama said, though, that all this guaranteed him when attempting to contact Hong was that Hong's door was open to him, that Hong would listen to him. For whatever reason, Hong did subsequently, either with the concurrence of or at the direction of Gov. Ariyoshi, file a brief with the US Supreme Court, supporting Hasegawa's position.

Not long after Fujiyama was retained by Hasegawa in 1982, he said he began casting about for people to help him in what, to a great extent, would be a political effort, a matter of mobilizing support. He said he hit upon the idea of asking Burt Tsuchiya for help. Tsuchiya was a former Kauai councilman whom Fujiyama said he had gotten to know in the early 1980s when they served together on the University of Hawaii Board of Regents. In an interview Fujiyama said that Tsuchiya was quite helpful in the subsequent efforts by Hasegawa and KFN to reverse the 1980 Nukolii referendum. Tsuchiya, in addition, for whatever reasons, became a member of the KFN Campaign Committee.

Back during the Land Use Commission's 1974 review, Masaru Yokouchi was spending a great deal of his time working on behalf of a client who was planning a large resort in Makena, Maui. In 1973 Yokouchi, representing Ulupalakua Ranch as a real estate broker, had sold 1,000 acres in Makena to Japan's Seibu Group Enterprises. At the request of Seibu and with the permission of the head of the ranch, Yokouchi agreed after the sale to help Seibu get set up on Maui, to gain initial government approvals. The first such approval would come from the Land Use Commission during the Commission's 1974 review. Yokouchi has said that in the course of helping Seibu in this way, he talked to a number of land use commissioners. When he did so, he said in an interview for this book, it would have been like him to also put in a good word for Nukolii. Yokouchi thought he probably did this; he stressed, though, that he could not specifically recall having done so. It should be noted that all LUC members serving in 1974 who were interviewed for this book said they had never been talked to by Yokouchi concerning Nukolii, or by anyone else outside the LUC, for that matter.

If in fact Yokouchi did lobby commissioners, he would probably have gotten a cordial hearing from most of them.

For example, since the mid-1960s Yokouchi had been chairman of the State Foundation on Culture and the Arts. For a while in the mid to late 1960s Eddie Tangen had represented the ILWU on the foundation's board. Yokouchi said that as a result he and Tangen had gotten to know each other. In 1974 Tangen was chairman of the Land Use Commission.

The Maui member of the LUC in 1974, Tanji Yamamura, had his seat because Yokouchi nominated him. In several interviews for this book, Yokouchi said that about 1969, the governor's office asked him to find a farmer from Maui to represent Maui County on the LUC. Yokouchi said he then asked around among farmers' organizations, was eventually given Yamamura's name, and in turn passed it on to Gov. Burns, who made the appointment. Yokouchi also said that prior to about 1969 he and Yamamura did not know each other, though by 1974 they were acquainted.

Another man sitting on the LUC in 1974, Sunao Kido, was born and raised on Maui. Yokouchi said he and Kido knew each other fairly well. As of 1974, for example, Yokouchi had been for 14 years a co-investor with Kido, his brother Mitsuyuki, and a number of other Maui-born *nisei* in Heeia Development Co., with its Bishop Estate development agreement.

A fourth commissioner, Stanley Sakahashi from Kauai, said he also knew Yokouchi by 1974, and that he believed he first got to know him when Sakahashi worked in the Legislature in the early 1960s for Yokouchi's close friend, Nadao Yoshinaga, then a senator from Maui.

Sakahashi also said he believed he first learned of Yokouchi's investment in Nukolii from Yamamura. Sakahashi said he recalled that sometime in 1974, Yamamura mentioned Yokouchi's investment to him, calling it "Pundy's baby." (Yokouchi's nickname was "Pundy.") Yamamura declined to be interviewed for this book on this or any other subject.

In discussing "insider ties" and Nukolii, there is also the matter of the Amfac sale of Nukolii to Yokouchi in the first place. As described elsewhere in this book, the sale occurred as a result of Amfac wanting to hire someone politically influential to help settle some community and labor problems that were inhibiting the expansion of the company's Kaanapali resort in the late 1960s. Although Yokouchi worked on these problems for Amfac without pay, he said in several interviews for this book that, nevertheless, he told an Amfac executive and others at the time that he did hope Amfac would show its gratitude toward him by doing business with him in the future. By this he meant that when Amfac was selling real estate, the company would consider him as a potential buyer.

Nukolii was one of several Amfac sales to Yokouchi that resulted.

At the same time, Yokouchi noted that these sales were, strictly speaking, not a *quid pro quo* arrangement. He has said, for example, that the first sale did not occur until several years after he had helped Amfac regarding Kaanapali; that invariably, when Amfac had real estate for sale, he had to contact Amfac, that Amfac people did not come looking for him; that he had to pay the going rate; and that, in general, Amfac never offered him what he considered the choicest properties that the company was selling at any one time. For example, at the time he negotiated for Nukolii in 1973, Amfac was negotiating a sale of the Lihue Shopping Center to Harry Weinberg. Yokouchi has said that he would have much preferred to buy the shopping center, but it was never offered to him.

Exactly what to say about the effects of all these and conceivably more insider ties on the evolution of the whole Nukolii episode is problematic. For one thing, there is no direct evidence that, but for these connections, the whole thing would have gone any differently.

Moreover, specifically with respect to Yokouchi, despite the harsh appraisals of his behavior made by many when they read of his unregistered *hui*, no evidence was uncovered in the course of research for this book that he had, in some consciously sinister way, attempted to manipulate government for private ends.

What he did do, with apparently the best of intentions, was make use of extremely good political connections that, in the end, led to Nukolii being sold to him, and may have, after he had already resold the property, helped ensure that his buyer could go forward with developing a resort there.

Yokouchi was known to put a high value on personal sincerity; he has indicated that he did these things with only honorable intentions.

Yet it was precisely the kind of excellent access to decision-makers that he had, and the suspicion that he was making use of this access, that led many to judge his behavior in the Nukolii matter so harshly. For example, it lent credence to the remark made in 1974 by a land use commissioner to a reporter, mentioned at the start of this chapter, to the effect that the LUC redistricting of Nukolii was going to go through because a "powerful man from Maui" was connected with it. And it was such suspicions that led CSN member Sally Jo Soares to say, on the occasion of James Dooley's *Honolulu Advertiser hui* story in 1980, that "the *Advertiser* report confirms what has been apparent to us all along: that the governmental approvals of the Nukolii resort were based on factors other than merit."[126]

Even some of Kauai's more conservative people joined Soares in this appraisal. For example, retired *Honolulu Star-Bulletin* Kauai bureau chief Harold W. Ching was a fairly conservative person. After the Dooley story in 1980, Ching wrote of the 1974 LUC redistricting that it "slipped down a well-greased path to open the door to our present dilemma. It was no secret to those at the marathon Land Use Commission public hearings, running late into the night and past midnight, how things work. A hui picked up the option-to-buy or an agreement-of-sale, then went to peddle the property for a big profit. If a rezoning wasn't put across and a rich buyer wasn't found, the hui would have had to take the loss of the downpayment, comparatively low, and had to start scurrying around for another deal."[127]

So pervasive was the belief of large-scale irregularities surrounding the

Yokouchi *hui* that Nukolii developers were at pains to dissociate themselves from it. Thus several days after Dooley's *Advertiser* story ran, the then-current developer, Hasegawa Komuten, one sale removed from the Amfac-Yokouchi-Pacific Standard transactions, ran an ad in *The Garden Island*, through a Hasegawa attorney. The ad said: "Don't link us with suggested improprieties in that earlier transaction."[128]

* * *

Nukolii had its legacy, one made up of many particularized segments, derived from all the individuals who in some way or other took part, even just as watchers from the sidelines who might have occasionally voted or signed a petition.

At the most obvious level, phase one of the project would be completed. Nukolii would have a resort.

To an extent Hawaii's blackened reputation in national and world business circles was redeemed by the second election.

Certain other reputations, however, were probably permanently damaged somewhat, whether fairly or not, most especially those of Masaru Yokouchi, who signed an agreement to buy Nukolii back in 1973, and the Amfac executive who handled preliminary contact with him on the transaction, Earl Stoner.

Several in government on Kauai whose responsibilities touched on land use and who dealt a good deal with the public, said Nukolii had ushered in a new era in their work, one of far greater sensitivity in dealing with the public, partly born of fear of ever having another uproar like Nukolii.

In 1984 the Legislature amended the law on absentee balloting so that it could never again be used as KFN had done.

In 1985 the Legislature passed and the governor signed a bill that went even further toward ensuring that nothing like Nukolii would ever happen again. The bill allowed counties to enter into agreements with developers which among other things would fix, at the point of signing, the developer's right to existing zoning, if he wanted it. The bill recited that its purpose "is to provide a means by which an individual may be assured at a specific point in time that having met or having agreed to meet all of the terms and conditions of the development agreement, the individual's rights to develop the property in a certain manner shall be vested." At the point when Hasegawa-Komuten bought an interest in Nukolii, the land was already fully zoned. Such a law might have meant that Hasegawa and the Kauai County government could have signed a contract under which, as long as Hasegawa met all the terms of the agreement, the zoning could never be taken away.

At the local political level, Nukolii represented perhaps the greatest clash yet between Kauai's old guard Democratic political establishment, heavily Japanese-led, and a rising group of younger, more liberal, environmentally-oriented people, many of whom were mainland *haole*. This was a conflict that was being played out in many settings statewide, part of a political readjustment statewide; it appeared to have a way to go.

As things stood at the conclusion of phase one of the Nukolii development, the old guard had withstood a major challenge, and had shoved the challengers back a few steps.

Many fell back extremely disillusioned. Julia O. Abben, born on Kauai and owner of a small store in Hanamaulu not far from Nukolii, was active in CSN. In late 1984 the *Honolulu Advertiser* ran an editorial saying it was time to let the wounds of Nukolii heal. She lashed back in a letter, asking why people should be expected to forget having taken such abuse. She ended on a bitter note: "And if you are ever unhappy with any governmental or corporate decisions, don't follow your heart and intelligence and the laws. Lay back and force yourself to say, Who cares?"[129]

It was not only CSN people who had ideals that they were attempting to realize in the course of the Nukolii episode. KFN people from their own standpoint were deeply and sincerely concerned about the economic future of their island and the state. For example, in an interview for this book Hasegawa attorney Wallace Fujiyama spoke movingly on this subject.

But in the end, no matter whether a person was for or against building at Nukolii, a deep-running suspicion lingered that the whole story had not been unearthed on possible manipulations of government decisions for private benefit. Half a year before the second election CSN had a professional pollster conduct an opinion survey of Kauai residents. At about this time KFN was having one of its several surveys run as well, each time finding clear majorities favoring completion of the project. The published results of the CSN survey did not include a finding on the question of completion; presumably CSN would have found what KFN was finding. The CSN survey did ask this question, though: "Would you like to see an outside and independent special investigator appointed who would try to get the truth and make a special report to the public before the referendum vote?" Replying "yes" were nearly 75% of those questioned, many of whom apparently later, weary of it all, went on to vote in favor of finishing the development anyway.[130]

Like so many controversies of this kind in Hawaii's Democratic years, whether there was or was not more to it than met the eye, would simply never be known.

12

ONE MAN'S CAREER: GEORGE ARIYOSHI

GEORGE R. Ariyoshi was born in 1926 into a relatively poor family of immigrants living in Honolulu's Chinatown.

Bright and ambitious, he struggled to overcome a speech impediment, worked hard in school, and was president of his senior class at McKinley High School in 1944.

He went into the army a few months before the end of World War II, and served briefly in occupied Japan as an interpreter. Afterwards he got his college education at the University of Hawaii and Michigan State University, and then a law degree at the University of Michigan.

Ariyoshi began his private law practice in Honolulu in early 1953. He has said that this was when, for the first time in his life, he encountered the way that Big Five domination of Hawaii made for a relative lack of career opportunities for the Islands' non-*haoles*, and that this discovery eventually propelled him into politics, to work for equal opportunity.[1]

In 1954 Ariyoshi, with the encouragement of John Burns, ran for the territorial House of Representatives and was elected as part of the first Democratic majority in Hawaii's history. Aged 28 at the start of the session, he was the youngest member of the first Legislature of the "Democratic revolution."

* * *

In 1955, following his first legislative session, Ariyoshi was invited to join the law firm of Kobayashi, Kono & Laureta.

This firm had a political cast to it. Over the Democratic years all the partners rose in the world of government. Bert T. Kobayashi Sr. was appointed a district court magistrate in 1952 and held that position until 1958. In 1962 he rose to be state attorney general and then, in 1969, was named an associate justice of the Hawaii Supreme Court. Russell K. Kono was elected to the House along with Ariyoshi. In 1959 he also was named a magistrate, and rose through the district court system on Oahu to become in 1970 administrative magistrate for the rural district courts, and later chief administrator for the entire Oahu system, a position he held until the mid-1980s. Alfred Laureta, Hawaii's first attorney of Filipino ancestry, in

1955 became a member of the Central Committee of the Democratic Party. From 1959 to 1962 he was an assistant to Congressman Daniel K. Inouye. In 1963 Laureta along with Kobayashi joined Gov. Burns' cabinet, as director of the Department of Labor and Industrial Relations. Thereafter he was named a state circuit court judge and then a federal judge in the Northern Marianas Islands.

On through Ariyoshi's years as a private attorney, his practice continued to include men who were on their way into Democratic politics and government. James E. T. Koshiba, who worked in his firm 1969–1970, became in 1979 a member and chairman of the State Judicial Selection Commission. Robert S. Toyofuku was in Ariyoshi's firm in 1970; he later became an aide to Congressman Cecil Heftel.

* * *

Ariyoshi stayed in the Legislature 16 years, moving up to the Senate in 1959.

In 1963–1964 he was chairman of the powerful Ways and Means Committee. He was majority leader 1965–1966, and majority floor leader 1969–1970.

Despite these leadership positions Ariyoshi was rarely in the limelight, preferring to work quietly behind the scenes. As Hawaii Democrats went, Ariyoshi was middle of the road, a moderate. In 1964 the *Honolulu Star-Bulletin* wrote that Ariyoshi had said in a recent speech that "he believes in moving ahead by small and safe steps."[2] From the late 1950s his personal election platforms stressed unexceptionable issues, often with a conservative cast to them: a balanced budget, governmental efficiency, an improved school system, promotion of local industry. More often than most Democrats he voted against labor legislation benefiting workers. As late as 1969 he voted with a group of conservative senators, most of them Republicans, to retain a state subversive activities commission, a vestige of the McCarthy era.

Specifically on the question of land and land reform, Ariyoshi was a moderate too. Unlike some of his contemporaries he had not started out on the left wing of the party, where the idea of land reform as social justice was important, and then drifted in a more conservative direction. He simply had never been a left-liberal, much less a radical, though there is evidence that during the 1950s and 1960s he shifted somewhat to the right of where he started. For example, as early as 1959, speaking at an election rally sponsored by the Honolulu Chamber of Commerce, Ariyoshi stressed that he would protect the rights of property, saying he would "fight any attempt to undermine the concept of land ownership."[3]

Like a good many other mainstream Democrats, Ariyoshi by the early 1960s was well on his way to a personal, professional, and business accommodation with Hawaii's old landed interests.

In his law practice in 1961 he had clients with a development agreement with Bishop Estate—to build a bowling alley on Dillingham Blvd. in Kapalama—and he represented these clients before the Honolulu City Council.

In 1963 he took a seat on the board of directors of the First National Bank of Hawaii (later renamed First Hawaiian Bank). Board members included executives of a number of old-line Hawaii corporations, and of course the bank dealt regularly with the old companies and estates.

First National had grown out of Bishop Bank, the bank of Samuel M. Damon of Moanalua. The Damon Estate owned a large block of the bank's stock, and four Damon trustees sat on the board. One of these was Dudley C. Lewis, who was among three Damon trustees who approached Ariyoshi about joining the board. Research for this book indicates that Lewis, prior to approaching Ariyoshi, asked another *nisei* Democrat attorney/senator to become a director. In an interview for this book, that man said he declined, citing to Lewis the fact that he was a director of a competing bank. Lewis, in an interview for this book, said it was he who put Ariyoshi's name to the bank board. Another Damon trustee and bank director, Republican Sen. D. Hebden Porteus, was a "key supporter" of the nomination, according to Lewis. Ariyoshi in an interview for this book said that it was these two plus a third trustee/director who came to see him in late 1962 to see if he would be willing to serve. Ariyoshi said he believed it had been mainly Porteus who pushed the idea of his selection, saying that he and Porteus had had "a very close friendship and rapport" going back to 1955 and the first legislative session in which they served together.

Ariyoshi and a local-Chinese businessman who was seated in the same year were the first two local-Asians ever chosen for the First National board. This put Ariyoshi among the first local-Asians to be picked as a director of such a major old-money firm.

Ariyoshi was selected largely because the old companies were coming to accept the permanence of the "Democratic revolution," and were seeking ties to its leaders. In the case of First National, the board of directors apparently believed they now needed a director who was a somewhat business-oriented, *nisei* Democratic senator who was also a lawyer.

In joining the bank board Ariyoshi was seated among the staunchest of the Republican old guard, men for whom the Democrats' land reform program verged on communism. It is an index of where Ariyoshi located himself as a Democrat and government policy-maker that the bank was comfortable with his appointment. In an interview for this book, Ariyoshi said that he himself was comfortable with the appointment, remaining on the board until 1970 when he ran for and was elected lieutenant governor.

Ariyoshi thereafter acquired two more directorships of establishment corporations: Honolulu Gas Co. in 1965; and in 1966 The Hawaiian Insurance & Guaranty Co. Ltd., a subsidiary of C. Brewer. In 1967 in his capacity as a private attorney Ariyoshi represented Brewer itself in a land use matter before the Honolulu City Council.

In the same years as Ariyoshi was serving on the boards of old-line firms, he was rising to the presidency of the Hawaii Bar Association. This was a high honor in itself, and a definite signal that a man was on the way up. The first local-Asian to reach the presidency was Masaji Marumoto in 1954; in 1956 he became the first local-Asian to serve on the territorial Supreme Court. The second was Ralph T. Yamaguchi in 1957; he subsequently became a board member of Hawaiian Electric Co., Hawaiian Telephone, and American Factors. Ariyoshi's law partner Bert T. Kobayashi was president in 1959; Kobayashi was named attorney general in 1962 and later an associate supreme court justice. William S. Richardson, president in 1961, was elected lieutenant governor in 1962, then appointed chief justice of the Supreme Court in 1966. In 1967 Ariyoshi was elected as the next year's Bar Association vice-president, which automatically carried with it the prestigious presidency for the following year.

* * *

Beginning about 1959–1960 Ariyoshi made a modest start in the land investment and development business on his own account. From then on as an investor, lawyer, and company director he was involved with a number of land and construction projects around the state, as Table 20 indicates.

———————————— **TABLE 20** ————————————

GEORGE ARIYOSHI DEVELOPMENT-RELATED INVESTMENTS, LEGAL WORK, AND BUSINESS ACTIVITIES

1959–1980s. Bought and held 2 lots, 3 acres each, in 2,500-lot subdivision Orchid Land Estates, Puna, Hawaii. Developer was Hilo Development Inc., whose president was Sen. Kazuhisa Abe.

1960–67. Member small hui that bought and later sold 2 adjacent lots totalling 60 acres Kula, Maui. Hui included Vincent H. Yano and Bert T. Kobayashi who, in 1963, became, respectively, a state senator and state attorney general.

1960. As attorney represented developer Norman N. Inaba before State Board of Agriculture and Forestry on forest reserve matter re Hilolani Acres, subdivision above Hilo, Hawaii.

1960. Formed hui George Ariyoshi & Associates that made offer to undertake large residential development Oahu. Two other hui members were engineer Chung Dho Ahn and realtor Edward Y.F. Tseu.

1960. Bought house lot Moanalua-Salt Lake from Clarence T.C. Ching's IDCo, and later resold.

1961. As attorney incorporated J&J Investments Ltd., which was to build bowling alley.

1961. As attorney represented Jack K. Taniyama and James H. Miyake in zoning matter re bowling alley before Honolulu City Council.

1962–73. Drafted partnership registration papers for Norman Inaba's Royal Gardens hui which developed 1,500-lot speculative subdivision on 1,807 acres Puna, Hawaii. As part of legal fee received share in hui, which business records show retained till 1973.

1962–73. Drafted partnership registration papers for Norman Inaba's Milolii Syndicate which developed 1,000-lot speculative subdivision on 423 acres South Kona, Hawaii. As with Royal Gardens received hui share, which held till 1973.

Early 1960s. As attorney represented Hawaiian Electric Co. in obtaining easement above Palolo Valley, Oahu.

1963–70. Elected to board of directors First National Bank of Hawaii, later renamed First Hawaiian. Much of bank's lending was development-related.

1963. Certified to State Contractors License Board that he knew and endorsed Norman Inaba in matter before board involving Inaba.

1963. As attorney prepared and signed document for Norman Inaba re Inaba's Hilolani Acres subdivision.

1964. Certified to State Contractors License Board that he knew and endorsed Futoshi Inaba in matter before board involving Inaba.

1964-68. With law partner Russell K. Kono bought from Clarence Ching's IDCo house lot Moanalua Valley, Oahu, later resold. Kono at that time was Honolulu district court magistrate.

1964–66. Member 4-man hui that bought lot near Queen's Hospital, Honolulu, built 18-unit apartment building, then sold building; hui included brother James Ariyoshi and Daniel R. Matsukage.

1965–70. Elected to board of directors Honolulu Gas Co. Ltd.

1965–1980s. With law partner Russell K. Kono bought 4 house lots at mouth Moanalua Valley; resold 1 late 1965, 1 1966, built houses on all 4.

1965. Was attorney for incorporation, secretary, a director and shareholder Hawaiian International Hotel Inc.

1965. As attorney represented contractor Henry Haitsuka in processing Land Court documents for 3-lot subdivision Kaneohe, Oahu.

1966–67. As attorney represented Mark Construction Inc. in civil lawsuit; president of company was Mark Y. Watase.

1966. As attorney represented Terrace Developers Ltd. before Honolulu City Council on improvement district matter; company was developing 13-story, 74-unit leasehold condomimium, Honolulu.

1966–69. With law partner Norman H. Suzuki bought and later resold Unit 8 in Terrace Apartments.

1966–70. Elected to board Hawaiian Insurance & Guaranty Co. Ltd., wholly-owned subsidiary C. Brewer. HIG was surety for numerous construction projects.

1967. As attorney represented C. Brewer in improvement district matter re Fort St., Honolulu, before Honolulu City Council.

1968. As attorney filed with State Real Estate Commission horizontal property regime report for 72-unit leasehold condominium The Coronet, Honolulu.

1960-1980s. Bought lot Nuuanu Valley, Honolulu, built house.

Late 1960s. Invested $5,000 in Reliance Industries Inc., which had several development-related subsidiaries.

1969–1980s. Bought house lot Milolii Beach Lots Subdivision, South Kona, Hawaii.

1969. As attorney represented contractor Henry Haitsuka before Honolulu City Council on rezoning matter Heeia, Oahu.

1969. As attorney represented developers Waikiki Gateway Hotel; was master of ceremonies for groundbreaking. Developers were Rodney Y. Inaba and Charles B. Kim.

1969. Certified to State Real Estate Commission that Jean S. Yokoyama was of good character.

1971–1980s. Bought 2 units in The Coronet condominium, resold 1 1972.

Sources: State of Hawaii, Department of Commerce and Consumer Affairs, Real Estate Commission; City and County of Honolulu, Finance Department, Real Property Assessment Division; personal financial disclosure statements by George Ariyoshi on file with State Ethics Commission; City and County of Honolulu, City Council, miscellaneous subject indices; State of Hawaii, Department of Commerce and Consumer Affairs, Business Registration Division; miscellaneous newspaper articles and periodicals.

As was common in the new Democratic establishment—just as it had been in the old Republican establishment—business roles had frequent overlaps. These were evident in Ariyoshi's dealings, as Table 21 indicates.

The bank and the insurance company on whose boards Ariyoshi sat, plus financial institutions with which his brother James was affiliated, often had financial involvements with construction projects where Ariyoshi was investing or doing legal work. At times Ariyoshi represented the project and/ or invested in it, and the bank or insurance company provided finance or bonding.

―――――――――――――― TABLE 21 ――――――――――――――

REAL ESTATE PROJECTS INVOLVING GEORGE ARIYOSHI AND FINANCIAL INSTITUTIONS WITH WHICH HE OR JAMES ARIYOSHI WERE AFFILIATED

1964–66. 18-unit apartment building near Queen's Hospital, Honolulu. Hawaii National Bank. George, James, and Daniel R. Matsukage were 3 of 4 members of developing hui. Bank provided interim financing. James was assistant bank cashier. Until year before Matsukage was bank V-P.

1966. House lot in Moanalua. Real Estate Finance Corporation (REFC). Ariyoshi and law partner bought lot. REFC later lent them purchase money. REFC president was Daniel R. Matsukage with whom Ariyoshi was then developing 18-unit apartment.

1966. Terrace Apartments. First National Bank of Hawaii. Ariyoshi represented developer before Honolulu City Council. He and law partner bought unit. First National Bank provided interim financing for construction of the building. Ariyoshi was bank director.

1968. The Coronet. Hawaiian Insurance & Guaranty Co. Ltd. George was project attorney before State Real Estate Commission. James was member of 5-man developing hui. George 1971 bought 2 units. George sat on board of Hawaiian Insurance, which bonded project.

1969. Waikiki Gateway Hotel. First Hawaiian Bank. Ariyoshi was developer's attorney. Also First Hawaiian director. First Hawaiian provided interim financing.

1969–70. Ulu Wehi (Hawaii Housing Authority project). Hawaiian Insurance & Guaranty Co. Ltd. Ariyoshi law firm represented developer. Ariyoshi owned stock in developer's parent company. Hawaiian Insurance bonded project. Ariyoshi was director Hawaiian Insurance.

Sources: State of Hawaii, Department of Commerce and Consumer Affairs, Real Estate Commission; City and County of Honolulu, Finance Department, Real Property Assessment Division; personal financial disclosure statements by George Ariyoshi on file with State Ethics Commission; City and County of Honolulu, City Council, miscellaneous subject indices; State of Hawaii, Department of Commerce and Consumer Affairs, Business Registration Division; miscellaneous newspaper articles and periodicals.

In these years as well, Ariyoshi as a senator repeatedly handled legislation that affected a company on whose board he sat, its competitors, and a state agency that regulated them.

From 1967 to 1970, while Ariyoshi was a director of Honolulu Gas Co., he was also chairman of the Senate Utilities Committee. Virtually the entire work of this committee pertained to the gas company, its competitors (such as Hawaiian Electric Co.), and the state Public Utilities Commission, which regulated utilities.

For example, Ariyoshi managed on the Senate floor or processed in his committee bills to: allow the expansion of operations of Kauai Electric Co.; repeal a three-year residency requirement for officers and directors of public utility companies; provide civil service status for several PUC staff positions; provide that the PUC had authority in rate-setting proceedings to investigate parent-subsidiary and brother-sister company relationships; make oil refining operations a public utility and therefore subject to PUC regulation; permit public utilities to issue securities for non-utility and non-rate base items; eliminate the possibility of sub-standard wages being paid to people working for public utilities' contractors and subcontractors; and have the PUC staff confer with electric companies about possibly lowering rates charged to farmers.

In apparently only one instance, in 1967, does the Senate Journal reflect that Ariyoshi publicly declared a conflict of interest. In that case he evidently did so only after his committee had finished handling the bill and reported it out to the full Senate with a recommendation that it should pass.

At issue was a development-related measure to allow Honolulu Gas Co. to take part more readily in the urbanization of the outer islands. Specifically, the company's franchise was to be extended from Honolulu and South Hilo to the whole state. In essence the bill would give the company power of eminent domain where it did not already have it, enabling the company to obtain easements and lay pipes anywhere in the state. With a statewide franchise the gas company could lay pipes in subdivisions, supplying gas at lower cost than if it had to be trucked in in cylinders. This would improve the company's position, for example, vis-a-vis Maui Electric Co., with which it was then in competition over providing such things as water heaters in an upcoming Alexander & Baldwin housing subdivision increment at Kahului, Maui.

With the permission of the Senate president, Ariyoshi voted for the bill despite his conflict of interest.[4]

* * *

As with many other attorney-legislators, Ariyoshi's family, law firm, and business associates lapped over into his legislative office.

People hired by Ariyoshi as office staff included his wife, his brother, his sister, and his sister-in-law. Also hired were a law partner and the wife of another law partner. He hired the secretary of a business associate of his brother; the associate had also been his brother's best man. He hired the wife of an architect who was a business associate of his. He hired a young man whose father organized development *huis* which Ariyoshi represented as an attorney and invested in. And he hired political supporters, from outside this circle of associates.

At times he also hired other young men on their way up in the political and business world of Hawaii in the 1950s and 1960s, creating yet another strand in the fabric that bound many of these men together. In 1957 Ariyoshi hired as a committee clerk James H. Wakatsuki, who himself was elected to the House in 1959, where he rose to be speaker in 1975. In 1980 Ariyoshi appointed Wakatsuki a circuit court judge, and in 1983 an associate justice of the state Supreme Court.

The political segment of Hawaii's new establishment was heavily Japanese. Nowhere was this more strongly reflected than in Ariyoshi's hiring. As reflected in the House and Senate journals, in his 16 years in the Legislature Ariyoshi made 43 office appointments. As Table 22 indicates, every one of the 43 went to a person with a Japanese last name.

——————————————— TABLE 22 ———————————————

GEORGE ARIYOSHI'S LEGISLATIVE AIDES DURING 16 YEARS IN THE LEGISLATURE

1955. ARIYOSHI, JAMES M. Committee clerk. Brother.

1957. WAKATSUKI, JAMES H. Committee clerk. Elected Representative 1959; later Speaker, circuit court judge, Supreme Court justice.

1957. KOBAYASHI, VICTORIA T. Committee clerk. Wife of law partner.

1959. ARIYOSHI, JEAN M. Secretary. Wife.

1959. INASE, HELEN Y. Secretary. Sister.

1959. TANIGUCHI, CHARLES T. Committee clerk.

1961. ARIYOSHI, ELEANOR K. L. Secretary. Sister-in-law.

1962. ARIYOSHI, ELEANOR K. L. Stenographer. Sister-in-law.

1963. ARIYOSHI, ELEANOR K. L. Stenographer. Sister-in-law.

1963. KANESHIRO, HARRIET H. Stenographer.

1963. DOMAI, HELEN T. Stenographer.

1963. KUNIYOSHI, ELAINE S. Secretary.

1963. SAKAI, HIROSHI. Chief clerk Senate Ways and Means Committee.

1963. UYEHARA, MITSUO. Research analyst.

1964. NISHIMURA, HELEN H. Secretary.

1964. UCHIMA, FRANCES. Stenographer.

1964. SUZUKI, DOROTHY M. Stenographer.

1964. KURATA, CAROL S. Stenographer.

1964. SAKAI, HIROSHI. Chief clerk Senate Ways and Means Committee.

1964. UYEHARA, MITSUO. Research analyst.

1965. OKAZAKI, NANCY Y. Secretary. Ariyoshi's law firm secretary.

1965. ARIYOSHI, JEAN M. Committee clerk. Wife.

1966. INABA, RODNEY Y. Committee clerk. Son of developer Norman N. Inaba who was client of Ariyoshi; Ariyoshi later represented Rodney Inaba in development of Waikiki Gateway Hotel.

1966. IKEDA, CYNTHIA Y. Secretary.

1967. OKAZAKI, NANCY Y. Secretary. Ariyoshi's law firm secretary.

1967. SUZUKI, NORMAN H. Research assistant. Law partner.

1967. INABA, RODNEY Y. Research assistant. (See 1966 Inaba above.)

1967. URABE, ALICE J. Committee clerk.

1967. OTANI, MARY H. Stenographer.

1968. IKEDA, CYNTHIA Y. Secretary.

1968. OTANI, MARY H. Secretary.

1968. YOSHIDA, VIOLET M. Committee clerk. Secretary to Francis H. Yamada, longtime supporter of Ariyoshi, best man and business associate of Ariyoshi's brother James.

1969. NAKAMURA, SANDRA S. Research assistant.

1969. ANBE, FLORENCE F. Committee clerk. Wife of architect Takashi Anbe, an Ariyoshi business associate and political supporter.

1969. OTANI, MARY H. Secretary.

1969. OKAZAKI, NANCY Y. Research assistant. Ariyoshi law firm secretary.

1969. IKEDA, CYNTHIA Y. Stenographer.

1969. YAMAGATA, KAREN R. Committee clerk. Daughter of insurance executive Walter Takeguchi, an Ariyoshi supporter.

1970. OTANI, MARY H. Secretary.

1970. NAKAMOTO, SYLVIA H. Clerk.

1970. NAKAMURA, SANDRA S. Research assistant.
1970. SAKATA, RONALD K. Clerk.
1970. MORITA, LENA W. A. Committee clerk.

Sources: Journals Territorial House of Representatives and Territorial and State Senate; Gwenfread E. Allen, ed., *Men and Women of Hawaii: A Biographical Directory of Noteworthy Men and Women of Hawaii* (Honolulu, 1966); Betty F. Buker, ed., *Men and Women of Hawaii 1972: A Biographical Directory of Noteworthy Men and Women of Hawaii* (Honolulu, 1972); State of Hawaii, Legislative Reference Bureau, *Directory of State, County and Federal Officials: Supplement to Guide to Government in Hawaii* (published occasionally, most recently annually); miscellaneous references in newspapers and periodicals.

Though not a developer in his own right, Ariyoshi in the years before he became lieutenant governor and then governor was nevertheless extensively involved with the development industry. He represented contractors and developers before state boards, before the Honolulu City Council, and in court. He was involved with the construction of hotels and residential condominiums. He invested in land on Maui, Oahu, and the Big Island. He owned shares in and did legal work for speculative lava-field subdivisions on the Big Island, including a subdivision that in the mid-1980s was partially inundated by lava.

Like many Democrats, Ariyoshi, together with members of his family, was involved in real estate-related matters with political associates who were at the same time personal friends, for instance James K. Takushi, Tom T. Ebesu, and Francis H. Yamada:

Takushi was an Ariyoshi campaign worker from the beginning. Ariyoshi's law firm handled Takushi's legal work, for example preparing in 1961 the articles of incorporation for Keehi Site Inc. Ariyoshi 1982–1983 appointed Takushi head of the State Department of Personnel Services and a member of the State Judicial Selection Commission.

Ebesu was a friend who in 1954 first urged Ariyoshi to run for office, and took him to meet John Burns. When Ariyoshi married in 1955, just before his first legislative session got under way, Ebesu was his best man. Ebesu continued to campaign actively for Ariyoshi and other Democrats. In the 1960s Ebesu was appointed executive director of the State Public Employees Health Plan. In 1978 his sister's husband invested in a four-person *hui* called 1525 Partners that included Ariyoshi's brother James, and James' best man, Francis Yamada.

Yamada had been a political supporter of Ariyoshi since 1954. In 1974 Ariyoshi appointed him to the State Civil Service Commission. Yamada and James Ariyoshi in 1978 organized 1525 Partners. Yamada in 1979 joined a James Ariyoshi *hui* called Kupono Associates which bought the Hale Kupono condominium in Kaneohe. Other *hui* members included the Ariyoshis' mother and their three sisters, plus a woman who had been a committee clerk of Ariyoshi's in 1968 when he was in the Senate.

Ariyoshi's overall real estate involvement put him in business with the usual broad range of politically well-connected people, including Republicans as well as Democrats:

In 1959 Ariyoshi bought two lots in Orchid Land Estates on the island of Hawaii from a company whose president was his fellow senator Kazuhisa Abe.

In 1960 he joined a small *hui* that bought 60 acres in Kula, Maui. Also a *hui* member was Vincent H. Yano, who in 1962 won a Senate seat and in 1970 ran unsuccessfully against Ariyoshi for lieutenant governor.

In the early 1960s Ariyoshi bought house lots in the Moanalua-Salt Lake area of Honolulu from International Development Co., headed by Gov. Burns' chief campaign fundraiser Clarence T.C. Ching.

Also in the early 1960s Ariyoshi as an attorney drew up the partnership registration papers for three Norman Inaba *huis* that between them bought large acreage on the Big Island. According to Ariyoshi, as part of his fees he accepted shares in the partnerships. In the *huis* along with Ariyoshi were Republican Sen. Clinton Shiraishi; the wife of Jack H. Mizuha, a Republican recently appointed an associate justice of the state Supreme Court; and Ralph K. Ajifu, a Republican who had been the first chairman of the Land Use Commission.

In the mid-1960s Ariyoshi joined a small *hui* that built an 18-unit apartment house near Queen's Hospital in Honolulu. The *hui* members were Ariyoshi, his brother James, Shigeo Matsui, and Daniel R. Matsukage (to be appointed a Honolulu planning commissioner in 1966). The *hui* bought the lot in 1964 from a part-Hawaiian woman for $55,000, on condition that in the apartment house to be built, one unit would be hers to live in for life. The *hui's* initial purchase and construction money was a loan from Hawaii National Bank, where James Ariyoshi was an assistant cashier and where Daniel Matsukage had been a vice-president until the previous year. A year later this loan was superseded by long-term financing from an insurance company, and Hawaii National was paid off in full. The apartment house was built, 18-units, hollow-tile. A little over a year after construction, Ariyoshi's *hui* sold out to a Chinese couple who owned the Dutch Girl Pastry Shoppe in Kalihi.

*   *   *

Crucial to the success of financially "small" people like Ariyoshi in land development was the boom-time fragmentation of real property into many house lots and small apartment deals as well as large condominimum projects, also the multiplicity of professional jobs connected with land development, and the organization of investment *huis*.

Ariyoshi participated by all these means, although overall his personal involvement with land and development was not the major part of his life, nor was he anything more than a small player in this field.

But if he was not a commanding figure in real estate development he was without doubt a representative figure. Many people in Hawaii, especially local-Asians, did what he he was doing—or wished they could.

* * *

Neither was Ariyoshi a commanding figure in politics in the 1950s and 1960s. He had risen quite far, but remained inconspicuous. For one with such an outstanding record of success at the polls, Ariyoshi on the floor of the Legislature kept a very low profile indeed.

In fact in his 16 years as a legislator he had but a single moment of high visibility, even notoriety, and this was substantially against his will.

Because that single occasion was central to Democratic land politics, it is worth examining for what it might reveal about Ariyoshi as a man on his way up in life, and as a Democrat on his way eventually to the highest office in the state.

In the legislative session of 1963, the Democrats were pushing a land reform measure commonly known as a "Maryland bill," named after the state where land reform of this particular kind had been a fact since the late nineteenth century.

The Maryland bill was designed to allow people who owned a home that stood on a leased lot to buy their lot and thus own it in fee simple.

This was a basic item in the Democrats' overall land program—none more basic. It was of continuing interest to the party, in varying degrees of intensity, from before they came to office in the 1950s right through to the 1980s.

Needless to say, the big estates, the big lessors, hated the idea of leasehold-to-fee conversion.

In 1963, a Maryland bill had passed the House. Now in the 25-member Senate it needed 13 "yes" votes to pass.

Those who counted the numbers could find 12 Democrats in favor. Against were all 10 Republican senators. Two Democrats were also against. One of these was Harry M. Field from Maui, a part-Hawaiian sympathetic to the Bishop Estate, a major lessor whose lands amounted to a kind of surviving Hawaiian patrimony. The other was Mitsuyuki Kido, the senator-developer who in 1959 had supported a bill to raise the pay of Bishop Estate trustees at the same time as he was negotiating a co-venture with the estate to develop 520 acres of its land in Heeia, Oahu.

As things stood in the Senate on the Maryland bill it was 12–12. The twenty-fifth vote would be decisive either way. That last vote was Ariyoshi's.

Ariyoshi was slow to declare himself, and was put under considerable pressure by fellow Democrats to follow the party line. A very high percentage of new houses coming onto the Oahu market around that time were on lease land. Since at least the early 1950s Democratic Party platforms had planks calling for more fee-simple ownership of houses and house lots throughout the Islands. The 1962 platform stated that "we pledge . . . the enactment of statutes requiring the insertion of options to purchase in residential leases."[5]

But on the final reading of the bill, Ariyoshi voted against. The Democrats were left that single vote short. The Maryland bill was lost.

It was a momentous defeat on an issue that was a cornerstone of the Democrats' program. They did not seriously try a Maryland bill again until 1967.

When Ariyoshi explained his stand, he said he was voting his conscience. He gave the media a list of reasons for his "no" vote including doubts about the constitutionality of the bill; the possible devaluation of approximately 7,500 existing leases; fears that rents would be forced up; and fears that construction of homes would slow down, damaging the economy. He also said that tremendous advances had been made in land reform without the necessity for this bill. The Burns administration's tax reassessment policy, he said, would force more lands onto the market for productive use. Landowners had already been "shaken to take a new look at their policies on land utilization," and Ariyoshi hoped they would "voluntarily make some effort to meet the desires of some of our people."[6] On the whole Ariyoshi stressed a single reason for his vote, having to do with the fact that the 1963 Maryland bill was to apply only to leases signed after the bill would come into effect. Ariyoshi essentially said this was not fair business practice. He argued that if future leaseholders were to benefit by being able to buy out their leases, then people on existing leases, which could not be bought out, were at a disadvantage, and the value of their property would drop.

Above and beyond all this detailed reasoning there is circumstantial evidence that Ariyoshi's "no" vote was part of a general defining or redefining of himself across the board, in business, in professional life, and in politics.

For example, in earlier years Ariyoshi had routinely signed major Democratic Party land reform bills for purposes of introduction. These came under a variety of headings: Maryland bills; omnibus tax reform bills; the "New Zealand plan" for government condemnation of privately-owned land at or near assessed tax value; a bill to abolish a forest reserve tax shelter; a bill to limit the percentage of real property a trust might hold as part of its total assets; the "Pittsburgh plan" to encourage land development by taxing land at higher rates than buildings; and bills to give the counties control of their own zoning.

In general in every session 1955–1959, Ariyoshi signed such bills.

In 1961 he signed none. In 1962 there were apparently none for him to sign. In 1963 there were; again he signed none of them.

In 1955 Ariyoshi had signed a Maryland bill for introduction. Research for this book indicates that on every occasion afterwards, down through 1963, when Maryland bills were introduced in whichever house he was then serving, Ariyoshi did not sign them.

Now, using the signing of bills for introduction as an indicator of broad political orientation is problematic. For one thing, a legislator might for whatever reasons simply not have been available the day a bill was sent around for signature. For another, though a legislator might not sign a bill for introduction he might nevertheless still vote for it. This Ariyoshi did in 1963 with the New Zealand and Pittsburgh bills, although the New Zealand bill as passed was considerably milder than as introduced.

On the other hand, the publicly available evidence suggests that Ariyoshi's pattern of signing or not signing major land reform bills indicated something about his evolving general attitude toward the subject:

The 1955–1963 legislative sessions were those of greatest activity for the Democrats' land reform program.

All the bills mentioned above were party bills. Normally they were discussed in pre-session Democratic caucuses, then signed for purposes of introduction by most Democrats in the respective houses into whose hoppers they were dropped. For example, there were two Maryland bills introduced in the Senate in 1963. One was signed by nine of the Senate's 15 Democrats, the other by 13. In those years, then, the lack of a Democratic legislator's signature on party land reform bills was unusual, and generally indicated reservations.

The 1963 Maryland bill on which Ariyoshi voted "no" was a House version; as mentioned it applied only to future leases. Both Senate bills applied to existing as well as to future leases. In other words, neither Senate bill contained that technical matter cited by Ariyoshi as a main reason for voting down the House version. Yet Ariyoshi signed neither of the Senate versions.

In an interview for this book, Ariyoshi said that he signed neither Senate bill because bills applying to existing leases had a potentially serious constitutional defect. He said that passing a law that affected existing leases between private parties might have violated the federal constitutional prohibition against impairment of contracts.

Whether Ariyoshi made a large issue in 1963 of this constitutional point is unclear. Whether he did or not, if the constitutional point he made in the interview is put together with the point about economics on which he rested his case in 1963, then apparently there was no Maryland bill he would vote for at the time.

The question arises: did his evolving position in Island society and business form any predisposition to see the points that he gave as his reasons for voting "no"? Or, why did George Ariyoshi see these problems as determinative when most other Democrats did not, when most others possibly did not even see them at all?

As mentioned, by 1963 Ariyoshi had ties to some of the big estates. Thereafter he was to develop yet other such affiliations. These expressed the reality that Ariyoshi had an outlook that estate trustees found at least relatively agreeable, and perhaps a mind that would be inclined to hesitate over land reform bills. These links also tended to bind Ariyoshi to men who were extremely anti-land reform.

It was only a month before the start of the 1963 session that Ariyoshi joined the board of First National Bank of Hawaii. As also mentioned the Damon Estate owned a good deal of the bank's stock, and it had been at the urging of Damon trustees that Ariyoshi had been elected a director. At the time the estate owned about 1,000 residential lease lots.

There was also evidence that some members of the Islands' old upper class believed Ariyoshi's "no" vote in 1963 was not based on technical objections, but on fundamental political reservations.

For example, in the early and mid-1960s Ariyoshi was one of the few Democratic politicians in some favor with the trustees of the Bishop Estate. In an interview Ariyoshi said that "right after that Maryland law was defeated, I had many conversations with [Bishop trustee] Frank Midkiff. I told him that to avoid these kinds of concerns that exist in the Legislature, that I felt that voluntary conversion would help." At some point over the next year or two, the Bishop trustees did decide to voluntarily sell the fee interests in some residential leases in Halawa Hills in leeward Oahu. According to Ariyoshi, Midkiff asked him to locate someone among the lessees with whom Bishop could negotiate. Ariyoshi said he contacted a young attorney of his acquaintance, Harry H. Masaki, who lived in the tract under discussion. Masaki set up a corporation to handle the sale to individual lessees in what was one of the first conversions of leasehold property to take place in Hawaii.

Ariyoshi has said that his role in the conversion was "to be [Masaki's] liaison with the estate," though without pay.

It was the observation of one of the lessees heavily involved in the negotiations that "the Bishop Estate thought very highly of George," and that "he was close to some of the Bishop Estate trustees."

If this was so, then it is hard to see how Ariyoshi could also have seriously favored Maryland bills, since Bishop trustees by and large abhorred them as forced condemnation of private property.

In general, members of the old *haole* establishment disliked Maryland bills. A number of these people may have thought that Ariyoshi did, too. Raymond R. "Doc" Lyons, board chairman of Maui Electric Co. in the 1960s, was interviewed for this book. He said that when Ariyoshi ran for reelection in 1964, fundraising among executives of major businesses was carried out in order to support Ariyoshi for having voted "no" on the Maryland bill the year before.

*   *   *

Ariyoshi took flak from many of his fellow-Democrats for his momentous vote against a basic party bill. Some spoke freely of him as having sold out.

During his 1964 campaign he was sharply attacked for his "no" vote.[7] Nevertheless, in the primary Ariyoshi ran a strong second in a field of four. Out of three candidates for two seats in the general, he finished first.

In 1967 a modified Maryland bill passed. This bill applied to both existing and future leases, though only those of long-term duration in tracts of at least five acres.

The fact that both existing and future leases were provided for meant that the major objection raised by Ariyoshi in 1963 was taken care of.

At the same time the years since 1963 had seen a shift in the attitudes of at least some estate trustees toward Maryland bills, which helped secure passage of one in 1967.

Of great significance was the fact that the 1967 bill differed enormously from that of 1963 in likely federal tax consequences. The IRS in 1967 rendered an informal opinion that income deriving from sales based on that session's bill would probably receive far more favorable tax treatment than, by implication, sales would have based on the 1963 bill.

Also, by 1967 some estate trustees were reportedly interested in selling lease lots in order to either diversify their investment portfolios or to raise capital for other types of development. Bishop Estate, for example, had begun planning a major resort on its land in Keauhou, Kona. According to *Honolulu Star-Bulletin* writer Byron Baker, Bishop was desirous of cash that could be obtained as a result of a Maryland bill in order to capitalize the resort: "So the Bishop Estate trustees were in the market for the type of land reform-by-condemnation legislation that this session produced."[8]

Ariyoshi signed the 1967 bill for purposes of introduction and voted for it as well.

*   *   *

Ariyoshi won re-election once more in 1968, this time without attracting great controversy. He was now in his fourteenth year as a legislator, undefeated at the polls.

Translated into the specific terms of electoral politics in Hawaii, this meant that Ariyoshi was a highly acceptable figure, even a reassuring figure, someone with whom a great many local-Asian voters could identify, perhaps even beyond his own senatorial district.

This became of great political interest at the end of the 1960s, when John Burns was getting ready to run for his third and final term as governor.

Ariyoshi in late 1969 was picked by leaders of the Burns organization to be Burns' running mate in the 1970 election. This meant that, should the team win, Ariyoshi would be formally first in line to succeed Burns.

Reportedly, Attorney General Bert T. Kobayashi, Ariyoshi's former law partner, was first approached to run with Burns, but declined. The name of Elmer F. Cravalho, now mayor of Maui, was also under serious consideration; but he also indicated a disinclination to run for lieutenant governor.

A former ILWU leader interviewed for this book said that the people most involved with selecting a running mate for Burns were inner-circle Burns Democrats and leaders of the ILWU, in consultation with executives of major local businesses. He said that after Ariyoshi's name became a serious possibility among inner-circle people and the ILWU, it was then run past business leaders, who found Ariyoshi acceptable. The ILWU man also said that through an intermediary, Burns made it known that Ariyoshi was acceptable to him as well. The ILWU man said that at that point several

ILWU leaders, together with Alexander & Baldwin public relations man Nelson Prather, went to Ariyoshi and asked him if he was willing to run. According to the union man, Ariyoshi replied that he would have to talk to Burns first.

Evidently at the time there were a number of people urging Ariyoshi to run. In an interview he indicated it was the urging of one person in particular, whom he declined to name, which was crucial. Ariyoshi said that when this person came to see him, he questioned the person as to how Burns felt about Ariyoshi running. The next day Ariyoshi got a call from Burns, asking him to meet Burns for breakfast soon. Ariyoshi also said that when he and Burns met, Burns asked him to run not only for lieutenant governor in 1970 but for governor in 1974.

In choosing Ariyoshi, the ILWU man said that of paramount importance was finding someone who was Japanese and who would be acceptable to the business establishment. He also said that the emphasis at that point was on getting Burns re-elected, that little or no attention was being paid to the likelihood that the lieutenant governor candidate in 1970 would likely be first in line to succeed Burns, should Burns win that year.

The fact that Ariyoshi was Japanese was extremely important in his being selected. The major contest looming in the 1970 gubernatorial race was in the Democratic primary. In that primary, although Hawaii's Japanese then accounted for only about 28% of the population, nearly half of the voters were going to be Japanese. Moreover, as it turned out, so moribund was the Republican Party by the 1970s that the two subsequent gubernatorial elections of the decade were also going to be decided in the Democratic primaries, where again a disproportionate number of voters were going to be Japanese.

Ariyoshi sat on the boards of three old-establishment companies, a clear indication that he was acceptable to businessmen.

Ariyoshi was a political moderate down the line, even known to vote at times with Republicans.

And Ariyoshi was extensively tied to the development business. Real-estate development had become one of the single greatest means of financial advancement for locally-born Asians, and leadership in development and in Democratic politics had become more or less the same.

In the politics of Hawaii, all this added up to a winning combination.

Obviously, by the time George Ariyoshi came to be considered and then chosen as a running mate for John Burns, he had come to embody in some central way much of what Democratic politics had come to mean in Hawaii, and what it would continue to mean throughout the 1970s and into the 1980s.

(As a parallel to the path Ariyoshi was following, it is worth considering the evolution of the law partnership which he joined when he was a freshman legislator in the mid-1950s. As of 1983 Bert Kobayashi was a kind of senior consultant to the firm; his oldest son was senior partner. The firm was now representing employers in labor-management matters. A 1983 lawyers' directory listed among the firm's representative clients three Big Five firms: Amfac, Castle & Cooke and C. Brewer. The firm also represented several major Japan companies developing land in Hawaii, such as the developers of the Mauna Lani Resort in South Kohala on the Big Island.)

Ariyoshi won the lieutenant governor's race in 1970. After Burns' retirement from active politics because of illness in 1973, Ariyoshi served as acting governor. In 1974 he ran for governor in his own right. He won. He ran again in 1978 and 1982, and won both times. By 1985, when he was in the last years of his final constitutionally allowable term as governor, George Ariyoshi had been a Democrat in elective politics for three decades—and he had never lost an election.

13

THE MARYLAND LAW

By the time the Democrats won control of the Legislature in 1954 there was a substantial middle class in Hawaii, mostly locally born Japanese and Chinese, especially on Oahu. Their numbers were growing all the time. They wanted homes to live in, and not in plantation camps any more, but single-family housing in the city of Honolulu and its suburbs. Those homes had to be built on land. And quite predictably these new middle-class householders of Hawaii—United States citizens working and paying their way on American soil—wanted to own the land on which their houses stood.

The Democrats were their voice in this matter as in so many others. "We feel," said a legislative committee report written by Democrats in 1959, "that a free citizen in a country such as ours should have the opportunity to own his own home and the land on which it stands. Home ownership in fee simple gives the owner a sense of permanence and status."[1]

But fee simple land for middle-class housing was not available in quantities equal to what many Democrats believed was effective demand. On Oahu much of the land suitable for urban and suburban housing was in the hands of a few large trust estates and a ranch company, and for a long time they sold very little land.

When the estates or the ranch did release land for housing on Oahu in the early days of rapid urbanizing, their strong preference was to keep title to the land, letting it out on a leasehold basis, charging their tenants a land or ground rent.

In Hawaii a far smaller percentage of people were able to afford their own home than in an average mainland state, and this had been the case for a long time. In 1950 only 26% of all housing units in the Islands were owner-occupied. Although that figure rose to 34% as of 1960, and to about 43% in 1970, still, by national standards Hawaii ranked consistently low in amount of owner-occupied housing. Indeed, in 1974, the State Department of Planning and Economic Development wrote that "home ownership rates in Hawaii are low, ranking fiftieth of the fifty states."[2] On Oahu this problem was sharpest. And life in a long-established plantation society where land was in the hands of a few big owners, meant that among those who managed to put together a down payment on a home, a number were making their mortgage payments on a house that stood on land that was not theirs, lease land, in most cases land still owned by a major landowner. Thus while in 1950 5% of all owner-occupied housing in Hawaii stood on lease land, by 1960 this had risen to 11%, and to 23% in 1970.[3] By Democratic lights this situation was not fair and it was not right. The Democrats meant to do something about it.

So housing and the leasing of residential land were vital areas where land development, land reform, and politics came together in a very pressing way in the Democratic years.

* * *

The Democrats took the attitude that residential leasehold land ought to be and could be turned into fee simple land. This would be by legislation authorizing a kind of condemnation of the fee simple interest on behalf of the lessee. Their attempts at this were embodied in measures often called "land reform bills" or "Maryland bills."

Maryland, especially around the city of Baltimore, had once been like Hawaii, a place where concentrated land ownership brought about the extensive leasing of residential land. This in turn led to the passage of state laws allowing people whose homes stood on lease land to buy the land from the owner. Maryland's first so-called "redemption act," enabling lessees to "redeem" the fee interest in their house lots from their landlords, was passed in 1884. Much later, in 1940, an article in the *Maryland Law Review* said that "Baltimore has time and again been called a city of homeowners, and it has been rather generally conceded that this accomplishment is due in large measure to the growth of the redeemable ground rent system . . ."[4]

The fact that Hawaii in the 1950s and beyond had a large number of residential leaseholds made the Islands very unusual in the nation at the time.

The issue of leasehold conversion was a matter of high priority for Hawaii Democrats—at times none higher.

They started pushing Maryland-type bills in the Legislature even before they came to power. (Oddly enough, apparently the very first such bill was introduced by a Republican, Joseph P. Andrews, as HB 277 in 1949. That session a Democrat, Charles E. Kauhane, also introduced a Maryland bill, HB 304. Thereafter most or all leasehold conversion bills were introduced by Democrats.)

With the great Democratic electoral victory of 1954 and big Democratic majorities in most legislative sessions from then on, it might have been expected that a Maryland bill would be quickly passed—along with other parts of the Democrats' land program in those years.

The Democrats controlled both houses of the Legislature from 1955-1959, and again in 1963 and ever since. But from the time that Democrats first controlled the Legislature till the time a Maryland-type bill passed, it took 12 years.

Not only that, even after a Maryland bill passed in 1967 the governor refused to sign it into law. And this was no longer an appointed governor of the old kind—so often tight with the old landed class—but the popularly-elected Democratic governor John Burns, the head of a political party that for about two decades had championed the idea of fee simple homes and land for Hawaii-born middle and working-class people.

The 1967 law came into effect without Burns' signature. And even then it was not implemented by Democratic state administrations until after several legislative acts in 1975—that is to say, after almost two continuous decades of Democrats in office.

Clearly there was more here than met the eye.

In fact, what happened concerning Maryland bills from start to finish, and what happened to the general idea of converting residential lease land to fee simple, is very instructive about what was happening overall in the politics of land in Hawaii.

In the course of the Democratic years the pressures for and against leasehold conversion went through some major shifts:

The Democratic Party leaders changed from their fairly liberal early days, turning into a politically moderate and conservative group of aging men with multiple ties to the landowning establishment, including ties to the trust estates that did most of the leasing.

Early in the Democratic years, about 40% of all lease lots were owned by a few charitable trusts, the balance by a few private trusts and corporations that were generating income for a handful of relatively wealthy individuals. In the mid-1960s one large private trust substantially or entirely divested itself of residential leaseholds. Then, beginning in the mid to late 1970s, virtually all of the other major lessors moved to do the same. By the early 1980s this left one charitable trust, Bishop Estate, owning about 75% of all existing lease lots. Bishop had as its beneficiaries a group of people who were among the Islands' most underprivileged—Hawaiian children.

If over time the composition of the lessors narrowed in one direction, that of lessees did so in another.

When Maryland bills were being debated through the 1950s and 1960s, the lessees were an ethnically and politically diverse group of middle and working-class people, spread all around the developed parts of Oahu. By the mid-1980s, the geographic, economic, social and political characteristics of lessees were more constricted. As mentioned, about three-quarters of all lessees were now living on Bishop Estate land, mostly in relatively desirable areas in east and windward Oahu. The majority were middle and upper-class *haoles* and local-Asians, and the districts where they lived tended to vote Republican.

What could in, say, 1960, have reasonably been called "land reform" through application of a Maryland-type law, redistributing land away from the more fortunate to the less, had by the 1980s come in a way to look like the opposite—a fairly prosperous group securing for itself by leasehold conversion a useful economic benefit, and over the objections of the representatives of a socially deprived and oppressed group.

For further complications, the five trustees of the Bishop Estate were no longer all old-line Republicans, members of the old *haole* elite. Most of them were appointees of a state Supreme Court that had been appointed by a Democratic governor; the majority of the trustees were men who had been part of the "Democratic revolution." Now, in the latter years of their public lives, they found themselves each being paid the better part of a quarter of a million dollars a year ($238,000 in fiscal 1983), in the course of defending one of the biggest single symbols of the old Republican land monopoly, against a heavily Republican group of tenants that wanted to force it to sell off its developed residential lands.

* * *

It was in the years before World War II that the practice arose in the Islands of major landowners leasing house lots rather than selling them. Then and especially later almost all of this took place on Oahu.

For decades Oahu had been Hawaii's most population-heavy island, thus the most land-scarce in terms of meeting effective demand for residential and other types of urban property.

During the early 1950s about a third of all new single family lots coming onto the Oahu market were leasehold. The overall average 1961-1981 was about 45%. In the early 1980s there was some tendency for the percentage to decline, however. In 1981, for example, the figure was 31%.[5]

To put this in some perspective: as of 1950 lease lots accounted for about 3% of the total single-family residential lots on Oahu. In 1963 the figure was 13%. An apparent high of 20.5% was reached in 1975. In 1980 it was down to 16%. Also, since the 1950s, housing on lease land accounted for between 5-10% of all types of residential units throughout the Islands.[6]

The major landowners on Oahu, in particular the Bishop, Damon and Campbell estates, plus Queen's Hospital and Harold K.L. Castle's Kaneohe Ranch Co., leased rather than sold for a complex of reasons:

First, like all large landowners in the Islands, they maintained for a long time the old view that their lands basically should not be sold but held indefinitely.

A connected matter was that a careful reading of the trusts' founding documents indicated to most trustees that, in general, they had been instructed not to sell real property; and of course as trustees they were not to do anything at all unless it directly benefitted the trust. Particularly in Bishop's case, where the trust was perpetual and the beneficiaries were native Hawaiians who over the years had lost so much land, trustees could reasonably believe the estate ought to preserve its lands intact.

Also inhibiting the trusts from selling were federal tax considerations. As merely passive holders of land, obtaining rental income and selling land only occasionally, the charitable trusts received their rental income tax-free. If a charitable trust, though, were to develop and sell masses of lots as though it was primarily a sales operation of some kind, then the IRS would tax the sales proceeds. In the case of the private trusts either they or their beneficiaries paid taxes at so-called "ordinary income" rates. If mass sales caused private trusts to appear to the IRS to be land sales businesses, they would still pay tax at ordinary income levels. But their tax brackets would jump. Estimates on how much income would thus be taken ranged up to 90%, virtually a confiscatory tax.

Along with the natural reluctance to sell land and these very real tax considerations, there went the perception that Oahu was going to grow markedly in population. This would put pressure on land, raising its value. So a number of large owners saw wisdom in holding onto land for long-term value appreciation.

An additional reason why most large owners went the leasing route was that they could reach a larger market than through fee simple sales. The buyer of a lease got less by way of property rights than the buyer of a fee simple lot; because leases were therefore cheaper, more people could buy them.

Whatever was in the minds of large owners, to the politically-left Democrats of the early post-World War II era, residential leaseholding was but another injustice worked by Hawaii's outmoded land system, where a handful of large trusts, corporations, wealthy individuals and the government owned virtually everything.

Thus in part the Democrats' drive for a Maryland bill was ideological, carrying over from grievances having nothing specifically to do with residential leaseholding. The lands in question belonged to or were managed by the old enemies: old-money *haole* businessmen who met in boardrooms on Merchant St. and lunched at the Pacific Club, who were using their commanding position in Oahu's land market to the arguable disadvantage of a segment of the island's middle and working classes.

The Democrats also made strictly economic arguments against lease lots:

They believed that fee ownership was a better long-term investment than having a lease. The 1959 Democratic legislative committee that talked about the essential right of Americans to a house and lot of their own, also noted that "land on Oahu is recognized as one of the best investments" a person could make.[7] A University of Hawaii researcher, Louis A. Vargha, wrote in 1964 that there were "long-run financial disadvantages which current leasehold tenure can have for the home owner." He said that although a person paid less for a lease interest than fee, he got proportionately even less by way of potential monetary return. Evidence of this was that lessees paid for site improvements, like sidewalks and gutters, which became the property of the landowner when at the end of the lease the lot reverted to the owner. Vargha also wrote that at the end of the lease the house had to be moved, abandoned, or possibly sold at an unfavorable price to the lessor. In addition, lessees were subject to rent increases during the life of the lease, unlike persons buying outright, who agreed to an overall purchase price and thus had mortgage payments that were normally fixed at the start. Finally, Vargha argued that lessees toward the end of the lease had diminished ability to borrow against the property since, with little time left on the lease, their lots had reduced value as collateral.[8]

Over the years many Democrats also argued that extensive leaseholding led to inflated prices for all types of residential property on Oahu. A 1963 Maryland bill said that there was a land monopoly on the island which "causes upward pressures on land prices," and that "such pressures are made more intensive" by the existence of a large amount of residential leasehold. A 1975 legislative bill explained exactly how these pressures might have connected to leaseholds. The bill said that the more leasehold around, the less fee simple, hence the higher the price for fee simple. As a result, "the high levels of fee simple residential unit prices have artificially raised the level of prices for leasehold units." Next, "the high prices commanded for leasehold units have encouraged the development of leasehold residential units and discouraged the development of fee simple units."[9]

This reasoning was complex; it may also have been circular. Louis Vargha, whose study of residential leaseholding in Hawaii was one of the most thorough ever conducted, and who endorsed Maryland bills in general, thought the fact of leasing *per se* did not affect land values. He wrote in 1964 that "the residential lease itself has not been a direct factor in land values."[10]

* * *

As mentioned, at least as early as 1949 Democratic legislators started introducing bills that would force lessors to sell to their lessees. Bills were introduced thereafter in most sessions that considered general legislation, until 1967 when a Maryland-type bill passed.

Passage took 18 years from 1949 for many reasons. In the first place, the Democrats did not control the Legislature until the 1955 session. Then through 1957 Democrats concentrated on tax issues. Thereafter until 1963, intra-party fighting, temporary loss of the Senate to the Republicans, and statehood, each at different times, hindered efforts to move such a bill.

In 1963 Democrats again controlled both houses of the Legislature, and for the first time ever the governor's mansion as well. By now the residential leasehold question had become larger. According to Vargha, 45% of all new lots coming on the Oahu market 1959-1960 were leasehold. From 1961 to 1963 the figure rose to 71%.[11]

But the 1963 bill went down to defeat on the tie-breaking Senate vote of George Ariyoshi. The Democrats did not seriously try again until 1967, when finally they were successful.

* * *

Most of the early Maryland bills applied to all residential leases, regardless of the number held by a particular landowner, as long as the leases were for at least 15 years and the land was occupied by the tenant as his sole residence for at least five years before he sought to buy it.

The 1963 Maryland bill would have applied only to leases made after the effective date of the law.

The bill that passed in 1967 applied only to tracts on Oahu of at least five contiguous acres in which at least half of the lessees were willing and able to buy. If these conditions were met, then the state's Hawaii Housing Authority (HHA) would buy the entire tract, resell lots to those residents who wanted to and could afford to buy, and become landlord to those who did not buy. Both pre-existing and future leases were covered. An existing lease had to have at least 35 years left on it. Future leases had to be for at least 20 years.

In some ways the version that finally passed in 1967 was no longer a Maryland bill. The acts of the Maryland Legislature, and all of Hawaii's previous leasehold condemnation bills which were closely patterned after those acts, had several essential differences with the 1967 law. For one thing, the acts of the Maryland Legislature applied only to future leases. Furthermore and perhaps most importantly, the 1967 law called for a government agency to condemn whole leasehold tracts, whereas previous Hawaii bills, as well as the laws adopted in Maryland, would insert options to buy in each individual lease. Under this option approach there was no government agency in between lessor and lessee, and each individual lessee acted alone in buying out his landlord.

To a great extent it was federal tax considerations that led to the Hawaii Legislature going a different route in 1967.

As mentioned, for years a major worry of the trust estates was that selling masses of houselots to their lessees might involve a nearly confiscatory tax. In consultation with the IRS, those who drafted the 1967 bill tailored it to avoid this result.

During or just before the 1967 legislative session, a delegation of legislators and representatives of the Bishop and Campbell estates and Kaneohe Ranch visited an IRS official in Washington, D.C. According to a report later made by the group, the IRS indicated that the Maryland bill then under consideration and subsequently adopted would make sales possible that would entail no tax to charitable estates. Private estates would have two tax options available, both of which were considerably better than paying tax at rates that ranged up to 90%.

The first was to simply pay tax at capital gains rates. This meant that the "basis" of the property was first exempted. The "basis" was what the property cost when initially acquired or as of 1913, the year in which the Internal Revenue Code took effect, whichever was later. Then a certain portion of the income—over the years it was usually 50%—was allowed as tax-free, and then the balance was taxed at ordinary income rates.

The second option was that if the sales proceeds were reinvested within a fixed period in other real property, then there would be no tax at all on the sales.

What did occur with the latter option was this: the basis of the property that was sold was transferred to the new property—the reinvestment property—if that basis was less than the current market value of the new property.

Typically the trusts' Hawaii property had been acquired before the effective date of the Internal Revenue Code, and so the basis was fixed as of 1913. Normally this basis was laughably tiny vis-a-vis say, the market value of an office building in California constructed by some corporation in 1980 on land it purchased in 1979. Therefore if, for example, a private Hawaii trust in 1981 sold residential lease lots and immediately reinvested the proceeds by buying the California office building and its lot, the basis of the building and lot would be the value of the Hawaii property as of 1913. But if and when that building was later sold by the Hawaii trust, a capital gains tax would be assessed, and its basis exemption would be miniscule.

On Maryland bills in Hawaii, what was pivotal to the IRS in 1967 was how much a bill would make the landowners appear as merely passive lessors who occasionally sold and did so only under threat of government condemnation, versus how much they looked like companies set up to sell land in the ordinary course of business. The more the lessors looked like just occasional sellers under threat, the better their tax treatment tended to be, and vice-versa.

What mattered to the IRS in the proposed 1967 bill was that sales by lessors would be few and occasional, because they would be in bulk. Also, sales would take place under the threat of, or actually by, government condemnation. The report of the group of Hawaii lawmakers and lessors' representatives who met with the IRS official, said that the "IRS has given the impression that it prefers the condemnation approach, provided the statute calls for condemnation in bulk."[12]

With the 1963 bill it is unknown how the IRS might have reacted, since there is no record of anyone officially asking for even an off-the-record opinion. But because the bill would have entailed many sales to individuals, the lessors would have looked more like land sale companies than under the 1967 plan.

In any event, the IRS indication that the 1967 bill would probably provide for favorable tax treatment may have helped persuade some estate trustees to quit fighting so hard against forced lease-to-fee conversion. At least there was the appearance that several trustees about this time softened their opposition to Maryland bills, though some trustees continued to oppose them strenuously.

Also important in understanding what happened in the Hawaii Legislature in 1967 was that this new approach on the tax ramifications of Maryland bills came at a time when some trustees were reportedly interested in selling residential lease land in order to diversify their portfolios, or to raise develop-

ment capital. Bishop Estate, for example, had begun planning a major resort
on its land in Keauhou, Kona, and, according to *Honolulu Star-Bulletin* writer
Byron Baker, was desirous of cash that could be obtained by way of a Maryland
bill: "So the Bishop Estate trustees were in the market for the type of land
reform-by-condemnation legislation that this session produced."[13]

* * *

When the Legislature passed a Maryland bill in 1967, Gov. Burns said
publicly: "I do not believe that his measure will bring about true land reform."[14] He had a veto message prepared, but then let the bill become law
without his signature. The legislation became known formally as the Hawaii Land Reform Act.

But if Burns would not kill the bill he would not use it either.

Immediately after the 1967 law's effective date, which was mid-1969, several groups of lessees petitioned the state's Hawaii Housing Authority to
begin sales.

The HHA was empowered by the law to float bonds in order to raise the
money needed to buy leasehold tracts. About the time the first petitions
came in, an HHA official said the money market was unfavorable. HHA
declined to float any bonds.[15]

For the next few years nothing happened. Then, four years after the bill
passed, William G. Among, head of the state department that contained
HHA, announced that the kind of bonds authorized by the law would not
work. So-called "revenue bonds" had been authorized. Among said such
bonds had to be fully repaid by the activity for which they were used. But he
said the way the Land Reform Act was then written, HHA would buy an
entire tract, resell to those lessees willing and able to buy, and become landlord to the rest. Recouping the bond money would take many years, since
part would be repaid by leaserent paid in over a long period of time. Conceivably the money could never be fully repaid if the return from the land
through rent was lower than the interest rate on the bond. Among said the
law needed rewriting so that general obligation bonds could be used, where
immediate repayment was not necessary.[16]

The Legislature complied during its next session, that of 1971.

Then, in 1972, a reporter, following up on whether the law was being
implemented, asked Burns whether he would now use it. Burns said he
would not.

Burns said he did not want the state to become landlord to all those lessees who would not or could not repurchase, and he did not want to tie up
state money in owning their lots.[17] At about this time the state's bond counsel also questioned the wisdom of risking the state's bond rating by floating
bonds to implement a law that some people believed was unconstitutional.[18]

* * *

There matters rested until George Ariyoshi ran for governor in 1974 as Burns' successor.

At that time Ariyoshi found himself having to cope with the fallout from a great many disputed rent renegotiations between Bishop Estate and its lessees.

In fact, in the mid-1970s, mostly because of Bishop's renegotiation policies, plus the Islands' spiraling property values and cost of living, there coalesced enough upset lessees so that a critical mass was generated sufficient to get the state government moving along the path of actually implementing the Maryland Law.

This is the way it happened:

Most leases were 55 years long, to conform to collateral requirements of the Federal Housing Administration, which was lending to many lessees. The typical lease fixed an annual rent for the first 25 to 40 years, after which the rent was renegotiated. Since the initial rent had been set in something of a buyers' market and at a time of relatively low land prices in Hawaii, by the early 1970s rents were very low in relation to market value. When renegotiated they increased dramatically.

Take, for example, a Bishop Estate lessee living in the fashionable Honolulu suburb of Waialae-Kahala. Not only had his initial rent been set at a time of comparatively low land values, but, in a subdivision like Waialae-Kahala Tract A, he had paid relatively little of the cost of so-called "off-site improvements" such as sidewalks and the installation of utilities. As a sales inducement in what was then moderately a buyers' market, landowners in early subdivisions had often asked for rather little of the cost of these things. They did this in the hope that more could be obtained on renegotiation when they would have captive tenants, and that anyway there would be long-term appreciation in land values.

Increases now asked by Bishop in Tract A averaged more than 1000%. For example, on one Tract A lot the ground rent as of 1974 was $290 a year. Bishop calculated the new rent, beginning in 1976, at $3,180.[19]

An important social dimension here was that many of the lessees whose rent was coming up for renegotiation were nearing retirement age, meaning their income was leveling off or declining at precisely the point where their lease rent was dramatically rising. The Tract A lease cited above was a case in point. According to a finding by a state circuit court judge in 1978, this particular lessee as of about 1975 was a married couple. The husband was 66 and recently retired from a management-level position in private industry. The wife was 60 and not working. After gauging the capacity of their financial resources to withstand the huge jump in rent, the judge wrote that "the lease rent . . . offered by Bishop Estate amounts to an eviction."[20]

The *Honolulu Star-Bulletin* in a series published in early 1973 said "there is a growing feeling of dissatisfaction with the leasehold system among some middle-class families."[21] By the fall of 1974 the feeling had become one of open anger.

At about the time of the 1974 election, the *Star-Bulletin* said that on the average, rents were going from $350 or $400 a year to $5,000.[22]

Lessees and the news media reacted accordingly.

George Ariyoshi responded by saying he supported the Maryland Law anyway. After being elected he instituted steps intended to lead to conversions.

The Legislature was also feeling the pressure, enabling some longtime proponents of the law like Sen. John J. Hulten Sr. to push for amendments that finally led to sales.

The Legislature in 1975 rewrote the law so that only 25 lessees within a tract need be willing/able to buy, instead of at least 50%. Also now the Hawaii Housing Authority need only condemn those lots whose tenants would purchase, rather than the whole tract.

Also, and very significantly, by a separate bill the Legislature put a ceiling on renegotiated rents, so that an annual rent could not be more than of 4% of the value of the lessor's interest in the lot.

From the tenants' standpoint, even with this ceiling there were later some renegotiated figures that were exorbitant and difficult to pay.

On the other side, for the landowner, from an investment standpoint 4% was a poor return. Actually, to say that the effective ceiling on return was 4% was to understate somewhat. Land in Hawaii was generally an asset that appreciated over time. Thus a landlord got his 4% plus appreciation. One estate staff member estimated that, with appreciation factored in, the effective ceiling on rate of return was about 5%.

But this was still quite low as compared to what most other urban-type rental property might produce. The Frank Russell Property Index for 1984, for example, said that nationwide on the average, the rate of return on investments in real property 1977–1979 had been 18%, and 1979–1983 14.2%.[23]

Lessors were also getting the message that the Legislature was at last taking action, even if slowly, to make residential leasing less profitable and perhaps eventually to end it.

The upshot of all this was that most lessors were now more inclined to sell.

Damon Estate had already sold off its roughly 1,000 lease lots back in the mid-1960s,[24] but in 1975 all of the other original, large lessors were still in the residential leasing business. Following that year's legislative amendments, however, negotiated sales began to occur.

* * *

As mentioned, what had apparently done the most to force the hand of the state government, in turn leading to sales, were large renegotiated rents demanded by the largest lessor, the Bishop Estate.

In proposing large rent increases, were the landlords, Bishop in particular, acting like cynical, gouging land barons as many of their lessees believed? Or were the landlords simply asking for their due, as determined by ordinary business standards, and what, in the case of Bishop, the trustees believed best for the Hawaiian children who were the estate's beneficiaries?

In establishing their policies on rent renegotiation, trustees and officers of the lessors, especially the large ones and most especially Bishop, had to pick their way through an exceedingly complex economic, social, legal and political maze:

They had their legal duties to their beneficiaries or shareholders. They had to be cognizant of the myriad factors that bore on land prices. They were operating within a political arena which included forces hostile to their interests. A wary eye had to be kept on what might trigger adoption or use of a Maryland law, or related legislation that might, say, limit rent. At the same time they had to be alert to the possibility that the higher the rent, the higher the price that could be sought in condemnation if it ever came to that, on the theory that rent levels were an indicator of market value. Connected to legislation were federal tax issues. And Bishop had its Hawaiian beneficiaries to consider as an added dimension.

From the start of the residential leasehold system through the mid-1960s, Bishop Estate had an established policy on the amount of rent to demand at renegotiation. In 1968 the trustees revised the policy. The approach adopted at that time was in effect during the early to mid-1970s, when big waves of rental renegotiations took place.

According to a 1968 Bishop staff memo, the existing policy at renegotiation had been to ask for 3.2% of the estate's interest in the house lot. The staff recommended an increase to somewhere between 3.6% and 4%. The trustees decided on 4.28%.

These numbers might appear small and differences between them negligible. Not so. In simple lay terms, for example, going from 3.2 to 4.28 represented an increase of 34%. And of course the 4.28% was applied to a land value that by the 1970s had increased hundreds of percent since the lease was first negotiated so long ago—hence the leap in actual dollars paid from hundreds to thousands per year.

William Van Allen of the Bishop staff oversaw preparation of the 1968 memo. He was quite prophetic about the possible social and political consequences of large renegotiated rent increases of the kind the trustees adopted, despite his recommendation to the contrary.

Van Allen wrote that "abrupt major changes in policy by a major landowner such as Bishop Estate can have very serious consequences on the economy of the State and can also arouse very serious public opposition. It is therefore important that revision of policy on such delicate matters as changes in the basic rent be made on a conservative basis." He also said that "in the long term, appreciation of land values is more significant in increasing Estate income than rate of return on leases."

Repeatedly and in the clearest language Van Allen warned the trustees: "A large increase in the base rent upon renegotiation will probably . . . raise a violent reaction." "A large increase will . . . arouse widespread public opposition . . ." "A policy change in one step to an excessively high rate of return may arouse public protest." "An immediate increase of more than 4% is likely to . . . arouse public indignation . . ."

As mentioned, the trustees raised the figure to 4.28%. Protest was indeed loud and sustained.

Van Allen also warned that a related effect of an excessive increase could be to "stimulate action under Act 307 [the 1967 Maryland bill] and possibly result in additional land reform legislation."[25]

Again he was right on target. It was mostly the lessees' reaction to Bishop's renegotiated rents in the early to mid-1970s that led to the additional legislation in 1975 that finally brought about sales.

*   *   *

Several of the attempts by Bishop lessees to buy their lots following the 1975 legislation brought about trials in state circuit court.

The findings in cases by Judge Herman T. F. Lum in 1978 with respect to Waialae-Kahala Tract A, and Judge Ronald B. Greig in 1983 concerning Kamiloiki Valley in Hawaii Kai, illustrated how many people, Bishop lessees in particular, considered the behavior of the large lessors as exploitative in general, and helped explain why so many lessees wanted to be free of their landlords.[26]

The Bishop Estate was a commanding figure in Oahu's residential land business, owning about 15% of Oahu, mostly in east and windward areas.

Judge Lum wrote that these were, respectively, Oahu's most and second most desirable areas for single family residential living.

Furthermore, in east Oahu 1961–1974, Lum said that 93% of all new single family units coming onto the market in tracts of at least 25 lots were on lease land. Most of this was Bishop's.

On the windward side, where 66% of such lots were leasehold, Castle and Bishop were the two largest private owners. All or almost all lease lots were theirs.

On Oahu overall during the 1960s, Bishop's lease lots accounted for 40% of all new lots coming on the market. From 1970 to 1975 the figure rose to 50%.

Lum took the view that the large owners, including Bishop, were just more or less dribbling out new land at a slow rate in order to keep prices high. He wrote that in east Oahu there were 975 vacant, residentially zoned acres, 824 of which Bishop owned. In windward Oahu he said there were 1,334 such acres, of which Bishop owned at least 350, plus some indeterminate amount of the balance. (Lum wrote that large owners also dominated the vacant residential land market in central and leeward Oahu, although there far more of the land coming on the market was fee simple.)

Lum wrote that the large owners, in order to keep prices up, were deliberately holding back on developing this already zoned land: "Overly restrictive residential zoning has not caused the shortage of single-family housing on Oahu. The existence of vacant land in rural and urban areas, already zoned for residential use, will not alleviate the shortage, because the development practices of the major landowners control the availability of land for housing." Judge Greig, for his part, wrote that "leasehold property prices are . . . kept high by the practice of incremental development."

Further evidence, to Lum, of large owners monopolistically withholding land was Hawaii's extremely low housing vacancy rate. He said that statewide 1950–1973 the rate for all types of units, multi-family as well as single-family, was less than 3%. Lum wrote this "indicates a tight market. A vacancy rate in excess of 10% would be indicative of a highly competitive market."

Lum and Greig thought all this left Bishop in a thoroughly commanding position vis-a-vis its lessees, especially when lessees were already living in their houses and it came time to renegotiate rent. Greig wrote: "The lessee is required to negotiate a rent escalation in the middle of the lease, when he is captive and has no real bargaining power." He also noted that "although the lessee may have the opportunity of removing the improvements on the land, houses built of single wall and rock wall on concrete slabs usually cannot be moved."

The judges believed that the resultant bargaining process was one-sided. Lum wrote that Bishop's development manager for east and windward Oahu, during testimony at trial, "could recall only one instance in his five years as manager when the lessee disputed the quoted lease rent on renegotiation and there was actual give and take negotiating."[27] (Similarly a Senate committee wrote in 1975: "In instances, lessor's terms are peremptorily submitted to the lessee in ultimatum form through letters rather than through any actual bargaining process." The committee believed this was a result of "unequal bargaining power" between lessors and lessees that flowed from the "oligopolistic land ownership in this State.")

Lessees' attorneys argued before Judge Greig that sections of a 1968 Bishop Estate staff report indicated collusion on the part of the largest lessors in establishing policies on renegotiated rent, which was offered as further evidence of a lopsided relationship between lessees and their landlords. What the memo depicted was also an apparently glaring violation of federal and state antitrust laws, according to the lessees' lawyers.

The memo stated that "the [Bishop] Staff contacted Kaneohe Ranch and the Campbell Estate to ascertain their policy on determining rents upon renegotiation." The memo then described the policies of these two lessors, as explained to the Bishop staff. In summarizing the "need for increasing base rent on renegotiation," the memo listed the "policies of other landowners" as one of five reasons calling for an increase. In discussing actual figures that Bishop might adopt, one figure was said to be "reasonable compared to that charged by the other landowners."

Lum believed that the renegotiated rents were unconscionable.

Waialae-Kahala Tract A residents on the average had been paying $250 a year. Lum said that if rents increased in line with Honolulu's median family income 1950–1974, the new rent should be about $1,000. Instead Bishop was asking nearly $3,000. Lum said this was "beyond the financial capacities of a substantial number of the Tract A lessees."[28] Judge Greig in 1983 wrote that "the new lease rents will not leave a sufficient amount in the family's budget deemed reasonable enough to pay for other necessary expenses of life."

As an additional criticism of Bishop Estate, Lum compared the proposed renegotiated rent for Waialae-Kahala Tract A with the new rent for Waialae-Iki View Lots Unit IV, a subdivision on a ridge above Tract A which was just coming on the market.

Lum said Unit IV was "a more desirable location than Tract A because it has better homes, a better view and is a higher quality development." In 1976–1977, according to Lum, the average price of a Unit IV home on the open market was $149,440, and the lease rents Bishop was asking for these lots were "the highest lease rents charged by Bishop Estate for any of its new subdivisions. Only beachfront lot rents are higher."

In 1976–1977 the average sale price of a Tract A home was $83,560— about 56% of what Unit IV homes were going for. But whereas Tract A lessees were being asked to pay nearly $3,000 a year, Unit IV lessees were being asked only $1,320 annually for the first 30 years. Thus "the residents of Tract A have been asked by the trustees to pay more than twice as much rent for Tract A lots which are worth considerably less than the Unit IV lots."

Lum also wrote that, of the two rents, Unit IV was probably a more accurate reflection of open market forces. He said it was fair to "presume [it to be] in balance with the income of Unit IV homeowners," because otherwise they could not obtain financing to buy in the first place.

The logical conclusion from all this was that Bishop as a renegotiating landlord had acted unreasonably, to say the least.

Bishop, with its own side of the story to tell, said that between the Tract A renegotiated rents and the Unit IV new rents there was an additional significant difference, not included in Judge Lum's findings. Bishop said that Unit IV buyers were paying much more up front for site improvements than did Tract A people when they first bought after World War II. Tract A purchasers paid about $800, which in 1976–1977 dollars would have been about $2,000, as compared with Unit IV people paying some $30,000.

These two figures were each part of initial purchase price. This meant that Tract A buyers had paid less up front and would tend to have to pay more in renegotiated rent than Unit IV buyers might pay in initial rent.[29]

Just how much difference these two figures might account for was hard to know. There was also the fact that Bishop and other lessors tended to set initial rents somewhat lower than the market would indicate, as an inducement to buy.

Also, Tract A lessees for years had been paying rents that were far below what market value indicated the rents should have been. As mentioned, this was because of relatively low land values when the initial rents were set; also because in the early years of Oahu's post-WWII development boom it was a buyers' market, and sellers often set rents particularly low to attract buyers. In the rent renegotiation controversy, lessees seldom acknowledged that for years they had been getting an exceptionally good deal. Their states of mind and household budgets, rather, were fixed at the level of their old rent, and neither financially nor emotionally were they prepared for a big jump.

* * *

There were also federal court decisions involving Hawaii's leasehold conversion legislation, and from a legal standpoint these were the main events.

Begun by a lawsuit filed in 1979 by Bishop Estate, there was a succession of three opinions, culminating with the US Supreme Court ruling in 1984 that it was constitutional to force transfer of the fee interest in the house lot from landlord to lessee.[30] This decision seemingly capped an era of contemporary land history in Hawaii (although the Hawaii Supreme Court still had pending before it a challenge to the law's constitutionality, and despite the US Supreme Court ruling the Hawaii Supreme Court could still find the law unconstitutional).

Bishop had attacked the law on several grounds. One of these involved the question: did the Hawaii Land Reform Act violate the US Constitution's fifth amendment?

The pertinent part of the fifth amendment reads: "[N]or shall private property be taken for public use, without just compensation." The section presumes that any private property condemned by the government must be for a valid public use. The question with the Hawaii leasehold conversion law was whether it deserved that presumption. More particularly: was there some constitutionally valid public purpose served in forcing a lessor to sell to his tenant the house lot under his tenant/homeowner's house, in a community where there was a substantial number of such tenants renting from a few large landlords?

Hawaii Federal District Court Judge Samuel P. King in 1979 ruled that the taking was for a constitutionally permissible public use, although he struck down provisions in the law relating to mandatory arbitration and a sale price formula.

The US Ninth Circuit Court of Appeals in 1983 reversed King on the public use question.

The Supreme Court in 1984 reversed the Ninth Circuit.

From the standpoint of legal reasoning there was in each of these decisions a threshold question on the structure of governmental authority in the United States. Did the legislative branch have near-exclusive right to decide whether the condemning of private property was for a valid public use? Or could the judicial branch conduct an extensive inquiry into whether a particular use was valid?

The two decisions that held that the proposed takings were for a valid public use did so mainly on the basis that courts had little to say on matters of this kind, that such things were largely a question for the legislative branch, whether Congress or state legislatures. Courts at most were to inquire whether the social objective of the condemnation was one over which Congress or a legislature had legitimate authority—the provision of an adequate housing supply for a community, for example—and whether the condemnation or the law authorizing it was a rational attempt to deal with a perceived problem in such an area. To be "rational" it was only necessary not to be arbitrary. Thus the US Supreme Court said "it will not substitute its judgment for a legislature's judgment as to what constitutes a public use unless the use be palpably without reasonable foundation." These were not hard tests, and with Judge King and the Supreme Court the Hawaii Land Reform Act had no trouble passing them.

The Ninth Circuit Court, on the other hand, said that if Congress in a condemnation matter determined that something was for public use, then courts had to be very deferential. But if a state legislature made the decision, then "this court must properly make the ultimate determination of whether the use is public." In that the Hawaii law was passed by the Hawaii Legislature, the Ninth Circuit went on to set up a standard by which to judge whether the law was for a legitimate public purpose. The court said that the law had no precedent within the whole range of condemnation laws found constitutional by various courts over the years, also that the law would simply transfer property from one private owner to another with no public benefit being effected in the process. The Ninth Circuit Court thus ruled the law unconstitutional.

There was some evidence that the legal reasoning in the three federal opinions was in part a function of general predispositions, of social and political outlooks held by the judges and justices. This could be seen in how the opinions dealt with questions of fairness, with who was the underdog, and with the act's social morality.

When King got down to talking about fairness and who was and was not being taken advantage of, he wrote mainly about lessees. He quoted extensively from legislative findings that portrayed Hawaii's residential leasehold system as socially abusive. He cited a Ninth Circuit Court case upholding a Guam urban renewal law that had as an objective the making of straight and even lot lines and streets. King wrote that "it is difficult for this Court to see how condemning land to have even streets is more for a public purpose than condemning land so that a large number of long-term lessees can have the opportunity to own the land they live on."

The Ninth Circuit, on the other hand, focused on lessors. It called the Land Reform Act a kind of "majoritarian tyranny" which the court said the country's founders had opposed. The court quoted James Madison at the Constitutional Convention: "In future times a great majority of the people will not only be without landed, but any sort of, property. These [may] . . . combine under the influence of their common situation; in which case, the rights of property & the public liberty [will not be safe in their hands]." The court wrote that the federal constitution and the Bill of Rights were in part designed in reaction to this fear, to give "protection to minority rights," such as those of Bishop Estate.

The Supreme Court also harked back to the nation's founding, but for support for the law: "The people of Hawaii have attempted, much as the settlers of the original 13 Colonies did, to reduce the perceived social and economic evils of a land oligopoly traceable to their monarchs."

In looking at the diverging views on who is the oppressed underdog and on what the country's founders thought about big landowners, some of the judicial reasoning takes on the appearance of social and political philoso-phizing in legal garb. If so, this would be nothing new. What was somewhat startling, though, was that a rather conservative US Supreme Court ruled for a mass of middle class and upper-class homeowners against a major landowner.

Whatever the reasons for the Supreme Court decision, in so holding it may have at last ended nearly 40 years of questions in Hawaii about the constitutionality of Maryland bills. (As mentioned, though, the Hawaii Su-preme Court still had a case pending, in which that court could hold the law unconstitutional.)

The US Supreme Court decision also appeared to signal a continued gradual decline in the practice of residential leaseholding in the Hawaiian Islands.

* * *

For many in Hawaii, reading their newspapers at the time of the Ninth Circuit decision, it was novel to see the Islands' large landowners character-ized as a victimized minority.

There were, however, several such ironies over the whole course of the residential-leasehold controversy, with the ordinary meaning of words turned around, and with apparently strange political behavior.

For one thing, there was the fact that the Legislature entitled the lease-hold conversion law the "Hawaii Land Reform Act."

On a world scale, the phrase "land reform" conjures up situations involv-ing widespread political oppression, sometimes provoking armed revolu-tionary movements, in parts of the world where tiny landlord classes live in relative luxury off the labor of impoverished, landless masses. Places like India and Central America come to mind.

China underwent extensive land reform beginning in the 1930s and con-tinuing into the 1950s. That program involved no politely-debated legisla-tion nor payment of fair-market value to the expropriated landlords. The Chinese landlord who was not killed was lucky.

There have of course also been less extreme cases, but with generally modest redistributions.

Now, by the 1980s the Hawaii lessees who were seeking to own the land on which their homes stood were mainly middle and upper class *haoles* and local-Asians. They were concentrated in east and windward Oahu, though there was also some residential leasehold around Pearl Harbor and in the Ewa Plain. An irony is that Americans of these socio-economic classes generally opposed political movements in the Third World that espoused land redistribution of the kind often associated with the words "land reform."

There is a related point, having to do with extremes of wealth and poverty in Hawaii itself:

As mentioned, in the years following World War II there were several major landowners heavily involved in the creation of leasehold tracts. Because most later came to believe they could make more money with other investments, and seeing condemnations coming, most major lessors substantially divested themselves through negotiated sales.

The beneficiaries of the Bishop Estate were ethnic Hawaiians. The Hawaiian community in general strongly opposed Bishop selling much or any of its land. So although Bishop sold off several thousand lots, the estate was especially adamant about getting the highest possible return on the lots it had to sell, and alone among the major lessors continued to try to hang on to most of its leaseholds. Thus while in 1963 Bishop owned 36% of all Oahu's lease lots, in 1984 it owned about 75%.

The Bishop Estate was a perpetual charitable trust whose beneficiary was a school for Hawaiian children. The school in 1984 had some 2,850 full-time Hawaiian students and about 6,000 part-time. (The school was established pursuant to a trust in the will of Bernice P. Bishop. The will did not say whether the students had to be Hawaiian, but it was assumed that they must. The only exception was for the children of teachers, who for a time were able to enroll irrespective of ethnicity. That practice was discontinued in the late 1960s.)

In socio-economic terms Hawaiian children were about the Islands' most underprivileged people, with among the most social problems.

As of the mid-1980s, then, the residential leasehold situation involved some of Hawaii's most privileged people seeking land redistribution from the least. To call this "land reform," as though it bore some similarity to land redistributions in the Third World, was an incongruous use of language.

From a historical standpoint there was irony in the role of Hawaiians:

During the 1963 legislative session, in which a Maryland bill nearly passed, a group of Hawaiians staged a torchlight parade around Iolani Palace, where the Legislature was in session. The pastor of Kawaiahao Church, Rev. Abraham K. Akaka, sermonized from the pulpit against the bill. The Honolulu Hawaiian Civic Club president wrote a scathing attack on the bill in the club newsletter. Akaka sermonized again in 1967 when a bill passed.[31]

Leaseholding's most vocal proponents were often Hawaiian because of Bishop Estate's major involvement. Hawaiians' statements in defense of the system tended to recall their peoples' loss of land in the nineteenth century. Akaka wrote in 1967: "Memories of the Great Mahele of 1848 come to mind. We feel that pressure for land reform then was due more to a rising generation of Western investors than from the native Hawaiian himself. We cannot but feel that pressure for land reform now is due not to the poorer man—among whom are a great many Hawaiians—but from a new generation of investors from East and West."[32]

The irony was that in defending leaseholds, Akaka and others were in *de facto* alliance with the descendants and successors of those people who in the nineteenth century did most to dispossess Hawaiians of their land and sovereignty.

The major lessors as of the 1960s were, as mentioned, the Bishop Estate, Harold K. L. Castle's Kaneohe Ranch, Damon Estate, and Campbell Estate. The founder of Damon Estate, two of the initial trustees of Bishop Estate, and the father and two uncles of Harold Castle, were deeply involved with the Committee of Safety, which in 1893 organized the overthrow of Queen Liliuokalani. Harold Castle's father, James, and his father's brothers William and George, belonged to the Committee of Safety, to a subcommittee, or to the revolutionary militia. Samuel M. Damon was also on a subcommittee. Less than a decade before the 1893 revolution, he had been bequeathed the *ahupua'a* of Moanalua by the queen's sister-by-adoption. On these lands the Damon Estate, created by a trust in Damon's will, later had residential lease lots. Damon was also one of the initial trustees of the Bishop Estate. Another of the initial trustees, William O. Smith, was also on the Committee of Safety. Another, Charles M. Cooke, in 1893 was appointed a representative of the post-revolutionary provisional government to propose to the US government that it annex Hawaii.[33]

The one apparent exception to this picture is that of James Campbell, who founded the Campbell Estate. In a biographical sketch appearing in the *Honolulu Star-Bulletin* in 1935, Campbell was said to have "been a partisan of Queen Liliuokalani at the time of the overthrow," and to have been "a royalist to the end of his days." Also, Liliuokalani wrote that Campbell's wife visited her during a period of imprisonment after the overthrow, and showed kindness to the deposed queen.[34]

The twentieth-century Hawaiians who made common cause with the descendants and successors of these men were, in part, forced into an alliance by circumstance. But some were establishment Hawaiians who had made their peace with the *haole* system and had ties to it that went beyond being thrown together by Maryland bills. For example, the person who in 1963 as Honolulu Hawaiian Civic Club president penned an attack on the Maryland Bill was Mrs. Parker Widemann. At the time she was secretary to D. Hebden Porteus, a Republican senator who was also a Damon Estate trustee.[35]

* * *

It was not just certain Hawaiians who were crossing strange lines when it came to residential leaseholds in post-World War II Hawaii. Many legislators did too.

Throughout the 1950s and 1960s most of the legislators pushing Maryland bills came from districts with little or no leasehold.

On the other hand many of those in opposition came from districts with high concentrations of lease land, particularly from east and windward

Oahu where roughly 50% of all residents lived on lease land. In the crucial votes in 1963 and 1967, 40% of all "no" votes came from lawmakers from east and windward districts. Furthermore, looking only at votes cast by legislators from these districts, for 1963 and 1967 combined, 61% were "no." For 1963 alone the figure was 77%. And—to make this really noteworthy— few or none of these politicians suffered noticeably at the polls as a result.

What was going on here was moderately complex:

In terms of proximity to Honolulu, and in terms of desirable natural environments for the new, suburban, single-family homes of the post-war era, east and windward Oahu were generally considered the prime locations.

The other major alternatives were west and central Oahu. The parts of these latter areas more or less near Honolulu, with its jobs and shopping and so on, were hot and dry, compared with east and windward locales. They were also close to Pearl Harbor, other military bases and industrial activities—things most people, if given a choice, would rather not live near. Then, to get to parts of west and central Oahu that were far from all this, was to be quite far from Honolulu.

Henry J. Kaiser, who in 1959 began his extremely large Hawaii Kai community on Bishop Estate land in east Oahu, used to say that suburbanites who drove to and from work preferred to live to the east of their workplaces so that the sun was not in their faces when commuting.[36]

For whatever reasons, then, as Honolulu's population grew after World War II and the suburban bedroom community came into vogue in the Islands, middle and upper-class prospective home buyers preferred east and windward areas.

In 1962 an attorney reviewing the business affairs of the Campbell Estate wrote that "the principal asset of the estate is real property strategically located athwart the main course of Hawaii's economy."[37] The same could be said of Bishop Estate and Harold Castle's Kaneohe Ranch in the post-war years with regard to east and windward Oahu. They owned most of the buildable land there.

As mentioned, Bishop and Castle generally leased. From the mid-1950s about half of all residents of east and windward Oahu lived on lease land, most of it belonging to Bishop and Castle.

The communities that grew up in east and windward Oahu were somewhat disproportionately *haole*. According to 1970 US Census data, 39% of the population statewide at the time was *haole*. In windward Oahu census tracts with large amounts of leasehold, on the average 47% of the people were *haole*. For all of east Oahu the figure was 50%.

The tendency for *haoles* to concentrate here was partly a matter of socioeconomic standing. Caucasians overall tended to be in Hawaii's middle and upper-income strata, and east and windward locales were considered fairly desirable for suburban living. Partly too, it was popularly believed that among Hawaii's local-Asians, who made up the other major ethnic grouping with large numbers of people able to buy into subdivisions, there was much greater emphasis on obtaining fee-simple property.

In Hawaii and elsewhere in the nation the affluent tended to vote Republican. And Republican politicians in Hawaii, because ideologically they opposed government regulation and/or interfering with private property rights, or for reasons of material self-interest, or for all of these reasons, opposed land reform almost across the board through the 1960s.

On balance it really was a classic case of voters not putting two and two together, because windward and east Oahu politicians voting against Maryland bills were apparently not suffering at the polls as a result.

In 1963 there were altogether 12 House members who voted "no." Seven of the eight windward and east representatives were among the 12. Five of the seven were Republicans.

Six of the seven were re-elected in 1964. The seventh ran for the Senate and lost. Two of the four candidates who ran ahead of him were Republicans who had also voted "no."

In 1967 there were 15 representatives voting "no." Again seven of the eight House members from east and windward were against. This time all seven were Republican. Again six of seven were subsequently re-elected. (The seventh did not run.)

That Maryland bills were not a burning popular issue in other districts either was suggested by the celebrated case of Sen. George Ariyoshi's 1964 re-election bid. In 1963 he had cast what was widely seen as the tie-breaking vote against that session's bill. Many Democratic leaders angrily accused him of selling out the party program, and his 1964 candidacy was viewed as a test of popular support for the bill. In the primary Ariyoshi ran a strong second in a field of four for two nominations. In the general he came in first out of three candidates for two seats.

As the years wore on and particularly as rental renegotiations started occurring, voters in east and windward districts began to temper fine old Republican principles with self-interest. Their legislators came around, and began supporting bills to force lessors to sell, and to do such things as regulate lease rent. The Republican legislative caucus in 1984 issued a statement relating to a lease rent bill, which pointed to the Republican change of heart: "While Republicans generally believe in the traditional GOP philosophy of private property rights, the situation in which we find ourselves has to be solved outside that conservative tradition."[38]

The start of the GOP shift can be seen in 1967. As mentioned, that year seven of windward and east Oahu's eight representatives voted "no," and all seven were Republican. But none of the seven senators whose districts included windward and east Oahu were against, and four of them were Republican. Then, on two bills passed in 1975 to lower threshold requirements for sales and to limit renegotiated rent, no one in either house from east or windward Oahu voted "no," and most of these legislators were Republicans.

* * *

Thus in the Legislature in the 1960s and 1970s there was underway a redefinition of what kind of lawmakers supported bills that came to the aid of lessees.

Overall what appeared to be happening was that material self-interest was displacing liberal political ideology as the primary generator of measures of these kinds, a trend related to what was happening in the private business lives óf legislators and others who were politically influential in Hawaii, and in the lives of a great many ordinary people as well.

Over the years that these bills were before the Legislature, a number of people high up in politics and government were developing private business ties with the major lessors.

For example, in 1959 the Bishop Estate agreed to enter into a development agreement with Sen. Mitsuyuki Kido covering 520 acres in Heeia, in windward Oahu. To develop the portion of those lands intended for residential leaseholds, Kido and others organized Heeia Development Co., a *hui* that contained a very large number of Democratic officeholders and people involved with the Burns wing of the party.

At about the same time, Campbell Estate entered into an agreement covering its lands in Makakilo with Republican US Sen. Hiram L. Fong's Finance Realty Co. Associated with Finance Realty in carrying out this agreement were a large number of local-Asian Republican officeholders in addition to Fong.

Both agreements were in force throughout the 1960s and 1970s.

At their inception both saw cases of benefit to the estates flowing from actions of the politicians involved. As mentioned in an earlier chapter, when in 1959 Sen. Kido was negotiating with Bishop for the Heeia lands, he was at the same time supporting a legislative bill that roughly doubled the commissions paid to Bishop trustees—a bill introduced by Republicans that could not have passed without the endorsement of key Democrats like Kido. At about the time in 1960 that Sen. Fong's Finance Realty was negotiating with Campbell for Makakilo, Fong was supporting federal action that resulted in a federal-aid highway linking Honolulu with the Makakilo area, which was then far out in the country.[39]

Research for this book turned up cases of legislators with other such ties voting on bills relating to residential leaseholds. In most cases the financial interests were not publicly disclosed.

The voting was both for and against; and generally it appears that, in terms of social origins and party affiliation, these men voted as might have been expected.

These then were not necessarily cases of lawmakers with hidden interests secretly manipulating legislation for their own ends. Rather, they were reflections of the myriad business interests that ran through the Legislature, which after a while helped brake enthusiasm for land-reform legislation on the part of Democrats.

The bills were all Democrat-sponsored. Most of the Democratic legislators studied who had financial interests in the bills voted for them.

One of two Democrats voting "no" was Ernest N. Heen Jr. Heen was part-Hawaiian, and frequently Hawaiians opposed Maryland bills for fear of hurting the Bishop Estate.

Two of the four who voted "no" were Republicans. In terms of party affiliation Republicans voted "no" far more often than Democrats.

The first year for which research for this book turned up cases of this sort was 1963.

One that year was openly acknowledged, that of Sen. Kido, who voted against. Research indicates that this was the only case mentioned in this book where the interest was publicly disclosed (though in one other case, that of Sen. D. Hebden Porteus, the interest was well-known).

As mentioned, Kido was a general partner of a *hui* that had a development agreement with Bishop Estate. Most of what would be developed were residential leaseholds, and the *hui* would share in the leaserent with Bishop. Kido asked the Senate president to be allowed to abstain from voting. His request was denied and he voted "no."

All cases discovered of legislators with interests voting "yes" involved investors in Kido's *hui*; for example, Sen. S. George Fukuoka, who voted in favor of the Maryland bill in 1963. These apparently were cases of legislators elevating principle and/or party allegiance over self-interest. On the other hand, in the case of the 1967 bill, a provision was included covering compensation to developers in the case of conversion, irrespective of whether the development agreement with the landowners had so provided: "Notwithstanding any contrary provision in any contract or lease, a developer or other person entitled to share in the lease rentals shall share in such compensation paid by the authority to the extent of his interest."[40]

Republican Sen D. Hebden Porteus in 1963 voted "no." He was a trustee of the Damon Estate at the time, which had about 1,000 residential leaseholds.

In an interview for this book, Porteus said that the estate as such took no interest in the 1963 Maryland bill, that Damon had no long-term plan to stay in residential leasing, and that several years later the estate voluntarily sold its lease lots. Porteus also pointed out that he voted in favor of the 1967 bill. In the meantime, though, Damon had sold off most or all of its lease lots. Furthermore the 1967 bill provided what was apparently much improved federal tax treatment for lessors as compared with the 1963 bill.

Democratic Rep. Ernest N. Heen Jr. also voted against the 1963 session's Maryland bill. At the time Heen was project coordinator for the principal developer of Kaneohe Ranch Co.'s extensive land holdings in windward Oahu. As of 1963 the ranch owned about 10,000 acres; its lands accounted for roughly 26% of Oahu's lease lots. In at least several tracts Heen's employer participated in the leases, meaning the developer shared leaserent income with Castle. Several attempts were made to interview Heen for this book; telephone calls placed to his office were not returned.

A more complicated case was that of Republican Sen. Wadsworth Y. H. Yee in 1967 and 1975: In 1967 Yee was one of only three senators to vote against that session's Maryland bill. In 1975 he was one of only two in the Senate to vote against a bill that imposed a ceiling on renegotiated rent.

Yee's aunt was married to Hiram L. Fong. In 1950 Yee joined the Fong constellation of development/finance/insurance/law firms and companies and Chinese/Japanese Republican politicians and appointed public officeholders, and remained part of it from then on.

One of the Fong companies, Finance Realty Co. Ltd., from 1960 through the mid-1970s was the principal developer of residential leaseholds on Campbell Estate land. This was in Makakilo, in the southern foothills of the Waianae Mountains. Beginning in the mid to late 1970s the company developed fee simple at Makakilo. Other related Fong businesses took part in the project throughout.

Although a Republican in a Democratic era, Hiram Fong was one of the most powerful politicians in post-World War II Hawaii. First elected to the territorial House in 1938, he was speaker 1949-1953. With statehood in 1959 Hawaii was entitled to two US senators. Fong was one of the first two elected and held the post until he retired in 1976.

Fong was also one of contemporary Hawaii's wealthiest individuals. The year he left Washington *Parade* magazine wrote that he was "perhaps the single richest man in the US Senate."[41]

Wadsworth Yee was a lawyer. From 1950 to 1953 he was a law clerk and then associate attorney in Fong's law firm. Yee then in 1953 obtained a Republican appointment as a deputy territorial attorney general. When he left that office in 1957 the Republican administration of the territory appointed him to the Board of Health. When also in 1957 Fong founded Grand Pacific Life Insurance Co. Ltd., Yee joined the company. Working for Grand Pacific became Yee's principal occupation. In 1962 he became executive vice-president and in 1971 president.

When Sen. Yee cast his "no" votes in 1967 and 1975 he had multiple indirect ties to the Fong company developing leasehold lots on Campbell land. Among other things, part of Yee's salary was paid by the developer's parent company.

In 1967 Fong was president of both Grand Pacific, for which Yee worked, and Finance Realty, the developer. In 1975 Fong was a director of Grand Pacific and president of Finance Realty.

Fong also in 1967 was president and in 1975 board chairman of Finance Factors Ltd., an industrial loan firm that was the parent of both companies. During 1967 Finance Factors owned 62.5% of Finance Realty and 54.7% of Grand Pacific. Finance Realty in turn owned 15% of Finance Factors. By 1975 the state government had ceased requiring corporations to list their stockholders in publicly-filed annual exhibits, so it is impossible to know from the public record the extent of interrelated ownership among these companies for that year.

As mentioned Finance Factors was the parent of the company doing the developing, and part of Yee's salary was paid by Finance Factors. In addition Finance Factors put up the bonds required by the city during subdivision. During 1967, for example, Finance Factors supplied a letter of credit in connection with the creation of Makakilo City Unit XII. Various other Finance Factors subsidiaries or related concerns took part in the development, including at various times Finance Home Builders Ltd., Highway Construction Co. Ltd., Mahalo Nui Loa Management, and Fong's law firm.

In addition during this period Yee was generally referred to in the media as Fong's chief political lieutenant in Hawaii. When Fong was first elected to the US Senate in 1959 he named Yee his chief Hawaii representative. Thereafter, as for example in the *Honolulu Star-Bulletin* in 1960, Yee was described as Fong's "top Hawaii political coordinator."[42] Yee by then, though, was no longer Fong's Hawaii representative in a formal sense, that post having passed to Herman Fong.

The bill which Yee voted against in 1967 stood to disrupt Finance Realty's development agreement with Campbell Estate.

During the legislative session Campbell board chairman Alan S. Davis said that were the bill to pass, Campbell might be forced out of the residential leasing business. Once the bill passed and while the governor was deciding what to do about it, Campbell "notified [Finance Realty] that the Trustees would issue no more leases" if the bill were not vetoed, according to the complaint in a lawsuit Campbell later filed.[43]

The Campbell trustees' main objection was the formula for determining how much the lessor would be paid in selling to lessees. Campbell in its suit said that existing leases provided in effect that Campbell, for an average lot, would receive not less than $4,160. The price formula in the law, on the other hand, would bring no more than $2,405, according to Campbell.

Campbell also alleged in its suit that Finance Realty had said that were the development agreement to be cancelled, Finance Realty stood to lose $2 million, and would thus sue Campbell to compel continuance.

About six months after the bill passed Bishop Estate filed suit challenging the law's constitutionality. A month later Campbell also sued, alleging unconstitutionality. Campbell's challenge was based on a claim that the law did not provide just compensation to the landowner. Campbell asked that either the law's sale price provisions be declared invalid, or that Campbell be excused from its agreement with Finance Realty, which the estate named as a defendant.[44]

Several months after Campbell filed, the 1968 Legislature amended the law as it pertained to the sale price formula, among other things. Thereafter but without public explanation, Bishop and Campbell withdrew their suits. Campbell at some point resumed carrying out its agreement with Finance Realty.

The 1975 Legislature passed two leasehold bills. One set a ceiling on rent when leases were renegotiated. This ceiling turned out to be perhaps the single most important factor in subsequently persuading lessors to begin offering to sell to their lessees. Yee was one of only two senators to vote against it.

Although the bill heavily impacted Campbell, the estate did not react as it had in 1967. Campbell objected to the legislation, but had had enough and wanted to get out of residential leasing. Thus this time there was no apparent disruption of its agreement with Finance Realty. Instead Campbell moved to start offering to sell to its lessees. The estate eventually sold most of its lease lots at prices its lessees generally considered very reasonable, if not cheap. In 1977–1978, for example, Campbell made an offering to over 1,000 Makakilo lessees to sell at $1.35 per square foot, at a time when, according to published reports, the market value was at least several dollars per square foot. The lessees' attorney, Dennis E. W. O'Connor, told them: "You're never going to see an offer like this again—not in Makakilo—not in Hawaii!" In general Campbell took the proceeds from selling off residential leaseholds and reinvested in greater income-producing property on the US mainland.[45]

Finance Realty was apparently less directly affected by the 1975 rent ceiling than by the 1967 law; the company's arrangement with Campbell did not call for it to participate in the rental income from the leases Finance Realty issued, unlike, say, Bishop's arrangement with Heeia Development Co. Finance Realty, rather, leased the land from Campbell, developed it, then conveyed the lease to the individual homeowner. After the sale Finance Realty was out of the picture, and would apparently be unaffected by rental rates. Furthermore Finance Realty went on being Campbell's developer at Makakilo, though of fee simple lots.[46]

If there was no disruption in the Finance Realty program and no apparent financial loss for the company either, Yee nevertheless had voted against a bill that arguably cost Campbell money, by influencing the estate to sell at a time and on terms other than the trustees might have otherwise chosen.

In an interview for this book, Yee explained that throughout his long years in the Legislature, he differentiated between bills that pertained solely to a business with which he was involved, and bills that impacted an industry which included a business with which he was involved. In the former situation he believed it better to not participate in legislation, whereas in the latter he generally believed it was alright. The Finance Realty/Makakilo case was of the latter variety.

Yee also said that whenever there was a question in his mind of a possible conflict of interest, he sought a ruling from the head of the legislative body in which he was then serving, and was guided by that opinion

*   *   *

A final case of overlapping public/private involvements in voting on leasehold bills concerns Sen. Duke T. Kawasaki in 1984:

Kawasaki that session as a member of the Housing and Urban Development Committee voted against a bill that would have lowered the ceiling on renegotiated leaserent.

At the time he was the manager of a general partnership, called Wiliwili Nui Ridge Subdivision, that was the developer of Waialae View Estates, on a ridge in east Oahu.

At one point the *hui* had 80 to 90 lots on Bishop Estate land, obtained raw in 1967 on a 75-year lease, although as of 1984 it had only about 12. Kawasaki's *hui* issued subleases for the lots to individual homeowners. The subleases, as was common practice, called for a period of fixed rent, and then after the period was up the rent would be renegotiated.

The bill which Kawasaki voted against would have lowered the amount of rent that landlords could obtain in renegotiations.

In an interview for this book Kawasaki said that per an unrecorded document, his partnership and Bishop had agreed that when the dozen or so leases came up for renegotiation, they would revert to Bishop. Thus there could be no direct benefit to his *hui* from his having voted as he did.

He was asked if, even so, ought he to have abstained from voting, since at the time he was signatory to an agreement with the entity most affected by his vote. (As mentioned, Bishop as of 1984 held about 75% of all residential leases in the state.) Kawasaki, a Democrat, answered that the only reason he voted as he did was that he had a strong belief in "the landlord's private property rights to charge whatever he wants."

* * *

As observed above, in the years when Maryland bills were before the Legislature, Democratic legislators were building up business interests in land, including land where leasehold conversion was an issue.

The following story sheds light on how these new relationships appeared to work in practice, and how differently they might be perceived, depending on whether the observer was in or out of political power:

Nadao Yoshinaga was a state senator from Maui. He was highly representative of the successful politician of the Democratic years. He was *nisei*, a veteran of the 442d Regiment, from an outer island, generally aligned with the Burns faction of the party though at times also its most vocal critic, and was a real estate broker who was also licensed to practice law. In addition he was a former ILWU attorney, and in politics he associated closely with the union.

In early 1965, Yoshinaga moved from Maui to Oahu because reapportionment was about to reduce the number of Maui County senators from five to two. He chose to relocate in Waipahu, which was basically a sugar plantation town. The senatorial district of which it was a part had a moderately large concentration of ILWU members, and it appeared Yoshinaga had a good chance of being elected from there. In fact he won a Senate seat in the following election, that of 1966.

Apparently by coincidence, at about the same time as Yoshinaga moved, one of Waipahu's largest landowners, American Factors, became one of Hawaii's first residential lessors to be willing to sell its lessees the fee interest in their lots. This involved 102 lots in the Wailani Rise Subdivision in Waipahu.[47]

Many of the lessees were ILWU members. One of them, in fact, was an

ILWU officer, Newton K. Miyagi. Miyagi later served as the ILWU's appointee on the State Land Board. Another lessee was Shinichi Nakagawa, who also served on the Land Board and, after that, on the State Land Use Commission.

Yoshinaga asked the American Factors subsidiary that held title to the lots, Oahu Sugar Co., to sell to him. He in turn would resell at a profit to individual lessees. The company was agreeable. Yoshinaga had a corporation formed, Ethereal Inc., as the vehicle to which Oahu Sugar would sell and which would in turn resell to lessees. In late 1965 the land was sold to Ethereal. ("Ethereal" means "heavenly." Yoshinaga corporations often had names that were out of the ordinary. He once named a company after the eighteenth-century French philosopher Jean Jacques Rousseau.)

Oahu Sugar for years had privately maintained a public park near the Waipahu mill, Hans L'Orange Park. By the 1960s this vestige of a paternalistic past was a burden to the company. Oahu Sugar wanted the government to take the cost off its hands and turn the place into a state or city park.

House and Senate bills were introduced in the 1965 Legislature to appropriate state money to give to the city to buy the park. The bills made it no farther than, respectively, the House Appropriations Committee and the Senate Ways and Means Committee. The latter was chaired by Yoshinaga.

In 1966 two bills were introduced in the Senate to enable acquisition of the park. One was offered by a group of senators from the affected district, the other by Yoshinaga (who was still sitting as a Maui senator, though by now he had moved to Waipahu). Both went into Senate Ways and Means, still chaired by Yoshinaga. In the state budget subsequently adopted there was an $105,000 appropriation for Hans L'Orange Park. (Eventually, in 1969, via condemnation, the city bought the park.)

In the fall of 1966 Yoshinaga for the first time stood for election to the Senate from Waipahu.

He was opposed by leaders of the Hawaii State Federation of Labor, AFL-CIO. This group was associated with a section of the Democratic Party identified with Thomas P. Gill, opposing the group Yoshinaga was allied with, the Burns faction, which included the ILWU. Yoshinaga won.

About the time of the general election, AFL-CIO leaders learned of both the $105,000 appropriation and the sale to Ethereal. In the weeks following the election they researched the sale and appropriation and then issued a news release charging the two were connected.[48]

They pointed out that all the people who comprised Ethereal were prominent Burns Democrats. Besides Yoshinaga, who was a particularly powerful senator as chairman of Ways and Means, there was Senate Lands and Natural Resources Committee Chairman John T. Ushijima, Senate Clerk Seichi "Shadow" Hirai, and Burns' chief campaign organizer and representative on Maui, Masaru Yokouchi.

Although not mentioned in the AFL-CIO news release, the grouping of these four men, irrespective of exactly what was going on with the Wailani

Rise Subdivision and Hans L'Orange Park, told a story about some of the roots of the contemporary Hawaii political establishment. Yoshinaga, Ushijima and Hirai had served together in the 442d Regiment, and they made one of those wartime vows to work for political change in postwar Hawaii. The fourth man in Ethereal, Yokouchi, was a close personal friend of Yoshinaga who, at Yoshinaga's prodding, also became deeply committed to progressive political change in postwar Hawaii.[49]

In any case, as the AFL-CIO release did point out, park acquisition bills introduced in early 1965 languished for whatever reason in committee. Then, that December, the sale to Ethereal took place. Yoshinaga a few months later authored one of the two bills introduced in the 1966 session to acquire the park. The committee which he chaired apparently treated the matter favorably, in that an appropriation was contained in the state budget adopted that session.

The AFL-CIO leaders added this all up and charged "potentially serious conflicts of interest."

Yoshinaga said that the AFL-CIO charges were politically motivated, that Waipahu residents wanted the park purchased, and that the sale and appropriation were two separate, unconnected events.[50] An Oahu Sugar executive involved in the sale to Ethereal, John E. Loomis, in an interview for this book pictured it the way Yoshinaga did.

Who had the accurate account? As is so often the case with stories of this kind, the answer by anyone looking from the outside can only be: who knows?

People connected to the Burns faction tended to take Yoshinaga's side. Gill people believed it to be a case of corruption; they talked about it for years afterward.

For his part, ILWU officer Newton Miyagi, who was a lessee, reportedly became angry at the idea of Yoshinaga's group making money by selling him and his neighbors their house lots. For whatever reason, in 1967 Ethereal sold the 102 lots back to Oahu Sugar at cost. The plantation in 1969 again sold them in bulk, this time to a non-profit corporation whose president was Miyagi. That corporation finally started selling lots to individual lessees.[51]

Regardless of where the exact truth might lie regarding the charge made by the AFL-CIO, an underlying reality was that the political power of the Burns group, especially following Burns' election as governor in 1962, gave them a substantial entree with the major landowners. Part of the reason Loomis of Oahu Sugar was willing to deal with Ethereal over Wailani Rise was the power that Yoshinaga and the Burns faction wielded. That power included the ability to deliver on acquisition funds for Hans L'Orange Park. Whether when Loomis and Yoshinaga negotiated the land sale they also mentioned or even thought about the park was, in a sense, immaterial. Ultimately there was no real separation between the park funds and the land sale.

By extension, this suggests that by the mid-1960s the "Democratic revolution" regarding land was pretty much over for many of the men close to John Burns. The ILWU's Jack Hall saw this trend in even broader terms. In 1965 he told the Kauai Chamber of Commerce that the "socio-political-economic revolution has just about exhausted itself."[52]

Through private arrangements, Burns Democrats and other successful politicians were able to obtain much of what they wanted from the major landowners and the old-money *haoles*. For their own purposes they had become part of the establishment. Any enthusiasm these politicians and their associates might have once had for things like forced conversion of residential leasehold land tended to decline proportionately.

*   *   *

The winding down of the enthusiasm of mainstream Democrats for Maryland-type bills was probably brought about to an extent by John Burns.

Behind technical objections to Maryland bills raised by Burns over the years were fundamental reservations on his part as to the whole idea of governmentally-forced sales. In interviews for this book, several persons close to Burns and familiar with this subject were asked about his basic attitude toward Maryland bills. These men included George Ariyoshi, Mitsuyuki Kido, and Burns' brother Edward, whom John appointed director of the State Department of Taxation 1962–1969. All said that during the different periods when each was in close contact with Burns and discussed the subject of land reform in Hawaii, he was very opposed to Maryland bills.

According to Ariyoshi, who in 1963 cast the decisive Senate vote against that year's bill, Burns was relieved that the bill failed, because defeat in the Legislature saved Burns from having to veto. Ariyoshi told interviewers in 1979 that "I think [Burns] probably would have" vetoed it. Ariyoshi also said that "after it was all over [Burns] indicated to me on a number of occasions that—he mentioned this at the time that I was lieutenant governor—that he was happy that the measure did not come to him for his disposition."[53]

How was it that Burns, the most powerful and respected single figure in the Democratic Party, opposed one of the party's key pieces of legislation in an area so fundamental to the social transformation of the Islands that the Democrats had set out to accomplish?

On the evidence, Burns apparently never had supported Maryland-type legislation, not from the very beginnings of the modern Democratic Party. Mitsuyuki Kido, who with Burns was part of the small founding group that used to meet around the end of World War II and talk about a Democratic political future, later said that Burns from the start opposed forced condemnation of land as a means to accomplish land reform in any of its manifestations.

For Burns this opposition to forced condemnation was connected to his personal style, to how he worked best with people and how he believed people were best motivated. He preferred to avoid confrontation. When in the governor's office, this approach translated into a political ideology of "consensus," of bringing together in a cooperative spirit leaders of the major segments of the Islands' power structure.

The years of opposition or ambivalence on the part of Burns and Ariyoshi may also have taken a toll in terms of the efficacy of the state agency charged with implementing the law, the Hawaii Housing Authority (HHA):

In a study of HHA's performance released in 1982, Legislative Auditor Clinton T. Tanimura wrote that "the whole approach of the HHA with respect to the leasehold to fee conversion program, was one of lack of enthusiasm." Tanimura also touched on the fact that over the years the HHA had raised a series of funding and constitutional questions bearing on the wisdom and legality of implementing the law. "These issues have been used by the HHA to shield it from its neglect to plan for the implementation of the [law]. The HHA professed that these issues posed formidable, if not insurmountable, obstacles to the implementation of the program, and that unless the issues were resolved, nothing could be done to implement the program. It then sat back and failed to deliberate on how the law might be implemented." The auditor overall said the HHA's performance "may be characterized as one of utter neglect."[54]

HHA countered by citing the number of lots that had been converted over the years and the number then in progress.[55]

In any event, as with George Ariyoshi's refusal in 1963 to vote for that session's Maryland bill, so with John Burns as governor there was probably more to it than Burns said publicly. On the record Burns only said that Maryland bills would not bring about true land reform, and that he did not want the state to tie up money in conversions, nor for the state to become landlord to lessees in condemned tracts who could not or would not repurchase from the state.[56]

Underlying much of Burns' political outlook was a desire to see the people he led, Hawaii's Japanese especially, "make it" financially. By the 1960s this was starting to happen. Included among those making it were many of those closest to him in politics, a number of whom had developed various kinds of business arrangements with major lessors. Having seen all this headway being made, Burns, who might not have inclined toward forced land reform anyway, may have been doubly disinclined to do something as radical, in his eyes, as condemning thousands of lease lots.

* * *

Following the 1967 passage of a Maryland Law it appeared as though this was going to be the last time a leasehold bill would occasion much debate and controversy in the Legislature. Supplemental legislation passed easily in 1975 and 1976, and sales began.

Then in 1984 bills were introduced in both houses that would lower the ceiling on renegotiated leaserent. Unexpectedly great argument occurred.

The House version reached the floor for final reading, passed by a wide margin and went over to the Senate. There it went into the Housing and

Urban Development Committee. The Senate version had already passed out of this committee and into the Senate Judiciary Committee; it was now put aside with the idea that the House bill would be the vehicle for considering what was roughly the same idea contained in both bills.

A storm occurred when Senate Housing Committee Chairperson Patsy K. Young announced that the House bill, which was now the only live version, would not be coming out of her committee.

It had been Young's committee, with her approval, that had favorably reported out the Senate version, which, had it passed the full Legislature in that form, would have meant even lower renegotiated rents than the House bill she now said was going to stay in committee.

Since having supported the Senate bill, Young said, she became aware of hazards that she had not perceived before. One concerned the fact that the Land Reform Act was then on appeal to the US Supreme Court and a decision appeared imminent. Young said she feared that although the Land Reform Act and the leaserent bill, which would amend an existing statute, had to do with entirely separate statutes, still the stated public purposes of both were roughly similar. If the Land Reform Act was found unconstitutional, she argued so also might rent ceilings be invalid.

About the time she was having her change of mind, Young said she determined from an informal poll that a majority of her committee no longer supported bills to lower renegotiated leaserent; at least there was no longer a majority to move a bill that session. She therefore announced that the House bill was not coming out of her committee. Instead, Young proposed a one-year moratorium on renegotiating rents, during which she hoped the Supreme Court would render a decision and the Legislature could conduct a study.[57]

Lessee groups were in a fury over Young's reversal, over her not having told them first of her change of position, and over her endorsement of a moratorium. An aide to Young said her office received some 60 phone calls from irate lessees, virtually all of whom were living on Bishop Estate land in east and windward Oahu.[58]

Lessees were incensed because either bill would of course have meant lower renegotiated rents. Lessee spokesmen also said that the formula in the House bill for determining renegotiated rent would have made for predictability, whereas they said there was little or no predictability in the current approach, based as it was in part on items that were matters of opinion.

The lessees said all this was not only a matter of paying less rent in the future, but of obtaining better terms if refinancing in the present. This was because the lower the future rent, the more money a person would have available to repay a loan, so the more the person could borrow. Lower and more predictable levels of renegotiated leaserent would also have meant lessees could have sold their homes more readily; since the renegotiated leaserent would have been lower and clearly ascertainable, the sale price could have been cheaper. Lessees objected to a moratorium because they

said that certain kinds of property transfers could not occur without renegotiating the rent.[59]

The upshot was that the idea of a legislatively-mandated moratorium
died. Instead there was a voluntary moratorium, to which some but not all
lessors agreed; and, between legislative sessions, a study of the whole issue
of renegotiated leaserent was to be carried out.[60]

Throughout this controversy party affiliations were interesting to observe. Most noteworthy, this was the first time in history that Democrats
constituted a majority of those in opposition to residential leasehold bills
that would benefit lessees.

The House bill had passed 46–5. All five who voted "no" were Democrats.

Sen. Young's committee had seven members—five Democrats, including
Young, and two Republicans. When the committee approved the Senate
bill, three members voted "no;" one was a Democrat, two were Republicans.
At the time Young announced that she was opposed to moving the House
bill, reportedly another Democrat joined her in opposition. When the
whole thing became highly controversial, the two Republicans on the committee announced they were switching their public positions, saying they
now supported bills to lower renegotiated leaserent. While it was hard to be
sure how to count the numbers at this point, on the record no Republicans
opposed the bill; the only people who certainly did were Democrats.

Also interesting was that those seeking legislative redress here over a
land and housing problem were to a great extent *haoles* from predominantly
Republican districts.

Landlord to most of them was a trust whose income, as mentioned, went
to educating children of perhaps the most disadvantaged of the Islands'
social groups. And most of the trustees were men who had been central to
the making of the "Democratic revolution," and were now as trustees being
paid nearly a quarter of a million dollars a year apiece, and stoutly defending that income as only what they deserved.

*　*　*

Times really had changed in Hawaii over the Democratic years. Just how
much so was illustrated by the appointment in 1984 of House Speaker
Henry H. Peters as a Bishop Estate trustee.

Peters, a Democrat and a part-Hawaiian, occasioned considerable controversy when he announced that as a trustee he would also seek re-election
to the House and would, if re-elected, not necessarily step down as speaker.

In the view of Peters' critics, being simultaneously chief officer of the
House of Representatives and a trustee of the Islands' largest landowner,
upon whose affairs legislation had manifold impacts, was too much of a
concentration of power in one person's hands—a sort of massive and ongoing conflict of interest.

Peters responded that if a legislator could also be, say, a banker, why then not also a Bishop trustee? "There is no conflict," he said. Moreover, he said "it adds to the balance" for someone to have a foot in each of the two worlds in which he would hold positions.[61]

From the standpoint of Hawaii history and the arc of Peters' political life there were two sizable ironies in what he was saying in the mid-1980s.

In 1971, when Peters was a grassroots community leader and director of a government poverty program in Waianae, possibly the most depressed community in Hawaii, he wrote a letter to the Honolulu City Council opposing approval of what became the Makaha Surfside condominium.

Two councilmen, Rudy Pacarro and James Y. Shigemura, both Democrats, had once worked for or been retained by one or both of the companies that had a stake in Makaha Surfside. Peters' letter urged that they therefore not vote.

Peters said he realized that Pacarro and Shigemura had filed disclosure statements, and had "thereby satisfied all state and local legal provisions regarding conflict." But, "as you are well aware, the state and local laws on this subject are woefully weak and inadequate," and the mere fact of disclosing "cannot sever ties that have developed over many years."

Peters also said that "it seems inevitable that should you vote . . . many citizens will see your vote as being influenced by your past [or present] relationships with one or another of the organizations involved in Makaha Surfside Development."

"As a public administrator," Peters went on, "I can speak from personal experience on the difficulty of encouraging people to believe their government and its elected and appointed officials are objective, unselfish, and devoted to serving the interests of the general public rather than their own selfish interests ... I believe your vote ... can only sow more distrust of government among our people."[62]

Both councilmen voted with the majority in favor of the project, which was ultimately built.

Peters' objections to what Pacarro and Shigemura were doing amounted to the perennial complaint of those out of power who are looking in at the institutions that dominate a power structure. Often outsiders notice the dense interconnections between those institutions, and wonder if the public interest is best served by so many close, overlapping relationships.

Insiders do not wonder so much about these things, and by the early 1970s leading Democrats like Pacarro and Shigemura were insiders.

By the 1980s Peters in his turn had become an insider. When he was pressed to justify his overlapping public roles as Bishop trustee/House Speaker, he argued that many others before him had done as he was doing. In support of his position, he pointed to the business and political careers of seven men. Four had been chief officer of either the House or the Senate, and at the same time a Bishop or Campbell trustee or vice-president of a Big Five firm. Another had been a territorial and state senator and a Bishop trustee. Two other elected politicians had been chief executive officer and president of major local businesses.

Noteworthy in this self-justification was that all seven men Peters identified with were old-time Republicans, members of that *haole*, Big Five-connected monied class whose powers and practices the "Democratic revolution" had set out to break.

Peters' use of pure old-line Republican precedent to show the respectability of his own position apparently did not injure him as a 1980s Democrat. He was re-elected in 1984, and for the session of 1985 he was able to summon up the numbers in the House to once again be chosen Speaker.

* * *

Looking back across the years, it was a strange legacy indeed that the idealistic lease-to-fee conversion program of the Democratic Party's early post-World War II years had bequeathed to the 1980s. The two men who became Democratic governors, holding office from 1963 through the mid-1980s, had shown ambivalence or outright opposition to forced conversion under Maryland-type laws (though George Ariyoshi later indicated support). This opposition may have been why there was no action or apparently sluggish action on the part of the state administration in implementing the program once it became law. In the beginning, most lessors were conspicuous "haves" and lessees in the main were equally obvious "have-nots." Over time, this was turned around so that most lessees of the 1980s were by all other socio-economic standards fairly conspicuous "haves," as compared with the Hawaiian children who were the beneficiaries of the Bishop Estate. Even before the 1980s, the old party of the "have-nots" was producing a fairly large group of politicians who lost strong interest and motivation for land reform, in part once their own financial future was provided for. From within the party a smaller and yet more privileged group emerged to be appointed to run the Bishop Estate, for the benefit of disadvantaged Hawaiian children, receiving in reward nearly a quarter of a million dollars a year each, and defending their right to this level of income.

As stories about reform went, this was one to meditate on. It had all kinds of twists and turns. Its raw materials were much of the land and many of the people of Hawaii. It was set for the most part in a time of unparalleled prosperity. And the outcome was determined in the long haul by an increasingly obvious commitment on the part of the most successful participants to quite narrowly defined material self-interest.

CONCLUSION

ONE of the opening observations of this book is worth repeating here at its conclusion:

There never was a ruling group in the history of Hawaii that did not base its power on land. This was true of every group in power before the Democrats. It was true of the Democrats in turn.

To distinguish the Democrats from their predecessors in at least one important respect, it is worth stressing that whatever the Democrats in power did about land was done with at least the tacit consent of the great majority of the governed. In traditional times, Hawaiian chiefs did not have to bother about consent. In mid-nineteenth century, it was the most highly placed Hawaiian chief, as monarch of the Hawaiian kingdom, who gave his royal consent to the introduction of a western property system that within half a century saw his people, the commoners, substantially dispossessed of their lands. In the first half of the twentieth century, the dominant Republicans did not have to bother greatly about broadly-based consent. They could generate a *haole* electoral majority out of a demographic minority, with the compliance of the native Hawaiians plus the fact of a large percentage of aliens, meaning non-voters, among the Asians. But the Democrats of 1954 were genuinely a party of the people, and to a degree they remained so.

As a popularly elected party, with collective responsibility for land matters, the Democrats at the state level kept getting returned to power, to the point where the Republican Party fell into conspicuous disarray and lost its ability to compete convincingly at the polls. So to whatever degree and for whatever reason, the governed of Hawaii consented sufficiently in what the Democrats did regarding land.

The underpinnings of this consent were certainly complex and perhaps not even primarily land-related. Without question the Democrats in their social programs earned the support of the majority of ordinary people in Hawaii, and this in itself should have been enough to get them re-elected.

But if the focus of discussion is concentrated upon land, a possible reason for continued support of the Democrats can be fairly stated in very straightforward and simple terms. During the boom years that were also the Democrats' great years, anybody at all who owned real property, even on the most modest scale, was profiting by a sharp rise in values. That is to say, life for them looked good, indeed never better. Many were able to go beyond the simple ownership of a home and look toward joining real estate *huis* on a small scale, for example taking out a share in an investment in a condominium unit with the idea of resale in a rising market, or putting money into a speculative lot on the Big Island for a few hundred dollars down and easy terms. Beyond this, a percentage of local people would have been invited to join an especially promising real estate *hui* organized by a well-connected Democrat. A larger percentage again would have known someone who knew someone who had been invited in. All this created an environment in which a great many ordinary middle-class people would have been looking forward to the chance to become property owners and small-scale real estate investors themselves, and it also created an atmosphere in which a great many more were looking forward to doing likewise. It is very likely true to say that if most Hawaii residents had the chance to get cut in on a direct share of the profits of the boom they would unhesitatingly have accepted the offer. So the Democrats not only earned consent but were additionally in the position of being able to purchase consent on terms that most people found highly attractive.

All this is speculative. In any case the Democrats as a party kept on getting returned to power. And certainly it is difficult to think of any individual Democratic politician at the state level whose career was adversely affected to any major extent by being strongly in favor of development.

Among those discussed in this book, no one could have been more strongly and directly identified with big development than Sen. John Ushijima was with Boise Cascade in the 1960s—on their payroll, sponsoring proposed legislation drafted by Boise attorneys, with voters ultimately being informed, at length, that this highly-placed senator was forwarding a big special interest in the Legislature. When the facts were made public, Ushijima was not seriously damaged. Far from it. Indeed, as detailed earlier, he rose after the Boise episode to become president of the Senate.

By contrast, it is possible to think of individuals of some capability and some standing whose careers between them spanned the Democratic years, who were variously critical of unrestrained development, and who wound up departing from electoral politics before their time, against their will, defeated at the polls or otherwise moved to call it a day. Jean S. King, a promising liberal Democrat, emerged in the 1970s as being moderately to strongly against the Burns-Ariyoshi consensus on development. She made something of a name for herself in the House and then the Senate, and later ran successfully for lieutenant governor, but went no further than that. As of 1983 she was out of office, with no certainty of returning. Also in the 1970s Republican Frederick W. Rohlfing, unusually for someone of his party, could be heard opposing the consequences that would follow the building of a federally funded interstate-standard highway linking windward Oahu with Honolulu, a project that would presumably have great impact on development on the windward side. Rohlfing over the years was a conscientious legislator, something of a bright light on his side of the House and the Senate. He was one of his party's best bets to run for federal office. He ran unsuccessfully for Congress in 1976. Following the 1984 Hawaii legislative session, in which he served in the House, Rohlfing moved to Maui, conceivably through with running for office.

Most significantly, the name that heads this list is that of Thomas P. Gill, a member of the territorial and then the state House 1959-1962, elected to the US Congress in 1962, a candidate for the US Senate in 1964, elected lieutenant governor in 1966, and finally in 1970 a serious candidate for governor.

Hawaii's leading liberal Democrat, Gill was the prime mover in the basic piece of Democratic legislation intended to regulate development statewide, the Land Use Law of 1961.

Long after the Democrats were ensconced in power, Gill continued to campaign for reform in land matters. But now he was in effect campaigning against Burns Democrats and their land dealings. For example, he made issues of Sen. Nadao Yoshinaga and Ethereal Inc. at Waipahu, and Land Use Commissioner Shiro "Sally" Nishimura profiting from the redistricting of land on Kauai in which he had a private interest.

Gill was able to advance his career and his causes only so far. In his 1964 US Senate race, he was beaten by the Republican Hiram Fong, who was the embodiment of the businessman-developer. In Gill's 1970 race for governor, he was beaten in the Democratic primary by John Burns, whose closest associates were closest to the politics of development.

Land development was not the only issue separating Gill from the Burns wing of the Democratic party. Far from it. But focusing once again on land, Gill was the man who during his 1970 campaign coined the sharp phrase "alarming friends" about Burns' political intimates, including Nishimura. This did not get Gill elected. Indeed a case can be made for saying it helped to get him beaten. As detailed earlier, public opinion was more than forgiving of the governor for having appointed Nishimura to the LUC.[1]

Looking at state-level politics from a slightly different angle, it is possible to note a handful of young Democratic politicians getting elected in the early 1970s, in the days of the national environmentalist movement, on a platform that included something resembling an anti-development or even a pro-environmentalist attitude, but then tempering this in favor of an accommodation with the business establishment and/or the pro-development Democratic mainstream. Russell Blair entered the House in 1975 as an environmentalist of sorts. He rose to be House majority leader in 1983, by which time he had also risen in his private law practice to represent a big resort development, making use as a private attorney of expertise on shoreline management which he had acquired as chairman of a House committee.[2] Richard Garcia in his first legislative session in 1971 was an outspoken environmentalist. Before he left elective politics at the end of the 1970s he had been on the payroll of one of the Big Five and indicated in his financial disclosure statements real property holdings valued at close to a million dollars.[3]

Perhaps all that the above indicates is that, across the political board, the Hawaii electorate from the 1950s to the 1980s had no real appetite for anything more demanding than the Burns version of Democratic politics: generous social programs and expanded business opportunities for local people. But again if the focus is concentrated upon land, a reasonable conclusion might be that in elective politics at the state level there was just no political percentage in being outspoken against development—in fact no political future at all.

At the level of county politics, on the outer islands Maui and Hawaii could never get enough of development.

On Oahu, the evidence indicates that it took until 1982 for large-scale sentiment against pro-development Councils to make itself evident at the polls.

In general conservationist terms, there were throughout the Democratic years a number of Honolulu-based respectable middle-class groups which conscientiously expressed anti-development opinions at public hearings, but which by themselves had no clearly decisive large-scale influence: the Conservation Council, the Audubon Society, the Outdoor Circle, and so on.

One Honolulu-based environmentalist group (as distinct from community groups) which was determinedly not "respectable," Life of the Land, made a sizable impact in the local media and even something of an impact in the courts in the early 1970s at the highwater mark of general environmental consciousness in Hawaii and the nation. But for a Hawaii-based organization, Life of the Land's style was overwhelmingly middle-class mainland-*haole*, and this in itself was enough to condemn the group to isolation from local community anti-development groups. Life of the Land's financial support, such as it was, came almost exclusively from a tiny percentage of the disposable income of a few hundred middle-class professionals and other such people, almost all of them Honolulu suburbanites. When the Hawaii economy began to sour somewhat along with the national economy in the mid-seventies, and disposable income became tighter, the majority of the group's early sympathizers decided that if they were to maintain other desirable elements of their lifestyle, environmentalism was something they could no longer afford. Something of the same sort was happening nationwide, and the environmental movement was losing impetus as a result. Life of the Land's constituency, small enough to begin with, shrank almost to nothing. In order to stay alive, the organization began looking for grant money from private and governmental sources. A condition of continued existence on grant money is an acceptance of political ineffectuality: the hand of the feeder must not be bitten. On these terms Life of the Land survived into the 1980s.[4]

At the local level, particular districts on Oahu where tenants were threatened with possible or actual mass eviction were able to generate community groups in opposition. At Kalama Valley, the landlord won outright. Elsewhere the picture was not so definite in favor of the developers. At Waiahole-Waikane, the residents substantially won. At Ota Camp in Waipahu, a relocation housing program was obtained. But these and other anti-development/anti-eviction efforts never coalesced into a sustained mass movement.

Of all the counties, Kauai was alone in generating an effective community-wide anti-development movement. But even there, no anti-development candidate could be elected mayor. And, as late as 1984 concerning Nukolii, enough votes could be mustered by whatever means to defeat serious, well-organized and sustained protest and guarantee the completion of a hotly disputed development.[5]

*   *   *

With all the above in mind—the near-absolute dominance of a development ethic and the very small and shifting political base of anti-development sentiment—it is interesting to note among Democratic politicians some significant absences from the lists of those who were on the public record as being financially involved in development.

To begin with the most obvious name of all: John Burns. He was keen for those around him to have the chance to make money out of real estate development, and was pleased when they succeeded. For example, Burns would never have criticized Nadao Yoshinaga over Wailani Rise and Hans L'Orange Park, and he publicly defended Shiro Nishimura on Kauai as no more than a man who took a gamble on an investment and saw it pay off. Members of Burns' immediate family benefited financially out of Clarence Ching's Salt Lake development, and from Nukolii. But on the evidence of the public record, Burns himself in his years in public office was present in land transactions only at the minimum level of house and lot and one or two other minor transactions.

Another very high-profile Democrat was likewise absent from the ranks of the long-term dealers in real estate. This was a local-Asian who rose to be a high-ranking US senator: Daniel K. Inouye. In his years in local politics he was quite closely associated with Democrats who worked steadily as developers' lawyers and who themselves invested in real estate development through *huis*. And in the early days of rezonings around Diamond Head, he himself for a time represented one of the developers. But over the years he apparently invested very little in real estate.

The other longtime local-Asian Democratic US representative and later senator, Spark M. Matsunaga, was also only minimally present in the public record on land development (in the same Diamond Head project as Inouye, to mention one instance).

Tom Gill, the liberal reformer, had the benefit of family property in Waikiki, but did not make large-scale real estate investments of the kind so common among Burns Democrats. Neither did another leading liberal Democrat, Patsy T. Mink (in the Hawaii House and Senate 1957–1959, 1963–1964, then in the US House 1965–1976). As attorneys, both Mink and Gill did a certain amount of real estate-related work, as was very common among all sorts of attorneys, without it being a substantial part of their practice.

It is perhaps not so surprising to find liberal reformists of a self-denying kind like Gill and Mink abstaining from participating in the profits of the Hawaii land boom. But it is at least interesting that mainstream Democrats like Inouye and Matsunaga did not take the *hui* investment route early on, as so many of their contemporaries did.

*   *   *

The *hui*, of course, was not the sole vehicle for real estate investment and development. A significant number of large developers did not use it as a vehicle, and studies remain to be made of their work—Henry Kaiser and Del Webb, to name only two. This book would have taken a somewhat different shape if such developers had been made the focus of the study, just as the book would have been different in certain ways if we had chosen different case studies—for example, West Oahu College rather than Salt Lake, Waiahole-Waikane rather than Nukolii, and so on. But it is unlikely that the conclusions to be drawn about connections between real estate development and politics would have been markedly different. The *hui* was made the center of the research for this book not because it was the only way to invest, but because it was a characteristic way, because its use was widespread in the community at large, and especially because it was used extensively by those in politics and government. In other words the connections between politics and land development could be most readily and widely observed by observing the formation and operation of real estate *huis*.

With all that in mind, it is extremely important not to end this book without stressing that by no means all *huis* formed in the Democratic years were on the public record.

For a variety of reasons, many perfectly legitimate, some perhaps less so, many *huis* were never registered. By the very fact that they were not registered, their number and extent cannot be known.

This takes us back to something mentioned in the introduction: that even careful research in the public record might leave the student of such matters in the position of the blind man unable to see the whole size and shape of the elephant.

Details of registered *huis* are there to be studied in the publicly accessible files of a state government agency. By contrast, papers of unregistered *huis* are locked away privately in lawyers' offices and safe deposit boxes.

It is rare for evidence of unregistered *huis* to emerge in public. Such a thing may happen, in some instances, only by misfortune or misadventure, after death, whether natural death or murder. Thus unregistered land investments may occasionally surface in probate files. This book has mentioned the case of a probate file revealing the fact of a sitting circuit court judge managing a land investment for a man who helped run illegal gambling and who was later killed in an apparent syndicate-related murder. There were several comparable cases in the Demócratic years. Whether all such cases have already come to light, or whether there are more, and if so how many, cannot be known, at least until every such possible case comes to probate.

In any case, here are some questions confronting the possible blind man who finds himself confronted by what might or might not be an elephant:

How many unregistered *huis* were in fact formed in the Democratic years? Who were the organizers? Who were the members? Why were these *huis* not registered? For quite legitimate reasons under existing laws, or from a wish to proceed quietly and unobserved regardless of what the law said? Were laws on registration of *huis* framed clearly and unambiguously in the public interest? Or might there be reason to think that the laws were limited in intent and application so as to make it easy to do extensive business in real estate without having to be concerned about public scrutiny? What has been the quality of state enforcement of existing laws on the registration of *huis*?[6] Finally: we have seen something of the connections between politics and land development in the case of registered *huis*. Would unregistered *huis* be more or less likely to show close connections between politics and land development?

These are questions that for the most part cannot be answered. But equally they are questions worth asking, and worth keeping in mind against the day when other probate files might yield evidence of unregistered *hui* investments by politically well-connected people.

*   *   *

Other groups besides members of unregistered *huis* are also significantly absent from the record on land investment in the Democratic years, but not because the record is partially hidden. Most notable in this regard are Hawaiians and Filipinos.

These missing groups simply did not get in on the land boom as investors, in part because they simply were not politically well-connected, for the rest because they were not financially well situated to begin with. And of course those two factors are connected.

By the same token there has been a strongly marked presence of Japanese names (and to a lesser degree Chinese names) in this book. This is because Japanese tended to dominate the Democratic Party from the 1950s to the mid-1980s. People who rose in politics tended strongly to come from the same groups that were rising in business, and the reasons for success in politics were largely the same as reasons for success in business. Moreover, people rising in each of these spheres of life could and did give each other a helping hand.

*   *   *

With this ethnic distribution of power and potential profit in mind, it is of interest that by the mid-1980s certain signs tended to suggest that the classic Democratic years, as defined by a local-Asian dominance under John Burns and his successor George Ariyoshi, were perhaps close to an end.

On the broad demographic scale, the Japanese dominance of Democratic politics appeared to be over. In the early Democratic years, Japanese were the single biggest element in the voting public. They were also without much question the best organized ethnic group in political terms. The combination of sheer numbers plus muscle developed by excellent organization meant that Japanese were markedly "over-represented" in elective politics, with a consequent flow-over into high government and judicial appointments. By the 1980s the demographic numbers were running conclusively against the Japanese, and not even continued good organization would be able to secure them continued over-representation on the old scale. Many of those who had come into office with Burns and Ariyoshi were already gone from the political scene.

With this in mind it is interesting to reflect that in the long run George Ariyoshi might turn out to be the sole local-Japanese ever elected to the governorship and kept there in significant part by the votes of local-Japanese.

*   *   *

There were some other highly visible signs worth reflecting on as possible indications that the long-familiar Democratic years were running to a close, in the sense that fatigue was apparently beginning to show among some of the prime beneficiaries of the system the Democrats had brought into being.

The Democrats had come into power just before the land boom. They rode the boom to the limit. By the mid-1980s the boom was long over (though real estate values in the Islands generally remained high, grossly inflated, continuing to cause severe difficulties for local people trying to meet exorbitant rent payments or attempting with even less hope to qualify for a mortgage). As detailed in previous chapters, among those who had done best out of the boom were politically well-connected local-Japanese developers. Now in the bad times of the later 1970s and 1980s, prominent among those who could not stay the course were several land-related industrial loan companies founded and run by local-Japanese. And among them were some politically well-connected individuals. One of the firms that failed was Hirotoshi Yamamoto's Manoa Finance Company Inc., closed by the State in 1983. For many years Yamamoto was associated in land and finance businesses with Democratic politicians Sakae Takahashi and Rudy Pacarro.[7] Another of the failed firms was Pacific Standard Investment and Loan Inc., headed at the time of its collapse in 1981 by Daniel R. Matsukage, in earlier years associated with George Ariyoshi in a real estate venture.[8] Hawaiian Finance and Investment Co. Ltd., which collapsed in 1982, was headed by Francis H. Yamada, a close political supporter of Ariyoshi since his first campaign for the Legislature, associated with Ariyoshi's brother James in real estate ventures, and appointed by Ariyoshi to the State Civil Service Commission in 1974. Yet another such firm which collapsed, closed by the State as bankrupt in 1983, was Great Hawaiian Financial Corporation, headed by Norman N. Inaba, with whom George Ariyoshi as a rising young attorney-politician had been regularly associated throughout the 1960s, and whose plans for speculative subdivisions on lava land on the Big Island were routinely given speedy approval by ranking civil servants of the Burns administration.[9]

These firms had typically done better than most in the boom years by virtue of an extra-heavy concentration on real estate, plus a more than average closeness to politically well-connected individuals, leading to benign treatment by supervisory and regulatory agencies, amounting overall to a sort of insider status. In the wake of repeated bankruptcies, it was possible to surmise that the same factors were perhaps typically causes of the fall. As the state official who closed Manoa Finance and Great Hawaiian said, they "were relying heavily on real estate investments that were made many years ago when Hawaii was experiencing its phenomenal development. The decline in the real estate market [since] and high interest rates proved to be insurmountable obstacles to the correction of their fiscal problems."[10] It was possible to detect as well in some cases a tendency, even a readiness, to make insider loans which were not sufficiently checked by state regulatory agencies. Looking at this situation in the long term, it might be argued that large-scale financial benefits accruing to a relatively few people in the earlier Democratic years by way of a close connection between politics and land development turned out in the late 1970s and 1980s to have catastrophic widespread costs associated with them.[11]

*   *   *

So some lives lived in the Democratic years were ending less well than others.

As stated at the very beginning, this book has been written from the public record, and those discussed in the book have been talked about only in terms of their public life. Now, public life is not all of life. Yet, apart from their participation in politics and related business, relatively little is known about most of the men of the Democratic first generation as individuals. A major oral history project being carried out at the University of Hawaii on John Burns and his associates has been yielding valuable information. A full-scale biography of ILWU leader Jack Hall has been published. A doctoral dissertation on Republican businessman/politician Hiram Fong has been completed, concentrating principally on his public life. Some few academic studies in the sociology of politics have been done.[12] But for the most part and for whatever reason, even the men who figure most prominently in this book have been known outside their immediate circle only as public names and not as whole people. Now that their generation has basically done its work, it would be of great interest to know more about the intersections between their public and private lives—how they saw themselves privately, as individuals, as they took on the weight of making the political and economic history of modern Hawaii.

For example, one man who figures largely in this book found himself at a critical time in his life to be medically uninsurable, and this was when he turned to real estate development as a way of securing a future for his family. Another man prominent in politics but not well provided for financially found himself involved in divorce proceedings, and it was not long afterwards that he asked for and accepted a sizable real estate-related favor from a highly-placed and well-connected Democrat. Another man was pressed by an old acquaintance to associate himself with a real estate venture which had illegal elements in its financing. He chose not to.

Every person has choices to make every day of his life, on the basis of a multitude of considerations, private as well as public. Faced with these choices, how did the first generation of Democrats choose? The evidence of loyalty to ethnic group, to class, to local community origins, to old friends, can be seen everywhere in the public record of the Democratic years. Some of that evidence has been set down in this book. But by its nature, this has been a book written from the outside, so to speak. It would be historically valuable, and humanly good, to hear about the experiences of those in the first generation of Democratic politics in Hawaii spelled out firsthand and from the inside, by those who have now made all their public choices and can reflect upon their lives.

* * *

It was essentially young local-Asians who made the modern Democratic Party what it was and what it became. Starting out in Democratic politics after World War II, into the 1950s and even the early 1960s, they were likely enough to do so on the basis of some sort of principled vision of a more open society in Hawaii. They were sure their cause was just, and this was what gave them energy and purpose. That many of them, some sooner than others, fell away from this elevated standard of political principle and social action was no more than human.

In the Hawaii of the mid-1980s it seemed more difficult to detect among most young people entering state-level politics a principled vision for the future of Hawaii. Political newcomers tended to give the appearance of being already reconciled to or even actively attracted by the power-broking aspects of politics, not to mention the opportunities for self-advancement.

Perhaps a symptomatic indication of changing times in Democratic politics came in the story of one young local-Asian making his first run for office in 1982.[13]

Outwardly Ross Segawa could be described in terms that made him sound very like a young Democrat of 1954. He was locally born, raised, and educated. At the time of the 1982 campaign he was on his way to a law degree at the University of Hawaii. He had a Japanese name and a sizable support group of others almost all with Japanese names, including most importantly an established Democratic politician, Clifford T. Uwaine, who in his early thirties was majority leader in the Senate.

Segawa was running in the primary election in the 19th House district on Oahu, Moiliili-Lower Manoa-Makiki, where the Japanese vote was still influential. By every indication he had excellent chances of success in the primary. This in turn meant he was almost certainly headed for the House in his mid-twenties, even younger than George Ariyoshi had been in 1954 when he was the youngest member to take a seat in that great year for the Democrats.

With all this in prospect, what Segawa and his close associates chose to do was to work a criminal scheme to pad his primary vote.

They recruited people from outside the 19th district—a total of 32 known names—and used false addresses to register them on the 19th district rolls. In doing this they drew on the cooperation of friends and acquaintances, several of whom served as volunteer voter registrars, others then working in political patronage jobs in the Legislature or in the office of the state attorney general, plus one person in the sheriff's office, others again who were in law school with Segawa, and family members, up to and including Sen. Uwaine's father, wife, sister, and brother-in-law.

The conspiracy was discovered and made public between the primary election and the general. Segawa's political career was over before it began; Uwaine's was ended at the next election.

In the wake of investigations, 18 individuals were indicted on misdemeanor charges. (As a matter of sociological interest, the names of two of their attorneys are worth mention, reflecting as they do certain important aspects of the Democratic years: Meyer Ueoka, Maui member of the Board of Education and an attorney highly active in work for developers and in real estate investment on his own account; and Asa Akinaka, one of the first two local-Asians to be admitted to the exclusive Pacific Club.)

Felony indictments for conspiracy and election fraud were brought down against Segawa and Uwaine (plus two others: Segawa's girlfriend and an aide of Uwaine). Segawa pled no contest and was sentenced to a year in jail. Uwaine's trial ended in a hung jury; as of early 1985 he had not been retried.

The law school, as part of the university, took its own steps to discipline a total of 10 students involved, seven of them classmates of Segawa in their final year. Three were reprimanded, six were suspended. Segawa was expelled, with the provision (comparable to the case of a disbarred attorney) that he could reapply for admission after five years.

It was, in the estimation of one of Honolulu's principal newspapers, the biggest election scandal ever in Hawaii's modern history, with Uwaine apparently the first sitting legislator ever indicted on a felony charge.

No one could feel good about any of this, and least of all mainstream Democrats—all the more so because the overwhelming majority of those involved (more than 80%) had Japanese names. Gov. Ariyoshi made only short, arm's-length comments to the media. US Sen. Daniel Inouye, having spoken privately to Segawa and Uwaine after the scandal broke, likewise made only the most general of remarks in public. Segawa contacted prominent attorney and former University of Hawaii Board of Regents member Wallace S. Fujiyama, an influential member of the Democratic establishment who had been closely involved in the founding and running of the law school. Ariyoshi, Inouye, and Fujiyama, all three, had started their successful careers with a law degree—each from a mainland school, because in their day there was no local law school. The law school of the University of Hawaii, a product of the high-water mark of the Democratic years, had been consciously envisioned as a place where locals could equip themselves for professional and public life without the necessity of leaving Hawaii for a mainland school. Fujiyama was as strong as any public figure in modern Hawaii on the entitlement of local people, perhaps especially Japanese, to be well represented in public life. Now Fujiyama said in substance that he could do nothing for Segawa.[14]

In grand jury testimony and in other comments made public, some of those involved said essentially that they were just friends helping out a friend. In other words Segawa, so to speak, had formed a *hui*. Now, *huis* were everywhere in Hawaii, in private as well as in public life. They were formed for a multitude of purposes, the vast majority perfectly honorable, some less so. To hear invoked in the Segawa case the notion of self-interested political action justified on the basis of friendship was a repetition of the sort of thing commonly said throughout the Democratic years by, for example, those who formed insider real estate *huis* on the basis of political connections, or those who while in public office maintained private real estate connections with organized criminals. Here in the Democratic politics of the mid-1980s the cynical and outright criminal activity of illegally registering voters was presented as being in the nature of a classic *hui*. It all sounded a long time away from 1954.

* * *

If it seemed clear by the mid-1980s that the political establishment created by the "Democratic revolution" was looking less and less able to sustain and perpetuate itself in its old form, it was not clear who would follow in power.

But no matter what might happen in the areas of land use and land development, or in the general arena of politics, it seemed certain that right at the center of land politics in the next phase of the history of Hawaii would be two specifically native-Hawaiian issues.

Both sprang from the central fact of Hawaiian history in the nineteenth and twentieth centuries—the dispossession of native Hawaiians from their lands:

First, Hawaiian groups were now demanding that their lands be returned to them, or at least that the Hawaiian people should be compensated by the federal government on a large scale for the loss of lands that followed the overthrow of the Hawaiian monarchy in 1893 in the presence of American troops and with the support of the United States minister to Hawaii. Hawaiians were making common cause with ethnic minorities on the US mainland—native-American Indians and Eskimoes—who had been successful in one way or another in getting land or a money settlement. No one in Hawaii in the mid-1980s was predicting an early resolution of this issue; more likely it would be around till the end of the century.

Second, and closely interrelated, there was the question of the future of the Bishop Estate, representing the principal remaining land patrimony of the Hawaiians. Relations between the estate and its Hawaiian beneficiaries had been complex and ambiguous, to say the least, in the entire century of the estate's existence. By the mid-1980s, for the first time, there was the clear prospect of a steady selling off of Bishop Estate residential land through leasehold-to-fee conversion. This too was an issue that would certainly be long in being resolved. The immediate response of many Hawaiians, understandably, was great perturbation. Also by the mid-1980s, for the first time ever, a majority of the Estate's trustees had Hawaiian blood. And also by the mid-1980s, for the first time since the Democrats came to power, there were signs of a determined Hawaiian attempt to organize culturally and politically, through the Office of Hawaiian Affairs, and through other community and activist organizations. And there were beginning to appear in elective politics Hawaiians who looked to be, in the classic American political phrase, "available" for high public office.

This combination of large-scale, Hawaiian-centered, land-related political problems and opportunities made it next to certain that part of the next chapter in the history of land and power in Hawaii would be written by, for, and about native Hawaiians.

*   *   *

At the same time, it was likely enough that *haoles* would be playing a larger part in the future politics of land. Not *haoles* of the old Big Five kind, but recent arrivals, in-migrating to Hawaii from the mainland. They would be a growing percentage of total population. They would be applying their own pressures to the real estate market, purchasing apartment units and house lots, and in some cases investing in development. There were enough of them in place by the mid-1980s to give a new tilt to the old ethnic balances, even to suggest something of an emerging new power bloc in politics.

*   *   *

Whoever the successors to the Burns-Ariyoshi Democrats might turn out to be, and whatever their party affiliation, there were some daunting issues in the area of land use and development that would confront them.

One of these was new to Hawaii, in the later Democratic years. It concerned marijuana. As previously noted in this book, marijuana by the 1980s was apparently yielding more dollars than sugar and pineapple put together. And it was a major use of land in several districts, especially Puna and Kona on the Big Island. Yet apparently no planning document aimed at the rest of the twentieth century acknowledged this. And apparently no serious public study of the connections between marijuana, land, and political power in Hawaii had ever been made. In a time of such fundamental uncertainty about future major uses of land in Hawaii, it was at least curious that such a major land use with such major economic implications was so regularly omitted from official calculations, at least on the public record.

There were other problems, more readily visible and more openly discussed but no easier to solve. There was no apparent solution to the acute problem of housing in Hawaii: fearsomely high costs for the home buyer, matched by equally daunting costs for the renter. Though it was by no means all the Democrats' fault, at the end of three decades of Democratic politics it was still no easier for an ordinary family in Hawaii to buy a home.

On a broader scale, there was the problem of the changing fortunes and problematic futures of all of Hawaii's modern land-related economic mainstays:

Tourism, with its heavy impact on land use in prime real estate areas, was projected to dominate the civilian economy for the rest of the twentieth century. Some scenarios called for a doubling of tourist numbers from four million in the early 1980s to eight million by the year 2000.

Tourism was dominant as much by default as by design. Those numbers, unthinkable at the start of the Democratic years, might well turn out to be necessary to sustain the state economy if sugar and pineapple continued their downward slide. Pineapple was already deeply and apparently terminally diminished. As for sugar, in the mid-1980s there were warnings about the future being sounded from Washington, in the form of proposed changes in farm legislation by the Reagan administration. If for whatever reason Hawaiian sugar could not sustain its share of the US market, the industry in the Islands was probably doomed. What the consequences might be for land use across all that agricultural acreage was scarcely thinkable—let alone the economic consequences for Big Five firms still in sugar and the social consequences for the entire population of Hawaii.

NOTES

GENERAL: The following sources offer useful context for the study of land and power in Hawaii in the Democratic years:

The twentieth-century background to the Democratic years is set out in some detail in Lawrence Fuchs, *Hawaii Pono: A Social History of Hawaii* (New York, 1961); more briefly in Gavan Daws, *Shoal of Time: A History of the Hawaiian Islands* (New York, 1968). For the ethnic base of present-day Hawaii society and politics, see Robert W. Gardner and Eleanor C. Nordyke, *The Demographic Situation in Hawaii* (Honolulu, 1974). For the general workings of politics in Hawaii: James C.F. Wang, *Hawaii's State and Local Politics* (Hilo, 1982). For the Democrats in office: Tom Coffman, *Catch A Wave: Hawaii's New Politics* (Honolulu, 1972); and Paul C. Phillips, *Hawaii's Democrats: Chasing the American Dream* (Washington, D.C. 1982). The ongoing John A. Burns Oral History Project (Hamilton Library, University of Hawaii, Honolulu, Hawaii), is building up a collection of taped and transcribed interviews on the Democratic years. Daniel Boylan is at work on a biography of John Burns. The only life of Jack Hall is Sanford Zalburg, *A Spark Is Struck! Jack Hall and the ILWU in Hawaii* (Honolulu, 1979). The two principal daily newspapers in Hawaii, the *Honolulu Advertiser* and the *Honolulu Star-Bulletin*, offer continuing coverage of land and politics. Partial indices of these newspapers are available at public libraries, and selective clipping files are maintained at the Hawaiian room of the main public library, King St., Honolulu. For the purposes of this book the work of reporters Tom Coffman, James Dooley, Walter Wright, Stirling Morita, Hugh Clark, and Edwin Tanji has been particularly useful. Over its brief existence 1973– 1978, the *Hawaii Observer* kept an eye on the Democrats in office and ran a number of long articles on various aspects of land and power, such as the development of windward Oahu, the record of the Bishop Estate, and so on; the work of Pete Thompson and Brian Sullam, among others, is to the point. In recent years, *Hawaii Business* has published many useful articles. TV and radio reporters pay attention to land, politics, labor, business, and organized crime; but no permanent audio or video record is kept beyond a short time. Levels of construction activity and those involved are recorded in *Pacific Business News* and in various publications of the major Hawaii banks. The State Department of Planning and Economic Development steadily publishes reports on land use and planning. Among individuals who have written at length on land ownership, use, and development are Robert H. Horwitz, who published with various collaborators several studies, including *Land and Politics in Hawaii* (East Lansing, 1963), and *Public Land Policy in Hawaii: Major Landowners* (Honolulu, 1967); Thomas H. Creighton, *The Lands of Hawaii: Their Use and Misuse* (Honolulu, 1978); David L. Callies, *Regulating Paradise: Land Use Controls in Hawaii* (Honolulu, 1984); Bryan Farrell, *Hawaii: The Legend that Sells* (Honolulu, 1982); and Gordon Kemmery Lowry, "Control and Consequence: The Implementation of Hawaii's Land Use Law," PhD dissertation, University of Hawaii, 1976. David DeLeon has written an as yet unpublished book of case studies of community action in relation to development. Noel J. Kent, *Hawaii: Islands Under the Influence* (New York, 1983) is, among other things, a radical critique of development.

STATISTICS: The most convenient source for basic statistics on land use and development, also election data and other political data, is the state's annual data book, published by the Department of Planning and Economic Development. Long series of statistics are consolidated in Robert C. Schmitt, *Historical Statistics of Hawaii* (Honolulu, 1977). Note: for the present book, some small surveys were carried out and statistics on particular questions were generated from original research.

BIOGRAPHICAL DETAIL: Careers of public figures, with posts held, can be traced in *Men and Women of Hawaii* (Honolulu, 1966 and 1972); and *Leaders of Hawaii* (Honolulu and Louisville, 1983).

RESEARCH METHODS: A great deal of the data for this book came from government records relating to real estate, business, and official actions concerning real estate and business. In general the real estate data came from the City and County of Honolulu, Department of Finance, Real Property Assessment Division; the State Ethics Commission; and the State of Hawaii Bureau of Conveyances. The business data came from the Hawaii State Department of Commerce and Consumer Affairs (DCCA), Business Registration Division; the DCCA Professional and Vocational Licensing Division; the DCCA Real Estate Commission; and the Hawaii State Archives. For readers of this book an important thing to note is that starting just with the name of a partnership or corporation, a visit to DCCA can bring out data on membership. Accordingly, in the text of the book, this sort of information is not normally footnoted: the name is sufficient information to allow its existence and membership to be ascertained— always provided, of course, that the business has been registered. Similarly, to track the real estate activities of a given partnership, the names of the general partners can be run through the indices at the Bureau of Conveyances, or through the alphabetical listings at the Real Property Division of the Department of Finance, which will generate a tax key number, which will lead to a tax field book page containing information on the history of a given piece of real estate, as well as precise citations to the Bureau of Conveyances, where original conveyance documents are held. Again, because of the straightforwardness of checking the source, normally this sort of information is not footnoted. The government agency files most often consulted regarding government regulation of real estate and business were those of the State Land Use Commission; the State Department of Land and Natural Resources; the Legislative Reference Bureau; the Hawaii state circuit courts; the Hawaii Supreme Court; the US District Court for the District of Hawaii; and the City and County of Honolulu Clerk's Office and Office of Council Services. A useful case study in investigative research in public documents is Beverly Keever, ed. *James Dooley as Detective of Documents: The Hui Connection* (Honolulu, n.d.).

Introduction

1 There are slightly varying estimates on exactly what percentage of the total surface area of the Hawaiian Islands was then accounted for by government and crown lands combined. Hawaii State Statistician Robert C. Schmitt indicated that, as of 1893, the total combined acreage was between 1,743,000 and 1,812,000 acres. (*Historical Statistics of Hawaii*, [Honolulu, 1977], 298.) Using the conventional, rounded figure of 4.1 million acres as the total surface area of the Hawaiian Islands, Schmitt's numbers put the percentage of crown and government lands combined as of 1893 at between 42.5% and 44.2%.

2 Schmitt, *Historical Statistics of Hawaii*, 607.

3 Vernon A. Mund, Fred C. Hung, *Interlocking Relationships in Hawaii and Public Regulation of Ocean Transportation* (Honolulu, 1961), 14, 27, 48-52.

4 Well into and indeed throughout the Democratic years this concentration of landowning persisted. From 1950-1964 the percentage accounted for by major owners actually increased. See State of Hawaii, Legislative Reference Bureau,

Public Land Policy in Hawaii: Major Landowners, Report No. 3 (Honolulu, 1967),
12-16.
5 Lawrence H. Fuchs, Hawaii Pono: A Social
History (New York, 1961), 334, 335.
6 HB 6 (1957) proposed a ceiling of 30%
for charitable trusts and 40% for private
trusts.
7 These were the so-called "New Zealand"
bills. See for example SB 25 (1963) and
HB 25 (1963).
8 Session Laws of Hawaii 1963, Act 143.
9 Legislative Reference Bureau, Public
Land Policy in Hawaii: Major Landowners,
97.
10 For population figures see Schmitt,
Historical Statistics of Hawaii, 8, 14. On the
value of building permits see State of
Hawaii, Department of Planning and
Economic Development, The State of
Hawaii Data Book (1968), 97.
11 For corporations and partnerships for
all but mid-1983 see Schmitt, Historical
Statistics of Hawaii, 564. For mid-1983 see
State of Hawaii, Department of Planning
and Economic Development, The State of
Hawaii Data Book 1983: A Statistical
Abstract, 420. That personal after-tax
income rose 125% was deduced by
taking the gross gain in per capita income
in Hawaii during the 1960s, and removing
an amount equal to the increase in the
Honolulu consumer price increase over
this period--removing that which was
accounted for by inflation, in other
words. For the unadjusted income
figures see Schmitt, 167. For the Honolulu CPI see Schmitt, 146. For automobile
registration see Schmitt, 431.
12 This hui was Pukalani Terrace Landco, a
partnership. The four people mentioned
are, respectively, Masaru Yokouchi,
Takeo Yamauchi, Asa F. Baldwin, and
Gerald K. Machida.
13 This was Pyramid Ranch Co. Its purpose
was to invest in land in California. The
investors mentioned are, respectively,
Hung Wo Ching, Philip E. Spalding Sr.
and Jr., Dai Ho Chun, William R.
Norwood, William S. Richardson, and
Amfac Inc.
14 This was the Nukolii hui. The governor's
children are Mary Beth Statts and James
S. Burns. The former Republican official
is John E.S. Kim. The state and county
officials from Maui include Wallace T.
Yanagi, Lanny H. Morisaki, and Charles
S. Ota. The ILWU official is Thomas S.
Yagi. The Big Five executive is C.
Earl Stoner Jr. The state department

director is Edwin H. Honda.
15 "East of Eden," Forbes, Jan 31 1983.
16 Honolulu Advertiser, Jan 25 1983. Cited
from now on as HA.

1/Land Reform

1 Honolulu Star-Bulletin Oct 10 1967. Cited
from now on as HSB.
2 HSB Feb 27 1957.
3 Lawrence H. Fuchs, Hawaii Pono: A Social
History (New York, 1961), 427.
4 HSB Dec 18 1958.
5 Fuchs, Hawaii Pono, 428.
6 Same as for note 5 above.
7 HSB Feb 27 1957.
8 US Bureau of Education, "A Survey of
Education in Hawaii" (1920), 105.
9 Daniel W. Tuttle Jr., The Hawaii Democratic
and Republican Party Platforms 1952-1962
(Honolulu, 1962), 16.
10 HA Apr 29 1960.
11 Tax Review Commission, State of Hawaii,
"Inflation and Hawaii Income Taxes,"
Staff Working Report No. 5 (revised Nov
1984); Robert M. Kamins, Richard L.
Pollock, Robert D. Ebel, Hawaii's Major
Taxes: A Time for Examination (Honolulu,
1973)—see table on unnumbered page
immediately following title page; Tax
Foundation of Hawaii, Government in
Hawaii (various years); United States
Department of Commerce, Bureau of
the Census, Governmental Finances (various years).
12 Same as for note 11 above.
13 Same as for note 11 above.
14 Same as for note 11 above.
15 Territory of Hawaii, Legislative Reference
Bureau, A Study of Large Land Owners in
Hawaii (Report No. 2, 1957), 1.
16 See for example, regarding residential
lessees, HB 30 (1955), HB 65 (1957), SB
627 (1961), SB 24 (1963); regarding
HLDA, SB 7 (1959); limiting assets in
real property, HB 6 (1957), SB 9 (1959);
tying assessment value to condemnation
price, SB 25 (1963); abolishing various
kinds of interlocking directorates, HB
27 (1961), HB 906 (1961).
17 HSB Feb 9 1962.
18 HSB Apr 23 1959; HSB May 5 1959.

2/Land and the New
Political Establishment

1 Rodney M. Fujiyama, "The Social Backgrounds of Hawaii's Legislators, 1945-

1967," unpublished paper, University of Hawaii (1967); Chamber of Commerce of Hawaii, *Who's Who in Government State of Hawaii* (various years).

2 Same as for note 1 above; also Robert C. Schmitt, *Historical Statistics of Hawaii* (Honolulu, 1977), 25; State of Hawaii, Department of Planning and Economic Development, *The State of Hawaii Data Book* (1981), 38.

3 Same as for note 2 above.

4 Same as for note 2 above.

5 Same as for note 2 above.

6 Same as for note 2 above; also Territory and State of Hawaii, House and Senate journals (various years).

7 Same as for note 2 above; also Gwenfread E. Allen, ed., *Men and Women of Hawaii: A Biographical Directory of Noteworthy Men and Women of Hawaii*, Vol. 8 (Honolulu, 1966); Betty F. Buker, ed., *Men and Women of Hawaii 1972: A Biographical Directory of Noteworthy Men and Women of Hawaii (Honolulu, 1972).*

8 Capital Investment Co. Ltd., "A Report to the Stockholders of Waianae Development Co. Ltd. et al" (1948).

9 See for example the following tax key parcels on Maui: 3-8-14:14-23.

10 Report of the master on the 1958 annual accounting of the trustees of the Campbell Estate, on file State of Hawaii, First-Circuit Court, Equity No. 2388.

11 Same as for note 10 above.

12 HSB Feb 27 1959.

13 The consortium was International Development Co. (IDCo), a large limited partnership. The sale was by Damon Estate through another entity, Territorial Investors. Ching was one of IDCo's general partners. Kido and Mau were among the limited partners. Kido was also, in turn, head of an unregistered sub-partnership within IDCo.

14 HA May 23 1959. The Kaiser-Lee work relationship was apparently short-lived, however.

15 For Kaneohe Ranch holdings see State of Hawaii, Legislative Reference Bureau, *Public Land Policy in Hawaii: Major Landowners (Honolulu, 1967),* 114. The developer was Centex-Trousdale Co. For the various public offices held see Allen, *Men and Women of Hawaii* (1966); Buker, *Men and Women of Hawaii* (1972); *Chamber of Commerce of Hawaii, Who's Who in Government State of Hawaii* (various years).

16 The number of bills introduced was determined by adding the House and Senate bills totals as reflected in compen-

diums of legislative bills introduced each session, on file with the Hawaii State Archives. The fact that about 400 were Republican and that, of these, 12 passed, was determined by research done for this book by Maria R. Patton.

17 The 12 legislative acts of the 1959 Territorial Legislature that were Republican measures were, in the order listed in the text of the book: act numbers 23, 61, 76, 89, 91, 100, 111, 131, 166, 239, 215, 169.

18 SB 42, Senate Standing Committee Report 241 (1943).

19 Same as for note 18 above; also Act 149 of 1943 that resulted from SB 42 (1943); annual reports of the trustees of the Bishop Estate (various years), on file with State of Hawaii, First Circuit Court, Equity No 2048.

20 Interview for this book with Mitsuyuki Kido, Mar 3 1983.

21 Same as for note 19 above.

22 HSB Dec 20 1963; *Honolulu Star-Bulletin & Advertiser* May 6 1984. Cited from now on as HSB & A.

23 HSB & A, May 6 1984.

24 Memorandum from City Planning Director Frank B. Skrivanek to Honolulu Planning Commission, Sept 18 1968, 1.

25 Harland Bartholomew and Associates, *A Comprehensive Development Plan for the Ahupuaa of Heeia* (Honolulu, 1957). This same planning firm in about 1949 also did a report for Bishop on its Heeia lands.

26 By this time it was well known that Kido was one of the principals of a *hui* that held a development agreement concerning Bishop Estate lands in Heeia, with the agreement calling for, among other things, creation of a large number of residential leasehold lots. His conflict-of-interest declaration, according to the Senate Journal, did not specifically mention the Heeia agreement, however.

27 As with a number of large partnerships, some of the partners' names appeared in business registration documents filed with the territorial and state governments, some did not. Those names that appeared and that are mentioned here are: Takabuki, Matsui, Yokouchi, Izumi, Hirai and Lee. The fact of the others' investments was learned in several ways. Fukuoka was discovered to have had an interest by reviewing the probate file of Stanley T. "Banjo" Tamura (State of Hawaii, Second Circuit Court, Prob. No. 6202). The fact of investing by Yamasaki and Kato is reflected in personal finan-

cial disclosure statements they filed as
legislators in the 1970s.

28 HA Apr 13 1982.

29 Same as note 28 above; also HSB Apr 12
1983.

30 Same as note 28 above.

31 Same as note 28 above.

32 See generally State of Hawaii, First
Circuit Court, Equity No. 2048, a running
file of court-supervised matters pertaining to Bishop Estate, including annual
reports by trustees, persons appointed as
masters, size of fees paid masters, etc.

33 Regarding court-appointed criminal
defense work, see Hawaii Revised Statutes sec. 802-5. The information regarding guardianship work was supplied by
the Hawaii state judiciary Public Information Office May 1 1985.

34 Esposito and Chikasuye shared Room
412 in the Trust Company Building, at
250 S. King St. For the record of the City
Council vote see generally City and
County of Honolulu, City Council, Ord.
No. 1885.

35 Mizuha was a Republican. In at least one
election campaign during the 1970s he
organized a group called "Republicans
for Fasi." Murai was one of a group of
five men, including John Burns, that
began meeting just after the close of
World War II, and became the nucleus of
the newly-invigorated, post-war Democratic Party.

36 His representation was of Kalua Koi
Corp., with regard to a road and other
facilities in connection with a condominium project at Kawakiu Bay, Molokai.
See Maui County Planning Department,
file numbers 80/SMA-23 and 24.

37 Several interviews for this book with
Masaru Yokouchi, including Apr 9 1985.

38 During this period the Leadership
executive in charge on Kauai, John
Slayter, was filing written weekly status
reports with his superiors. A block of
reports was obtained by opponents of the
Leadership project in Poipu and given to
the news media. A report dated June 21
1974 made the claim that Shiraishi at
the time that he was representing Leadership before Kauai County and the LUC,
was also handling five other LUC matters
in which sitting LUC members had
interests: "I discovered that five of the
eight petitions for reclassification [being
handled by Shiraishi] were on behalf of
State Land Use Commission members
themselves." As mentioned Shiraishi
later denied this, and there was never

any other known evidence contradicting
his denial.

39 The following is a sampling of persons
who were in office on Kauai at the time
of investing in a Shiraishi venture or who
attained office while holding an invest-
ment: Councilman Jerome Y. K. Hew in
White Rock Ltd. Partnership; Planning
Commissioner Arthur S. Fujita in Lucky
Twenty-Five; County Water Department
Chief Engineer Walter L. Briant in
Wailua Haven Inc.; District Court Judge
Clifford L. Nakea in Kauai-Kamuela
Associates; State Department of Hawaiian
Home Lands Project Manager Juliet K.
Aiu in White Rock; Dean of Student
Services at Kauai Community College
Guy Y. Fujiuchi in Kaumualii Investment
Co.; Fifth Circuit Court Administrative
Assistant Mildred K. Hiramoto in
Waipouli Ltd. Partnership; Board of
Water Supply member Ronald B.Iida in
Poipu Sands Ltd. Partnership; Board of
Supervisors Chairman Raymond X. Aki
in Kauai Resorts Development Inc.

40 For a more complete discussion of these
events see Chapter 5 of this book, "Land
and Labor: The ILWU."

41 Weekly status reports filed with the
Leadership executive in charge on Kauai.
See note 38 above.

42 HSB Feb 21 1970.

43 For Ushijima's representation of Boise
before the Land Use Commission, see
LUC file (A)68-194. At the Big Island
County level Ushijima represented the
company before the Planning Commission. As mentioned McClung may have
assisted Ushijima with regard to the
Boise project, or they may have coordinated their work, each on behalf of his
own respective client. While doing
research for this book, there was discovered a handwritten note in the Boise
LUC file, indicating that an employee of
McClung's, first name Blanche, had
apparently hand-delivered a letter to the
LUC from a Boise executive, Robert B.
Pummill. The letter provided supplemen-
tary information regarding the Boise
LUC application. After an author of this
book questioned an LUC staff member
about the note, it was removed from the
file. In any case, regarding McClung's
work on behalf of Signal, see HSB June
12 1969.

44 HSB June 12 1969.

45 HSB Feb 18 1970.

46 In general see Chapter 8 of this book,
"Hawaii: Subdividing Lava Fields."

47 Interview for this book Feb 8 1984 with Raymond Suefuji, who at the time of the Boise presentation was county planning director.
48 State of Hawaii, Land Use Commission file (A)68-194.
49 Same as for note 48 above.
50 HSB Feb 19 1970.
51 Same as for note 48 above.
52 Same as for note 48 above.
53 On Southward see HSB & A July 5 1970. Note that Sheehan had also, in 1969, been appointed to the Honolulu Planning Commission, though for whatever reason left the Commission soon after his appointment. For background on Sheehan see Buker, *Men and Women of Hawaii* (1972).
54 HSB Feb 21 1970.
55 Same as for note 45 above.
56 See Davies and Castle & Cooke annual reports to shareholders for pertinent years.
57 HSB & A June 28 1970.
58 Same as for note 48 above.
59 Same as for note 54 above; also HA June 20 1969.
60 HSB June 18 1969.
61 Same as for note 54 above.
62 Same as for note 54 above. The California deputy state attorney general interviewed was Marshall S. Mayer.
63 SBs 1951, 1950.
64 HA Oct 9 1976.
65 HSB Nov 23 1971.
66 Same as for note 65 above.
67 State of Hawaii, State Ethics Commission, Ops. Nos. 26-28(1969). Note that the opinions do not include the names of the people whose behavior was being reviewed. Upon public release of opinions 26-28, however, Ushijima, McClung and Shigemura all acknowledged that the opinions pertained to them.
68 Session Laws of Hawaii 1972, Act 163.
69 American Bar Association, *Canons of Professional Ethics, Annotated* (1967), Opinion No. 296.
70 HSB Nov 9 1973; *Hawaii Observer* May 28 1974.

3 / The Land Use Commission

1 G. Kem Lowry Jr., "Evaluating State Land Use Control: Perspectives and Hawaii Case Study," *Urban Law Annual* Vol. 18 (1980), 93.
2 HSB Nov 18 1967.
3 State of Hawaii, Department of Planning and Economic Development, *The State of Hawaii Data Book* (1983), 190.
4 Same as for note 3 above.
5 See HB 1279 (1961) in Senate Journal: Chamber of Commerce of Honolulu, *Who's Who in Government State of Hawaii* (1961); C. Brewer annual report to shareholders 1961; for Damon Estate see State of Hawaii, First Circuit Court Equity No. 2816, a running file on all court-supervised matters regarding the estate, including the appointment of trustees.
6 They were each filed twice, hence there are two LUC application numbers for each applicant: Robinson Trusts— (A)67-158, (A)68-197; Bishop Estate— (A)67-161, (A)68-201; Austin Estate— (A)67-162, (A)68-202.
7 Same as for note 6 above.
8 HSB Sept 13 1969; HA Dec 6 1969.
9 Same as for note 6 above; also, for Lemke and Ho as Robinson trustees, see Allen, *Men and Women of Hawaii* (1966) and Buker, *Men and Women of Hawaii* (1972); for Stuart Ho sharing law offices with Takabuki see the attorneys section in the yellow pages of the Oahu telephone directories for pertinent years; for Kanazawa also having shared law offices with Takabuki see Takabuki disclosure of interest statements on file with Honolulu City Clerk; for Pao and Ferry see Allen, *Men and Women of Hawaii* (1966) and interview for this book with Ferry, Apr 22 1985; for Omori and Murakami see HSB Nov 18 1967; for Omori and Inouye see Buker, *Men and Women of Hawaii* (1972).
10 Same as for note 6 above.
11 Same as for note 6 above; also, HSB Sept 13 1969 and interview for this book with former ILWU officer with understanding that his name not be used.
12 HA July 14 1974.
13 State of Hawaii, Department of Planning and Economic Development, Land Use Commission, *Report to the People on the Second Five-Year District Boundaries and Regulations Review of the State of Hawaii Land Use Commission* (Feb 1975), 25.
14 HA Jan 18 1975.
15 HSB Oct 14 1975. Note that these remarks were as paraphrased by HSB.
16 HA Oct 10 1975.
17 *Town v. Land Use Commission*, 55 Haw. 538 (1974).
18 HA Feb 28 1975.
19 HB 1870 (1975) as introduced.
20 Harvey S. Kawakami, as told through

Tom Coffman, *From Japan to Hawaii, My Journey* (Honolulu, 1976), 64.

21 Buker, *Men and Women of Hawaii* (1972); Chamber of Commerce of Hawaii, *Who's Who in Government State of Hawaii* (1975-1976); financial disclosure statements on file with the Hawaii State Ethics Commission; State Department of Commerce and Consumer Affairs, Business Registration Division.

22 HSB Sept 25 1961.

23 HSB Apr 12 1962.

24 See Table this chapter, listing all land use commissioners 1963-1984, together with brief biographical data and any known personal involvement with land and development.

25 HSB May 5 1967.

26 HA Mar 27 1975.

27 *Honolulu*, Dec 1978.

28 HA Oct 30 1970.

29 HSB Aug 14 1970.

30 Interview with Ramon A. Duran Apr 22 1985. At the time of the Nishimura matter Duran was head of the LUC staff.

31 HA Aug 15 1970.

32 Same as for note 29 above.

33 See publicly-filed business records of Hui o Kauai I; purchase and resale documents regarding Lawai land on file with the Hawaii Bureau of Conveyances Regular System (Hui o Kauai I purchase—book 6470 page 92, resale—book 6955 page 55).

34 *Doe v. State Ethics Commission, State of Hawaii*, First Circuit Court, Civ. 32745 (1970); *Doe v. State Ethics Commission*, 53 Haw. 373 (1972). Note that the court records do not reflect the names of the people involved; due to requirements of state law, proceedings of this sort did not reveal actual names of current or former government officials who were the objects of State Ethics Commission proceedings. Nishimura, however, in an interview for this book Jan 24 1985, said that there had been court cases concerning him and the State Ethics Commission. He also provided sufficient detail about the cases, which, when combined with details the case files did provide that in turn could be matched with information provided by newspaper stories and other sources, made it was possible to determine with reasonable certainty that the above-cited cases pertained to him.

35 HSB Aug 15 1970.

36 HA Oct 30 1970.

37 HSB Oct 14 1970.

38 *Doe v. State Ethics Commission*, 53 Haw. 373, 375 fn 1 (1972).

39 HA Aug 15 1970.

40 Tom Coffman, *Catch A Wave: A Case Study of Hawaii's New Politics* (Honolulu, 1972), 148.

41 Coffman, *Catch A Wave*, 11, 148.

42 Same as for note 36 above.

43 Same as for note 36 above.

44 HA Aug 20 1970; see also City and County of Honolulu, Building Department, building permit section, file referenced by tax key number 2-5-20: 7.

45 See note 44 above regarding building permit file.

46 Same as for note 45 above.

47 Same as for note 44 above.

48 HSB Mar 21 1970.

49 Wilbert H.S. Choi to Ramon A. Duran, July 22 1969, letter, on file with Land Use Commission, files pertaining to 1969 Land Use Districts and Regulations Review.

50 Same as for note 45 above.

51 Same as for note 45 above.

52 Same as for note 45 above.

53 Same as for note 45 above.

54 Same as for note 45 above.

55 HA Aug 20 1970.

56 Coffman, *Catch A Wave*, 146.

57 Coffman, *Catch A Wave*, 150, 151.

58 See LUC file for Kauai, 1969 Land Use Districts and Regulations Review.

59 As mentioned, the Olomana matter was voted on simultaneously with all proposed Oahu redistrictings at the end of the Oahu phase of the 1969 review. The vote was 7-1 in favor, with Commissioner Mark the one voting "no," and Commissioner Burns absent. At the time the intended developer of Mount Olomana was Hawaiian Pacific Industries Inc., of which Mitsuyuki Kido was a director, according to HPI's publicly-filed business records and a newspaper account (HSB Dec 26 1970). The leeward Oahu matter, although approved in 1969, was prior to and separate from the boundary review, hence it was handled on an individual basis. (See LUC file 69–210.) In this instance, the developer was to be a partnership, Pearl Harbor Heights Developers, of which HPI was a partner. An attempt was made to interview Sunao Kido as to whether, at the time of these two votes, as well as at the time of the Kauai vote which included the Kalaheo/Lawai property, he was aware of his brother's involvement. Sunao declined the interview before there was a chance to indicate to him what the interview would have consisted of.

60 HSB Dec 26 1970.

61 State of Hawaii, Land Use Commission, file (A)72-330.
62 State of Hawaii, Land Use Commission, file (T)64-71.
63 See portion of note 9 above regarding Omori and Murakami.
64 State of Hawaii, Land Use Commission files (A)68-208, (A)70-263, (A)71-292. Note that with respect to (A)70-263 Commissioner Inaba made a conflict-of-interest statement, though the LUC file does not reflect the basis for the statement. In the other two files cited here there were apparently no such statements.
65 Lowry, "Evaluating State Land Use Control: Perspectives and Hawaii Case Study."
66 Same as for note 65 above, 109.
67 HSB Feb 13 1980.
68 Same as for note 66 above.
69 "East of Eden," *Forbes*, Jan 31 1983.

4/The Honolulu City Council

1 Robert C. Schmitt, *Historical Statistics of Hawaii* (Honolulu, 1977), 11. Note that the Hawaii population numbers as presented by Schmitt contain, as explained in his footnote 1, figures for several sparsely-inhabited islands that are, strictly speaking, not part of the Hawaiian Islands. For purposes of the population statistics here referenced these figures have been removed.
2 Interview with Council member Marilyn Bornhorst Sept 24 1981.
3 Revised Laws of Hawaii 1955, sec. 149-197(b); HSB Apr 22 1953.
4 HSB Apr 22 1953; HSB Apr 7 1956; Charter of the City and County of Honolulu 1959.
5 City and County of Honolulu, Office of the Clerk, personal disclosure file of Matsuo Takabuki.
6 Interview with Matsuo Takabuki Nov 9 1981; State of Hawaii, Department of Commerce and Consumer Affairs, Business Registration Division; Hawaii State Archives; HSB Mar 30 1965; HA Aug 30 1965.
7 HSB Sept 30 1960; Lawrence H. Fuchs, *Hawaii Pono: A Social History* (New York, 1961), 343; HA Nov 11 1962; HSB Oct 3 1963.
8 Hawaii State Bar Association, directories of attorneys for miscellaneous years; interview with Matsuo Takabuki Nov 9 1981; HSB Jan 25 1952; Hawaiian Telephone Co. Oahu directories yellow pages for attorneys (note that in the years discussed here it is often necessary to match up telephone numbers and addresses in order to know that two lawyers are sharing offices or are in some other and more formal way associated in the practice of law); City and County of Honolulu, Office of the Clerk, personal disclosure file of Matsuo Takabuki.
9 City and County of Honolulu, City Council, subject indexes, various years.
10 Same as for note 9 above.
11 Same as for note 9 above; also interview with Matsuo Takabuki Nov 9 1981.
12 Same as for note 9 above.
13 Hawaiian Telephone Co. Oahu directories yellow pages for attorneys; City and County of Honolulu, City Council, subject indexes; Hawaii State Bar Association, directories of attorneys for various years.
14 Same as for note 9 above; Betty F. Buker, ed., *Men and Women of Hawaii 1972: A Biographical Directory of Noteworthy Men and Women of Hawaii* (Honolulu, 1972).
15 HSB Apr 3 1978; State of Hawaii, Department of Commerce and Consumer Affairs, Business Registration Division; Hawaii State Archives.
16 Same as for note 9 above.
17 Same as for note 9 above.
18 City and County of Honolulu, Office of the Clerk, personal disclosure file of Matsuo Takabuki.
19 HA Oct 16 1965.
20 American Bar Association, *Canons of Professional and Judicial Ethics: Opinions of Committee on Professional Ethics and Grievances* (1957), Op. No. 104.
21 Same as for note 19 above.
22 Same as for note 19 above; Hawaiian Telephone Co. Oahu directories attorneys section of yellow pages.
23 City and County of Honolulu, City Council, subject indexes for 1968, 1969.
24 Tom Coffman, *Catch A Wave: A Case Study of Hawaii's New Politics* (Honolulu, 1972), 125; regarding Akinaka see HSB Apr 17 1968, HA Apr 18 1968.
25 Interview with Herman G. P. Lemke Sept 21 1981.
26 City and County of Honolulu, Office of the Clerk, personal disclosure file of Herman G. P. Lemke; Gwenfread E. Allen, ed., *Men and Women of Hawaii: A Biographical Directory of Noteworthy Men and Women of Hawaii*, Vol. 8 (Honolulu, 1966); State of Hawaii, Department of Commerce and Consumer Affairs, Business Registration Division; Hawaii State Archives.

27 City and County of Honolulu, Office of the Clerk, personal disclosure file of Clesson Y. Chikasuye; State of Hawaii, Department of Commerce and Consumer Affairs, Business Registration Division; Hawaii State Archives.

28 City and County of Honolulu, City Council, Ord. No. 1885 (1960) and connected files.

29 HA Sept 11 and 12 1974.

30 City and County of Honolulu, City Council, subject index 1962, see various references to zoning matter concerning Tadashi Fukunaga as applicant.

31 Same as for note 9 above.

32 City and County of Honolulu, City Council, subject index 1970, see miscellaneous references to Heeia light industrial zoning matter.

33 Kaito also was appointed a Damon Estate guardian (1975) and a Campbell Estate master and guardian (1977-1978). See discussion of such appointments in Chapter 2 of this book, "Land and the New Political Establishment."

34 HSB Nov 16 1972; City and County of Honolulu, Office of the Clerk, personal disclosure file of George M. Koga.

35 Same as for note 9 above.

36 HSB Apr 3 1978.

37 Same as for note 36 above.

38 City and County of Honolulu, Office of the Clerk, personal disclosure file of George G. Akahane; State of Hawaii, Bureau of Conveyances, Regular System, miscellaneous entries in grantor and grantee indexes regarding State Savings and Loan Association.

39 HSB Oct 29 1981.

40 The property is identified as TMK 1-4-14: 26. See transactions concerning this property referenced by this TMK in field book of City and County of Honolulu, Department of Finance, Real Property Assessment Division.

41 Same as for note 39 above.

42 City and County of Honolulu, City Council, Special Committee of the Whole, "Report of the Kukui Plaza Urban Renewal Project" (1978), 59-116; HA May 25 1976. Note that Joseph Gum was also in partnership with Pacarro with regard to this lease.

43 City and County of Honolulu, Office of the Clerk, personal disclosure file of Toraki Matsumoto.

44 City and County of Honolulu, Office of the Clerk, personal disclosure file of Daniel G. Clement Jr.

45 HSB Nov 5 1981.

46 See law firm of Fong and Miho in Hawaii section of Martindale-Hubbell Law Directory (1982); for Hobron see HSB Feb 27 1979, HA Feb 28 1979. See also HSB Nov 5 1981.

47 City and County of Honolulu, Office of the Clerk, personal disclosure file of Yoshiro Nakamura; State of Hawaii, Department of Commerce and Consumer Affairs, Business Registration Division.

48 HSB Apr 14 1971; regarding Signal Oil see discussion in Chapter 2 of this book, "Land and the New Political Establishment."

49 For Kennedy see City and County of Honolulu, Office of the Clerk, personal disclosure file of Eugene F. Kennedy; for George see records pertaining to Flave George in State of Hawaii, Department of Commerce and Consumer Affairs, Professional and Vocational Licensing Division; for Casey see personal disclosure file of Brian L. Casey; for Holck see discussion in Chapter 10 of this book, "Oahu: Salt Lake;" for Loo see personal disclosure file of Frank W.C. Loo.

50 Bornhorst did own a part-interest in a macadamia nut farm on the Big Island, however. See HSB Apr 13 1978.

51 Others labeled "right-wing Democrats" by the *Star-Bulletin* were Charles E. Kauhane, who had been in the territorial House for most of the time since 1943, and Ingram M. Stainback, governor of Hawaii 1942-1951. Regarding Heen's life in general see HA Oct 11 1965, HSB Oct 11 1965.

52 Buker, *Men and Women of Hawaii* (1972); HSB June 16 1978; Legislative Reference Bureau, *Directory of State, County and Federal Officials: Supplement to Guide to Government in Hawaii* (published occasionally, most recently annually); HA Apr 21 and May 7 1982.

53 Interview for this book with Walter M. Heen Nov 10 1981.

54 Marion was also at various times a Democratic Party officer and a director of the HGEA. Shim also practiced law with David C. McClung, and was an attorney for the International Brotherhood of Electrical Workers.

55 HSB Sept 4 1951.

56 HSB June 1 1973; HA June 2 1973. Note that these are articles regarding William Heen's life in general, published on the occasion of his death.

57 State of Hawaii, Department of Commerce and Consumer Affairs, Professional and Vocational Licensing Division;

City and County of Honolulu, City Council, subject index for 1958 (see "Yoshikawa Development Co.").

58 State of Hawaii, Department of Commerce and Consumer Affairs, Professional and Vocational Licensing Division; regarding Centex-Trousdale see City and County of Honolulu, City Council, subject indexes various years, under headings of "Centex-Trousdale," "Kaneohe," "Kaneohe Ranch Co.," "Kawainui."

59 City and County of Honolulu, Office of the Clerk, personal disclosure file of Walter M. Heen; HSB & A May 24 1964.

60 City and County of Honolulu, City Council, subject indexes various years.

61 City and County of Honolulu, City Council, subject index 1961 (see "Yoshikawa Development Co.").

62 According to the Council subject indexes, Mink's work on behalf of Yoshikawa involved fairly routine processing of documents. There is no indication in the indexes of her having represented the company in the matter of a major city action, such as a rezoning.

63 HA Feb 6 1963.

64 City and County of Honolulu, City Council, Res. No. 153 (1962); Res. No. 40 (1963); Ord. No. 2366 (1963); Ord. No. 2438 (1964).

65 City and County of Honolulu, City Council, subject index 1960 (see "Ilikai"); Office of the Clerk, personal disclosure file of Matsuo Takabuki.

66 City and County of Honolulu, City Council, subject index 1961 (see matters referenced under "Waianae").

67 Same as for note 66 above.

68 City and County of Honolulu, City Council, subject indexes as follows: for Bryan see "Bryan" and/or "Wailupe;" for individual in 1962 see "William K.W. Auyong;" for Brown see "Pacific Network" and/or "Kaiser Teleprompter;" for Akiona see "Moses Akiona Ltd."

69 Same as for note 68 above: for Imperial Hotel see "Imperial Hotel;" for apartment zoning on Dole St. see Ord. No. 3882; for Diamond Head see "Diamond Head" and/or "Richard K. Kimball."

70 Prior relations with Koga and Kaito outlined in an interview for this book with Walter M. Heen Nov 10 1981.

71 City and County of Honolulu, City Council, subject index for 1961 (see "Diamond Head").

72 City and County of Honolulu, Finance Department, Real Property Assessment Division, see Oahu field book pages referenced by TMK 3-1-35: 19.

73 Same as for note 72 above, see TMK 3-1-36: 1.

74 HSB Oct 4 1961.

75 Hawaii State Archives, card index under "Diamond Head;" Gordon A. Macdonald, Agatin T. Abbott, Frank L. Peterson, *Volcanoes in the Sea: The Geology of Hawaii* (Honolulu, 1983), 444.

76 State of Hawaii, Department of Planning and Economic Development, *The State of Hawaii Data Book* (1983), 625.

77 Ralph S. Kuykendall, *The Hawaiian Kingdom*, Vol. III, 1874–1893, The Kalakaua Dynasty (Honolulu, 1967), 112.

78 Paul T. Yardley, *Millstones and Milestones: The Career of B.F. Dillingham* (Honolulu, 1981), 302; HA Jan 4 1959; HSB May 7 1974.

79 Kuykendall, *The Hawaiian Kingdom*, Vol. III, 113.

80 Makalei Heights: see State of Hawaii, Bureau of Conveyances, Land Court System, File Plan 292; Diamond Head Terrace: HSB May 22 1965.

81 City and County of Honolulu, Planning Commission, Res. No. 10 (1940); Res. No. 74 (1942); Res. No. 207 (1946).

82 City and County of Honolulu, Planning Commission, Res. No. 902 (1957) and prior connected matters referenced in file on this resolution.

83 Same as for note 82 above.

84 Same as for note 82 above.

85 City and County of Honolulu, City Council, Ord. No. 1949 (1961).

86 A realtor named Ronald H. Deisseroth was the promoter. By July 1960 the owners of approximately 70 of Diamond Head Terrace's 85 houses and lots had reportedly agreed to jointly list their property with Deisseroth's Hawaii Housing Corporation.

87 State of Hawaii, Bureau of Conveyances, Land Court System, Doc. 256348.

88 See in general Chapter 10 of this book, "Oahu: Salt Lake."

89 Allen, *Men and Women of Hawaii* (1966), viii.

90 HA June 27 1962.

91 State of Hawaii, First Circuit Court, *Bowen v. City and County of Honolulu*, Civ. No. 10274 (1963).

92 Interview with Frederick K.F. Lee Sept 29 1981.

93 *Bowen v. City and County of Honolulu*, Hawaii Supreme Court No. 4403 (1964).

94 Citizens Advisory Committee to the Waikiki-Diamond Head Development

Plan, *The Waikiki Plan* (Honolulu, 1966).
95 HA Dec 12 1967.
96 City and County of Honolulu, City Council, subject index for 1967, see miscellaneous entries under "Diamond Head."
97 In its editorial the *New York Times* wrote that "the national landmark will be hopelessly scarred if the builders defeat the conservationists in a battle that is now being joined." (As reprinted in HSB July 14 1967.)
98 City and County of Honolulu, Development Plan for the Primary Urban Center, Ord. No. 81-79 (1981); zoning was accomplished by Ord. No. 82-58, zoning map no. 3 (1982).
99 Capital Investment Co. Ltd., *A Report to the Stockholders of Waianae Development Co. Ltd. et al* (1948).
100 Fuchs, *Hawaii Pono*, 399.
101 Same as for note 82 above.
102 Interview with David A. Benz Aug 21 1984; interview with Sally Sheehan Dec 17 1981.
103 See for example, HSB Sept 19 1961; also City and County of Honolulu, City Council, subject index for 1962 (see "Diamond Head").
104 State of Hawaii, Department of Commerce and Consumer Affairs, Business Registration Division; Hawaii State Archives.
105 City and County of Honolulu, City Council, subject index for 1957 (see "Diamond Head").
106 City and County of Honolulu, City Council, subject indexes for various years (see "Diamond Head").
107 City and County of Honolulu, City Council, subject index for 1962 (see "Diamond Head").
108 Same as for note 107 above.
109 HSB May 7 and 14 1965.
110 State of Hawaii, First Circuit Court, State v. Fasi, Cr. No. 50047 (1977).
111 Same as for note 94 above.
112 HA Jan 10 1968.
113 Same as for note 82 above.
114 For the DHIA and businesses mentioned see State of Hawaii, Department of Commerce and Consumer Affairs, Business Registration Division; Hawaii State Archives.
115 HSB Nov 30 1960.
116 HSB Sept 14 1960.
117 HSB Mar 29 1961.
118 HSB May 11 1965.
119 As occurred with other contested rezonings, among those opposed were several councilmen; in general these were outside the ruling blocs. In the Ewa case one who dissented was Councilman Frank Fasi.
120 HSB Oct 27 1971.
121 HA Aug 12 1976.
122 HSB Nov 5 1981.
123 City and County of Honolulu, City Council, subject index for 1960 (see "Waialae-Kahala" and/or "Pietsch" and/or "Hilton").
124 HSB July 6 and 7 1960.
125 HSB July 6 1960.
126 HSB June 28 1961.
127 HSB Nov 11 1964
128 Same as for note 127 above.
129 Aikahi: HSB Aug 25 1965, Sept 8 1965; Pao: Sept 27 and 30 1966; Foster Village: HSB Nov 2 1966; Kaneohe: HSB Nov 29 1967.
130 HSB Apr 14 1971.
131 HA Sept 8 1971.
132 State of Hawaii, First Circuit Court, *Makaha Surfside Development Co. v. City and County of Honolulu*, Civ. No. 34672 (1971).
133 HSB June 22 1971; State of Hawaii, Department of Commerce and Consumer Affairs, Business Registration Division; Hawaii State Archives.
134 HSB Aug 5 and Nov 3 1971.
135 HA Nov 12 1975.
136 HA Oct 28 1981; HSB Nov 2 1981.
137 Same as for note 122 above.
138 HSB Nov 5 1969; HA May 24 1980.
139 HA Nov 3 1977.
140 Interview with Yoshiro Nakamura Sept 25 1981.
141 HSB June 29 1966.
142 In light of the subsequent careers of councilmen Doi, Takabuki and Kaito, it will be interesting to observe the late life careers of councilmen Akahane and Pacarro, two of the most powerful councilmen of the 1970s and early 1980s. Akahane and Pacarro were still on the Council in early 1985 when this book was finalized.
143 HA Nov 6 1979.
144 This was according to a study done for this book. For the years up to 1974 the sources on campaign expenditures were generally miscellaneous newspaper articles. Beginning in 1974 the sources were campaign spending reports filed with the Hawaii State Campaign Spending Commission. Election results were obtained from reports prepared by the Office of the Lieutenant Governor. A typical report is Result of Votes Cast,

General Election, Tuesday, November 7, 1978, State of Hawaii.

145 Same as for note 144 above.

146 Reports on election results prepared by the Office of the Lieutenant Governor. A typical report is Result of Votes Cast, General Election, Tuesday, November 7, 1978, State of Hawaii.

147 Chamber of Commerce of Hawaii, *Who's Who in Government State of Hawaii* (various years).

148 Same as for note 147 above.

149 Same as for note 146 above; population figures derived from miscellaneous publications of State of Hawaii, Department of Planning and Economic Development.

150 Same as for notes 147-149 above.

151 Same as for note 146 above.

5/Land and Labor: The ILWU

1 Sanford Zalburg, *A Spark Is Struck! Jack Hall and the ILWU in Hawaii* (Honolulu, 1979). Zalburg wrote on page 141 that as of 1946 there were 25,383 sugar workers in ILWU bargaining units, and on pages 135-136 that at about the same time there were approximately 7,200 pineapple workers. Sugar and pineapple combined thus totalled about 32,583 ILWU members. This apparently was the first year for which he provided these kinds of numbers; it also was the first or about the first year in which these two industries were substantially organized by the ILWU. Also, already by this time due to mechanization, the numbers employed in sugar and pineapple were in fairly steady decline. The year 1946 was about a high point, then, in terms of numbers of workers in sugar and pineapple who were represented by the ILWU. Interviews for this book with various ILWU leaders from that era indicate that, by adding in ILWU members from industries other than sugar and pineapple — longshore in particular—an accurate grand total number of ILWU members as of this period might have been about 37,000.

2 Zalburg, *A Spark Is Struck!*, 230.

3 Interestingly the ILWU itself may not have kept numbers of this kind. For this book several inquiries were made of current and former ILWU leaders as to the percentage of aliens in the union over the years. Each time the response was that the ILWU did not know. What-

ever the numbers were, presumably they declined over time.

4 State of Hawaii, Office of the Lieutenant Governor. The lieutenant governor as the state's chief elections administrator prepares and maintains in several forms the results of all voting for public office that takes place in Hawaii. In general what was used for this book was a publication by that office entitled, to take one year as an example, Result of Votes Cast, Primary Election, Saturday, October 7, 1978, State of Hawaii.

5 Henry A. Walker Jr., "Remarks to the ILWU Regional Convention," Sept 21 1983.

6 Interviews with two former ILWU leaders with the understanding that their names not be used.

7 As Tangen and several other former ILWU leaders pointed out in interviews, in general it was not difficult to promote diversified agriculture without harming sugar and pineapple. During this period the amount of land that diversified farming could conceivably make use of was very small; not enough to put diversified agriculture in serious competition with plantation agriculture, for the most part. In the case of Moloaa the lands eyed for papaya were Amfac lands that had been but were no longer in sugar and pineapple.

8 Zalburg, *A Spark Is Struck!*, 476-479.

9 The study, "Community Power Structure: A Case Study of Honolulu," was by a University of Hawaii honors student in political science, Diane L. Nosse (later Dods). It is unpublished. Nosse's work was astute and could have been considered good even if done by an instructor. Her research approach was a combination of a methodology developed by political scientist Floyd Hunter, called the "reputational technique," together with the "decisional method" derived from the work of political scientist Robert A. Dahl. To simplify: Nosse's approach was to first ask a group of 14 staff officers from a sample of institutions whom they thought were Oahu's most powerful people in general. She did this by asking a "reputational" question: "Suppose a major project were before the community, one that required decision by a group of leaders whom nearly everyone would accept. Which persons would you choose to make up this group—regardless of whether or not you know them personally?" These officers' top 43

choices became Nosse's leadership group, and they were then asked the same question. The leaders were also asked three "decisional" questions, ones that were similar to the reputational except that they named a specific project area: planning, education, industry. In answering the general, "reputational" question the 43 ranked as second most powerful a labor leader. In that Nosse did not use real names one must surmise in each case whom is being referred to. In those years no labor leader came near Hall in terms of stature and power, and there would seem to be no logical conclusion as to whom this unnamed union leader could be except Hall. Likewise Burns is not mentioned by name, but it is hard to imagine what other governmental figure of that time this could have been.

10 Same as for note 6 above.

11 Same as for note 6 above.

12 For Yagi see edition of May 1983; for Castillo see Aug 1984; for Takamine see Nov 1983. The *Hawaii Business* writer relied heavily on interviews with leaders and with people presumably knowledgable as to who was influential in the communities studied. Apparently at times the way the magazine ranked an particular influential person did not jibe with that person's self-image. Takamine, for example, in an interview for this book, said that characterizing him as the Big Island's single most influential person was "ridiculous."

13 HA Aug 7 1971.

14 Two plantation camps cited by the State Health Department were an Amfac camp at Kealia, Kauai, and a Maui Land and Pineapple Co. camp at Honolua, Maui. In both cases raw sewage was being allowed to flow into the ocean. Both camps were closed in the early to mid-1970s.

15 State of Hawaii, Land Use Commission, file (A)67-158.

16 HSB Sept 13 1969.

17 Bryan H. Farrell, *Hawaii: The Legend That Sells* (Honolulu, 1982), 98-112.

18 Alexander & Baldwin Inc., *Ampersand* (Winter 1983-1984), 5.

19 Same as for note 18 above, 8.

20 Same as for note 19 above.

21 Same as for note 19 above.

22 Gilbert E. Cox to Mayor Elmer F. Cravalho, letter, Sept 20 1978.

23 Tavares was involved with the talks. At the time he was a vice-president for community relations. Often his duties involved dealing with government agencies. Sasaki was a vice-president in properties. As such he had major responsibility for the development of Maui Lani.

24 Same as for note 19 above.

25 HA Sept 4 1980; interview with Robert K. Sasaki Feb 26 1985; *The Maui News* Mar 23 1981.

26 "Testimony of Eddie Tangen on Behalf of ILWU, Hawaii State Land Use Commission, Docket A80-483, Kahului, Maui, Sept 3 1980."

27 Same as for note 26 above.

28 HA Sept 4 1980.

29 State of Hawaii, Land Use Commission, Special Permit App. No. 80-351.

30 Same as for note 26 above.

31 State of Hawaii, Land Use Commission file (A)80-483.

32 State of Hawaii, Land Use Commission file (A)82-535, written testimony of Donald Rickard, Oct 6 1982.

33 Same as for note 32 above.

34 Same as for note 18 above, 9.

35 Same as for note 5 above.

36 For the initial numbers see note 1 above. For the latter numbers see ILWU, Sixteenth Biennial Convention, "Statement in Support of ILWU Members in the Sugar Industry" (1983) and "Statement in Support of ILWU Members in the Pineapple Industry" (1983).

37 From the standpoint of generating job opportunities for Hawaii-born people, the tourist industry had its down side, too. In 1972, the Hawaii State Department of Planning and Economic Development (DPED) published its two-volume *Tourism in Hawaii*, that contained some harsh assessments regarding tourism and the extent to which it might benefit the Hawaii-born workforce. For one thing, DPED said that tourism wages were often low, chances for advancement poor, and, as a result, a large portion of the tourist industry labor force was made up of in-migrants. Looking toward the then-probable future expansion of the industry, DPED wrote: "Most of the jobs generated will be low paying with small chance for advancement." (Vol. 1, 84). Regarding place of origin of existing workers, the study said that "according to a recent survey, about 45% of workers in the hotel industry were born outside of Hawaii." (Vol. 1, 80).

38 What Ariyoshi favored instead was the state, using its power of eminent domain, condemning a leasehold interest in the

lands, then subleasing to farmers. About this time however, a good number of the investors began to be foreclosed by C. Brewer or by a Brewer subsidiary. As Brewer was regaining title or not long afterwards, the company suggested that the leasehold condemnation plan be dropped. Brewer proposed instead that it would attempt large-scale guava and prawn operations on portions of the land, and sell off the rest as genuine agricultural lots. The title documents to the lots would have conditions that would tend to restrict the use of the land to farming, though not necessarily guarantee bona fide agriculture. Ariyoshi, finding the Brewer plan acceptable, dropped his leasehold condemnation proposal.

39 Interview with former ILWU leader on Kauai with the understanding that his name not be used.

40 State of Hawaii, Office of the Lieutenant Governor, Result of Votes Cast, General Election, Tuesday, November 7, 1978, State of Hawaii.

41 Leadership Homes of Hawaii Inc., weekly status reports by John Slayter, report dated May 10 1974.

42 Same as for note 41 above, report dated June 21 1974.

43 HA June 3 1968.

44 HA July 25 1974.

45 For example, ILWU International Representative Eddie Tangen in mid-1977, as chairman of the Land Use Commission, proposed a compromise in a heated dispute between tenants and an intended developer of Waikane Valley. For the contents of his suggestion Tangen was verbally attacked by the tenants. What happened was that the governor had recently proposed that the state buy a good portion of neighboring Waiahole Valley, to forestall plans there for mass evictions and residential development. Some leading legislators, such as Senate President John T. Ushijima, questioned the legality of what Ariyoshi was proposing, namely to use Hawaii Housing Authority funds, which ostensibly were for housing projects, to buy what were rural lands. The intended developer of Waiahole, Windward Partners, which held an option to buy, was also to be the developer of Waikane. Windward Partners was saying that it might mount a legal challenge to the governor's condemnation plan, conceivably based on the kind of issue that Ushijima raised. Re-

garding Waikane, Windward Partners had pending with the LUC a redistricting application, asking that 429 acres be changed from agricultural to urban. The Waiahole-Waikane Community Association (WWCA) opposed the redistricting. As an attempt at overall compromise, Tangen proposed that Windward Partners and the WWCA agree that the *hui* be allowed to urbanize 200 acres in Waikane, in exchange for Windward Partners dropping any thought of a legal challenge to the governor's plan for Waiahole. WWCA members said that Tangen's proposal was the same or about the same as an offer recently put directly or indirectly to them by the man who was then heading Windward Partners, Harold Lewis. The WWCA was angry at Tangen for suggesting a compromise which they thought had come from the developer, and which would lead, in the eyes of the WWCA, to a large and unacceptable amount of urbanization in Waikane. They also believed that Lewis, who was head of the Operating Engineers union in Hawaii and thus with Tangen was a sort of fellow union leader, had in some way conspired against the WWCA. At an LUC hearing WWCA members and supporters carried signs and angrily chanted "Tangen, Lewis made a deal!"

46 The other two men in the photo were also labor leaders—Jack C. Reynolds of the AFL-CIO Building and Construction Trades Council, and Art Rutledge.

47 The ILWU, because it had to fight so hard to bring itself into existence, because it underwent a certain amount of political persecution in the 1940s and 1950s, and because in its early years it faced a media establishment that generally favored employers, became by nature highly disciplined and secretive in general; persons who had no need to know something were not told. Also, in becoming a part of the establishment and dealing regularly with business executives and politicians, ILWU leaders found themselves bargaining with men who often wanted whatever was discussed to be kept strictly among those in the discussion, or, if others would be told, then very few. Inevitably ILWU leaders made agreements that they did not talk about with reporters, nor did they always tell even their own rank and file.

48 There was primarily one community organization opposing Leadership, the

Ohana o Mahaulepu. That and the
Niumalu-Nawiliwili Tenants Association
obtained the memos. The fullest airing
of the memos' contents came in *The
Garden Island,* Oct 7 1974.
49 Same as for note 42 above.
50 Same as for note 42 above.
51 Same as for note 41 above, report of July
1 1974.
52 Same as for note 41 above, report of July
19 1974.
53 Same as for note 52 above.
54 Same as for note 42 above.
55 See, for example, HSB Oct 4 1974.
56 By the time the organizations that
released the reports were in a position to
do so, the LUC had already turned
Leadership down. Several outside observers thus saw nothing, or nothing much,
to be gained as against Leadership by
releasing the reports at the time; the
memos might have been held until the
day when Leadership was again before a
government agency seeking development
approval. From the activists' viewpoint
there was a bit to be gained against
Leadership; releasing the reports at the
time they were let out might discredit
Leadership so much that it would leave
Hawaii. Part of the activists' motivation
in releasing the memos was general
public education about what they saw as
government officials secretly collaborat-
ing with a major developer to get approval for an unpopular project. To the
extent that public education was the
motivation for release, and given that,
although Leadership's proposed redistricting was dead, still many others that
activists opposed were alive, then the
sooner the reports were released the
better. Also, by the time the community
organizations who had the reports were
in a position to release them, it was just a
month before the 1974 general election.
Incumbent Mayor Francis M.F. Ching
was in a tough re-election fight against
Councilman Eduardo E. Malapit. Malapit
was somewhat more palatable to anti-
development activists than Ching. Given
that Ching was extensively named in the
memos as having promised to help
Leadership obtain its government approvals even though he was claiming on the
record to be non-committal vis-a-vis
Leadership, and given that the memos
tended to show that the activists were
right in saying that Ching was heavily
tied up with developers, there thus
seemed to be something to be gained by

releasing the memos during the election
in an effort to discredit Ching. Ultimately,
probably the largest single material
result of the whole Leadership memos
episode was the apparent fact that release
of the reports prior to the 1974 general
election did indeed play a role in Ching's
defeat.
57 Same as for note 42 above.
58 These included two of the children of
John Burns, then in the last year of his
last term as governor; Burns' representative on Maui, Masaru Yokouchi, who was
also chairman of the State Foundation
on Culture and the Arts; Charles S. Ota,
Maui member of the University of Hawaii
Board of Regents; Wallace T. Yanagi,
deputy administrator of the state's Maui
Memorial Hospital; and the director of
the State Department of Regulatory
Agencies, Edwin H. Honda.
59 In general see Chapter 11 of this book.
60 HA Oct 26 1980.
61 This was Masaru Yokouchi, who negotiated the purchase of Nukolii from Amfac,
then organized the *hui.* He functioned
as the *hui* manager, hence its spokesman.
62 This was a large limited partnership
entitled Windward Partners. Opposition
surfaced in 1974, during the State Land
Use Commission's statewide five year
review. Windward Partners' publicly-
filed partnership registration statement
indicated that the partnership was not
organized until 1975.
63 The reporter he was interviewed by was
James B. Dooley. SB & A June 7 1981.
64 Same as for note 63 above. See also State
of Hawaii, Department of Commerce
and Consumer Affairs, Business Registration Division.
65 US Bureau of Labor Statistics, Directory
of National Unions and Employee Associations (various years); Robert C. Schmitt,
Historical Statistics of Hawaii (Honolulu,
1977) 111-142; State of Hawaii, Department of Planning and Economic Development, *The State of Hawaii Data Book 1983:
A Statistical Abstract* (1983), 310-336.
66 Same as for note 65 above.
67 "Union Blues," *Hawaii Business,* Mar
1983.
68 Same as for note 67 above; also, data
supplied by Hawaii Employers Council.
69 Same as for note 67 above.
70 According to files of the National Labor
Relations Board in Honolulu, at the
time of the representation election that
resulted in a win for the ILWU, there
were 715 employees. According to ILWU

records this number thereafter grew to about 1,000.

71 Same as for note 67 above.
72 HA May 9 1984.
73 HSB May 9 1984.
74 HSB June 6 1978.
75 HSB Nov 5 1983.
76 HA July 13 1984; interview with Assistant US Attorney Les Osborn Jan 29 1985.
77 Uwaine had, however, been reindicted. Whether he would ultimately be acquitted or found guilty was unknown as of early 1985 when work on this book ceased.
78 Interview of Walter Kupau by Gay Eastman for this book, in early Oct 1984. At the time Eastman, a paralegal, was working for the authors of this book as a research assistant.
79 HA Apr 4 1981.
80 Same as for note 79 above.
81 HA Feb 18, 19, 20 1973.
82 Same as for note 81 above.
83 Same as for note 81 above.
84 State of Hawaii, Department of Planning and Economic Development, *The State of Hawaii Data Book 1983: A Statistical Abstract* (1983), 306.
85 HA Dec 13 1983.
86 HA July 15 1967; HSB Nov 2 and 3 1967.
87 Same as for note 86 above.
88 Interview with Robert T. Chuck July 31 1984. Chuck was manager/chief engineer for the Water and Land Development Division of the State Department of Land and Natural Resources.
89 HA Mar 9 1973.
90 HSB Mar 22 1972.
91 State of Hawaii, Board of Land and Natural Resources (DLNR), minutes of meeting Jan 12 1973, Item D-4; see also DLNR, Division of Water and Land Development (DOWALD) file pertaining to Kalua Koi application.
92 Same as for note 88 above.
93 Same as for note 88 above.
94 National Labor Relations Board, Kepuhi Partnership dba Sheraton Molokai Hotel, Employer, and ILWU Local 142, Petitioner, Case No. 37-RC-2349. Although this case pertained to the hotel, the case file contains background on the matter of the golf course.
95 Same as for note 94 above.
96 Voice of the ILWU Apr 1977.
97 Same as for notes 94 and 96 above.
98 Note that the sequence of the decisions to close may not have been the same as that of the public announcements. For

simplicity's sake this book used the dates of the public announcements.
99 HA Sept 6 1984.
100 Same as for note 5 above.
101 University of Hawaii at Manoa, Industrial Relations Center, Occasional Publication No. 147, Helene S. Tanimoto, *Duration of Collective Bargaining Agreements in Hawaii* (1984).
102 Same as for note 65 above.

6/Land and Big Business: The Example of Amfac

1 Frederick Simpich Jr., *Anatomy of Hawaii* (New York, 1971), 168.
2 Simpich, *Dynasty in the Pacific* (New York, 1974), 3-5.
3 Theodore Morgan, *Hawaii: A Century of Economic Change 1778-1876* (Cambridge, 1948), 186.
4 Gavan Daws, *Shoal of Time: A History of the Hawaiian Islands* (New York, 1968), 312.
5 Lawrence H. Fuchs, *Hawaii Pono: A Social History* (New York, 1961), 241, 242.
6 Same as for note 5 above, 242.
7 Fuchs, *Hawaii Pono*, 388; Governor's Agriculture Coordinating Committee, "Response of Governor's Agriculture Coordinating Committee, Office of the Governor, State of Hawaii, to House Resolution No. 656", H.D. 1, Eleventh Legislature of the State of Hawaii (1982), 12.
8 Practically the only plantation that owned most or all of its own lands, and which Amfac owned substantially or entirely during the post-World War II period, and that did not have significant urbanizing potential, was in Puna, on the Big Island.
9 Interview with Colin C. Cameron Feb 28 1985. Cameron was president of Maui Land and Pineapple Co.
10 Interview with Kenneth F. Brown Feb 28 1985. Brown was a descendant of John Papa Ii.
11 That Brewer's and Davies' lands did not begin to have the urbanizing potential of, say, Amfac's, was apparently fortuitous; it is hard to imagine, as factor/plantation relations began to be formed in the mid-nineteenth century, and even as land purchases for agricultural uses occurred down through about World War II, that anybody could really have foreseen the urban value which, for example, Kaanapali would one day have.

12 Simpich, *Dynasty in the Pacific*; HSB Mar 31 1983.

13 "Goodbye Big Five," *Hawaii Business* (Jan 1984), 37; HSB & A Aug 5 1984.

14 "Goodbye Big Five," 37.

15 Same as for note 14 above, 39.

16 The SEC document is popularly known as a "10-K," after a subsection of the federal Securities and Exchange Act of 1934 that, in general, required publicly traded corporations to annually prepare and file with the SEC rather factual annual reports. By and large when researching corporations for whatever purpose, a 10-K statement is much preferable to an annual report to shareholders. Reports to shareholders tend to contain fairly general, public-relations-oriented statements.

17 Amfac Inc., annual report to shareholders for 1973, 11.

18 HSB Mar 12 1974.

19 The Hawaii State Legislature in 1961 passed HB 27, which in general barred the interlocking of competitors. There after the state attorney general's office proceeded against interlocked competitors in the real estate finance field. About this time the US Department of Justice for apparently the first time in history began using federal laws long in place to attempt, successfully as it turned out, the disinterlocking of the Big Five.

20 The fact that, throughout this period, ownership of the Big Five was steadily slipping away to persons and organizations based outside of Hawaii, with no prospect of reversal in sight, seemed to mean that Hawaii-born non-*haoles* would probably never attain top executive positions.

21 HSB Mar 18 1960.

22 HSB Jan 27 1961.

23 HA Jan 8 1982.

24 "East of Eden," *Forbes*, Jan 31 1983.

25 Bryan H. Farrell, *Hawaii: The Legend That Sells* (Honolulu, 1982), 92.

26 Through the 1970s as well, Amfac agreed to housing programs for its employees at Pioneer Mill and also at Kaanapali, in part as conditions of ILWU and state and county support for the continued expansion of Kaanapali.

27 See Code of the County of Maui (1980), Title 19, Art. III, Maui County Historic Districts.

28 Interview with George Takeuchi Nov 29 1983; also, for Maui TMK 4-6-9:6, see state conveyance tax and Bureau of Conveyances references, contained on field book page for this parcel, in City and County of Honolulu, Finance Department, Real Property Assessment Division.

29 HA Oct 26 1980.

30 The study was done by a special investigative committee, made up of three members of the Amfac board of directors who, according to Amfac, had had no involvement with the sale to Yokouchi. Following completion of their study Amfac said that the three had found the sale "fair to the company." HA Feb 10 1981. A copy of the report was requested from Amfac by an author of this book, in a letter dated June 17 1983 from George Cooper to Robert H. Ozaki of Amfac Corporate Communications. The letter asked a variety of other questions as well. By a return letter from Amfac Board Chairman Henry A. Walker Jr., dated July 7 1983, the request was denied. Walker did, however, answer most of the other questions posed in the letter from Cooper.

31 State of Hawaii, Department of Commerce and Consumer Affairs, Business Registration Division; Gwenfread E. Allen, ed., *Men and Women of Hawaii: A Biographical Directory of Noteworthy Men and Women of Hawaii* (Honolulu, 1966); Betty F. Buker, ed., *Men and Women of Hawaii 1972: A Biographical Directory of Noteworthy Men and Women of Hawaii* (Honolulu, 1972); State of Hawaii, Legislative Reference Bureau, *Directory of State, County and Federal Officials: Supplement to Guide to Government in Hawaii* (published occasionally, most recently annually); Hawaii State Archives; miscellaneous references in newspapers and periodicals.

32 HSB Jan 26 1979; *State v. Reis*, Hawaii Intermediate Court of Appeals, No. 8799 (1983).

33 Weekly status reports by John Slayter, report of June 21 1974.

34 The Poipu hotel story was an involved one. In its plans to build a new Waiohai hotel, Amfac applied twice for permission to exceed Kauai County's building height limit of four stories. The first time Amfac asked for eight stories. In 1975 the Kauai Planning Commission voted this down. The second time the company proposed six stories. This time the Commission approved. A citizens action committee then appealed the decision to circuit court on Kauai, and a related citizens group made the first use ever of the Kauai charter's then recently-

adopted initiative provision. An initiative ballot item was certified, one that would strip the Commission of authority to allow buildings to exceed the height limit. With the suit and election both pending, Amfac, exasperated, called it quits in June of 1978. The six story plan was withdrawn. In its place a four story building was proposed, approved and ultimately built. As it turned out the initiative item lost by 38 votes in the 1978 general election.

35 Diane L. Nosse, "Community Power Structure: A Case Study of Honolulu," unpublished paper, University of Hawaii at Manoa, 1967.

36 "Goodbye Big Five," *Hawaii Business* (Jan 1984).

7/Organized Crime

1 Hawaii Crime Commission, *Organized Crime in Hawaii* (1978), 13, 14.

2 Same as for note 1 above, 8, 9.

3 Same as for note 1 above, 13.

4 *US* v. *Pulawa et al*, US District Court for the District of Hawaii, Crim No. 13194, testimony of Roy R. Ryder Sr.

5 HA Aug 19 1984.

6 HSB June 6 1978.

7 Same as for note 4 above.

8 HA May 30 1973; HSB May 30 1973.

9 Both are on file in Second Circuit Court, on Maui. Matsuoka's is SE 1580-2; Tamura's is Prob. 6202.

10 State of Hawaii, Legislative Reference Bureau, *Directory of State, County and Federal Officials: Supplement to Guide to Government in Hawaii* (published occasionally, most recently annually); HSB June 13 1962; HA Mar 21 1979; HA Dec 15 1969; HA June 29 1970.

11 HSB & A June 15 1980.

12 In a more general way, the Hawaii Crime Commission indicated that it, too, believed Tamura's death was syndicate-related. See *Organized Crime in Hawaii*, 27.

13 HSB Mar 15 1979.

14 Same as for note 13 above.

15 Same as for note 11 above.

16 HA Dec 21 1972.

17 HA Mar 30 1978.

18 HSB May 26 1978; HA May 27 1978.

19 HA Mar 21 1979.

20 See note 9 above regarding Tamura probate.

21 HA Dec 15 1969.

22 HA Jan 27 1979.

23 Feb 19 1963; HA Mar 15 1968 and Oct 15 1968; HSB June 3 1982.
   The outcomes of the various cases in general were learned from interviews with police and prosecutors.

24 HA Dec 24 1981. Outcomes were learned in an interview May 23 1984 with the Maui deputy prosecuting attorney assigned to the cases, Lawrence Goya.

25 HSB Feb 13 1981. See also HA June 27 1980.

26 Interview with Lawrence Goya May 23 1984.

27 Roosevelt High School annual for 1952, on file at Roosevelt High School.

28 HA July 20 1984.

29 Same as for note 28 above.

30 Same as for note 28 above.

31 HA Aug 28 1984.

32 HA Jan 24 1974.

33 SB & A July 15 1979.

34 Same as for note 4 above.

35 *US* v. *Pulawa*, testimony of Sherwin K. "Sharkey" Fellezs.

36 Alu Like Inc., *Study on Native Hawaiians in the Criminal Justice System* (Honolulu, 1977); George K. Ikeda, *A Report on Native Hawaiian Youth Employment and Training Needs* (Honolulu, 1980); Alu Like Inc., *A Report on Mental Health and Substance Abuse Among the Native Hawaiian Population* (Honolulu, 1979).

37 Same as for note 35 above.

38 Same as for note 6 above.

39 HSB Jan 7 1977.

40 Some of the social and political dynamics were like those seen a few years before in US mainland civil rights organizations. Many of those involved in the Kalama Valley struggle felt it necessary to not only take a stand against evictions, but, internally, for Kokua Kalama/Hawaii to be part of a revolutionary process as well. That meant that whites, who at least culturally belonged to the dominant/oppressive majority in the US, should be excluded from membership in the organization, but could, if they wanted, take part in support work outside of the valley. Moreover, it was decided that to be in leadership a person ought to be at least part-Hawaiian, since ethnic Hawaiians were considered the most oppressed group in the Islands, their lands taken mainly by whites.

41 Same as for note 6 above.

42 Same as for note 39 above.

43 Same as for note 1 above, 11.

44 Same as for note 1 above, 12.

45 Interviews for this book with members

and/or supporters of Protect Kahoolawe Ohana, with understanding that their names not be used.

46 This was a stand similar to those taken by several members of the Protect Kahoolawe Ohana when prosecuted for trespassing on Kahoolawe. Such stands were of course purely symbolic.

47 Wilford K. Pulawa, "To The Hawaiian People of Hawaii," open letter, Aug 13 1978.

48 *Hawaii Observer*, Mar 10 1977, 12.

49 HA June 24 1977.

50 HSB July 12 1978; *Mehau v. Gannett*, 66 Haw. 134 (1983).

51 HA Sept 22 1980.

52 HSB Aug 12 and Oct 9 1958.

53 HSB Sept 11 1960.

54 HA Oct 3 1957.

55 Same as for note 53 above.

56 HA July 31 1984.

57 SB and A July 15 1979.

58 HA Dec 5 1980.

8 / Hawaii: Subdividing Lava Fields

1 State of Hawaii, Department of Commerce and Consumer Affairs, Business Registration Division; Hawaii State Archives; HSB Nov 12 1958; HA Mar 15 1959.

2 A good summary as to the state of existing and planned resort development in west Hawaii as of 1972 is provided in State of Hawaii, Department of Planning and Economic Development, West Hawaii: *Hawaii Tourism Impact Plan*, Vol. 2, regional (1972).

3 Larry K. Stephenson, Jean I. Nishida, "Little Pieces of Paradise: Remote Subdivision Ownership in Puna, Hawaii," *Geographical Survey*, Vol. 8, 1 (Jan 1979), 27. Stephenson and Nishida state that 4,636 was the number of speculative lots in Puna owned by persons or organizations with Big Island addresses as of 1974. This was based on Nishida and her sister having personally reviewed state real property tax records for every or nearly every speculative subdivision lot in Puna. Stephenson and Nishida do not indicate whether there were many instances of one person or organization owning more than one lot. In reviewing tax maps and tax field books for this book, however, in general it did not appear that there had been a great many cases of a person or organization buying more than one lot each. For this book it

was assumed, then, that the number of individual buyers in the 4,636 figure was 4,000. Next it was necessary to extrapolate from the fact that Stephenson and Nishida studied Puna lots only, which constituted about two-thirds of the Big Island speculative subdivision total. That meant that the number of individual Big Island buyers was an estimated 6,000. As of about the time that Nishida and her sister did their research, the population of the Big Island was approximately 78,000, meaning there were about 19,500 families, using a State Department of Planning and Economic Development estimate of four people to a family. Next, dividing 19,500 by 6,000 yielded an estimated one family in three owning a speculative subdivision lot. To be on the safe side, this number was changed to one in four, as a rounded lower limit number of the extent to which Big Island families took part in investing in speculative subdivisions.

4 Same as for note 3 above.

5 American Society of Planning Officials, *Subdividing Rural America: Impacts of Recreational Lot and Second Home Development*, (Washington, 1976), 6.

6 Quoted in HSB June 25 1958.

7 SB & A Oct 16 1960.

8 Same as for note 7 above.

9 State of Hawaii, Department of the Attorney General, Opinion 62-33.

10 Session Laws of Hawaii 1969, Act 232.

11 HSB Mar 22 1962.

12 See SB 548 (1963) and SB 358 (1964).

13 Brochure entitled "Royal Gardens," on file with Hawaii County Planning Department in files on Royal Gardens subdivision.

14 Betty White to Sumio Nakashima, Apr 18 1961, letter in possession of Arthur U. Ishimoto.

15 Jean I. Nishida, Larry K. Stephenson, "Patterns of Expected Use of Hawaii's Remote Subdivisions," *Erdkunde* Vol. 31, 1 (Mar 1977), 67. Nishida and Stephenson here report the findings of a sample survey conducted in the mid-1970s of owners of lots within four Puna subdivisions. They state that 69.9% of those responding indicated they had not seen their lot prior to purchase.

16 For a study of this phenomenon in general see a three volume work, the overall title of which is *Promised Lands*. Volume I is separately titled *Subdivisions in Deserts and Mountains*, by Leslie Allan, Beryl Kuder, and Sarah L. Oakes (New

York, 1976). Volume II is entitled *Subdivisions in Florida's Wetlands*, by the same three authors (New York, 1977). Volume III is entitled *Subdivisions and the Law*, by Allan and Kuder, also Patricia A. Simko and Jean Schreier (New York, 1978).

17 Same as for note 16 above.

18 US Department of Agriculture, Soil Conservation Service, Soil Survey of Island of Hawaii, State of Hawaii (1973), map sheet nos. 34, 43, 154. For an old map that includes waterholes, see State of Hawaii, Department of Land and Natural Resources, Survey Office, map by A. B. Loebenstein, Nov 1893.

19 Interview with R. Eugene Platt, Sept 20 1982.

20 Soil Survey of Island of Hawaii, 55.

21 Hawaii County, Planning Department, file on Royal Gardens.

22 Donald R. Mullineaux, Donald W. Peterson, *Volcanic Hazards on the Island of Hawaii* (1974), 5, 17.

23 Same as for note 22 above; HA Nov 7 1983; interviews with Hawaii County Civil Defense Director Harry Kim June 25 1984 and Apr 29 1985.

24 Same as for note 16 above, Vol. 1, 17.

25 The figure 60% is an estimate done for this book. It was derived by overlaying a US Geological Survey (USGS) map showing volcanic hazard zones, onto maps indicating subdivisions. For a USGS map see Mullineaux and Peterson in note 22 above, 7. For maps indicating subdivisions see "The Big Island's Best Bargains," *Hawaii Business* Oct 1982, 82 (showing Puna only); and James A. Bier, *Map of Hawaii: The Big Island* (3rd ed.) (showing major subdivisions throughout island).

26 State of Hawaii, Department of Commerce and Consumer Affairs, subdivision registration section, files on Royal Gardens.

27 Same as for note 21 above.

28 One Big Island subdivision banned from being sold in California for non-registration was another Norman Inaba project, Milolii Beach Lots Subdivision. See State of California, Department of Real Estate, "To Great Hawaiian Realty Inc. et al, Order to Desist and Refrain," No. H-17502 LA (1967).

29 Same as for note 13 above.

30 Kenneth P. Emory et al, *Natural and Cultural History Report on Kalapana Extension of the Hawaii Volcano National Park* (1959), 4.

31 HA Mar 29 1961.

32 Same as for note 21 above.

33 Same as for note 21 above.

34 State of Hawaii, Land Use Commission, file (A)69-228.

35 Same as for note 34 above.

36 HSB July 6 1962.

37 Same as for note 36 above.

38 Same as for note 36 above; HSB Apr 24 1964.

39 Visit to Milolii Beach Lots Subdivision by Laureen K.K. Wong and George Cooper Aug 13 1982.

40 HSB Apr 24 1964.

41 Same as for note 26 above.

42 In possession of Arthur U. Ishimoto. Ishimoto was a limited partner in Royal Gardens, the partnership.

43 Raymond Suefuji, Hawaii County Planning Director, to Frank De Luz III, Chairman Hawaii County Council Planning, Research, Development and Legislative Committee, letter, Jan 20 1975.

44 Harland Bartholomew and Associates, *Land Use Districts for the State of Hawaii* (1963), 91.

45 Louis A. Vargha, Harold L. Baker, *Urban Development on the Island of Hawaii, 1946-1963* (LSB Bull. No. 5, Mar 1965), 8.

46 Interview with Raymond Suefuji June 25 1984.

47 HSB Dec 5 1966.

48 Revised Ordinances of the County of Hawaii 1967, Ord. No. 62.

49 "Guns, Grass—And Money," *Newsweek* (Oct 25 1982) 42; HA Oct 18 1984.

50 "Puna Goes to Pot," *Hawaii Business* (Oct 1982), 67.

51 Sheet of paper entitled "Green Harvest & Maintenance Statistics," given George Cooper by Big Island Police Department vice squad head Charles S. K. Wakita June 1984.

52 Shown to George Cooper June 1984 by person who placed the ad; shown on the condition that person's name not be used.

9/Maui: Developing Kihei

1 Honolulu Stock Exchange, Manual of Hawaiian Securities, statements of 1960 and 1961; Frederick Simpich Jr., *Dynasty in the Pacific* (New York, 1974).

2 Simpich, *Dynasty in the Pacific*, 197.

3 See miscellaneous Amfac annual reports to shareholders in early and mid-1980s.

4 This was to Consolidated Oil and Gas Co. The resort was also named Princeville.

5 As of 1980, according to the US Census Bureau as indicated in a state of Hawaii report, Maui County had a little more than twice the condominiums that Kauai and Hawaii counties had combined. State of Hawaii, Department of Planning and Economic Development, *The State of Hawaii Data Book 1983: A Statistical Abstract* (1983), 559. The island of Maui was rapidly expanding its condominium supply at that point, so that by about three years later it would have about 16,500 units, whereas, according to the US Census, Maui County (including Molokai and Lanai) in 1980 held only about 10,400. Kauai and Hawaii did not begin to keep pace with this growth; by about 1983 the island of Maui held three to four times the condominiums that all other outer islands had put together. (For the 16,500 figure see Guidelines Corporation, *Maui Condominiums* [1982] 6.) As indicated in Maui Condominiums, as of January 1982, of the total condominiums in existence and under construction on Maui, about half were along the Kihei coast.

6 Same as for note 5 above.

7 Noboru Kobayashi, Howard K. Nakamura, Robert O. Ohata, *Kihei Civic Development Plan* (1970), 35.

8 In general this information was developed by, first, reviewing real property tax field book sheets for the entire Kihei coast. At times information indicated on the sheets was checked or further developed by looking at references on the sheets to documents on file with the Hawaii Bureau of Conveyances. Also used was a condominium reference book compiled by the Guidelines Corp., *Maui Condominiums* (Jan 1982).

9 Same as for note 7 above, 87, 48.

10 *The Maui News* Dec 7 1983.

11 HA Mar 17 1975.

12 Same as for note 11 above.

13 "Maui: The 20 Most Influential People," *Hawaii Business*, May 1983.

14 Announced HA July 9 1974.

15 Interview Mar 5 1985 with person who was project manager for one of landowners, with understanding that person's name not be used.

16 Miscellaneous Maui County Planning Department, County Clerk, and County Council files.

17 Same as for note 16 above; also HA May 8 1980.

18 Same as for note 16 above; also State of Hawaii, Department of Commerce and Consumer Affairs, Business Registration Division; Hawaii Bureau of Conveyances.

19 Same as for note 16 above.

20 Same as for note 16 above.

21 Same as for note 16 above.

22 Same as for note 16 above; also State of Hawaii, Land Use Commission, file (A)78-437.

23 The lawyer was Allen W. Wooddell. See his letter to the Land Use Commission, Oct 17 1974, in LUC Maui files for 1974 boundary review, docket number M74-25.

24 Staff report to Maui Planning Commission regarding Makena Surf, July 10 1979.

25 HA May 22 1980.

26 Same as for note 25 above.

27 Interview Feb 16 1983; interview was conducted with the understanding that person's name not be used.

10/Oahu: Salt Lake

1 Reverend Daniel Tyerman, George Bennet, compiled by James Montgomery, *Journal of Voyages and Travels*, Vol. 1 (London, 1831), 460.

2 Same as for note 1 above.

3 Frederick D. Bennett, *Narrative of a Whaling Voyage Round the Globe*, Vol. 1 (London, 1840) 398.

4 "Oahu's Salt Lake Turns Fresh," *The Friend* (Apr 1927), 91; "Hawaiian Salt Making," *Hawaiian Annual for 1924*, 115.

5 HA Aug 12 1958.

6 HSB Jan 8 1964.

7 Same as for note 1 above.

8 *The Friend* (Apr 1927), 91.

9 In general see State of Hawaii, Department of Land and Natural Resources, planning office, Conservation District Use Application OA-66-6-30-36, applicant International Development Co.

10 HSB May 16 1973.

11 HSB July 15 1966.

12 John A. Burns to Mrs. Harold R. Erdman, president, The Outdoor Circle, letter, July 20 1966, in file referenced in note 9 above.

13 HA Sept 10 1966.

14 Same as for note 13 above.

15 Franklin Y. K. Sunn to Raymond Yamashita, Executive Officer, State Land Use Commission, letter, June 12 1964, in file referenced in note 9 above; HSB Aug 26 1966.

16 HA July 1 1965.

17 HSB Mar 7 1972.

18 Same as for note 9 above; also State of Hawaii, Land Use Commission, file (A)72-330.
19 Same as for note 9 above; also HSB Aug 13 1966.
20 Legislative Auditor of the State of Hawaii, Financial Audit of the State Department of Budget and Finance (1969), Part II, 13.
21 Andrew T.F. Ing to Clinton T. Tanimura, Auditor, letter, Feb 13 1969, appended to report cited in note 20 above.
22 Interview with James P. Ferry Aug 26 1983.
23 Same as for note 9 above.
24 HA Mar 20 1973.
25 Same as for note 9 above.
26 Same as for note 9 above.
27 Interview with Wilfred M. Oka Aug 23 1983.
28 Needless to say, there were endless situations where the picture was less sharp than this, on which city, county and state ethics commissions were asked for opinions or initiated cases. See, for example, City and County of Honolulu, City Ethics Commission, Ops. Nos. 1-89 (1979).
29 HSB Nov 16 1972.
30 City and County of Honolulu, Office of the Clerk, personal disclosure file of George M. Koga.
31 HA Apr 19 1978.
32 State of Hawaii, Land Use Commission, file (A)72-330.
33 Same as for note 32 above.
34 State of Hawaii, First Circuit Court, Equity No. 2816, which is a running file on all court-supervised matters involving Damon Estate.
35 HA Apr 13 1971; HA Jan 17 1973.
36 HA Jan 17 1973.

11/Kauai: Nukolii

1 State of Hawaii, Department of Land and Natural Resources, map of Lihue-Hanamaulu area of Kauai, prepared by M. D. Monsarrat, dated 1900, on file with survey office.
2 University of Hawaii, Land Study Bureau, *Detailed Land Classification – Island of Kauai* (1967), map 101.
3 County of Kauai, Office of the Clerk, Ord. 26-79 and connected files. The attorney was Walton D. Y. Hong. Nukolii's near-shore waters were good for certain water activities—things like surfing and diving for fish—though these were

activities that tourists generally did not engage in.
4 Appraisal by General Appraisal Co., as part of appraisal of large number of Amfac properties. Nukolii was indicated to be "parcel #100" in the General Appraisal work. The appraisal is undated, however in the concluding section under the heading "Final Estimate of Value," it is indicated that the suggested value is as of November 30, 1972. The appraisal was given an author of this book by a former Amfac executive.
5 HA Sept 8 1984.
6 EDAW Inc., Muroda and Associates Inc., Morris G. Fox, Roger Lee Associates, *Lihue Development Plan* (1976).
7 The core of the Lihue Development Plan were the plan's specific land use changes. They were adopted via two ordinances, Ord. No. 334, which pertained to the county general plan, and Ord. No. 335, which concerned county zoning maps. They were adopted by the Council and signed into law by the mayor in 1977.
8 County of Kauai, Planning Department, Lihue Development Plan file, CAC minutes for meeting of July 10 1975.
9 Same as for note 8 above.
10 The landowner was Kanoa Estate Inc.
11 This was the first or about the first development issue that the Wong sisters of nearby Koloa took part in. At the start of the Poipu Beach expansion controversy Napua, Tamara and Paula Wong were all under 20. They would be among the leaders of the Ohana o Mahaulepu which in 1974 defeated one of the nation's largest homebuilders in its bid to construct a major resort at Mahaulepu, adjacent to Poipu.
12 Kanoa was planning a resort and some light industrial development where a good many of its tenants in Niumalu lived; Kanoa thus wanted the tenants out. As a relocation housing plan, Kanoa offered to sell the tenants some semi-swampland in Niumalu at a nominal price. The tenants would have had to bear the cost of making the land buildable. Because the tenants feared the development cost would be prohibitive, because they said that a Kanoa representative or representatives had for years promised to give them the first chance to buy their existing houses and lots if Kanoa were ever to sell, and because the tenants had grown attached to their homes, they rejected the Kanoa offer. When they did so, Kanoa sent eviction

notices to about half of its 40 or so tenant households in Niumalu and Nawiliwili. As it turned out, about a decade later the tenants accepted something similar to the swamp offer. The latter plan, however, provided that the swampland would be given the tenants free if the state and county governments allowed Kanoa to develop about 40 acres overlooking the Menehune (Alakoko) Fishpond, and if the tenants supported the Kanoa application before government agencies. If the 40 acre-plan was not approved, then the tenants would have to buy the swampland. Also, under the latter plan several tenant households would get their existing houses and lots free or have to buy them, again depending on what happened with the 40 acres. As of early 1985 when this book was completed, the tenants had begun filing applications to build on the edge of the swamp. Neither Kanoa nor a Kanoa developer had yet filed an application concerning the 40 acres overlooking the fishpond.

13 HA Dec 30 1972.

14 The report was written by George K. Houghtailing's Community Planning Inc. Houghtailing is extensively mentioned elsewhere in this book, as a former Honolulu planning director who, after he left city government, had an extensive practice as a consultant representing landowners and developers before government agencies.

15 *The Garden Island* Mar 2 1977. On the public relations front, in an effort to discredit the developer in the business community and with government agencies, the tenants did research and issued a news release on the subject of the developer's apparent financial difficulties. In a release dated June 7 1976, the NNTA wrote that the developer "is paying none of its bills, is being sued right and left by its creditors, and—very importantly—has been unable to get construction financing. Also, [the developer] is about eight months over the deadline given by the Planning Commission in September of 1974 to start 'substantial construction of the units within one year.' All indications are that [the developer] is about to go under." In fact the developer did go under; subsequently its lender foreclosed on the Nawiliwili project.

16 HSB Sept 21 1976.

17 HSB Nov 18 1976.

18 Hawaii Crime Commission, *Organized*

Crime in Hawaii (1978), 42, 43.

19 HSB Oct 24 1970; HA May 6 1972.

20 HSB Feb 15 1979; HSB Aug 21 1979.

21 *The Garden Island* May 2 1977.

22 Same as note 18 above, 28.

23 *The Garden Island* May 18 1977.

24 Same as for note 23 above.

25 The accord was first announced in detail several months after it was reached. See *The Garden Island* Aug 1 1977.

26 *The Garden Island* Apr 22 1977.

27 Same as for note 26 above.

28 Regarding the graveyard see *The Garden Island* June 8 1977; regarding the Poipu resort see State of Hawaii, Land Use Commission, file (A)76-418.

29 Office of the Lieutenant Governor, Result of Votes Cast, General Election, Tuesday, November 2, 1976, State of Hawaii.

30 Unemployment statistics derived from State of Hawaii, Department of Planning and Economic Development, *The State of Hawaii Data Book 1983: A Statistical Abstract* (Honolulu, 1983), 306. Hotel occupancy rate figures supplied by Hawaii Visitors Bureau research section.

31 HSB Dec 9 1974.

32 One of the most famous/infamous attacks occurred in Hanalei in February 1976. Four local men attacked or fought with one or two *haoles*. At least one of the locals used a four-by-four piece of lumber to beat one of the *haoles*. The attack/fight included one of the locals holding the head of one of the *haoles* under water in a taro patch ditch.

33 See County of Kauai, Finance Department, Real Property Tax Division, field book entries for TMK 3-7-3-7 and miscellaneous transactions referenced there.

34 *The Garden Island* July 20 1977.

35 HA Feb 2 1979.

36 See Kauai County Charter Article V, which contained the provisions regarding initiative and referendum. These provisions were enacted in 1976.

37 *County of Kauai v. Pacific Standard Life Insurance Co.*, 65 Haw. 318, 321 (1982).

38 Same as for note 37 above, 322.

39 See County of Kauai, County Council, Bill 689 (1980).

40 Same as for note 39 above.

41 HSB Sept 25 1980.

42 Same as for note 41 above.

43 Interview with Hasegawa attorney Edward A. Jaffe Jan 2 1985.

44 According to the contractor's vice-president for administration, Frederick

Fleischmann, "the damage was not done by a group of juveniles but by people who knew what they were doing."

45 Same as for note 37 above, 322.

46 *The Garden Island* Nov 10 1980.

47 HA Oct 26 1980.

48 HA Feb 10 1981.

49 SB & A June 7 1981.

50 Same as for note 47 above.

51 HA Apr 18 1974.

52 Same as for note 30 above.

53 Office of the Lieutenant Governor, Result of Votes Cast, General Election, Tuesday, November 4, 1980, State of Hawaii, 165.

54 The vandalism this time was mostly or entirely spraypainting things like pipes at the construction site. Among what was painted on were "4 sale cheap" and "The people has decided."

55 Same as for note 37 above, 322.

56 The spokeman was Stanford Achi, leader of the Niumalu-Nawiliwili Tenants Association. His warning to Malapit was in turn relayed by Malapit in a letter to the Nukolii development project manager. Malapit wrote that Achi indicated that "violence is imminent." In his letter Malapit also cited the recent arrest or detaining of an unemployed construction worker, Arthur DeFries, who had been shouting at people demonstrating against construction at Nukolii. In addition Malapit cited the instances of vandalism that had occurred and a small, unexploded bomb that had recently been found at the construction site at Nukolii.

57 HA Feb 2 1981.

58 Information on the 31 supplied by Jane Kawasaki, employee of State of Hawaii District Court of the Fifth Circuit; information on the remaining defendant supplied by defendant herself, Georgette Meyers.

59 HA Jan 3 1981.

60 Information on the results supplied by Jane Kawasaki, employee of State of Hawaii District Court of the Fifth Circuit.

61 HA Feb 2 1981.

62 For a sleepy place, Kauai was now quite tense. Death threats, a bombing, civil disobedience arrests, what for Kauai was mass picketing, all created an atmosphere where a bomb threat at a hotel was now not so unusual.

63 Same as for note 37 above, 322.

64 He was Sidney M. Wolinsky. In an interview December 13, 1984, Wolinsky said that Public Advocates was non-profit, and that its greatest emphasis was on

representing socially disadvantaged groups, in particular among the elderly and disabled. Wolinsky also said that at the time of the interview, the firm had a case pending in the California Supreme Court against General Foods, having to do with the amount of sugar the company was using in children's breakfast cereals. In Hawaii, Public Advocates represented leprosy patients who unsuccessfully resisted relocation from an old facility called Hale Mohalu, at Pearl City on Oahu. Wolinsky was the commencement speaker for the 1985 graduation ceremonies for the University of Hawaii William S. Richardson School of Law.

65 For Malapit initially saying he would go along with downzoning see HA June 25 1981; for his reversal see HA Mar 18 1982; for Council override see HSB Apr 21 1982.

66 HA Sept 8 1982.

67 HSB Sept 8 1982.

68 Same as for note 67 above.

69 Same as for note 37 above, 325.

70 Same as for note 37 above, 339.

71 He was Turk Tokita. He was interviewed on this point Nov 30 1984.

72 The poll was apparently done by Hawaii Opinion Inc., for this firm did KFN's later polling. A member of KFN showed an author of this book the results of one of the Hawaii Opinion polls.

73 The Cades law firm was an outgrowth of what for Hawaii was an old firm, one that entirely or nearly entirely throughout its existence represented the Islands' major businesses, such as Amfac. Cades Schutte was heavily *haole*, though in recent years hired a number of young local Asians. The Fujiyama firm was of more recent origin; it was heavily Japanese. Perhaps partly as a consequence, Fujiyama was often sought out by major Japan companies seeking to establish themselves in Hawaii, though this was probably also a function of the general perception in the community that Wallace Fujiyama was politically influential, in addition to being a very good attorney.

74 460 US 1077 (1983).

75 The fact of the US Supreme Court's refusal to take the case prompted CSN member Julia O. Abben to say to a reporter, who had apparently asked for her reaction: "I'm speechless. Oh, I just thought of something. It's settled once and for all." (*The Garden Island* Apr 18 1983.)

76 Kent M. Keith, Director, Hawaii State

Department of Planning and Economic Development, "Nukolii and Hawaii's Future," a paper presented to Kauai Rotary Club, Kauai Surf Hotel, Sept 30 1983.

77 HA Sept 2 1983; HA Sept 8 1983; HA Sept 21 1983.

78 SB & A Nov 20 1983; HA Feb 4 1984.

79 Robert K. Yotsuda to Kauai County Council, May 29 1980, letter.

80 *Committee to Save Nukolii v. County of Kauai*, State of Hawaii, Supreme Court, No. 9747, Complaint (1984), 20, 21.

81 State of Hawaii, Campaign Spending Commission, reports filed by Kauaians for Nukolii, Kauaians for Nukolii Campaign Committee, and Committee to Save Nukolii, plus reports filed by miscellaneous Kauai mayoral candidates for elections in 1980, 1982, 1984.

82 Same as for note 81 above.

83 Interviews with two KFN officers with understanding that their names not be used.

84 HA Apr 19 1983.

85 *The Garden Island* Apr 19 1983.

86 HA Apr 20 1983.

87 *The Garden Island* Apr 22 1983.

88 Same as for note 86 above.

89 Regarding the whole shoreline question see State of Hawaii, Department of Land and Natural Resources, planning office, Conservation District Use Application, File No. KA-10/15/81-1419; State of Hawaii, Land Use Commission, (A)83-546.

90 *The Garden Island* Jan 30 1984.

91 *The Garden Island* July 18 1983.

92 *Kauai Times* Feb 29 1984.

93 Part IV in *Kauai Times* Feb 15 1984; Part III in *Kauai Times* Feb 8 1984.

94 *Kauai Times* June 15 1983.

95 Henry A. Walker Jr., "Remarks to ILWU Regional Convention, September 21, 1983."

96 What appears to be the fact that Iwa had this effect is a judgment based on interviewing and simply talking with many people on Kauai in the course of researching the Nukolii chapter of this book, in December 1984.

97 A KFN officer allowed an author of this book to review the results of this poll. The results were accompanied by a cover letter dated Sept 24 1983.

98 Jerome Y. K. Hew, County Clerk, County of Kauai, "Results of Votes Cast, County Special Election—February 4, 1984."

99 Same as for note 80 above, 5.

100 Same as for note 80 above, Decision.

101 *Soules v. Kauaians for Nukolii Campaign Committee*, US District Court for the District of Hawaii, Civ. No. 84-0297, order entered Nov 30 1984, 15.

102 Same as for note 37 above, 340 fn 22.

103 *County of Kauai v. Pacific Standard Life Insurance Co.*, State of Hawaii, Fifth Circuit Court, Civ. No. 2388, Decision, entered Dec 7 1984.

104 Same as for note 103 above, "Position Statement of County of Kauai," filed Aug 16 1983; "Position Statement of County of Kauai," filed Aug 15 1984.

105 HA May 8, May 12; SB & A May 25, June 15 1980.

106 Beverly Keever, ed., *James Dooley as Detective of Documents: The Hui Connection* (undated), 29.

107 "East of Eden," *Forbes* Jan 31 1983.

108 Interview with Wallace S. Fujiyama Mar 25 1985.

109 Fujiyama was to be president, Trask secretary-treasurer. Prominent Honolulu attorney Alvin T. Shim was to be a director.

110 HSB Sept 13 1978.

111 *Honolulu* Oct 1982.

112 On another occasion in 1982, Fujiyama was reported to have attended a small breakfast meeting that included Ariyoshi, several other lawyers and businessmen, also Frank Hata, who was the or one of the principal campaign fundraisers for Ariyoshi.

113 HA Dec 16 1981.

114 Same as for note 37 above.

115 HA Jan 31 and Feb 2 1979.

116 Interview with Ariyoshi media aide Robert Wernet Dec 27 1984, who was relaying comments made by Ariyoshi in response to questions posed in a letter from George Cooper to Wernet Dec 3 1984.

117 Same as for note 76 above.

118 Interview with Stanford H. Achi May 8 1985.

119 *The Garden Island* July 5 1983.

120 Same as for note 37 above, 323.

121 State of Hawaii, County of Kauai, Department of Public Works, Building Division, building permit applications on file for both hotels.

122 State of Hawaii, Department of Health, Environmental Protection and Health Services Division, miscellaneous files maintained in connection with sewage system for Nukolii resort.

123 Same as for note 122 above.

124 Same as for note 122 above.

125 Same as for note 122 above.

126 In making a statement like this Soares was echoing what many others said as well. For example, in 1983 a Kauai Rotary Club president, veterinarian Walter R. Haas, said "the general public has a nasty taste about Nukolii" because of "lies" and "shady deals."
127 HSB Nov 19 1980.
128 *The Garden Island* Nov 3 1980.
129 HA Jan 5 1984.
130 *The Garden Island* Aug 10 1983.

12/One Man's Career: George Ariyoshi

1 Transcript of interview with George R. Ariyoshi, John A. Burns Oral History project, on file with University of Hawaii Hamilton Library, Hawaiian/Pacific Collection.
2 HSB May 9 1964.
3 HA July 24 1959.
4 See SB 1018 (1967) and its progress through Senate, in Senate Journal for 1967.
5 Daniel W. Tuttle Jr., ed. *The Hawaii Democratic and Republican Party Platforms 1952-1962* (Honolulu, 1962).
6 HSB Apr 30 1963; HA May 1 1963.
7 What made Ariyoshi's performance at the polls of even greater note was that the 1964 primary was a so-called "closed" primary, meaning only persons registered as Democrats could vote for Democratic candidates. The Maryland Bill had been solidly a Democratic Party measure; presumably more Democrats were for it than Republicans. Yet Ariyoshi did quite well in both the primary and general elections.
8 HSB May 31 1967.

13/The Maryland Law

1 SB 7, House Select Committee Report 1 (1959 Regular Session).
2 Robert C. Schmitt, *Historical Statistics of Hawaii* (Honolulu, 1977), 393; State of Hawaii, Department of Planning and Economic Development, "Housing Statistics for Hawaii, 1973," 3.
3 Schmitt, *Historical Statistics of Hawaii*, 393.
4 Frank A. Kaufman, "The Maryland Ground Rent—Mysterious But Beneficial," V *Maryland Law Review* 1 (Dec 1940), 68.
5 Regarding 1950s see Louis A. Vargha,

An Economic View of Leasehold and Fee Simple Tenure of Residential Land in Hawaii (Honolulu, 1964), 10; regarding figures 1961-1981 see *Hawaii Housing Authority* v. *Midkiff* (later v. *Lyman*), State of Hawaii, First Circuit Court, Civ. No. 63408, "Defendant Trustees' Proposed Findings of Fact and Conclusions of Law," filed June 20, 1983; regarding 31% see Bank of Hawaii, *Construction in Hawaii* (1982).
6 Regarding percentages of lots on Oahu at various times accounted for by lease-hold, see Hawaii Housing Authority in note 5 above; regarding percentage of all housing units in Hawaii 1950s through mid-1980s on lease land, see State of Hawaii, Department of Planning and Economic Development, state data books for various years, sections on housing.
7 Same as for note 1 above.
8 Vargha, *An Economic View of Leasehold and Fee Simple Tenure of Residential Land in Hawaii*, 15-30.
9 HB 24 HD 3 SD 1 (1963); SB 1200 Act 184 (1975).
10 Same as for note 8 above, 49 fn 107.
11 Same as for note 8 above, 10.
12 Hawaii State Legislature, Special Committee Report No. 1 (1967), done in conjunction with SB 1128 (1967).
13 HSB May 31 1967.
14 HA June 16 1967.
15 HSB Sept 1 1970.
16 HA Jan 13 1971.
17 HA Nov 17 1972.
18 Legislative Auditor of the State of Hawaii, *Management Audit of the Leasehold to Fee Conversion Program of the Hawaii Housing Authority* (1982), 10.
19 *Midkiff* v. *Amemiya*, State of Hawaii, First Circuit Court, Civ. No. 47103, "Findings of Fact and Conclusions of Law," entered June 29, 1978.
20 Same as for note 19 above.
21 HSB Mar 14 1973.
22 HSB Sept 24 1974.
23 According to the Frank Russell Property Index, the rate of return on a group of 500 selected stocks had likewise been better than 5%. For 1977-1979 the rate had been 7.8%. In 1979-1983 it had been 16.4%.
24 Interview with Damon Estate Trustee D. Hebden Porteus Mar 7 1984.
25 Bernice P. Bishop Estate, staff report, "Comprehensive Review of Bishop Estate Leasing Policies" (1968), included as Exhibit L-37 in Hawaii Housing Authority in note 5 above.

26 Midkiff in note 19 above; Hawaii Housing Authority in note 5 above, "Findings of Fact and Conclusions of Law."

27 Same as for note 19 above.

28 Same as for note 19 above.

29 Interview with Bishop Estate staff member with understanding that staff member's name not be used.

30 *Midkiff* v. *Tom*, 471 F. Supp. 871 (1979); 702 F.2d 788 (1983); *Hawaii Housing Authority* v. *Midkiff*, 52 USLW 4673.

31 Robert H. Horwitz, Norman Meller, *Land and Politics in Hawaii* (Honolulu, 1966), 53; HA Apr 4, 12 1963; HSB Apr 24, 30 1963.

32 HA May 3 1967.

33 Also interesting is the extent to which the estate founders and trustees who were also revolutionaries were in addition missionary descendants. The Castles mentioned were sons of the missionary Samuel N. Castle. Charles Cooke, also mentioned, was son of missionary Amos S. Cooke. Samuel Damon's father was a missionary. Another Bishop trustee, Rev. Charles M. Hyde, was in 1893 the Hawaii representative of the American Board of Missions. He apparently did not take part in overthrowing the queen, although Queen Liliuokalani indicated he had helped create an atmosphere conducive to the overthrow. She wrote later that he held "prejudices against the native people of the Hawaiian Islands and against their queen." (Liliuokalani, *Hawaii's Story by Hawaii's Queen* [Rutland, 1973], 244.)

34 HSB Aug 3 1935; Liliuokalani, *Hawaii's Story By Hawaii's Queen*, 290.

35 Prior to the evictions that took place in Kalama Valley in 1971, the land issue that brought the greatest number of Hawaiians to the fore publicly in the post World War II era had to do with Maryland bills in the 1960s, specifically in 1963 and 1967. In 1963 activities included a torchlight parade around Iolani Palace, where in those days the Legislature met.

36 Interview with senior staff member of Bishop Estate with understanding that staff member's name not be used.

37 State of Hawaii, First Circuit Court, Equity No. 2388, report of the master on the 1960 annual account of the trustees of the Campbell Estate, master's report filed June 12, 1962, 2.

38 HA Mar 24 1984.

39 Regarding Finance Realty and Makakilo see *Davis* v. *Finance Realty Co. Ltd.*, State

of Hawaii, Supreme Court, No. 4735 (1968); regarding Fong and the highway see H. Kusumoto, Division Administrator, Federal Highway Administration, US Department of Transportation, letter to George Cooper, Sept 24 1981, and two accompanying memoranda dated Mar 31 and Apr 28 1960 that discuss lobbying efforts of a Fong aide, obtained for this book pursuant to Freedom of Information Act request.

40 Sec. 15 Act 307 (1967).

41 *Parade* edition contained in SB & A May 23 1976.

42 HSB Nov 20 1969.

43 Davis, same as for note 39 above.

44 Same as for note 43 above.

45 HA Jan 6 1978.

46 For underlying agreement between Campbell and Finance Realty see copy of agreement in file referenced in note 43 above, attached to complaint as Exhibit B.

47 HSB Dec 2 1966; HA Dec 6 1966.

48 Same as for note 47 above.

49 Probably the best-known of those stories about Hawaii *nisei* soldiers in World War II and vows to work for progressive social change in the Islands after the war, concerns Daniel K. Inouye and Sakae Takahashi. See Lawrence H. Fuchs, *Hawaii Pono: A Social History* (New York, 1961), 308.

50 Same as for note 47 above.

51 State of Hawaii, Bureau of Conveyances, Land Court System, docs. 432963 (back to Oahu Sugar Co.), 481130 (to Wailani Rise Association Inc.), 483908 (as an example of one to an individual lessee).

52 It was at about this time that the ILWU turned a certain amount of attention to quality of life issues. Regarding this see Sanford Zalburg, *A Spark Is Struck! Jack Hall and the ILWU in Hawaii* (Honolulu, 1979), 476-479.

53 University of Hawaii, Hamilton Library, Hawaiian/Pacific Collections, John A. Burns Oral History Project, transcript of George R. Ariyoshi.

54 Same as for note 18 above, 7, 9.

55 Same as for note 18 above, attachment 2.

56 HA June 16 1967; HA Nov 17 1972.

57 Patsy K. Young, form letter to persons inquiring as to her actions regarding bill in 1984 legislative session on changing the ceiling on renegotiated leaserent, Mar 22 1984, copy of letter supplied by staff of Sen. Young; see also HA Apr 13 1984.

58 Information supplied by member of staff of Sen. Patsy K. Young.
59 Interview with Robert B. Schieve, Chairman of the Hawaii Leaseholders Equity Coalition, Mar 13 1985.
60 HA Apr 13 1984. Note that not all lessors agreed to moratorium, though Bishop Estate did.
61 HA May 5 1984.
62 Henry Peters to Councilman Rudy Pacarro, letter, Dec 6 1971.

Conclusion

1 Tom Coffman, *Catch A Wave: A Case Study of Hawaii's New Politics* (Honolulu, 1972), 148.
2 County of Maui, Planning Department, file 80/SMA-23.
3 HSB Dec 21 1978.
4 One of the authors of this book was able to observe Life of the Land from its beginnings in 1970 until the start of this period of grant-getting.
5 See in general Chapter 11 of this book, "Kauai: Nukolii."
6 For a general discussion of investigating unregistered *huis* and a collection of newspaper articles on the subject, see Beverly Keever, ed., *James Dooley as Detec-*
tive of Documents: The Hui Connection (Honolulu, n.d.).
7 HSB Oct 29 1981.
8 Matsukage, Ariyoshi, Ariyoshi's brother, plus one other man, in the mid-1960s erected and sold an 18-unit apartment building near Queen's Hospital in Honolulu.
9 See in general discussion in Chapter 8 of this book, "Hawaii: Subdividing Lava Fields."
10 HSB Feb 10 1983.
11 See a seven-part series by James Dooley in the *Honolulu Advertiser* on failures of industrial loan companies in Hawaii, beginning in the *Sunday Honolulu Star-Bulletin & Advertiser* Mar 24 1985.
12 The oral history project is simply called The John A. Burns Oral History Project. Copies of transcripts are available for public inspection in the University of Hawaii Hamilton Library, in the Hawaiian-Pacific Collection. The study on Hall is *A Spark Is Struck!: Jack Hall and the ILWU in Hawaii* (Honolulu, 1979), by Sanford Zalburg. The dissertation on Fong is by Michaelyn P. Chou.
13 The Segawa-Uwaine case was steadily in the newspapers for several months beginning October 1982. See the printed indices of the *Advertiser* and the *Star-Bulletin*.
14 Same as for 13 above.

INDEX

less zeal for change 1967, 154
real estate development, 14
resistant to change, 166
state banking deposit policy, 310
successors unclear 1980s, 457
take over Honolulu City Council, 124
ties to landowning establishment, 412
Democrats
   as developers, 11
   as real estate *hui* members, 12
   attorneys appointed to review internal
      business, 62
   invest with Republicans, 12
   leaders privately involved with develop-
      ment, 55
   profit from land boom, 12
Denver, 259
Depression, 210
Develco Corp., 286
Development
   California, 81
   outside developers' representatives, 69
   outside money flows into Hawaii 1960s,
      1970s, 69
Devens, Paul, 19, 233
Devereux, Dorothy, 20
Diamond Head, 18, 27, 58, 133, 142-144,
   151, 152, 154-157, 369, 450
   ILWU opposes high-rises 1967, 173
   Kainalu rezoning approved 1957, 146
   National Natural Landmark, 150
   anti-development groups, 145, 149
   attempted rezonings Diamond Head
      Terrace 1947-1957, 145
   citizens advisory committee zoning rec-
      ommendations, 149
   development politics, 150, 154
   general plan classification, 148
   not to be developed 1967, 150
   pro-development groups, 145, 146
   residents' attitude to development, 147
   rezoning 1940, 145
   rezoning 1961, 147
   rezonings in Diamond Head Terrace
      1959-1961, 146
   zoned high-density, 148
Diamond Head Improvement Association,
   18, 149, 151, 153, 155
Diamond Head Road, 146, 149, 150, 152
Diamond Head Terrace, 144, 145-147, 149,
   150-152, 155
Dillingham Corp., 3, 191, 214
Dillingham Investment Co., 97
Dillingham, Benjamin F. II, 61
Dillingham, Harold, 147
Dillingham, Louise G., , 155
Dillingham, Lowell S., 191
Dillingham, Walter F., 147
Dillingham, Walter F. and Louise G., 144
Dillingham family, 145, 146, 147
Disneyland, 239

Dodge, Robert G., 64, 138
Doi, Herbert T., 20, 348
Doi, Masato, 64, 158, 163
Doi, Nelson K., 20, 55, 57, 109, 266
Doi, Reginald Y., 20
Dole Co., 136, 201, 206
Dole Corporation, 97, 211
Dole, James D., 210
Dole, Sanford B., 210
Domai, Helen T., 400
Donaldson, Samuel, 83
Donho Inc., 251
Doo, Leigh-Wai, 165
Dooley, James, 67, 195, 242, 258, 346, 347,
   348, 350-352, 370, 389
Dream City, 177
Duke, Charles W., 112
Dunes, 240
Duplanty, Ronald K., 75
Dura Constructors Inc., 29, 58
Duran, Ramon A., 20, 91, 114
Dutch Girl Pastry Shoppe, 402
Duty Free Shoppers Ltd., 374
Dyer, John F., 65
Dynamic Industries Corporation, 318

East-West Center, 13, 17, 19
East-West Center, Board of Governors, 29
Eastern Building Co., 25
Ebesu, Tom T., 401
Economic boom, 1950s-1970s, 9
Eden Roc, 33, 267
Ehlers, B.F., 211
Elbert, Samuel H., 326
Electric Sales & Service Ltd., 130
Elko Terrace Development Co. of Hawaii, 24
Elks Club, 145, 150
Elysium Corp., 18
Enchanted Lake, 218, 219
Enchanted Lake Partners, 22, 25, 196
Environmental Land Concerns Inc., 31
Environmentalism, 154, 341, 365
Equal Rights Amendment, 5
Esmeralda, 190
Esposito, O. Vincent, 20, 44, 55, 57, 70, 72,
   75, 100, 129, 131, 133, 157, 168
Estates, major
   attorneys review internal business af-
      fairs, 62
   courts oversee trusts, 63
   divesting lease lots 1960s-1970s, 412
   do not favor selling land, 413
   favor holding title to housing land, 410
   founded by dispossessing Hawaiians, 429
   forced breakup, 6
   founders and trustees in overthrowing
      monarchy, 429
   inclined to sell lease lots mid-1970s, 420
   property tax assessments, 7
   real property assets, 6
   trustees as elected politicians, 444